Analysis of Real-World Security Protocols in a Universal Composability Framework

DISSERTATION

Submitted to

FACHBEREICH IV – INFORMATIK/WIRTSCHAFTSINFORMATIK
UNIVERSITÄT TRIER

for the degree of

DOCTOR OF SCIENCE
(DR. RER. NAT.)

by

MAX TUENGERTHAL

Dipl.-Inf., born August 13, 1981 in Frankfurt am Main

accepted on the recommendation of

Prof. Dr. Ralf Küsters, examiner
Dr. Jan Camenisch, co-examiner

2013

Bibliografische Information der Deutschen Nationalbibliothek

Die Deutsche Nationalbibliothek verzeichnet diese Publikation in der
Deutschen Nationalbibliografie; detaillierte bibliografische Daten sind
im Internet über http://dnb.d-nb.de abrufbar.

ISBN 978-3-8325-3468-4

Logos Verlag Berlin GmbH
Comeniushof, Gubener Str. 47,
10243 Berlin
Tel.: +49 (0)30 42 85 10 90
Fax: +49 (0)30 42 85 10 92
INTERNET: http://www.logos-verlag.de

Acknowledgments

First of all, I would like to thank Ralf Küsters for being such an exceptionally good advisor. He is such a dedicated researcher and has the ability to always ask the right questions. Without him, this work would not have been possible. The atmosphere in his group was always warm and welcoming, also because Ralf is such a kind and friendly person. I also want to thank Jan Camenisch for co-refereeing this thesis.

As to the group, I would like to thank all the people I worked with, Nicole Trouet-Schartz, Tomasz Truderung, Andreas Vogt, Daniel Fett, Guido Schmitz, and Enrico Scapin, not only for having lunch and playing darts with me, but also for many interesting discussions about work and other things. Especially, I want to thank Nicole for her helping hands and for taking care of most administrative matters, which made working at the University of Trier non-bureaucratic for me; Tomasz for many interesting discussions about research and life in general and for his very fine humor; and Andreas for always being interested in details and elegant proofs when preparing exercises and for being a great climbing partner.

I would like to thank my friends Stefan Gulan and Martin Taphorn for enriching my life in Trier. Stefan especially for "bäckern" (coffee and pastry) and many endless, though not pointless, discussions about almost everything. Martin especially for the challenging badminton matches, although I seldom won.

I would like to thank my parents, Inge and Gert Tuengerthal, for their unlimited trust in me and for their love. Last but not least, I want to thank my future wife, Gesine Möller, for her support, patience, and encouragement, especially in the final stage of writing up this thesis, and for her love.

Würzburg, June 2013   *Max Tuengerthal*

Abstract

Security protocols employed in practice, such as SSL/TLS, SSH, IPsec, DNSSEC, IEEE 802.11i, etc., are used in our everyday life and we heavily depend on their security. The complexity of these protocols still poses a big challenge on their comprehensive analysis. To cope with this complexity, a promising approach is modular security analysis based on universal composability frameworks. Universal composition theorems, such as the one in Canetti's Universal Composability (UC) model, and composition theorems with joint state, such as the one by Canetti and Rabin, are useful and widely employed tools for the modular design and analysis of cryptographic protocols. This appealing approach has, however, only very rarely been applied to the analysis of (existing) real-world protocols. One obstacle is the lack of suitable ideal functionalities for the most basic cryptographic primitives. While for many cryptographic tasks, such as public-key encryption; digital signatures; authentication; key exchange; and many other more sophisticated tasks, ideal functionalities have been formulated in universal composability frameworks, along with their realizations, surprisingly, however, no such functionality exists for symmetric encryption and many other basic symmetric cryptographic primitives, except for a more abstract Dolev-Yao style functionality. Another crucial obstacle is that all universal and joint state composition theorems, that have been obtained so far, assume that parties participating in a protocol session have pre-established a unique session identifier (SID). While the use of such SIDs is a good design principle, existing protocols, in particular real-world security protocols, typically do not use pre-established SIDs, at least not explicitly and not in the particular way stipulated by the theorems. As a result, the composition theorems cannot be applied to the analysis of such protocols in a modular and faithful way; at most for analyzing idealized variants of the original protocols.

The main goal of this thesis therefore is to push modular protocol analysis as far as possible, but without giving up on accurate modeling.

In this thesis, we propose an ideal functionality for symmetric encryption, that also supports a mechanism for key derivation (which is used by almost every real-world security protocol); public-key encryption; and message authentication codes (MACs), and we show that it can be realized based on standard cryptographic assumptions and constructions. This functionality, which can be combined with other ideal functionalities, including those of interest for real-word protocols (e.g., digital signatures or certification of public keys), is widely applicable and provides a solid foundation for faithful, composable cryptographic analysis of real-world security protocols.

The main application of this new ideal functionality is to analyze protocols directly in a cryptographic setting, and we will demonstrate its usefulness in various applications. At first, however, we use it in the field of computational soundness of formal analysis. Formal analysis of security protocols based on symbolic models has been very successful in finding flaws in published protocols and proving protocols secure, using automated tools. An important question is whether this kind of formal analysis implies the strong security guarantees as defined by modern cryptography. Initiated by the seminal work of Abadi and Rogaway, this question has been investigated and numerous positive results showing this so-called computational soundness of formal analysis have been obtained. However, for the case of active adversaries and protocols that use symmetric encryption computational soundness has remained a challenge. In this thesis, we present the first general computational soundness result for key exchange protocols with symmetric encryption, along the lines of a paper by Canetti and Herzog on protocols with public-key encryption. More specifically, we develop a symbolic, automatically checkable criterion, based on observational equivalence, and show that a key exchange protocol that satisfies this criterion realizes an ideal key exchange functionality in terms of universal composability. Our results hold under standard cryptographic assumptions. To show our computational soundness result, we use our new ideal functionality to abstract from symmetric encryption and we apply composition with joint state to obtain multi-session security from single-session security, which greatly simplifies the proof.

In order to demonstrate the usefulness of our new ideal functionality for the analysis of real-world cryptographic protocols directly in a universal composability framework, we identify a sufficient criterion for protocols to provide secure, universally composable key exchange. Since this criterion is based on the new functionality, checking the criterion requires merely information-theoretic or even only syntactical arguments, rather than involved reduction arguments. As a case study, we use our method to analyze two central protocols of the IEEE standard 802.11i, namely the 4-Way Handshake Protocol and the CCM Protocol, proving composable security properties. As to the best of our knowledge, this constitutes the first rigorous cryptographic analysis of these protocols.

To mitigate the second of the above mentioned obstacles, we then present universal and joint state composition theorems which do not assume pre-established SIDs. In our joint state composition theorem, the joint state is our new ideal functionality. We demonstrate the usefulness of our composition theorems by case studies on the real-world security protocols SSL/TLS, IEEE 802.11i, SSH, IPsec, and EAP-PSK. While our applications focus on real-world security protocols, our theorems, models, and techniques should be useful beyond this domain.

Zusammenfassung

Sicherheitsprotokolle, wie SSL/TLS, SSH, IPsec, DNSSEC, IEEE 802.11i, etc., sind aus unserem Alltag nicht mehr wegzudenken und wir verlassen uns stark auf ihre Sicherheit. Die Komplexität dieser Protokolle stellt immer noch eine große Herausforderung bei ihrer ausführlichen Sicherheitsanalyse dar. Ein erfolgversprechender Ansatz, dieser Komplexität zu begegnen ist die modulare Sicherheitsanalyse in sogenannten "universal composability" (UC) Modellen. Universelle Kompositionstheoreme, z. B. das aus Canettis UC-Modell, und Kompositionstheoreme mit geteiltem Zustand (*joint state*), z. B. das von Canetti und Rabin, sind nützliche und weit verbreitete Hilfsmittel für den modularen Entwurf und die modulare Analyse von kryptographischen Protokollen. Trotzdem wurde dieser Ansatz bisher nur selten für die Analyse von in der Praxis verwendeten Sicherheitsprotokollen verwendet. Ein Hindernis ist das Fehlen einer geeigneten idealen Funktionalität für grundlegende kryptographische Primitive. Obwohl ideale Funktionalitäten für viele kryptographische Aufgaben, wie asymmetrische Verschlüsselung, digitale Signaturen, Authentifizierung, Schlüsselaustausch und viele andere Aufgaben in UC-Modellen formuliert wurden, zusammen mit ihren Realisierungen, existiert überraschenderweise bisher keine solche Funktionalität für symmetrische Verschlüsselung und viele andere grundlegende symmetrische kryptographische Verfahren, mit Ausnahme einer abstrakteren Dolev-Yao-artigen Funktionalität. Ein anderes entscheidendes Hindernis ist, dass alle bisher vorgestellten Kompositionstheoreme annehmen, dass Parteien, welche an einer gemeinsamen Protokollsitzung teilnehmen, eine im Vorfeld ausgehandelte Sitzungskennung (SID) verwenden. Zwar ist das Verwenden solch einer SID ein gutes Konstruktionsprinzip, aber existierende Protokolle, insbesondere in der Praxis verwendete, benutzen solche SID typischerweise nicht. Zumindest nicht explizit und in der Art und Weise wie von den Theoremen gefordert. Daher können die Kompositionstheoreme nicht für die modulare und präzise Analyse von solchen Protokollen verwendet werden. Allenfalls idealisierte Varianten der Orginalprotokolle können mit ihnen analysiert werden.

Das Hauptziel dieser Arbeit ist es daher Hilfsmittel zur Verfügung zu stellen, welche eine modulare Protokollanalyse erlauben ohne deren Genauigkeit einzuschränken.

In dieser Arbeit stellen wir dazu zunächst eine ideale Funktionalität für symmetrische Verschlüsselung vor, welche außerdem Verfahren zum Ableiten von Schlüsseln, asymmetrische Verschlüsselung und Message Authentication Codes (MAC) unterstützt. Außerdem zeigen wir, dass sie mit gängigen Annahmen und Konstruktionen realisiert werden kann. Diese Funktionalität, welche mit anderen idealen Funktionalitäten, insbesondere für reale Protokolle relevante (z. B. digitale Signaturen), kombiniert werden kann, hat ein weites Anwendungsfeld und bietet eine gute Basis für präzise und modulare kryptographische Analyse von praxisrelevanten Sicherheitsprotokollen.

Die Hauptanwendung dieser neuen idealen Funktionalität ist die Analyse von Protokollen direkt in einem kryptographischen Modell und wir stellen ihre Nützlichkeit in verschiedenen Anwendungen dar. Zunächst nutzen wir sie allerdings auf dem Gebiet der berechenbaren Korrektheit (*computational soundness*) formaler Analyse. Formale Analyse von Sicherheitsprotokollen basierend auf symbolischen Modellen wurde sehr erfolgreich eingesetzt, um Schwachstellen in existierenden Protokollen zu finden und Sicherheit mit automatischen Methoden zu beweisen. Eine dabei wichtige Frage ist, ob diese Art der formalen Analyse Sicherheitsgarantien im Sinne der modernen Kryptographie bietet. Initiiert durch die grundlegende Arbeit von Abadi und Rogaway wurde diese Frage untersucht und viele positive Ergebnisse zeigen diese sogenannte berechenbare Korrektheit formaler Analyse. Für den Fall von aktiven Angreifern und Protokollen welche symmetrische Verschlüsselung verwenden blieb dies allerdings eine Herausforderung. In dieser Arbeit stellen wir das erste allgemeine Ergebnis zur berechenbaren Korrektheit formaler Analyse für Schlüsselaustauschprotokolle, die symmetrische Verschlüsselung verwenden, vor. Wir folgen dabei in groben Zügen einer Arbeit von Canetti und Herzog über Protokolle mit asymmetrischer Verschlüsselung. Genauer gesagt, entwickeln wir ein symbolisches, automatisch verifizierbares Kriterium und zeigen, dass Schlüsselaustauschprotokolle, welche dieses Kriterium erfüllen, sicher im Sinne von UC-Modellen sind. Unser Ergebnis gilt unter gängigen kryptographischen Annahmen. Um den Beweis dieses Ergebnisses zu vereinfachen, nutzen wir unsere neue ideale Funktionalität (zur Abstraktion von symmetrischer Verschlüsselung) und wir verwenden Kompositionstheoreme mit geteiltem Zustand (um Sicherheit für mehrere Protokollsitzungen aus der Sicherheit einer einzelnen Protokollsitzung zu folgern).

Um den Nutzen unserer neuen idealen Funktionalität für die Analyse von praxisrelevanten Sicherheitsprotokollen direkt in einem UC-Modell zu demonstrieren, ermitteln wir ein Kriterium für Schlüsselaustauschprotokolle, welches hinreichend für ihre Sicherheit im Sinne von UC-Modellen ist. Da dieses Kriterium auf der neuen Funktionalität basiert, erfordert es lediglich informationstheoretische oder gar nur syntaktische Argumente, anstatt aufwendiger Reduktionsargumente, um das Kriterium zu zeigen. Als Fallstudie nutzen wir unsere Methode, um zwei zentrale Protokolle des IEEE Standards 802.11i, nämlich das 4-Way Handshake Protokoll und das CCM Protokoll, zu analysieren und deren Sicherheit zu beweisen. Nach unserem besten Wissen stellt dies die erste fundierte kryptographische Analyse dieser Protokolle dar.

Um dem zweiten angesprochenen Hinderniss zu begegnen, stellen wir ein universelles Kompositionstheorem und eines mit geteiltem Zustand vor, welche keine vorherbestimmten SID annehmen oder verwenden. Der geteilte Zustand im Kompositionstheorem ist unsere neue ideale Funktionalität. Wir demonstrieren den Nutzen unserer Kompositionstheoreme in mehreren Fallstudien, in denen wir die Sicherheitsprotokolle SSL/TLS, IEEE 802.11i, SSH, IPsec und EAP-PSK betrachten. Obwohl sich unsere Anwendungen auf praxisrelevante Protokolle konzentrieren, sollten unsere Theoreme und Techniken darüber hinaus von Interesse sein.

Contents

1. Introduction

Security protocols employed in practice, such as SSL/TLS, SSH, IPsec, DNSSEC, IEEE 802.11i, Kerberos, and many others, are used in our everyday life and we heavily depend on their security. While many attacks on such protocols have been uncovered (see, e.g., [CJS+08, DP10, APW09, TB09, RD09] for recent examples), their comprehensive analysis still poses a big challenge, as is often pointed out in the literature (see, e.g., [RS09, Kra03, CK02a]). A central problem is the complexity of these protocols.

To cope with this complexity, a viable approach is composable security analysis based on a framework of simulation-based security; in particular universal composability/reactive simulatability, [Can01, PW01]: Higher-level components of a protocol are designed and analyzed based on lower-level idealized components, called ideal functionalities. Composition theorems then allow for the replacement of the ideal functionalities by their realizations, altogether resulting in a system without idealized components. Typically, the higher-level components are shown to realize idealized functionalities themselves. Hence, they can be used as lower-level idealized components in even more complex systems. Moreover, universal composition theorems, such as Canetti's composition theorem in the UC model [Can01] and Küsters' composition theorems in the IITM model [Küs06], allow us to obtain security for multiple sessions of a protocol by analyzing just a single protocol session.

This appealing approach has been used widely in cryptography to design (new) protocols in a modular way (see [Can06] for an overview). However, it has only very rarely been applied to the analysis of (existing) real-world protocols (see the related work in Section 7.8). Crucial obstacles are the lack of *(i)* suitable idealized functionalities and corresponding realizations for the most basic cryptographic primitives and *(ii)* composition theorems that are applicable to real-world protocols. They prevented analyses from being fully modular or forced them to be imprecise, i.e., not the original but only severely modified protocols could be analyzed.

The main goal of this thesis is therefore to overcome these obstacles and to push modular protocol analysis as far as possible but without giving up on accurate modeling. We will now discuss the above mentioned obstacles and our contributions in more detail.

Ideal Functionalities for Symmetric Cryptographic Primitives

Ideal functionalities for cryptographic primitives provide higher-level protocols with the functionality of the primitive (e.g., encryption and decryption) and guarantee security in an ideal way (e.g., ciphertexts are generated independently of the encrypted plaintexts). They are useful for modular protocol analysis because, in the analysis of a protocol, one can use the properties that are syntactically guaranteed by the ideal functionalities instead of doing reduction proofs to the security of the underlying cryptographic primitives. Then, using composition theorems, one can replace the ideal functionality by its realization to obtain security for the original protocol.

While ideal functionalities for public-key encryption and digital signatures have been proposed early on [Can01, PW01, KT08], similar ideal functionalities for symmetric primitives, in particular for symmetric encryption, are still missing; there only exists an abstract Dolev-Yao style functionality [BP04] (see Section 5.5 for the discussion of related work). Compared to a functionality for public-key encryption, one faces several challenges when devising a functionality for symmetric key encryption: In case of public-key encryption, it is reasonable to assume that the private key never leaves the functionality, making it relatively easy to formulate and provide certain security guarantees. However, symmetric keys, in particular session keys, typically have to travel between parties, as in, e.g., Kerberos. Although, of course, a symmetric encryption functionality cannot just give out these keys because no security guarantees could be provided. So, clearly a user must not get his/her hands on these keys directly, but should only be able to refer to these keys by pointers [BP04]. A user should, for instance, be able to instruct the functionality to encrypt a message m with the key corresponding to a pointer ptr, where m itself may contain pointers to keys; these keys can then travel (securely) encapsulated in the ciphertext to m. This implies that an ideal symmetric encryption functionality has to keep track of who knows which keys and which keys have been revealed, e.g., due to corruption or encryption with a previously revealed key. The functionality also has to provide mechanisms for bootstrapping symmetric encryption. For example, by such a mechanism it should be possible to distribute symmetric keys using encryption under long-term pre-shared keys or public-key encryption. Finally, one has to deal with two technical problems: key cycles [GM84, AR00] and the commitment problem [BP04, CF01, DDM$^+$06]. A key cycle occurs if an encryption under a key k_1 depends on a key k_2 and vice versa, e.g., if a key is encrypted under itself. In the context of symmetric encryption, the commitment problem occurs in simulation-based approaches if a key is revealed after it was used to encrypt a message.

Contribution. In Chapter 5, we present an ideal functionality $\mathcal{F}_{\text{crypto}}$ for symmetric and public-key encryption, MACs, and key derivation that allows parties to generate fresh and pre-shared symmetric keys and public/private keys and to use these keys for ideal encryption and decryption, MAC generation and verification, and key derivation. The encrypted messages may contain symmetric and public keys and parties are given the actual ciphertexts, as bit strings. Support for other cryptographic primitives, such as digital signatures, can easily be added by combining $\mathcal{F}_{\text{crypto}}$ with other ideal functionalities. We show that, for a reasonable class of environments (basically, environments that do not produce key cycles or cause the commitment problem), $\mathcal{F}_{\text{crypto}}$ can be realized based on standard cryptographic assumptions and constructions: IND-CCA secure or authenticated encryption, UF-CMA secure MACs, and pseudorandom functions for key derivation, which are common also in implementations of real-world protocols.

Since $\mathcal{F}_{\text{crypto}}$ is a rather low-level ideal functionality and its realization is based on standard cryptographic assumptions and constructions, it is widely applicable and allows for a precise modeling of real-word security protocols, including precise modeling of message formats on the bit level. We will demonstrate the usefulness of $\mathcal{F}_{\text{crypto}}$ in several applications (see below). Its main application is to analyze protocols directly in a universal composability framework, i.e., to show that a protocol that uses one or more of the primitives provided by $\mathcal{F}_{\text{crypto}}$ realizes some ideal functionality (e.g., an ideal key exchange functionality). Another application of $\mathcal{F}_{\text{crypto}}$ is, for example, to obtain so-called computational soundness of formal analysis (see below).

We note that the functionality $\mathcal{F}_{\text{crypto}}$ is a further development of joint work with Küsters [KT09b, KT11b] that generalizes some aspects of [KT11b], yielding a functionality that is applicable to a slightly broader class of protocols and allows for easier modeling of protocols.

Computational Soundness for Protocols with Symmetric Encryption

Formal analysis of security protocols based on symbolic models, also called Dolev-Yao models [DY83], has been very successful in finding flaws in published protocols and proving protocols secure, using fully automated or interactive tools (see, e.g., [MSS98, MSC04, BMP05, BFGT06, ABB+05, Bla01]). While formal analysis in symbolic models is appealing due to its relative simplicity and rich tool support (ranging from finite state model checking, over fully or semi-automatic special purpose tools, to general purpose theorem provers), an important question is whether analysis results obtained in the symbolic model carry over to the realm of modern cryptography with its strong security notions. Initiated by the seminal work of Abadi and Rogaway [AR00], this so-called *computational soundness* problem has attracted a lot of attention in the last few years and many positive results have been obtained (see, e.g., [AR00, BPW03, MW04, CW05, CKKW06, KM07, BU08]).

However, as further discussed in Chapter 6, establishing computational soundness results for protocols with symmetric encryption in presence of active adversaries has turned out to be non-trivial. Most results for symmetric encryption assume passive or at most adaptive adversaries (see, e.g., [AR00, KM07]). Conversely, results for active adversaries mostly consider asymmetric cryptography, e.g., public-key encryption and digital signatures (see, e.g., [MW04, CW05, CKKW06, CH06, BU08]).

Contribution. In Chapter 6, we present a computational soundness result for key exchange protocols that use symmetric keys in presence of active adversaries, with standard cryptographic assumptions. This computational soundness result is joint work with Küsters [KT09a].

To obtain our computational soundness result, we develop a natural symbolic, automatically checkable criterion for key exchange protocols. Our computational soundness result states that, if a symbolic key exchange protocol satisfies our symbolic criterion, then this protocol (more precisely, its computational interpretation), realizes a standard ideal key exchange functionality (in terms of universal composability), which is a very strong security guarantee. We first prove this result for the case where symmetric encryption is performed based on the ideal crypto functionality $\mathcal{F}_{\mathrm{crypto}}$ (see above). We then, using composition theorems, replace this functionality by its realization based on secure authenticated symmetric encryption, resulting in a computational interpretation of the protocol without idealized components. This last step requires that the protocol does not produce key-cycles and does not cause the commitment problem (see above). We propose symbolic, automatically checkable criteria for these properties.

Protocol Analysis Without Pre-Established Session Identifiers

Universal composition theorems, such as Canetti's composition theorem in the UC model [Can01] and Küsters' composition theorems in the IITM model [Küs06], allow to obtain security for multiple sessions of a protocol by analyzing just a single protocol session. These theorems assume that different protocol sessions have disjoint state; in particular, each session has to use fresh randomness. This can lead to inefficient and impractical protocols, since, for example, every session has to use fresh long-term symmetric and public/private keys. Canetti and Rabin [CR03] therefore proposed to combine universal composition theorems with what they called composition theorems with joint state. As the name suggests, such theorems yield systems in which different sessions may use some joint state, e.g., the same long-term and public/private keys.

However, these theorems, both for universal and joint state composition, assume that parties participating in a protocol session have pre-established a unique session identifier (SID), and as a result (as we will see in Section 7.1), make heavy use of this SID in a specific way stipulated by the universal and joint state composition theorems. On the one hand, the use of such SIDs is a good design principle and, as discussed by Canetti [Can05] and Barak et al. [BLR04], establishing such SIDs is simple. On the other hand, many existing protocols, including most real-world security protocols, do not make use of such pre-established SIDs, at least not explicitly and not in the particular way stipulated by the theorems. As a result, these theorems cannot be used for the faithful modular analysis of such protocols; at most for analyzing idealized variants of the original protocols, which is unsatisfactory and risky because attacks on the original protocols might be missed (as demonstrate in Section 7.6). The problems resulting from pre-established SIDs in the existing composition theorems do not seem to have been brought out in previous work.

Contribution.   In Chapter 7, we devote ourselves to protocols that do not make use of pre-established SIDs. This allows us to analyze a much broader class of protocols, including many real-world protocols, without giving up on precise modeling.

In Section 7.4, in joint work with Küsters [KT11b], we develop a criterion to prove universally composable security for key exchange protocols that use our ideal crypto functionality $\mathcal{F}_{\text{crypto}}$ (see above). This criterion is based on $\mathcal{F}_{\text{crypto}}$ and can therefore be checked merely using information-theoretic arguments, rather than more involved and harder to manage reduction proofs; often even purely syntactic arguments suffice, without reasoning about probabilities. Indeed, the use of $\mathcal{F}_{\text{crypto}}$ tremendously simplifies proofs in the context of real-world security protocols, as we demonstrate by a case study on the wireless networking protocol WPA2 (IEEE standard 802.11i [IEE07, IEE04]). More precisely, we show that two central components, namely the 4-Way Handshake (4WHS) protocol and the CCM Protocol (CCMP), of the pre-shared key mode of WPA2 (WPA2-PSK) are secure. As to the best of our knowledge, this constitutes the first rigorous cryptographic analysis of these protocols.

However, the criterion presented in Section 7.4 needs to be proved directly in a multi-session setting and, hence, does not exploit the full potential of modular analysis. Therefore, in Sections 7.5 and 7.6, in joint work with Küsters [KT11a], we present a general universal composition theorem and a composition theorem with joint state, respectively, that do not assume pre-established SIDs and their use in cryptographic protocols, and hence, enable fully modular, yet faithful analysis of protocols without the need to modify/idealize these protocols.

Our universal composition theorem without pre-established SIDs states that if a protocol realizes an ideal functionality in a single-session setting, then it also realizes the ideal functionality in a multi-session setting, subject to mild restrictions on the single-session simulator. The important point is that a party invokes a protocol instance simply with a *local* SID, locally chosen and managed by the party itself, rather than with an SID pre-established with other parties for that session. This not only provides the party with a more common and convenient interface, where the party addresses her protocol instances with the corresponding local SIDs, but, more importantly, frees the real protocol from the need to use pre-established SIDs and allows for realizations that faithfully model existing (real-world) protocols. In [KT11a], the restrictions put on the single-session simulator basically force the protocol to provide mutual authentication. In this thesis, we mitigate these restrictions such that the theorem is even applicable to protocols that do not provide authentication.

In our joint state composition theorem without pre-established SIDs, we consider protocols that use the ideal crypto functionality $\mathcal{F}_{\text{crypto}}$. It states that, under a certain condition on the protocol, which we call *implicit (session) disjointness*, it suffices to show that a protocol realizes an ideal functionality in a single-session setting in order to obtain security for multiple sessions of the protocol, where all sessions may use the *same* ideal crypto functionality $\mathcal{F}_{\text{crypto}}$; again we put restrictions on the single-session simulator. So, $\mathcal{F}_{\text{crypto}}$ (or its realization), with the keys stored in it, constitutes a joint state across sessions. As in the case of the universal composition theorem, users again invoke protocol instances with locally chosen and managed SIDs. Unlike joint state composition theorems with pre-established SIDs, our joint state composition theorem does not modify/idealize the original protocol. The restrictions on the single-session simulator basically force the protocol to provide mutual authentication but, for protocols providing this, the restrictions are mild. Moreover, as we discuss in the conclusion, we think that they can be relaxed such that our joint state composition theorem becomes applicable to protocols that do not provide authentication.

Given our composition theorems, (real-world) security protocols can be analyzed with a high degree of modularity and without giving up on precision: Once implicit disjointness is established for a protocol—first proof step—, it suffices to carry out single-session analysis for the protocol—second proof step—in order to obtain multi-session security with joint state for the original protocol, not just an idealized version with pre-established SIDs added in various places. We emphasize that, due to the use of $\mathcal{F}_{\text{crypto}}$, in all proof steps often merely information-theoretic or purely syntactical reasoning suffices, without reduction proofs.

In Section 7.7, in joint work with Küsters [KT11a], we demonstrate the usefulness of our composition theorems and approach by several case studies on real-world security protocols, namely (subprotocols of) SSL/TLS, WPA2 (IEEE 802.11i), SSH, IPsec, and EAP-PSK. More precisely, we show that all these protocols satisfy implicit disjointness, confirming our believe that this property is satisfied by many (maybe most) real-world security protocols. While proving implicit disjointness requires to reason about multiple sessions of a protocol, this step is nevertheless relatively easy. In fact, as demonstrated by our case studies, to prove implicit disjointness, typically the security properties of only a few primitives used in the protocol need to be considered. For example, to prove that the SSH key exchange protocol satisfies implicit disjointness, only collision resistance of the hash function is needed, but not the security of the encryption scheme, the MAC, or the Diffie-Hellman key exchange used in SSH. Since the above mentioned protocols satisfy implicit disjointness, to now show that these protocols are secure key exchange or secure channel protocols, single-session analysis suffices. Performing this single-session analysis for these protocols is out of the scope of this thesis. The main point of this thesis is to provide a machinery for faithful and highly modular analysis, not to provide a full-fledged analysis of these protocols.

Structure of this Thesis

All results presented in this thesis are formulated in Küsters' IITM model [Küs06], which has recently been updated by Küsters and Tuengerthal [KT13] and which we recall in Chapter 2. In Chapter 3, we introduce preliminaries that are used throughout the thesis. In Chapter 4, we describe how the IITM model is used in this thesis to model protocols. We also present basic ideal functionalities for several cryptographic primitives and protocol tasks that are used in this thesis. Our ideal crypto functionality $\mathcal{F}_{\text{crypto}}$ and its realization are presented in Chapter 5. In Chapter 6, we present our computational soundness result for key exchange protocols that use symmetric encryption. Our results about protocol analysis without pre-established session identifiers are presented in Chapter 7. We conclude in Chapter 8.

2. The IITM Model

In this chapter, we recall the IITM model [Küs06, KT13], a simple and expressive model for universal composability. More precisely, we recall the IITM model as presented in [KT13], which equips the original IITM model [Küs06] with a more general notion of runtime, namely one that is based on notions proposed by Hofheinz et al. [HUMQ09], which allows us to formulate protocols and ideal functionalities in an intuitive way, without technical artifacts.

While being in the spirit of Canetti's UC model [Can05], the IITM model resolves some technical problems of the UC model caused by the way the runtime of interactive Turing machines is defined (see, e.g., discussions in [Küs06, KT08, HUMQ09, HS11, KT13]). As pointed out in [KT08, HS11], these problems also affect the universal and joint state composition theorems in the UC model.

2.1. The General Computational Model

In the IITM model, security notions and composition theorems are formalized based on a simple, expressive general computational model, in which IITMs (inexhaustible interactive Turing machines) and systems of IITMs are defined.

Inexhaustible interactive Turing machines. An *inexhaustible interactive Turing machine (IITM)* is a probabilistic Turing machine with named input and output tapes as well as an associated polynomial. The tape names determine how different machines are connected in a system of IITMs (see below). Tapes named start and decision serve a particular purpose when running a system of IITMs. It is required that only input tapes can be named start and only output tapes can be named decision. Tapes named start are used to provide a system with external input and to trigger an IITM if no other IITM was triggered. An IITM is triggered by another IITM if the latter sends a message to the former. An IITM with an input tape named start is called *master IITM*. On tapes named decision the final output of a system of IITMs will be written. An IITM runs in one of two modes, CheckAddress and Compute. The CheckAddress mode is used as a generic mechanism for addressing copies of IITMs in a system of IITMs, as explained below. In this mode, an IITM may perform, in every activation, a deterministic polynomial-time computation in the length of the security parameter plus the length of the current input plus the length of its current configuration, where the polynomial is the one associated with the IITM. The IITM is supposed to output "accept" or "reject" at the end of the computation in this mode, indicating whether the received message is processed further or ignored. The actual processing of the message, if accepted, is done in mode Compute. In this mode, a machine may only output at most one message on an output tape (and hence, only at most one other machine is triggered). The runtime in this mode is not a priori bounded. Later the runtime of systems and their subsystems will be defined in such a way that the overall runtime of a system of IITMs is polynomially bounded in the security parameter. We note that in both modes, an IITM cannot be exhausted (hence, the name): in every activation it can perform actions and cannot be forced to stop. This property, while not satisfied in all other models, is crucial to obtain a reasonable model for universal composability (see, e.g., [KT13]).

Systems of IITMs.   A *system* S of IITMs is of the form

$$S = M_1 \mid \cdots \mid M_k \mid !M'_1 \mid \cdots \mid !M'_{k'}$$

where M_i, $i \in \{1, \ldots, k\}$, and M'_j, $j \in \{1, \ldots, k'\}$, are IITMs such that, for every tape name c, at most two of these IITMs have a tape named c and, if two IITMs have a tape named c, this tape is an input tape in one of the machines and an output tape in the other. That is, two IITMs can be connected via tapes with the same name and opposite directions. These tapes are called *internal* and all other tapes are called *external*. The IITMs M'_j are said to be in the scope of a bang operator. This operator indicates that in a run of a system an unbounded number of (fresh) copies of a machine may be generated. Conversely, machines which are not in the scope of a bang operator may not be copied. Systems in which multiple copies of a machine may be generated are often needed, e.g., in case of multi-party protocols or in case a system describes the concurrent execution of multiple instances of a protocol. The above conditions imply that in every system only at most one IITM may be a master IITM, i.e., may have an input tape named start; there may be several copies of such a machine in a run of a system though.

Running a system.   In a run of a system S for some security parameter η and bit string a as external input, such a system is denoted by $S(1^\eta, a)$, at any time only one (copy of an) IITM is active and all other IITMs wait for new input. The active copy, say M', which is a copy of a machine M defined in S, may write at most one message, say m, on one of its output tapes, say c. This message is then delivered to another (copy of an) IITM with an input tape named c, say N is the machine specified in S with an input tape named c.[1] In the current configuration of the system, there may be several copies of N. In the order of creation, the copies of N are run in mode CheckAddress with input m. Once one copy accepts m, this copy gets to process m, i.e., it runs in mode Compute with input m, and in particular, may produce output on one output tape, which is then sent to another copy and so

---

[1]By the convention on the names of input tapes in systems of IITMs there can be at most one such machine.

on. If no copy of N accepts m and N is in the scope of a bang, a fresh copy of N is created and run in mode CheckAddress. If this copy accepts m, it gets to process m in mode Compute. Otherwise, the new copy of N is deleted, m is dropped, and a master IITM is activated (with empty input). If N is not in the scope of a bang (and—the only copy of—N does not accept m), then too a master IITM is activated. The first IITM to be activated in a run is a master IITM. It gets a as external input (on tape start). A master IITM is also activated if the currently active machine does not produce output (i.e., stops in its activation without writing to any output tape). A run stops if a master IITM, after being activated, does not produce output or output was written by some machine on an output tape named decision. In the first case, the *overall output* of the run is defined to be the empty bit string and, in the latter case, it is defined to be the message that is output on decision. The probability that, in runs of $\mathcal{S}(1^\eta, a)$, the overall output is $m \in \{0,1\}^*$ is denoted by

$$\Pr\left[\mathcal{S}(1^\eta, a) = m\right] .^2$$

To illustrate runs of systems, consider, for example, the system $\mathcal{S} = M_1 \mid !M_2$ and assume that M_1 has an output tape named c, M_2 has an input tape named c, and M_1 is the master IITM. (There may be other tapes connecting M_1 and M_2.) Furthermore, assume that in the run of $\mathcal{S}$ executed so far, two copies of M_2, say M_2' and M_2'', have been generated, with M_2' generated before M_2'', and that M_1 just sent a message m on tape c. This message is delivered to M_2' (as the first copy of M_2). First, M_2' runs in mode CheckAddress with input m; as mentioned, this is a deterministic computation in polynomial time which outputs "accept" or "reject". If M_2' accepts m, then M_2' gets to process m in mode Compute and could, for example, send a message back to M_1. Otherwise, m is given to M_2'' which then runs in mode CheckAddress with input m. If M_2'' accepts m, then M_2'' gets to process m in mode Compute. Otherwise (if both M_2' and M_2'' do not accept m), a new copy M_2''' of M_2 with fresh randomness is generated and M_2''' runs in mode CheckAddress with input m. If M_2''' accepts m, then M_2''' gets to process m. Otherwise, M_2''' is removed again, the message m is dropped, and the master IITM is activated (with empty input), in this case M_1, and so on.

Equivalence/indistinguishability of systems. First, negligible functions are defined following [Can05].

Definition 2.1. *A function* $f\colon \{1\}^* \times \{0,1\}^* \to \mathbb{R}_{\geq 0}$ *is called* negligible *if for all* $c, d \in \mathbb{N}$ *there exists* $\eta_0 \in \mathbb{N}$ *such that for all* $\eta > \eta_0$ *and all* $a \in \bigcup_{\eta' \leq \eta^d} \{0,1\}^{\eta'}$: $f(1^\eta, a) < \eta^{-c}.^3$

---

[2] Formally, $\mathcal{S}(1^\eta, a)$ is a random variable that describes the overall output of runs of $\mathcal{S}(1^\eta, a)$, based on a standard probability space for runs of systems, see [KT13] for details.

[3] This definition is equivalent to the following: f is negligible if and only if for all positive polynomials $p(\eta)$ and $q(\eta)$ in $\eta \in \mathbb{N}$ (i.e., $p(\eta) > 0$ and $q(\eta) > 0$ for all $\eta \in \mathbb{N}$) there exists $\eta_0 \in \mathbb{N}$ such

A function $f\colon \{1\}^* \times \{0,1\}^* \to [0,1]$ *is called* overwhelming *if* $1-f$ *is negligible.*[4]

Two systems that produce overall output 1 with almost the same probability are called equivalent or indistinguishable:

Definition 2.2 ([KT13]). *Let* $f\colon \{1\}^* \times \{0,1\}^* \to \mathbb{R}_{\geq 0}$ *be a function. Two systems* $\mathcal{P}$ *and* $\mathcal{Q}$ *are called* f-equivalent *or* f-indistinguishable *(*$\mathcal{P} \equiv_f \mathcal{Q}$*) if and only if for every security parameter* $\eta \in \mathbb{N}$ *and external input* $a \in \{0,1\}^*$:

$$\left| \Pr\left[\mathcal{P}(1^\eta, a) = 1\right] - \Pr\left[\mathcal{Q}(1^\eta, a) = 1\right]\right| \leq f(1^\eta, a) \ .$$

Two systems $\mathcal{P}$ *and* $\mathcal{Q}$ *are called* equivalent *or* indistinguishable *(*$\mathcal{P} \equiv \mathcal{Q}$*) if and only if there exists a negligible function* f *such that* $\mathcal{P} \equiv_f \mathcal{Q}$.

It is easy to see that for every two functions f, f' as in Definition 2.2 the relation $\equiv_f$ is reflexive and that $\mathcal{P} \equiv_f \mathcal{Q}$ and $\mathcal{Q} \equiv_{f'} \mathcal{S}$ implies $\mathcal{P} \equiv_{f+f'} \mathcal{S}$. In particular, $\equiv$ is reflexive and transitive.

2.2. Polynomial Time and Properties of Systems

So far, the runtime of IITMs in mode Compute has not been restricted in any way. To define notions of universal composability, it has to be enforced that systems run in polynomial time (except maybe with negligible probability). This will be done based on the following runtime notions.

A system $\mathcal{S}$ is called *strictly bounded* if there exists a polynomial p such that, for every security parameter η and external input a, the overall runtime of $\mathcal{S}$ in mode Compute is bounded by $p(\eta + |a|)$ in every run of $\mathcal{S}(1^\eta, a)$. If this holds only for an overwhelming set of runs, $\mathcal{S}$ is still called *almost bounded*. As shown in [KT13], every almost/strictly bounded system can be simulated (except maybe with a negligible error) by a polynomial-time Turing machine.

A system $\mathcal{E}$ is called *universally bounded* if there exists a polynomial p such that, for every security parameter η; external input a; and system $\mathcal{S}$ that can be connected to $\mathcal{E}$ (i.e., $\mathcal{E} \mid \mathcal{S}$ is defined), the overall runtime of $\mathcal{E}$ in mode Compute is bounded by $p(\eta + |a|)$ in every run of $(\mathcal{E} \mid \mathcal{S})(1^\eta, a)$. (We note that environmental systems will be universally bounded, see below.)

A system $\mathcal{P}$ is called *environmentally (almost) bounded* if $\mathcal{E} \mid \mathcal{P}$ is almost bounded for every universally bounded system $\mathcal{E}$ that can be connected to $\mathcal{P}$. Similarly, $\mathcal{P}$ is called *environmentally strictly bounded* if $\mathcal{E} \mid \mathcal{P}$ is strictly bounded for every

---

that for all $\eta > \eta_0$ and all $a \in \bigcup_{\eta' \leq q(\eta)} \{0,1\}^{\eta'}$: $f(1^\eta, a) < \frac{1}{p(\eta)}$. Negligible functions have the following properties: *(i)* If f and g are negligible, then $f+g$ is negligible. *(ii)* If f is negligible and p is a positive polynomial, then $g(1^\eta, a) := p(\eta + |a|) \cdot f(1^\eta, a)$ for all η, a is negligible.

[4]By $[0,1]$ we denote the interval of all real numbers x such that $0 \leq x \leq 1$.

universally bounded system $\mathcal{E}$ that can be connected to $\mathcal{P}$.[5] (We note that protocol systems will be environmentally bounded. Therefore, it will be guaranteed that a protocol, together with an environment, runs in polynomial time, see below.)

We now recall two properties of systems that allow us to replace a subsystem by a single IITM that simulates the subsystem. These properties are useful in proofs and essential for many general results in the IITM model, such as the composition theorems.

Lemma 2.1 ([KT13]). *For every system S there exists an IITM M such that the following conditions are satisfied:*

1. *M and S have the same external tapes.*

2. *M accepts every message in mode CheckAddress.*

3. *For every system Q that can be connected to S (i.e., $S \mid Q$ is defined):*

   a) *$S \mid Q \equiv_0 M \mid Q$ and*

   b) *$S \mid Q$ is almost/strictly bounded if and only if $M \mid Q$ is almost/strictly bounded.*

The following lemma shows how one subsystem of an almost bounded system can be replaced by one universally bounded IITM.

Lemma 2.2 ([KT13]). *Let S and Q be two systems such that S can be connected to Q (i.e., $S \mid Q$ is defined), $S \mid Q$ is almost bounded, and S contains a master IITM (i.e., start is an input tape of S). Then there exists an IITM M such that the following conditions are satisfied:*

1. *M and S have the same external tapes.*

2. *M accepts every message in mode CheckAddress.*

3. *M is universally bounded.*

4. *$M \mid Q$ is almost bounded.*

5. *$M \mid Q \equiv S \mid Q$.*

---

[5] As discussed in [KT13], since the runtime of universally bounded systems is polynomially bounded, the definition of environmentally almost/strictly bounded is equivalent to the following: $\mathcal{P}$ is environmentally almost/strictly bounded iff, for every universally bounded system $\mathcal{E}$, there exists a polynomial p such that, for every η and a, the overall runtime of $\mathcal{P}$ in mode Compute is bounded by $p(\eta + |a|)$ in every run of $(\mathcal{E} \mid \mathcal{P})(1^\eta, a)$ (except for a negligible set of runs).

2.3. Notions of Universal Composability

The following terminology is needed. For a system S, the external tapes are grouped into *I/O* and *network tapes*. Three different types of systems are considered: protocol systems, adversarial systems, and environmental systems, modeling *(i)* real and ideal protocols/functionalities, *(ii)* adversaries and simulators, and *(iii)* environments, respectively. *Protocol systems*, *adversarial systems*, and *environmental systems* are systems which have an I/O and network interface, i.e., they may have I/O and network tapes. Environmental systems have to be universally bounded and protocol systems have to be environmentally bounded.[6] Protocol systems and adversarial systems may not have a tape named start or decision; only environmental systems may have such tapes, i.e., environmental systems may contain a master IITM and may determine the overall output of a run. Furthermore, for every IITM M that occurs in a protocol system and is not in the scope of a bang, it is required that M accepts every incoming message in mode CheckAddress.[7]

To define notions of universal composability, the following sets of systems are used. Given a system S, the set of all environmental systems that connect to S (on the network or I/O interface) is denoted by $\mathrm{Env}(S)$. For two protocol systems P and F, $\mathrm{Sim}^{P}(F)$ denotes the set of all adversarial systems A such that A can be connected to F, the set of external tapes of A is disjoint from the set of I/O tapes of F (i.e., A only connects to the network interface of F), $A \,|\, F$ and P have the same external network and I/O interface, and $A \,|\, F$ is environmentally bounded.

We now recall the definition of strong simulatability; other, equivalent, security notions, such as UC and dummy UC, are defined in a similar way.

Definition 2.3 ([KT13]). *Let P and F be protocol systems, the real and ideal protocol, respectively. Then, P realizes F ($P \leq F$) if and only if there exists a simulator $S \in \mathrm{Sim}^{P}(F)$ (also called ideal adversary) such that $\mathcal{E} \,|\, P \equiv \mathcal{E} \,|\, S \,|\, F$ for every environment $\mathcal{E} \in \mathrm{Env}(P)$.*

As shown in [KT13], this relation is reflexive and transitive.

---

[6] We note that protocol systems, as defined in [KT13], per se are not required to be environmentally bounded. Instead, to obtain more general results, this is explicitly stated where needed. However, in most applications and throughout this thesis protocol systems are always environmentally bounded (or even environmentally strictly bounded). Therefore, we simply require protocol systems to be environmentally bounded.

[7] The motivation behind this condition is that if M does not occur in the scope of a bang, then, in every run of the protocol system (in some context), there will be at most one copy of M. Hence, there is no reason to address different copies of M, and therefore, in mode CheckAddress, M should accept every incoming message. This condition is needed in the proofs of the composition theorems for unbounded self-composition.

2.4. Composition Theorems

The first composition theorem handles concurrent composition of a fixed number of (possibly different) protocol systems. The second one guarantees secure composition of an unbounded number of copies of a protocol system.

Theorem 2.1 ([KT13]). *Let $k \geq 1$. Let $\mathcal{Q}, \mathcal{P}_1, \ldots, \mathcal{P}_k, \mathcal{F}_1, \ldots, \mathcal{F}_k$ be protocol systems such that they connect only via their I/O interfaces, $\mathcal{Q} \mid \mathcal{P}_1 \mid \cdots \mid \mathcal{P}_k$ is environmentally bounded, and $\mathcal{P}_i \leq \mathcal{F}_i$, for $i \in \{1, \ldots, k\}$. Then, $\mathcal{Q} \mid \mathcal{P}_1 \mid \cdots \mid \mathcal{P}_k \leq \mathcal{Q} \mid \mathcal{F}_1 \mid \cdots \mid \mathcal{F}_k$.*

Note that this theorem does not require that the protocols $\mathcal{P}_i / \mathcal{F}_i$ are subprotocols of $\mathcal{Q}$, i.e., that $\mathcal{Q}$ has matching external I/O tapes for all of these protocols. How these protocols connect to each other via their I/O interfaces is not restricted in any way, even the environment could connect directly to (the full or the partial) I/O interface of these protocols. Clearly, the theorem also holds true if the system $\mathcal{Q}$ is dropped.

For the following composition theorem, we introduce the notion of a session version of a protocol in order to be able to address copies of the protocol. Given an IITM M, the *session version* $\underline{M}$ of M is an IITM which internally simulates M and acts as a "wrapper" for M. In the CheckAddress mode, $\underline{M}$ accepts an incoming message only if *(i)* the message is prefixed with some specific identifier (ID), e.g., a session ID (SID) or a party ID (PID), and hence, the message is of the form (id, m),[8] and *(ii)* the internally simulated M accepts m in mode CheckAddress. The ID id that $\underline{M}$ expects is the one with which $\underline{M}$ was first activated. If $\underline{M}$ accepts a message (id, m) (in mode CheckAddress), then, in mode Compute it strips off the ID id and gives the actual message m to its internally simulated M, i.e., M is simulated in mode Compute with input m. If M outputs a message, $\underline{M}$ prefixes the ID id to that message and outputs the message.

For example, if M specifies an ideal functionality, then $!\underline{M}$ denotes a multi-session version of M, i.e., a system in which an unbounded number of copies of M can be created where every copy of M can be addressed by a unique ID, where the ID could be a PID (then an instance of $\underline{M}$ might model one party running M), an SID (then an instance of $\underline{M}$ models one session of M), or it could have a more complex structure, e.g., (sid, pid) (then $\underline{M}$ models an instance of party pid running M in session sid).

Given a system $\mathcal{S}$, its *session version* $\underline{\mathcal{S}}$ is obtained by replacing all IITMs in $\mathcal{S}$ by their session version. For example, we obtain $\underline{\mathcal{S}} = \underline{M} \mid !\underline{M'}$ for $\mathcal{S} = M \mid !M'$.

Now, the following composition theorem says that if a protocol $\mathcal{P}$ realizes $\mathcal{F}$, then the multi-session version of $\mathcal{P}$ realizes the multi-session version of $\mathcal{F}$.

Theorem 2.2 ([KT13]). *Let $\mathcal{P}$ and $\mathcal{F}$ be protocol systems such that $!\underline{\mathcal{P}}$ is environmentally bounded and $\mathcal{P} \leq \mathcal{F}$. Then, $!\underline{\mathcal{P}} \leq !\underline{\mathcal{F}}$.*

---

[8] Clearly, one could specify other forms as well. Everything checkable by a polynomial-time machine works. In particular, it is sometimes required that the ID belongs to a specific domain. Messages with IDs not belonging to that domain are rejected.

We note that the extra proof obligation that $!\mathcal{P}$ is environmentally bounded is typically easy to show. In particularly, it holds if $\mathcal{P}$ is environmentally strictly bounded (see below).

Theorems 2.1 and 2.2 can be applied iteratively to construct more and more complex systems. For example, as a corollary of the above theorems, one immediately obtains that for any protocol system $\mathcal{Q}$: $\mathcal{P} \leq \mathcal{F}$ implies $\mathcal{Q} \mid !\mathcal{P} \leq \mathcal{Q} \mid !\mathcal{F}$, provided that $\mathcal{Q} \mid !\mathcal{P}$ is environmentally bounded. In words: $\mathcal{Q}$ using an unbounded number of copies of $\mathcal{P}$ realizes $\mathcal{Q}$ using an unbounded number of copies of $\mathcal{F}$.

When addressing a session version $\underline{M}$ of a machine M, the machine M simulated within $\underline{M}$ is not aware of its ID and cannot use it. For example, it cannot put the ID into a message that M creates. However, sometimes this is desirable. Therefore another, more general, composition theorem is considered, where machines are aware of their IDs. While these IDs can, as already mentioned above, be interpreted in different ways, they will often be referred to as SIDs.

To this end, [KT13] first generalized the notion of a session version. They consider (polynomial-time computable) *session identifier (SID) functions* which, given a message and a tape name, output a SID (a bit string) or $\perp$. For example, the following function takes the prefix of a message as its SID: $\sigma_{\mathrm{prefix}}(m, c) := s$ if $m = (s, m')$ for some s, m' and $\sigma_{\mathrm{prefix}}(m, c) := \perp$ otherwise, for all m, c. Clearly, many more examples are conceivable. The reason that σ, besides a message, also takes a tape name as input is that the way SIDs are extracted from messages may depend on the tape a message is received on.

Given an SID function σ, an IITM M is called a σ-*session machine* (or a σ-*session version*) if the following conditions are satisfied: *(i)* M rejects (in mode CheckAddress) a message m on tape c if $\sigma(m, c) = \perp$. *(ii)* If m_0 is the first message that M accepted (in mode CheckAddress), say on tape c_0, in a run, then, M will reject all messages m received on some tape c (in mode CheckAddress) with $\sigma(m, c) \neq \sigma(m_0, c_0)$. *(iii)* Whenever M outputs a messages m on tape c, then $\sigma(m, c) = \sigma(m_0, c_0)$, with m_0 and c_0 as before.

It is easy to see that session versions are specific forms of σ-session versions: given an IITM M, we have that $\underline{M}$ is a σ_{prefix}-session version. The crucial difference is that while σ-session versions look like session version from the outside, inside they are aware of their SID.

Before the composition theorem can be stated, a notion of single-session realizability needs to be introduced.

An environmental system $\mathcal{E}$ is called σ-*single session* if it only outputs messages with the same SID according to σ. Hence, when interacting with a σ-session version, such an environmental system invokes at most one protocol session. Given a system $\mathcal{S}$ and an SID function σ, $\mathrm{Env}_{\sigma\text{-single}}(\mathcal{S})$ denotes the set of all environments $\mathcal{E} \in \mathrm{Env}(\mathcal{S})$ such that $\mathcal{E}$ is σ-single session, i.e., $\mathrm{Env}_{\sigma\text{-single}}(\mathcal{S})$ is the set of all σ-single session environmental systems that can be connected to $\mathcal{S}$.

For two protocol systems $\mathcal{P}$ and $\mathcal{F}$ and an SID function σ, $\mathrm{Sim}^{\mathcal{P}}_{\sigma\text{-single}}(\mathcal{F})$ denotes the set of all adversarial systems $\mathcal{A}$ such that $\mathcal{A}$ can be connected to $\mathcal{F}$, the set of external tapes of $\mathcal{A}$ is disjoint from the set of I/O tapes of $\mathcal{F}$ (i.e., $\mathcal{A}$ only connects to the network interface of $\mathcal{F}$), $\mathcal{A}\,|\,\mathcal{F}$ has the same external tapes as $\mathcal{P}$, and $\mathcal{E}\,|\,\mathcal{A}\,|\,\mathcal{F}$ is almost bounded for every $\mathcal{E} \in \mathrm{Env}_{\sigma\text{-single}}(\mathcal{A}\,|\,\mathcal{F})$. We note that $\mathrm{Sim}^{\mathcal{P}}(\mathcal{F}) \subseteq \mathrm{Sim}^{\mathcal{P}}_{\sigma\text{-single}}(\mathcal{F})$; the only difference between these two sets is that the runtime condition on $\mathcal{A}\,|\,\mathcal{F}$ is relaxed in $\mathrm{Sim}^{\mathcal{P}}_{\sigma\text{-single}}(\mathcal{F})$.

Let $\mathcal{P}$ and $\mathcal{F}$ be protocol systems, which in the setting considered here would typically describe multiple sessions of a protocol. Moreover, we assume that $\mathcal{P}$ and $\mathcal{F}$ are σ-session versions. Now, it is defined what it means that a single session of $\mathcal{P}$ realizes a single session of $\mathcal{F}$. This is defined just as $\mathcal{P} \leq \mathcal{F}$ (Definition 2.3), with the difference that only σ-single session environments are considered, and hence, environments that invoke at most one session of $\mathcal{P}$ and $\mathcal{F}$.

Definition 2.4 ([KT13]). *Let σ be an SID function and let $\mathcal{P}$ and $\mathcal{F}$ be protocol systems, the* real *and* ideal *protocol, respectively, such that $\mathcal{P}$ and $\mathcal{F}$ are σ-session versions. Then, $\mathcal{P}$ single-session realizes $\mathcal{F}$ w.r.t. σ ($\mathcal{P} \leq_{\sigma\text{-single}} \mathcal{F}$) if and only if there exists $\mathcal{S} \in \mathrm{Sim}^{\mathcal{P}}_{\sigma\text{-single}}(\mathcal{F})$ such that $\mathcal{E}\,|\,\mathcal{P} \equiv \mathcal{E}\,|\,\mathcal{S}\,|\,\mathcal{F}$ for every σ-single session environment $\mathcal{E} \in \mathrm{Env}_{\sigma\text{-single}}(\mathcal{P})$.*

Now, analogously to Theorem 2.2, the following theorem says that if $\mathcal{P}$ realizes $\mathcal{F}$ w.r.t. a single session, then $\mathcal{P}$ realizes $\mathcal{F}$ w.r.t. multiple sessions. As mentioned before, in the setting considered here $\mathcal{P}$ and $\mathcal{F}$ would typically model multi-session versions of a protocol/functionality.

Theorem 2.3 ([KT13]). *Let σ be an SID function and let $\mathcal{P}$ and $\mathcal{F}$ be protocol systems such that $\mathcal{P}$ and $\mathcal{F}$ are σ-session versions, and $\mathcal{P} \leq_{\sigma\text{-single}} \mathcal{F}$. Then, $\mathcal{P} \leq \mathcal{F}$.*

Clearly, this theorem can be combined with the other composition theorems to construct more and more complex systems.

As discussed in [KT13], the composition of two environmentally bounded systems is not necessarily environmentally bounded. However, in applications this is typically the case and easy to see. We now recall two simple lemmas that show that the composition of environmentally strictly bounded protocol systems with disjoint tapes is environmentally strictly bounded.[9]

Lemma 2.3 ([KT13]). *Let $\mathcal{P}$ and $\mathcal{Q}$ be two environmentally strictly bounded protocol systems such that the sets of external tapes of $\mathcal{P}$ and $\mathcal{Q}$ are disjoint. Then, $\mathcal{P}\,|\,\mathcal{Q}$ is environmentally strictly bounded.*

Lemma 2.4 ([KT13]). *Let $\mathcal{S}$ be an environmentally strictly bounded protocol system. Then, $!\underline{\mathcal{S}}$ is environmentally strictly bounded.*

---

[9]We note that these lemmas do not hold for environmentally almost bounded systems, see [KT13].

3. Preliminaries

In this chapter, we present preliminaries that are used throughout this thesis.

3.1. Notation for the Definition of IITMs

In this section, we describe notational conventions that we use to define IITMs.

3.1.1. Pseudocode

To define IITMs (and algorithms in general), we use standard pseudocode with an obvious semantics.

By $x := y$ we denote deterministic assignment of the variable or constant y to variable x. By $x \leftarrow A$ we denote probabilistic assignment to the variable x according to the distribution of algorithm A. By $x \overset{\$}{\leftarrow} S$ we denote that x is chosen uniformly at random from the finite set S.

All values that are manipulated are bit strings or special symbols such as the error symbol $\bot$.

We only use very basic data structures. For example, we often use tuples and sets (of bit strings). A tuple of bit strings $x_1, \ldots, x_n$ is denoted by $(x_1, \ldots, x_n)$. We assume that tuples have a simple bit string representation and that converting a tuple to its bit string representation and vice versa is efficient. We do not distinguish between a tuple and its bit string representation. We assume an efficient implementation of sets (e.g., by lists) that allows us *(i)* to add a bit string to a set, *(ii)* to remove a bit string from a set, *(iii)* to test if a bit string is an element of a set, and *(iv)* to iterate over all elements of a set. Sometimes we use functions as data structures. Initially, such functions map every bit string to $\bot$. (This function can be interpreted as a partial function with empty input domain.) We consider them as syntactic sugar for sets: A function f represents the set $S_f = \{(x, y) \mid f(x) = y \neq \bot\}$. The term $f(x)$ evaluates to y if $(x, y) \in S_f$ for some y and to $\bot$ otherwise. By $f(x) := y$ we denote that S_f is updated: $(x, f(x))$ is removed from S_f (if $f(x) \neq \bot$) and (x, y) is added to S_f.

3.1.2. Parts of IITMs

Most of our definitions of IITMs are divided into six parts (where some are optional): *Parameters, Tapes, State, CheckAddress, Initialization,* and *Compute*.

Parameters. In this part, we list all parameters of the IITM. That is, when defining a system that contains this IITM, these parameters have to be instantiated. This part is omitted if the IITM has no parameters.

For example, our ideal functionalities are typically parameterized by a number $n > 0$ that defines the I/O interface (more precisely the number of I/O tape pairs, see below).

Tapes. This part lists all input and output tapes. Unless otherwise stated, I/O tapes are named io_x^y and network tapes are named net_x^y for some decorations x, y. The IITMs we define in this thesis have a corresponding output tape for every input tape. The intuition is that, upon receiving a message on some input tape, the response is sent on the corresponding output tape. Furthermore, we typically give a name (this name is independent of the tape names) to every such pair of input and output tapes: We write "from/to z: (c, c')" to denote that the pair of tapes (c, c') is named z. Then, we refer to the input tape c by "from z" and to the output tape c' by "to z". We use the generic names IO and NET to refer to general I/O and network tapes where an environment or adversary/simulator, respectively, connects to that is not otherwise specified. If the tapes connect to a known machine/system, we typically use the name of this machine/system.

For example, the ideal public-key encryption functionality $\mathcal{F}_{\mathrm{pke}}$ (see Section 4.2.1) has the I/O input tapes $\mathsf{io}_{\mathrm{pke}_r}^{\mathrm{in}}$ (for all $r \leq n$ where the number n is a parameter of $\mathcal{F}_{\mathrm{pke}}$) and the network input tape $\mathsf{net}_{\mathcal{F}_{\mathrm{pke}}}^{\mathrm{in}}$ and the corresponding output tapes $\mathsf{io}_{\mathrm{pke}_r}^{\mathrm{out}}$ and $\mathsf{net}_{\mathcal{F}_{\mathrm{pke}}}^{\mathrm{out}}$. We give the name IO_r to the pair $(\mathsf{io}_{\mathrm{pke}_r}^{\mathrm{in}}, \mathsf{io}_{\mathrm{pke}_r}^{\mathrm{out}})$ and the name NET to $(\mathsf{net}_{\mathcal{F}_{\mathrm{pke}}}^{\mathrm{in}}, \mathsf{net}_{\mathcal{F}_{\mathrm{pke}}}^{\mathrm{out}})$. So, "from IO_r" refers to the tape $\mathsf{io}_{\mathrm{pke}_r}^{\mathrm{in}}$, "to NET" refers to $\mathsf{net}_{\mathcal{F}_{\mathrm{pke}}}^{\mathrm{out}}$, etc. A machine M that uses $\mathcal{F}_{\mathrm{pke}}$ (i.e., connects to the I/O interfaced of $\mathcal{F}_{\mathrm{pke}}$) would have the input tape $\mathsf{io}_{\mathrm{pke}_r}^{\mathrm{out}}$ (for some $r \leq n$) and the corresponding output tape $\mathsf{io}_{\mathrm{pke}_r}^{\mathrm{in}}$ and the pair $(\mathsf{io}_{\mathrm{pke}_r}^{\mathrm{out}}, \mathsf{io}_{\mathrm{pke}_r}^{\mathrm{in}})$ would get the name $\mathcal{F}_{\mathrm{pke}}$. So, in M, by "to $\mathcal{F}_{\mathrm{pke}}$" we refer to $\mathsf{io}_{\mathrm{pke}_r}^{\mathrm{in}}$ and by "from $\mathcal{F}_{\mathrm{pke}}$" we refer to $\mathsf{io}_{\mathrm{pke}_r}^{\mathrm{out}}$. See Section 4.4 for an example protocol.

State. Here, we list all state variables of the machine. These are variables that define the state of this copy of the IITM and are saved on its work tapes (i.e., they are local to the copy of the IITM and cannot be accessed by other copies). These state variables are set to some initial value when a copy of this machine is created. Typically, the initial value is $\bot$ (undefined) for bit strings and tuples of bit strings and the empty set $\emptyset$ for sets. In mode Compute, the machine may modify the values of these variables. We always use sans-serif font for state variables.

For example, many machines that we define in this thesis have a state variable $\mathsf{corr} \in \{0, 1\}$ which holds the corruption status of (this copy of) the machine.

CheckAddress. In this part, we define the mode CheckAddress of the machine.

Initialization. This part is optional. If it exists and (this copy of) the machine is activated for the first time in mode Compute, then the machine executes the code in this part. When the code finishes, the machine then processes the incoming message as defined in the part *Compute*, see below.

Initialization is used for example to tell the adversary (or simulator) that a new copy of this machine has been created and to allow her to corrupt this copy of the machine right from the start.

Compute. The description in mode Compute, consists of a sequence of blocks where every block is of the form "**recv** m_t **on** c **s.t.** $\langle condition \rangle$: $\langle code \rangle$" where m_t is an input template (see below), c is an input tape (see above), $\langle condition \rangle$ is a condition on the input, and $\langle code \rangle$ is the code of this block, that is executed if the input template matches and the condition is satisfied (see below).

An *input template* is recursively defined as follows: It is either an unbound variable, a constant bit string, a state variable (see above), or a tuple of input templates. We say that a bit string m *matches* an input template m_t if there exists a mapping σ from the unbound variables in m_t to bit strings such that m equals m_t' where m_t' is obtained from m_t by replacing every unbound variable x in m_t by the bit string $\sigma(x)$ and every state variable x in m_t by the value of the state variable (according to the state of the machine). We say that σ is the *matcher* of m and m_t. To distinguish unbound variables from constant bit strings and state variables, we use sans-serif font for constant bit strings and state variables and *cursive font* for unbound variables. For example, the input template (Enc, x) is matched by every tuple that consists of the constant bit string Enc and an arbitrary bit string.

Upon activation, the blocks are checked one after the other. The (copy of the) machine executes the code of the first block that matches the input (see below). If no block matches the input, the machine stops for this activation without producing output. In the next activation, the machine will again go through the sequence of blocks, starting with the first one, and so on.

A block, as above, *matches some input*, say message m on input tape c', if $c = c'$, m matches m_t (as defined above), and $\langle condition \rangle$ is satisfied. The condition may use state variables of the machine and the unbound variables contained in m_t (these are instantiated by the matcher σ of m and m_t). Similarly, when executing the code, the unbound variables contained in m_t are instantiated by the matcher σ of m and m_t.

Every execution of code ends with a send command: **send** m **to** c, where m is a bit string and c is an output tape. This means that the machine outputs the message m on tape c and stops for this activation. In the next activation the machine will not proceed at the point where it stopped, but again go through the sequence of blocks, starting with the first one, as explained above. However, if the send command is followed directly by a receive command, such as **send** m **on** c; **recv** m_t **on** c' **s.t.** $\langle condition \rangle$ (where m_t is an input template, c' an input tape, and $\langle condition \rangle$ a condition, as above), then the machine does the following: It outputs m on tape c

and stops for this activation. In the next activation, it will check whether it received a message on input tape c' and check whether this message matches m_t and the condition is satisfied (as above). If it does, the computation continues at this point in the code. Otherwise, the machine stops for this activation without producing output. In the next activation, it will again check whether it received a message on input tape c' and whether this message matches m_t and the condition is satisfied and behaves as before, and so on, until it receives an expected message.

For named pairs of input and output tapes, as described above in the *Tapes* part, we use the following notation: Let z be the name of the pair (c, c') of an input tape c and an output tape c'. Then, we write "**recv** m_t **from** z **s.t.** $\langle condition \rangle$" for "**recv** m_t **on** c **s.t.** $\langle condition \rangle$" and "**send** m **to** z" for "**send** m **on** c'".

3.1.3. Running External Code

Sometimes, an IITM M obtains the description of an algorithm A as input on some tape and has to execute it (e.g., most of our ideal functionalities for cryptographic primitives receive algorithms from the adversary/simulator). We write $y \leftarrow A^{(p)}(x)$, where p is a polynomial, to say that M simulates algorithm A on input x for $p(\eta + |x|)$ steps, where η is the security parameter and $|x|$ the length of x. The random coins that might be used by A are chosen by M uniformly at random. The variable y is set to the output of A if A terminates after at most $p(\eta + |x|)$ steps. Otherwise, y is set to the error symbol $\perp$. If we want to enforce that M simulates A in a deterministic way, we write $y := A^{(p)}(x)$. In the simulation of A, M sets the random coins of A to zero.

Typically, we are interested in environmentally bounded systems. If such a system contains an IITM M that executes external code A (e.g., A is provided by the adversary or simulator), then M is only allowed to perform a polynomial number of steps for executing the algorithm A (except with negligible probability). So, M has to be parameterized by a polynomial p and simulates A as described above. We note that at least the degree of the polynomial that bounds the runtime of the algorithm has to be fixed in advance because it must not depend on the security parameter. This holds true for any definition of polynomial time and is not a limitation of the definition of polynomial time in the IITM model.

3.2. Standard Security Notions for Cryptographic Primitives

In this section, we recall standard security notions for cryptographic schemes. They will be used to realize the ideal functionalities for cryptographic primitives that we present in this thesis.

Traditionally, security notions for cryptographic primitives are defined with respect to adversaries that do not obtain external input, except for the security parameter.

Universal composability frameworks such as the UC model [Can05] or the IITM model deal with environments that receive external input (and where the runtime of the environment might depend on the security parameter and the length of the external input). In order to realize ideal functionalities for cryptographic primitives, reduction proofs to the security of the underlying primitives are necessary, and hence, the notions have to be compatible. We chose to adapt the standard notions of security, i.e., we formulate them with respect to adversaries that receive external input. We note, however, that all our results carry over to the setting without external input, i.e., where all environments and adversaries do not receive external input (except for the security parameter).

To define the security notions, as usual in cryptographic literature, we use the following notation: By

$$\Pr\left[y \leftarrow A(x) : B\right]$$

we denote the probability of an event B where the probability distribution is given by a probabilistic algorithm A with input x: y is a random variable that is distributed according to the probability distribution induced by A. This notion is extended naturally to allow for a sequence of algorithms $A_1, \ldots, A_n$ instead of A. For example, given algorithms gen, enc, and A; a security parameter $\eta \in \mathbb{N}$; and a bit string x, the probability that A on input y outputs 1 where (the probability distribution of) y is obtained from running gen on input 1^η (to obtain k) and then running enc on input k and x is denoted by

$$\Pr\left[k \leftarrow \mathsf{gen}(1^\eta); y \leftarrow \mathsf{enc}(k, x) : A(y) = 1\right] \ .$$

Furthermore, we use the notion of negligible functions as used in the IITM model (Definition 2.1).

3.2.1. Symmetric Encryption

In this section, following [BN00], we recall standard notions for symmetric encryption schemes.

Definition 3.1. *A symmetric encryption scheme $\Sigma = (\mathsf{gen}, \mathsf{enc}, \mathsf{dec})$ consists of three polynomial-time algorithms. The probabilistic key generation algorithm gen expects a security parameter (in unary form) and returns a key. The probabilistic encryption algorithm enc expects a key and a plaintext and returns a ciphertext. The deterministic decryption algorithm dec expects a key and a ciphertext and returns a plaintext if decryption succeeds. Otherwise, it returns the special error symbol $\bot$.*

It is required that, for every security parameter η, key k generated by $\mathsf{gen}(1^\eta)$, plaintext x, and ciphertext y generated by $\mathsf{enc}(k, x)$, it holds that $\mathsf{dec}(k, y) = x$.

In this thesis, we only consider stateless encryption schemes but this could be extended easily. Also, we do not restrict the domain of plaintexts, i.e., any bit string is a valid plaintext. Our results could easily be extended to deal with other domains.

To define security notions for symmetric encryption, we first define a left-right choice function LR. For every $b \in \{0, 1\}$ and $x_0, x_1 \in \{0, 1\}^*$: $\mathrm{LR}(x_0, x_1, b) := x_b$ if $|x_0| = |x_1|$. Otherwise, $\mathrm{LR}(x_0, x_1, b) := \bot$.

Definition 3.2 (IND-CPA security). *A symmetric encryption scheme Σ is called IND-CPA secure (indistinguishability of encryptions under adaptive chosen-plaintext attacks) if for every probabilistic, polynomial-time algorithm $A^{O(\cdot,\cdot)}$ with access to an oracle O, the IND-CPA advantage of A with respect to Σ*

$$\mathrm{adv}_{A,\Sigma}^{\mathrm{ind\text{-}cpa}}(1^\eta, a) := \left| \Pr\left[k \leftarrow \mathsf{gen}(1^\eta) : A^{\mathsf{enc}(k, \mathrm{LR}(\cdot, \cdot, 1))}(1^\eta, a) = 1 \right] \right.$$
$$\left. - \Pr\left[k \leftarrow \mathsf{gen}(1^\eta) : A^{\mathsf{enc}(k, \mathrm{LR}(\cdot, \cdot, 0))}(1^\eta, a) = 1 \right] \right|$$

is negligible (as a function in 1^η and a).

Definition 3.3 (IND-CCA2 security). *A symmetric encryption scheme Σ is called IND-CCA2 secure (indistinguishability of encryptions under adaptive chosen-ciphertext attacks) if for every probabilistic, polynomial-time algorithm $A^{O_1(\cdot,\cdot), O_2(\cdot)}$ with access to two oracles O_1, O_2 which never queries O_2 with a bit string returned by O_1, the IND-CCA2 advantage of A with respect to Σ*

$$\mathrm{adv}_{A,\Sigma}^{\mathrm{ind\text{-}cca2}}(1^\eta, a) := \left| \Pr\left[k \leftarrow \mathsf{gen}(1^\eta) : A^{\mathsf{enc}(k, \mathrm{LR}(\cdot, \cdot, 1)), \mathsf{dec}(k, \cdot)}(1^\eta, a) = 1 \right] \right.$$
$$\left. - \Pr\left[k \leftarrow \mathsf{gen}(1^\eta) : A^{\mathsf{enc}(k, \mathrm{LR}(\cdot, \cdot, 0)), \mathsf{dec}(k, \cdot)}(1^\eta, a) = 1 \right] \right|$$

is negligible (as a function in 1^η and a).

We note that the above notion IND-CCA2 is called IND-CCA in [BN00].

Definition 3.4 (INT-CTXT secure). *A symmetric encryption scheme Σ is called INT-CTXT secure if for every probabilistic, polynomial-time algorithm $A^{O_1(\cdot), O_2(\cdot)}$ with access to two oracles O_1, O_2, the INT-CTXT advantage of A with respect to Σ*

$$\mathrm{adv}_{A,\Sigma}^{\mathrm{int\text{-}ctxt}}(1^\eta, a) := \Pr[k \leftarrow \mathsf{gen}(1^\eta) : A^{\mathsf{enc}(k, \cdot), \mathsf{dec}(k, \cdot)}(1^\eta, a) \text{ queries } \mathsf{dec}(k, \cdot) \text{ with } y$$
$$\text{such that } \mathsf{dec}(k, y) \neq \bot \text{ and } y \text{ was not previously returned by } \mathsf{enc}(k, \cdot)]$$

is negligible (as a function in 1^η and a).

3.2.2. Public-Key Encryption

In this section, following [BDPR98], we recall standard notions for public-key encryption schemes.

Definition 3.5. *A public-key encryption scheme $\Sigma = (\mathsf{gen}, \mathsf{enc}, \mathsf{dec})$ consists of three polynomial-time algorithms. The probabilistic key generation algorithm gen expects a* security parameter (in unary form) and returns a pair of keys (pk, sk), the public key pk and the private key sk. The probabilistic encryption algorithm enc expects a public key and a plaintext and returns a ciphertext. The deterministic decryption algorithm dec expects a private key and a ciphertext and returns a plaintext if decryption succeeds. Otherwise, it returns the special error symbol $\perp$.

It is required that, for every security parameter η, public/private key pair (pk, sk) generated by $\mathsf{gen}(1^\eta)$, plaintext x, and ciphertext y generated by $\mathsf{enc}(pk, x)$, it holds that $\mathsf{dec}(sk, y) = x$.

As for symmetric encryption schemes, we note that we only consider stateless encryption schemes and that we do not restrict the domain of plaintexts. However, our results could easily be extended to take such stipulations into account.

Recall the left-right choice function LR from above. That is, for every $b \in \{0, 1\}$ and $x_0, x_1 \in \{0, 1\}^*$: $\mathrm{LR}(x_0, x_1, b) = x_b$ if $|x_0| = |x_1|$. Otherwise, $\mathrm{LR}(x_0, x_1, b) = \perp$.

Definition 3.6 (IND-CCA2 security). *A public-key encryption scheme Σ is called IND-CCA2 secure (indistinguishability of encryptions under adaptive chosen-ciphertext attacks) if for every probabilistic, polynomial-time algorithm $A^{O_1(\cdot, \cdot), O_2(\cdot)}$ with access to two oracles O_1, O_2 which never queries O_2 with a bit string returned by O_1, the IND-CCA2 advantage of A with respect to Σ*

$$
\mathrm{adv}_{A,\Sigma}^{\text{ind-cca2}}(1^\eta, a)
$$
$$
:= \left| \Pr\left[(pk, sk) \leftarrow \mathsf{gen}(1^\eta) : A^{\mathsf{enc}(pk, \mathrm{LR}(\cdot, \cdot, 1)), \mathsf{dec}(sk, \cdot)}(1^\eta, a, pk) = 1 \right] \right.
$$
$$
\left. - \Pr\left[(pk, sk) \leftarrow \mathsf{gen}(1^\eta) : A^{\mathsf{enc}(pk, \mathrm{LR}(\cdot, \cdot, 0)), \mathsf{dec}(sk, \cdot)}(1^\eta, a, pk) = 1 \right] \right|
$$

is negligible (as a function in 1^η and a).

We note that this notion is called IND-CCA-SE in the taxonomy of [BHK09].

3.2.3. Digital Signatures

In this section, following [GMR88], we recall standard notions for digital signature schemes.

Definition 3.7. *A (digital) signature scheme $\Sigma = (\mathsf{gen}, \mathsf{sig}, \mathsf{ver})$ consists of three polynomial-time algorithms. The probabilistic key generation algorithm gen expects a security parameter (in unary form) and returns a pair of keys (pk, sk), the public key pk and the private key sk. The (possibly) probabilistic signing algorithm sig expects a private key and a message and returns a signature. The deterministic verification algorithm ver expects a public key, a message, and a signature and returns 1 (verification succeeds) or 0 (verification fails).*

It is required that, for every security parameter η, public/private key pair (pk, sk) generated by $\mathsf{gen}(1^\eta)$, message m, and signature σ generated by $\mathsf{sig}(sk, m)$, it holds that $\mathsf{ver}(pk, m, \sigma) = 1$.

As for symmetric and public-key encryption schemes, we note that we only consider stateless signature schemes and that we do not restrict the domain of messages. However, our results could easily be extended to take such stipulations into account.

Definition 3.8 (UF-CMA security). *A* digital signature scheme Σ *is called* existentially unforgeable under adaptive chosen-message attacks (UF-CMA secure) *if for every probabilistic, polynomial-time algorithm* $A^{O(\cdot)}$ *with access to a signing oracle* O, *the* advantage *of* A *with respect to* Σ

$$\mathrm{adv}^{\mathrm{sig}}_{A,\Sigma}(1^\eta, a) := \Pr\left[(pk, sk) \leftarrow \mathsf{gen}(1^\eta); (m, \sigma) \leftarrow A^{\mathsf{sig}(sk,\cdot)}(1^\eta, a, pk) : \right.$$

$$\left. \mathsf{ver}(pk, m, \sigma) = 1 \text{ and } A \text{ has not queried } \mathsf{sig}(sk, \cdot) \text{ with } m\right]$$

is negligible (as a function in 1^η *and* a).

3.2.4. Message Authentication Codes

In this section, following [BKR94, BKR00],[10] we recall standard notions for message authentication codes (MACs).

Definition 3.9. *A* message authentication code (MAC) $\Sigma = (\mathsf{gen}, \mathsf{mac})$ *consists of two polynomial-time algorithms. The probabilistic key generation algorithm* gen *expects a security parameter (in unary form) and returns a key. The deterministic MAC generation algorithm* mac *expects a key and a message and returns a message authentication code (or tag).*

We note that sometimes stateful or probabilistic message authentication schemes are considered (see, e.g., [BGM04] and references therein). The results of this thesis could easily be extended to consider such schemes.

Definition 3.10 (UF-CMA security). *A MAC* Σ *is called* existentially unforgeable under adaptive chosen-message attacks (UF-CMA secure) *if for every probabilistic, polynomial-time algorithm* $A^{O(\cdot)}$ *with access to an oracle* O, *the* UF-CMA advantage *of* A *with respect to* Σ

$$\mathrm{adv}^{\mathrm{uf\text{-}cma}}_{A,\Sigma}(1^\eta, a) = \Pr\left[k \leftarrow \mathsf{gen}(1^\eta); (m, \sigma) \leftarrow A^{\mathsf{mac}(k,\cdot)}(1^\eta, a) : \right.$$

$$\left. \mathsf{mac}(k, m) = \sigma \text{ and } A \text{ has not queried } \mathsf{mac}(k, \cdot) \text{ with } m\right]$$

is negligible (as a function in 1^η *and* a).

---

[10]We note that UF-CMA security for MACs has first been defined in [BKR94], based on the security notion for digital signatures from [GMR88].

3.2.5. Pseudorandom Functions

Variable-length output pseudorandom functions are extensions of regular pseudo-random functions (PRFs). They take an additional length parameter and output a pseudorandom bit string of that length. They are usually built using regular PRFs and output extension (see, e.g., [Kra10] and the references therein). Formally, they are defined as follows.

Definition 3.11. *A* variable-length output pseudorandom function (VLO-PRF) *is polynomial-time computable function* PRF^* *that takes as input a key (of some length $l(\eta)$ that might depend on the security parameter η), a bit string x (as salt), and a length $l' \in \mathbb{N}$ and outputs a bit string of length l'.*

Following [Kra10], we define security for VLO-PRFs as follows.[11]

Definition 3.12. *Let* PRF^* *be a VLO-PRF with key length $l(\eta)$ for every security parameter η. We say that* PRF^* *is secure if for every adversary $A = (A_1, A_2)$ that is a pair of probabilistic, polynomial-time algorithms such that:*

1. $A_1^{O(\cdot,\cdot)}$ *expects* $1^\eta, a$ *as input, has access to an oracle O, and produces output of the form $(x^*, 1^{l^*}, st)$ such that O has never been queried with input x^* as the first argument, and*

2. $A_2^{O(\cdot,\cdot)}$ *expects a salt x^*, a state $st \in \{0,1\}^*$, and a bit string $y \in \{0,1\}^*$ as input, has access to an oracle O but never queries O with input x^* as the first argument, and outputs a bit $b' \in \{0,1\}$,*

the following advantage is negligible (as a function in 1^η and a):

$$\text{adv}_{A,\text{PRF}^*}(1^\eta, a) := 2 \cdot \left| \frac{1}{2} - \Pr\left[k \xleftarrow{\$} \{0,1\}^{l(\eta)}; (x^*, 1^{l^*}, st) \leftarrow A_1^{\text{PRF}^*(k,\cdot,\cdot)}(1^\eta, a); \right.\right.$$

$$y_0 \xleftarrow{\$} \{0,1\}^{l^*}; y_1 := \text{PRF}^*(k, x^*, l^*); b \xleftarrow{\$} \{0,1\};$$

$$\left.\left. b' \leftarrow A_2^{\text{PRF}^*(k,\cdot,\cdot)}(x^*, st, y_b) : b = b' \right] \right| .$$

3.3. Leakage Algorithms

In this section, we introduce leakage algorithms that are used by our ideal function-alities for public-key and symmetric encryption. In these functionalities, instead of the actual plaintexts, their *leakages* are encrypted. These leakages are computed by leakage algorithms and capture the amount of information that may at most be leaked about the plaintexts.

---

[11] We note that Krawczyk [Kra10] defines security for VLO-PRFs in the concrete (or exact) security setting. We adapt Krawczyk's definition in a straightforward way to the asymptotic setting.

Definition 3.13. A leakage algorithm L *is a probabilistic, polynomial-time algorithm which takes as input a security parameter (in unary form) and a message* $x \in \{0,1\}^*$ *and returns a bit string that represents the information that may be leaked about* x.

Example 3.1. Typical examples of leakage algorithms are *(i)* $L(1^\eta, x) = 0^{|x|}$ and *(ii)* the algorithm that returns a random bit string of length $|x|$. They both leak exactly the length of a message.

We sometimes require leakage algorithms to have the following properties.

Leakage algorithms are length preserving if the leakage has the same length as the message:

Definition 3.14. *We call a leakage algorithm* L length preserving *if it holds that* $\Pr\left[|L(1^\eta, x)| = |x|\right] = 1$ *(the probability is over the random coins of* L*) for all* $\eta \in \mathbb{N}$ *and* $x \in \{0,1\}^*$.

Leakage algorithms *leak at most the length (of a message)* if the leakage of a message does not reveal any information about the actual bits of the message. Formally, this is defined as follows:

Definition 3.15. *We say that a leakage algorithm* L leaks at most the length (of a message) *if there exists a probabilistic, polynomial-time algorithm* T *such that the probability distribution of* $T(1^\eta, 1^{|x|})$ *equals the probability distribution of* $L(1^\eta, x)$, *i.e.,* $\Pr[T(1^\eta, 1^{|x|}) = \overline{x}] = \Pr[L(1^\eta, x) = \overline{x}]$ *for all* $\overline{x} \in \{0,1\}^*$ *(the probability is over the random coins of* T *and* L*, respectively), for all* $\eta \in \mathbb{N}$ *and* $x \in \{0,1\}^*$.

Definition 3.16. *We say that a leakage algorithm* L leaks exactly the length (of a message) *if it is length preserving and leaks at most the length.*

Leakage algorithms have *high entropy* if collisions of the leakage occur only with negligible probability. For length preserving leakage algorithms, of course, this cannot be guaranteed for "short" messages. Therefore, in the following definition, we only require that collisions are rare for a certain domain of messages (e.g., messages that have length at least η).

Definition 3.17. *We say that a leakage algorithm* L has high entropy w.r.t. a domain *of messages* $D = \{D(\eta)\}_{\eta \in \mathbb{N}}$ *if it holds that the probability of collisions*

$$\Pr\left[\overline{x} \leftarrow L(1^\eta, x), \overline{x}' \leftarrow L(1^\eta, x') : \overline{x} = \overline{x}' \wedge x, x' \in D(\eta)\right]$$

(the probability is over the random coins of L*) is negligible (as a function in* η*) for all* $x, x' \in \{0,1\}^*$.

Example 3.2. Both leakage algorithms from Example 3.1 are length preserving and leak at most the length, i.e., they leak exactly the length. Moreover, the second leakage algorithm has high entropy w.r.t. the domain of "long" messages:

$D(\eta) := \{x \in \{0,1\}^* \mid |x| \geq \eta\}$.[12] We note that deterministic leakage algorithms (e.g., the first leakage algorithm from Example 3.1) do not have high entropy w.r.t. to any non-empty domain.

Usefulness of leakage algorithms with high entropy. Leakage algorithms with high entropy are sometimes useful when reasoning about protocols. In the following, we describe why. As mentioned above, leakage algorithms are used in our ideal (public-key and symmetric) encryption functionalities: Instead of the actual plaintexts, their leakages are encrypted.

Let enc and dec be arbitrary algorithms that both take as input a bit string. The algorithm enc may be probabilistic but dec must be deterministic. (The intuition is that enc is an encryption algorithm and dec is a decryption algorithm where the public/private or symmetric key is already part of the algorithms.) Now, let $\bar{x} \leftarrow L(1^\eta, x)$ be the leakage of a "plaintext" x, $y \leftarrow \text{enc}(\bar{x})$ be the "encryption" of the leakage $\bar{x}$, and $\bar{x}' := \text{dec}(y)$ be the "decryption" of the "ciphertext" y. If the "decryption" of the "ciphertext" yields the leakage again (i.e., $\bar{x}' = \bar{x}$, a property satisfied by all encryption schemes), then it is guaranteed that the "ciphertext" y contains not only at most the information of the leakage $\bar{x}$ but exactly the information of $\bar{x}$. In particular, it contains all the randomness introduced by the leakage algorithm. If the leakage algorithm L has high entropy w.r.t. a domain that contains x, then y is sufficiently random. Just like a nonce, the probability that y collides with any set of polynomially many bit strings is negligible (in the security parameter). Also, an adversary cannot "guess" y (without given any information about y).

For example, these properties can be useful when reasoning about protocols that use nested encryption. One might be able to argue that the adversary cannot guess (except with negligible probability) a ciphertext that is hidden inside another encryption. This kind of reasoning is, for example, used in our computational soundness result for symmetric encryption in Chapter 6 to prove a mapping lemma from concrete to symbolic traces (Lemma 6.4). Furthermore, these properties can be used to show that collisions among ciphertexts occur only with negligible probability. This argument is, for example, used in our computational soundness result in Chapter 6 (Lemma 6.1) and to prove our joint state composition theorem that does not rely on pre-established SIDs in Section 7.6 (Lemma D.2 in the appendix).

---

[12]The probability of collisions of leakages is $1/2^l$ for messages that have the same length l and 0 if they have different lengths. That is, the probability in Definition 3.17 is at most $1/2^\eta$.

4. Modular Protocol Analysis in the IITM Model

In this chapter, we provide a profound introduction to how we use the IITM model in this thesis to model (multi-party) cryptographic protocols, including the addressing of multiple sessions as well as the modeling of subprotocols and corruption.[13] In Chapter 7, we will deviate from this modeling. Nevertheless, many aspects of the modeling described here are still relevant in that chapter and provide the reader with a good background.

A general description of our modeling of protocols is provided in Section 4.1. Therein, we also explain how such protocols can be analyzed in a modular way using universal and joint state composition theorems. An important role in universal composability frameworks (such as the IITM model) play ideal functionalities. Therefore, we define ideal functionalities for common cryptographic primitives (Section 4.2) and protocol tasks (Section 4.3). To illustrate our approach, we model and analyze a simple example protocol in Section 4.4.

We note that, for the protocol tasks, we focus on key exchange and secure channel protocols but the general ideas apply to all kind of cryptographic protocols. We further note that most of the ideal functionalities we present here are closely related to previous work. The only new ideal functionalities that we present are the ones for the primitives symmetric encryption, message authentication codes (MACs), and key derivation and the one for the protocol task key usability. The functionalities for symmetric encryption and MACs are straightforward adaptions of functionalities for public-key encryption and digital signatures, respectively, from the literature. Although the functionalities for symmetric key primitives (symmetric encryption, MAC, and key derivation) can be useful for protocol analysis (see, e.g., Section 4.4), they are only applicable to a very limited class of protocols. Therefore, for us, their main purpose is to use them in the definition of key usability functionalities (see Section 4.3.2) and to establish a basis for Chapter 5, where we combine (variants of) these functionalities to obtain an ideal crypto functionality for several cryptographic primitives.

---

[13]Since the IITM model is a very flexible and expressive model, it allows us to model protocols in various ways; depending on the kind of setting, other approaches might be favorable.

4.1. Modeling Protocols

A protocol with n roles can be modeled in the IITM model as the following protocol
system:

$$\mathcal{P} := !M_1 \mid \cdots \mid !M_n \tag{4.1}$$

where M_i, for $i \in \{1, \ldots, n\}$, is an IITM which models the i-th role. Every machine
is in the scope of a bang operator to model multiple sessions of the protocol (see
below). Moreover, every machine M_i has I/O and network tapes. The network tapes
are used to communicate with other machines over the (untrusted) network. As
usual, the network is controlled by the adversary, and hence, all messages sent on
a network tape go directly to the adversary and all message received on a network
tape come from the adversary. Network tapes are also used to model corruption
(see below). The I/O tapes are not controlled by the adversary. They are used by
a machine M_i to communicate with the environment, such as (honest) users of the
protocol or higher-level protocols. For example, if $\mathcal{P}$ is a key exchange protocol, then
an I/O tape would be used to output a successfully established session key (to some
user or, for example, to an instance of a secure channel protocol). Potentially, the
I/O tapes can also be used by a machine M_i to communicate with other roles directly,
rather than through the adversary or environment. In this case, M_i would directly
be connected with another machine, say M_j, via I/O tapes. However, this would
constitute an ideal channel of communication between two parties, which would
typically be modeled as an ideal functionality serving as an (ideal) subprotocol of
$\mathcal{P}$ (see below). Nevertheless, the IITM model is flexible enough to model such ideal
channels.

4.1.1. Addressing of Multiple Sessions

Due to the general concept of the mode CheckAddress there are many possible ways
of how multiple sessions of a protocol can be addressed. We now describe one such
approach, which is based on globally unique session identifiers (SIDs); we refer the
reader to Chapter 7 for an addressing mechanism with *locally* chosen and managed
SIDs.

To address multiple instances of a machine (role) M_i, and hence, multiple sessions
of $\mathcal{P}$, by using (global) SIDs, M_i can be defined as follows: In mode CheckAddress,
the machine M_i accepts an incoming message only if it is of the form (sid, m) for
some SID sid and some message m. In mode Compute the machine M_i records
the SID in the first accepted message. Later it will only accept messages in mode
CheckAddress which are prefixed with the recorded SID sid. Moreover, in mode
Compute the machine M_i will only output messages that are prefixed by sid.

This guarantees that in a run of $\mathcal{P}$ (with some environment) there is at most one
copy of every M_i for every SID sid; we denote such a copy by $M_i[sid]$ and say that
this copy is *addressed by* sid. The instances $M_1[sid], \ldots, M_n[sid]$ (or a subset thereof
if not all instances are present in a run) form a session of the protocol $\mathcal{P}$, the *session*

with SID sid. We say that $M_i[sid]$ *belongs to session sid.* Note that all instances within one session share the same SID. This SID is globally unique, is given to an instance from outside the protocol, and is pre-established by the parties participating in one session, in the sense that the SID is established before the actual protocol starts to run.

We note that, with the notion from Section 2.4, $\mathcal{P}$ is an σ_{prefix}-session version.[14] In particular, the composition theorems can be applied, and hence, it suffices to reason about $\mathcal{P}$ in a single-session setting (see below). Note that, by modeling M_i to be an σ_{prefix}-session version, an instance $M_i[sid]$ of M_i addressed by *sid* may be aware of its SID *sid*, i.e., it can use *sid* in its computation, and for example, include it in messages to be signed/encrypted. If this is not necessary, one could model M_i as a session version of some IITM M_i', i.e., $M_i = \overline{M_i'}$ (see Section 2.4). In this case, M_i would be completely oblivious to its SID.

Typically, an SID is structured and contains, in addition to the actual SID, the names of the parties involved in the session. For example, to model that in one session s the i-th role is played by party pid_i the SID would be of the form $sid = (sid', pid_1, \ldots, pid_n)$ and a machine M_i would be defined in such a way that an instance $M_i[sid]$ would run the i-th role as party pid_i. (Clearly, this can be generalized to let several parties run one role in one session of the protocol.)

4.1.2. Security Proofs Using Composition Theorems

In universal composability frameworks, security of a protocol $\mathcal{P}$, as modeled above, typically means that it realizes some appropriate ideal protocol/functionality $\mathcal{F}$ (e.g., in case of a key exchange protocol, an ideal key exchange functionality), i.e., $\mathcal{P}$ is considered secure (w.r.t. $\mathcal{F}$) if $\mathcal{P} \leq \mathcal{F}$. Of course, one can attempt to prove $\mathcal{P} \leq \mathcal{F}$ directly. But this would require a proof which has to consider multiple concurrent sessions. Using the composition theorems for unbounded self-composition (Theorem 2.2, if the protocol does not depend on the SIDs, i.e., $M_i = \overline{M_i'}$ for some M_i'; or Theorem 2.3 if the protocol depends on the SIDs) simplifies this proof because one has to consider only a single session of the protocol: For example, by Theorem 2.3, except for some (typically simple) checks concerning the runtime of the system, one has to show only that $\mathcal{P} \leq_{\sigma_{\text{prefix}}\text{-single}} \mathcal{F}$ to obtain that $\mathcal{P} \leq \mathcal{F}$. Hence, roughly speaking, it suffices to show that $M_1[sid] \mid \cdots \mid M_n[sid]$ realizes $\mathcal{F}[sid]$ for one session *sid*.

4.1.3. Subprotocols and Ideal Functionalities

Complex protocols can often be/are often structured into a hierarchy of higher- and lower-level protocols. For example, a secure channel protocol might use a key exchange protocol or an authenticated channel as a subprotocol, and cryptographic

---

[14]Recall that, for all messages m and tapes c, $\sigma_{\text{prefix}}(m, c) := sid$ if $m = (sid, m')$ for some sid, m' and $\sigma_{\text{prefix}}(m, c) := \bot$ otherwise.

primitives (such as encryption or digital signatures) could be modeled as subprotocols (see below).

For the sake of the discussion here, let $\mathcal{P}' = !M_1' \mid \cdots \mid !M_n'$ be a subprotocol of $\mathcal{P}$ with the same structure as $\mathcal{P}$ and where the addressing of machines is defined just as for $\mathcal{P}$. Since $\mathcal{P}'$ is supposed to be a subprotocol of $\mathcal{P}$, the machines in $\mathcal{P}'$ typically connect via I/O tapes to the corresponding machines in $\mathcal{P}$, i.e., M_i' and M_i are connected via I/O tapes. By the addressing defined above for $\mathcal{P}$ and $\mathcal{P}'$, every instance $M_i[sid]$ will, via the I/O tapes, only interact with $M_i'[sid]$. Instead of the subprotocol $\mathcal{P}'$, $\mathcal{P}$ might be connected to an ideal protocol (or ideal functionality) $\mathcal{F}'$ that provides the same I/O interface as $\mathcal{P}'$ but provides the functionality of $\mathcal{P}'$ in an ideal way (e.g., an ideal key exchange or an ideal cryptographic primitive).

Structuring a protocol like this again simplifies the proof of security of a (complex) protocol because the subprotocol can be analyzed in separation and then $\mathcal{P}$ can be analyzed based on the ideal protocol as follows: To prove that $\mathcal{P} \mid \mathcal{P}'$ is secure, i.e., $\mathcal{P} \mid \mathcal{P}' \leq \mathcal{F}$ for some ideal protocol/functionality $\mathcal{F}$, it suffice to show that:

$$\mathcal{P}' \leq_{\sigma_{\text{prefix-single}}} \mathcal{F}'$$

for some appropriate ideal protocol/functionality $\mathcal{F}'$ and that:

$$\mathcal{P} \mid \mathcal{F}' \leq_{\sigma_{\text{prefix-single}}} \mathcal{F} .$$

From this, using the composition theorems (Theorems 2.1 and 2.3) and transitivity of $\leq$, it follows that $\mathcal{P} \mid \mathcal{P}' \leq \mathcal{F}$. We note that both proof steps require merely single-session reasoning and that the second proof step is further simplified because the subprotocol/functionality used by $\mathcal{P}$ is idealized.

We note that the IITM model and the composition theorems are flexible enough to deal with much more complex scenarios than the one described above:

1. The reasoning can be iterated: $\mathcal{P}'$ itself could use subprotocols and the composition theorems can be used to simplify the proof of $\mathcal{P}' \leq_{\sigma_{\text{prefix-single}}} \mathcal{F}'$, just as in the case of $\mathcal{P}$ above.

2. $\mathcal{P}$ might use more than just one subprotocol in parallel.

3. $\mathcal{P}$ could use multiple sessions of $\mathcal{P}'$ per session. In this case, the sessions of $\mathcal{P}'$ could, for instance, be addressed by a hierarchical SID (sid, sid', m) where sid is the SID that $\mathcal{P}$ uses and sid' is an extra SID that is used to address the sessions of $\mathcal{P}'$ within a session of $\mathcal{P}$. However, again single-session reasoning would suffice for both $\mathcal{P}$ and $\mathcal{P}'$ to establish security properties for $\mathcal{P}$ (in composition with $\mathcal{P}'$) for multiple sessions.

4. $\mathcal{P}'$ is not restricted to have the same structure as $\mathcal{P}$. For example, $\mathcal{P}'$ could be a two-party/two-role protocol and $\mathcal{P}$ could be an n-party/n-role protocol where every two parties of one session in $\mathcal{P}$ use one session of $\mathcal{P}'$. This way, for example, an n-party key exchange protocol could be build from a two-party key exchange protocol.

4.1.4. Modeling Corruption

In the IITM model, the way corruption is modeled is not fixed and hard-wired into the model but is part of the specification of protocols, with the advantage that *(i)* the IITM model is simple, *(ii)* general theorems proven in the IITM model, such as composition theorems, hold true independently of how corruption is modeled, and *(iii)* corruption can be modeled in a very flexible way.

We now describe one possible way of modeling corruption: The adversary (or environment) who connects to the network interface of a protocol $\mathcal{P}$ may send a special *corrupt* message to a network tape of (some instance of) a machine M_i in $\mathcal{P}$. When M_i receives such a message it considers itself corrupted and outputs its complete configuration to the adversary (clearly other options are conceivable and useful as well, see below). From then on M_i forwards all messages between the I/O and network interface, i.e., the adversary is in full control of the corrupted instance. If $\mathcal{P}$ uses subprotocols/functionalities, as described above, the adversary would also gain access to the I/O interface of the subprotocols because $\mathcal{P}$ also forwards messages from the adversary to the subprotocols and vice versa. This models fully adaptive, active corruption of single instances. We note that, as always in universal composability settings, the distinguishing environment should have the possibility to know which instances are corrupted because, otherwise, a simulator could always corrupt instances in the ideal world and then perfectly simulate the real world, i.e., every protocol system would realize every other protocol system (with the same I/O interface). Therefore, a machine M_i should be defined in such a way that, on the I/O interface, it accepts *corruption status requests* of the form Corr? and answers 1 if it is has been corrupted, i.e., if it has received a *corrupt* message on the network interface before, and 0 otherwise. As a result, an environment can ask whether or not an instance is corrupted.

If $\mathcal{P}$ uses subprotocols/functionalities, then, typically, the corruption status of a machine in $\mathcal{P}$ also depends on the corruption status of the subprotocol. That is, an instance of a machine M_i might consider itself corrupted also if one of its subprotocol instances is corrupted (a fact that M_i itself can check by sending a corruption status request to its subprotocol). Note, however, that even if M_i returns to the environment that it is corrupted (e.g., because some part of the subprotocol is corrupted), then this does not necessarily mean that M_i has to consider itself completely controlled by the adversary. (Clearly, if desired, M_i could be modeled in such a way that in this case it considers itself to be fully controlled by the adversary.)

For example, if M_i models an instance of a key exchange protocol and uses a functionality for public-key encryption, then M_i, if asked whether it is corrupted, would return 1 if it has been corrupted directly or if its public-key functionality has been corrupted (modeling that its public/private key has been corrupted), because in this case it could not provide security guarantees. It makes sense to model M_i in such a way that, even though the public-key functionality that M_i uses is corrupted, it still follows its prescribed protocol: the fact that the private key was stolen by the adversary does not necessarily mean that every instance that uses the key is completely controlled by the adversary. However, if desired, one could also model M_i in such a way that if one of its subprotocols is corrupted, then M_i considers itself controlled by the adversary. This depends on the kind of corruption one would like to consider. Conversely, the adversary could corrupt only M_i but not the public-key functionality that M_i uses, which would model that the private key of M_i is still not known by the adversary (e.g., because it is stored on a smart card), but the process (the instance of M_i) that uses the private key is corrupted.

It should be clear that the way of corruption sketched above allows for a very fine-grained and flexible modeling of corruption, ranging from the corruption of single instances to the corruption of complete parties: The adversary can corrupt every instance of M_i (and subprotocol instances used by this instance) that belong to the party an adversary wants to control. For such a form of corruption, instances would typically check whether one of their subprotocols are corrupted and then consider themselves completely controlled by the adversary as well. If one wants to make sure that if an instance is corrupted, then also all its subinstances are corrupted, an instance could check that if it has been explicitly corrupted by the adversary that then all its subinstances have been corrupted as well (and if this is not the case it could wait until the adversary has explicitly corrupted all subinstances).

So far we did not restrict when corruption can occur, and hence, we modeled adaptive corruption. Clearly, static corruption can be modeled as well: For this, upon its first activation (an instance of a) machine could first ask the adversary whether she wants to corrupt the machine. Subsequent corrupt messages would be ignored by the machine.

While, as introduced above, explicit corruption meant that a machine provides its complete configuration to the adversary, other forms of corruption where a machine gives away, for example, merely its long-term or ephemeral keys are conceivable as well.

4.1.5. Composition with Joint State

The composition theorems for unbounded self-composition allow us to conclude that a protocol is secure in a setting with multiple sessions, given that the protocol is secure in a single-session setting. However, these composition theorems assume that protocol sessions are completely disjoint: there does not exist a joint state between different sessions, i.e., between instances of the M_i's with different SIDs. Such a joint state is, however, often desirable/required. For example, one would like to use the same long-term keys, such as public/private key pairs or shared long-term symmetric keys, in every protocol session. Such long-term keys constitute a joint state between different protocol sessions. Using fresh long-term keys in every session would be completely impractical.

We emphasize that it is, of course, straightforward to model a (practical) protocol in such a way that different instances make use of joint state. In particular, a protocol $\mathcal{P}$ of the form $!M_1 \mid \cdots \mid !M_n$ as introduced above could, for example, be extended by a subprotocol, an ideal functionality $\mathcal{F}$ (or its realization), say, such that in every run all instances of M_i access the same instance of $\mathcal{F}$. The point is that with such a joint state the composition theorems for unbounded self-composition would not be applicable anymore, and hence, the security of such a protocol would have to be proven directly in the multi-session setting.

To be able to analyze protocols that use joint state in a single-session setting and still obtain security in the multi-session setting, Canetti and Rabin [CR03] where the first to propose composition theorems that allow for joint state—so-called joint state composition theorems; see [KT08, KT13] for a discussion of [CR03].

In [CR03], Canetti and Rabin first propose a general joint state theorem (in Canetti's UC model). In [KT08], this theorem was stated in the IITM model and it was shown that, in the IITM model it is a direct consequence of the composition theorem for a constant number of systems (Theorem 2.1). Formulated in the IITM model, the general joint state theorem states that if $\mathcal{P}' \leq \mathcal{F}'$, then $\mathcal{P} \,|\, \mathcal{P}' \leq \mathcal{P} \,|\, \mathcal{F}'$, where $\mathcal{F}'$ models some multi-session version of some ideal functionality and $\mathcal{P}'$ is supposed to be a realization of $\mathcal{F}'$ that utilizes some joint state across the sessions, e.g., $\mathcal{P}'$ uses only a single copy of $\mathcal{F}'$ for all sessions.

The general joint state theorem by itself does not say how a joint state realization looks like. The main challenge is always to find suitable joint state realizations for concrete ideal functionalities. As an example, we consider the joint state realization for public-key encryption, following [KT08] (see also Section 4.2.1 where we restate this result from [KT08]). In [KT08], an ideal functionality $\mathcal{F}_{\mathrm{pke}}$ for public-key encryption is defined; the details of this functionality are not important for this discussion (see Section 4.2.1). This functionality is the "encryption/decryption-box" modeling one public/private key pair (that belongs to some party) and can be used to encrypt and decrypt messages under this key pair. In particular, it encapsulates the key pair, where the private key stays in the functionality (except if the functionality is corrupted) and the public key is given out, and hence, can be distributed. The system $!\mathcal{F}_{\mathrm{pke}}$ describes the *multi-key* version of $\mathcal{F}_{\mathrm{pke}}$ where every instance of $\mathcal{F}_{\mathrm{pke}}$ is addressed by a public/private key name. In every run there is at most one instance $\mathcal{F}_{\mathrm{pke}}[name]$ of $\mathcal{F}_{\mathrm{pke}}$ per public/private key name *name*.[15] For example, *name* is a party name (the name of the party the public/private key encapsulated in $\mathcal{F}_{\mathrm{pke}}[name]$ belongs to) or a party name plus a counter, to model that parties may have multiple public/private keys. The system $!\mathcal{F}_{\mathrm{pke}}$ models the multi-session version of $!\mathcal{F}_{\mathrm{pke}}$, i.e, there may be multiple sessions per key pair and instances of $\mathcal{F}_{\mathrm{pke}}$ are addresses by identifiers of the form $(sid, name)$, denoting the key pair *name* in session *sid*. In [KT08], a joint state realization $!\mathcal{P}_{\mathrm{pke}}^{\mathrm{js}} \,|\, !\mathcal{F}_{\mathrm{pke}}$ is proposed (which is restated in Section 4.2.6), where $\mathcal{P}_{\mathrm{pke}}^{\mathrm{js}}$ is a kind of multiplexer which handles multiple sessions

---

[15]We note that previous work defined $\mathcal{F}_{\mathrm{pke}}$ in the IITM model to only captured a single public/private key. The multi-key version was then described by the system $!\mathcal{F}_{\mathrm{pke}}$ (as defined in Section 2.4).

In this thesis (see Section 4.2.1), we define $\mathcal{F}_{\mathrm{pke}}$ to capture directly the multi-key setting because this makes it less technical to model protocols that use $\mathcal{F}_{\mathrm{pke}}$. Apart from that, there is no difference and both approaches are just as expressive.

per key pair but where encryption and decryption of all sessions of one key pair *name* are handled by the instance $\mathcal{F}_{\text{pke}}[name]$ for that key pair. The basic idea is that SIDs are added to messages to be encrypted. Upon decryption in session *sid*, it is checked whether the decrypted plaintext contains *sid*. By this, it is prevented that ciphertexts created in one session can be used in other sessions. In [KT08] (see also Section 4.2.6), it has been proved that the proposed joint state realization in fact realizes the multi-session version of $!\mathcal{F}_{\text{pke}}$:

$$!\mathcal{P}^{\text{js}}_{\text{pke}} \mid !\mathcal{F}_{\text{pke}} \leq !\mathcal{F}_{\text{pke}} . \tag{4.2}$$

With such a joint state realization it is possible to prove that a protocol $\mathcal{P}$ that uses public-key encryption is secure in a multi-session setting where the same public/private keys are used across all sessions by reasoning about just a single session of $\mathcal{P}$. To illustrate this, let $\mathcal{P}$ be a protocol of the form (4.1) that uses $!\mathcal{P}^{\text{js}}_{\text{pke}} \mid !\mathcal{F}_{\text{pke}}$ for encryption and decryption such that the key pair names are simply the party names of the owners of the key pairs (i.e., every instance of $\mathcal{F}_{\text{pke}}$ is addressed by a party name). Recall that an instance of M_i is addresses by an SID of the form $(sid, pid_1, \dots, pid_n)$. If such an instance wants to encrypt a message m for party pid_j (i.e., under the public key of party pid_j, the party that plays role j in this protocol session), it would send an encryption request containing the message m to $!\mathcal{P}^{\text{js}}_{\text{pke}} \mid !\mathcal{F}_{\text{pke}}$. For addressing purposes, this request also contains the SID $(sid, pid_1, \dots, pid_n)$ and the party name pid_j. Since $\mathcal{P}^{\text{js}}_{\text{pke}}$ adds the SID to the message before encryption, the message $((sid, pid_1, \dots, pid_n), m)$ is encrypted using the instance $\mathcal{F}_{\text{pke}}[pid_j]$.

Now, assume that we want to prove that $\mathcal{P} \mid !\mathcal{P}^{\text{js}}_{\text{pke}} \mid !\mathcal{F}_{\text{pke}}$ realizes $\mathcal{F}$, where $\mathcal{F}$ is some ideal functionality. Then it suffices to show that:

$$\mathcal{P} \mid !\mathcal{F}_{\text{pke}} \leq_{\sigma_{\text{prefix-single}}} \mathcal{F} . \tag{4.3}$$

From this, using the joint state composition theorem for public-key encryption (4.2), the composition theorems (Theorems 2.1 and 2.3), and transitivity of $\leq$, it follows that:

$$\mathcal{P} \mid !\mathcal{P}^{\text{js}}_{\text{pke}} \mid !\mathcal{F}_{\text{pke}} \leq \mathcal{F} . \tag{4.4}$$

Moreover, if $!\mathcal{P}_{\text{pke}}$ is a realization of $!\mathcal{F}_{\text{pke}}$, i.e., $!\mathcal{P}_{\text{pke}} \leq !\mathcal{F}_{\text{pke}}$, basically an IND-CCA2 secure public-key encryption scheme (see Theorem 4.1), we obtain by Theorem 2.1 that:

$$\mathcal{P} \mid !\mathcal{P}^{\text{js}}_{\text{pke}} \mid !\mathcal{P}_{\text{pke}} \leq \mathcal{F} . \tag{4.5}$$

Note that to prove (4.3) only a single session $(sid, pid_1, \dots, pid_n)$ of $\mathcal{P}$ needs to be analyzed. Such a session might contain n instances of $\mathcal{F}_{\text{pke}}$, one for each pid_i. Such an analysis is further simplified due to the use of $\mathcal{F}_{\text{pke}}$, i.e., *ideal* public-key encryption.

Note that in the realization $\mathcal{P} \mid !\mathcal{P}^{\text{js}}_{\text{pke}} \mid !\mathcal{P}_{\text{pke}}$ the SIDs $(sid, pid_1, \dots, pid_n)$ are added to all encrypted messages (this is what $\mathcal{P}^{\text{js}}_{\text{pke}}$ does). While this is a good design principle, existing, in particular real-world protocols, typically do not follow this pattern. Hence, such protocols cannot be analyzed with the joint state theorem sketched above without severely modifying the protocols: adding SIDs to plaintexts is a severe modification of a protocol, which can turn an insecure protocol into a secure one. In order to analyze a protocol without modifying it, one could resort to multi-session analysis, with the disadvantage that the analysis is more complex and one does not make full use of modular analysis. Therefore, in Chapter 7 composition and joint state theorems are proposed which allow for establishing the security of a protocol w.r.t. multiple sessions by analyzing only a single session of the protocol, but without requiring to change the protocol by adding SIDs in messages or in any other way.

Remark 4.1. Canetti et al. [CDPW07] extended Canetti's UC model by a concept called *global setup*, which allows for modeling protocols that use a globally available trusted setup assumption such as a public-key infrastructure (PKI) or a common reference string (CRS). "Globally available" means that everybody, including the attacker and other protocols, has access to the setup assumption. This is in contrast to composition with joint state where not everybody but only the analyzed protocol has access to the joint state. For example, all sessions of the protocol $\mathcal{P}$ described above have access to the same copy of the public-key encryption functionality but no other protocol (or the environment) has (direct) access to this copy of the public-key encryption functionality. Global setup for public-key encryption would mean that everybody has access to the same copy of the public-key encryption functionality (since it is globally available). For public-key encryption this would typically break security of the protocol because everybody (even the attacker) can use it to decrypt all messages. But for other tasks, such as a PKI or a CRS, modeling a global setup functionality can be desirable. If, as described, all components have permanently access to a global setup functionality, the composition theorems need to be adjusted accordingly.

Due to the flexibility of the IITM model, global setup can also be considered in the IITM model in an elegant and simple way, as discussed in [KT13]. Since global setup is not useful in the context of the kind of cryptographic primitives (such as public-key encryption) and protocol tasks that we consider in this thesis, we do not go into detail here and refer to [KT13] instead.

4.2. Ideal Functionalities for Cryptographic Primitives

In this section, we present ideal functionalities for public-key and symmetric encryption, digital signatures, MACs, and key derivation. As explained in Section 4.1, they can be used by protocols to simplify the analysis of the protocol. In the analysis of the protocol, one can use the properties that are syntactically guaranteed by the ideal functionalities instead of doing reduction proofs to the security of the underlying cryptographic primitives. Then, using the composition theorems, one can replace the ideal functionality by its realization to obtain security for the original protocol.

The ideal functionalities for asymmetric cryptographic primitives (i.e., public-key encryption) model public/private key pairs (of some parties). Likewise, the ideal functionalities for symmetric cryptographic primitives (i.e., symmetric encryption, MACs, and key derivation) model symmetric keys (that are shared between the users of the functionality). These functionalities, that we call *long-term key functionalities* because they model long-term keys or key pairs (see below), allow their users (i.e., the users/parties of a protocol that uses these functionalities) to perform the respective cryptographic operations in an ideal way (e.g., ciphertexts are computed independently of the plaintexts and decryption is done by table look-up). We also show that these functionalities capture their respective standard cryptographic security notions (IND-CCA2, authenticated encryption, UF-CMA), i.e., they are realizable by the respective cryptographic scheme if and only if the scheme is secure. Key derivation is realized by pseudorandom functions.

While users of these functionalities, and their realization, obtain the actual public keys (in case of asymmetric primitives), they do not get their hands on the actual private and symmetric keys stored in the functionalities, since otherwise no security guarantees could be provided. For asymmetric primitives this is no real disadvantage because the private key is typically never used except for the cryptographic operations. In particularly, it is typically not sent around and encrypted with other keys. This however means that the functionalities for symmetric primitives are only useful for modeling so-called *long-term* or *pre-shared* keys, keys that are shared between parties before the protocol starts. In particularly, these are not keys that are established in one protocol session and they cannot be sent around and encrypted under other keys. As mentioned in the introduction, in Chapter 5, we present an ideal crypto functionality $\mathcal{F}_{\mathrm{crypto}}$ that overcomes this problem and models symmetric keys that can be part of plaintexts to be encrypted under other symmetric and public keys.

To simplify the analysis of multiple protocol sessions that use the same long-term key (i.e., long-term key functionality) in every session, as explained in Section 4.1.5, we propose joint state realizations for our long-term key functionalities in Section 4.2.6.

Finally, in Section 4.2.7, we introduce a simple ideal functionality for nonces.

We note that all ideal functionalities presented in this section, upon a request from a user (e.g., to encrypt a message), immediately produce output, i.e., the output is computed locally within the functionality without communication with the adversary/simulator. This reflects that these operations are local operations that do not involve interaction and is in line with [Can05, KT08]. As mentioned in [Can05], to obtain realizations by distributed protocol where the adversary may delay the output, the functionalities need to be relaxed appropriately. Functionalities with local computation are sometimes needed in applications, see below.

We further note that all our functionalities can handle an unbounded number of requests with the messages, ciphertexts, MACs, etc. being arbitrary bit strings of arbitrary length. We leave it up to the protocol that uses the functionalities how to interpret (parts of) bit strings, e.g., as length fields, nonces, ciphertexts, MACs, digital signatures, non-interactive zero-knowledge proofs, etc. Since users of all our functionalities are provided with actual bit strings, the functionalities can be combined with other functionalities too, including those of interest for real-word protocols, e.g., certification of public keys (see, e.g., [Can04]).

4.2.1. Public-Key Encryption

Several ideal functionalities for public-key encryption have been proposed in the literature (see, e.g., [Can05, PW01, CH06, KT08]). The ideal public-key encryption functionality $\mathcal{F}_{\text{pke}}$ that we present below is similar to ones proposed in [Can05, KT08] and follows most closely the one in [KT08].

Our ideal functionality $\mathcal{F}_{\text{pke}}$ models public/private key pairs that can be used for (ideal) encryption and decryption. The encryption and decryption algorithms and the key pairs that are used in $\mathcal{F}_{\text{pke}}$ are provided by the adversary (or simulator). To ideally guarantee that ciphertexts do not leak (undesired) information about the plaintexts, the functionality is parameterized by a leakage algorithm (see Section 3.3) that returns the amount of information about a message that may be leaked (e.g., only the length of the message). Then, instead of the actual messages, the leakage of the messages are encrypted. The message/ciphertext pairs are recorded and decryption is done by table look-up. As mentioned above, ciphertexts are determined by local computations, and hence, a priori do not reveal ciphertexts. For example, this might be needed in applications to reason about nested encryption: if a secret message is encrypted under a corrupted key and the ciphertext is then encrypted under an uncorrupted key, the secret message is still not revealed.

In previous works (see, e.g., [Can05, KT08]), it has been shown (for similar ideal functionalities) that a public-key encryption scheme realizes $\mathcal{F}_{\text{pke}}$ (w.r.t. static corruptions) if and only if the scheme is IND-CCA2 secure (Definition 3.6). Of course, this only holds for appropriate leakage algorithms, see below. That is, $\mathcal{F}_{\text{pke}}$ exactly captures the standard security notion IND-CCA2. This also holds for our ideal functionality $\mathcal{F}_{\text{pke}}$. Moreover, it is shown in [KT08] that there is a joint state realization of $\mathcal{F}_{\text{pke}}$ (in Section 4.2.6 we restate this result for our version of $\mathcal{F}_{\text{pke}}$). This distinguishes our version of $\mathcal{F}_{\text{pke}}$ and the one in [KT08] from other functionalities for public-key encryption, see [KT08].

The Ideal Public-Key Encryption Functionality $\mathcal{F}_{\text{pke}}$

The ideal functionality $\mathcal{F}_{\text{pke}}$ is a single IITM with n I/O input tapes and n I/O output tapes (n is a parameter of $\mathcal{F}_{\text{pke}}$). These I/O tapes allow (machines of) a protocol to send encryption and decryption requests to $\mathcal{F}_{\text{pke}}$ (and to receive the responses).[16] Furthermore, $\mathcal{F}_{\text{pke}}$ has one network input and one network output tape to communicate with the adversary/simulator. In mode CheckAddress, $\mathcal{F}_{\text{pke}}$

---

[16]For example, these tapes can be used by a protocol of the form $\mathcal{P} = !M_1 | \cdots | !M_n$, as described in Section 4.1, that uses $\mathcal{F}_{\text{pke}}$ (i.e., connects to its I/O interface) such that machine M_i connects to the i-th I/O input and output tape of $\mathcal{F}_{\text{pke}}$. We note that these tapes are only for addressing purposes, to allow n different machines to connect to $\mathcal{F}_{\text{pke}}$; $\mathcal{F}_{\text{pke}}$ does not interpret input on

is defined such that it accepts only messages of the form $(id, name, m)$ on the I/O tapes and messages of the form $(name, m)$ on the network tape, where the identifier (ID) id, the key pair name $name$, and the message m are arbitrary bit strings; m is the actual request and id and $name$ are used for addressing. The key pair name serves like an SID for $\mathcal{F}_{pke}$: Upon the first activation with some message of this form, (an instance of) $\mathcal{F}_{pke}$ records the key pair name $name$ and from then on only accepts messages with this key pair name. That is, in a run of $!\mathcal{F}_{pke}$ (with some protocol/environment), multiple instances of $\mathcal{F}_{pke}$ can be addressed by different key pair names. We denote the instance of $\mathcal{F}_{pke}$ that is addressed by $name$ by $\mathcal{F}_{pke}[name]$. Every instance of $\mathcal{F}_{pke}$ models a single public/private key pair (of some party). For example, the name to address instances of $\mathcal{F}_{pke}$ can be a party's name and, then, $\mathcal{F}_{pke}[pid]$ models the key pair of party (with name/identifier) pid. The ID id that is included in every message sent on an I/O tape is useful for addressing the response to the (instance of the) machine that sent the request. Whenever $\mathcal{F}_{pke}$ receives a request, i.e., a message of the form $(id, name, m)$, it returns a response of the form $(id, name, m')$. This allows multiple machines that are addressed by IDs (e.g., for protocols as described in Section 4.1 this ID is the SID of the machines in a protocol) to send requests to $\mathcal{F}_{pke}$ on the same tape and to receive the responses. In Section 4.4, this is illustrated in detail for an example protocol (this protocol uses $\mathcal{F}_{senc}$ instead of $\mathcal{F}_{pke}$ but the concept is the same).

As mentioned above, $\mathcal{F}_{pke}$ is parameterized by a leakage algorithm L. Furthermore, as usual for machines that run external code (see Section 3.1.3), $\mathcal{F}_{pke}$ is parameterized by a polynomial p. It is used to bound the runtime of the encryption and decryption algorithms that are provided by the adversary and guarantees that $!\mathcal{F}_{pke}$ is environmentally strictly bounded. To emphasize the parameters of $\mathcal{F}_{pke}$, we write $\mathcal{F}_{pke}(n, p, L)$ to denote $\mathcal{F}_{pke}$ with n I/O input and output tapes, polynomial p, and leakage algorithm L. However, we usually omit at least n because it is clear from the context.

The functionality $\mathcal{F}_{pke}$ is defined in pseudocode in Figure 4.1 (see Section 3.1 for notational conventions). We now describe the operations that an instance of $\mathcal{F}_{pke}$, say $\mathcal{F}_{pke}[name]$, provides in more detail. Upon the first request (initialization), $\mathcal{F}_{pke}[name]$ asks the adversary for a (probabilistic) encryption and (deterministic) decryption algorithm, a public/private key pair, and whether it is corrupted (this models static corruption per instance of $\mathcal{F}_{pke}$). Then, it continues processing the first request as all later requests, which is as follows. In the following description, we omit the ID id and the key pair name $name$ that are included in every message sent/received on the I/O tapes.

Public key request GetPubKey: Upon this request on an I/O input tape, $\mathcal{F}_{pke}[name]$ returns (on the corresponding I/O output tape) the recorded public key (provided by the adversary upon initialization). This request allows the "owner" of the pub-

---

different I/O tapes differently. If a request is sent on the i-th I/O input tape, $\mathcal{F}_{pke}$ outputs the response on the i-th I/O output tape.

Parameters: – $n > 0$ *{number of I/O tape pairs}*
   – p *{polynomial bounding the runtime of the algorithms provided by adversary}*
   – L *{leakage algorithm}*

Tapes: from/to IO_r $(r \le n)$: $(\mathsf{io}^{in}_{\mathsf{pke}_r}, \mathsf{io}^{out}_{\mathsf{pke}_r})$; from/to NET: $(\mathsf{net}^{in}_{\mathcal{F}_{\mathsf{pke}}}, \mathsf{net}^{out}_{\mathcal{F}_{\mathsf{pke}}})$

State: – name $\in \{0,1\}^* \cup \{\bot\}$ *{public/private key pair name; initially $\bot$}*
   – enc, dec, pk, sk $\in \{0,1\}^* \cup \{\bot\}$ *{algorithms, key pair (provided by adversary); initially $\bot$}*
   – $\mathsf{H} \subseteq \{0,1\}^* \times \{0,1\}^*$ *{recorded plaintext/ciphertext pairs; initially $\emptyset$}*
   – corr $\in \{0,1\}$ *{corruption status; initially 0}*

CheckAddress: *Accept* input m from IO_r *iff* $m = (id, name, m')$ *for some* $id, name, m'$ *and* $(name = \bot$ *or* $name = name)$. *Accept* input m from NET *iff* $m = (name, m')$ *for some* m'.

Initialization: Upon receiving the first message $(id, name, m')$ in mode Compute do:

  name $:= name$ *{record key pair name (used to address multiple instances of $\mathcal{F}_{\mathsf{pke}}$)}*
  send (name, Init) **to** NET   ⎧ *get algorithms and*
  recv (name, corr, e, d, pk, sk) **from** NET s.t. corr $\in \{0,1\}$ ⎨ *key pair from adversary,*
  corr $:= corr$; enc $:= e$; dec $:= d$; pk $:= pk$; sk $:= sk$ ⎩ *allow corruption*

  Then, continue processing the first request in mode Compute.

Compute: In the following, by "**recv** m **from** $\mathsf{IO}_r[id]$" we denote "**recv** $(id, name, m)$ **from** IO_r" and by "**send** m **to** $\mathsf{IO}_r[id]$" we denote "**send** $(id, name, m)$ **to** IO_r".

  recv GetPubKey **from** $\mathsf{IO}_r[id]$: **send** pk **to** $\mathsf{IO}_r[id]$ *{return public key}*
  recv (Enc, pk, x) **from** $\mathsf{IO}_r[id]$:
    if corr $= 0 \wedge pk = $ pk: *{i.e., uncorrupted and correct public key}*
      $\overline{x} \leftarrow L(1^\eta, x)$; $y \leftarrow \mathsf{enc}^{(p)}(\mathsf{pk}, \overline{x})$; $\overline{x}' := \mathsf{dec}^{(p)}(\mathsf{sk}, y)$ *{encrypt leakage of x (and decrypt)}*
      if $y = \bot \vee \overline{x}' \ne \overline{x}$: **send** $\bot$ **to** $\mathsf{IO}_r[id]$ *{error: encryption or decryption test failed}*
      add (x, y) **to** H; **send** y **to** $\mathsf{IO}_r[id]$ *{record (x, y) for decryption, return y}*
    else: *{i.e., corrupted or wrong public key}*
      $y \leftarrow \mathsf{enc}^{(p)}(pk, x)$; **send** y **to** $\mathsf{IO}_r[id]$ *{encrypt x, return y}*
  recv (Dec, y) **from** $\mathsf{IO}_r[id]$:
    if corr $= 0 \wedge \exists x : (x, y) \in$ H:
      if $\exists x, x' : x \ne x' \wedge (x, y), (x', y) \in$ H: **send** $\bot$ **to** $\mathsf{IO}_r[id]$ *{error: decryption not possible}*
      let x s.t. $(x, y) \in$ H   *{this x always exists and is unique in this case}*
      send x **to** $\mathsf{IO}_r[id]$ *{return x}*
    else:
      $x := \mathsf{dec}^{(p)}(\mathsf{sk}, y)$; **send** x **to** $\mathsf{IO}_r[id]$ *{decrypt y, return x}*
  recv Corr? **from** $\mathsf{IO}_r[id]$: **send** corr **to** $\mathsf{IO}_r[id]$ *{corruption status request}*

Figure 4.1.: The ideal public-key encryption functionality $\mathcal{F}_{\mathsf{pke}}$.

lic/private key pair to obtain its public key (e.g., to distribute it) and can also be used to model certain setup assumptions such as a public key infrastructure (see Remark 4.2).

Encryption (Enc, pk, x): Upon an encryption request for message x with public key pk on an I/O input tape, $\mathcal{F}_{\mathsf{pke}}[name]$ does the following. If $\mathcal{F}_{\mathsf{pke}}[name]$ is corrupted or pk is not the recorded public key, $\mathcal{F}_{\mathsf{pke}}[name]$ encrypts x with pk (using the encryption algorithm provided by the adversary upon initialization) and returns the ciphertext to the user. Otherwise, $\mathcal{F}_{\mathsf{pke}}[name]$ generates the ciphertext by encrypting the leakage

$\overline{x} \leftarrow L(1^\eta, x)$ of x. Then, $\mathcal{F}_{\mathrm{pke}}[name]$ checks that the decryption of the ciphertext yields the leakage $\overline{x}$ again. If this check fails, $\mathcal{F}_{\mathrm{pke}}[name]$ returns an error message. (We refer to Remark 4.3 for an explanation why this decryption test is useful and sometimes needed.) Otherwise, $\mathcal{F}_{\mathrm{pke}}[name]$ records the message x for that ciphertext (for later decryption) and returns the ciphertext.

Decryption (Dec, y):   Upon a decryption request for ciphertext y on an I/O input tape, $\mathcal{F}_{\mathrm{pke}}[name]$ does the following. If $\mathcal{F}_{\mathrm{pke}}[name]$ is corrupted or there is no recorded message for y, $\mathcal{F}_{\mathrm{pke}}[name]$ decrypts y with the recorded private key (using the decryption algorithm; key and algorithm were provided by the adversary upon initialization) and returns the resulting plaintext. Otherwise, the message that is recorded for y is returned to the user (an error message is returned if there is more than one recorded plaintext for y because unique decryption is not possible in this case).

Corruption status request Corr?:   Upon a corruption status request on an I/O input tape, $\mathcal{F}_{\mathrm{pke}}[name]$ returns 1 if it is corrupted and 0 otherwise. See Section 4.1.4 for a discussion of corruption status requests.

This concludes the description of $\mathcal{F}_{\mathrm{pke}}$.

Remark 4.2. As mentioned above, the ideal functionality $!\mathcal{F}_{\mathrm{pke}}$ models multiple public/private key pairs. For example, the key pair of party pid could be modeled by the instance $\mathcal{F}_{\mathrm{pke}}[pid]$. The definition of $\mathcal{F}_{\mathrm{pke}}$, does not restrict how $\mathcal{F}_{\mathrm{pke}}[pid]$ is used by a protocol. In particularly, it is not enforced that only party pid sends decryption requests to $\mathcal{F}_{\mathrm{pke}}[pid]$ (which should be the case of course). This has to be enforced by the protocol (which is easily possible). So, when modeling a protocol, one has to make sure that the usage of $\mathcal{F}_{\mathrm{pke}}[pid]$ is meaningful. Similarly, $\mathcal{F}_{\mathrm{pke}}[pid]$ allows everybody to ask for the public key stored in $\mathcal{F}_{\mathrm{pke}}[pid]$. If the protocol is defined such that all parties may ask $\mathcal{F}_{\mathrm{pke}}[pid]$ for the public key, i.e., not only party pid, this models a setup assumption such as a public key infrastructure or that pid's public key is distributed in a trusted way.

Remark 4.3. Every reasonable encryption scheme satisfies that the decryption of the encryption yields the plaintext again. However, as we do not put any restrictions on the algorithms provided by the adversary, $\mathcal{F}_{\mathrm{pke}}$ does not know whether they have this property. The decryption test that is performed upon encryption (to check that the decryption of the ciphertext yields the leakage $\overline{x}$ again) guarantees that the ciphertext contains not only at most the information of $\overline{x}$ but exactly the information of $\overline{x}$. This is needed for the joint state realization in Section 4.2.6 (to prevent collisions among ciphertexts from different sessions). Furthermore, when the leakage algorithm has high entropy, then this decryption test gives use the advantages mentioned in Section 3.3 about the usefulness of leakage algorithms with high entropy.

Parameters: – $n > 0$ {*number of I/O tape pairs*

     – $\Sigma = (\mathsf{gen}, \mathsf{enc}, \mathsf{dec})$ {*public-key encryption scheme*

Tapes: from/to IO_r ($r \leq n$): $(\mathsf{io}^{\mathsf{in}}_{\mathsf{pke}_r}, \mathsf{io}^{\mathsf{out}}_{\mathsf{pke}_r})$; from/to NET: $(\mathsf{net}^{\mathsf{in}}_{\mathcal{P}_{\mathsf{pke}}}, \mathsf{net}^{\mathsf{out}}_{\mathcal{P}_{\mathsf{pke}}})$

State: – name $\in \{0,1\}^* \cup \{\bot\}$ {*public/private key pair name; initially* $\bot$

     – pk, sk $\in \{0,1\}^* \cup \{\bot\}$ {*public and private key; initially* $\bot$

     – corr $\in \{0,1\}$ {*corruption status; initially* 0

CheckAddress: *Accept* input m from IO_r iff $m = (id, name, m')$ for some $id, name, m'$ and (name $= \bot$ or name $= name$). *Accept* input m from NET iff $m = (name, m')$ for some m'.

Initialization: Upon receiving the first message $(id, name, m')$ in mode Compute do:

     name $:= name$ {*record key pair name (used to address multiple instances of* $\mathcal{F}_{\mathsf{pke}}$)

     send (name, Init) **to** NET; **recv** (name, corr, pk, sk) **from** NET {*ask adversary for corruption*

     if $corr = 1$: corr $:= 1$; pk $:= pk$; sk $:= sk$ {*use key pair provided by adversary*

     else: $(\mathsf{pk}, \mathsf{sk}) \leftarrow \mathsf{gen}(1^\eta)$ {*generate fresh key pair*

     Then, continue processing the first request in mode Compute.

Compute: In the following, by "**recv** m **from** $\mathsf{IO}_r[id]$" we denote "**recv** $(id, name, m)$ **from** IO_r" and by "**send** m **to** $\mathsf{IO}_r[id]$" we denote "**send** $(id, name, m)$ **to** IO_r".

     recv GetPubKey **from** $\mathsf{IO}_r[id]$: **send** pk **to** $\mathsf{IO}_r[id]$ {*return public key*

     recv (Enc, pk, x) **from** $\mathsf{IO}_r[id]$: $y \leftarrow \mathsf{enc}(pk, x)$; **send** y **to** $\mathsf{IO}_r[id]$ {*encrypt* x, *return ciphertext*

     recv (Dec, y) **from** $\mathsf{IO}_r[id]$: $x \leftarrow \mathsf{dec}(sk, y)$; **send** x **to** $\mathsf{IO}_r[id]$ {*decrypt* y *with* sk, *return plaintext*

     recv Corr? **from** $\mathsf{IO}_r[id]$: **send** corr **to** $\mathsf{IO}_r[id]$ {*corruption status request*

Figure 4.2.: The realization $\mathcal{P}_{\mathsf{pke}}$ of $\mathcal{F}_{\mathsf{pke}}$.

Realization by Public-Key Encryption Schemes

A public-key encryption scheme $\Sigma = (\mathsf{gen}, \mathsf{enc}, \mathsf{dec})$ yields a straightforward realization $!\mathcal{P}_{\mathsf{pke}}(n, \Sigma)$ (often just called $!\mathcal{P}_{\mathsf{pke}}$) of $!\mathcal{F}_{\mathsf{pke}}$. The IITM $\mathcal{P}_{\mathsf{pke}}$ is defined as $\mathcal{F}_{\mathsf{pke}}$ except that it generates its own public/private key pair using the key generation algorithm of Σ and that it always encrypts and decrypts the actual messages/ciphertexts using the algorithms of Σ. It is defined in pseudocode in Figure 4.2. We define $\mathcal{P}_{\mathsf{pke}}$ to be only statically corruptible (see Remark 4.5 where we discuss why $\mathcal{F}_{\mathsf{pke}}$ is not realizable under standard assumptions w.r.t. adaptive corruption): The adversary can corrupt $\mathcal{P}_{\mathsf{pke}}$ upon initialization, in which case she provides the public/private key pair. It is easy to see that $!\mathcal{P}_{\mathsf{pke}}$ is environmentally strictly bounded.

The following theorem shows that $\mathcal{F}_{\mathsf{pke}}$ exactly captures the standard security notion IND-CCA2 (Definition 3.6), if the leakage algorithm leaks exactly the length (Definition 3.16). The proof of the corresponding theorem in [KT08] can easily be adapted to the definition of $\mathcal{F}_{\mathsf{pke}}$ we consider in this thesis.

Theorem 4.1. *Let $n > 0$, Σ be a public-key encryption scheme, p be a polynomial that bounds the runtime of the algorithms in Σ (in the length of their inputs), and L be a leakage algorithm that leaks exactly the length (e.g., one from Example 3.1). Then, Σ is IND-CCA2 secure if and only if $!\mathcal{P}_{\mathsf{pke}}(n, \Sigma) \leq !\mathcal{F}_{\mathsf{pke}}(n, p, L)$.*

The direction from left to right holds for any length preserving leakage algorithm

and the one from right to left holds for any leakage algorithm that leaks at most the
length.

We note that, using Theorem 2.3, the above theorem can be proved by only
reasoning about a single instance of $\mathcal{P}_{\text{pke}}$ and $\mathcal{F}_{\text{pke}}$ (it suffices to show that basically
$\mathcal{P}_{\text{pke}}[name]$ realizes $\mathcal{F}_{\text{pke}}[name]$ for every $name$).[17]

Remark 4.4. We note that if Σ is only IND-CPA secure [BDPR98] (indistinguisha-
bility of encryptions under chosen-plaintext attacks), then $!\mathcal{P}_{\text{pke}}$ still realizes $!\mathcal{F}_{\text{pke}}$
for a restricted class of environments, namely environments that, in runs with $!\mathcal{F}_{\text{pke}}$,
ask an uncorrupted instance of $\mathcal{F}_{\text{pke}}$ to decrypt a ciphertext that has not previously
been output by this instance only with negligible probability.[18] For example, this
restriction on the environment might be enforced by a higher-level protocol that uses
$!\mathcal{F}_{\text{pke}}$ and authenticates ciphertexts using digital signatures or MACs.

Remark 4.5. Theorem 4.1 only holds for static corruption (more precisely, $\mathcal{P}_{\text{pke}}$ is
defined such that it only allows static corruption). If we would allow the adversary to
adaptively corrupt instances of $\mathcal{P}_{\text{pke}}$ (and $\mathcal{F}_{\text{pke}}$), upon corruption, the simulator would
have to come up with a key such that the ciphertexts (which are encryptions of the
leakage of messages) produced so far decrypt to the original messages. However, this
is typically not possible under standard assumptions about the encryption scheme.
To tackle this problem, one could use different encryption schemes and/or stronger
security assumptions (see, e.g., the discussion in [Can05]). However, real-world
protocols do not rely on such encryption schemes. Therefore, we only allow static
corruption.

Remark 4.6. In [BHK09], two notions (namely IND-CCA-BP and IND-CCA-BE)
are defined that are shown to be strictly weaker than IND-CCA2 security (which
is called IND-CCA-SE in the taxonomy of [BHK09]). We note that Theorem 4.1
shows that these weaker notions do not suffice to realize $!\mathcal{F}_{\text{pke}}$ (if L leaks at most
the length).

4.2.2. Digital Signatures

Several ideal functionalities for digital signatures have been proposed in the literature
(see, e.g., [Can05, BPW03, Can04, BH04, KT08]). They all share the same basic
ideas. The ideal functionality $\mathcal{F}_{\text{sig}}$ for digital signatures, that we present in this
section is similar to the ones proposed in [Can05, KT08] and follows most closely the
one in [KT08].

---

[17]It is easy to see that both $!\mathcal{F}_{\text{pke}}$ and $!\mathcal{P}_{\text{pke}}$ are σ-session versions for the following SID function
σ: For all messages m and tapes c: $\sigma(m, c) := name$ if c is an I/O tape and $m = (id, name, m')$
or c is a network tape and $m = (name, m')$ (for some $id, name, m'$). Otherwise, $\sigma(m, c) := \bot$.
Then, $!\mathcal{P}_{\text{pke}} \leq_{\sigma\text{-single}} !\mathcal{F}_{\text{pke}}$ implies (by Theorem 2.3) $!\mathcal{P}_{\text{pke}} \leq !\mathcal{F}_{\text{pke}}$.

[18]If the environment is restricted like this, it is easy to see that the IND-CCA2 adversary that is
constructed in the proof of Theorem 4.1 only uses its decryption oracle with negligible probability.
Hence, it can easily be transformed into a successful IND-CPA adversary.

Similar to the public-key functionality $\mathcal{F}_{\text{pke}}$ (see above), it models public/private key pairs that can be used for (ideal) signature generation and verification. The signature generation and verification algorithms are provided by the adversary (or simulator). To perfectly prevent forgery, $\mathcal{F}_{\text{sig}}$ records all messages that are signed. Upon verification, if a signature verifies but the message has not been recorded, an error message is returned. As mentioned above, signatures are determined by local computations, and hence, the signatures and the signed messages are a priori not revealed to the adversary. This is, for example, needed to reason about protocols where the signatures and the signed messages remain secret, e.g., because they are always encrypted.

In previous works (see, e.g., [Can05, KT08]), it has been shown (for similar ideal functionalities) that a signature scheme realizes $\mathcal{F}_{\text{sig}}$ if and only if the signature scheme is UF-CMA secure (existential unforgeability under adaptive chosen-message attacks; see Section 3.8). That is, $\mathcal{F}_{\text{sig}}$ exactly captures this standard security notion for signature schemes. This also holds for our ideal functionality $\mathcal{F}_{\text{sig}}$. Moreover, it is shown in [KT08] that there is a joint state realization of $\mathcal{F}_{\text{sig}}$ (in Section 4.2.6 we restate this result for our version of $\mathcal{F}_{\text{sig}}$). This distinguishes our version of $\mathcal{F}_{\text{sig}}$ and the one in [KT08] from other functionalities for digital signatures in the literature, see [KT08].

The Ideal Digital Signature Functionality $\mathcal{F}_{\text{sig}}$

The ideal functionality $\mathcal{F}_{\text{sig}}$ is a single IITM similar to $\mathcal{F}_{\text{pke}}$ (see above). As $\mathcal{F}_{\text{pke}}$, it has n I/O input and n I/O output tapes and one network input and one network output tape. Mode CheckAddress is defined exactly as for $\mathcal{F}_{\text{pke}}$. Hence, for every public/private key pair name $name$, in runs with $!\mathcal{F}_{\text{sig}}$, there exists (at most) one instance of $\mathcal{F}_{\text{sig}}$, denoted by $\mathcal{F}_{\text{sig}}[name]$, that is addressed by $name$. As described for $\mathcal{F}_{\text{pke}}$, all messages sent to/by $\mathcal{F}_{\text{sig}}[name]$ on the I/O tapes are of the form $(id, name, m)$, where m is the actual request/response and the ID id is used to address the response to the machine that sent the request. All messages sent to/by $\mathcal{F}_{\text{sig}}[name]$ on the network tapes are of the form $(name, m)$. As usual for machines that run external code (see Section 3.1.3), $\mathcal{F}_{\text{sig}}$ is parameterized by a polynomial p that is used to bound the runtime of the signature generation and verification algorithms that are provided by the adversary. It guarantees that $!\mathcal{F}_{\text{sig}}$ is environmentally strictly bounded. To emphasize the parameters of $\mathcal{F}_{\text{sig}}$, we write $\mathcal{F}_{\text{sig}}(n, p)$ to denote $\mathcal{F}_{\text{sig}}$ with n I/O input and output tapes and polynomial p. However, we usually omit at least n because it is clear from the context.

The functionality $\mathcal{F}_{\text{sig}}$ is defined in pseudocode in Figure 4.3 (see Section 3.1 for notational conventions). We now describe the operations that an instance of $\mathcal{F}_{\text{sig}}$, say $\mathcal{F}_{\text{sig}}[name]$, provides in more detail. Upon the first request (initialization), $\mathcal{F}_{\text{sig}}[name]$ first asks the adversary for a (probabilistic) signature generation and a (deterministic) verification algorithm, a public/private key pair, and whether it is corrupted (this allows corruption upon initialization but later corruption is allowed too, see below). Then, it continues processing the first request as all later requests, which is as follows.

Parameters: $- \; n > 0$ {*number of I/O tape pairs*
   $- \; p$ {*polynomial bounding the runtime of the algorithms provided by adversary*

Tapes: from/to IO_r ($r \leq n$): $(\mathsf{io}^{\mathrm{in}}_{\mathrm{sig}_r}, \mathsf{io}^{\mathrm{out}}_{\mathrm{sig}_r})$; from/to NET: $(\mathsf{net}^{\mathrm{in}}_{\mathcal{F}_{\mathrm{sig}}}, \mathsf{net}^{\mathrm{out}}_{\mathcal{F}_{\mathrm{sig}}})$

State: $-$ name $\in \{0,1\}^* \cup \{\bot\}$ {*public/private key pair name; initially* $\bot$

   $-$ sig, ver, pk, sk $\in \{0,1\}^* \cup \{\bot\}$ {*algorithms, key pair (provided by adversary); initially* $\bot$

   $-$ H $\subseteq \{0,1\}^*$ {*recorded messages; initially* $\emptyset$

   $-$ corr $\in \{0,1\}$ {*corruption status; initially* 0

CheckAddress: *Accept input* m *from* IO_r *iff* $m = (id, name, m')$ *for some* $id, name, m'$ *and* (name $= \bot$ *or* name $= name$). *Accept input* m *from* NET *iff* $m = (name, m')$ *for some* m'.

Initialization: *Upon receiving the first message* $(id, name, m')$ *in mode* **Compute** *do:*

   name $:= name$ {*record key pair name (used to address multiple instances of* $\mathcal{F}_{\mathrm{sig}}$)

   send (name, Init) **to** NET   ⎰ *get algorithms and*

   recv (name, *corr*, *s*, *v*, *pk*, *sk*) **from** NET **s.t.** *corr* $\in \{0,1\}$ ⎱ *key pair from adversary,*

   corr $:= corr$; sig $:= s$; ver $:= v$; pk $:= pk$; sk $:= sk$ *allow corruption*

    Then, continue processing the first request in mode **Compute**.

Compute: *In the following, by* "**recv** m **from** $\mathsf{IO}_r[id]$" *we denote* "**recv** $(id, name, m)$ **from** IO_r" *and by* "**send** m **to** $\mathsf{IO}_r[id]$" *we denote* "**send** $(id, name, m)$ **to** IO_r".

   recv GetPubKey **from** $\mathsf{IO}_r[id]$: **send** pk **to** $\mathsf{IO}_r[id]$ {*return public key*

   recv (Sign, x) **from** $\mathsf{IO}_r[id]$:

     $\sigma \leftarrow \mathsf{sig}^{(p)}(\mathsf{sk}, x)$; $b := \mathsf{ver}^{(p)}(\mathsf{pk}, x, \sigma)$ {*sign* x *(and verify)*

     if $\sigma = \bot \lor (b \neq 1 \land \mathsf{corr} = 0)$: **send** $\bot$ **to** $\mathsf{IO}_r[id]$ {*error: signing or test verification failed*

     add x **to** H; **send** σ **to** $\mathsf{IO}_r[id]$ {*record* x *for verification and return signature*

   recv (Verify, pk, x, σ) **from** $\mathsf{IO}_r[id]$:

     $b := \mathsf{ver}^{(p)}(pk, x, \sigma)$ {*verify signature*

     if corr $= 0 \land pk = \mathsf{pk} \land b = 1 \land x \notin$ H: **send** $\bot$ **to** $\mathsf{IO}_r[id]$ {*prevent forgery, return error*

     send b **to** $\mathsf{IO}_r[id]$ {*return verification result*

   recv Corr? **from** $\mathsf{IO}_r[id]$: **send** corr **to** $\mathsf{IO}_r[id]$ {*corruption status request*

   recv (name, Corr) **from** NET: corr $:= 1$; **send** (name, Ack) **to** NET   {*adaptive corruption*

Figure 4.3.: The ideal digital signature functionality $\mathcal{F}_{\mathrm{sig}}$.

In the following description, we omit the ID *id* and the key pair name *name* that are included in every message sent/received on the I/O tapes. Similarly, we omit the key pair name *name* that is included in every message sent to/received on the network tapes.

Public key request GetPubKey: Just as for $\mathcal{F}_{\mathrm{pke}}$, upon this request on an I/O input tape, $\mathcal{F}_{\mathrm{sig}}[name]$ returns the recorded public key (on the corresponding I/O output tape). This allows to model setup assumptions such as a public key infrastructure (see Remark 4.2 for $\mathcal{F}_{\mathrm{pke}}$, which applies here as well).

Signature generation (Sign, x): Upon a signature generation request on an I/O input tape, $\mathcal{F}_{\mathrm{sig}}[name]$ computes a signature for the message x using the recorded signature generation algorithm and private key (both provided by the adversary upon initialization). Then, $\mathcal{F}_{\mathrm{sig}}[name]$ checks that the signature verifies (using the recorded verification algorithm and public key). If this check fails and $\mathcal{F}_{\text{sig}}[name]$ is uncorrupted (note that upon corruption, $\mathcal{F}_{\text{sig}}[name]$ does not guarantee anything, not even that the public and private key belong together), $\mathcal{F}_{\text{sig}}[name]$ returns an error message.[19] Otherwise, $\mathcal{F}_{\text{sig}}[name]$ records the message x (to prevent forgery, see below) and returns the signature.

Verification (Verify, pk, x, σ):   Upon a signature verification request on an I/O input tape, $\mathcal{F}_{\text{sig}}[name]$ verifies the signature σ for x using the provided public key pk and the recorded verification algorithm (provided by the adversary). If the verification succeeds but $\mathcal{F}_{\text{sig}}[name]$ is not corrupted, pk equals the recorded public key (provided by the adversary), and x has not been recorded (upon signature generation), then $\mathcal{F}_{\text{sig}}[name]$ returns an error message. This ideally prevents forgery (if $\mathcal{F}_{\text{sig}}[name]$ is uncorrupted and the correct public key is used) because it guarantees that signatures only verify if the message has previously been signed using $\mathcal{F}_{\text{sig}}[name]$. Otherwise, $\mathcal{F}_{\text{sig}}[name]$ returns the verification result.

Corruption status request Corr?:   Upon a corruption status request on an I/O input tape, $\mathcal{F}_{\text{sig}}[name]$ returns 1 if it is corrupted and 0 otherwise. See Section 4.1.4 for a discussion of corruption status requests.

Corruption request Corr: Upon a corruption request on the network input tape (i.e., from the adversary), $\mathcal{F}_{\text{sig}}[name]$ records itself as corrupted and returns an acknowledgment message (on the network output tape). This models adaptive corruption. We could have defined $\mathcal{F}_{\text{sig}}[name]$ to output its entire state (in particularly all recorded messages) to the adversary upon corruption. However, this would only make the simulator stronger and it is not needed to realize $!\mathcal{F}_{\text{sig}}$, as we will see below.

This concludes the description of $\mathcal{F}_{\text{sig}}$.

As mentioned for $\mathcal{F}_{\text{pke}}$ (Remark 4.2), it is up to the protocol that uses $\mathcal{F}_{\text{sig}}$ that the modeling is meaningful. For example, that only the party that owns the key pair modeled by one instance of $\mathcal{F}_{\text{sig}}$ uses this instance of $\mathcal{F}_{\text{sig}}$ to generate signatures.

Realization by Digital Signature Schemes

Similarly to public-key encryption, a digital signature scheme $\Sigma = (\text{gen}, \text{sig}, \text{ver})$ yields the straightforward realization $\mathcal{P}_{\text{sig}}(n, \Sigma)$ (often just called $\mathcal{P}_{\text{sig}}$) of $\mathcal{F}_{\text{sig}}$ which is given in Figure 4.4. We define $\mathcal{P}_{\text{sig}}$ to be adaptively corruptible: If the adversary decides to corrupt an instance of $\mathcal{P}_{\text{sig}}$ upon initialization, she provides the public/private

---

[19]Note that every reasonable digital signature scheme satisfies that this check never fails. However, as we do not put any restrictions on the algorithms provided by the adversary, $\mathcal{F}_{\text{sig}}[name]$ does not know whether they have this property. Because of this test, it is guaranteed that every verification request to $\mathcal{F}_{\text{sig}}[name]$ succeeds for signatures that have been created by $\mathcal{F}_{\text{sig}}[name]$ (if the proper message is provided upon verification).

Parameters: – $n > 0$ {*number of I/O tape pairs*
      – $\Sigma = (\text{gen}, \text{sig}, \text{ver})$ {*digital signature scheme*

Tapes: from/to IO_r $(r \leq n)$: $(\text{io}^{\text{in}}_{\text{sig}_r}, \text{io}^{\text{out}}_{\text{sig}_r})$; from/to NET: $(\text{net}^{\text{in}}_{\mathcal{P}_{\text{sig}}}, \text{net}^{\text{out}}_{\mathcal{P}_{\text{sig}}})$

State, CheckAddress, and Initialization: As for $\mathcal{P}_{\text{pke}}$ (Figure 4.2).

Compute: In the following, by "**recv** m **from** $\text{IO}_r[id]$" we denote "**recv** (id, name, m) **from** IO_r" and by "**send** m **to** $\text{IO}_r[id]$" we denote "**send** (id, name, m) **to** IO_r".

    recv GetPubKey **from** $\text{IO}_r[id]$: **send** pk **to** $\text{IO}_r[id]$ {*return public key*

    recv (Sign, x) **from** $\text{IO}_r[id]$: $\sigma \leftarrow \text{sig}(\text{sk}, x)$; **send** σ **to** $\text{IO}_r[id]$ {*sign x with sk, return signature*

    recv (Verify, pk, x, σ) **from** $\text{IO}_r[id]$: $b \leftarrow \text{ver}(pk, x, \sigma)$; **send** b **to** $\text{IO}_r[id]$ {*verify, return result*

    recv Corr? **from** $\text{IO}_r[id]$: **send** corr **to** $\text{IO}_r[id]$ {*corruption status request*

    recv (name, Corr) **from** NET: corr := 1; **send** (name, pk, sk) **to** NET   {*adaptive corruption*

Figure 4.4.: The realization $\mathcal{P}_{\text{sig}}$ of $\mathcal{F}_{\text{sig}}$.

key pair. Otherwise, the instance generates a fresh key pair itself. If the adversary decides to corrupt an instance of $\mathcal{P}_{\text{sig}}$ after initialization, she obtains this key pair. It is easy to see that $!\mathcal{P}_{\text{sig}}$ is environmentally strictly bounded.

The following theorem shows that $\mathcal{F}_{\text{sig}}$ exactly captures the standard security notion UF-CMA for digital signatures (Definition 3.8). The proof of the corresponding theorem in [KT08] can easily be adapted to our definition of $\mathcal{F}_{\text{sig}}$.

Theorem 4.2. *Let $n > 0$, Σ be a digital signature scheme, and p be a polynomial that bounds the runtime of the algorithms in Σ (in the length of their inputs). Then, Σ is UF-CMA secure if and only if $!\mathcal{P}_{\text{sig}}(n, \Sigma) \leq !\mathcal{F}_{\text{sig}}(n, p)$.*

As for public-key encryption, we note that, using Theorem 2.3, the above theorem can be proved by only reasoning about a single instance of $\mathcal{P}_{\text{sig}}$ and $\mathcal{F}_{\text{sig}}$ (basically, it suffices to show that $\mathcal{P}_{\text{sig}}[name]$ realizes $\mathcal{F}_{\text{sig}}[name]$ for every $name$).

4.2.3. Symmetric Encryption

The ideal functionality $\mathcal{F}_{\text{senc}}$ for symmetric encryption that we present in this section models symmetric keys that can be used for (ideal) encryption and decryption.[20] Similar to the ideal public-key encryption functionality $\mathcal{F}_{\text{pke}}$, encryption and decryption algorithms and keys are provided by the adversary/simulator and, to ideally guarantee that ciphertexts do not leak (undesired) information about the plaintexts, $\mathcal{F}_{\text{senc}}$ is parameterized by a leakage algorithm (see Section 3.3) and instead of the actual messages the leakage of the messages are encrypted. The message/ciphertext pairs are recorded and decryption is done by table look-up. The functionality $\mathcal{F}_{\text{senc}}$ has two modes: *authenticated* (referred to by $\mathcal{F}^{\text{auth}}_{\text{senc}}$) and *unauthenticated encryption* (referred to by $\mathcal{F}^{\text{unauth}}_{\text{senc}}$). In $\mathcal{F}^{\text{auth}}_{\text{senc}}$, it is syntactically guaranteed that only ciphertext produced within $\mathcal{F}^{\text{auth}}_{\text{senc}}$ decrypt (decryption of other ciphertexts yields a decryption error). This captures ciphertext integrity (INT-CTXT).

---

[20]We note that it is similar to the ideal functionality $\mathcal{F}_{\text{ltsenc}}$ for symmetric encryption with long-term keys defined in [KT09b].

We then show that *(i)* a symmetric encryption scheme realizes $\mathcal{F}_{\text{senc}}^{\text{auth}}$ if and only if the scheme is a secure authenticated encryption scheme (i.e., IND-CPA and INT-CTXT secure) and *(ii)* a symmetric encryption scheme realizes $\mathcal{F}_{\text{senc}}^{\text{unauth}}$ if and only if the scheme is IND-CCA2 secure. Of course, these statements hold for appropriate leakage algorithms and static corruption only, see below. That is, $\mathcal{F}_{\text{senc}}$ exactly captures these standard security notions for symmetric encryption schemes. We refer to Section 3.2.1 for definitions of the security notions IND-CPA, IND-CCA2, and INT-CTXT.

The Ideal Symmetric Encryption Functionality $\mathcal{F}_{\text{senc}}$

The ideal functionality $\mathcal{F}_{\text{senc}}$ is a single IITM similar to $\mathcal{F}_{\text{pke}}$ (see above). As $\mathcal{F}_{\text{pke}}$, $\mathcal{F}_{\text{senc}}$ has n I/O input and n I/O output tapes and one network input and one network output tape. Mode CheckAddress is defined exactly as for $\mathcal{F}_{\text{pke}}$. However, *name* is now not interpreted as a public/private key name but as a symmetric long-term key name (see below). For every long-term key name *name*, in runs with $!\mathcal{F}_{\text{senc}}$, there exists (at most) one instance of $\mathcal{F}_{\text{senc}}$, denoted by $\mathcal{F}_{\text{senc}}[name]$, that is addressed by *name*. As described for $\mathcal{F}_{\text{pke}}$, all messages sent to/by $\mathcal{F}_{\text{senc}}[name]$ on the I/O tapes are of the form $(id, name, m)$, where m is the actual request/response and the ID *id* is used to address the response to the machine that sent the request. All messages sent to/by $\mathcal{F}_{\text{senc}}[name]$ on the network tapes are of the form $(name, m)$. Every instance of $\mathcal{F}_{\text{senc}}$ models a single long-term key (shared between parties). For example, the name to address instances of $\mathcal{F}_{\text{senc}}$ can be a pair of party names $name = (pid_1, pid_2)$. This models that (the key modeled by) $\mathcal{F}_{\text{senc}}[(pid_1, pid_2)]$ is shared between the two parties pid_1 and pid_2. The protocol that uses $!\mathcal{F}_{\text{senc}}$ would then be defined such that only party pid_1 and pid_2 use $\mathcal{F}_{\text{senc}}[(pid_1, pid_2)]$. A more detailed example is given in Section 4.4, where we use $!\mathcal{F}_{\text{senc}}$ to analyze an example protocol.

As mentioned above, $\mathcal{F}_{\text{senc}}$ is parameterized by a leakage algorithm L and has two modes: *authenticated* and *unauthenticated encryption*. Furthermore, as usual for machines that run external code (see Section 3.1.3), $\mathcal{F}_{\text{senc}}$ is parameterized by a polynomial p that is used to bound the runtime of the encryption and decryption algorithms that are provided by the adversary. It guarantees that $!\mathcal{F}_{\text{senc}}$ is environmentally strictly bounded. To emphasize the parameters of $\mathcal{F}_{\text{senc}}$, we write $\mathcal{F}_{\text{senc}}^{\text{auth}}(n, p, L)$ to denote $\mathcal{F}_{\text{senc}}$ in mode *authenticated encryption* with n I/O input and output tapes, polynomial p, and leakage algorithm L. Similarly, we write $\mathcal{F}_{\text{senc}}^{\text{unauth}}(n, p, L)$ to denote $\mathcal{F}_{\text{senc}}$ in mode *unauthenticated encryption* with the given parameters. However, we usually omit at least n because it is clear from the context.

The functionality $\mathcal{F}_{\text{senc}}$ is defined in pseudocode in Figure 4.5 (see Section 3.1 for notational conventions). We now describe the operations that an instance of $\mathcal{F}_{\text{senc}}$, say $\mathcal{F}_{\text{senc}}[name]$, provides in more detail. Upon the first request (initialization), $\mathcal{F}_{\text{senc}}[name]$ first asks the adversary for a (probabilistic) encryption and a (deterministic) decryption algorithm, a symmetric key, and whether it is corrupted (this models static corruption). Then, it continues processing the first request as all later requests, which is as follows.

Parameters: – $mode \in \{\text{auth}, \text{unauth}\}$ {*modeling un-/authenticated encryption*}
     – $n > 0$ {*number of I/O tape pairs*}
     – p {*polynomial bounding the runtime of the algorithms provided by adversary*}
     – L {*leakage algorithm*}

Tapes: from/to IO_r $(r \leq n)$: $(\mathsf{io}^{\text{in}}_{\text{senc}_r}, \mathsf{io}^{\text{out}}_{\text{senc}_r})$; from/to **NET**: $(\mathsf{net}^{\text{in}}_{\mathcal{F}_{\text{senc}}}, \mathsf{net}^{\text{out}}_{\mathcal{F}_{\text{senc}}})$

State: – $\text{name} \in \{0,1\}^* \cup \{\bot\}$ {*long-term key name; initially* $\bot$}
     – $\text{enc}, \text{dec}, \mathsf{k} \in \{0,1\}^* \cup \{\bot\}$ {*algorithms and key (provided by adversary); initially* $\bot$}
     – $\mathsf{H} \subseteq \{0,1\}^* \times \{0,1\}^*$ {*recorded plaintext/ciphertext pairs; initially* $\emptyset$}
     – $\text{corr} \in \{0,1\}$ {*corruption status; initially* 0}

CheckAddress: *Accept* input m from IO_r *iff* $m = (id, name, m')$ *for some* $id, name, m'$ and $(\text{name} = \bot$ *or* $\text{name} = name)$. *Accept* input m from **NET** *iff* $m = (name, m')$ *for some* m'.

Initialization: Upon receiving the first message $(id, name, m')$ in mode **Compute** do:
     $\text{name} := name$ {*record long-term key name (used to address multiple instances of* $\mathcal{F}_{\text{senc}}$}
     send $(name, \mathsf{Init})$ **to NET**   {*get algorithms from adversary, allow corruption*}
     recv $(name, corr, e, d, k)$ **from NET s.t.** $corr \in \{0,1\}$; $\text{corr} := corr$; $\text{enc} := e$; $\text{dec} := d$; $\mathsf{k} := k$

     Then, continue processing the first request in mode **Compute**.

Compute: In the following, by "**recv** m **from** $\mathsf{IO}_r[id]$" we denote "**recv** $(id, name, m)$ **from** IO_r" and by "**send** m **to** $\mathsf{IO}_r[id]$" we denote "**send** $(id, name, m)$ **to** IO_r".

recv (Enc, x) **from** $\mathsf{IO}_r[id]$:
     if $\text{corr} = 0$:
         $\bar{x} \leftarrow L(1^\eta, x)$; $y \leftarrow \text{enc}^{(p)}(\mathsf{k}, \bar{x})$; $\bar{x}' := \text{dec}^{(p)}(\mathsf{k}, y)$ {*encrypt leakage of* x *(and decrypt)*}
         if $y = \bot \lor \bar{x}' \neq \bar{x}$: **send** $\bot$ **to** $\mathsf{IO}_r[id]$ {*error: encryption failed or decryption test failed*}
         add (x, y) **to** H; **send** y **to** $\mathsf{IO}_r[id]$ {*record* (x,y) *for decryption, return* y}
     else:
         $y \leftarrow \text{enc}^{(p)}(\mathsf{k}, x)$; **send** y **to** $\mathsf{IO}_r[id]$ {*encrypt* x, *return* y}

recv (Dec, y) **from** $\mathsf{IO}_r[id]$:
     if $\text{corr} = 0 \land (mode = \text{auth} \lor \exists x: (x, y) \in \mathsf{H})$:
         if $\exists x, x': x \neq x' \land (x, y), (x', y) \in \mathsf{H}$:
             send $\bot$ **to** $\mathsf{IO}_r[id]$ {*error: unique decryption not possible*}
         else if $\exists x: (x, y) \in \mathsf{H}$:
             send x **to** $\mathsf{IO}_r[id]$ {*this* x *is unique in this case*}
         else: {*this case may occur only in authenticated encryption mode (mode* = auth*)*}
             send $\bot$ **to** $\mathsf{IO}_r[id]$ {*error: prevent forgery (ciphertext not recorded)*}
     else:
         $x := \text{dec}^{(p)}(\mathsf{k}, y)$; **send** x **to** $\mathsf{IO}_r[id]$ {*decrypt* y}

recv $\mathsf{Corr?}$ **from** $\mathsf{IO}_r[id]$: **send** corr **to** $\mathsf{IO}_r[id]$ {*corruption status request*}

Figure 4.5.: The ideal symmetric encryption functionality $\mathcal{F}_{\text{senc}}$.

Encryption (Enc, x): Upon an encryption request for message x on an I/O input tape, $\mathcal{F}_{\text{pke}}[name]$ does the following. Such encryption requests are handled similarly to encryption requests in $\mathcal{F}_{\text{pke}}$. If $\mathcal{F}_{\text{senc}}[name]$ is corrupted, it encrypts x (using the recorded key and encryption algorithm; both provided by the adversary upon initialization). Otherwise, it encrypts the leakage of x and records x for the resulting ciphertext (for decryption).[21] The resulting ciphertext is returned.

---

[21] As in $\mathcal{F}_{\text{pke}}$, upon encryption, it is tested whether the decryption of the ciphertext yields the leakage again. An error is returned if this test fails. This decryption test is performed for the

Decryption (Dec, y): Upon a decryption request for ciphertext y on an I/O input tape, $\mathcal{F}_{\text{senc}}[name]$ does the following. If $\mathcal{F}_{\text{senc}}[name]$ is corrupted, it decrypts y (using the recorded key and decryption algorithm) and returns the resulting plaintext. Otherwise, $\mathcal{F}_{\text{senc}}[name]$ distinguishes the following cases: *(i)* If there exist two different plaintexts x, x' such that both x and x' have been recorded for y (upon encryption), then $\mathcal{F}_{\text{senc}}[name]$ returns an error message (unique decryption is not possible). *(ii)* If there exists exactly one plaintext x such that x has been recorded for y, then $\mathcal{F}_{\text{senc}}[name]$ returns x. *(iii)* If there does not exist a plaintext that has been recorded for y, then $\mathcal{F}_{\text{senc}}^{\text{auth}}[name]$ (i.e., in mode *authenticated encryption*) returns an error (modeling that decryption should fail when an authenticated encryption scheme is used and the ciphertext has not been generated honestly) and $\mathcal{F}_{\text{senc}}^{\text{unauth}}[name]$ (i.e., in mode *unauthenticated encryption*) decrypts y (using the recorded key and decryption algorithm) and returns the resulting plaintext.

We note that decryption in mode *unauthenticated encryption* is as in $\mathcal{F}_{\text{pke}}$.

Corruption status request Corr?: Upon a corruption status request on an I/O input tape, $\mathcal{F}_{\text{senc}}[name]$ returns 1 if it is corrupted and 0 otherwise. See Section 4.1.4 for a discussion of corruption status requests.

This concludes the description of $\mathcal{F}_{\text{senc}}$.

Realization by Symmetric Encryption Schemes

Similarly to public-key encryption, a symmetric encryption scheme $\Sigma = (\text{gen}, \text{enc}, \text{dec})$ yields the straightforward realization $\mathcal{P}_{\text{senc}}(n, \Sigma)$ (often just called $\mathcal{P}_{\text{senc}}$) of $\mathcal{F}_{\text{senc}}$ which is given in Figure 4.6. We note that this realization relies on the setup assumption that the symmetric keys are shared between the users of $\mathcal{P}_{\text{senc}}$. It is only statically corruptible because, otherwise, it would not realize $\mathcal{F}_{\text{senc}}$ under standard assumptions on Σ (see Remark 4.8). That is, the adversary can corrupt an instance of $\mathcal{P}_{\text{senc}}$ only upon initialization, in which case she provides the key. It is easy to see that $!\mathcal{P}_{\text{senc}}$ is environmentally strictly bounded.

The following theorem shows that $\mathcal{F}_{\text{senc}}^{\text{unauth}}$ exactly captures the standard security notion IND-CCA2 and that $\mathcal{F}_{\text{senc}}^{\text{auth}}$ exactly captures the standard security notion for authenticated encryption (IND-CPA and INT-CTXT security), if the leakage algorithm leaks exactly the length (Definition 3.16); the notions IND-CCA2, IND-CPA, and INT-CTXT are recalled in Section 3.2.1. We provide a proof in Appendix A.1.

Theorem 4.3. *Let $n > 0$, Σ be a symmetric encryption scheme, p be a polynomial that bounds the runtime of the algorithms in Σ (in the length of their inputs), and L be a leakage algorithm that leaks exactly the length (e.g., one from Example 3.1). Then, the following two statements hold:*

---

same reasons as explained for $\mathcal{F}_{\text{pke}}$ (see Remark 4.3): It is needed for our joint state realization in Section 4.2.6 and, when using leakage algorithms with high entropy, sometimes useful for reasoning about protocols as mentioned in Section 3.3.

Parameters: – $n > 0$ *{number of I/O tape pairs*
        – $\Sigma = (\mathsf{gen}, \mathsf{enc}, \mathsf{dec})$ *{symmetric encryption scheme*
Tapes: from/to IO_r $(r \leq n)$: $(\mathsf{io}^{\mathrm{in}}_{\mathsf{senc}_r}, \mathsf{io}^{\mathrm{out}}_{\mathsf{senc}_r})$; from/to NET: $(\mathsf{net}^{\mathrm{in}}_{\mathcal{P}_{\mathsf{senc}}}, \mathsf{net}^{\mathrm{out}}_{\mathcal{P}_{\mathsf{senc}}})$
State: – $\mathsf{name} \in \{0,1\}^* \cup \{\bot\}$ *{long-term key name; initially $\bot$*
       – $\mathsf{k} \in \{0,1\}^* \cup \{\bot\}$ *{symmetric key; initially $\bot$*
       – $\mathsf{corr} \in \{0,1\}$ *{corruption status; initially 0*
CheckAddress: *Accept* input m from IO_r iff $m = (id, name, m')$ for some $id, name, m'$ and ($\mathsf{name} = \bot$ or $\mathsf{name} = name$). *Accept* input m from NET iff $m = (name, m')$ for some m'.
Initialization: Upon receiving the first message $(id, name, m')$ in mode Compute do:
     $\mathsf{name} := name$ *{record long-term key name (used to address multiple instances of $\mathcal{P}_{\mathsf{senc}}$)*
     send $(\mathsf{name}, \mathsf{Init})$ **to** NET; **recv** $(\mathsf{name}, corr, k)$ **from** NET   *{ask adversary for corruption*
     if $corr = 1$: $\mathsf{corr} := 1$; $\mathsf{k} := k$ **else:** $\mathsf{k} \leftarrow \mathsf{gen}(1^\eta)$ *{use key from adversary or fresh key*

     Then, continue processing the first request in mode Compute.
Compute: In the following, by "**recv** m **from** $\mathsf{IO}_r[id]$" we denote "**recv** (id, name, m) **from** IO_r" and by "**send** m **to** $\mathsf{IO}_r[id]$" we denote "**send** (id, name, m) **to** IO_r".
     recv (Enc, x) **from** $\mathsf{IO}_r[id]$: $y \leftarrow \mathsf{enc}(\mathsf{k}, x)$; **send** y **to** $\mathsf{IO}_r[id]$ *{encrypt x with k, return ciphertext*
     recv (Dec, y) **from** $\mathsf{IO}_r[id]$: $x \leftarrow \mathsf{dec}(\mathsf{k}, y)$; **send** x **to** $\mathsf{IO}_r[id]$ *{decrypt y with k, return plaintext*
     recv $\mathsf{Corr?}$ **from** $\mathsf{IO}_r[id]$: **send** corr **to** $\mathsf{IO}_r[id]$ *{corruption status request*

Figure 4.6.: The realization $\mathcal{P}_{\mathsf{senc}}$ of $\mathcal{F}_{\mathsf{senc}}$.

1. Σ *is IND-CCA2 secure if and only if* $!\mathcal{P}_{\mathsf{senc}}(n, \Sigma) \leq !\mathcal{F}^{\mathrm{unauth}}_{\mathsf{senc}}(n, p, L)$.

2. Σ *is IND-CPA and INT-CTXT secure if and only if* $!\mathcal{P}_{\mathsf{senc}}(n, \Sigma) \leq !\mathcal{F}^{\mathrm{auth}}_{\mathsf{senc}}(n, p, L)$.

The directions from left to right hold for any length preserving leakage algorithm and the directions from right to left hold for any leakage algorithm that leaks at most the length.

As for public-key encryption, we note that, using Theorem 2.3, the above theorem can be proved by only reasoning about a single instance of $\mathcal{P}_{\mathsf{sig}}$ and $\mathcal{F}_{\mathsf{sig}}$ (basically, it suffices to show that $\mathcal{P}_{\mathsf{sig}}[name]$ realizes $\mathcal{F}_{\mathsf{sig}}[name]$ for every $name$).

Remark 4.7. We note that IND-CPA security alone is sufficient to realize $!\mathcal{F}_{\mathsf{senc}}$ if it is guaranteed that every instance of $\mathcal{F}_{\mathsf{senc}}$ is only asked to decrypt ciphertexts that have previously been generated within this instance. See Remark 4.4, where we explain this for public-key encryption, for details.

Remark 4.8. The realization $!\mathcal{P}_{\mathsf{senc}}$ is only statically corruptible (per instance). If we would allow the adversary to adaptively corrupt instances of $\mathcal{P}_{\mathsf{senc}}$ (and $\mathcal{F}_{\mathsf{senc}}$), we could not prove that $!\mathcal{P}_{\mathsf{senc}}$ realizes $!\mathcal{F}_{\mathsf{senc}}$ because of the so-called commitment problem. This is similar to public-key encryption, see Remark 4.5. In the context of symmetric encryption, the commitment problem occurs if a key is revealed after it was used to encrypt a message. Before the key is revealed, messages encrypted under this key are encrypted ideally, i.e., the leakage of the message is encrypted. When the key is revealed, the simulator would have to come up with a key such that the ciphertexts produced so far decrypt to the original messages. However, this is typically not possible (see, e.g., [BP04]). To tackle this problem, one could make a stronger assumption about the security of the encryption scheme, such as deniable encryption (see, e.g., [CDNO97]). However, real-world protocols do not rely on such encryption schemes. Therefore, we only allow static corruption.

4.2.4. Message Authentication Codes

The ideal functionality $\mathcal{F}_{\mathrm{mac}}$ for (deterministic) message authentication codes (MACs) that we present in this section models symmetric keys that can be used to create and verifies MACs such that forgery is ideally prevented. It is similar to the ideal functionality $\mathcal{F}_{\mathrm{sig}}$ for digital signatures from Section 4.2.2. The MAC algorithms and keys that are used in $\mathcal{F}_{\mathrm{mac}}$ are provided by the adversary/simulator. To perfectly prevent forgery, the functionality records all messages that are MACed. Then, upon MAC verification, if a MAC verifies but the message has not been recorded, an error is returned. We note that MACs are determined by local computations. As mentioned for digital signatures, this is sometimes needed because the MACs and messages are not a priory revealed to the adversary.

We then show that a MAC realizes $\mathcal{F}_{\mathrm{mac}}$ if and only if the MAC is UF-CMA secure (unforgeability against chosen-message attacks; see Definition 3.10). That is, $\mathcal{F}_{\mathrm{mac}}$ captures this standard security notion for MACs. This even holds for adaptive corruption.

The Ideal MAC Functionality $\mathcal{F}_{\mathrm{mac}}$

The ideal functionality $\mathcal{F}_{\mathrm{mac}}$ is a single IITM. As the above functionalities, it has n I/O input and n I/O output tapes and one network input and one network output tape. Mode CheckAddress is defined exactly as for $\mathcal{F}_{\mathrm{senc}}$. Hence, for every long-term key name $name$, in runs with $!\mathcal{F}_{\mathrm{mac}}$, there exists (at most) one instance of $\mathcal{F}_{\mathrm{mac}}$, denoted by $\mathcal{F}_{\mathrm{mac}}[name]$, that is addressed by $name$. As described for $\mathcal{F}_{\mathrm{senc}}$, all messages sent to/by $\mathcal{F}_{\mathrm{mac}}[name]$ on the I/O tapes are of the form $(id, name, m)$, where m is the actual message and the ID id is used to address the response to the machine that sent the request. All messages sent to/by $\mathcal{F}_{\mathrm{mac}}[name]$ on the network tapes are of the form $(name, m)$.

As usual for machines that run external code (see Section 3.1.3), $\mathcal{F}_{\mathrm{mac}}$ is parameterized by a polynomial p that is used to bound the runtime of the MAC algorithm that is provided by the adversary. It guarantees that $!\mathcal{F}_{\mathrm{mac}}$ is environmentally strictly bounded. To emphasize the parameters of $\mathcal{F}_{\mathrm{mac}}$, we write $\mathcal{F}_{\mathrm{mac}}(n, p)$ to denote $\mathcal{F}_{\mathrm{mac}}$ with n I/O input and output tapes and polynomial p. However, we usually omit at least n because it is clear from the context.

The functionality $\mathcal{F}_{\mathrm{mac}}$ is defined in pseudocode in Figure 4.7 (see Section 3.1 for notational conventions). We now describe the operations that an instance of $\mathcal{F}_{\mathrm{mac}}$, say $\mathcal{F}_{\mathrm{mac}}[name]$, provides in more detail. Upon the first request (initialization), $\mathcal{F}_{\mathrm{mac}}[name]$ first asks the adversary for a (deterministic) MAC algorithm, a symmetric

Parameters: $-\ n > 0$ 　　　　　　　　　　　　　　　　　　　　　　　　　*{number of I/O tape pairs*
　　　　$-\ p$ 　　　　　　　*{polynomial bounding the runtime of the algorithm provided by adversary*
Tapes: from/to IO_r $(r \leq n)$: $(\mathsf{io}^{\mathrm{in}}_{\mathrm{mac}_r}, \mathsf{io}^{\mathrm{out}}_{\mathrm{mac}_r})$; from/to **NET**: $(\mathsf{net}^{\mathrm{in}}_{\mathcal{F}_{\mathrm{mac}}}, \mathsf{net}^{\mathrm{out}}_{\mathcal{F}_{\mathrm{mac}}})$
State: $-$ name $\in \{0,1\}^* \cup \{\bot\}$ 　　　　　　　　　　　*{long-term key name; initially $\bot$*
　　　　$-$ mac, k $\in \{0,1\}^* \cup \{\bot\}$ 　　　　　*{algorithm and key (provided by adversary); initially $\bot$*
　　　　$-$ H $\subseteq \{0,1\}^*$ 　　　　　　　　　　　　　*{recorded messages; initially $\emptyset$*
　　　　$-$ corr $\in \{0,1\}$ 　　　　　　　　　　　　　　*{corruption status; initially 0*
CheckAddress: *Accept input m from* IO_r *iff* $m = (id, name, m')$ *for some $id, name, m'$ and*
(name $= \bot$ *or* name $= name$). *Accept input m from* **NET** *iff* $m = (name, m')$ *for some m'.*
Initialization: *Upon receiving the first message* $(id, name, m')$ *in mode* **Compute** *do:*
　　　name $:=$ name 　　　　*{record long-term key name (used to address multiple instances of $\mathcal{F}_{\mathrm{mac}}$)*
　　　send (name, Init) **to NET** 　　　　　*{get algorithm and key from adversary, allow corruption*
　　　recv (name, corr, mac, k) **from NET s.t.** corr $\in \{0,1\}$; corr $:=$ corr; mac $:=$ mac; k $:=$ k

　　　Then, continue processing the first request in mode **Compute**.
Compute: *In the following, by* "**recv** m *from* $\mathsf{IO}_r[id]$" *we denote* "**recv** $(id, name, m)$ *from* IO_r"
and by "**send** m *to* $\mathsf{IO}_r[id]$" *we denote* "**send** $(id, name, m)$ *to* IO_r".
　　　recv (MAC, x) **from** $\mathsf{IO}_r[id]$:
　　　　　$\sigma := \mathrm{mac}^{(p)}(\mathrm{k}, x)$ 　　　　　　　　　　　　　　　　　　　　　*{MAC x*
　　　　　if $\sigma = \bot$: **send** $\bot$ **to** $\mathsf{IO}_r[id]$ 　　　　　　　　　*{error: MACing failed*
　　　　　add x **to** H; **send** σ **to** $\mathsf{IO}_r[id]$ 　　　*{record x for verification and return MAC*
　　　recv (Verify, x, σ) **from** $\mathsf{IO}_r[id]$:
　　　　　$\sigma' := \mathrm{mac}^{(p)}(\mathrm{k}, x)$ 　　　　　　　　　　　　　　　　　　　　　*{MAC x*
　　　　　if $\sigma = \sigma' \neq \bot$: $b := 1$ **else:** $b := 0$ 　　*{verification succeeds iff $\sigma = \sigma' \neq \bot$*
　　　　　if corr $= 0 \wedge b = 1 \wedge x \notin$ H: **send** $\bot$ **to** $\mathsf{IO}_r[id]$ 　*{prevent forgery, return error*
　　　　　send b **to** $\mathsf{IO}_r[id]$ 　　　　　　　　　　　　　　　*{return verification result*
　　　recv Corr? **from** $\mathsf{IO}_r[id]$: **send** corr **to** $\mathsf{IO}_r[id]$ 　　　　*{corruption status request*
　　　recv (name, Corr) **from NET**: corr $:= 1$; **send** (name, Ack) **to NET** 　*{adaptive corruption*

Figure 4.7.: The ideal MAC functionality $\mathcal{F}_{\mathrm{mac}}$.

key, and whether it is corrupted (this allows corruption upon initialization but later corruption is allowed too, see below). Then, it continues processing the first request as all later requests, which is as follows. In the following description, we omit the ID id and the key name *name* that are included in every message sent/received on the I/O tapes. Similarly, we omit the key name *name* that is included in every message sent to/received on the network tapes.

MAC (MAC, x): Upon a MAC request for a message x on an I/O input tape, $\mathcal{F}_{\mathrm{mac}}[name]$ computes the MAC for x (using the recorded key MAC algorithm, both provided by the adversary), records the message x (to prevent forgery upon verification, see below), and returns the MAC.

Verification (Verify, x, σ): Upon a MAC verification request for a message x and a MAC σ on an I/O input tape, $\mathcal{F}_{\mathrm{mac}}[name]$ computes the MAC for x (using the recorded key and MAC algorithm) and compares it with σ. Verification succeeds if and only if σ is equal to the computed MAC. If verification succeeds but $\mathcal{F}_{mac}[name]$ is not corrupted and x has not been recorded upon MACing, $\mathcal{F}_{mac}[name]$ returns an error message. This prevents forgery (if $\mathcal{F}_{mac}[name]$ is uncorrupted) because it guarantees that MACs only verify if the message has previously been MACed using $\mathcal{F}_{mac}$. Otherwise, $\mathcal{F}_{mac}$ returns the verification result.

Corruption status request Corr?:   Upon a corruption status request on an I/O input tape, $\mathcal{F}_{mac}[name]$ returns 1 if it is corrupted and 0 otherwise. See Section 4.1.4 for a discussion of corruption status requests.

Corruption request Corr: Upon a corruption request on the network input tape (i.e., from the adversary), $\mathcal{F}_{mac}[name]$ records itself as corrupted and returns an acknowledgment message (on the network output tape). This models adaptive corruption. We could have defined $\mathcal{F}_{mac}[name]$ to output its entire state (in particularly all recorded messages) upon corruption. However, this would only make the simulator stronger and is not needed to realize $!\mathcal{F}_{mac}$, as we will see below.

This concludes the description of $\mathcal{F}_{mac}$.

We note that $\mathcal{F}_{mac}$ models deterministic message authentication schemes. One could easily extend $\mathcal{F}_{mac}$ to also consider probabilistic message authentication schemes (see, e.g., [KT11b]). Such a functionality would be similar to the digital signature functionality $\mathcal{F}_{sig}$ and it would precisely capture the security notion defined in [BGR95] (an extension of UF-CMA security where the adversary also obtains a verification oracle). A discussion of different security notions for probabilistic message authentication schemes can be found in [BGM04].

Realization by MACs

A MAC $\Sigma = (\mathsf{gen}, \mathsf{mac})$ yields the straightforward realization $\mathcal{P}_{mac}(n, \Sigma)$ (often just called $\mathcal{P}_{mac}$) of $\mathcal{F}_{mac}$ which is given in Figure 4.8. We note that this realization relies on the setup assumption that the symmetric key is shared between the users of $\mathcal{P}_{mac}$. We define $\mathcal{P}_{mac}$ to be adaptively corruptible: If the adversary decides to corrupt an instance of $\mathcal{P}_{mac}$ upon initialization, she provides the key. Otherwise, a fresh key is generated within $\mathcal{P}_{mac}$. If the adversary decides to corrupt an instance of $\mathcal{P}_{mac}$ after initialization, she obtains this key. It is easy to see that $!\mathcal{P}_{mac}$ is environmentally strictly bounded.

The following theorem shows that $\mathcal{F}_{mac}$ exactly captures the standard security notion UF-CMA for MACs (Definition 3.10). Its proof, that we provide in Appendix A.2, is similar to the proof of Theorem 4.2 ($!\mathcal{P}_{sig} \leq !\mathcal{F}_{sig}$).

Theorem 4.4. *Let $n > 0$, Σ be a MAC, and p be a polynomial that bounds the runtime of the algorithms in Σ (in the length of their input). Then, Σ is UF-CMA secure if and only if $!\mathcal{P}_{mac}(n, \Sigma) \leq !\mathcal{F}_{mac}(n, p)$.*

Parameters: – $n > 0$ {*number of I/O tape pairs*
     – $\Sigma = (\mathsf{gen}, \mathsf{mac})$ {*MAC scheme*

Tapes: from/to IO_r ($r \leq n$): ($\mathsf{io}^{\mathrm{in}}_{\mathrm{mac}_r}, \mathsf{io}^{\mathrm{out}}_{\mathrm{mac}_r}$); from/to NET: ($\mathsf{net}^{\mathrm{in}}_{\mathcal{P}_{\mathrm{mac}}}, \mathsf{net}^{\mathrm{out}}_{\mathcal{P}_{\mathrm{mac}}}$)

State, CheckAddress, and Initialization: As for $\mathcal{P}_{\mathrm{senc}}$ (Figure 4.6).

Compute: In the following, by "**recv** m **from** $\mathsf{IO}_r[id]$" we denote "**recv** (id, name, m) **from** IO_r" and by "**send** m **to** $\mathsf{IO}_r[id]$" we denote "**send** (id, name, m) **to** IO_r".

    recv (MAC, x) **from** $\mathsf{IO}_r[id]$: $\sigma := \mathsf{mac}(k, x)$; **send** σ **to** $\mathsf{IO}_r[id]$ {*compute and return MAC*

    recv $(\mathsf{Verify}, x, \sigma)$ **from** $\mathsf{IO}_r[id]$:

        if $\sigma = \mathsf{mac}(k, x)$: **send** 1 **to** $\mathsf{IO}_r[id]$ **else**: **send** 0 **to** $\mathsf{IO}_r[id]$ {*verify MAC and return result*

    recv $\mathsf{Corr}?$ **from** $\mathsf{IO}_r[id]$: **send** corr **to** $\mathsf{IO}_r[id]$ {*corruption status request*

    recv $(\mathit{name}, \mathsf{Corr})$ **from** NET: $\mathsf{corr} := 1$; **send** (name, k) **to** NET   {*adaptive corruption*

Figure 4.8.: The realization $\mathcal{P}_{\mathrm{mac}}$ of $\mathcal{F}_{\mathrm{mac}}$.

4.2.5. Key Derivation

The ideal functionality $\mathcal{F}_{\mathrm{derive}}$ for key derivation, that we present in this section, models symmetric keys that can be used for (ideal) key derivation.[22] Different keys can be derived from the key derivation key (that is modeled by an instance of $\mathcal{F}_{\mathrm{derive}}$) by providing different non-secret bit strings as *salts*. Instead of actually deriving keys, $\mathcal{F}_{\mathrm{derive}}$ generates fresh keys (and records them, to return the same keys upon a later request with the same salt). This models *ideal* key derivation.

We then show that $\mathcal{F}_{\mathrm{derive}}$ can be realized by secure variable-length output pseudorandom functions (VLO-PRFs); we recall notions for VLO-PRFs in Section 3.2.5. Of course, this holds for static corruption only, see below.

The Ideal Key Derivation Functionality $\mathcal{F}_{\mathrm{derive}}$

The ideal functionality $\mathcal{F}_{\mathrm{derive}}$ is a single IITM. Similar to the ideal functionalities defined above, it has n I/O input and n I/O output tapes and one network input and one network output tape. Mode CheckAddress is defined exactly as for $\mathcal{F}_{\mathrm{senc}}$ and $\mathcal{F}_{\mathrm{mac}}$. Hence, for every long-term key name *name*, in runs with $!\mathcal{F}_{\mathrm{derive}}$, there exists (at most) one instance of $\mathcal{F}_{\mathrm{derive}}$, denoted by $\mathcal{F}_{\mathrm{derive}}[\mathit{name}]$, that is addressed by *name*. As described for $\mathcal{F}_{\mathrm{senc}}$, all messages sent to/by $\mathcal{F}_{\mathrm{derive}}[\mathit{name}]$ on the I/O tapes are of the form (id, name, m), where m is the actual message and the ID *id* is used to address the response to the machine that sent the request. All messages sent to/by $\mathcal{F}_{\mathrm{derive}}[\mathit{name}]$ on the network tapes are of the form (name, m).

The functionality $\mathcal{F}_{\mathrm{derive}}$ is parameterized by a polynomial-time computable function parse: $\{1\}^* \times \{0, 1\}^* \to \mathbb{N}^* \cup \{\bot\}$ that takes as input a security parameter (in unary form) and a salt and outputs a list of key lengths $l_1, \ldots, l_m \in \mathbb{N}$ (for some

---

[22] We note that, in this thesis, we always consider the case where the source keying material (i.e., the key derivation key) is assumed to be a cryptographically strong key (i.e., a random or pseudorandom key) that can directly be used as input to a pseudorandom function. In particularly, we do not consider the case where the key derivation key is a password from which one has to first extract the randomness (see, e.g., [Kra10] for key derivation from passwords).

$m \in \mathbb{N}$ that may depend on the input). This *salt parsing function* is used to determine how many keys of which length shall be derived. We assumes that the salt carries this information. This assumption is quite natural for most practical protocols, e.g., because they prefix the salt with a constant that determines the purpose of the derived keys (and this definitely is a good design practice). For example, in the 4-Way Handshake protocol of WPA2 (see Section 7.4.3), three keys (the KCK, KEK and TK) are derived from the Pairwise Master Key (PMK) using a salt that is prefixed by the string `"Pairwise key expansion"` and a PMK identifier (PMKID) is derived from the PMK using a salt that is prefixed by the string `"PMK Name"`. So, for this protocol, we would define:

$$
\mathsf{parse}(1^\eta, x) := \begin{cases} (l_{\text{KCK}}, l_{\text{KEK}}, l_{\text{TK}}) & \text{if } \exists x': x = \texttt{"Pairwise key expansion"} \| x' \\ (l_{\text{PMKID}}) & \text{if } \exists x': x = \texttt{"PMK Name"} \| x' \\ \varepsilon & \text{otherwise (where } \varepsilon \text{ is the empty list)} \end{cases}
$$

where l_{KCK} is the length of the key KCK, l_{KEK} is the length of the key KEK, etc. (See also Section 7.7.2 for more examples.) To emphasize the parameters of $\mathcal{F}_{\text{derive}}$, we write $\mathcal{F}_{\text{derive}}(n, \mathsf{parse})$ to denote $\mathcal{F}_{\text{derive}}$ with n I/O input and output tapes and the salt parsing function parse. However, we usually omit at least n because it is clear from the context.

The functionality $\mathcal{F}_{\text{derive}}$ is defined in pseudocode in Figure 4.9 (see Section 3.1 for notational conventions). We now describe the operations that an instance of $\mathcal{F}_{\text{derive}}$, say $\mathcal{F}_{\text{derive}}[name]$, provides in more detail. Upon the first request (initialization), $\mathcal{F}_{\text{derive}}[name]$ first asks the adversary whether it is corrupted (this models static corruption). Then, it continues processing the first request as all later requests, which is as follows. In the following description, we omit the ID *id* and the key name *name* that are included in every message sent/received on the I/O tapes.

Key derivation (Derive, x): Upon a key derivation request with a salt x on an I/O input tape, $\mathcal{F}_{\text{derive}}[name]$ first checks if it has previously derived keys with the salt x. If this is the case, $\mathcal{F}_{\text{derive}}[name]$ returns these keys. Otherwise, $\mathcal{F}_{\text{derive}}[name]$ parses the salt x using the salt parsing function parse. This yields key lengths $l_1, \ldots, l_m$. If $\mathcal{F}_{\text{derive}}[name]$ is corrupted, it asks the adversary to provide keys $k_1, \ldots, k_m$ such that the length of k_i is l_i, for all $i \leq m$. If $\mathcal{F}_{\text{derive}}[name]$ is not corrupted, it freshly generates these keys (i.e., $\mathcal{F}_{\text{derive}}[name]$ chooses k_i uniformly at random from the set of bit strings of length l_i, for all $i \leq m$). If corrupted or not corrupted, $\mathcal{F}_{\text{derive}}[name]$ then records the keys $k_1, \ldots, k_m$ for the salt x and returns them.

Corruption status request Corr?: Upon a corruption status request on an I/O input tape, $\mathcal{F}_{\text{derive}}[name]$ returns 1 if it is corrupted and 0 otherwise. See Section 4.1.4 for a discussion of corruption status requests.

This concludes the description of $\mathcal{F}_{\text{derive}}$. We note that it is easy to see that $!\mathcal{F}_{\text{derive}}$ is environmentally strictly bounded.

Parameters: – $n > 0$ *{number of I/O tape pairs*
  – parse: $\{1\}^* \times \{0,1\}^* \to \mathbb{N}^*$ *{salt parsing function*
Tapes: from/to IO_r $(r \leq n)$: $(\mathsf{io}^{\mathrm{in}}_{\mathrm{derive}_r}, \mathsf{io}^{\mathrm{out}}_{\mathrm{derive}_r})$; from/to NET: $(\mathsf{net}^{\mathrm{in}}_{\mathcal{F}_{\mathrm{derive}}}, \mathsf{net}^{\mathrm{out}}_{\mathcal{F}_{\mathrm{derive}}})$
State: – name $\in \{0,1\}^* \cup \{\bot\}$ *{long-term key name; initially $\bot$*
  – derived: $\{0,1\}^* \to (\{0,1\}^*)^* \cup \{\bot\}$ *{recorded derived keys; initially $\forall x$: derived$(x) = \bot$*
  – corr $\in \{0,1\}$ *{corruption status; initially 0*
CheckAddress: *Accept* input m from IO_r *iff* $m = (id, name, m')$ *for some* $id, name, m'$*and*
  (name $= \bot$ *or* name $=$ *name*). *Accept* input m from NET *iff* $m = (name, m')$ *for some* m'.
Initialization: Upon receiving the first message $(id, name, m')$ in mode Compute do:
    name $:=$ *name*   *{record long-term key name (used to address multiple instances of $\mathcal{F}_{\mathrm{derive}}$)*
    send (name, Init) **to** NET   *{ask adversary for corruption*
    recv (name, corr) **from** NET **s.t.** corr $\in \{0,1\}$; corr $:=$ corr

Then, continue processing the first request in mode Compute.
Compute: In the following, by "**recv** m **from** $\mathsf{IO}_r[id]$" we denote "**recv** $(id, name, m)$ **from** IO_r"
  and by "**send** m **to** $\mathsf{IO}_r[id]$" we denote "**send** $(id, name, m)$ **to** IO_r".
  recv (Derive, x) **from** $\mathsf{IO}_r[id]$:
      if derived$(x) = \bot$:
          $(l_1, \ldots, l_m) :=$ parse$(1^\eta, x)$ *{parse the salt x to obtain key lengths*
          if corr $= 0$:
              for all $i \in \{1, \ldots, m\}$ **do:** $k_i \xleftarrow{\$} \{0,1\}^{l_i}$ *{generate fresh keys if uncorrupted*
          else:
              send (name, Derive, x) **to** NET   *{adversary provides keys if corrupted*
              recv (name, $k_1, \ldots, k_m$) **from** NET **s.t.** $\forall i \leq m$: $|k_i| = l_i$
          derived$(x) := (k_1, \ldots, k_m)$ *{record derived keys*
      send derived(x) **to** $\mathsf{IO}_r[id]$ *{return recorded derived keys*
  recv Corr? **from** $\mathsf{IO}_r[id]$: **send** corr **to** $\mathsf{IO}_r[id]$ *{corruption status request*

Figure 4.9.: The ideal key derivation functionality $\mathcal{F}_{\mathrm{derive}}$.

Realization by Variable-Length Output Pseudorandom Functions

A variable-length output pseudorandom function (VLO-PRF) PRF^* (as introduced in Section 3.2.5) and a salt parsing function parse (see above) yield the straightforward realization $\mathcal{P}_{\mathrm{derive}}(n, \mathrm{PRF}^*, \mathrm{parse})$ (often just called $\mathcal{P}_{\mathrm{derive}}$) of $\mathcal{F}_{\mathrm{derive}}$ which is given in Figure 4.10. We note that this realization relies on the setup assumption that the key derivation key is shared between all users of $\mathcal{P}_{\mathrm{derive}}$. The salt parsing function parse determines the lengths of the keys that shall be derived. Then, PRF^* is used to derive a pseudorandom bit string of appropriate length and this bit string is split into the derived keys. We define $\mathcal{P}_{\mathrm{derive}}$ to be only statically corruptible (see Remark 4.10 about adaptive corruption): The adversary can corrupt instances of $\mathcal{P}_{\mathrm{derive}}$ upon initialization, in which case she provides the key. It is easy to see that $!\mathcal{P}_{\mathrm{derive}}$ is environmentally strictly bounded.

The following theorem shows that $\mathcal{F}_{\mathrm{derive}}$ can be realized by secure VLO-PRFs. Security for a VLO-PRF means that it in fact produces pseudorandom output, i.e.,

---

Parameters: $-\ n > 0$ *{number of I/O tape pairs*
- parse: $\{1\}^* \times \{0,1\}^* \to \mathbb{N}^*$ *{salt parsing function*
- PRF^* *{VLO-PRF with key length $l(\eta)$ for every security parameter η*

Tapes: from/to IO_r $(r \le n)$: $(\mathsf{io}^{\mathrm{in}}_{\mathrm{derive}_r}, \mathsf{io}^{\mathrm{out}}_{\mathrm{derive}_r})$; from/to NET: $(\mathsf{net}^{\mathrm{in}}_{\mathcal{P}_{\mathrm{derive}}}, \mathsf{net}^{\mathrm{out}}_{\mathcal{P}_{\mathrm{derive}}})$

State, CheckAddress, and Initialization: As for $\mathcal{P}_{\mathrm{senc}}$ (Figure 4.6), except that $\mathsf{k} \leftarrow \mathsf{gen}(1^\eta)$ is replaced by $\mathsf{k} \xleftarrow{\$} \{0,1\}^{l(\eta)}$.

Compute: In the following, by "**recv** m **from** $\mathsf{IO}_r[id]$" we denote "**recv** (id, name, m) **from** IO_r" and by "**send** m **to** $\mathsf{IO}_r[id]$" we denote "**send** (id, name, m) **to** IO_r".

recv (Derive, x) **from** $\mathsf{IO}_r[id]$:
   $(l_1, \ldots, l_m) := \mathsf{parse}(1^\eta, x)$ *{parse the salt x to obtain key lengths*
   $y := \mathrm{PRF}^*(\mathsf{k}, x, l_1 + \cdots + l_m)$ *{derive y of length $l_1 + \cdots + l_m$ from k with salt x*
   let $k_1, \ldots, k_m$ s.t. $y = k_1 \| \cdots \| k_m \wedge \forall i \le m \colon |k_i| = l_i$ *{split y into keys*
   send $(k_1, \ldots, k_m)$ **to** $\mathsf{IO}_r[id]$ *{return derived keys*
   recv Corr? **from** $\mathsf{IO}_r[id]$: **send** corr **to** $\mathsf{IO}_r[id]$ *{corruption status request*

Figure 4.10.: The realization $\mathcal{P}_{\mathrm{derive}}$ of $\mathcal{F}_{\mathrm{derive}}$.

output computationally indistinguishable from random output (see Section 3.2.5 for a formal security definition). We provide a proof in Appendix A.3.

Theorem 4.5. *Let $n > 0$, PRF^* be a secure VLO-PRF, and parse be a salt parsing function. Then,* $!\mathcal{P}_{\mathrm{derive}}(n, \mathrm{PRF}^*, \mathsf{parse}) \le !\mathcal{F}_{\mathrm{derive}}(n, \mathsf{parse})$.

Remark 4.9. Other realizations of $!\mathcal{F}_{\mathrm{derive}}$ with different assumptions (i.e., realizations not based on VLO-PRFs) are possible of course. For example, if $\mathsf{parse}(1^\eta, x) = l'(\eta) \in \mathbb{N}$ for all η, x, i.e., only a single key of fixed length is derived (not possibly multiple keys of possibly different lengths), then $!\mathcal{F}_{\mathrm{derive}}$ can be realized by regular pseudorandom functions. We note that the above realization (i.e., based on VLO-PRFs) is what is done in many existing protocols, see Sections 7.4.3 and 7.7.2 for examples.

Remark 4.10. Instances of the realization $\mathcal{P}_{\mathrm{derive}}$ are only statically corruptible. If we would allow the adversary to adaptively corrupt instance of $\mathcal{P}_{\mathrm{derive}}$ (and $\mathcal{F}_{\mathrm{derive}}$), we could not prove that $!\mathcal{P}_{\mathrm{derive}}$ realizes $!\mathcal{F}_{\mathrm{derive}}$ because the simulator would have to come up with a key k such that all keys that were ideally derived from k (i.e., freshly generated) are now really derived from k. This is not possible under standard assumptions about pseudorandom functions.

4.2.6. Joint State Realizations

Joint state realizations of ideal functionalities, as introduced in Section 4.1.5, are useful because they allow us to deduce multi-session security from single-session security, although the realization has state that is shared with other sessions, such as long-term symmetric or public/private keys. Canetti and Rabin [CR03] where the first to present a joint state realization of a cryptographic primitive, namely digital signatures (for an interactive digital signature functionality, i.e., where the simulator is asked to provide signatures). In [KT08], similar joint state realizations have been presented for digital signature and public-key encryption functionalities similar to the ones presented above. In this section, we recall these joint state realizations from [KT08] and adapt them to our formulations of the functionalities. We also present new joint state realizations for symmetric encryption, MACs, and key derivation, which are straightforward adaptions of the joint state realizations for digital signatures and public-key encryption. They all have in common that SIDs are added to messages (or salts, in case of key derivation) to prevent that different sessions interfere with each other. While this idea is simple, several subtleties have to be taken care of, which were overlooked in other works, see [KT08]. We note that we use these joint state realizations in Section 5.4 to obtain a joint state realization of our crypto functionality $\mathcal{F}_{\mathrm{crypto}}$.

Public-Key Encryption

In this section, we briefly recall the joint state realization for public-key encryption from [KT08] and adapt it to our formulation of $\mathcal{F}_{\mathrm{pke}}$; see [KT08] for details.

Recall from Section 4.1.5 that $!\mathcal{F}_{\mathrm{pke}}$ (the multi-session version of $!\mathcal{F}_{\mathrm{pke}}$) is used as follows: All messages sent to $!\mathcal{F}_{\mathrm{pke}}$ are prefixed by an SID sid and a public/private key name $name$ (e.g., the owner's party name) and are received by the instance $\mathcal{F}_{\mathrm{pke}}[sid, name]$. Vice versa, $\mathcal{F}_{\mathrm{pke}}[sid, name]$ prefixes all output by sid and $name$. We now present a realization of $!\mathcal{F}_{\mathrm{pke}}$ that, for every public/private key name, uses only one instance of $\mathcal{F}_{\mathrm{pke}}$ for all sessions.

The joint state realization. The joint state realization of $!\mathcal{F}_{\mathrm{pke}}$ is the protocol system $!\mathcal{P}_{\mathrm{pke}}^{\mathrm{js}} \mid !\mathcal{F}_{\mathrm{pke}}$ (formally, I/O tapes have to be renamed to guarantee that $!\mathcal{P}_{\mathrm{pke}}^{\mathrm{js}} \mid !\mathcal{F}_{\mathrm{pke}}$ and $!\mathcal{F}_{\mathrm{pke}}$ have the same external I/O interface). Mode CheckAddress of the IITM $\mathcal{P}_{\mathrm{pke}}^{\mathrm{js}}$ is defined such that, for every public/private key pair name $name$, at most one copy of $\mathcal{P}_{\mathrm{pke}}^{\mathrm{js}}$, referred to by $\mathcal{P}_{\mathrm{pke}}^{\mathrm{js}}[name]$, is created in a run with $!\mathcal{P}_{\mathrm{pke}}^{\mathrm{js}} \mid !\mathcal{F}_{\mathrm{pke}}$. Also, $\mathcal{P}_{\mathrm{pke}}^{\mathrm{js}}[name]$ invokes only one instance of $\mathcal{F}_{\mathrm{pke}}$, namely $\mathcal{F}_{\mathrm{pke}}[name]$. That is, $\mathcal{P}_{\mathrm{pke}}^{\mathrm{js}}[name]$ handles all requests to $\mathcal{F}_{\mathrm{pke}}[name]$ in all sessions, and serves as a multiplexer. It strips off the SID before forwarding a request to $\mathcal{F}_{\mathrm{pke}}[name]$ and adds the SID before forwarding a response from $\mathcal{F}_{\mathrm{pke}}[name]$.

However, $\mathcal{F}_{\mathrm{pke}}[name]$ does not only forward messages but modifies encryption requests and responses to decryption requests as follows. When forwarding an encryption request to $\mathcal{F}_{\mathrm{pke}}[name]$, say for a plaintext x in session sid, $\mathcal{P}_{\mathrm{pke}}^{\mathrm{js}}[name]$ replaces the plaintext by (sid, x) (i.e., it adds the SID to the plaintext before encryption). Here, we assume that (sid, x) is some efficient encoding of a pair of bit strings such that the length of (sid, x) only depends on the length of sid and x (i.e., $|(sid, x)| = |(sid', x')|$ for all sid, sid', x, x' such that $|sid| = |sid'|$ and $|x| = |x'|$). This is needed below, to obtain length preserving leakage algorithms, see Remark 4.11.

When forwarding the response to a decryption request, say a plaintext x in session sid, then $\mathcal{P}_{\text{pke}}^{\text{js}}[name]$ checks if x is of the form (sid, x') for some bit string x'. If this check succeeds, $\mathcal{P}_{\text{pke}}^{\text{js}}[name]$ forwards x'. Otherwise, $\mathcal{P}_{\text{pke}}^{\text{js}}[name]$ outputs an error message (i.e., decryption fails).

Following the above description, it is easy to define $\mathcal{P}_{\text{pke}}^{\text{js}}$ formally, see [KT08] for details. We note that $!\mathcal{P}_{\text{pke}}^{\text{js}} \mid !\mathcal{F}_{\text{pke}}$ is environmentally strictly bounded. Finally, we emphasize two technical details of $\mathcal{P}_{\text{pke}}^{\text{js}}$ that are necessary for the joint state theorem to hold. The first one is concerned with the order in that the environment sends messages to $!\mathcal{P}_{\text{pke}}^{\text{js}} \mid !\mathcal{F}_{\text{pke}}$. When the environment sends the first request to $\mathcal{P}_{\text{pke}}^{\text{js}}[name]$, for some key pair name $name$ and in some session sid, then $\mathcal{P}_{\text{pke}}^{\text{js}}[name]$ forwards it to $\mathcal{F}_{\text{pke}}[name]$ which in turn sends an initialization request to the adversary (i.e., on the network tape) and waits for a response from her (because this is the first request send to it). Now, while waiting for this response, the environment might send another request to $\mathcal{P}_{\text{pke}}^{\text{js}}[name]$, in some other session $sid' \neq sid$. When this happens, $\mathcal{F}_{\text{pke}}[name]$ is still blocked because it is waiting for a response from the adversary. In the ideal world (i.e., in an interaction of the environment with $!\mathcal{F}_{\text{pke}}$ and a simulator) now there would be two copies, namely $\mathcal{F}_{\text{pke}}[sid, name]$ and $\mathcal{F}_{\text{pke}}[sid', name]$ waiting for a response to the initialization request from the simulator. To make the joint state realization indistinguishable from the ideal world in this case, we define $\mathcal{P}_{\text{pke}}^{\text{js}}[name]$ to record sid' as *blocked* and to ignore this last request, i.e., to end this activation without producing output. All later requests in sessions with a blocked SID are also ignored. The simulator will accordingly be defined to never complete initialization for $\mathcal{F}_{\text{pke}}[sid', name]$. This guarantees that the environment cannot exploit such race conditions to distinguish between the joint state realization and the ideal world.

The second technical detail of $\mathcal{P}_{\text{pke}}^{\text{js}}$ that is important has to do with the length of SIDs. The length of SIDs has to be polynomially bounded in the security parameter. This is needed because the algorithms that are provided by the adversary/simulator and executed by $\mathcal{F}_{\text{pke}}$ get different inputs. In the joint state realization, they obtain input (sid, x) and in the ideal world, they just obtain input x and have to add the SID. See [KT08] for details. Hence, $\mathcal{P}_{\text{pke}}^{\text{js}}$ will simply block (as above) all sessions with long SIDs.

We note that these two technical problems could have been solved easily by restricting the environment. For example, we could require that the environment only uses SIDs of length at most $p(\eta)$ for some fixed polynomial p (i.e., the simulator may depend on p) and that the environment always directly replies to the initialization request from $\mathcal{F}_{\text{pke}}$. This would not overly restrict the environment and would make the joint state realization less technical.

The joint state theorem. We now state the joint state theorem for $!\mathcal{F}_{\text{pke}}$. The joint state realization $\mathcal{P}_{\text{pke}}^{\text{js}}(n)$ (the parameter $n > 0$ defines the I/O interface just as for $\mathcal{F}_{\text{pke}}$) is based on $!\mathcal{F}_{\text{pke}}$ that will use the leakage L' that in addition to the leakage L in the ideal world ($!\mathcal{F}_{\text{pke}}$) also leaks the SID of the session in which a message was encrypted. This, in conjunction with the decryption test performed in $\mathcal{F}_{\mathrm{pke}}$ (upon encryption of a leakage, $\mathcal{F}_{\mathrm{pke}}$ checks that the decryption of the ciphertext yields the leakage again), will guarantee that ciphertexts generated in different sessions are different, which is crucial for the joint state theorem to hold. The leakage algorithm L' is defined as follows.

Definition 4.1. *Let L be a leakage algorithm. By L' we denote the leakage algorithm that additionally leaks the SID. It is obtained from L as follows: Upon input 1^η and x, L' checks if x is of the form (sid, x') for some bit strings sid, x'. If this is the case, then L' computes $\bar{x}' \leftarrow L(1^\eta, x')$ and returns $(sid, \bar{x}')$. Otherwise, L' returns x (see Remark 4.11).*

Remark 4.11. We note that if L is probabilistic, then L' is probabilistic too and L' uses its own random coins to compute $L(1^\eta, x')$. We further note that it is irrelevant what value is returned if x is not of the form (sid, x') because, by definition of $\mathcal{P}_{\mathrm{pke}}^{\mathrm{js}}$, L' will only be applied to messages of this form. Since we have chosen to output x in this case, L' is length preserving (Definition 3.14) if L is length preserving. This argument also requires that the length of (sid, x') only depends on the length of sid and x', as we required above. Furthermore, if L has high entropy w.r.t. to a domain of messages $D = \{D(\eta)\}_{\eta \in \mathbb{N}}$ (Definition 3.17), then L' has high entropy w.r.t. the domain $D' := \{D'(\eta)\}_{\eta \in \mathbb{N}}$ where $D'(\eta) := \{(sid, x) \mid sid \in \{0,1\}^*, x \in D(\eta)\}$ for all $\eta \in \mathbb{N}$.

The proof of the joint state theorem for public-key encryption in [KT08] can easily be adapted to prove the following theorem.

Theorem 4.6. *For every polynomial p there exists a polynomial p' such that for every $n > 0$ and leakage algorithm L:*

$$!\mathcal{P}_{\mathrm{pke}}^{\mathrm{js}}(n) \mid !\mathcal{F}_{\mathrm{pke}}(n, p, L') \ \leq \ !\mathcal{F}_{\mathrm{pke}}(n, p', L)$$

where L' is the leakage algorithm that additionally leaks the SID (Definition 4.1).

Using the composition theorems (Theorem 2.1; and transitivity of $\leq$), we can replace the ideal functionality in the joint state realization by its realization as stated in Theorem 4.1, resulting in an actual joint state realization (without any ideal functionality).

Corollary 4.1. *Let $n > 0$, Σ be an IND-CCA2 secure public-key encryption scheme, p be a polynomial that bounds the runtime of the algorithms in Σ (in the length of their inputs), p' be the polynomial that is given by Theorem 4.6 (and that depends on p), and L be a length preserving leakage algorithm (e.g., one from Example 3.1). Then:*

$$!\mathcal{P}_{\mathrm{pke}}^{\mathrm{js}}(n) \mid !\mathcal{P}_{\mathrm{pke}}(n, \Sigma) \ \leq \ !\mathcal{F}_{\mathrm{pke}}(n, p', L) \ .$$

Digital Signatures

In [KT08], a joint state realization for digital signatures has been proposed that is similar to the one for public-key encryption. We now briefly recall their results for our formulation of $\mathcal{F}_{\text{sig}}$. The joint state realization is of the form $!\mathcal{P}_{\text{sig}}^{\text{js}} \mid !\mathcal{F}_{\text{sig}}$ where $\mathcal{P}_{\text{sig}}^{\text{js}}$ is similar to $\mathcal{P}_{\text{pke}}^{\text{js}}$ (see above). The only difference is the following: When forwarding a signing or verification request to $\mathcal{F}_{\text{sig}}[name]$, say in session sid, for a message x, $\mathcal{P}_{\text{sig}}^{\text{js}}[name]$ replaces the message by (sid, x) (i.e., it adds the SID to the message before signature generation or verification). The joint state theorem from [KT08] can now be stated as follows in our setting (the proof carries over).

Theorem 4.7. *For every polynomial p exists a polynomial p' such that for every $n > 0$:*

$$!\mathcal{P}_{\text{sig}}^{\text{js}}(n) \mid !\mathcal{F}_{\text{sig}}(n, p) \leq \underline{!\mathcal{F}_{\text{sig}}(n, p')} \ .$$

As mentioned for public-key encryption, by the composition theorems, we can replace the ideal functionality in the joint state realization by its realization as stated in Theorem 4.2, resulting in an actual joint state realization (without any ideal functionality).

Corollary 4.2. *Let $n > 0$, Σ be an UF-CMA secure signature scheme, p be a polynomial that bounds the runtime of the algorithms in Σ (in the length of their inputs), and p' be the polynomial that is given by Theorem 4.7 (and that depends on p). Then:*

$$!\mathcal{P}_{\text{sig}}^{\text{js}}(n) \mid !\mathcal{P}_{\text{sig}}(n, \Sigma) \leq \underline{!\mathcal{F}_{\text{sig}}(n, p')} \ .$$

Symmetric Encryption

The joint state realization for symmetric encryption is similar to the one for public-key encryption. It is of the form $!\mathcal{P}_{\text{senc}}^{\text{js}} \mid !\mathcal{F}_{\text{senc}}$ where $\mathcal{P}_{\text{senc}}^{\text{js}}$ is similar to $\mathcal{P}_{\text{pke}}^{\text{js}}$ (see above). That is, the SID is added to the plaintext before encryption and upon decryption it is tested that the plaintext is prefixed by the correct SID. We omit the proof of the following theorem because it is similar to the proof of the joint state theorem for public-key encryption.

Theorem 4.8. *For every polynomial p there exists a polynomial p' such that for every $n > 0$, $mode \in \{\text{auth}, \text{unauth}\}$, and leakage algorithm L:*

$$!\mathcal{P}_{\text{senc}}^{\text{js}}(n) \mid !\mathcal{F}_{\text{senc}}^{mode}(n, p, L') \leq \underline{!\mathcal{F}_{\text{senc}}^{mode}(n, p', L)}$$

where L' is the leakage algorithm that additionally leaks the SID (Definition 4.1).

As mentioned for public-key encryption, using the composition theorems, we can replace the ideal functionality in the joint state realization by its realization as stated in Theorem 4.3, resulting in an actual joint state realization (without any ideal functionality).

Corollary 4.3. *Let $n > 0$, Σ be a symmetric encryption scheme, p be a polynomial that bounds the runtime of the algorithms in Σ (in the length of their inputs), p' be the polynomial that is given by Theorem 4.8 (and that depends on p), and L be a length preserving leakage algorithm (e.g., one from Example 3.1).*

1. If Σ is IND-CCA2 secure, then:

$$!\mathcal{P}^{js}_{senc}(n) \,|\, !\mathcal{P}_{senc}(n, \Sigma) \;\leq\; !\mathcal{F}^{unauth}_{senc}(n, p', L) \;.$$

2. If Σ is IND-CPA and INT-CTXT secure, then:

$$!\mathcal{P}^{js}_{senc}(n) \,|\, !\mathcal{P}_{senc}(n, \Sigma) \;\leq\; !\mathcal{F}^{auth}_{senc}(n, p', L) \;.$$

MACs

The joint state realization for MACs is similar to the one for digital signatures. It is of the form $!\mathcal{P}^{js}_{mac} \,|\, !\mathcal{F}_{mac}$ where $\mathcal{P}^{js}_{mac}$ is similar to $\mathcal{P}^{js}_{sig}$ (see above). That is, SIDs are added to messages before MAC generation and verification. We omit the proof of the following theorem because it is similar to the proof of Theorem 4.7.

Theorem 4.9. *For every polynomial p exists a polynomial p' such that for every $n > 0$:*

$$!\mathcal{P}^{js}_{mac}(n) \,|\, !\mathcal{F}_{mac}(n, p) \;\leq\; !\mathcal{F}_{mac}(n, p') \;.$$

As mentioned for public-key encryption, using the composition theorems, we can replace the ideal functionality in the joint state realization by its realization as stated in Theorem 4.4, resulting in an actual joint state realization (without any ideal functionality).

Corollary 4.4. *Let $n > 0$, Σ be a UF-CMA secure MAC, p be a polynomial that bounds the runtime of the algorithms in Σ (in the length of their inputs), and p' be the polynomial that is given by Theorem 4.9 (and that depends on p). Then:*

$$!\mathcal{P}^{js}_{mac}(n) \,|\, !\mathcal{P}_{mac}(n, \Sigma) \;\leq\; !\mathcal{F}_{mac}(n, p') \;.$$

Key Derivation

We now present a joint state realization for key derivation. Similar to the joint state realizations above, it is of the form $!\mathcal{P}^{js}_{derive} \,|\, !\mathcal{F}_{derive}$ where $\mathcal{P}^{js}_{derive}$ is similar to $\mathcal{P}^{js}_{pke}$ (see above). The only difference is the following: When forwarding a key derivation request to $\mathcal{F}_{derive}[name]$, say in session sid, for a salt x, $\mathcal{P}^{js}_{derive}[name]$ replaces the salt by (sid, x) (i.e., it adds the SID to the salt).[23]

We now state the joint state theorem for $\mathcal{F}_{derive}$. The joint state realization $\mathcal{P}^{js}_{derive}$ is based on $\mathcal{F}_{derive}$ that will use the salt parsing function parse' that behaves as the

---

[23] We note that we do not need to require polynomially bounded SIDs (see above for $\mathcal{P}^{js}_{pke}$) because $\mathcal{F}_{derive}$, in contrast to $\mathcal{F}_{pke}$, does not run external code.

salt parsing function in the ideal world ($!\mathcal{F}_{\text{derive}}$), except that it ignores the SID. Formally, given parse, parse$'$ is defined as follows: $\text{parse}'(1^\eta, (sid, x)) := \text{parse}(1^\eta, x)$ for every security parameter η, SID sid, and salt x. For salts not of the form (sid, x), the definition of parse$'$ is irrelevant because $\mathcal{P}_{\text{derive}}^{\text{js}}$ guarantees that parse$'$ is never called for such salts. For example, in this case, we define the outcome of parse$'$ to be the empty list ε.

Theorem 4.10. *Let $n > 0$, parse be a salt parsing function (as defined in Section 4.2.5), and parse$'$ be defined as above. Then:*

$$!\mathcal{P}_{\text{derive}}^{\text{js}}(n) \mid !\mathcal{F}_{\text{derive}}(n, \text{parse}') \ \leq \ !\mathcal{F}_{\text{derive}}(n, \text{parse}) \ .$$

Proof sketch. By Theorem 2.3 (note that $!\mathcal{P}_{\text{derive}}^{\text{js}} \mid !\mathcal{F}_{\text{derive}}$ and $!\mathcal{F}_{\text{derive}}$ are σ-session version for an appropriate SID function σ that outputs the key name *name* as the SID), it suffice to show that $!\mathcal{P}_{\text{derive}}^{\text{js}} \mid !\mathcal{F}_{\text{derive}}$ realizes $!\mathcal{F}_{\text{derive}}$ for environments that only use a single key name, i.e., only create copies of $\mathcal{P}_{\text{derive}}^{\text{js}}[name]$ and $\mathcal{F}_{\text{derive}}[name]$ or $\mathcal{F}_{\text{derive}}[sid, name]$, respectively, for a single key name and (possibly) multiple SIDs sid.

First, we sketch a simulator $\mathcal{S}$. Because we are in the "single-key setting", $\mathcal{S}$ just simulates one copy of $\mathcal{F}_{\text{derive}}$, namely $\mathcal{F}_{\text{derive}}[name]$ for some key name *name*. When this copy gets corrupted upon initialization (recall that corruption is static), then $\mathcal{S}$ corrupts $\mathcal{F}_{\text{derive}}[sid, name]$ for all SIDs sid and, upon key derivation, simply forwards the corrupted keys. It is easy to see that upon corruption, an environment cannot distinguish between the *joint-state world* (i.e., an interaction with $!\mathcal{P}_{\text{derive}}^{\text{js}} \mid !\mathcal{F}_{\text{derive}}(\text{parse}')$) and the *ideal world* (i.e., an interaction with $\mathcal{S} \mid !\mathcal{F}_{\text{derive}}(\text{parse})$).

In the uncorrupted case, by the definition of $\mathcal{P}_{\text{derive}}^{\text{js}}$, it is easy to see that, it never happens that the same salt is used in different sessions (because salts are prefixed by SIDs). Hence, keys derived in one session are independent from all other sessions. It is now easy to see that an environment cannot distinguish between the joint-state world and the ideal world. $\square$

We note that the above theorem (just as all joint state theorems above) even holds for unbounded environments.

As mentioned for public-key encryption, by the composition theorems, we can replace the ideal functionality in the joint state realization by its realization as stated in Theorem 4.5, resulting in an actual joint state realization (without any ideal functionality).

Corollary 4.5. *Let $n > 0$, PRF^* be a secure VLO-PRF, parse be a salt parsing function (as defined in Section 4.2.5), and parse$'$ be defined as above. Then:*

$$!\mathcal{P}_{\text{derive}}^{\text{js}}(n) \mid !\mathcal{P}_{\text{derive}}(n, \text{PRF}^*, \text{parse}') \ \leq \ !\mathcal{F}_{\text{derive}}(n, \text{parse}) \ .$$

4.2.7. Nonces

The ideal functionality $\mathcal{F}_{\text{nonce}}$ for nonces that we present in this section models ideal nonces that never collide. It is different from the long-term key functionalities

---

Parameters: $n > 0$ {*number of I/O tape pairs*

Tapes: from/to IO_r ($r \leq n$): $(\mathsf{io}^{in}_{nonce_r}, \mathsf{io}^{out}_{nonce_r})$; from/to NET: $(\mathsf{net}^{in}_{\mathcal{F}_{nonce}}, \mathsf{net}^{out}_{\mathcal{F}_{nonce}})$

State: $\mathsf{H} \subseteq \{0,1\}^*$ {*recorded nonces; initially* $\emptyset$

CheckAddress: Accept every input on every tape.

Compute:

  recv $(id, \mathsf{NonceGen})$ **from** IO_r:

    send $\mathsf{NonceGen}$ **to** NET; **recv** x **on** NET **s.t.** $x \notin \mathsf{H}$ {*get nonce from adversary*

    add x **to** H; **send** (id, x) **to** IO_r {*record and return* x

---

Figure 4.11.: The ideal nonce functionality $\mathcal{F}_{nonce}$.

above because it does not encapsulate keys. In particularly, there will only be one instance of $\mathcal{F}_{nonce}$ in every run with $\mathcal{F}_{nonce}$ (i.e., $\mathcal{F}_{nonce}$ accepts all messages in mode CheckAddress). For example, $\mathcal{F}_{nonce}$ can be realized by randomly choosing bit strings of appropriate length, see below.

The Ideal Nonce Functionality $\mathcal{F}_{nonce}$

The ideal functionality $\mathcal{F}_{nonce}$ is a single IITM with n I/O input tapes and n I/O output tapes (n is a parameter of $\mathcal{F}_{nonce}$) that is defined in pseudocode in Figure 4.11 (see Section 3.1 for notational conventions). We denote $\mathcal{F}_{nonce}$ parameterized by n by $\mathcal{F}_{nonce}(n)$. However, we usually omit n because it is clear from the context. As for the long-term key functionalities above, the I/O tapes allow (machines of) a protocol to send requests to $\mathcal{F}_{nonce}$ (and to receive the response).

The functionality $\mathcal{F}_{nonce}$ offers only one operation, namely to generate a fresh nonce $(id, \mathsf{NonceGen})$: Upon receiving this nonce generation request on an I/O input tape, $\mathcal{F}_{nonce}$ asks the adversary to provide an arbitrary bit string that has not been recorded before. Then, $\mathcal{F}_{nonce}$ records this nonce and returns it. This guarantees that $\mathcal{F}_{nonce}$ always outputs a fresh nonce. The identifier id contained in the request (and response), as for the long-term key functionalities above, allows multiple machines that are addressed by IDs to send requests to $\mathcal{F}_{nonce}$ on the same tape and to receive the responses, i.e., it is for addressing purposes only.

It is easy to see that $\mathcal{F}_{nonce}$ is environmentally strictly bounded.

Realization by Randomly Choosing Nonces

The ideal functionality $\mathcal{F}_{nonce}$ can, for example, be realized by choosing nonces uniformly at random from a large enough domain such that collisions among nonces occur only with negligible probability. For example, the realization $\mathcal{P}_{nonce}(n)$ (or simply $\mathcal{P}_{nonce}$) of $\mathcal{F}_{nonce}(n)$ that chooses nonces of length η (where η is the security parameter) is given in Figure 4.12. It is easy to see that $\mathcal{P}_{nonce}$ is environmentally strictly bounded. We omit the proof of the following theorem because it is straightforward.

Parameters: $n > 0$ *{number of I/O tape pairs*

Tapes: from/to IO_r $(r \leq n)$: $(\mathsf{io}^{\mathrm{in}}_{\mathrm{nonce}_r}, \mathsf{io}^{\mathrm{out}}_{\mathrm{nonce}_r})$; from/to NET: $(\mathsf{net}^{\mathrm{in}}_{\mathcal{P}_{\mathrm{nonce}}}, \mathsf{net}^{\mathrm{out}}_{\mathcal{P}_{\mathrm{nonce}}})$

CheckAddress: Accept every input on every tape.

Compute:

    recv $(id, \mathsf{NonceGen})$ **from** IO_r: $x \xleftarrow{\$} \{0, 1\}^\eta$; **send** (id, x) **to** IO_r

---

Figure 4.12.: The realization $\mathcal{P}_{\mathrm{nonce}}$ of $\mathcal{F}_{\mathrm{nonce}}$.

Theorem 4.11. $\mathcal{P}_{\mathrm{nonce}}(n) \leq \mathcal{F}_{\mathrm{nonce}}(n)$ *for all* $n \in \mathbb{N}$.

We note that, for the realization $\mathcal{P}_{\mathrm{nonce}}$, a joint state realization of $\mathcal{F}_{\mathrm{nonce}}$ is not required because $\mathcal{P}_{\mathrm{nonce}}$ does not have any (joint) state.

4.3. Ideal Functionalities for Key Exchange and Secure Channel Protocols

In this section, we define ideal functionalities for key exchange and secure channel protocols that capture their security properties. We also introduce ideal functionalities for key usability that are supposed to be realizable by key exchange protocols even if the exchanged session key does not satisfy key indistinguishability because the session key has been used during the key exchange (e.g., for key confirmation).

4.3.1. Key Exchange

We now define a standard ideal functionality $\mathcal{F}_{\mathrm{ke}}$ for key exchange (see, e.g., [CK02b]). This functionality describes one session of an ideal key exchange between n parties/roles (typically, $n = 2$). It is defined in pseudocode in Figure 4.13 (see Section 3.1 for notational conventions).

The functionality $\mathcal{F}_{\mathrm{ke}}$ has n sets of I/O tapes, one for each role. It first waits to receive session establish requests of the form $(\mathsf{Establish}, m)$ from a role. In this, m is an arbitrary bit string that is not interpreted by the functionality. It may be used by the role to specify options for the session that are used in a protocol that is meant to realize $\mathcal{F}_{\mathrm{ke}}$, e.g., the name of a key server or the role's choice of algorithms it wants to use in this protocol session. Of course, m can be omitted (or forced to be the empty bit string ε) if it is not required by a realization of $\mathcal{F}_{\mathrm{ke}}$. The simulator (ideal adversary) is informed about such requests. If the simulator sends a message for one role to establish the session $((\mathsf{Establish}, r, k)$ for role $r \in \{1, \dots, n\}$ and key $k \in \{0, 1\}^\eta)$, $\mathcal{F}_{\mathrm{ke}}$ outputs k to that role if $\mathcal{F}_{\mathrm{ke}}$ is corrupted and, otherwise, outputs the session key to that role, where the session key is chosen uniformly at random from $\{0, 1\}^\eta$ by $\mathcal{F}_{\mathrm{ke}}$ (η is the security parameter). (Of course, another domain and distribution could be used for the session key.) The simulator has the ability to corrupt $\mathcal{F}_{\mathrm{ke}}$, by sending a special corrupt message (Corr) to it before any of the roles

---

Parameters: $n > 0$ *{number of I/O tape pairs*

Tapes: from/to IO_r $(r \leq n)$: $(\mathsf{io}_{\mathsf{ke}_r}^{\mathsf{in}}, \mathsf{io}_{\mathsf{ke}_r}^{\mathsf{out}})$; from/to NET: $(\mathsf{net}_{\mathcal{F}_{\mathsf{ke}}}^{\mathsf{in}}, \mathsf{net}_{\mathcal{F}_{\mathsf{ke}}}^{\mathsf{out}})$

State: – key $\in \{0,1\}^\eta \cup \{\bot\}$ *{exchanged session key; initially $\bot$*

  – $\forall r \leq n$: $\mathsf{st}_r \in \{\mathsf{inactive}, \mathsf{active}, \mathsf{established}\}$ *{status of role r; initially* inactive

  – corr $\in \{0,1\}$ *{corruption status; initially 0*

CheckAddress: Accept every input on every tape.

Compute:

Session establishment:
  recv (Establish, m) **from** IO_r **s.t.** $\mathsf{st}_r = $ inactive: $\mathsf{st}_r := $ active; **send** (Establish, m, r) **to** NET
  recv (Establish, r, k) **from** NET **s.t.** $\mathsf{st}_r = $ active $\wedge$ $k \in \{0,1\}^\eta$:
    $\mathsf{st}_r := $ established
    if corr $= 1$:
      send (Established, k) **to** IO_r *{output key provided by adversary if corrupted*
    else:
      if key $= \bot$: key $\xleftarrow{\$} \{0,1\}^\eta$ *{generate session key (if not done before)*
      send (Established, key) **to** IO_r *{output session key*

Corruption:
  recv Corr **from** NET **s.t.** $\forall r \leq n$: $\mathsf{st}_r \neq$ established: *{static corruption*
    corr $:= 1$; **send** Ack **to** NET
  recv Corr? **from** IO_r: **send** corr **to** IO_r *{corruption status request*

Figure 4.13.: The ideal key exchange functionality $\mathcal{F}_{\mathsf{ke}}$.

has output a key. Altogether, an uncorrupted $\mathcal{F}_{\mathsf{ke}}$ guarantees that the key a role receives is a freshly generated key that is only given to the roles involved in the key exchange. The key is indistinguishable from random for an adversary even if the key is output by one role before the end of the protocol. Also, if another role receives a key, the two keys are guaranteed to coincide. Conversely, a corrupted $\mathcal{F}_{\mathsf{ke}}$ does not provide any security guarantees; the keys the roles obtain (if any) are determined by the simulator and they do not need to coincide. As usual (see Section 4.1.4), the environment may ask whether $\mathcal{F}_{\mathsf{ke}}$ has been corrupted (Corr?).

As mentioned, $\mathcal{F}_{\mathsf{ke}}$ captures only a single key exchange between n roles (played by arbitrary parties). Key exchange for an unbounded number of sessions and between an unbounded number of parties can be described by the multi-session version $!\mathcal{F}_{\mathsf{ke}}$ of $\mathcal{F}_{\mathsf{ke}}$. For example, the domain of SIDs that $\mathcal{F}_{\mathsf{ke}}$ accepts can be defined to be SIDs of the form $sid = (sid', pid_1, \ldots, pid_n)$ for party names $pid_1, \ldots, pid_n$. Intuitively, an instance of $\mathcal{F}_{\mathsf{ke}}$ addressed by such an SID would be an ideal functionality for the key exchange between the parties $pid_1, \ldots, pid_n$ in session sid'. (Note that by this, there can be multiple sessions for the key exchange between the same list of parties.)

We note that $\mathcal{F}_{\mathsf{ke}}$ does not model authentication, i.e., one role might receive a key although not all roles have sent session establish requests to $\mathcal{F}_{\mathsf{ke}}$ (to start the protocol). (Still, $\mathcal{F}_{\mathsf{ke}}$ guarantees that the key this role receives is indistinguishable from random.) For example, to model mutual authentication, which is often required from key exchange protocols, we could consider a variant $\mathcal{F}_{\mathsf{ake}}$ of $\mathcal{F}_{\mathsf{ke}}$ where the simulator may only send a message for one role to establish a session if all roles have previously sent their session establish requests to $\mathcal{F}_{\mathrm{ake}}$ or if $\mathcal{F}_{\mathrm{ake}}$ is corrupted. Of course, other forms of authentication are also conceivable (e.g., where it is only guaranteed that a certain subset of roles have sent their session establish requests before one role can establish a session).

We further note that $\mathcal{F}_{\mathrm{ke}}$ only allows static corruption (corruption is only possible until some role received a key). This could be relaxed and adaptive corruption could be allowed. Then, the simulator should obtain the session key upon corruption. Furthermore, we could define corruption such that individual roles are corruptible. However, this is not needed in this thesis.

In Section 4.4, we analyze an example protocol and show that it realizes $\mathcal{F}_{\mathrm{ke}}$. Furthermore, in Chapter 6 and Section 7.4 we propose criteria for key exchange protocols and prove that they are sufficient to show that a protocol realizes $\mathcal{F}_{\mathrm{ke}}$. (The criterion in Chapter 6 is a symbolic one.)

4.3.2. Key Usability

We now propose an ideal functionality $\mathcal{F}_{\mathrm{keyuse}}$ for key usability. It is a generalization of the key usability functionality proposed in [KT11a] and is inspired by the notion of key usability proposed in [DDMW06]. It is very similar to a standard key exchange functionality. However, parties do not obtain the actual exchanged key but only a message that a session has been established (i.e., that a key has been exchanged). They can then use this session (i.e., this key) to perform *ideal* cryptographic operations, e.g., encryption, MACing, key derivation, etc. Compared to the standard key exchange functionality, $\mathcal{F}_{\mathrm{keyuse}}$ has two advantages: *(i)* One can reason about the session key (and keys derived from it) still in an *ideal* way, which greatly simplifies the analysis when used in higher-level protocols. *(ii)* $\mathcal{F}_{\mathrm{keyuse}}$ can be realized by key exchange protocols which use the session key during the key exchange, e.g., for key confirmation.

More precisely, $\mathcal{F}_{\mathrm{keyuse}}$ is defined based on an arbitrary ideal functionality $\mathcal{F}$ that has n pairs of I/O tapes, one for each role. The idea is that $\mathcal{F}$ captures the usage of a single symmetric key. Basically, $\mathcal{F}_{\mathrm{keyuse}}$ is a wrapper around $\mathcal{F}$ that makes its interface similar to that of key exchange protocols.

For example, $\mathcal{F}$ is one of the long-term key functionalities $\mathcal{F}_{\mathrm{senc}}$, $\mathcal{F}_{\mathrm{mac}}$, or $\mathcal{F}_{\mathrm{derive}}$ defined in Section 4.2. But $\mathcal{F}$ might be more complex, such as the ideal crypto functionality $\mathcal{F}_{\mathrm{crypto}}$ proposed in Chapter 5. In this case, $\mathcal{F}$ would basically be set up as a copy of $\mathcal{F}_{\mathrm{crypto}}$ with one designated key (of some type, e.g., an encryption key or a key derivation key), the established session key, that allows all operations that $\mathcal{F}_{\mathrm{crypto}}$ allows (such as generating fresh keys, encrypting or MACing messages, or deriving keys). In particular, the established session key can be used for these operations (depending on its type).

Formally, the ideal key usability functionality $\mathcal{F}_{\mathrm{keyuse}}^{\mathcal{F}}$ w.r.t. $\mathcal{F}$ is defined as

$$\mathcal{F}_{\mathrm{keyuse}}^{\mathcal{F}} := \mathcal{F}_{\mathrm{keyuse}} \mid \mathcal{F}$$

Parameters: $n > 0$ *{number of I/O tape pairs*

Tapes: $\forall r \leq n$: from/to IO_r: $(\mathsf{io}_r^{in}, \mathsf{io}_r^{out})$; from/to IO_r': $(\mathsf{io}_r^{out'}, \mathsf{io}_r^{in'})$; from/to NET: $(\mathsf{net}^{in}, \mathsf{net}^{out})$

State: $\forall r \leq n$: $\mathsf{st}_r \in \{\text{inactive, active, established}\}$ *{status of role r; initially* inactive

CheckAddress: Accept every input on every tape.

Compute:

Session establishment:
> **recv** (Establish, m) **from** IO_r **s.t.** $\mathsf{st}_r = $ inactive: $\mathsf{st}_r := $ active; **send** (Establish, m, r) **to** NET
> **recv** (Establish, r) **from** NET **s.t.** $\mathsf{st}_r = $ active: $\mathsf{st}_r := $ established; **send** Established **to** IO_r

Key usage:
> **recv** m **from** IO_r **s.t.** $\mathsf{st}_r = $ established: **send** m **to** IO_r' *{forward m from IO_r to $\mathcal{F}$*
> **recv** m **from** IO_r' **s.t.** $\mathsf{st}_r = $ established: **send** m **to** IO_r *{forward m from $\mathcal{F}$ to IO_r*

Corruption:
> **recv** Corr? **from** IO_r **s.t.** $\mathsf{st}_r \neq $ established: *{corruption status request*
>   **send** Corr? **to** IO_r'; **recv** *corr* **from** IO_r'; **send** *corr* **to** IO_r *{return corruption status of $\mathcal{F}$*

Figure 4.14.: The IITM $\mathcal{F}_{\text{keyuse}}$. It is used to define the ideal key usability function-ality $\mathcal{F}_{\text{keyuse}}^{\mathcal{F}} := \mathcal{F}_{\text{keyuse}} \,|\, \mathcal{F}$ for an ideal functionality $\mathcal{F}$ with I/O input tapes $\mathsf{io}_1^{in'}, \ldots, \mathsf{io}_n^{in'}$ and I/O output tapes $\mathsf{io}_1^{out'}, \ldots, \mathsf{io}_n^{out'}$.

where $\mathcal{F}_{\text{keyuse}}$ is an IITM defined in pseudocode in Figure 4.14 (see Section 3.1 for notational conventions) and described below.

The IITM $\mathcal{F}_{\text{keyuse}}$ is defined such that it provides a similar I/O interface as $\mathcal{F}$ (i.e., there is one pair of I/O tapes for each role) and connects to the I/O interface of $\mathcal{F}$. It also has network tapes to connect to the simulator (ideal adversary). Just like $\mathcal{F}_{\text{ke}}$, $\mathcal{F}_{\text{keyuse}}$ waits to receive session establish requests from roles. The simulator is informed about such requests. If the simulator sends a message for one role to establish a session (($\mathsf{Establish}, r$) for role $r \in \{1, \ldots, n\}$), $\mathcal{F}_{\text{keyuse}}$ sends a message (Established) to the environment for this role, to inform it that the session has been established. From then on, $\mathcal{F}_{\text{keyuse}}$ forwards all messages for this role between the environment and $\mathcal{F}$. Corruption is not (and does not need to be) modeled in $\mathcal{F}_{\text{keyuse}}$; this is left to the definition of $\mathcal{F}$. For example, $\mathcal{F}$ might define static corruption (as $\mathcal{F}_{\text{senc}}$ or $\mathcal{F}_{\text{derive}}$) or adaptive corruption (as $\mathcal{F}_{\text{mac}}$). As usual (see Section 4.1.4), the environment may ask whether $\mathcal{F}_{\text{keyuse}}$ has been corrupted (Corr?). This request is forwarded to $\mathcal{F}$ (even if the role for which this request is sent has not established the session yet) and the response is returned to the environment. That is, the environment obtains the corruption status of $\mathcal{F}$.

It is easy to see that $\mathcal{F}_{\text{keyuse}}^{\mathcal{F}}$ is environmentally (strictly) bounded if $\mathcal{F}$ is environ-mentally (strictly) bounded because $\mathcal{F}_{\text{keyuse}}$ only forwards messages.

We note that, similarly to $\mathcal{F}_{\text{ke}}$, $\mathcal{F}_{\text{keyuse}}^{\mathcal{F}}$ does not model authentication. For example, mutual authentication, which is often required from key exchange protocols, could be modeled by a variant $\mathcal{F}_{\text{auth-keyuse}}^{\mathcal{F}}$ of $\mathcal{F}_{\text{keyuse}}^{\mathcal{F}}$ where the simulator may only send a message for one role to establish a session if all roles have previously sent their session establish requests to $\mathcal{F}^{\mathcal{F}}_{\text{auth-keyuse}}$ or if $\mathcal{F}$ is corrupted.[24] As mentioned for $\mathcal{F}_{\text{ke}}$, other forms of authentication are also conceivable.

As mentioned for $\mathcal{F}_{\text{ke}}$, $\mathcal{F}^{\mathcal{F}}_{\text{keyuse}}$ captures only a single key exchange between n roles (played by arbitrary parties). Key usability for an unbounded number of sessions and between an unbounded number of parties can be described by the multi-session version $!\mathcal{F}^{\mathcal{F}}_{\text{keyuse}}$ of $\mathcal{F}_{\text{keyuse}}$.

The realizations $\mathcal{P}_{\text{senc}}$, $\mathcal{P}_{\text{mac}}$, and $\mathcal{P}_{\text{derive}}$, given in Section 4.2, combined with a key exchange protocol $\mathcal{P}$ that realizes $\mathcal{F}_{\text{ke}}$ induce realizations of $\mathcal{F}^{\mathcal{F}_{\text{senc}}}_{\text{keyuse}}$, $\mathcal{F}^{\mathcal{F}_{\text{mac}}}_{\text{keyuse}}$, and $\mathcal{F}^{\mathcal{F}_{\text{derive}}}_{\text{keyuse}}$, respectively. Where the key established using $\mathcal{P}$ is then used in the realizations $\mathcal{P}_{\text{senc}}$, $\mathcal{P}_{\text{mac}}$, and $\mathcal{P}_{\text{derive}}$, respectively. Of course, other realizations exist. As mentioned above, $\mathcal{F}^{\mathcal{F}}_{\text{keyuse}}$ is realizable by key exchange protocols that use the key during the key exchange (e.g., for key confirmation), and hence, do not realize $\mathcal{F}_{\text{ke}}$. For example, a key exchange protocol $\mathcal{P}$ that does not provide authentication (i.e., it realizes $\mathcal{F}_{\text{ke}}$ as defined above and not a variant of $\mathcal{F}_{\text{ke}}$ that provides authentication) might be turned into a protocol that realizes a variant of $\mathcal{F}_{\text{keyuse}}$ that provides authentication by adding a key confirmation phase to $\mathcal{P}$ in which the established session key is used.

In Section 7.4, we propose a criterion for key exchange protocols that can be used to show that a protocol realizes $\mathcal{F}_{\text{keyuse}}$.

4.3.3. Secure Channel

In this section, we define ideal functionalities for secure channels. First, we note that there is not *the* ideal secure channel functionality because every secure channel protocol has slightly different security goals, e.g., concerning reordering of messages, see also Remark 4.12. We define two ideal secure channel functionalities $\mathcal{F}_{\text{sc}}$ and $\mathcal{F}^+_{\text{sc}}$ that capture typical security properties of secure channel protocols. While both functionalities do not allow that messages are replayed or reordered, $\mathcal{F}_{\text{sc}}$ allows that messages are dropped while $\mathcal{F}^+_{\text{sc}}$ prevents message loss. We note that $\mathcal{F}^+_{\text{sc}}$ is similar to the ideal secure channel functionality in [Can05].

The ideal secure channel functionalities $\mathcal{F}_{\text{sc}}$ and $\mathcal{F}^+_{\text{sc}}$ for a single session are defined in pseudocode in Figure 4.15 (see Section 3.1 for notational conventions) and described below. As $\mathcal{F}_{\text{ke}}$ and $\mathcal{F}_{\text{keyuse}}$, the machines $\mathcal{F}_{\text{sc}}$ and $\mathcal{F}^+_{\text{sc}}$ are parameterized by a number $n > 0$ that defines the number of I/O tapes and thus roles (typically, $n = 2$).

Just like $\mathcal{F}_{\text{ke}}$ and $\mathcal{F}_{\text{keyuse}}$, $\mathcal{F}_{\text{sc}}$ waits to receive session establish requests from roles. The simulator (ideal adversary) is informed about such requests. If the simulator sends a message for one role to establish a session ((Establish, r) for role $r \in \{1, \ldots, n\}$), $\mathcal{F}_{\text{sc}}$ sends a message (Established) to the environment for this role to inform it that the session has been established. That is, session establishment is defined exactly as for $\mathcal{F}_{\text{keyuse}}$. From then on, $\mathcal{F}_{\text{sc}}$ allows this role to send messages to other roles ((Send, r', x)). These messages are recorded in a queue (there is one queue

---

[24]We note that, to define $\mathcal{F}_{\text{auth-keyuse}}$ like this, $\mathcal{F}_{\text{auth-keyuse}}$ has to know the corruption status of $\mathcal{F}$ and it is able to learn it by sending a corruption status request to $\mathcal{F}$ on its own behalf.

Parameters: $n > 0$　　　　　　　　　　　　　　　　　　　*{number of I/O tape pairs}*

Tapes: from/to IO_r $(r \leq n)$: $(\mathsf{io}_{\mathrm{sc}_r}^{\mathrm{in}}, \mathsf{io}_{\mathrm{sc}_r}^{\mathrm{out}})$; from/to NET: $(\mathsf{net}_{\mathcal{F}_{\mathrm{sc}}}^{\mathrm{in}}, \mathsf{net}_{\mathcal{F}_{\mathrm{sc}}}^{\mathrm{out}})$

State: $-$ $\forall r, r' \leq n$: $\mathsf{q}_{r,r'}$　　　　　　　*{queue of messages from role r to r'; initially empty}*

　　　　$-$ $\forall r \leq n$: $\mathsf{st}_r \in \{\mathrm{inactive}, \mathrm{active}, \mathrm{established}\}$　　*{status of role r; initially inactive}*

　　　　$-$ $\mathrm{corr} \in \{0, 1\}$　　　　　　　　　　　　　*{corruption status; initially 0}*

CheckAddress: Accept every input on every tape.

Compute:

Session establishment:
　　recv $(\mathsf{Establish}, m)$ **from** IO_r **s.t.** $\mathsf{st}_r = \mathrm{inactive}$: $\mathsf{st}_r := \mathrm{active}$; **send** $(\mathsf{Establish}, m, r)$ **to** NET
　　recv $(\mathsf{Establish}, r)$ **from** NET **s.t.** $\mathsf{st}_r = \mathrm{active}$: $\mathsf{st}_r := \mathrm{established}$; **send** $\mathsf{Established}$ **to** IO_r

Secure channel usage:
　　recv (Send, r', x) **from** IO_r **s.t.** $\mathsf{st}_r = \mathrm{established} \wedge r' \neq r$:
　　　　if $\mathrm{corr} = 0$:
　　　　　　add x **to** $\mathsf{q}_{r,r'}$; **send** $(\mathsf{Send}, r, r', 0^{|x|})$ **to** NET　　*{append x at the end of the queue $\mathsf{q}_{r,r'}$}*
　　　　else:
　　　　　　send $(\mathsf{Send}, r, r', x)$ **to** NET　　　　　　　　　*{give x to adversary}*
　　recv $(\mathsf{Deliver}, r, r', x)$ **from** NET **s.t.** $\mathsf{st}_{r'} = \mathrm{established} \wedge r' \neq r$:
　　　　if $\mathrm{corr} = 0$:
　　　　　　if $\mathsf{q}_{r,r'}$ is empty: **send** $\perp$ **to** NET　　　　　　　*{return error}*
　　　　　　remove the first message from $\mathsf{q}_{r,r'}$; let x' be this message
　　　　　　send $(\mathsf{Received}, r, x')$ **to** $\mathsf{IO}_{r'}$　　　*{deliver first message from queue}*
　　　　else:
　　　　　　send $(\mathsf{Received}, r, x)$ **to** $\mathsf{IO}_{r'}$　　*{deliver message from adversary if corrupted}*
　　recv (Drop, r, r') **from** NET **s.t.** $\mathsf{q}_{r,r'}$ is not empty:
　　　　remove the first message from $\mathsf{q}_{r,r'}$; **send** Ack **to** NET　　　　*{drop message}*

Corruption:
　　recv Corr **from** NET **s.t.** $\forall r \leq n$: $\mathsf{st}_r \neq \mathrm{established}$:　　　*{static corruption}*
　　　　$\mathrm{corr} := 1$; **send** Ack **to** NET
　　recv $\mathsf{Corr?}$ **from** IO_r: **send** corr **to** IO_r　　　*{corruption status request}*

Figure 4.15.: The ideal secure channel functionality $\mathcal{F}_{\mathrm{sc}}$. Its strengthened variant
　　　　　　$\mathcal{F}_{\mathrm{sc}}^{+}$ differs from $\mathcal{F}_{\mathrm{sc}}$ only in that drop requests are ignored.

per ordered pair of roles, the sender and the receiver). Upon such a request, $\mathcal{F}_{\mathrm{sc}}$ informs the simulator about this request. If corrupted $\mathcal{F}_{\mathrm{sc}}$ also gives the message to the simulator. Otherwise, $\mathcal{F}_{\mathrm{sc}}$ only gives the length of the message to the simulator (this is typically required to obtain realizability but it could be modified to capture security guarantees of secure channels that hide the length of messages). If $\mathcal{F}_{\mathrm{sc}}$ is corrupted, the simulator can tell $\mathcal{F}_{\mathrm{sc}}$ to deliver arbitrary messages. Otherwise, the simulator can only tell $\mathcal{F}_{\mathrm{sc}}$ to deliver or to drop messages from the queues. Upon delivery, $\mathcal{F}_{\mathrm{sc}}$ removes the oldest message in the queue and sends it to the receiving role. If the simulator tells $\mathcal{F}_{\mathrm{sc}}$ to drop a message, $\mathcal{F}_{\mathrm{sc}}$ simply removes the oldest message from the queue but does not deliver it. The simulator has the ability to statically corrupt $\mathcal{F}_{\mathrm{sc}}$ just as for $\mathcal{F}_{\mathrm{ke}}$, i.e., $\mathcal{F}_{\mathrm{sc}}$ is corruptible until one role established a session. Altogether, an uncorrupted $\mathcal{F}_{\mathrm{sc}}$ guarantees that messages are delivered in the correct order and unaltered (see also Remark 4.12); however, some messages might have been dropped. Furthermore, the simulator only obtains the length of the messages. Conversely, a corrupted $\mathcal{F}_{sc}$ does not provide any security guarantees; all messages are forwarded to the simulator and the simulator may deliver arbitrary messages. As usual (see Section 4.1.4), the environment may ask whether $\mathcal{F}_{sc}$ has been corrupted (Corr?).

The strengthened variant $\mathcal{F}_{sc}^+$ is defined just as $\mathcal{F}_{sc}$, except that the simulator cannot drop messages. Clearly, $\mathcal{F}_{sc}^+ \leq \mathcal{F}_{sc}$ because the simulator can block all drop requests.

Just like $\mathcal{F}_{ke}$ and $\mathcal{F}_{keyuse}$, $\mathcal{F}_{sc}$ and $\mathcal{F}_{sc}^+$ capture only a single secure channel between n roles (played by arbitrary parties). Secure channels for an unbounded number of sessions and between an unbounded number of parties can be described by the multi-session versions $!\underline{\mathcal{F}_{sc}}$ of $\mathcal{F}_{sc}$ and $!\underline{\mathcal{F}_{sc}^+}$ of $\mathcal{F}_{sc}^+$.

Remark 4.12. We note that $\mathcal{F}_{sc}$ and $\mathcal{F}_{sc}^+$ prevent reordering of messages between every pair of roles. In the usual case with two roles this means that it is guaranteed that the messages from one role to the other are delivered in the correct order (messages may or may not be dropped). However, the order of message in different directions is not guaranteed. For example, if the first role sends a message to the second role and then the second role sends a message to the first role, it is not guaranteed in which order these messages are delivered. Of course, one can define variants of $\mathcal{F}_{sc}$ and $\mathcal{F}_{sc}^+$ that prevent this kind of reordering. Moreover, if the secure channel does not guarantee replay protection or does not guarantee that messages arrive in the correct order, one could easily weaken the functionality appropriately.

Furthermore, we note that, similarly to $\mathcal{F}_{ke}$ and $\mathcal{F}_{keyuse}$, $\mathcal{F}_{sc}$ and $\mathcal{F}_{sc}^+$ do not model authentication. Several forms of authentication could be modeled by appropriately modifying $\mathcal{F}_{sc}$ and $\mathcal{F}_{sc}^+$; see the explanations for $\mathcal{F}_{ke}$.

Which variant of the secure channel functionality should be considered depends on the protocol under analysis. In general, one should consider the variant that precisely captures the security guarantees the protocol provides (or should provide).

Remark 4.13. Similarly, one could define ideal functionalities for authenticated channels; similar to the ideal functionality $\mathcal{F}_{AUTH}$ in [Can05]: Instead of $0^{|x|}$, the actual message x would be sent to the simulator even if the functionality is not corrupted.

4.4. Security Analysis of an Example Protocol

We now present a concrete example of a protocol in order to illustrate the modeling described in Section 4.1 and the usage of the ideal functionalities introduced above. More specifically, we show how to model a simple key exchange protocol based on symmetric encryption. We also prove the security of this protocol along the lines sketched in Section 4.1 using the ideal functionality for symmetric encryption $\mathcal{F}_{senc}$

(see Section 4.2.3) and its joint state realization (see Section 4.2.6). Security for this protocol means that it realizes a standard ideal key exchange functionality; more precisely, the multi-session version $!\mathcal{F}_{ke}$ of the functionality $\mathcal{F}_{ke}$ (see Section 4.3.1). Finally, we illustrate how to build a secure channel from an ideal key exchange functionality (or a protocol that realizes it).

4.4.1. Our Simple Key Exchange Protocol (OSKE)

The example protocol that we now model and analyze is a simple key exchange protocol based on symmetric encryption. We call it *Our Simple Key Exchange Protocol (OSKE)*. It can informally be described as follows. There are two roles A and B with party names pid_A and pid_B, respectively, that share a symmetric long-term key k_{AB}. We assume that the two parties have already established this key (it is shared across all sessions) and a unique SID $sid = (sid', pid_A, pid_B)$ for a session of the protocol. That is, sid is only used once for a session between the parties pid_A and pid_B with pid_A playing role A and pid_B playing role B. This SID can for example be established by exchanging nonces.[25] Now, to exchange a fresh session key k in session sid, A generates k and sends the concatenation of sid and k, encrypted under k_{AB}, to B. That is, this protocol consists of only one protocol step:

$$A \to B: \ \{sid, k\}_{k_{AB}} \ .$$

4.4.2. Modeling OSKE in the IITM Model

We now model OSKE in the IITM model. It is straightforward to specify OSKE as a protocol system $\mathcal{P}_{oske} = !M_A \,|\, !M_B$, as described in Section 4.1, which relies on $!\mathcal{P}_{senc}$ (the realization of the ideal symmetric encryption functionality $!\mathcal{F}_{senc}$, see Section 4.2.3) for encryption and decryption with k_{AB}. That is, every copy of M_A and M_B is addressed by a structured SID of the form $sid = (sid', pid_A, pid_B)$ and every message received and output by copies of M_A and M_B is prefixed by their SID. We denote the instance of M_A that is addressed by sid by $M_A[sid]$. Instance of M_B are denoted similarly. For simplicity, we assume that sid', pid_A, and pid_B have length η (where η is the security parameter). That is, sid could simply be the concatenation of these bit strings: $(sid', pid_A, pid_B) = sid' \| pid_A \| pid_B$. The protocol $\mathcal{P}_{oske}$ uses $!\mathcal{P}_{senc}$ as a subprotocol for encryption and decryption under the long-term key k_{AB}. More precisely, $M_A[sid]$ (i.e., the instance of M_A with SID $sid = (sid', pid_A, pid_B)$) uses the instance $\mathcal{P}_{senc}[k_{AB}^{name}(sid)]$ (i.e., the instance of $\mathcal{P}_{senc}$ that is addressed by $k_{AB}^{name}(sid)$ and models the long-term key with name $k_{AB}^{name}(sid)$) where $k_{AB}^{name}(sid) := (\min\{pid_A, pid_B\}, \max\{pid_A, pid_B\})$ (we assume some total order on bit strings, such as lexicographical order). Analogous for instances of M_B. This guarantees that the same long-term key is used in every session with the same

---

[25] As explained in [BLR04], a unique, pre-established SID can be established as follows: Both parties send nonces N_A, N_B in plain to each other. The SID then is the concatenation of the nonces and the party names, e.g., $sid = (N_A, N_B, pid_A, pid_B)$.

parties (no matter in what roles). We note that this usage of $!\mathcal{P}_{\text{senc}}$ models the setup assumption that every two parties share a long-term key.

Formally, OSKE can be modeled by the protocol system

$$\mathcal{P}_{\text{oske}} := !M_A \mid !M_B \mid !\mathcal{P}_{\text{senc}}(\Sigma)$$

where Σ is a symmetric encryption scheme (in the following, we often omit Σ) and M_A and M_B are defined in pseudocode in Figures 4.16 and 4.17 (see the notational conventions given in Section 3.1) and described below. A run of this system is depicted in Figure 4.18. It is easy to see that $\mathcal{P}_{\text{oske}}$ is environmentally strictly bounded.

We now discuss how corruption is modeled. Static corruption of instances of M_A is defined as follows (corruption of instances of M_B is defined analogously). The adversary may corrupt $M_A[sid]$ at the beginning (when the adversary is informed about the key exchange request that $M_A[sid]$ got) by sending a corrupt message to it. We require however that, when the adversary corrupts $M_A[sid]$, then its long-term key must be corrupted, i.e., $\mathcal{P}_{\text{senc}}[k_{AB}^{\text{name}}(sid)]$ must be corrupted (this restriction is enforced by $M_A[sid]$ itself by checking the corruption status of $\mathcal{P}_{\text{senc}}[k_{AB}^{\text{name}}(sid)]$). We note that it is natural to assume that long-term keys of corrupted instances are corrupted.[26] If corrupted, $M_A[sid]$ allows the adversary to determine the session key. We note that, additionally, $M_A[sid]$ could allow the adversary to encrypt and decrypt messages using $\mathcal{P}_{\text{senc}}[k_{AB}^{\text{name}}(sid)]$. However, since $\mathcal{P}_{\text{senc}}[k_{AB}^{\text{name}}(sid)]$ has to be corrupted anyway in this case this does not give additional power to the adversary.

The environment has the ability to ask whether a session of $!\mathcal{F}_{\text{ke}}$ is corrupted, since $\mathcal{P}_{\text{oske}}$ has to provide the same I/O interface as $!\mathcal{F}_{\text{ke}}$, upon such a corruption status request by the environment, say for session sid, $M_A[sid]$ or $M_B[sid]$, respectively, return 1 if and only if they are corrupted or the long-term key they use is corrupted (i.e., $\mathcal{P}_{\text{senc}}[k_{AB}^{\text{name}}(sid)]$). We note that the adversary has the ability to corrupt $\mathcal{P}_{\text{senc}}[k_{AB}^{\text{name}}(sid)]$ without explicitly corrupting $M_A[sid]$ or $M_B[sid]$, and hence, these instances will still follow the prescribed protocol. However, they report to the environment that they are corrupted if $\mathcal{P}_{\text{senc}}[k_{AB}^{\text{name}}(sid)]$ is corrupted because the key exchange protocol does not guarantee security in this situation.

4.4.3. Security of OSKE

We now show that OSKE, as modeled above, is secure in the sense that it realizes an ideal key exchange functionality. More precisely, we show that it realizes the

---

[26]We note that, alternatively, one could define $M_A[sid]$ to be corruptible although $\mathcal{P}_{\text{senc}}[k_{AB}^{\text{name}}(sid)]$ is not corrupted. Then, the adversary should be given access to $\mathcal{P}_{\text{senc}}[k_{AB}^{\text{name}}(sid)]$ via the corrupted instance. However, then all sessions that use $\mathcal{P}_{\text{senc}}[k_{AB}^{\text{name}}(sid)]$, i.e., for the same two parties, must be considered corrupted because no security guarantees can be provided. For modeling corruption it is thus easier to assume that $\mathcal{P}_{\text{senc}}[k_{AB}^{\text{name}}(sid)]$ is corrupted if $M_A[sid]$ is corrupted.

Tapes: from/to IO: $(io_{ke_1}^{in}, io_{ke_1}^{out})$; from/to $\mathcal{P}_{senc}$: $(io_{senc_1}^{out}, io_{senc_1}^{in})$; from/to NET: $(net_{M_A}^{in}, net_{M_A}^{out})$

State: – sid $\in \{0,1\}^* \cup \{\bot\}$ *{the SID (see Initialization); initially $\bot$*

     – name $\in \{0,1\}^* \cup \{\bot\}$ *{name of the long-term key k_{AB} (see Initialization); initially $\bot$*

     – key $\in \{0,1\}^\eta \cup \{\bot\}$ *{exchanged session key; initially $\bot$*

     – st $\in \{inactive, active_1, active_2, established\}$ *{status; initially inactive*

     – corr $\in \{0,1\}$ *{corruption status; initially 0*

CheckAddress: *Accept* input m on any tape iff $m = ((sid', pid_A, pid_B), m')$ for some $sid', pid_A, pid_B \in \{0,1\}^\eta, m' \in \{0,1\}^*$ and $(sid = \bot$ or $sid = (sid', pid_A, pid_B))$.

Initialization: Upon receiving the first message $((sid', pid_A, pid_B), m')$ in mode **Compute** do:
$sid := (sid', pid_A, pid_B)$; name $:= (\min\{pid_A, pid_B\}, \max\{pid_A, pid_B\})$.

     Then, continue processing the first message in mode **Compute**.

Compute:

Protocol steps:
   recv $(sid, (Establish, \varepsilon))$ **from** IO s.t. st $= inactive$: $\left\{ \begin{array}{l} \varepsilon \text{ is the empty bit string, i.e., no} \\ \text{options are used (see Section 4.3.1)} \end{array} \right.$
     st $:= active_1$; **send** $(sid, Establish)$ **to** NET
   recv $(sid, Continue)$ **from** NET s.t. st $= active_1 \wedge corr = 0$:

     st $:= active_2$; key $\overset{\$}{\leftarrow} \{0,1\}^\eta$ *{update status, generate session key*
     send $(sid, name, (Enc, (sid, key)))$ **to** $\mathcal{P}_{senc}$ *{encrypt (sid, key) using $\mathcal{P}_{senc}[name]$*
     recv $(sid, name, y)$ **from** $\mathcal{P}_{senc}$ *{wait for receiving ciphertext*
     send (sid, y) **to** NET   *{send ciphertext via network/adversary*
   recv $(sid, Continue)$ **from** NET s.t. st $= active_2 \wedge corr = 0$:
     st $:= established$; **send** $(sid, (Established, key))$ **to** IO   *{update status, output session key*

Corruption:
   recv $(sid, Corr)$ **from** NET s.t. st $= active_1$:   *{static corruption*
     send $(sid, name, Corr?)$ **to** $\mathcal{P}_{senc}$ *{get corruption status of $\mathcal{P}_{senc}[name]$*
     recv $(sid, name, corr)$ **from** $\mathcal{P}_{senc}$
     if $corr = 0$: **send** $(sid, \bot)$ **to** NET   *{error: $\mathcal{P}_{senc}[name]$ must have been corrupted first*
     $corr := 1$; **send** (sid, Ack) **to** NET   *{update status*
   recv $(sid, Establish, k)$ **from** NET s.t. st $= active_1 \wedge corr = 1 \wedge k \in \{0,1\}^\eta$:
     st $:= established$; **send** $(sid, (Established, k))$ **to** IO   *{output key provided by adversary*
   recv $(sid, Corr?)$ **from** IO: *{corruption status request*
     send $(sid, name, Corr?)$ **to** $\mathcal{P}_{senc}$ *{get corruption status of $\mathcal{P}_{senc}[name]$*
     recv $(sid, name, corr)$ **from** $\mathcal{P}_{senc}$; **send** $(sid, corr)$ **to** IO   *{note that corr $= 1$ if corr $= 1$*

Figure 4.16.: Implementation M_A of role A of OSKE.

multi-session version $!\mathcal{F}_{ke}$ of $\mathcal{F}_{ke}$ (see Section 4.3.1). Of course, this does not hold if unauthenticated encryption is used (i.e., IND-CCA2 security does not suffice).[27]

---

[27] It can be shown that, under the assumption that IND-CCA2 secure public-key encryption schemes exist, there exists an IND-CCA2 secure symmetric encryption scheme such that OSKE, using this scheme, is insecure. The basic idea to show this is that the public-key encryption scheme can be turned into a symmetric one that allows the adversary to encrypt arbitrary messages without knowing the symmetric key. Then, the adversary can simply make up a session key, encrypt it for B (along with an SID), and B will accept this key as the session key. This clearly breaks security of the protocol for any reasonable security definition. In particularly, this attack can easily be turned into an environment that distinguishes between $\mathcal{P}_{oske}$ and $\mathcal{S} \,|\, !\mathcal{F}_{ke}$ for any simulator $\mathcal{S}$.

Tapes: from/to IO: $(\mathsf{io}^{\text{in}}_{\text{ke}_2}, \mathsf{io}^{\text{out}}_{\text{ke}_2})$; from/to $\mathcal{P}_{\text{senc}}$: $(\mathsf{io}^{\text{out}}_{\text{senc}_2}, \mathsf{io}^{\text{in}}_{\text{senc}_2})$; from/to NET: $(\mathsf{net}^{\text{in}}_{M_B}, \mathsf{net}^{\text{out}}_{M_B})$

State: As for M_A (Figure 4.16), except that $\text{st} \in \{\text{inactive}, \text{active}, \text{established}\}$.

CheckAddress and **Initialization:** As for M_A (Figure 4.16).

Compute:

Protocol steps:
  recv (sid, (Establish, ε)) **from** IO **s.t.** st = inactive: st := active; **send** (sid, Establish) **to** NET
  recv (sid, Continue, y) **from** NET **s.t.** st = active $\wedge$ corr = 0:
    send (sid, name, (Dec, y)) **to** $\mathcal{P}_{\text{senc}}$; **recv** (sid, name, x) **from** $\mathcal{P}_{\text{senc}}$ {*decrypt y with $\mathcal{P}_{\text{senc}}$[name]*}
    if $x = $ (sid, k) for some $k \in \{0,1\}^\eta$:   {*check format of plaintext*}
      st := established; key := k {*update status, record received session key*}
      send (sid, (Established, key)) **to** IO   {*output session key*}
    else:
      send (sid, $\bot$) **to** NET   {*error: decryption failed or plaintext has wrong format*}

Corruption: As for M_A (Figure 4.16), except that active$_1$ is replaced by active.

Figure 4.17.: Implementation M_B of role B of OSKE.

Theorem 4.12. *If Σ (recall that $\mathcal{P}_{\text{senc}}$ in $\mathcal{P}_{\text{oske}}$ is parameterized by Σ) is a secure authenticated symmetric encryption scheme (i.e., IND-CPA and INT-CTXT secure):*

$$\mathcal{P}_{\text{oske}} \leq !\mathcal{F}_{\text{ke}} .$$

To prove this theorem, we want to make full use of the composition theorems and the composition theorem with joint state for symmetric encryption, as described in Section 4.1.5. Therefore, we first transform the protocol $\mathcal{P}_{\text{oske}} = !M_A \mid !M_B \mid !\mathcal{P}_{\text{senc}}(\Sigma)$ into an equivalent protocol

$$\mathcal{P}'_{\text{oske}} := !M'_A \mid !M'_B \mid !\mathcal{P}^{\text{js}}_{\text{senc}} \mid !\mathcal{P}_{\text{senc}}(\Sigma)$$

that uses the joint state realization for symmetric encryption proposed in Section 4.2.6 (instead of $!\mathcal{P}_{\text{senc}}$ directly). By equivalent we mean here that $\mathcal{E} \mid \mathcal{P}_{\text{oske}} \equiv \mathcal{E} \mid \mathcal{P}'_{\text{oske}}$ for every environment $\mathcal{E}$ for $\mathcal{P}_{\text{oske}}$. It is very easy to obtain M'_A and M'_B from M_A and M_B, respectively. In the definition of M_A, we only have to replace the plaintext (sid, key) by key, i.e., only key (without the SID) is encrypted using $!\mathcal{P}^{\text{js}}_{\text{senc}} \mid !\mathcal{P}_{\text{senc}}$. In the definition of M_B, we only have to change the test after the decryption of the received ciphertext y, say x is the resulting plaintext: M'_B only checks that $x \in \{0,1\}^\eta$. If this is the case, M'_B sets key := x and outputs it as the session key. Otherwise, M'_B returns an error to the adversary. It is very easy to see that this does not actually change the protocol because the joint state realization, upon encryption, adds the SID and, upon decryption, performs the test that the plaintext is prefixed by the correct SID and only then returns the plaintext (with the SID removed); otherwise it returns an error. We note that $\mathcal{P}'_{\text{oske}}$ is environmentally strictly bounded. We obtain:

Lemma 4.1. *For every environment $\mathcal{E} \in \text{Env}(\mathcal{P}_{\text{oske}})$:*

$$\mathcal{E} \mid \mathcal{P}_{\text{oske}} \equiv \mathcal{E} \mid \mathcal{P}'_{\text{oske}} .$$

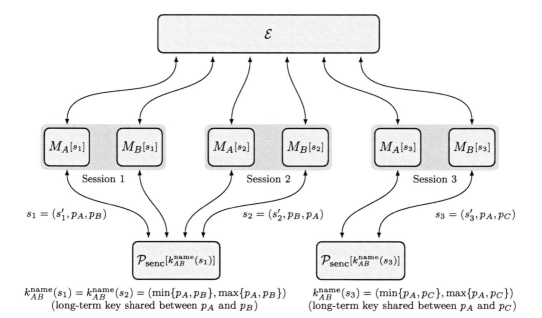

$k_{AB}^{\text{name}}(s_1) = k_{AB}^{\text{name}}(s_2) = (\min\{p_A, p_B\}, \max\{p_A, p_B\})$ $k_{AB}^{\text{name}}(s_3) = (\min\{p_A, p_C\}, \max\{p_A, p_C\})$
(long-term key shared between p_A and p_B)   (long-term key shared between p_A and p_C)

Figure 4.18.: Illustration of instances of machines created in a run of $\mathcal{E} \,|\, \mathcal{P}_{\text{oske}}$ (for some environment $\mathcal{E}$) and their connections. In this run, $\mathcal{E}$ created three sessions: (1) party p_A in role A and p_B in role B, (2) party p_B in role A and p_A in role B, and (3) party p_A in role A and p_C in role B. Every box denotes an instance created in this run. For example, $M_A[s_1]$ is the instance of M_A that is addressed by s_1 (i.e., party p_A in role A talking to p_B in session s_1) and $\mathcal{P}_{\text{senc}}[k_{AB}^{\text{name}}(s_1)]$ is the instance of $\mathcal{P}_{\text{senc}}$ that is addressed by $k_{AB}^{\text{name}}(s_1)$ (modeling the long-term key shared between p_A and p_B). Arrows denote (possible) communication between the instances via I/O tapes. All instances may also communicate with $\mathcal{E}$ via network tapes, but this is not displayed.

We note that the above lemma even holds for unbounded environments and when the encryption scheme Σ is insecure.

Next, we replace the joint state realization by the multi-session version of $\mathcal{F}_{\text{senc}}^{\text{auth}}$. More precisely, we use $\mathcal{F}_{\text{senc}}^{\text{auth}}(p', L)$ parameterized by the leakage algorithm $L(1^\eta, x) := 0^{|x|}$ (i.e., the algorithm that returns the all-zero bit string of the length of the message) and the polynomial p' that is given by Corollary 4.3 (i.e., such that $!\mathcal{P}_{\text{senc}}^{\text{js}} \,|\, !\mathcal{P}_{\text{senc}} \leq \,!\mathcal{F}_{\text{senc}}^{\text{auth}}(p', L)$).[28] We obtain the protocol system

$$\mathcal{P}_{\text{oske}}'' := \,!M_A' \,|\, !M_B' \,|\, !\mathcal{F}_{\text{senc}}^{\text{auth}}(p', L) \ .$$

---

[28] We note that we could have used any leakage algorithm that leaks exactly the length (Definition 3.16). We further note that the polynomial p' depends on the runtime of the encryption

We note that it is easy to see that $\mathcal{P}''_{\text{oske}}$ is environmentally strictly bounded. Using the composition theorem with joint state for symmetric encryption, we obtain the following:

Lemma 4.2. *If Σ (recall that $\mathcal{P}_{\text{senc}}$ in $\mathcal{P}'_{\text{oske}}$ is parameterized by Σ) is a secure authenticated symmetric encryption scheme (i.e., IND-CPA and INT-CTXT secure):*

$$\mathcal{P}'_{\text{oske}} \leq \mathcal{P}''_{\text{oske}} .$$

Proof. Since Σ is IND-CPA and INT-CTXT secure (and because of our choice of p' and L), by Corollary 4.3, we obtain that $!\mathcal{P}^{\text{js}}_{\text{senc}} \mid !\mathcal{P}_{\text{senc}}(\Sigma) \leq !\mathcal{F}^{\text{auth}}_{\text{senc}}(p', L)$. From this, by the composition theorem for a constant number of systems (Theorem 2.1), we conclude $\mathcal{P}'_{\text{oske}} \leq \mathcal{P}''_{\text{oske}}$. $\quad\square$

Next, we show that a $\mathcal{P}''_{\text{oske}}$ single-session realizes $!\mathcal{F}_{\text{ke}}$ (i.e., w.r.t. environments that create only a one session). We note that $\mathcal{P}''_{\text{oske}}$ is a σ_{prefix}-session version because every message is prefixed by an SID.[29]

Lemma 4.3. $\mathcal{P}''_{\text{oske}} \leq_{\sigma_{\text{prefix}}\text{-single}} !\underline{\mathcal{F}_{\text{ke}}}$.

Before we prove the above lemma, we use it to prove Theorem 4.12 ($\mathcal{P}_{\text{oske}} \leq !\underline{\mathcal{F}_{\text{ke}}}$):

Proof of Theorem 4.12. By Lemma 4.3, using the composition theorem for unbounded self-composition of SID dependent protocols (Theorem 2.3), we obtain that $\mathcal{P}''_{\text{oske}} \leq !\underline{\mathcal{F}_{\text{ke}}}$. From this, by Lemmas 4.1 and 4.2 (and because $\equiv$ and $\leq$ are transitive), we obtain that $\mathcal{P}_{\text{oske}} \leq !\underline{\mathcal{F}_{\text{ke}}}$. $\quad\square$

Since the proofs of Lemmas 4.1 and 4.2 are trivial (as we have seen above), the only real effort in proving security of OSKE (Theorem 4.12) lies in the proof that $\mathcal{P}''_{\text{oske}}$ single-session realizes a $!\underline{\mathcal{F}_{\text{ke}}}$ (Lemma 4.3). However, this proof is simple because we only have to consider a single protocol session and encryption is idealized using $\mathcal{F}^{\text{auth}}_{\text{senc}}$.

Proof of Lemma 4.3. We first define a (single-session) simulator $\mathcal{S}$. Let sid be the SID that is used by the environment in this session ($\mathcal{S}$ learns this SID when it receives the first message). The simulator $\mathcal{S}$ simulates $\mathcal{P}''_{\text{oske}} = !M'_A \mid !M'_B \mid !\mathcal{F}^{\text{auth}}_{\text{senc}}$ (i.e., one session with SID sid) and sends an Establish message to $\mathcal{F}_{\text{ke}}[sid]$ (the instance of $\mathcal{F}_{\text{ke}}$ with SID sid) if $\mathcal{P}''_{\text{oske}}$ (i.e., the simulated $M'_A[sid]$ or $M'_B[sid]$) outputs a session key. Upon corruptions of any party or the long-term key, the simulator corrupts $\mathcal{F}_{\text{ke}}[sid]$ and then is free to complete with exactly the same key as in the real world. We note that this is always possible because corruption in $\mathcal{P}''_{\text{oske}}$ is only possible before $\mathcal{P}''_{\text{oske}}$ outputs a session key. Hence, in case of corruption nothing is to show. We further

---

and decryption algorithms in Σ and on the length of SIDs. The length of SIDs is $3 \cdot \eta$ because we assume that every SID is of the form $sid = sid' \| pid_A \| pid_B$ for some $sid', pid_A, pid_B \in \{0,1\}^\eta$.

[29]Recall that σ_{prefix} is the SID function (see Section 2.4) that, for all messages m and tapes c, is defined as $\sigma_{\text{prefix}}(m, c) := sid$ if $m = (sid, m')$ for some sid, m' and $\sigma_{\text{prefix}}(m, c) := \bot$ otherwise.

note that it is easy to see that $\mathcal{S} \mid !\mathcal{F}_{\text{ke}}$ is environmentally strictly bounded. Hence, $\mathcal{S} \in \text{Sim}^{\mathcal{P}''_{\text{oske}}}_{\sigma_{\text{prefix-single}}}(!\mathcal{F}_{\text{ke}})$.

For the uncorrupted case, first note that, by definition of $\mathcal{F}^{\text{auth}}_{\text{senc}}$, the only plaintexts returned by $\mathcal{F}^{\text{auth}}_{\text{senc}}$ upon decryption are the ones "inserted" upon encryption.[30] Now, in every run of $\mathcal{E} \mid \mathcal{P}''_{\text{oske}}$ (without corruption) for some σ_{prefix}-single session environment $\mathcal{E}$ (i.e., $\mathcal{E} \in \text{Env}_{\sigma_{\text{prefix-single}}}(\mathcal{P}''_{\text{oske}})$ invokes only a single session w.r.t. σ_{prefix}), we have that only $M'_A[sid]$ uses $\mathcal{F}^{\text{auth}}_{\text{senc}}[sid, k^{\text{name}}_{AB}(sid)]$ (the copy of $\mathcal{F}^{\text{auth}}_{\text{senc}}$ addressed by sid and $k^{\text{name}}_{AB}(sid)$) for encryption, so, $\mathcal{F}^{\text{auth}}_{\text{senc}}[sid, k^{\text{name}}_{AB}(sid)]$ contains at most the session key key that has been generated by $M'_A[sid]$. Hence, if $M'_B[sid]$ establishes a session key, then this session key has to be key. Furthermore, $\mathcal{E}$'s view on a run is information theoretically independent of key because the ciphertext depends only on the length of key (because, instead of key, its leakage 0^η is encrypted), i.e., on the security parameter η. But then, $\mathcal{E}$ cannot distinguish between the session key key output by $\mathcal{P}''_{\text{oske}}$ in runs of $\mathcal{E} \mid \mathcal{P}''_{\text{oske}}$ and the session key generated and output by $!\mathcal{F}_{\text{ke}}$ in runs of $\mathcal{E} \mid \mathcal{S} \mid !\mathcal{F}_{\text{ke}}$ (recall that $\mathcal{E}$ only invokes a single session). Therefore, it is easy to establish a one-to-one correspondence between runs of $\mathcal{E} \mid \mathcal{P}''_{\text{oske}}$ and runs of $\mathcal{E} \mid \mathcal{S} \mid !\mathcal{F}_{\text{ke}}$ such that corresponding runs have the same probability and overall output. We obtain $\mathcal{E} \mid \mathcal{P}''_{\text{oske}} \equiv \mathcal{E} \mid \mathcal{S} \mid !\mathcal{F}_{\text{ke}}$, and hence, $\mathcal{P}''_{\text{oske}} \leq_{\sigma_{\text{prefix-single}}} !\mathcal{F}_{\text{ke}}$.   □

We note that due to the usage of $\mathcal{F}^{\text{auth}}_{\text{senc}}$, the above proof of Lemma 4.3 is completely syntactical. We also remark that Lemma 4.3 even holds in an information theoretic setting with unbounded environments, as the above proof shows.

4.4.4. Building Secure Channels from Key Exchange Protocols

To illustrate how more complex protocols can be built from lower-level functionalities (or realizations thereof) using the composition theorems, we consider the case of secure channel protocols based on key exchange protocols.

Based on $\mathcal{F}_{\text{keyuse}}$ (see Section 4.3.2), say for authenticated symmetric encryption (i.e., $\mathcal{F}_{\text{keyuse}} = \mathcal{F}^{\mathcal{F}^{\text{auth}}_{\text{senc}}}_{\text{keyuse}}$), it is very easy to design a secure channel protocol $\mathcal{P}_{\text{sc}}$ such that $\mathcal{P}_{\text{sc}} \mid \mathcal{F}_{\text{keyuse}}$ realizes $\mathcal{F}_{\text{sc}}$ (or $\mathcal{F}^+_{\text{sc}}$). For example, $\mathcal{P}_{\text{sc}}$ adds sender/receiver information and a counter to the messages that should be transmitted through the secure channel and then sends these messages, ideally encrypted using $\mathcal{F}_{\text{keyuse}}$, over the network (adversary). Upon receiving a ciphertext from the network (adversary), it is decrypted and output to the party, but only if the sender/receiver information and the counter value are as expected (to prevent, in particularly, reordering; replaying; and, if desired, message loss). We note that a similar secure channel protocol is proposed in Section 7.7.2 (see also Appendix D.3.2). Proving $\mathcal{P}_{\text{sc}} \mid \mathcal{F}_{\text{keyuse}} \leq \mathcal{F}_{\text{sc}}$ is straightforward because $\mathcal{F}_{\text{keyuse}}$ provides ideal authenticated encryption and decryption and only a

---

[30] We note that this argument would not be valid if we would use $\mathcal{F}^{\text{unauth}}_{\text{senc}}$ instead of $\mathcal{F}^{\text{auth}}_{\text{senc}}$, which reflects that the protocol is insecure if unauthenticated encryption is used (as mentioned above).

single session has to be considered. From this, by Theorem 2.2, we directly obtain security in the multi-session setting:

$$!\mathcal{P}_{sc} \mid !\mathcal{F}_{keyuse} \leq !\mathcal{F}_{sc} \, .^{31}$$

That is, we obtain a realization of the multi-session ideal secure channel functionality $!\mathcal{F}_{sc}$. Given any realization $\mathcal{P}_{ke}$ of $!\mathcal{F}_{keyuse}$ (i.e., $\mathcal{P}_{ke} \leq !\mathcal{F}_{keyuse}$), using Theorem 2.1 and transitivity of $\leq$, we then directly obtain that

$$!\mathcal{P}_{sc} \mid \mathcal{P}_{ke} \leq !\mathcal{F}_{sc} \, .$$

That is, the real protocol $!\mathcal{P}_{sc} \mid \mathcal{P}_{ke}$ is secure, in a strong universally composable sense. For example, as mentioned in Section 4.3.2, every protocol that realizes $!\mathcal{F}_{ke}$, such as $\mathcal{P}_{oske}$ (see Theorem 4.12), can be turned into a protocol that realizes $!\mathcal{F}_{keyuse}$. This variant of the key exchange protocol does not output the session key but, instead, allows the higher-level protocol (in our case the secure channel protocol) to use it, e.g., as the key in a secure authenticated symmetric encryption scheme.

---

[31] We note that if $\mathcal{P}_{sc}$ needs to make use of the session identifiers, e.g., because they contain information that needs to be included in protocol messages, then we can formulate $\mathcal{P}_{sc}$ directly in the multi-session setting (e.g., similar to $\mathcal{P}_{oske}$). Even in this case, single-session analysis of $\mathcal{P}_{sc}$ suffices because we can still use Theorem 2.3.

5. An Ideal Functionality for Cryptographic Primitives

In this chapter, we present an ideal functionality $\mathcal{F}_{\text{crypto}}$ for symmetric and public-key encryption, MACs, and key derivation that allows parties to generate fresh and pre-shared symmetric keys and public/private keys and to use these keys for ideal encryption and decryption, MAC generation and verification, and key derivation. We then show that, for a reasonable class of environments, $\mathcal{F}_{\text{crypto}}$ can be realized based on standard cryptographic assumptions and constructions. Furthermore, we give a joint state realization of $\mathcal{F}_{\text{crypto}}$ that is based on SIDs. (We note that, in Section 7.6, we provide another joint state realization of $\mathcal{F}_{\text{crypto}}$ that does not rely on SIDs and can therefore be used to analyze a broader class of protocols.) As mentioned in the introduction, a functionality like $\mathcal{F}_{\text{crypto}}$ is useful for the modular analysis of security protocols, in particular real-world protocols, and was missing in the literature; there only existed an abstract Dolev-Yao style functionality [BP04], see Section 5.5 for the discussion of related work.

The ideal crypto functionality $\mathcal{F}_{\text{crypto}}$ combines the ideal long-term key functionalities for symmetric and public-key encryption, MACs, and key derivation that were given in Section 4.2 such that all symmetric and public keys can now be part of plaintexts to be encrypted under other symmetric and public keys and derived keys can be used just as other symmetric keys. As mentioned above, the long-term key functionalities itself are not applicable to many protocols because symmetric keys cannot be part of plaintexts. Parties can use $\mathcal{F}_{\text{crypto}}$ *(i)* to generate symmetric keys, including pre-shared keys (i.e., symmetric keys shared among several parties), *(ii)* to derive symmetric keys from other symmetric keys, *(iii)* to encrypt and decrypt messages (public-key encryption and both unauthenticated and authenticated symmetric encryption is supported), and *(iv)* to compute and verify MACs, where all the above operations are done in an ideal way. We note that $\mathcal{F}_{\text{crypto}}$ can handle an unbounded number of requests for an unbounded number of parties with the messages, ciphertexts, MACs, etc. being arbitrary bit strings of arbitrary length. We leave it up to the protocol that uses $\mathcal{F}_{\text{crypto}}$ how to interpret (parts of) bit strings, e.g., as length fields, nonces, ciphertexts, MACs, non-interactive zero-knowledge proofs, etc. Since users of $\mathcal{F}_{\text{crypto}}$ are provided with actual bit strings, $\mathcal{F}_{\text{crypto}}$ can be combined with other functionalities too, including those of interest for real-word protocols, e.g., digital signatures and nonces (see Remark 5.4) or certification of public keys (see, e.g., [Can04]).

As mentioned in the introduction, since $\mathcal{F}_{\text{crypto}}$ is a rather low-level ideal functionality and its realization is based on standard cryptographic assumptions and constructions (IND-CCA secure or authenticated encryption, UF-CMA secure MACs, and pseudorandom functions for key derivation), it is widely applicable and allows for a precise modeling of real-word security protocols, including precise modeling of message formats on the bit level. In this thesis, $\mathcal{F}_{\text{crypto}}$ is used in Chapter 6 to obtain a computational soundness result for symmetric encryption. Furthermore, it is used in Section 7.4 to formulate a criterion for key exchange protocols to be secure. Since this criterion is based on $\mathcal{F}_{\text{crypto}}$ it can be checked merely using information-theoretic arguments, rather than involved and harder to manage reduction proofs.

We note that, compared to the ideal functionality $\mathcal{F}_{\text{crypto}}$ presented in joint work with Küsters [KT11b], the further development of $\mathcal{F}_{\text{crypto}}$ presented in this chapter provides a more liberal and, at the same time, simpler way to define message formats for plaintexts (message formats are needed because $\mathcal{F}_{\text{crypto}}$ needs to identify keys contained in plaintexts, see below) and allows to model more general key derivation functions. The formulation in [KT11b] only allows to derive one key from another key (per salt). However, many protocols (e.g., WPA2, see Section 7.4.3) derive multiple keys at once. For example, they use a variable-length output pseudorandom function (see Section 3.2.5) to derive a pseudorandom bit string and then split this bit string into several keys. This cannot be modeled directly using $\mathcal{F}_{\text{crypto}}$ from [KT11b] but a faithful modeling seems to be often possible (e.g., see the modeling of WPA2 in [KT11b]). Such key derivation can now be directly and faithfully modeled in an intuitive way, without (more or less) complicated constructions. Furthermore, in [KT11b], $\mathcal{F}_{\text{crypto}}$ only supported one cryptographic scheme per primitive. Now, $\mathcal{F}_{\text{crypto}}$ supports multiple schemes per primitive; one per key type, see below.

5.1. Preliminaries

Before we present our ideal crypto functionality $\mathcal{F}_{\text{crypto}}$, we start with some preliminaries.

5.1.1. Key Types and Domains

In $\mathcal{F}_{\text{crypto}}$, symmetric keys will be equipped with types and $\mathcal{F}_{\text{crypto}}$ will be parameterized by finite sets of key types: $\mathcal{T}_{\text{senc}}^{\text{auth}}$, $\mathcal{T}_{\text{senc}}^{\text{unauth}}$, $\mathcal{T}_{\text{derive}}$, and $\mathcal{T}_{\text{mac}}$. Keys that may be used for authenticated encryption have a type in $\mathcal{T}_{\text{senc}}^{\text{auth}}$, those for unauthenticated encryption one in $\mathcal{T}_{\text{senc}}^{\text{unauth}}$. We have the types $\mathcal{T}_{\text{mac}}$ for MAC keys and $\mathcal{T}_{\text{derive}}$ for keys from which new keys (of arbitrary type) can be derived. All sets of types are disjoint, i.e., a key can only have one type, reflecting common practice that a symmetric key only serves one purpose. For example, a MAC key is not used for encryption and keys from which other keys are derived are typically not used as encryption or MAC keys. We also note that standard security definitions for cryptographic primitives (see Section 3.2) do not capture the case where the same key is used for different tasks, so, security might be breached in this case.

We define $\mathcal{T}_{\mathrm{senc}} := \mathcal{T}_{\mathrm{senc}}^{\mathrm{auth}} \cup \mathcal{T}_{\mathrm{senc}}^{\mathrm{unauth}}$ to be the set of all encryption key types and we define $\mathcal{T} := \mathcal{T}_{\mathrm{senc}} \cup \mathcal{T}_{\mathrm{derive}} \cup \mathcal{T}_{\mathrm{mac}}$ to be the set of all key types.

Furthermore, $\mathcal{F}_{\mathrm{crypto}}$ will be parameterized by key domains: $\mathcal{D}_{\mathrm{keys}}^t = \{\mathcal{D}_{\mathrm{keys}}^t(\eta)\}_{\eta \in \mathbb{N}}$ for all key types $t \in \mathcal{T}$. For every key type t and security parameter η, $\mathcal{D}_{\mathrm{keys}}^t(\eta) \subseteq \{0,1\}^*$ is the set of all keys of type t (w.r.t. the security parameter η) and we require that it can be decided in polynomial time (in the security parameter η) whether a bit string is in this set. Typically, $\mathcal{D}_{\mathrm{keys}}^t(\eta) = \{0,1\}^{l_t(\eta)}$ for some key length $l_t(\eta)$, e.g., $l_t(\eta) = \eta$ for all η.

Definition 5.1. *Given a key type $t \in \mathcal{T}$ and a key $k \in \mathcal{D}_{\mathrm{keys}}^t$, the pair $\kappa := (t, k)$ is called a typed key. By $\kappa.t$ we denote its type t, by $\kappa.k$ we denote the actual key k.*

We also define the following domains of typed keys:

1. $\mathcal{D}_{\mathrm{senc}}^{\mathrm{auth}} := \{\mathcal{D}_{\mathrm{senc}}^{\mathrm{auth}}(\eta)\}_{\eta \in \mathbb{N}}$ *where* $\mathcal{D}_{\mathrm{senc}}^{\mathrm{auth}}(\eta) := \{(t, k) \mid t \in \mathcal{T}_{\mathrm{senc}}^{\mathrm{auth}}, k \in \mathcal{D}_{\mathrm{keys}}^t\}$.

2. $\mathcal{D}_{\mathrm{senc}}^{\mathrm{unauth}} := \{\mathcal{D}_{\mathrm{senc}}^{\mathrm{unauth}}(\eta)\}_{\eta \in \mathbb{N}}$ *where* $\mathcal{D}_{\mathrm{senc}}^{\mathrm{unauth}}(\eta) := \{(t, k) \mid t \in \mathcal{T}_{\mathrm{senc}}^{\mathrm{unauth}}, k \in \mathcal{D}_{\mathrm{keys}}^t\}$.

3. $\mathcal{D}_{\mathrm{senc}} := \{\mathcal{D}_{\mathrm{senc}}(\eta)\}_{\eta \in \mathbb{N}}$ *where* $\mathcal{D}_{\mathrm{senc}}(\eta) := \mathcal{D}_{\mathrm{senc}}^{\mathrm{auth}}(\eta) \cup \mathcal{D}_{\mathrm{senc}}^{\mathrm{unauth}}(\eta)$.

4. $\mathcal{D}_{\mathrm{derive}} := \{\mathcal{D}_{\mathrm{derive}}(\eta)\}_{\eta \in \mathbb{N}}$ *where* $\mathcal{D}_{\mathrm{derive}}(\eta) := \{(t, k) \mid t \in \mathcal{T}_{\mathrm{derive}}, k \in \mathcal{D}_{\mathrm{keys}}^t\}$.

5. $\mathcal{D}_{\mathrm{mac}} := \{\mathcal{D}_{\mathrm{mac}}(\eta)\}_{\eta \in \mathbb{N}}$ *where* $\mathcal{D}_{\mathrm{mac}}(\eta) := \{(t, k) \mid t \in \mathcal{T}_{\mathrm{mac}}, k \in \mathcal{D}_{\mathrm{keys}}^t\}$.

6. $\mathcal{D} := \{\mathcal{D}(\eta)\}_{\eta \in \mathbb{N}}$ *where* $\mathcal{D}(\eta) := \mathcal{D}_{\mathrm{senc}}(\eta) \cup \mathcal{D}_{\mathrm{derive}}(\eta) \cup \mathcal{D}_{\mathrm{mac}}(\eta)$.

5.1.2. Plaintext Formatting and Parsing

As mentioned above, keys may be part of plaintexts. To construct plaintexts that contain keys and to extract keys from plaintexts, $\mathcal{F}_{\mathrm{crypto}}$ will be parameterized by (plaintext) formatting and parsing functions. Basically, a formatting function takes a message and a list of (typed) keys and returns a plaintext. Vice versa, a parsing function takes a plaintext and returns the original message and the list of keys.

Definition 5.2. *A* (plaintext) formatting function format *is a polynomial-time computable function that takes as input a security parameter 1^η, a message $x \in \{0,1\}^*$, and a (possibly empty) list of typed keys $\kappa_1, \ldots, \kappa_n$ (for some $n \geq 0$) and returns a message $x' \in \{0,1\}^*$ or the error symbol $\perp$ (indicating that formatting failed). We require that, if format does not fail (i.e., does not return $\perp$) for some list of typed keys, then it does not fail for any list of typed keys with the same types. Formally: If $\mathrm{format}(1^\eta, x, \kappa_1, \ldots, \kappa_n) \neq \perp$ for some $\eta \in \mathbb{N}$, $x \in \{0,1\}^*$, and list of typed keys $\kappa_1, \ldots, \kappa_n$ (for some $n \geq 0$), then $\mathrm{format}(1^\eta, x, \kappa_1', \ldots, \kappa_n') \neq \perp$ for all typed keys $\kappa_1', \ldots, \kappa_n'$ such that κ_i and κ_i' have the same type, for all $i \leq n$.*

Given a formatting function format, *a corresponding* (plaintext) parsing function parse *is a polynomial-time computable function that takes as input a security parameter 1^η and a message $x' \in \{0,1\}^*$ and returns $\perp$ (indicating a parsing error) or a message*

x and a (possibly empty) list of typed keys $\kappa_1, \ldots, \kappa_n$ (for some $n \geq 0$) such that parsing a formatted message does not fail and returns the original message and the typed keys. Formally, we require that, for every security parameter $\eta \in \mathbb{N}$, messages $x, x' \in \{0, 1\}^*$, and list of typed keys $\kappa_1, \ldots, \kappa_n$ (for some $n \geq 0$) such that $x' = \mathsf{format}(1^\eta, x, \kappa_1, \ldots, \kappa_n)$, it holds that $\mathsf{parse}(1^\eta, x') = (x, \kappa_1, \ldots, \kappa_n)$.

We define the *range* of a formatting function format to be the domain of all plaintexts that can be constructed using format. More formally, we define:

$$\mathrm{rng}(\mathsf{format})(\eta) := \{ x' \mid \exists x, x' \in \{0, 1\}^*, n \geq 0, \kappa_1, \ldots, \kappa_n \in \mathcal{D}(\eta) :$$
$$x' = \mathsf{format}(1^\eta, x, \kappa_1, \ldots, \kappa_n) \}$$

for every security parameter $\eta \in \mathbb{N}$ (where $\mathcal{D}(\eta)$ is the domain of all typed keys for security parameter η, see above). The range of formatting functions is important for Theorem 5.1, to obtain that security of the encryption schemes is necessary to realize $\mathcal{F}_{\mathrm{crypto}}$.

Simple plaintext formatting and parsing functions can, for example, be defined based on a tagging mechanism that tags keys in messages, see, e.g., Section 6.3. However, formatting and parsing functions are much more powerful. This is often needed when analyzing a protocol using $\mathcal{F}_{\mathrm{crypto}}$. Then, we need to define these functions such that the constructed plaintexts model the plaintext formats that are used in the protocol. Since the above definitions only impose very mild constraints on formatting and parsing functions, for real-world protocols it is typically possible to find such functions such that the plaintext formats used in these protocols are captured precisely on the bit level; see, e.g., Section 7.4.3 where we use $\mathcal{F}_{\mathrm{crypto}}$ to analyze the 4-Way Handshake protocol of WPA2 (IEEE 802.11i). We further note that $\mathcal{F}_{\mathrm{crypto}}$ is not only parameterized by one formatting function (and a corresponding parsing function) but it is parameterized by a formatting function $\mathsf{format}^t_{\mathrm{senc}}$ for every symmetric encryption key type $t \in \mathcal{T}_{\mathrm{senc}}$ and a formatting function $\mathsf{format}^{name}_{\mathrm{pke}}$ for every public/private key pair name $name \in \{0, 1\}^*$ (and corresponding parsing functions $\mathsf{parse}^t_{\mathrm{senc}}, \mathsf{parse}^{name}_{\mathrm{pke}}$).[32] That is, the plaintext formats can even depend on the types of the keys (or public/private key pair names) that are used to encrypt the plaintexts.

Below, to realize $\mathcal{F}_{\mathrm{crypto}}$ (Theorem 5.1), we need to require that leakage algorithms (see Section 3.3) hide the keys in plaintexts. This is defined formally by saying that (the distribution of) the leakage of x' equals the leakage of x'' where x' and x'' are plaintexts obtained from formatting the same message x but with different keys:

Definition 5.3. *We say that a leakage algorithm L is* keys hiding (or hides keys) *w.r.t. a formatting function* format *if, for every security parameter $\eta \in \mathbb{N}$, messages*

---

[32]We note that, since $\{0, 1\}^*$ is an infinite set, this would mean that $\mathcal{F}_{\mathrm{crypto}}$ is parameterized by infinitely many functions. This is of course not possible. So, we assume that $\mathsf{parse}^{name}_{\mathrm{pke}}$ and $\mathsf{format}^{name}_{\mathrm{pke}}$, for all public/private key pair names $name$, can be computed by two polynomial-time algorithms $\mathsf{parse}_{\mathrm{pke}}$ and $\mathsf{format}_{\mathrm{pke}}$ where $name$ is an additional input. Formally, $\mathcal{F}_{\mathrm{crypto}}$ is parameterized by these two algorithms instead of infinitely many.

$x, x', x'' \in \{0,1\}^*$, number $n \geq 0$, typed keys $\kappa_1, \kappa'_1, \ldots, \kappa_n, \kappa'_n$ such that κ_i and κ'_i have the same type, $x' = \mathsf{format}(1^\eta, x, \kappa_1, \ldots, \kappa_n)$, and $x'' = \mathsf{format}(1^\eta, x, \kappa'_1, \ldots, \kappa'_n)$, it holds that the probability distribution of $L(1^\eta, x')$ equals the probability distribution of $L(1^\eta, x'')$, i.e., $\Pr\left[L(1^\eta, x') = \overline{x}\right] = \Pr\left[L(1^\eta, x'') = \overline{x}\right]$ for all $\overline{x} \in \{0,1\}^*$ (where the probabilities are over the random coins of L).

For example, both leakage algorithms defined in Example 3.1 are keys hiding w.r.t. all formatting functions format that are length regular in the sense that the length of the formatted plaintext does not depend on the actual bits of the keys. Formally, we say that format is *length regular* if $|x'| = |x''|$ for all $\eta \in \mathbb{N}$, $x, x', x'' \in \{0,1\}^*$, $n \geq 0$, typed keys $\kappa_1, \kappa'_1, \ldots, \kappa_n, \kappa'_n$ such that κ_i and κ'_i have the same type, $x' = \mathsf{format}(1^\eta, x, \kappa_1, \ldots, \kappa_n)$, and $x'' = \mathsf{format}(1^\eta, x, \kappa'_1, \ldots, \kappa'_n)$. We note that formatting functions typically are length regular.

5.1.3. Salt Parsing

The functionality $\mathcal{F}_{\mathrm{crypto}}$ allows users to derive new (symmetric) keys from key derivation keys (i.e., keys of some type $t \in \mathcal{T}_{\mathrm{derive}}$). How many keys are derived and their types are determined by the salt that is used to derive the keys. This is similar to our functionality $\mathcal{F}_{\mathrm{derive}}$ for deriving keys from a long-term key (see Section 4.2.5) and, as mentioned their, assumes that the salt carries this information, which is reasonable to assume for most practical protocols (see Sections 7.4.3 and 7.7.2 for examples). Therefore, $\mathcal{F}_{\mathrm{crypto}}$ will be parameterized by a salt parsing function $\mathsf{parse}_{\mathrm{salt}}^t$, for every $t \in \mathcal{T}_{\mathrm{derive}}$, that takes a salt and returns a list of key types.

Definition 5.4. *A salt parsing function (for $\mathcal{F}_{\mathrm{crypto}}$) is a polynomial-time computable function that takes as input a security parameter 1^η and a salt $x \in \{0,1\}^*$ and produces a (possibly empty) list of key types $t_1, \ldots, t_n \in \mathcal{T}$.*

5.2. The Ideal Crypto Functionality

We are now ready to define our ideal crypto functionality $\mathcal{F}_{\mathrm{crypto}}$.

5.2.1. Parameters

The ideal functionality $\mathcal{F}_{\mathrm{crypto}}$ is parameterized by a set of parameters Π and we write $\mathcal{F}_{\mathrm{crypto}}(\Pi)$ to denote $\mathcal{F}_{\mathrm{crypto}}$ parameterized by Π. However, we often leave the set of parameters implicit and just write $\mathcal{F}_{\mathrm{crypto}}$. The set Π contains the following parameters:

1. *Number of I/O tape pairs:* $n > 0$ – this number defines the I/O interface of $\mathcal{F}_{\mathrm{crypto}}$ where users can connect to. Similar to our long-term key functionalities (see Section 4.2), for every $r \in \{1, \ldots, n\}$, $\mathcal{F}_{\mathrm{crypto}}$ has an I/O input tape and an I/O output tape. $\mathcal{F}_{\mathrm{crypto}}$ accepts requests on the input tape and sends responses

on the corresponding output tape. This allows n different machines (e.g., a protocol with n roles where each role is modeled by a different machine) to use $\mathcal{F}_{\text{crypto}}$.

2. *Key types:* $\mathcal{T}_{\text{senc}}^{\text{auth}}$, $\mathcal{T}_{\text{senc}}^{\text{unauth}}$, $\mathcal{T}_{\text{derive}}$, $\mathcal{T}_{\text{mac}}$ – disjoint, finite sets of key types for (un-)authenticated symmetric encryption, key derivation, and MAC, see Section 5.1.1. We define $\mathcal{T}_{\text{senc}} := \mathcal{T}_{\text{senc}}^{\text{auth}} \cup \mathcal{T}_{\text{senc}}^{\text{unauth}}$ and $\mathcal{T} := \mathcal{T}_{\text{senc}} \cup \mathcal{T}_{\text{derive}} \cup \mathcal{T}_{\text{mac}}$.

3. *Key domains:* $\mathcal{D}_{\text{keys}}^{t}$ for all $t \in \mathcal{T}$ – domains of keys (per type), see Section 5.1.1. We note that, in Definition 5.1, we define domains of typed keys $\mathcal{D}$, $\mathcal{D}_{\text{senc}}^{\text{auth}}$, etc.

4. *Plaintext formatting and parsing functions:* $\text{format}_{\text{senc}}^{t}$ and $\text{parse}_{\text{senc}}^{t}$ for all $t \in \mathcal{T}_{\text{senc}}$, $\text{format}_{\text{pke}}^{name}$ and $\text{parse}_{\text{pke}}^{name}$ for all $name \in \{0,1\}^*$ – plaintext formatting and parsing functions, see Section 5.1.2.[33]

5. *Salt parsing functions:* $\text{parse}_{\text{salt}}^{t}$ for all $t \in \mathcal{T}_{\text{derive}}$ – salt parsing functions, see Section 5.1.3.

6. *Leakage algorithms:* L_{senc}^{t} for all $t \in \mathcal{T}_{\text{senc}}$, L_{pke}^{name} for all $name \in \{0,1\}^*$ – leakage algorithms for symmetric and public-key encryption, respectively, as defined in Section 3.3.[34]

7. *Polynomial:* p – a polynomial. As usual for machines that run external code (see Section 3.1.3), the polynomial p is used to bound the runtime of the algorithms that are provided by the adversary and executed by $\mathcal{F}_{\text{crypto}}$, see below. The polynomial guarantees that $\mathcal{F}_{\text{crypto}}$ is environmentally strictly bounded.[35]

5.2.2. Brief Description

As mentioned in Section 5.1.1, in $\mathcal{F}_{\text{crypto}}$, symmetric keys are equipped with the above mentioned types and all sets of types are disjoint, i.e., a key can only have one type, reflecting common practice that a symmetric key only serves one purpose. In fact, this is important to realize $\mathcal{F}_{\text{crypto}}$ under standard assumptions about the cryptographic primitives.

While users of $\mathcal{F}_{\text{crypto}}$, and its realization, are provided with the actual public keys generated within $\mathcal{F}_{\text{crypto}}$ (the corresponding private keys remain in $\mathcal{F}_{\text{crypto}}$), they do not get their hands on the actual symmetric keys stored in the functionality, but only on pointers to these (typed) keys, since otherwise no security guarantees

---

[33] We refer to footnote 32 on page 86 for a discussion about how to deal with the infinitely many formatting and parsing functions for public-key encryption.

[34] As mentioned in footnote 32 on page 86 for plaintext formatting and parsing functions, since $\{0,1\}^*$ is an infinite set, $\mathcal{F}_{\text{crypto}}$ would be parameterized by infinitely many leakage functions for public-key encryption, which is not possible. So, as explained for formatting and parsing functions, we assume that there exists a polynomial-time algorithm that takes a public/private key name as additional input and computes the leakage algorithms.

[35] We note that one could use a different polynomial for every key type.

could be provided. Upon encryption with $\mathcal{F}_{\text{crypto}}$, the user provides a message and a list of pointers. The plaintext that is actually encrypted is constructed using the plaintext formatting functions with the keys the pointers refer to. Upon decryption of a ciphertext, first the plaintext is parsed (using the plaintext parsing functions). This results in a message and a list of keys (recall that parsing inverts formatting). Pointers are created for these keys and the message along with the created pointers is returned to the user. As mentioned in Section 5.1.2, it is typically possible to define formatting and parsing functions such that they precisely capture the plaintext formats of real-world protocols.

A *user* of $\mathcal{F}_{\text{crypto}}$ is identified, within $\mathcal{F}_{\text{crypto}}$, by a user identifier $uid \in \{0,1\}^*$. In particular, $\mathcal{F}_{\text{crypto}}$ expects every request to be prefixed by a user identifier uid and conversely $\mathcal{F}_{\text{crypto}}$ prefixes responses with uid. The user identifiers are chosen and managed by the users (i.e., the protocols/machines that use $\mathcal{F}_{\text{crypto}}$) themselves. For example, they could be the name of a party or a role. Or, if parties access $\mathcal{F}_{\text{crypto}}$ in multiple sessions and every party wants to be treated as a different user by $\mathcal{F}_{\text{crypto}}$, they can use user identifiers of the form $uid = (sid, pid)$ where sid is a SID and pid is the party's name. We note that $\mathcal{F}_{\text{crypto}}$ does not interpret user identifiers. Any interpretation is completely up to protocol that use $\mathcal{F}_{\text{crypto}}$.

The functionality $\mathcal{F}_{\text{crypto}}$ keeps track of which user has access to which symmetric (typed) keys, via pointers, and which keys are known to the environment/adversary, i.e., have been corrupted; have been explicitly retrieved by the user (see below); or have been encrypted under a known key, and as a result became known. For this purpose, among others, $\mathcal{F}_{\text{crypto}}$ maintains a set $\mathcal{K}$ of all symmetric (typed) keys stored within $\mathcal{F}_{\text{crypto}}$ and a set $\mathcal{K}_{\text{known}} \subseteq \mathcal{K}$. We say that keys that are in $\mathcal{K}_{\text{known}}$ are *marked known (in $\mathcal{F}_{\text{crypto}}$)* and that the keys that are in $\mathcal{K}$ but not in $\mathcal{K}_{\text{known}}$ are *marked unknown.*

Before a cryptographic operation can be performed under a symmetric key (or a public/private key pair), $\mathcal{F}_{\text{crypto}}$ expects to receive (descriptions of) algorithms from the adversary (or simulator) for this key (or key pair), i.e., encryption/decryption algorithms for encryption keys and a MAC algorithm for MAC keys. In case of public-key encryption, the adversary also provides a public/private key pair. That is, if desired, the adversary can choose different algorithms for every key (resp., public/private key pair). However, she will typically use the same algorithms per key type. The adversary may decide to statically corrupt a public/private key at the moment she provides it to $\mathcal{F}_{\text{crypto}}$. In this case $\mathcal{F}_{\text{crypto}}$ records this public/private key pair as corrupted. We do not put any restrictions on these algorithms and keys; all security guarantees that $\mathcal{F}_{\text{crypto}}$ provides are made explicit within $\mathcal{F}_{\text{crypto}}$ without relying on specific properties of these algorithms. As a result, when using $\mathcal{F}_{\text{crypto}}$ in the analysis of systems, one can abstract from these algorithms entirely.

5.2.3. Detailed Description

We now describe $\mathcal{F}_{\mathrm{crypto}}$ in more detail. The ideal crypto functionality $\mathcal{F}_{\mathrm{crypto}}$ is defined to be the following protocol system:

$$\mathcal{F}_{\mathrm{crypto}} := !\mathcal{F}_{\mathrm{crypto}}^{\mathrm{user}} \mid \mathcal{F}_{\mathrm{crypto}}^{\mathrm{keys}} \mid !\mathcal{F}_{\mathrm{crypto}}^{\mathrm{keysetup}} \mid !\mathcal{F}_{\mathrm{crypto}}^{\mathrm{senc}} \mid !\mathcal{F}_{\mathrm{crypto}}^{\mathrm{derive}} \mid !\mathcal{F}_{\mathrm{crypto}}^{\mathrm{mac}} \mid !\mathcal{F}_{\mathrm{crypto}}^{\mathrm{pke}}$$

where $\mathcal{F}_{\mathrm{crypto}}^{\mathrm{user}}$, $\mathcal{F}_{\mathrm{crypto}}^{\mathrm{keys}}$, etc. are IITMs that we describe in the following.

The machine $\mathcal{F}_{\mathrm{crypto}}^{\mathrm{user}}$. Every copy of the machine $\mathcal{F}_{\mathrm{crypto}}^{\mathrm{user}}$ represents one user of $\mathcal{F}_{\mathrm{crypto}}$ and, for every user uid (as mentioned above), there exists at most one copy of $\mathcal{F}_{\mathrm{crypto}}^{\mathrm{user}}$ (in a run of $\mathcal{F}_{\mathrm{crypto}}$ with some environment), by definition of the mode CheckAddress, that is addressed by uid. More precisely, uid serves as an SID and every message to and from $\mathcal{F}_{\mathrm{crypto}}^{\mathrm{user}}$ is prefixed by uid. By $\mathcal{F}_{\mathrm{crypto}}^{\mathrm{user}}[uid]$ we denote the copy of $\mathcal{F}_{\mathrm{crypto}}^{\mathrm{user}}$ for user uid. It keeps track of the keys this user has access to via pointers. Therefore, it maintains a mapping key from pointers to typed keys. Furthermore, $\mathcal{F}_{\mathrm{crypto}}^{\mathrm{user}}[uid]$ allows the user uid to execute several commands on these keys. Therefore, $\mathcal{F}_{\mathrm{crypto}}^{\mathrm{user}}$ uses, as sub-functionalities, the other machines. The users do not have direct access to the other machines, only via $\mathcal{F}_{\mathrm{crypto}}^{\mathrm{user}}$. The machine $\mathcal{F}_{\mathrm{crypto}}^{\mathrm{keysetup}}$ is used by $\mathcal{F}_{\mathrm{crypto}}^{\mathrm{user}}$ to obtain pre-shared keys, i.e., keys that are shared between several users, see below.

The machine $\mathcal{F}_{\mathrm{crypto}}^{\mathrm{keys}}$. The machine $\mathcal{F}_{\mathrm{crypto}}^{\mathrm{keys}}$ (there is only one copy of this machine in every run of $\mathcal{F}_{\mathrm{crypto}}$) keeps track of which keys are known to the environment/adversary and maintains the above mentioned sets $\mathcal{K}$ and $\mathcal{K}_{\mathrm{known}}$. It allows the other machines ($\mathcal{F}_{\mathrm{crypto}}^{\mathrm{user}}$, $\mathcal{F}_{\mathrm{crypto}}^{\mathrm{keysetup}}$, etc.) to perform the following requests.

Request (Status, κ): to obtain the status (known or unknown) of a (typed) key κ. Upon this request, $\mathcal{F}_{\mathrm{crypto}}^{\mathrm{keys}}$ returns known if $\kappa \in \mathcal{K}_{\mathrm{known}}$ and unknown otherwise.

Request (MarkKnown, $\kappa_1, \ldots, \kappa_n$): to mark the keys $\kappa_1, \ldots, \kappa_n$ known. Upon this request, $\mathcal{F}_{\mathrm{crypto}}^{\mathrm{keys}}$ adds $\kappa_1, \ldots, \kappa_n$ to $\mathcal{K}_{\mathrm{known}}$ and returns an acknowledgment message.

Request (Add, $status$, $\kappa_1, \ldots, \kappa_n$): to add the keys $\kappa_1, \ldots, \kappa_n$ as new keys to $\mathcal{F}_{\mathrm{crypto}}^{\mathrm{keys}}$ such that their status is $status \in \{\mathrm{known}, \mathrm{unknown}\}$. For example, this request is used by $\mathcal{F}_{\mathrm{crypto}}^{\mathrm{user}}$ and $\mathcal{F}_{\mathrm{crypto}}^{\mathrm{keysetup}}$ when new keys are generated.

Upon this request with $status = \mathrm{unknown}$, $\mathcal{F}_{\mathrm{crypto}}^{\mathrm{keys}}$ returns an error message ($\perp$), indicating that this request failed, if $\kappa_i \in \mathcal{K}$ for some $i \leq n$, i.e., one of the keys is not fresh, it collides with an already recorded key. Otherwise, $\mathcal{F}_{\mathrm{crypto}}^{\mathrm{keys}}$ adds $\kappa_1, \ldots, \kappa_n$ to $\mathcal{K}$ and returns an acknowledgment message (indicating that this request succeeded). This models that a freshly generated key that is honestly generated (only then it should be marked unknown) should not collide with any other key.

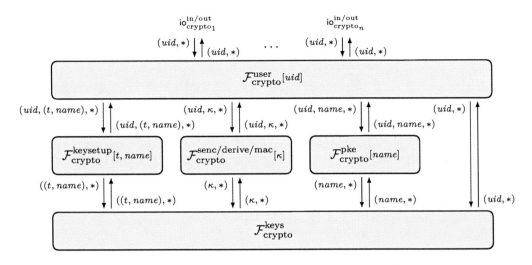

Figure 5.1.: Overview of $\mathcal{F}_{\text{crypto}}$. Only I/O tapes but no network tapes are displayed. The external I/O tapes of $\mathcal{F}_{\text{crypto}}$ are pairs of input and output tapes $\text{io}^{\text{in}}_{\text{crypto}_r}, \text{io}^{\text{out}}_{\text{crypto}_r}$ for $r = 1, \ldots, n$ (where n is a parameter of $\mathcal{F}_{\text{crypto}}$). There is only one copy of $\mathcal{F}^{\text{keys}}_{\text{crypto}}$. For every user uid there is one copy of $\mathcal{F}^{\text{user}}_{\text{crypto}}$, for every pair $(t, name)$ of a key type $t \in \mathcal{T}$ and a pre-shared key name $name$ there is one copy of $\mathcal{F}^{\text{keysetup}}_{\text{crypto}}$, for every typed key κ there is one copy of $\mathcal{F}^{\text{senc}}_{\text{crypto}}/\mathcal{F}^{\text{derive}}_{\text{crypto}}/\mathcal{F}^{\text{mac}}_{\text{crypto}}$, and for every public/private key pair name $name$ there is one copy of $\mathcal{F}^{\text{pke}}_{\text{crypto}}$. Every tape is labeled with the message formats that are used for addressing.

Upon this request with $status =$ known, $\mathcal{F}^{\text{keys}}_{\text{crypto}}$ returns an error message if $\kappa_i \in \mathcal{K} \setminus \mathcal{K}_{\text{known}}$ for some $i \leq n$, i.e., one of the keys is marked unknown. Otherwise, $\mathcal{F}^{\text{keys}}_{\text{crypto}}$ adds $\kappa_1, \ldots, \kappa_n$ to $\mathcal{K}$ and $\mathcal{K}_{\text{known}}$ and returns an acknowledgment message. Since all keys that are added using this command are provided by the environment/adversary (at least, this is the pessimistic assumption, see below), this models that keys marked unknown cannot be guessed by the environment/adversary, i.e., the environment/adversary cannot provide a key that collides with an unknown key.

For addressing purposes (to guarantee that the response is received by the sender of the request), all requests and responses to/from $\mathcal{F}^{\text{keys}}_{\text{crypto}}$ are prefixed by an identifier. For example, $\mathcal{F}^{\text{user}}_{\text{crypto}}[uid]$ (i.e., the copy of $\mathcal{F}^{\text{user}}_{\text{crypto}}$ for user uid) uses the identifier uid, as illustrated in Figure 5.1.

The machine $\mathcal{F}^{\text{keysetup}}_{\text{crypto}}$. Every copy of the machine $\mathcal{F}^{\text{keysetup}}_{\text{crypto}}$ represents one pre-shared key that is ideally distributed among several users and, for every key type

t and pre-shared key name *name*, there exists at most one copy of $\mathcal{F}_{\text{crypto}}^{\text{keysetup}}$, that is addressed by $(t, name)$ and that we denote by $\mathcal{F}_{\text{crypto}}^{\text{keysetup}}[t, name]$. More precisely, all messages sent between $\mathcal{F}_{\text{crypto}}^{\text{keysetup}}$ and $\mathcal{F}_{\text{crypto}}^{\text{user}}$ are of the form $(uid, (t, name), m)$ for some m and all messages sent between $\mathcal{F}_{\text{crypto}}^{\text{keysetup}}$ and $\mathcal{F}_{\text{crypto}}^{\text{keys}}$ are of the form $((t, name), m)$, as illustrated in Figure 5.1. That is, $\mathcal{F}_{\text{crypto}}^{\text{user}}[uid]$ can send requests of the form $(uid, (t, name), m)$ to $\mathcal{F}_{\text{crypto}}^{\text{keysetup}}[t, name]$ and the response, of the form $(uid, (t, name), m')$, will be received by $\mathcal{F}_{\text{crypto}}^{\text{user}}[uid]$.

The pre-shared key name *name* is chosen and managed by the users themselves and allows users to obtain pointers to the same keys (see below). Upon initialization, $\mathcal{F}_{\text{crypto}}^{\text{keysetup}}[t, name]$ asks the adversary to provide a key for the pre-shared key $(t, name)$. The adversary may corrupt $\mathcal{F}_{\text{crypto}}^{\text{keysetup}}[t, name]$ upon initialization (static corruption). When initialization is completed, $\mathcal{F}_{\text{crypto}}^{\text{keysetup}}[t, name]$ provides two requests to instances of $\mathcal{F}_{\text{crypto}}^{\text{user}}$: GetPSK, to obtain the pre-shared key $(t, name)$ (that has been provided by the adversary upon initialization), and Corr?, to asks for the corruption status of $\mathcal{F}_{\text{crypto}}^{\text{keysetup}}[t, name]$. We describe initialization and these requests in detail below.

The machines $\mathcal{F}_{\text{crypto}}^{\text{senc}}$, $\mathcal{F}_{\text{crypto}}^{\text{derive}}$, $\mathcal{F}_{\text{crypto}}^{\text{mac}}$, and $\mathcal{F}_{\text{crypto}}^{\text{pke}}$. The (ideal) cryptographic operations are performed in the machines $\mathcal{F}_{\text{crypto}}^{\text{senc}}$, $\mathcal{F}_{\text{crypto}}^{\text{derive}}$, or $\mathcal{F}_{\text{crypto}}^{\text{mac}}$, depending on the key type; or in $\mathcal{F}_{\text{crypto}}^{\text{pke}}$ for public-key encryption.

These machines are similar to the ideal long-term key functionalities from Section 4.2. We first describe $\mathcal{F}_{\text{crypto}}^{\text{senc}}$. For every symmetric encryption key κ, there exists at most one copy of $\mathcal{F}_{\text{crypto}}^{\text{senc}}$, that is addressed by κ and that we denote by $\mathcal{F}_{\text{crypto}}^{\text{senc}}[\kappa]$. More precisely, all messages sent between $\mathcal{F}_{\text{crypto}}^{\text{senc}}$ and $\mathcal{F}_{\text{crypto}}^{\text{user}}$ are of the form (uid, κ, m) for some m and all messages sent between $\mathcal{F}_{\text{crypto}}^{\text{senc}}$ and $\mathcal{F}_{\text{crypto}}^{\text{keys}}$ are of the form (κ, m), as illustrated in Figure 5.1. That is, $\mathcal{F}_{\text{crypto}}^{\text{user}}[uid]$ can send a request (e.g., to encrypt a message) of the form (uid, κ, m) to $\mathcal{F}_{\text{crypto}}^{\text{senc}}[\kappa]$ and the response, of the form (uid, κ, m'), will be received by $\mathcal{F}_{\text{crypto}}^{\text{user}}[uid]$. Analogously, for every key derivation and MAC key κ, there are is at most one copy of $\mathcal{F}_{\text{crypto}}^{\text{derive}}$ or $\mathcal{F}_{\text{crypto}}^{\text{mac}}$, respectively. For $\mathcal{F}_{\text{crypto}}^{\text{pke}}$ addressing is done similarly but instead of the typed key κ the public/private key name *name* is used.

A difference to the long-term key functionalities is that the machines $\mathcal{F}_{\text{crypto}}^{\text{senc}}$, $\mathcal{F}_{\text{crypto}}^{\text{derive}}$, and $\mathcal{F}_{\text{crypto}}^{\text{mac}}$ use a typed key for addressing (instead of a long-term key name) and this key is also used for the cryptographic operations. Furthermore, they are not corruptible by the adversary ($\mathcal{F}_{\text{crypto}}^{\text{pke}}$ is corruptible just as $\mathcal{F}_{\text{pke}}$). Instead, they connect to $\mathcal{F}_{\text{crypto}}^{\text{keys}}$, to obtain the known/unknown status of the key, which is used instead of the corruption status. That is, if the key is marked unknown, the cryptographic operation is performed ideally (e.g., only the leakage of a message is encrypted), otherwise, it is performed as in the realization (e.g., the actual message is encrypted). Another difference is that, upon encryption with a key that is marked known, the keys contained in the plaintext are marked known in $\mathcal{F}_{\text{crypto}}^{\text{keys}}$ (using the MarkKnown command provided by $\mathcal{F}_{\text{crypto}}^{\text{keys}}$), see below for details.

The machine $\mathcal{F}_{\text{crypto}}^{\text{derive}}$ is quite different from $\mathcal{F}_{\text{derive}}$. It does not generate fresh keys (uniformly at random) but instead lets the adversary choose derived keys similar to a symmetric key generation request (KeyGen), see below.

5.2.4. Detailed Description of the Provided Operations

We now describe the operations that $\mathcal{F}_{\text{crypto}}$ provides in more detail. This description contains all necessary details to understand how $\mathcal{F}_{\text{crypto}}$ works. Nevertheless, in Appendix B.1 we provide a formal specification of $\mathcal{F}_{\text{crypto}}$ in pseudocode that is sometimes convenient in proofs. As mentioned above, requests (and responses) from users to $\mathcal{F}_{\text{crypto}}$ are prefixed by a user identifier uid and all requests are sent to $\mathcal{F}_{\text{crypto}}^{\text{user}}$ (i.e., to the copy $\mathcal{F}_{\text{crypto}}^{\text{user}}[uid]$ for user uid). In the following description, we keep these user identifiers implicit, i.e., we state the requests without uid.

Generating fresh, symmetric keys (KeyGen, t): A user uid can ask $\mathcal{F}_{\text{crypto}}^{\text{user}}[uid]$ to generate a new key of some type $t \in \mathcal{T}$. This request is forwarded to the adversary who is supposed to provide such a key k (i.e., $k \in \mathcal{D}_{\text{keys}}^{t}(\eta)$, where $\mathcal{D}_{\text{keys}}^{t}(\eta)$ is the domain of keys of type t for security parameter η). Then, $\mathcal{F}_{\text{crypto}}^{\text{keysetup}}[t, name]$ sends the Add request (Add, unknown, (t, k)) to $\mathcal{F}_{\text{crypto}}^{\text{keys}}$, to add the typed key (t, k) as a new key that is marked unknown. By definition of $\mathcal{F}_{\text{crypto}}^{\text{keys}}$, this fails if (t, k) is not fresh (i.e., it is already in $\mathcal{K}$). If this fails, then $\mathcal{F}_{\text{crypto}}^{\text{user}}[uid]$ returns an error to the user. This models that the key must be fresh and guarantees that the key is marked unknown (it can however become known later, e.g., when encrypted under a key that is marked known). If no failure occurs, $\mathcal{F}_{\text{crypto}}^{\text{user}}[uid]$ creates a new pointer ptr to (t, k) and returns ptr to the user. The value of the pointer (i.e., ptr) does not need to be secret. In fact, new pointers are created by increasing a counter. Every instance of $\mathcal{F}_{\text{crypto}}^{\text{user}}$ uses a different counter, so, a user cannot tell how many keys have been created by other users from observing its pointers.

We emphasize that the difference between keys marked known or unknown is not whether the adversary knows the value of a key (she provides these values anyway). As mentioned above, the point is that if (t, k) is marked unknown, cryptographic operations with it are performed ideally (e.g., the leakage of a message is encrypted under the key k instead of the message itself). Conversely, if (t, k) is known, the cryptographic operation is performed as in the real world (e.g., the actual message is encrypted under k). So, no security guarantees are provided in this case. In the realization of $\mathcal{F}_{\text{crypto}}$, however, keys corresponding to keys that are marked unknown will of course not be known to the adversary.

Store (Store, κ): A user uid can ask $\mathcal{F}_{\text{crypto}}^{\text{user}}[uid]$ to store a typed key $\kappa \in \mathcal{D}(\eta)$ (i.e., $\kappa = (t, k)$ for some key type t and key k). Then, $\mathcal{F}_{\text{crypto}}^{\text{user}}[uid]$ sends the Add request

(Add, known, (t, k)) to $\mathcal{F}_{\text{crypto}}^{\text{keys}}$, to add the typed key (t, k) as a new key that is marked known. By definition of $\mathcal{F}_{\text{crypto}}^{\text{keys}}$, this fails if (t, k) is marked unknown (i.e., (t, k) is in $\mathcal{K} \setminus \mathcal{K}_{\text{known}}$). If this fails, then $\mathcal{F}_{\text{crypto}}^{\text{user}}[uid]$ returns an error to the user. This models that keys marked unknown cannot be guessed. If no failure occurs, $\mathcal{F}_{\text{crypto}}^{\text{user}}[uid]$ creates a new pointer ptr to κ (as above), and returns ptr to the user.

Retrieve (Retrieve, ptr): A user uid can ask $\mathcal{F}_{\text{crypto}}^{\text{user}}[uid]$ to retrieve a typed key κ pointer ptr points to. Then, $\mathcal{F}_{\text{crypto}}^{\text{user}}[uid]$ sends (MarkKnown, κ) to $\mathcal{F}_{\text{crypto}}^{\text{keys}}$ to mark κ as known (i.e., to add κ to $\mathcal{K}_{\text{known}}$). Then, $\mathcal{F}_{\text{crypto}}^{\text{user}}[uid]$ returns κ to the user.

Equality test (Equal?, ptr_1, ptr_2): A user uid can ask $\mathcal{F}_{\text{crypto}}^{\text{user}}[uid]$ whether two of its pointers ptr_1, ptr_2 refer to the same key (i.e., same key type and same actual key). Then, $\mathcal{F}_{\text{crypto}}^{\text{user}}[uid]$ returns 1 if the pointers refer to the same key and 0 otherwise.

Establishing pre-shared keys (GetPSK, $(t, name)$): A user uid can ask $\mathcal{F}_{\text{crypto}}^{\text{user}}[uid]$ to obtain a pointer to the pre-shared key of type $t \in \mathcal{T}$ and name (or identifier) $name$. Then, $\mathcal{F}_{\text{crypto}}^{\text{user}}[uid]$ sends a GetPSK request to $\mathcal{F}_{\text{crypto}}^{\text{keysetup}}[t, name]$ (i.e., to the instance of $\mathcal{F}_{\text{crypto}}^{\text{keysetup}}$ that is addressed by $(t, name)$ and handles the pre-shared key of type t and name $name$), waits for receiving a key k, and then creates a new pointer ptr to (t, k) (as above) and returns ptr to the user.

We now describe how the instance $\mathcal{F}_{\text{crypto}}^{\text{keysetup}}[t, name]$ responds to GetPSK requests from $\mathcal{F}_{\text{crypto}}^{\text{user}}[uid]$. Upon the first request (from any copy of $\mathcal{F}_{\text{crypto}}^{\text{user}}$), $\mathcal{F}_{\text{crypto}}^{\text{keysetup}}[t, name]$ asks the adversary to either provide a key or to corrupt $\mathcal{F}_{\text{crypto}}^{\text{keysetup}}[t, name]$. If the adversary provides a key k, then $\mathcal{F}_{\text{crypto}}^{\text{keysetup}}[t, name]$ sends (Add, unknown, (t, k)) to $\mathcal{F}_{\text{crypto}}^{\text{keys}}$, to add (t, k) as an unknown key (as upon a KeyGen request). If this fails (because (t, k) is not fresh), this process is iterated, i.e., the adversary is asked again to provide a key or to corrupt, until the adversary provided a fresh key or corrupted $\mathcal{F}_{\text{crypto}}^{\text{keysetup}}[t, name]$. In the end, this guarantees that $\mathcal{F}_{\text{crypto}}^{\text{keysetup}}[t, name]$ is corrupted or the (last) key k provided by the adversary is marked unknown. This key k is recorded. Then, $\mathcal{F}_{\text{crypto}}^{\text{keysetup}}[t, name]$ proceeds as in the case of a second or later request, which is as follows: If $\mathcal{F}_{\text{crypto}}^{\text{keysetup}}[t, name]$ is uncorrupted, then $\mathcal{F}_{\text{crypto}}^{\text{keysetup}}[t, name]$ returns the recorded key k to $\mathcal{F}_{\text{crypto}}^{\text{user}}[uid]$. Otherwise, $\mathcal{F}_{\text{crypto}}^{\text{keysetup}}[t, name]$ asks the adversary to provide a key k and then sends (Add, known, (t, k)) to $\mathcal{F}_{\text{crypto}}^{\text{keys}}$, to add the typed key (t, k) as a known key (as upon a Store request). If this fails (because (t, k) is marked unknown and guessing is prevented), $\mathcal{F}_{\text{crypto}}^{\text{keysetup}}[t, name]$ asks the adversary again until she provides a key where the Add request does not fail. Finally (i.e., no error and (t, k) is now marked known), $\mathcal{F}_{\text{crypto}}^{\text{keysetup}}[t, name]$ returns k to $\mathcal{F}_{\text{crypto}}^{\text{user}}[uid]$.

The pre-shared key name $name$ is chosen and managed by the users themselves and allows users to obtain pointers to the same keys. These names serve the same purpose as the key names for multi-key versions as described in Section 4.1.5, see also the example in Section 4.4. For example, this name could be a pair of two party names to model a long-term key shared between these two parties. More precisely, two parties (with party names) pid and pid' can obtain pointers to a key (t, k) shared between each other by each sending the request $(\mathsf{GetPSK}, (t, (pid, pid')))$ to $\mathcal{F}_{\mathrm{crypto}}$. Both parties then obtain pointers to the same key (t, k). This even holds for all users of the parties, e.g., to model that this key is shared across sessions. If party pid (and pid') uses $\mathcal{F}_{\mathrm{crypto}}$ with multiple users (e.g., $uid_1 = (sid_1, pid)$, $uid_2 = (sid_2, pid)$, etc. for SIDs sid_1, sid_2, etc.), then all these users obtain pointers to the same key (t, k). Another example is WPA2-PSK (see Section 7.4.3), where requests of supplicants (e.g., laptops) and authenticators (e.g., access points) are of the form $(\mathsf{GetPSK}, (t_{\mathrm{PMK}}, name_{\mathrm{PMK}}))$, with $name_{\mathrm{PMK}}$ being a name (instances of) suppliers and authenticators obtain from the environment (e.g., a system administrator) upon initialization.

We further note that, upon corruption, the adversary can choose different keys for every user; corrupted pre-shared keys are marked known and may collide with known keys but not with unknown keys. On the other hand, $\mathcal{F}_{\mathrm{crypto}}$ guarantees that new, uncorrupted pre-shared keys do not collide with any other key. Upon generation, uncorrupted pre-shared keys are marked unknown (they can however become known later, e.g., when encrypted under a key that is marked known).

Corruption status request for pre-shared keys $(\mathsf{CorrPSK?}, (t, name))$:   The environment can ask, for a user uid, whether the pre-shared key of some type $t \in \mathcal{T}$ and name $name$ is corrupted. Then, $\mathcal{F}_{\mathrm{crypto}}^{\mathrm{user}}[uid]$ sends $\mathsf{Corr?}$ to $\mathcal{F}_{\mathrm{crypto}}^{\mathrm{keysetup}}[t, name]$, to obtain the corruption status of $\mathcal{F}_{\mathrm{crypto}}^{\mathrm{keysetup}}[t, name]$, and forwards the corruption status to the environment. Upon the request $\mathsf{Corr?}$, $\mathcal{F}_{\mathrm{crypto}}^{\mathrm{keysetup}}[t, name]$ returns 1 if it has been corrupted upon initialization (see above) and 0 otherwise.

This request is important because the corruption status of a user of a protocol that uses $\mathcal{F}_{\mathrm{crypto}}$ might depend on the corruption status of the user's pre-shared keys; see also Section 4.1.4.

Encryption under symmetric keys $(\mathsf{Enc}, ptr, x, ptr_1, \ldots, ptr_l)$:   A user uid can ask $\mathcal{F}_{\mathrm{crypto}}^{\mathrm{user}}[uid]$ to encrypt a message x (an arbitrary bit string) under a typed key $\kappa = (t, k) \in \mathcal{D}_{\mathrm{senc}}(\eta)$ (i.e., $t \in \mathcal{T}_{\mathrm{senc}}$) a pointer ptr refers to. The plaintext is formatted such that it includes the keys the pointers $ptr_1, \ldots, ptr_l$ refer to. Then, $\mathcal{F}_{\mathrm{crypto}}^{\mathrm{user}}[uid]$ constructs the plaintext x' using the plaintext formatting function $\mathrm{format}_{\mathrm{senc}}^t$ as described in Section 5.1.2. More precisely, $x' := \mathrm{format}_{\mathrm{senc}}^t(1^\eta, x, \kappa_1, \ldots, \kappa_l)$ where κ_i is the typed key pointer ptr_i refers to, for all $i \le l$. If this fails (i.e., $x' = \bot$), then $\mathcal{F}_{\mathrm{crypto}}^{\mathrm{user}}[uid]$ returns an error to the user. Otherwise, $\mathcal{F}_{\mathrm{crypto}}^{\mathrm{user}}[uid]$ encrypts x' using $\mathcal{F}_{\mathrm{crypto}}^{\mathrm{senc}}[\kappa]$, i.e., it sends the encryption request (Enc, x') to $\mathcal{F}_{\mathrm{crypto}}^{\mathrm{senc}}[\kappa]$ (the copy of $\mathcal{F}_{\mathrm{crypto}}^{\mathrm{senc}}$ that is addressed by κ and handles all encryption and decryption requests for the key κ) and waits for receiving a ciphertext y as response (if an error occurs, then $y = \bot$). Then, $\mathcal{F}_{\mathrm{crypto}}^{\mathrm{user}}[uid]$ returns y to the user.

We now describe how $\mathcal{F}_{\mathrm{crypto}}^{\mathrm{senc}}[\kappa]$ handles the encryption request (Enc, x'). Upon the first request (any request, i.e., also counting decryption requests, from any copy of $\mathcal{F}_{\mathrm{crypto}}^{\mathrm{user}}$), $\mathcal{F}_{\mathrm{crypto}}^{\mathrm{senc}}[\kappa]$ asks the adversary to provide encryption and decryption algorithms. These algorithms are recorded. Then, $\mathcal{F}_{\mathrm{crypto}}^{\mathrm{senc}}[\kappa]$ proceeds as in the case of a second or later request, which is as follows. Encryption with $\mathcal{F}_{\mathrm{crypto}}^{\mathrm{senc}}[\kappa]$ is done as in $\mathcal{F}_{\mathrm{senc}}$ except that instead of the corruption status, the known/unknown status of κ is used and that the keys contained in the plaintext (i.e., $\kappa_1, \ldots, \kappa_l$) are marked known if κ is marked known.

More precisely: If κ is marked unknown ($\mathcal{F}_{\mathrm{crypto}}^{\mathrm{senc}}[\kappa]$ determines this by sending $(\mathsf{Status}, \kappa)$ to $\mathcal{F}_{\mathrm{crypto}}^{\mathrm{keys}}$), the leakage $\overline{x} \leftarrow L_{\mathrm{senc}}^{t}(1^\eta, x')$ of x' is computed. Then, $\overline{x}$ is encrypted (using the recorded encryption algorithm and key k; recall that $\kappa = (t, k)$) and it is tested that the decryption of the ciphertext yields the leakage again. If this test fails, an error is returned.[36] Otherwise, the plaintext x' is recorded for the ciphertext (for decryption) and the ciphertext is returned. If κ is marked known, then the plaintext x' is parsed using the plaintext parsing function $\mathsf{parse}_{\mathrm{senc}}^{t}$. By our requirements on parsing functions (see Section 5.1.2), this yields exactly the typed keys $\kappa_1, \ldots, \kappa_l$ from above. Then, $\mathcal{F}_{\mathrm{crypto}}^{\mathrm{user}}[uid]$ marks the typed keys $\kappa_1, \ldots, \kappa_l$ as known (i.e., it sends $(\mathsf{MarkKnown}, \kappa_1, \ldots, \kappa_l)$ to $\mathcal{F}_{\mathrm{crypto}}^{\mathrm{keys}}$), encrypts the actual plaintext x', and returns the ciphertext.

Decryption under symmetric keys (Dec, ptr, y):   A user uid can ask $\mathcal{F}_{\mathrm{crypto}}^{\mathrm{user}}[uid]$ to decrypt a ciphertext y (an arbitrary bit string) under a typed key $\kappa = (t, k) \in \mathcal{D}_{\mathrm{senc}}(\eta)$ (i.e., $t \in \mathcal{T}_{\mathrm{senc}}$) a pointer ptr refers to. Then, $\mathcal{F}_{\mathrm{crypto}}^{\mathrm{user}}[uid]$ decrypts y using $\mathcal{F}_{\mathrm{crypto}}^{\mathrm{senc}}[\kappa]$, i.e., it sends the encryption request (Dec, y) to $\mathcal{F}_{\mathrm{crypto}}^{\mathrm{senc}}[\kappa]$ and waits for receiving an error message or a plaintext x. If an error is received, $\mathcal{F}_{\mathrm{crypto}}^{\mathrm{user}}[uid]$ returns an error to the user. Otherwise, $\mathcal{F}_{\mathrm{crypto}}^{\mathrm{user}}[uid]$ parses x, using the plaintext parsing function $\mathsf{parse}_{\mathrm{senc}}^{t}$ (see Section 5.1.2). If parsing fails, $\mathcal{F}_{\mathrm{crypto}}^{\mathrm{user}}[uid]$ returns an error to the user. Otherwise, parsing yields a message x' and a (possibly empty) list of typed keys $\kappa_1, \ldots, \kappa_l$. Then, $\mathcal{F}_{\mathrm{crypto}}^{\mathrm{user}}[uid]$ creates new pointers to the keys $\kappa_1, \ldots, \kappa_l$ and returns x' and the pointers to the user.

We now describe how $\mathcal{F}_{\mathrm{crypto}}^{\mathrm{senc}}[\kappa]$ handles the decryption request (Enc, y). As mentioned above, when $\mathcal{F}_{\mathrm{crypto}}^{\mathrm{senc}}[\kappa]$ is activated the first time, it asks the adversary to provide encryption and decryption algorithms. Then, $\mathcal{F}_{\mathrm{crypto}}^{\mathrm{senc}}[\kappa]$ proceeds as in the case of a second or later request, which is as follows. Decryption with $\mathcal{F}_{\mathrm{crypto}}^{\mathrm{senc}}[\kappa]$ is done as in $\mathcal{F}_{\mathrm{senc}}$ except that instead of the corruption status, the known/unknown status of κ is used and "guessing unknown keys" is prevented, see below.

More precisely, if κ is marked unknown (determined by sending $(\mathsf{Status}, \kappa)$ to $\mathcal{F}_{\mathrm{crypto}}^{\mathrm{keys}}$) and some plaintext x has been recorded for y upon encryption, then x is returned if x is unique, otherwise, an error is returned. If κ is marked unknown

---

[36] This decryption test is performed for the same reasons as explained for $\mathcal{F}_{\mathrm{pke}}$ and $\mathcal{F}_{\mathrm{senc}}$ (see Remark 4.3): It is needed for our joint state realization in Section 5.4 and, when using leakage algorithms with high entropy, it is sometimes useful for reasoning about protocols as mentioned in Section 3.3.

but no plaintext has been recorded for y, two cases are distinguished: If $t \in \mathcal{T}_{\text{senc}}^{\text{auth}}$ (authenticated encryption), an error is returned (modeling that decryption should fail for ciphertext not produced by $\mathcal{F}_{\text{crypto}}^{\text{senc}}[\kappa]$). If $t \in \mathcal{T}_{\text{senc}}^{\text{unauth}}$, y is decrypted (using the decryption algorithm provided by the adversary and the key k). Then, in contrast to $\mathcal{F}_{\text{senc}}$, the resulting plaintext, say x, is parsed (using $\text{parse}_{\text{senc}}^t$ as above). This yields a (possibly empty) list of typed keys $\kappa_1, \ldots, \kappa_l$. Then, $\mathcal{F}_{\text{crypto}}^{\text{senc}}[\kappa]$ sends (Add, known, $\kappa_1, \ldots, \kappa_l$) to $\mathcal{F}_{\text{crypto}}^{\text{keys}}$ to add the typed keys $\kappa_1, \ldots, \kappa_l$ as a known keys. If this fails (because κ_i for some $i \leq l$ is marked unknown and guessing is prevented), $\mathcal{F}_{\text{crypto}}^{\text{senc}}[\kappa]$ returns an error to $\mathcal{F}_{\text{crypto}}^{\text{user}}[uid]$. Otherwise (i.e., no error and $\kappa_1, \ldots, \kappa_l$ are now marked known), $\mathcal{F}_{\text{crypto}}^{\text{senc}}[\kappa]$ returns the plaintext x to $\mathcal{F}_{\text{crypto}}^{\text{user}}[uid]$.

If κ is marked known, y is decrypted (using the decryption algorithm provided by the adversary and the key k). Then, as above, the plaintext is parsed and $\mathcal{F}_{\text{crypto}}^{\text{keys}}$ is called to add the containing keys as known keys. If this fails (because guessing is prevented), an error is returned. Otherwise, the plaintext is returned.

Key derivation (Derive, ptr, x): A user uid can ask $\mathcal{F}_{\text{crypto}}^{\text{user}}[uid]$ to derive keys from a typed key $\kappa = (t, k) \in \mathcal{D}_{\text{derive}}(\eta)$ (i.e., $t \in \mathcal{T}_{\text{derive}}$) a pointer ptr refers to. The salt x is an arbitrary bit string. Then, $\mathcal{F}_{\text{crypto}}^{\text{user}}[uid]$ sends the key derivation request (Derive, x) to $\mathcal{F}_{\text{crypto}}^{\text{derive}}[\kappa]$ (the copy of $\mathcal{F}_{\text{crypto}}^{\text{derive}}$ that is addressed by κ and handles all key derivation requests for the key κ) and waits for receiving a list of typed keys $\kappa_1, \ldots, \kappa_l$ or an error message. If an error is returned, $\mathcal{F}_{\text{crypto}}^{\text{user}}[uid]$ returns an error to the user. Otherwise, $\mathcal{F}_{\text{crypto}}^{\text{user}}[uid]$ creates new pointers to the keys $\kappa_1, \ldots, \kappa_l$ and returns the pointers to the user.

We now describe how $\mathcal{F}_{\text{crypto}}^{\text{derive}}[\kappa]$ handles the key derivation request (Derive, x). We note that this differs from $\mathcal{F}_{\text{derive}}$ in that the ideally derived keys are not chosen uniformly at random but instead they are obtained from the adversary just as upon key generation. The derived keys will also be marked known if and only if the key derivation key is marked known. More precisely, $\mathcal{F}_{\text{crypto}}^{\text{derive}}[\kappa]$ behaves as follows.

If keys have already been derive for this salt x (these keys are recorded, see below), $\mathcal{F}_{\text{crypto}}^{\text{derive}}[\kappa]$ returns the keys recorded for x. Otherwise, $\mathcal{F}_{\text{crypto}}^{\text{derive}}[\kappa]$ parses the salt using the salt parsing function $\text{parse}_{\text{salt}}^t$. As described in Section 5.1.3, this yields a list of key types $t_1, \ldots, t_l \in \mathcal{T}$. (We refer to Section 5.1.3 for an explanation why it is reasonable to use parsing functions to determine the types of the derived keys.) Then, $\mathcal{F}_{\text{crypto}}^{\text{derive}}[\kappa]$ gives the salt x and the known/unknown status of κ (determined by sending (Status, κ) to $\mathcal{F}_{\text{crypto}}^{\text{keys}}$) to the adversary and asks her to provide keys $k_1, \ldots, k_l$ such that, for all $i \leq l$, k_i is a key of type t_i (i.e., $k_i \in \mathcal{D}_{\text{keys}}^{t_i}(\eta)$). (We note that telling the adversary the known/unknown status of κ is important for our realization of $\mathcal{F}_{\text{crypto}}$.) If κ is marked known, $\mathcal{F}_{\text{crypto}}^{\text{derive}}[\kappa]$ sends (Add, known, $(t_1, k_1), \ldots, (t_l, k_l)$) to $\mathcal{F}_{\text{crypto}}^{\text{keys}}$ to add the typed keys as known keys. Otherwise, $\mathcal{F}_{\text{crypto}}^{\text{derive}}[\kappa]$ sends (Add, unknown, $(t_1, k_1), \ldots, (t_l, k_l)$) to $\mathcal{F}_{\text{crypto}}^{\text{keys}}$ to add the typed keys as unknown keys. As explained above, this might fail in both cases. If κ is marked known, it fails if some typed key is marked unknown, because guessing is prevented. If κ is marked unknown, it fails if some typed key is not fresh. Upon failure, $\mathcal{F}_{\text{crypto}}^{\text{derive}}[\kappa]$ asks the adversary again until it provides keys such that the Add request does not fail. Finally, $\mathcal{F}_{\text{crypto}}^{\text{derive}}[\kappa]$ records the keys $(t_1, k_1), \ldots, (t_l, k_l)$ for the salt x and returns them to $\mathcal{F}_{\text{crypto}}^{\text{user}}[uid]$.

We note that the above, ideal implementation of key derivation guarantees the following properties: *(i)* Key derivation is deterministic, i.e., using the same salt yields the same keys (or pointers to the same keys). *(ii)* Keys derived from a key marked unknown are fresh and marked unknown when they are derived for the first time (they may later become known, e.g., when encrypted under a known key). *(iii)* Keys derived from a key marked known do not collide with keys marked unknown (guessing is prevented) but the adversary/simulator is free to choose any fresh key or any key already marked known.

MAC (MAC, ptr, x): A user uid can ask $\mathcal{F}_{\text{crypto}}^{\text{user}}[uid]$ to compute a MAC for a message x (an arbitrary bit string) using a typed key $\kappa = (t, k) \in \mathcal{D}_{\text{mac}}(\eta)$ (i.e., $t \in \mathcal{T}_{\text{mac}}$) a pointer ptr refers to. Then, $\mathcal{F}_{\text{crypto}}^{\text{user}}[uid]$ computes the MAC using $\mathcal{F}_{\text{crypto}}^{\text{mac}}[\kappa]$, i.e., it sends the MAC request (MAC, x) to $\mathcal{F}_{\text{crypto}}^{\text{mac}}[\kappa]$ (the copy of $\mathcal{F}_{\text{crypto}}^{\text{mac}}$ that is addressed by κ and handles all MAC and verify requests for the key κ) and waits for receiving a MAC σ as response. Then, $\mathcal{F}_{\text{crypto}}^{\text{user}}[uid]$ returns σ to the user.

We now describe how $\mathcal{F}_{\text{crypto}}^{\text{mac}}[\kappa]$ handles the MAC request (MAC, x). As $\mathcal{F}_{\text{crypto}}^{\text{senc}}[\kappa]$, upon the first request (any request, i.e., also counting verification requests, from any copy of $\mathcal{F}_{\text{crypto}}^{\text{user}}$), $\mathcal{F}_{\text{crypto}}^{\text{mac}}[\kappa]$ asks the adversary to provide a MAC algorithm. This algorithm is recorded. Then, $\mathcal{F}_{\text{crypto}}^{\text{senc}}[\kappa]$ proceeds as in the case of a second or later request, which is as follows. MAC generation with $\mathcal{F}_{\text{crypto}}^{\text{mac}}[\kappa]$ is done as in $\mathcal{F}_{\text{mac}}$. That is, the MAC σ is computed using the algorithm provided by the adversary and the key k, the message x is recorded, and σ is returned.

MAC verification (Verify, ptr, x, σ): A user uid can ask $\mathcal{F}_{\text{crypto}}^{\text{user}}[uid]$ to verify a MAC σ for a message x using a typed key $\kappa = (t, k) \in \mathcal{D}_{\text{mac}}(\eta)$ (i.e., $t \in \mathcal{T}_{\text{mac}}$) a pointer ptr refers to. Then, $\mathcal{F}_{\text{crypto}}^{\text{user}}[uid]$ verifies the MAC using $\mathcal{F}_{\text{crypto}}^{\text{mac}}[\kappa]$, i.e., it sends the verification request (Verify, x, σ) to $\mathcal{F}_{\text{crypto}}^{\text{mac}}[\kappa]$ and waits for receiving the verification result, which then is returned to the user.

We now describe how $\mathcal{F}_{\text{crypto}}^{\text{mac}}[\kappa]$ handles the verification request (Verify, x, σ). As mentioned above, when $\mathcal{F}_{\text{crypto}}^{\text{mac}}[\kappa]$ is activated the first time, it asks the adversary to provide a MAC algorithm. Then, $\mathcal{F}_{\text{crypto}}^{\text{mac}}[\kappa]$ proceeds as in the case of a second or later request, which is as follows. MAC verification is done as in $\mathcal{F}_{\text{mac}}$ except that instead of the corruption status, the known/unknown status of κ is used. That is, $\mathcal{F}_{\text{crypto}}^{\text{mac}}[\kappa]$ computes the MAC σ' of x (as above). If $\sigma = \sigma'$, the MAC verifies and $\mathcal{F}_{\text{crypto}}^{\text{mac}}[\kappa]$ returns 1. Otherwise, 0 is returned. However, if κ is marked unknown (determined by sending (Status, κ) to $\mathcal{F}_{\text{crypto}}^{\text{keys}}$) and the MAC verifies although x has not been recorded, an error is returned instead of 1 (this prevents forgery).

Public/private key requests: A user uid can send the following public/private key requests to $\mathcal{F}_{\text{crypto}}^{\text{user}}[uid]$: *(i)* (GetPubKey, $name$): To obtain the public key that belongs to the public/private key pair (with name) *name*. The name *name* is chosen and managed by the users themselves and allows users to refer to multiple public/private key pairs. It serves the same purpose as the key names for the multi-key version of $\mathcal{F}_{pke}$, as described in Section 4.1.5 (see also Remark 4.2). For example, *name* = *pid* for a party name *pid* to refer to the public/private key pair of party *pid*. *(ii)* (EncPKE, *name*, *pk*, *pid*, x, $ptr_1, \ldots, ptr_l$): To encrypt a message x (an arbitrary bit string) under the public key *pk* that belongs to the public/private key pair *name*. The plaintext is formatted such that it includes the keys the pointers $ptr_1, \ldots, ptr_l$ refer to. *(iii)* (DecPKE, *name*, y): To decrypt a ciphertext y with the private key that belongs to the public/private key pair *name*. *(iv)* (CorrPKE?, *name*): To obtain the corruption status of the public/private key pair *name*.

Upon a GetPubKey or a corruption status request, $\mathcal{F}_{crypto}^{user}[uid]$ simply forwards the request to $\mathcal{F}_{crypto}^{pke}[name]$ (the copy of $\mathcal{F}_{crypto}^{pke}$ that is addressed by *name* and handles all requests for the public/private key pair *name*) and returns the response (i.e., the public key or the corruption status, respectively) to the user. Encryption and decryption requests are handled by $\mathcal{F}_{crypto}^{user}[uid]$ just as for symmetric encryption and decryption, respectively, except for the following differences: *(i)* The plaintext formatting function $format_{pke}^{name}$ and parsing function $parse_{pke}^{name}$ is used instead of $format_{senc}^{t}$ and $parse_{senc}^{t}$, respectively. *(ii)* The copy $\mathcal{F}_{crypto}^{pke}[name]$ is used for encryption and decryption instead of $\mathcal{F}_{crypto}^{senc}[\kappa]$. *(iii)* The encryption request sent to $\mathcal{F}_{crypto}^{pke}[name]$ contains the public key *pk* as an extra argument.

We now describe how $\mathcal{F}_{crypto}^{pke}[name]$ handles requests. It handles them just as $\mathcal{F}_{pke}$ (see Section 4.2.1), except that: *(i)* Upon encryption, if $\mathcal{F}_{crypto}^{pke}[name]$ is corrupted or the provided public key *pk* is not the correct public key, then the keys the pointers $ptr_1, \ldots, ptr_l$ refer to are marked known (just as encryption with $\mathcal{F}_{crypto}^{senc}[\kappa]$ when κ is marked known). *(ii)* Upon decryption, if the decryption is not done by table look-up but the decryption algorithm is used to decrypt y (i.e., $\mathcal{F}_{crypto}^{pke}[name]$ is corrupted or no plaintext has been recorded for y), then the computed plaintext is parsed (using $parse_{pke}^{name}$) and $\mathcal{F}_{crypto}^{keys}$ is called to add the containing keys as known keys. If this fails (because some of these keys are marked unknown and guessing is prevented), an error is returned. Otherwise, the plaintext is returned. (We note that this is just as decryption with $\mathcal{F}_{crypto}^{senc}[\kappa]$ when κ is marked known.)

5.2.5. Remarks

We conclude the description of $\mathcal{F}_{crypto}$ with several remarks.

Remark 5.1. As explained for encryption requests, if a message x (that is formatted to include keys) is encrypted under a key marked known (or under a corrupted public key), all keys in x are marked known in $\mathcal{F}_{crypto}$. Yet, if in an application the ciphertext y for x is encrypted again under a key marked unknown and y is always kept encrypted under keys marked unknown, the keys in x might not be revealed from the point of view of the application. While in such a case, $\mathcal{F}_{crypto}$ would be too pessimistic concerning the known/unknown status of keys, this case does typically not seem to occur: First, ciphertexts are typically sent unencrypted at some point. We are, in fact, not aware of any key exchange or secure channel protocol where this is not the case. Second, if in a session of a protocol symmetric keys known to the adversary are used, typically no security guarantees are provided for that session anyway.

Remark 5.2. Corruption in $\mathcal{F}_{\text{crypto}}$ is only modeled for pre-shared keys and public/private key pairs. They are corruptible when they are created (i.e., used for the first time). This models static corruption on a per key basis and allows to model many types of corruption, including corruption of single sessions and of complete parties (e.g., see the modeling of WPA2 in Section 7.4.3). We note that we could have defined $\mathcal{F}_{\text{crypto}}$ such that the adversary also has the ability to corrupt freshly generated symmetric keys (i.e., keys generated using the KeyGen request). In [KT11b], this was done: The adversary, when providing such keys, has the ability to corrupt them, in which case they are marked known instead of unknown. However, since this kind of key generation models a local process, it is reasonable to assume that keys generated by honest users are not corrupted. Furthermore, this typically would not give extra power to the adversary if corruption is defined reasonably in the protocol that uses $\mathcal{F}_{\text{crypto}}$ (see, e.g., Section 7.4.3). If this form of corruption is essential, it can be modeled in the protocol that uses $\mathcal{F}_{\text{crypto}}$ using the Store request: Before key generation, a user could always ask the adversary whether she wants to corrupt the key that the user is about to generate. If this is the case, the adversary provides a corrupted key and the user stores it in $\mathcal{F}_{\text{crypto}}$. Otherwise, the user simply generates a new key using $\mathcal{F}_{\text{crypto}}$.

Remark 5.3. In $\mathcal{F}_{\text{crypto}}$, user names/identifiers and public/private key pair names are arbitrary bit strings that are not interpreted by $\mathcal{F}_{\text{crypto}}$ in any form. In [KT11b] the user names where of the form $(pid, lsid)$ where pid is the party name of the user and $lsid$ is a (local) session identifier that can be used to allow the same party to act as different users. Furthermore, the public/private key pair names where party names, i.e., every party had exactly one public/private key pair. Then, in [KT11b], $\mathcal{F}_{\text{crypto}}$ only allowed decryption with a private key of some party, say pid, for users of that party, i.e., users with a name of the form $(pid, lsid)$ for arbitrary $lsid$. Of course, such a modeling is reasonable but, in this thesis, we decided to remove these restrictions from $\mathcal{F}_{\text{crypto}}$ because they are not necessary. Instead, the protocol that uses $\mathcal{F}_{\text{crypto}}$ has to use $\mathcal{F}_{\text{crypto}}$ in a reasonable way (e.g., to guarantee that only users that have access to a private key may use it for decryption).

Remark 5.4. As mentioned above, since users of $\mathcal{F}_{\text{crypto}}$ are provided with actual bit strings, $\mathcal{F}_{\text{crypto}}$ can easily be combined with other functionalities.

For example, to analyze a protocol that, in addition to the operations provided by $\mathcal{F}_{\text{crypto}}$, uses digital signatures, this protocol can be modeled such that it uses $\mathcal{F}_{\text{crypto}} \,|\, !\mathcal{F}_{\text{sig}}$ (where $\mathcal{F}_{\text{sig}}$ is the ideal digital signature functionality from Section 4.2.2). (We note that $\mathcal{F}_{\text{crypto}}$ and $!\mathcal{F}_{\text{sig}}$ have pairwise disjoint tapes, so, there is no direct communication between these two systems.) The protocol can then use $\mathcal{F}_{\text{sig}}$ to sign (and verify) arbitrary bit strings. Of course, these bit strings may depend on any bit strings returned by $\mathcal{F}_{\text{crypto}}$, e.g., ciphertexts generated by $\mathcal{F}_{\text{crypto}}$ can be signed. Conversely, since $\mathcal{F}_{\text{sig}}$ returns the actual signatures (as bit strings), these signatures may, e.g., be part of plaintexts encrypted using $\mathcal{F}_{\text{crypto}}$. However, $\mathcal{F}_{\text{sig}}$ cannot be used to sign (unknown) keys that are stored in $\mathcal{F}_{\text{crypto}}$. (Of course, keys can be retrieved from $\mathcal{F}_{\text{crypto}}$ and then signed, but retrieved keys are marked known.) One could extend $\mathcal{F}_{\text{crypto}}$ by digital signatures to allow this (just as for encryption, before signature generation, messages would be formatted to include keys that were referred to by pointers) but this extension would not be realizable under standard cryptographic assumptions about digital signatures because they do not guarantee secrecy of signed messages.

Similarly, $\mathcal{F}_{\text{crypto}}$ can be combined with the ideal nonce functionality $\mathcal{F}_{\text{nonce}}$ (see Section 4.2.7) to model a protocol that uses ideal nonces that do not collide.

When we say that a protocol uses $\mathcal{F}_{\text{crypto}}$ *extended by digital signatures and nonces*, we mean that the protocol uses $\mathcal{F}_{\text{crypto}} \,|\, !\mathcal{F}_{\text{sig}} \,|\, \mathcal{F}_{\text{nonce}}$.

5.3. Realization of the Ideal Crypto Functionality

We now present a realization $\mathcal{P}_{\text{crypto}}$ of $\mathcal{F}_{\text{crypto}}$ that uses standard cryptographic schemes to implement the cryptographic operations that $\mathcal{F}_{\text{crypto}}$ provides. Then, we prove that $\mathcal{P}_{\text{crypto}}$ realizes $\mathcal{F}_{\text{crypto}}$ (for a reasonable class of environments) if and only if the schemes are secure. That is, just as the long-term key functionalities presented in Section 4.2, $\mathcal{F}_{\text{crypto}}$ precisely captures standard security notions.

5.3.1. The Realization

The basic idea of the realization $\mathcal{P}_{\text{crypto}}$ is simple: Just as for the realizations of the long-term key functionalities (Section 4.2), we use symmetric encryption schemes, MACs, and (variable-length output) pseudorandom functions to realize the symmetric key operations in a straightforward way. We use potentially different encryption schemes, MACs, and pseudorandom functions per key type. That is, key types can not only be used to gain more flexibility for formatting and parsing plaintexts (i.e., to define the plaintext formats of the protocol that uses $\mathcal{F}_{\text{crypto}}/\mathcal{P}_{\text{crypto}}$, see Section 5.1.2) but also allow a protocol to use different encryption schemes, MACs, and pseudorandom functions.

Just as the ideal functionality $\mathcal{F}_{\text{crypto}}$, its realization $\mathcal{P}_{\text{crypto}}$ is parameterized by a similar set of parameters Π and we write $\mathcal{P}_{\text{crypto}}(\Pi)$ to denote $\mathcal{P}_{\text{crypto}}$ parameterized by Π. However, we often leave the set of parameters implicit and just write $\mathcal{P}_{\text{crypto}}$. The set Π for $\mathcal{P}_{\text{crypto}}$ contains the following parameters:

1. *Number of I/O tape pairs:* $n > 0$ – this number defines the I/O interface of $\mathcal{P}_{\text{crypto}}$; just as for $\mathcal{F}_{\text{crypto}}$.

2. *Key types:* $\mathcal{T}_{\text{senc}}^{\text{auth}}$, $\mathcal{T}_{\text{senc}}^{\text{unauth}}$, $\mathcal{T}_{\text{derive}}$, $\mathcal{T}_{\text{mac}}$ – disjoint, finite sets of key types; just as for $\mathcal{F}_{\text{crypto}}$. (Recall that $\mathcal{T}_{\text{senc}} = \mathcal{T}_{\text{senc}}^{\text{auth}} \cup \mathcal{T}_{\text{senc}}^{\text{unauth}}$ and $\mathcal{T} = \mathcal{T}_{\text{senc}} \cup \mathcal{T}_{\text{derive}} \cup \mathcal{T}_{\text{mac}}$.)

3. *Key domains:* $\mathcal{D}_{\text{keys}}^{t}$ for all $t \in \mathcal{T}$ – domains of keys (per type); just as for $\mathcal{F}_{\text{crypto}}$. For simplicity of presentation (see footnote 37), we assume here that all keys of type $t \in \mathcal{T}$ have a fixed length $l_t(\eta) \in \mathbb{N}$ that depends on the security parameter η, i.e., $\mathcal{D}_{\text{keys}}^{t}(\eta) = \{0,1\}^{l_t(\eta)}$. (Of course, to obtain an efficient realization, these lengths must be polynomial in η.)

4. *Plaintext formatting and parsing functions:* $\text{format}_{\text{senc}}^{t}$ and $\text{parse}_{\text{senc}}^{t}$ for all $t \in \mathcal{T}_{\text{senc}}$, $\text{format}_{\text{pke}}^{name}$ and $\text{parse}_{\text{pke}}^{name}$ for all $name \in \{0,1\}^*$ – plaintext formatting and parsing functions; just as for $\mathcal{F}_{\text{crypto}}$.

5. *Salt parsing functions:* $\text{parse}_{\text{salt}}^{t}$ for all $t \in \mathcal{T}_{\text{derive}}$ – salt parsing functions; just as for $\mathcal{F}_{\text{crypto}}$.

6. *Symmetric encryption schemes and MACs:* Σ_t for all $t \in \mathcal{T}_{\text{senc}} \cup \mathcal{T}_{\text{mac}}$ – where $\Sigma_t = (\text{gen}_t, \text{enc}_t, \text{dec}_t)$, for all $t \in \mathcal{T}_{\text{senc}}$, is a symmetric encryption scheme (as defined in Section 3.2.1) and $\Sigma_t = (\text{gen}_t, \text{mac}_t)$, for all $t \in \mathcal{T}_{\text{mac}}$, is a MAC (as defined in Section 3.2.4). For simplicity of presentation, we assume that symmetric encryption and MAC keys are generated by choosing them uniformly at random from the respective key domain. That is, $\text{gen}_t(1^\eta)$, for all $t \in \mathcal{T}_{\text{senc}} \cup \mathcal{T}_{\text{mac}}$, chooses keys uniformly at random from $\mathcal{D}_{\text{keys}}^{t}(\eta) = \{0,1\}^{l_t(\eta)}$.[37]

7. *Public-key encryption scheme:* Σ_{pke} – where $\Sigma_{\text{pke}} = (\text{gen}_{\text{pke}}, \text{enc}_{\text{pke}}, \text{dec}_{\text{pke}})$ is a public-key encryption scheme (as defined in Section 3.2.2). We note that we could use different public-key encryption schemes (e.g., based on the public/private key pair names or by introducing types for key pairs) to realize $\mathcal{F}_{\text{crypto}}$. For simplicity of presentation, we only use one public-key encryption scheme.

8. *Variable-length output pseudorandom functions (VLO-PRFs):* PRF_t^* for all $t \in \mathcal{T}_{\text{derive}}$ – PRF_t^*, for all $t \in \mathcal{T}_{\text{derive}}$, is a VLO-PRF (as defined in Section 3.2.5) with key length $l_t(\eta)$ for security parameter η (recall that $l_t(\eta)$ is the length of keys of type t).

As mentioned above, $\mathcal{P}_{\text{crypto}}$ basically uses the cryptographic schemes to perform the cryptographic tasks. For setting up pre-shared keys, it uses an ideal key setup functionality $\mathcal{F}_{\text{keysetup}}$ as setup assumption (see below). For key derivation, the

---

[37]We mainly rely on the assumption that keys have a fixed length and are chosen uniformly at random when we directly use (variable-length output) pseudorandom functions for key derivation. If keys where generated by arbitrary (probabilistic, polynomial-time) key generation algorithms, then, for key derivation, we could use pseudorandom functions to derive (enough) random coins and use these coins as the randomness of the key generation algorithms to generate the derived keys. However, symmetric keys have a fixed length in typical applications, and hence, we make this assumption for the sake of simplicity.

VLO-PRFs are used similar to the (long-term key) key derivation realization $\mathcal{P}_{\text{derive}}$ from Section 4.2.5.

More formally, $\mathcal{P}_{\text{crypto}}$ is defined to be the following protocol system:

$$\mathcal{P}_{\text{crypto}} := !\mathcal{P}_{\text{crypto}}^{\text{user}} \mid !\mathcal{P}_{\text{pke}} \mid !\mathcal{F}_{\text{keysetup}}$$

where $\mathcal{P}_{\text{pke}}$ is the realization (with parameter Σ_{pke}) of the ideal public-key encryption functionality $\mathcal{F}_{\text{pke}}$, see Section 4.2.1. We now describe the IITM $\mathcal{P}_{\text{crypto}}^{\text{user}}$ and the ideal key setup functionality $\mathcal{F}_{\text{keysetup}}$.

The machine $\mathcal{P}_{\text{crypto}}^{\text{user}}$. The machine $\mathcal{P}_{\text{crypto}}^{\text{user}}$ is defined as $\mathcal{F}_{\text{crypto}}^{\text{user}}$ with the following differences: *(i)* Keys are now generated inside $\mathcal{P}_{\text{crypto}}^{\text{user}}$; *(ii)* all calls to $\mathcal{F}_{\text{crypto}}^{\text{keys}}$ are removed (and the tapes to connect to $\mathcal{F}_{\text{crypto}}^{\text{keys}}$ are removed as well); *(iii)* for pre-shared keys, instead of $\mathcal{F}_{\text{crypto}}^{\text{keysetup}}$, $\mathcal{F}_{\text{keysetup}}$ is used; *(iv)* symmetric encryption/decryption and MAC generation/verification is done locally using Σ_t for the appropriate key type t (and all tapes to connect to $\mathcal{F}_{\text{crypto}}^{\text{senc}}$ or $\mathcal{F}_{\text{crypto}}^{\text{mac}}$ are removed); *(v)* key derivation from keys of type t is done locally using PRF_t^* (and all tapes to connect to $\mathcal{F}_{\text{crypto}}^{\text{derive}}$ are removed); and *(vi)* for public/private key operations, instead of $\mathcal{F}_{\text{crypto}}^{\text{pke}}$, $\mathcal{P}_{\text{pke}}$ is used. More formally, the differences are as follows:

1. Request (KeyGen, t): Instead of asking the adversary for a key, a fresh key is generated: $k \xleftarrow{\$} \{0,1\}^{l_t(\eta)}$ (recall that $l_t(\eta)$ denotes the length of keys of type t for security parameter η). Also, no Add request is sent to $\mathcal{F}_{\text{crypto}}^{\text{keys}}$.

2. Request (Store, κ): No Add request is sent to $\mathcal{F}_{\text{crypto}}^{\text{keys}}$.

3. Request $(\mathsf{Retrieve}, ptr)$: No $\mathsf{MarkKnown}$ request is sent to $\mathcal{F}_{\text{crypto}}^{\text{keys}}$.

4. $(\mathsf{GetPSK}, (t, name))$ and $(\mathsf{CorrPSK?}, (t, name))$: Instead of $\mathcal{F}_{\text{crypto}}^{\text{keysetup}}$, $\mathcal{F}_{\text{keysetup}}$ is used. In fact, nothing has to be changed because $\mathcal{F}_{\text{crypto}}^{\text{keysetup}}$ and $\mathcal{F}_{\text{keysetup}}$ have the same I/O interface.

5. $(\mathsf{Enc}, ptr, x, ptr_1, \ldots, ptr_l)$ and (Dec, ptr, y): Instead of using $\mathcal{F}_{\text{crypto}}^{\text{senc}}[\kappa]$ (where $\kappa = (t, k)$ is the key referred to by ptr), the plaintext x' (recall that $x' = \mathsf{format}_{\text{senc}}^t(1^\eta, x, \kappa_1, \ldots, \kappa_l)$) is encrypted using enc_t (i.e., $y \leftarrow \mathsf{enc}_t(k, x')$) and the ciphertext y is decrypted using dec_t (i.e., $x' := \mathsf{dec}_t(k, y)$), respectively.

6. $(\mathsf{Derive}, ptr, x)$: Instead of using $\mathcal{F}_{\text{crypto}}^{\text{derive}}[\kappa]$ (where $\kappa = (t, k)$ is the key referred to by ptr), the typed keys $\kappa_1, \ldots, \kappa_l$ are derived as follows:

   $(t_1, \ldots, t_l) := \mathsf{parse}_{\text{salt}}^t(1^\eta, x)$ {*parse the salt x to obtain key types*

   $y := \text{PRF}_t^*(k, x, l_{t_1}(\eta) + \cdots + l_{t_l}(\eta))$ {*derive y from k with salt x*

   let $k_1, \ldots, k_l$ **s.t.** $y = k_1 \| \cdots \| k_l \wedge \forall i \leq l : |k_i| = l_{t_i}(\eta)$ {*split y into keys*

   for all $i \leq l$ **do**: $\kappa_i := (t_i, k_i)$ {*construct typed keys*

We note that this usage of VLO-PRFs for key derivation is similar to their usage in Section 4.2.5, to realize key derivation for long-term keys.

7. (MAC, ptr, x) and (Verify, ptr, x, σ): Instead of using $\mathcal{F}^{\mathrm{mac}}_{\mathrm{crypto}}[\kappa]$ (where $\kappa = (t, k)$ is the key referred to by ptr), the message x is MACed using mac_t (i.e., $\sigma :=$ $\mathrm{mac}_t(k, x)$). The MAC σ for x is verified by computing the MAC of x as above and comparing it with σ.

8. GetPubKey, EncPKE, DecPKE, and CorrPKE?: Instead of $\mathcal{F}^{\mathrm{pke}}_{\mathrm{crypto}}$, $\mathcal{P}_{\mathrm{pke}}$ is used. In fact, nothing has to be changed because $\mathcal{F}^{\mathrm{pke}}_{\mathrm{crypto}}$ and $\mathcal{P}_{\mathrm{pke}}$ have the same I/O interface (only tape names have to be adapted).

The ideal key setup functionality $\mathcal{F}_{\mathrm{keysetup}}$. The ideal functionality $\mathcal{F}_{\mathrm{keysetup}}$ for key setup provides the commands GetPSK and CorrPSK? to $\mathcal{P}^{\mathrm{user}}_{\mathrm{crypto}}$. It is similar to $\mathcal{F}^{\mathrm{keysetup}}_{\mathrm{crypto}}$ except that uncorrupted keys are now freshly generated inside $\mathcal{F}_{\mathrm{keysetup}}$ and $\mathcal{F}^{\mathrm{keys}}_{\mathrm{crypto}}$ is not used. We now describe $\mathcal{F}_{\mathrm{keysetup}}$ in more detail (it is formally defined in pseudocode in Figure B.9 in the appendix).

The machine $\mathcal{F}_{\mathrm{keysetup}}$ is parameterized by a set of types $\mathcal{T}$ and key lengths $l_t(\eta)$ for all $t \in \mathcal{T}$ and security parameter η. We only consider $\mathcal{F}_{\mathrm{keysetup}}$ as part of $\mathcal{P}_{\mathrm{crypto}}$ and then these parameters are defined by the corresponding parameters of $\mathcal{P}_{\mathrm{crypto}}$, i.e., by the set Π as described above.

Just as for $\mathcal{F}^{\mathrm{keysetup}}_{\mathrm{crypto}}$, every copy of $\mathcal{F}_{\mathrm{keysetup}}$ represents one pre-shared key that is ideally distributed among several users and, for every key type t and pre-shared key name $name$, there exists at most one copy of $\mathcal{F}_{\mathrm{keysetup}}$, that is addressed by $(t, name)$ and that we denote by $\mathcal{F}_{\mathrm{keysetup}}[t, name]$. (We note that the role of the name $name$ and how this can be used to model security protocols is described in Section 5.2.) Upon initialization (i.e., when $\mathcal{F}_{\mathrm{keysetup}}[t, name]$ receives the first request from some instance of $\mathcal{P}^{\mathrm{user}}_{\mathrm{crypto}}$), $\mathcal{F}_{\mathrm{keysetup}}[t, name]$ asks the adversary whether the pre-shared key $(t, name)$ is corrupted (static corruption). If it is not corrupted, $\mathcal{F}_{\mathrm{keysetup}}[t, name]$ generates a fresh key of type t, i.e., it chooses k uniformly at random from $\{0, 1\}^{l_t(\eta)}$, and records this key. When initialization is completed, upon a GetPSK request from some user, $\mathcal{F}_{\mathrm{keysetup}}[t, name]$ returns the recorded key k if it is not corrupted. If it is corrupted, $\mathcal{F}_{\mathrm{keysetup}}[t, name]$ asks the adversary to provide a key of type t (i.e., some $k \in \{0, 1\}^{l_t(\eta)}$). Then, $\mathcal{F}_{\mathrm{keysetup}}[t, name]$ returns the key provided by the adversary to the user. Upon a corruption status request Corr?, $\mathcal{F}_{\mathrm{keysetup}}[t, name]$ returns 1 if it has been corrupted upon initialization and 0 otherwise.

We note that the adversary is in full control over corrupted pre-shared keys. She can even decide to return different keys upon different GetPSK requests with the same type and name. For uncorrupted pre-shared keys, however, $\mathcal{F}_{\mathrm{keysetup}}$ guarantees that these keys are honestly generated and ideally distributed (i.e., every GetPSK request with the same type and name returns the same key).

5.3.2. Proof of Realization

We would like to prove that $\mathcal{P}_{\mathrm{crypto}}$ realizes $\mathcal{F}_{\mathrm{crypto}}$ without restricting the environments and under standard assumptions about the cryptographic schemes (symmetric and public-key encryption, MACs, VLO-PRFs). However, it is easy to see that such a theorem does not hold in the presence of environments that may produce so-called key cycles (see, e.g., [BRS02, BP04]) or cause the so-called commitment problem (see, e.g., [BP04] and Remark 4.8).[38] Therefore, similar to [BP04], we restrict the class of environments that we consider, basically, to those environments that do not produce key cycles or cause the commitment problem.

More precisely, to formulate such a class of environments that captures what is typically encountered in applications, we observe, as was first pointed in [BP04], that once a key has been used in a protocol to encrypt a message, this key is typically not encrypted anymore in the rest of the protocol. Let us call these protocols *standard*; for example, many real-world protocols such as WPA2 can easily be seen to be standard (see Section 7.4.3). This observation can be generalized to *used-order respecting environments*, which we formulate based on $\mathcal{F}_{\mathrm{crypto}}$: An environment $\mathcal{E}$ (for $\mathcal{F}_{\mathrm{crypto}}$) is called *used-order respecting* if it happens only with negligible probability that, in a run of $\mathcal{E} \mid \mathcal{F}_{\mathrm{crypto}}$, an unknown key κ (i.e., κ is marked unknown in $\mathcal{F}_{\mathrm{crypto}}$) which has been used at some point (for encryption or key derivation, in case of keys of type $t \in \mathcal{T}_{\mathrm{senc}}^{\mathrm{unauth}}$ also for decryption) is encrypted itself by an unknown key κ' used for the first time later than κ. Clearly, such environments do not produce key cycles among unknown keys (except with negligible probability). (We do not need to prevent key cycles among known keys.) Note that MAC keys are not problematic because they cannot be used to MAC other keys.

We say that an environment $\mathcal{E}$ *does not cause the commitment problem (is non-committing)*, if it happens only with negligible probability that, in a run of $\mathcal{E} \mid \mathcal{F}_{\mathrm{crypto}}$, after an unknown encryption or key derivation key κ has been used (as above), κ becomes known later on in the run, i.e., is marked known by $\mathcal{F}_{\mathrm{crypto}}$. It is easy to see that for standard protocols, as introduced above, the commitment problem does not occur if corruption is defined appropriately, see below.

In the theorem, stated below, instead of explicitly restricting the class of environments described above, we introduce a functionality $\mathcal{F}^*$ that provides exactly the same I/O interface as $\mathcal{F}_{\mathrm{crypto}}$ (and hence, $\mathcal{P}_{\mathrm{crypto}}$), but before forwarding requests to $\mathcal{F}_{\mathrm{crypto}}/\mathcal{P}_{\mathrm{crypto}}$ checks whether the used-order is still respected and the commitment problem is not caused. Otherwise, $\mathcal{F}^*$ raises an error flag and from then on blocks all messages, i.e., effectively stops the run. It is easy to see that all information needed to perform these checks can be obtained from observing the I/O interface of $\mathcal{F}_{\mathrm{crypto}}$.

We can now state the theorem which shows that, $\mathcal{P}_{\mathrm{crypto}}(\Pi)$ realizes $\mathcal{F}_{\mathrm{crypto}}(\Pi')$ if the parameter sets Π and Π' are compatible (see below) and the cryptographic

---

[38]We note that one could make stronger assumptions about the security of the encryption schemes, such as deniable encryption (see, e.g., [CDNO97]) or key-dependent message (KDM) security (see [MTY11] for a survey about KDM security). However, real-world protocols do not rely on such encryption schemes.

primitives in Π are secure (where we use the standard security notions that are recalled in Section 3.2). Furthermore, the theorem also shows that if $\mathcal{P}_{\mathrm{crypto}}(\Pi)$ realizes $\mathcal{F}_{\mathrm{crypto}}(\Pi')$ (where Π and Π' are compatible), then the primitives in Π are secure (for encryption, additionally, we have to assume that the domain of plaintexts is contained in the range of the plaintext formatting functions; see Remark 5.6). In other words, $\mathcal{F}_{\mathrm{crypto}}$ exactly captures the standard security notions: IND-CCA2 security for public-key and unauthenticated encryption, IND-CPA and INT-CTXT for authenticated encryption, and UF-CMA security for MACs.

Definition 5.5. *Let Π and Π' be sets of parameters for $\mathcal{P}_{\mathrm{crypto}}$ and $\mathcal{F}_{\mathrm{crypto}}$, respectively, as defined above. We say that Π and Π' are* compatible *iff these two conditions are satisfied:*

1. *Π and Π' agree on the parameter that they have in common. That is, they have the same number n, sets of key types, domains of keys, plaintext formatting and parsing functions, and salt parsing functions.*

2. *The runtime of the algorithms in Σ_{pke} and Σ_t, for all $t \in \mathcal{T}_{\mathrm{senc}} \cup \mathcal{T}_{\mathrm{mac}}$, are bounded by the polynomial p (that is a parameter in Π') in the length of their input.*

Theorem 5.1. *Let Π be a set of parameters for $\mathcal{P}_{\mathrm{crypto}}$ with symmetric encryption schemes Σ_t for all $t \in \mathcal{T}_{\mathrm{senc}}$, MACs Σ_t for all $t \in \mathcal{T}_{\mathrm{mac}}$, VLO-PRFs PRF_t^* for all $t \in \mathcal{T}_{\mathrm{derive}}$, and public-key encryption scheme Σ_{pke}. Further, let Π' be a set of parameters for $\mathcal{F}_{\mathrm{crypto}}$ with leakage algorithms L_{senc}^t (for all $t \in \mathcal{T}_{\mathrm{senc}}$) and L_{pke}^{name} (for all $name \in \{0,1\}^*$) such that Π and Π' are compatible. Then:*

1. *If Σ_t is IND-CPA and INT-CTXT secure for all $t \in \mathcal{T}_{\mathrm{senc}}^{\mathrm{auth}}$, Σ_t is IND-CCA2 secure for all $t \in \mathcal{T}_{\mathrm{senc}}^{\mathrm{unauth}}$, Σ_{pke} is IND-CCA2 secure, Σ_t is UF-CMA secure for all $t \in \mathcal{T}_{\mathrm{mac}}$, and PRF_t^* is secure for all $t \in \mathcal{T}_{\mathrm{derive}}$, and all leakage algorithms are length preserving (Definition 3.14) and keys hiding (Definition 5.3),[39] then:*

$$\mathcal{F}^* \mid \mathcal{P}_{\mathrm{crypto}} \leq \mathcal{F}^* \mid \mathcal{F}_{\mathrm{crypto}} .$$

2. *If $\mathcal{F}^* \mid \mathcal{P}_{\mathrm{crypto}} \leq \mathcal{F}^* \mid \mathcal{F}_{\mathrm{crypto}}$, then:*

   (a) *Σ_t is UF-CMA secure, for all $t \in \mathcal{T}_{\mathrm{mac}}$,*

   (b) *Σ_t is IND-CPA and INT-CTXT secure, for all $t \in \mathcal{T}_{\mathrm{senc}}^{\mathrm{auth}}$, if L_{senc}^t leaks at most the length (Definition 3.15) and the domain of plaintexts of Σ_t is contained in the range of $\mathrm{format}_{\mathrm{senc}}^t$ (the range of formatting functions is defined in Section 5.2), and*

   (c) *Σ_t is IND-CCA2 secure, for all $t \in \mathcal{T}_{\mathrm{senc}}^{\mathrm{unauth}}$, if L_{senc}^t leaks at most the length and the domain of plaintexts of Σ_t is contained in the range of $\mathrm{format}_{\mathrm{senc}}^t$.*

---

[39] More precisely, L_{senc}^t hides keys w.r.t. the plaintext formatting function $\mathrm{format}_{\mathrm{senc}}^t$ (for all $t \in \mathcal{T}_{\mathrm{senc}}$) and L_{pke}^{name} hides keys w.r.t. $\mathrm{format}_{\mathrm{pke}}^{name}$ (for all $name \in \{0,1\}^*$), as defined in Section 5.1.2.

(d) Σ_{pke} *is IND-CCA2 secure if* L_{pke}^{name}, *for all* $name \in \{0,1\}^*$, *leaks at most the length and the domain of plaintexts of* Σ_{pke} *is contained in the range of* $\mathsf{format}_{\mathrm{pke}}^{name}$.

Before we prove the above theorem, we make the following remarks.

Remark 5.5. It does not hold that $\mathcal{F}^* \,|\, \mathcal{P}_{\mathrm{crypto}} \leq \mathcal{F}^* \,|\, \mathcal{F}_{\mathrm{crypto}}$ implies that PRF_t^* is secure, for all $t \in \mathcal{T}_{\mathrm{derive}}$. That is, the assumption that PRF_t^* is secure is sufficient but not necessary to realize $\mathcal{F}^* \,|\, \mathcal{F}_{\mathrm{crypto}}$. For example, if a symmetric encryption scheme does not use the first bit of its keys, $\mathcal{F}^* \,|\, \mathcal{P}_{\mathrm{crypto}} \leq \mathcal{F}^* \,|\, \mathcal{F}_{\mathrm{crypto}}$ could hold even if PRF_t^* sets the first bit of all these keys to zero. Clearly, such a PRF_t^* would not be secure.

Remark 5.6. The condition about the plaintext domain in the above theorem implies that the environment can use $\mathcal{F}_{\mathrm{crypto}}/\mathcal{P}_{\mathrm{crypto}}$ to encrypt any plaintext. This is needed to deduce that Σ_t (or Σ_{pke}) is secure because $\mathcal{F}_{\mathrm{crypto}}/\mathcal{P}_{\mathrm{crypto}}$ can only be used to encrypt plaintext that are in the range of the formatting function. Hence, nothing could be said about the security of Σ_t for plaintexts that cannot be construced using the formatting function. We further note that, in Sections 3.2.1 and 3.2.2, we defined the domain of plaintexts to be $\{0,1\}^*$ (the set of all bit strings). As mentioned there, this could be relaxed of course.

We now present a proof sketch for the above theorem (see Appendix B.2 for a full proof). Since derived keys can be encrypted and used as encryption keys, the security of encryption depends on the security of key derivation and vice versa. Therefore, we need to carry out a single hybrid argument, intertwining both encryption and key derivation.

Proof of Theorem 5.1 (sketch). We first prove statement 2.: For MACs, it is easy to see that the environment can use a single MAC key (e.g., generated with the KeyGen request) to perform basically the same operations as with $\mathcal{F}_{\mathrm{mac}}$ (the ideal long-term key MAC functionality from Section 4.2.4). Also, $\mathcal{P}_{\mathrm{mac}}$ (the realization of $\mathcal{F}_{\mathrm{mac}}$) basically provides the same operations as $\mathcal{P}_{\mathrm{crypto}}$ for MAC keys. Statement 2. (a) then follows from Theorem 4.4 (Σ is UF-CMA secure if $\mathcal{P}_{\mathrm{mac}}(\Sigma) \leq \mathcal{F}_{\mathrm{mac}}$). Statements 2. (b), 2. (c), and 2. (d), follow similarly from Theorem 4.3 (Σ is IND-CPA and INT-CTXT secure if $\mathcal{P}_{\mathrm{senc}}(\Sigma) \leq \mathcal{F}_{\mathrm{senc}}^{\mathrm{auth}}$ and Σ is IND-CCA2 secure if $\mathcal{P}_{\mathrm{senc}}(\Sigma) \leq \mathcal{F}_{\mathrm{senc}}^{\mathrm{unauth}}$) and Theorem 4.1 ($\Sigma$ is IND-CCA2 secure if $\mathcal{P}_{\mathrm{pke}}(\Sigma) \leq \mathcal{F}_{\mathrm{pke}}$), respectively, but here we need that the environment is able to encrypt any plaintext and to obtain the actual plaintext upon decryption (recall that $\mathcal{F}_{\mathrm{crypto}}/\mathcal{P}_{\mathrm{crypto}}$ applies the plaintext formatting and parsing functions upon encryption and decryption). Since the environment can use the Retrieve request, it is easy to see that it can reconstruct the actual plaintext (i.e., the formatted plaintext that might contains keys) upon decryption. As explained in Remark 5.6, for being able to encrypt any plaintext, it is required that the domain of plaintexts is contained in the range of the plaintext formatting function $\mathsf{format}_{\mathrm{senc}}^t$ (or $\mathsf{format}_{\mathrm{pke}}^{name}$). Now, using the Store request, the environment can actually use $\mathcal{F}_{\text{crypto}}/\mathcal{P}_{\text{crypto}}$ to encrypt any plaintext, as we explain now:

Let $x \in \{0,1\}^*$ be a plaintext and η be a security parameter. Since x is in the range of $\text{format}^t_{\text{senc}}$, as defined in Section 5.1.2, there exists a message x' and typed keys $\kappa_1, \ldots, \kappa_l \in \mathcal{D}(\eta)$ (for some $l \geq 0$) such that $x = \text{format}^t_{\text{senc}}(1^\eta, x', \kappa_1, \ldots, \kappa_l)$. Now, the environment can insert the keys $\kappa_1, \ldots, \kappa_l$ into $\mathcal{F}_{\text{crypto}}/\mathcal{P}_{\text{crypto}}$ (using the Store request). (We note that $\mathcal{F}_{\text{crypto}}$ might return an error upon storing keys but this can only happen with negligible probability because $\mathcal{F}^* | \mathcal{P}_{\text{crypto}} \leq \mathcal{F}^* | \mathcal{F}_{\text{crypto}}$ and $\mathcal{P}_{\text{crypto}}$ never returns an error upon storing keys.) Then, the environment can ask $\mathcal{F}_{\text{crypto}}/\mathcal{P}_{\text{crypto}}$ to encrypt x' and provides the pointers obtained upon storing the keys $\kappa_1, \ldots, \kappa_l$ (note that $\mathcal{F}^*$ will not block this request because all these keys are marked known). Upon such a request $\mathcal{F}_{\text{crypto}}/\mathcal{P}_{\text{crypto}}$ will construct exactly the plaintext $x = \text{format}^t_{\text{senc}}(1^\eta, x', \kappa_1, \ldots, \kappa_l)$, encrypt it, and return the ciphertext.

To prove statement 1. ($\mathcal{F}^* | \mathcal{P}_{\text{crypto}} \leq \mathcal{F}^* | \mathcal{F}_{\text{crypto}}$), we first replace public-key encryption ($\mathcal{P}_{\text{pke}}$) by ideal public-key encryption ($\mathcal{F}_{\text{pke}}$). By Theorem 4.1 and the composition theorem for a constant number of systems (Theorem 2.1), we obtain that $\mathcal{F}^* | \mathcal{P}_{\text{crypto}} \leq \mathcal{F}^* | \mathcal{P}'_{\text{crypto}}$ where

$$\mathcal{P}'_{\text{crypto}} := {!}\mathcal{P}^{\text{user}}_{\text{crypto}} \, | \, {!}\mathcal{F}_{\text{pke}} \, | \, {!}\mathcal{F}_{\text{keysetup}} \ .$$

We note that, formally, we have to consider a variant of $\mathcal{F}_{\text{pke}}$ here where the leakage algorithm of $\mathcal{F}_{\text{pke}}$ depends on the public/private key pair name such that the instance $\mathcal{F}_{\text{pke}}[name]$ for the key pair name $name$ uses the leakage algorithm L^{name}_{pke}. Theorem 4.1 directly carries over to this variant of $\mathcal{F}_{\text{pke}}$.

The proof proceeds as follows. Roughly speaking, the simulator $\mathcal{S}$ that we use to show $\mathcal{F}^* | \mathcal{P}'_{\text{crypto}} \leq \mathcal{F}^* | \mathcal{F}_{\text{crypto}}$ answers requests from $\mathcal{F}_{\text{crypto}}$ in such a way that they match the behavior of $\mathcal{P}'_{\text{crypto}}$ except that $\mathcal{S}$ generates a fresh key upon key derivation from an unknown key (instead of using the pseudorandom function for key derivation). The rest of the proof proceeds by a hybrid argument:

We define hybrid systems $\mathcal{F}^{(j)}_{\text{crypto}}$ for every $j \in \mathbb{N}$. The j-th hybrid $\mathcal{F}^{(j)}_{\text{crypto}}$ behaves like $\mathcal{F}_{\text{crypto}}$ except for the following: $\mathcal{F}^{(j)}_{\text{crypto}}$ keeps track of the order in which unknown (typed) keys are first used for encryption, key derivation, or decryption (in case of unauthenticated encryption). The first key used for one of these operations has *used-order* 1, the second has *used-order* 2, and so on. Now, all keys that have used-order less than j are treated *ideal*, i.e., as in $\mathcal{S} | \mathcal{F}_{\text{crypto}}$, while the others are treated *real*, i.e., as in $\mathcal{P}'_{\text{crypto}}$. All MAC keys are treated real; we replace real MACs by ideal MACs in a later step. Then, we show that the 0-th hybrid is indistinguishable from the real system and that the p-th hybrid (where p is a polynomial, in the security parameter and length of the external input, that bounds the number of keys that are used) is indistinguishable from the ideal system. The latter requires a hybrid argument itself to replace real MACs by ideal MACs. Finally, we show that the j-th hybrid is indistinguishable from the $(j+1)$-th hybrid: The two hybrids only differ in the handling of the j-th key, say κ, which is treated ideal and real, respectively. If κ was obtained by key derivation, it was derived by one of the keys with used-order $< j$, and hence, it was derived in an ideal way, distributed just like a fresh key. Moreover, κ is at most encrypted by keys with used-order $< j$, and hence, encrypted ideally. This allows the reduction to the indistinguishability games for encryption (if κ is of type $t \in \mathcal{T}_{\text{senc}}$) and key derivation (if κ is of type $t \in \mathcal{T}_{\text{derive}}$). $\qquad\qquad\square$

Theorem 5.1, together with the composition theorems, yields the following corollary, which gets rid of the functionality $\mathcal{F}^*$, assuming that $\mathcal{F}_{\text{crypto}}$ is used by what we call a non-committing, used-order respecting protocol. A protocol system $\mathcal{P}$ that uses $\mathcal{F}_{\text{crypto}}$ (i.e., $\mathcal{P}$ connects to the I/O interface of $\mathcal{F}_{\text{crypto}}$) is called *non-committing* and *used-order respecting* if the probability that in a run of $\mathcal{E} \mid \mathcal{P} \mid \mathcal{F}^* \mid \mathcal{F}_{\text{crypto}}$ the functionality $\mathcal{F}^*$ raises the error flag is negligible for any environment $\mathcal{E} \in \text{Env}(\mathcal{P} \mid \mathcal{F}^* \mid \mathcal{F}_{\text{crypto}})$. As mentioned above, most protocols have this property and this can typically be easily checked by inspection of the protocol. For example, standard protocols (see above) are non-committing and used-order respecting because unknown keys are never encrypted (by other keys) after they have been used. In particular, if the key is unknown at the moment it is first used, it will remain unknown. We note that corruption of whole parties (or users) where the adversary controls the party can be defined in such a way that a corrupted party cannot obtain a pointer to a key marked unknown. Thus, even for such a modeling of corruption, a protocol can be standard, and hence, non-committing and used-order respecting (e.g., see Section 7.4.3).

Corollary 5.1. *Let* Π *and* Π' *be given as in Theorem 5.1. Let* $\mathcal{P}$ *be a non-committing and used-order respecting protocol system. If all cryptographic schemes are secure and all leakage algorithms are length preserving and keys hiding (as in Theorem 5.1, statement 1.), then:*

$$\mathcal{P} \mid \mathcal{P}_{\text{crypto}} \leq \mathcal{P} \mid \mathcal{F}_{\text{crypto}} \ .$$

As demonstrated in the following chapters, with Theorem 5.1 and Corollary 5.1 protocols can first be analyzed based on $\mathcal{F}_{\text{crypto}}$ and then $\mathcal{F}_{\text{crypto}}$ can be replaced by its realization $\mathcal{P}_{\text{crypto}}$.

In Section 4.2, we mentioned that the long-term key functionalities for public-key and symmetric encryption ($!\mathcal{F}_{\text{pke}}$ and $!\mathcal{F}_{\text{senc}}$) are realizable by IND-CPA secure encryption schemes if the environment is restricted appropriately (Remarks 4.4 and 4.7). The restriction to the environment is that it only asks the functionalities to decrypt ciphertexts produced by the functionalities and can, for example, be enforced using digital signatures or MACs. This also holds for $\mathcal{F}_{\text{crypto}}$. That is, although encryption is only IND-CPA secure, $\mathcal{F}^* \mid \mathcal{P}_{\text{crypto}}$ realizes $\mathcal{F}^* \mid \mathcal{F}_{\text{crypto}}$ w.r.t. environments that, in runs with $\mathcal{F}^* \mid \mathcal{F}_{\text{crypto}}$, ask $\mathcal{F}_{\text{crypto}}$ to decrypt ciphertexts not produced by $\mathcal{F}_{\text{crypto}}$ only with negligible probability.

5.4. Joint State Realization of the Ideal Crypto Functionality

We already introduced composition with joint state in Section 4.1.5 and presented joint state realizations for long-term key functionalities in Section 4.2.6. It is also desirable to obtain a joint state realization of $\mathcal{F}_{\text{crypto}}$, more precisely of its multi-session version $!\mathcal{F}_{\text{crypto}}$, where long-term keys (i.e., pre-shared keys and public/private key pairs) are shared across sessions. This allows to model a protocol based on $!\mathcal{F}_{\text{crypto}}$. Then, it suffices to show single-session security of this protocol, i.e., security in a setting where there is only one session of the protocol that uses one instance of $\mathcal{F}_{\text{crypto}}$, to obtain security of the protocol in the multi-session setting by replacing $!\mathcal{F}_{\text{crypto}}$ by its joint state realization. In this section, we describe such a joint state realization that is based on SIDs.

In the proof of Theorem 5.1, statement 1. ($\mathcal{F}^* \mid \mathcal{P}_{\text{crypto}} \leq \mathcal{F}^* \mid \mathcal{F}_{\text{crypto}}$), we showed that (under the assumptions of Theorem 5.1, statement 1.):

$$\mathcal{F}^* \mid !\mathcal{P}_{\text{crypto}}^{\text{user}} \mid !\mathcal{F}_{\text{pke}} \mid !\mathcal{F}_{\text{keysetup}} \ \leq \ \mathcal{F}^* \mid \mathcal{F}_{\text{crypto}} \ .^{40} \tag{5.1}$$

Hence, using the joint state realization $!\mathcal{P}_{\text{pke}}^{\text{js}} \mid !\mathcal{P}_{\text{pke}}$ for public-key encryption from [KT08] (restated in Section 4.2.6) and the composition theorems, we directly obtain the following joint state realization of $!\mathcal{F}_{\text{crypto}}$:

$$!\underline{\mathcal{F}^*} \mid !\mathcal{P}_{\text{crypto}}^{\text{user}} \mid !\mathcal{P}_{\text{pke}}^{\text{js}} \mid !\mathcal{P}_{\text{pke}} \mid !\mathcal{F}_{\text{keysetup}}$$

$$\leq \ !\underline{\mathcal{F}^*} \mid !\mathcal{P}_{\text{crypto}}^{\text{user}} \mid !\mathcal{F}_{\text{pke}} \mid !\mathcal{F}_{\text{keysetup}} \quad \text{(by Corollary 4.1: } !\mathcal{P}_{\text{pke}}^{\text{js}} \mid !\mathcal{P}_{\text{pke}} \leq !\mathcal{F}_{\text{pke}}\text{)}$$

$$\leq \ !\underline{\mathcal{F}^*} \mid !\mathcal{F}_{\text{crypto}} \quad \text{(by Equation (5.1)).}$$

In this joint state realization ($!\underline{\mathcal{F}^*} \mid !\mathcal{P}_{\text{crypto}}^{\text{user}} \mid !\mathcal{P}_{\text{pke}}^{\text{js}} \mid !\mathcal{P}_{\text{pke}} \mid !\mathcal{F}_{\text{keysetup}}$) indeed all public/private key pairs are shared across all sessions. We note that the joint state realization $!\mathcal{P}_{\text{pke}}^{\text{js}} \mid !\mathcal{P}_{\text{pke}}$ adds the SID to a plaintext before encryption and, upon decryption, checks that the plaintext is prefixed by the correct SID. For example, if some user in session sid encrypts a message m under the public key for key pair $name$, then, in fact, (sid, m) is encrypted under the public key for key pair $name$ (i.e., using $\mathcal{P}_{\text{pke}}[name]$).

This joint state realization already deals well with public-key encryption. However, it does not deal at all with symmetric long-term keys (i.e., pre-shared keys generated using $\mathcal{F}_{\text{keysetup}}$). Every session uses a different copy of $\mathcal{F}_{\text{keysetup}}$, and hence, every symmetric long-term key is generated freshly in every session. We now describe a joint state realization that assumes that every symmetric long-term key is never encrypted under any other key. This joint state realization will reuse the joint realizations for

---

[40] Recall that $\mathcal{P}_{\text{crypto}} = !\mathcal{P}_{\text{crypto}}^{\text{user}} \mid !\mathcal{P}_{\text{pke}} \mid !\mathcal{F}_{\text{keysetup}}$ and the system $\mathcal{P}'_{\text{crypto}}$, constructed in the proof of Theorem 5.1, is $\mathcal{P}'_{\text{crypto}} = !\mathcal{P}_{\text{crypto}}^{\text{user}} \mid !\mathcal{F}_{\text{pke}} \mid !\mathcal{F}_{\text{keysetup}}$.

long-term key functionalities from Section 4.2.6. Therefore, we first describe a variant of $\mathcal{F}_{\text{crypto}}$ where symmetric long-term keys are not generated using $\mathcal{F}_{\text{keysetup}}$ but instead $\mathcal{F}_{\text{crypto}}$ uses the long-term key functionalities $!\mathcal{F}_{\text{senc}}$, $!\mathcal{F}_{\text{mac}}$, and $!\mathcal{F}_{\text{derive}}$.[41] Just as for public-key encryption, users now refer to these long-term keys by always using the long-term key name. (Recall that originally, users obtained pointers also for long-term keys and then used these pointers to refer to them.) For example, when a user wants to encrypt a message x under a long-term key (with name) *name*, it sends the new request $(\text{EncLT}, \textit{name}, x)$ to $\mathcal{F}_{\text{crypto}}$. Similarly, $\mathcal{F}_{\text{crypto}}$ supports new request for all other operations for symmetric long-term keys. We note that we cannot directly use $\mathcal{F}_{\text{senc}}$ and $\mathcal{F}_{\text{derive}}$ because interaction with $\mathcal{F}_{\text{crypto}}^{\text{keys}}$ is needed, e.g., when encrypting (short-term) keys under a corrupted long-term key, then these keys have to be marked known. So, we consider a variant of $\mathcal{F}_{\text{senc}}$ similar to $\mathcal{F}_{\text{crypto}}^{\text{pke}}$ and also a similar variant of $\mathcal{F}_{\text{derive}}$. These variants are like $\mathcal{F}_{\text{senc}}$ and $\mathcal{F}_{\text{derive}}$, respectively, but perform requests to $\mathcal{F}_{\text{crypto}}^{\text{keys}}$ just as $\mathcal{F}_{\text{crypto}}^{\text{senc}}$ and $\mathcal{F}_{\text{crypto}}^{\text{derive}}$. Formally, this variant of $\mathcal{F}_{\text{crypto}}$ is defined to be the following protocol system:

$$\mathcal{F}'_{\text{crypto}} := \mathcal{F}_{\text{crypto}}^{\text{ST}} \mid !\mathcal{F}_{\text{crypto}}^{\text{LT-senc}} \mid !\mathcal{F}_{\text{crypto}}^{\text{LT-derive}} \mid !\mathcal{F}_{\text{mac}}$$

where

$$\mathcal{F}_{\text{crypto}}^{\text{ST}} := !\mathcal{F}_{\text{crypto}}^{\text{user}'} \mid \mathcal{F}_{\text{crypto}}^{\text{keys}} \mid !\mathcal{F}_{\text{crypto}}^{\text{senc}} \mid !\mathcal{F}_{\text{crypto}}^{\text{derive}} \mid !\mathcal{F}_{\text{crypto}}^{\text{mac}} \mid !\mathcal{F}_{\text{crypto}}^{\text{pke}} \ ,$$

$\mathcal{F}_{\text{crypto}}^{\text{user}'}$ is the variant of $\mathcal{F}_{\text{crypto}}^{\text{user}}$ extended by the requests for symmetric long-term keys, and $\mathcal{F}_{\text{crypto}}^{\text{LT-senc}}$ and $\mathcal{F}_{\text{crypto}}^{\text{LT-derive}}$ are the above described variants of $\mathcal{F}_{\text{senc}}$ and $\mathcal{F}_{\text{derive}}$, respectively. That is, $\mathcal{F}_{\text{crypto}}^{\text{ST}}$ is basically $\mathcal{F}_{\text{crypto}}$ but it handles only short-term keys. All long-term keys are handled using $!\mathcal{F}_{\text{crypto}}^{\text{LT-senc}} \mid !\mathcal{F}_{\text{crypto}}^{\text{LT-derive}} \mid !\mathcal{F}_{\text{mac}}$.

Now, the proof of Theorem 5.1 can easily be extended to obtain that:

$$\mathcal{F}^* \mid \mathcal{P}_{\text{crypto}}^{\text{ST}} \mid !\mathcal{F}_{\text{senc}} \mid !\mathcal{F}_{\text{derive}} \mid !\mathcal{F}_{\text{mac}} \ \leq \ \mathcal{F}^* \mid \mathcal{F}'_{\text{crypto}}$$

where $\mathcal{P}_{\text{crypto}}^{\text{ST}}$ is a variant of $\mathcal{P}_{\text{crypto}}$ that is obtained from $\mathcal{P}_{\text{crypto}}$ as $\mathcal{F}_{\text{crypto}}^{\text{ST}}$ is obtained from $\mathcal{F}_{\text{crypto}}$. That is, $\mathcal{P}_{\text{crypto}}^{\text{ST}}$ is basically $\mathcal{P}_{\text{crypto}}$ but symmetric long-term keys are handled using $!\mathcal{F}_{\text{senc}} \mid !\mathcal{F}_{\text{derive}} \mid !\mathcal{F}_{\text{mac}}$.

Finally, we can apply the composition theorems with joint state for symmetric encryption, key derivation, and MACs from Section 4.2.6; as we did for public-key encryption. Using Corollaries 4.3, 4.4, and 4.5 (and the composition theorems), we obtain that:

$$!\underline{\mathcal{F}^*} \mid \mathcal{P}_{\text{crypto}}^{\text{js}} \ \leq \ !\underline{\mathcal{F}^*} \mid !\underline{\mathcal{F}'_{\text{crypto}}}$$

where the joint state realization $\mathcal{P}_{\text{crypto}}^{\text{js}}$ is defined as:

$$\mathcal{P}_{\text{crypto}}^{\text{js}} := !\underline{\mathcal{P}_{\text{crypto}}^{\text{ST}}} \mid !\mathcal{P}_{\text{senc}}^{\text{js}} \mid !\mathcal{P}_{\text{senc}} \mid !\mathcal{P}_{\text{derive}}^{\text{js}} \mid !\mathcal{P}_{\text{derive}} \mid !\mathcal{P}_{\text{mac}}^{\text{js}} \mid !\mathcal{P}_{\text{mac}} \ .$$

---

[41] We note that this variant of $\mathcal{F}_{\text{crypto}}$ is similar to the ideal functionality for symmetric encryption as defined in [KT09b]. However, [KT09b] is only concerned with symmetric and public-key encryption (MACs and key derivation are not considered).

In this joint state realization indeed all symmetric long-term keys are shared across all sessions. We note that this joint state realization adds the SID to every message before encryption or MAC generation and to every salt upon key derivation. Of course, the joint state realization for public-key encryption, as described above, can be applied in addition.

In analogy to Section 5.3.2, we call a protocol system $\mathcal{P}$ *non-committing and used-order respecting w.r.t.* $!\mathcal{F}'_{\text{crypto}}$ if the probability that, in a run of $\mathcal{E} \mid \mathcal{P} \mid !\underline{\mathcal{F}^*} \mid !\mathcal{F}'_{\text{crypto}}$, some instance of $\underline{\mathcal{F}^*}$ (i.e., in some session) raises the error flag is negligible for any environment $\mathcal{E}$.[42] Similar to Corollary 5.1, for such a protocol $\mathcal{P}$, we obtain that:

$$\mathcal{P} \mid \mathcal{P}^{\text{js}}_{\text{crypto}} \leq \mathcal{P} \mid !\mathcal{F}'_{\text{crypto}} \ .$$

Finally, we note that the assumption that symmetric long-term keys are not encrypted under other keys is reasonable for most protocols because such keys are typically not sent around. Nevertheless, in Section 7.6, we present a different joint-state realization for $\mathcal{F}_{\text{crypto}}$ that allows this and, more importantly, has the advantage that it does not add SIDs to messages before encryption and MACing and is therefore suitable for analyzing a broader class of protocols.

5.5. Related Work

Backes et al. [BPW03, BP04] proposed a Dolev-Yao style cryptographic library. The main purpose of the library is to provide a Dolev-Yao style abstraction to the user, in the spirit of computational soundness results [MW04, CKKW06, BDK07, KT09a]. In contrast, our functionality provides a much lower-level idealization, aiming at wide applicability and faithful treatment of cryptographic primitives. More specifically, unlike $\mathcal{F}_{\text{crypto}}$, based on the Dolev-Yao library only those protocols can be analyzed which merely use operations provided by the library (since the user, except for payload data, only gets his/her hands on pointers to Dolev-Yao terms in the library, rather than on the actual bit strings, internally everything is represented as terms too) and these protocols can only be shown to be secure w.r.t. non-standard encryption schemes (since, e.g., extra randomness and tagging with key identifiers is assumed for encryption schemes) and assuming specific message formats (all types of messages— nonces, ciphertexts, pairs of messages etc.—, are tagged in the realization). While the Dolev-Yao library considers symmetric encryption [BP04], among other primitives (but key derivation is not considered), it is an open problem whether it has a reasonable realization; the original proof of the realization of the Dolev-Yao library in [BP04] is flawed, as examples presented in [CLC08a] illustrate (see below).

---

[42] We note that, to show that a protocol system $\mathcal{P}$ that is a σ_{prefix}-session version (e.g., $\mathcal{P} = !\mathcal{P}'$ for some protocol system $\mathcal{P}'$) is non-committing and used-order respecting w.r.t. $!\mathcal{F}'_{\text{crypto}}$, it suffices to consider only a single session (i.e. environments $\mathcal{E} \in \text{Env}_{\sigma_{\text{prefix}}\text{-single}}(\mathcal{P} \mid !\underline{\mathcal{F}^*} \mid !\mathcal{F}'_{\text{crypto}})$). This follows from the composition theorems for unbounded self-composition (Theorems 2.2 and 2.3).

Other works concerned with abstractions of symmetric encryption include [AR00, Lau04, CLC08b]. However, these works do not consider universal composability and, just as the work by Backes and Pfitzmann, aim at computational soundness of Dolev-Yao style reasoning. In the full version [CLC08a] of the work by Comon-Lundh and Cortier [CLC08b], several examples are presented pointing out a problem that forced the authors to make the rather unrealistic assumption that the adversary cannot fabricate keys, except for honestly running the key generation algorithm. In other words, dishonestly generated keys are disallowed. Indeed these examples demonstrate that the original proof of the realization of the crypto library in [BP04] is flawed and suggest that dishonestly generated keys also have to be forbidden for the cryptographic library, in case symmetric encryption is considered. We note that, in our setting, dishonestly generated keys do not cause problems, since, as mentioned above, our functionality provides a lower level of abstraction of symmetric encryption.

In [DDMW06], a formal logic that enjoys a computational, game-based semantics is used to reason about protocols that use symmetric encryption. In [DDM+06], Datta et al. prove that certain variants of symmetric encryption cannot have realizable ideal functionalities.

We finally mention the tool CryptoVerif [Bla06] by Blanchet for analyzing protocols that, for example, employ symmetric encryption in a game-based cryptographic setting.

6. Computational Soundness for Key Exchange Protocols with Symmetric Encryption

Computational soundness of formal analysis, as already mentioned in the introduction, has attracted a lot of attention in the last few years and many positive results have been obtained. However, as further discussed in Section 6.6, establishing computational soundness results for protocols with symmetric encryption in presence of active adversaries has turned out to be non-trivial. One reason that the combination of symmetric encryption and active adversaries in computational soundness results is challenging is that, unlike private keys in asymmetric settings, symmetric keys may "travel" between parties and some of these keys may be dishonestly generated by the adversary. The behavior of encryption and decryption under dishonestly generated keys is almost arbitrary (see, e.g., [CLC11]), and hence, hard to map to symbolic settings, as cryptographic definitions do not consider dishonestly generated keys. The only other work that we are aware of that deals with dishonestly generated symmetric encryption keys without unrealistic assumptions is the work by Comon-Lundh et al. [CLCS12]. They introduce complex deduction rules into their symbolic model in order to capture the behavior of dishonestly generated keys. The drawback of these deduction rules is that symbolic analysis becomes more complicated, especially automation might be impossible. In contrast, security in our symbolic model is automatically provable using existing tools, such as ProVerif, see below.

In this chapter, we present a computational soundness result for key exchange protocols that use symmetric keys in presence of active adversaries, with standard cryptographic assumptions. More precisely, the contributions presented in this chapter are as follows.

We first propose a class of symbolic key exchange protocols (Section 6.2) based on the applied pi calculus [AF01] (which we recall in Section 6.1), with pairing, symmetric encryption, and nonces as well as branching via general if-then-else statements. These symbolic protocols are given an obvious computational interpretation (Section 6.3), with, compared to other works, only very mild tagging requirements; basically, only pairs and keys are tagged. In particular, we do not require ciphertexts to carry any auxiliary information.

For the main result of this chapter, the computational soundness result (which we present in Section 6.4, with a proof given in Section 6.5), we develop a natural symbolic criterion for key exchange protocols. This criterion requires *(i)* that the symbolic key exchange protocol is observationally equivalent [AF01] to its randomized version in which instead of the actual session key a new nonce is output and *(ii)* that all keys used within one session of the symbolic key exchange protocol remain secret in case the session is uncorrupted. The first condition is the natural symbolic counterpart of cryptographic key indistinguishability. The second condition also seems well justified from an intuitive point of view: It is hard to imagine a reasonable key exchange protocol where in an uncorrupted session the keys used in the session become known to the adversary. This second condition will enable us, unlike other work (see Section 6.6 for a discussion of related work), to deal with dishonestly generated keys. We note that the symbolic criterion only talks about *one* session of a protocol. Hence, it is particularly simple to check by automatic tools, e.g., [Bla01, BAF05] (see also [Bau05] for related decidability results).

The main result of this chapter is that if a symbolic key exchange protocol satisfies our symbolic criterion, then this protocol (more precisely, the computational interpretation of this protocol), realizes a standard ideal key exchange functionality (more precisely, the key exchange functionality $\mathcal{F}_{ke}$ from Section 4.3.1). This is a very strong security guarantee. It a priori only talks about one session of the protocol, but the composition theorems imply that polynomially many concurrent copies of this protocol can be used securely as key exchange protocols in *every* (probabilistic, polynomial-time) environment. While the composition theorems assume independent copies of protocols, a joint state theorem for symmetric encryption can be employed to obtain an implementation where symmetric long-term keys are shared across sessions. Our computational soundness result works for any symmetric encryption scheme that guarantees authenticated encryption, i.e., IND-CPA and INT-CTXT security.

To obtain our computational soundness result, we first prove it for the case where symmetric encryption is performed based on the ideal crypto functionality $\mathcal{F}_{crypto}$ (Chapter 5), which in particularly supports symmetric encryption. We then, using the composition theorem (with joint state), replace this functionality by its (joint state) realization based on secure authenticated symmetric encryption. This last step requires that the protocol does not produce key-cycles and does not cause the so-called commitment problem. We propose symbolic, automatically checkable criteria for these properties. We note that the ideal functionality $\mathcal{F}_{crypto}$ also supports other cryptographic primitives such as public-key encryption, MACs, and key derivation. Therefore it should be easy to extend the results presented here to protocols that use these other cryptographic primitives in addition to symmetric encryption.

6.1. The Symbolic Model

Our symbolic model is an instance of the applied π-calculus [AF01], similar to the one in [CLC08b].

6.1.1. Syntax

Let Σ be a finite set of function symbols, the *signature*. The set of *terms* $\mathcal{T}(\mathcal{N}, \mathcal{X})$ over Σ and infinite sets $\mathcal{N}$ and $\mathcal{X}$ of *names* and *variables*, respectively, is defined as usual. The set of *ground* terms, i.e., terms without variables, is $\mathcal{T}(\mathcal{N})$. In what follows, $s, t, \ldots$ and x, y, z denote terms and variables, respectively. We use $\alpha, \beta, \ldots$ to denote meta-variables that range over variables and names.

For our computational soundness result, we consider the signature

$$\Sigma = \{\langle \cdot, \cdot \rangle, \pi_1(\cdot), \pi_2(\cdot), \{\cdot\}_{\cdot}^{\cdot}, \mathrm{dec}_{\cdot}(\cdot), \mathrm{sk}(\cdot)\} ,$$

where, as usual, $\langle t_1, t_2 \rangle$ is the pairing of the terms t_1 and t_2, $\pi_1(t)$ and $\pi_2(t)$ are the projections to the first and second component of t (in case t is a pair), respectively, $\{t\}_k^r$ stands for the ciphertext obtained by encrypting t under the key k using randomness r, $\mathrm{dec}_k(t)$ is the plaintext obtained by decrypting t with k (in case t is a ciphertext under k), and $\mathrm{sk}(k)$ is used to tag symmetric keys. Accordingly, Σ is associated with the following equational theory E:

$$\pi_1(\langle x, y \rangle) = x , \quad \pi_2(\langle x, y \rangle) = y , \quad \mathrm{dec}_y(\{x\}_y^z) = x .$$

We denote by $=_E$ the congruence relation on terms induced by E. We say that a term t is *reduced* or in *normal form*, if it is not possible to apply one of the above equations from left to right. Obviously, every term has a unique normal form. For example, for $t_{\mathrm{ex}} := \mathrm{dec}_{\mathrm{sk}(k)}(\pi_2(\langle a, \{b\}_{\mathrm{sk}(k)}^r \rangle))$ we have that $t_{\mathrm{ex}} =_E b$ which is its normal form.

We also consider the following predicate symbols over ground terms, which may be used in if-then-else statements in processes:

1. M is a unary predicate such that $M(t)$ is true iff the normal form of t does not contain $\pi_1(\cdot)$, $\pi_2(\cdot)$, and $\mathrm{dec}.(\cdot)$, and for every subterm of t of the form $\{t_1\}_{t_2}^{t_3}$, there exists t_2' such that $t_2 =_E \mathrm{sk}(t_2')$.

2. EQ is a binary predicate such that $\mathrm{EQ}(s, t)$ is true iff $s =_E t$, $M(s)$, and $M(t)$.

3. P_{pair} is a unary predicate such that $P_{\mathrm{pair}}(t)$ is true iff t is a pair, i.e., $t =_E \langle t_1, t_2 \rangle$ for some terms t_1, t_2.

4. P_{enc} is a unary predicate such that $P_{\mathrm{enc}}(t)$ is true iff t is a ciphertext, i.e., $t =_E \{t_1\}_{t_2}^{t_3}$ for some terms t_1, t_2, t_3.

5. P_{key} is a unary predicate such that $P_{\mathrm{key}}(t)$ is true iff t is a key, i.e., $t =_E \mathrm{sk}(t')$ for some term t'.

For example, the predicates $M(t_{\mathrm{ex}})$ and $\mathrm{EQ}(t_{\mathrm{ex}}, b)$ are true, while $M(\pi_1(\{a\}_k^r))$ is false. We remark that the above predicates can be encoded in ProVerif [Bla01, BAF05] (see, e.g., Appendix C.2).

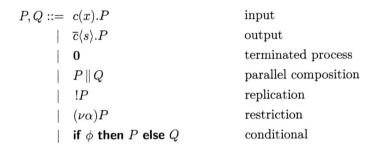

$$
\begin{aligned}
P, Q ::=\ & c(x).P & & \text{input} \\
\mid\ & \bar{c}\langle s\rangle.P & & \text{output} \\
\mid\ & 0 & & \text{terminated process} \\
\mid\ & P \parallel Q & & \text{parallel composition} \\
\mid\ & !P & & \text{replication} \\
\mid\ & (\nu a)P & & \text{restriction} \\
\mid\ & \text{if } \phi \text{ then } P \text{ else } Q & & \text{conditional}
\end{aligned}
$$

Figure 6.1.: Syntax of (plain) processes.

We call $M(t), \mathrm{EQ}(s,t), P_{\mathrm{pair}}(t), P_{\mathrm{enc}}(t), P_{\mathrm{key}}(t)$ for terms s and t (possibly with variables) *atoms*. A *condition* ϕ is a Boolean formula over atoms. For example, $\phi = M(s) \wedge M(t) \wedge \neg \mathrm{EQ}(s,t)$ says that s and t both satisfy the predicate M but are not equivalent modulo E. If ϕ contains only ground terms, then the truth value of ϕ is defined in the obvious way. If ϕ holds true, we write $\models \phi$.

Now, *(plain) processes* and *extended processes* are defined in Figure 6.1 and 6.2, respectively. For extended processes, there should be at most one active substitution for a variable and the set of active substitutions should be cycle-free, e.g., $\{x \mapsto x\}$ is not allowed. Extended processes basically extend plain processes by what is called a frame. A *frame* φ is of the form $(\nu \bar{n})\sigma$, where σ denotes a substitution, i.e., a set $\{x_1 \mapsto s_1, \ldots, x_l \mapsto s_l\}$, and $\bar{n}$ stands for a list of names, which are restricted via ν to σ. The *domain* $\mathrm{dom}(\varphi)$ of φ is the domain of σ, i.e., $\mathrm{dom}(\varphi) = \{x_1, \ldots, x_l\}$. A frame can also be considered as a specific extended process where the only plain process is $\mathbf{0}$. Every extended process A induces a frame $\varphi(A)$ which is obtained from A by replacing every plain process embedded in A by $\mathbf{0}$. Intuitively, a frame captures the knowledge of the attacker (who has access to the variables x_i), where the restricted names $\bar{n}$ are a priori not known to the attacker. The *domain* $\mathrm{dom}(A)$ of A is the domain of $\varphi(A)$.

By $\mathrm{fn}(A)$ and $\mathrm{fv}(A)$ we denote the sets of free names and free variables, respectively, in the process A, i.e., the variables and names not bound by a ν or an input command $c(x)$. Note that, for example, x is free in the process $\{x \mapsto s\}$, while it is bound in $(\nu x)\{x \mapsto s\}$. We call names that occur free in a process, excluding channel names, *global constants*. An extended process A is *closed* if the set $\mathrm{fv}(A)$ excluding variables assigned in active substitutions in A is empty, i.e., $\mathrm{fv}(A) = \mathrm{dom}(\varphi(A))$. Renaming a bound name or variable into a fresh name or variable, respectively, is called *α-conversion*. The process $A\{x \mapsto s\}$ is the process A in which free occurrences of x have been replaced by s.

An *evaluation context* C is an extended process with a hole, i.e., it is of the form

$$A, B ::= \quad P \qquad\qquad\qquad\qquad \text{(plain) process}$$
$$\mid \quad A \parallel B \qquad\qquad\qquad \text{parallel composition}$$
$$\mid \quad (\nu\alpha)A \qquad\qquad\qquad \text{restriction}$$
$$\mid \quad \{x \mapsto s\} \qquad\qquad \text{active substitution}$$

Figure 6.2.: Syntax of extended processes.

$(\nu\overline{\alpha})([\cdot] \parallel A)$, where A is an extended process. We write $\mathcal{C}[B]$ for $(\nu\overline{\alpha})(B \parallel A)$. A context $\mathcal{C}$ *closes* a process B if $\mathcal{C}[B]$ is closed.

6.1.2. Operational Semantics

To define the semantics of processes it is convenient to first define a *structural equivalence* relation $\equiv$ of processes, which captures basic properties of the operators, such as commutativity and associativity of $\parallel$. We define $\equiv$ to be the smallest equivalence relation on extended processes closed under α-conversion on both names and variables and closed under application of evaluation contexts such that the equations in Figure 6.3 are true.

For example, given an extended process A, we always find a list of names $\overline{n}$ and a substitution σ such that $(\nu\overline{n})\sigma$ is structural equivalent to the frame induced by A $((\nu\overline{n})\sigma \equiv \varphi(A))$.

Internal computation steps of a process, i.e., internal communication and evaluation of if-then-else statements, is defined by the *internal reduction relation* $\rightarrow$ which is the smallest relation on closed extended processes closed under structural equivalence $\equiv$ and closed under application of evaluation contexts such that the following is true, where ϕ contains only ground terms:

$$c(x).P \parallel \overline{c}\langle s\rangle.Q \quad \rightarrow \quad P\{x \mapsto s\} \parallel Q$$
$$\textbf{if } \phi \textbf{ then } P \textbf{ else } Q \quad \rightarrow \quad P \qquad\qquad\qquad \text{if } \models \phi$$
$$\textbf{if } \phi \textbf{ then } P \textbf{ else } Q \quad \rightarrow \quad Q \qquad\qquad\qquad \text{if } \not\models \phi \ .$$

By $\rightarrow^*$ we denote the reflexive and transitive closure of $\rightarrow$.

To describe communication of a process with its environment, we use the *labeled operational semantics* of a process in order to make the interaction with the environment, which typically represents the adversary, visible through labels and frames. The labeled operational semantics is defined by the relation $\xrightarrow{a}$, see Figure 6.4, over closed extended processes, where a is a *label* is of form $a = c(s)$, $a = \overline{c}\langle\alpha\rangle$, or $a = (\nu\alpha)\overline{c}\langle\alpha\rangle$ for a term s, channel name c, and variable or channel name α. For example, $c(x).P \xrightarrow{c(s)} P\{x \mapsto s\}$ describes an input action.

$$A \,\|\, \mathbf{0} \equiv A$$
$$A \,\|\, B \equiv B \,\|\, A$$
$$(A \,\|\, B) \,\|\, C \equiv A \,\|\, (B \,\|\, C)$$
$$(\nu\alpha)(\nu\beta)A \equiv (\nu\beta)(\nu\alpha)A$$
$$(\nu\alpha)(A \,\|\, B) \equiv A \,\|\, (\nu\alpha)B \qquad \text{if } \alpha \notin \mathrm{fn}(A) \cup \mathrm{fv}(A)$$
$$(\nu x)\{x \mapsto s\} \equiv \mathbf{0}$$
$$(\nu\alpha)\mathbf{0} \equiv \mathbf{0}$$
$$!P \equiv P \,\|\, !P$$
$$\{x \mapsto s\} \,\|\, A \equiv \{x \mapsto s\} \,\|\, A\{x \mapsto s\}$$
$$\{x \mapsto s\} \equiv \{x \mapsto t\} \qquad \text{if } s =_E t$$

Figure 6.3.: Structural equivalence.

We also have, for instance, $\bar{c}\langle s \rangle.0 \xrightarrow{(\nu x)\bar{c}\langle x \rangle} \{x \mapsto s\}$, for a ground term s, since $\bar{c}\langle s \rangle.0 \equiv (\nu x)(\bar{c}\langle x \rangle.0 \,\|\, \{x \mapsto s\}) \xrightarrow{(\nu x)\bar{c}\langle x \rangle} \{x \mapsto s\}$. In fact, since labels of the form $\bar{c}\langle t \rangle$ for a term t are not allowed, one is forced to store terms to be output into a frame, hence, make them accessible to the adversary.

Definition 6.1. *A (symbolic) trace t (from A_0 to A_n) is a finite derivation $t = A_0 \xrightarrow{a_1} A_1 \cdots \xrightarrow{a_n} A_n$ where each A_i is a closed extended process and each a_i is either ε (empty label representing an internal action $\rightarrow$) or a label as above, with $\mathrm{fv}(a_i) \subseteq \mathrm{dom}(A_{i-1})$, for all $i \leq n$.*

We call B a *successor* of A if there is a trace from A to B.

6.1.3. Deduction, Static Equivalence, and Labeled Bisimilarity

We define terms that an adversary can derive from a frame and the view an adversary has on frames, extended processes, and traces.

Definition 6.2. *We say that a ground term s is* deducible *from a frame $\varphi = (\nu\bar{n})\sigma$ (written $\varphi \vdash s$) if $\sigma \vdash s$ can be inferred by the following rules:*

1. *If there exists $x \in \mathrm{dom}(\sigma)$ such that $x\sigma = s$ or $s \in \mathcal{N} \setminus \bar{n}$, then $\sigma \vdash s$.*

2. *If $\sigma \vdash s_i$ for $i \leq l$ and $f \in \Sigma$, then $\sigma \vdash f(s_1, \ldots, s_l)$.*

3. *If $\sigma \vdash s$ and $s =_E s'$, then $\sigma \vdash s'$.*

$$c(x).P \xrightarrow{c(s)} P\{x \mapsto s\}$$

$$\frac{A \xrightarrow{a} A' \quad \alpha \text{ does not occur in } a}{(\nu\alpha)A \xrightarrow{a} (\nu\alpha)A'}$$

$$\bar{c}\langle\alpha\rangle.P \xrightarrow{\bar{c}\langle\alpha\rangle} P$$

$$\frac{A \xrightarrow{a} A' \quad \begin{array}{l} \text{bv}(a) \cap \text{fv}(B) = \emptyset \\ \text{bn}(a) \cap \text{fn}(B) = \emptyset \end{array}}{A \parallel B \xrightarrow{a} A' \parallel B}$$

$$\frac{A \xrightarrow{\bar{c}\langle\alpha\rangle} A' \quad c \neq \alpha}{(\nu\alpha)A \xrightarrow{(\nu\alpha)\bar{c}\langle\alpha\rangle} A'}$$

$$\frac{A \equiv B \quad B \xrightarrow{a} B' \quad B' \equiv A'}{A \xrightarrow{a} A'}$$

Figure 6.4.: Labeled semantics.

Let φ be a frame, p be a predicate (i.e., M, EQ, P_{pair}, P_{enc}, or P_{key}), and $s_1, \ldots, s_l$ be terms. We write $\varphi \models p(s_1, \ldots, s_l)$ if there exists $\bar{n}$ and σ such that $\varphi \equiv (\nu\bar{n})\sigma$, $\text{fn}(s_i) \cap \bar{n} = \emptyset$ for all $i \leq l$, and $\models p(s_1, \ldots, s_l)\sigma$. For example, consider the frame $\varphi_{\text{ex}} = (\nu n)\{x_1 \mapsto b, x_2 \mapsto t_{\text{ex}}, x_3 \mapsto n\}$, with t_{ex} as above, then $\varphi_{\text{ex}} \models \text{EQ}(x_1, x_2)$, but $\varphi_{\text{ex}} \not\models \text{EQ}(x_1, x_3)$.

Definition 6.3. *Two frames φ and φ', are* statically equivalent, *denoted $\varphi \sim_s \varphi'$, if their domains are equal and for all predicates p and terms $s_1, \ldots, s_l$ it holds $\varphi \models p(s_1, \ldots, s_l)$ iff $\varphi' \models p(s_1, \ldots, s_l)$.*

Two closed extended processes A and B are statically equivalent, *denoted $A \sim_s B$, if their frames $\varphi(A)$ and $\varphi(B)$ are statically equivalent.*

For example, $(\nu n_1, n_2, n_3)\{x_1 \mapsto b, x_2 \mapsto \{n_1\}_{\text{sk}(n_2)}^{n_3}\} \sim_s (\nu n_1, n_2)\{x_1 \mapsto b, x_2 \mapsto \{b\}_{\text{sk}(n_1)}^{n_2}\}$.

We now recall the definition of labeled bisimulation, which as shown in [AF01], is equivalent to observational equivalence. Intuitively, two process are labeled bisimilar, if an adversary cannot distinguish between them.

Definition 6.4. *Labeled bisimilarity $\sim_l$ is the largest symmetric relation $\mathcal{R}$ on closed extended processes such that $(A, B) \in \mathcal{R}$ implies:*

1. $A \sim_s B$,

2. *if $A \to A'$, then $B \to^* B'$ and $(A', B') \in \mathcal{R}$ for some B', and*

3. *if $A \xrightarrow{a} A'$ and $\text{fv}(a) \subseteq \text{dom}(A)$ and $\text{bn}(a) \cap \text{fn}(B) = \emptyset$, then $B \to^* \xrightarrow{a} \to^* B'$ and $(A', B') \in \mathcal{R}$ for some B'.*

6.2. Symbolic Protocols

We now define the class of key exchange protocols that we consider, called symbolic protocols. In Section 6.3, these protocols are given a computational interpretation. We restrict ourselves to two-party/role key exchange protocols, i.e., protocols where two parties (playing two different roles) want to exchange a session key. However, these two parties may use other parties (playing extra roles such as key distribution servers) to accomplish this, see below. Furthermore, we note that this restriction could be lifted easily.

We fix the following names for channels: c_{net}^{in}, c_{net}^{out}, and c_{io}^{out}. (Later we also consider certain decorations of these names.) Processes receive input from the network (the adversary) via c_{net}^{in}, send output on the network via c_{net}^{out}, and output session keys on c_{io}^{out}.

Symbolic protocols describe key exchange protocols and will essentially be a parallel composition of certain processes, called symbolic roles. A symbolic role first waits for input, then after performing some checks, by a sequence of if-then-else statements, produces output. The role may then terminate or wait for new input, and so on. A symbolic role R is defined by the following grammar:

$$R ::= \mathbf{0}$$
$$| \quad c_{net}^{in}(x).R'$$
$$R', R'' ::= \textbf{if } \phi \textbf{ then } \overline{c_{net}^{out}}\langle 1\rangle.R' \textbf{ else } \overline{c_{net}^{out}}\langle 0\rangle.R''$$
$$| \quad \overline{c}[s].c_{net}^{in}(x).R'$$
$$| \quad \overline{c}[s].\mathbf{0}$$

where $x \in \mathcal{X}$, $s \in \mathcal{T}(\mathcal{N}, \mathcal{X})$, $c \in \{c_{net}^{out}, c_{io}^{out}\}$, and ϕ may contain only the predicates M and EQ. The expression "$\overline{c}[s].B$" is an abbreviation for "$\textbf{if } M(s) \textbf{ then } \overline{c_{net}^{out}}\langle 1\rangle.\overline{c}\langle s\rangle.B$ $\textbf{else } \overline{c_{net}^{out}}\langle 0\rangle.\overline{c_{net}^{out}}\langle\bot\rangle.\mathbf{0}$", where $\bot, 1, 0$ are special globally known names (or constants). Note that the predicates P_{pair}, P_{enc}, and P_{key} may not be used by principles. However, they may be used by the adversary to enhance her power to distinguish processes. The reason for writing 1 and 0 on the network in if-then-else statements is that for our computational soundness result to hold, a symbolic adversary should be able to tell whether conditions in if-then-else statements are evaluated to true or to false. In other words, we force observationally different behavior for then- and else-branches of if-then-else statements. In protocol specifications then- and else-branches would in most cases exhibit observationally different behavior anyway: For example, if in the else-branch the protocol terminates but in the if-branch the protocol is continued, then this is typically observable by the adversary.

Now, a symbolic protocol is essentially a parallel composition of symbolic roles, specifying one session of a key exchange protocol. For example, in a key exchange protocol with an initiator, responder, and key distribution server, symbolic roles R_1, R_2, and R_3 would describe the behavior of these three entities, respectively.

Formally, a *symbolic (key exchange) protocol* Π is a tuple

$$\Pi = (\mathcal{P}, \mathcal{N}_{\mathrm{lt}}, \mathcal{N}_{\mathrm{st}}, \mathcal{N}_{\mathrm{rand}}, \mathcal{N}_{\mathrm{nonce}}) \ ,$$

with

$$\mathcal{P} = (\nu \overline{n})(R_1 \| \cdots \| R_l)$$

where $l \geq 2$ and $\overline{n}$ is the union of the *disjoint* sets of names $\mathcal{N}_{\mathrm{lt}}$ (long-term keys), $\mathcal{N}_{\mathrm{st}}$ (short-term keys), $\mathcal{N}_{\mathrm{rand}}$ (randomness for encryption), and $\mathcal{N}_{\mathrm{nonce}}$ (nonces).[43] As mentioned, R_i, $i \leq l$, are symbolic roles. We require that $\mathcal{P}$ is closed (i.e., it has no free variables) and R_i uses the channel names $c_{\mathrm{net}}^{\mathrm{in},i}$, $c_{\mathrm{net}}^{\mathrm{out},i}$, and $c_{\mathrm{io}}^{\mathrm{out},i}$, instead of $c_{\mathrm{net}}^{\mathrm{in}}$, $c_{\mathrm{net}}^{\mathrm{out}}$, and $c_{\mathrm{io}}^{\mathrm{out}}$, respectively, so that the adversary can easily interact with every single role. Other channel names are not used by R_i and the set $\overline{n}$ may not contain channel names or the special globally known names (or constants) $\perp, 1, 0, n_1, \ldots, n_l$ (i.e., $\perp, 1, 0, n_i, c_{\mathrm{net}}^{\mathrm{in},i}, c_{\mathrm{net}}^{\mathrm{out},i}, c_{\mathrm{io}}^{\mathrm{out},i} \notin \mathcal{N}_{\mathrm{lt}} \cup \mathcal{N}_{\mathrm{st}} \cup \mathcal{N}_{\mathrm{rand}} \cup \mathcal{N}_{\mathrm{nonce}}$ for all $i \leq l$). The special names $n_1, \ldots, n_l$ may be used by all roles and represent the names of the parties that are involved in the protocol session: n_i represents the name of the party that plays role R_i, for all $i \leq l$. For simplicity, we assume that all bound names and variables in $\mathcal{P}$ that occur in different contexts have different names (by α-conversion, this is w.l.o.g.). We often do not distinguish between Π and $\mathcal{P}$.

The roles R_1 and R_2 are the two "main roles" of the protocol, i.e., the roles that want to exchange a session key (with the help of the other roles). Only these roles may at most once output a session key on channel $c_{\mathrm{io}}^{\mathrm{out},1}$ and $c_{\mathrm{io}}^{\mathrm{out},2}$, respectively. That is, the roles R_i for $i \geq 3$ never use the channel $c_{\mathrm{io}}^{\mathrm{out},i}$.

We assume further syntactic restrictions on $\mathcal{P}$ in order for $\mathcal{P}$ to have a reasonable computational interpretation: Names in $\mathcal{N}_{\mathrm{st}}$, $\mathcal{N}_{\mathrm{rand}}$, and $\mathcal{N}_{\mathrm{nonce}}$ should occur in exactly one symbolic role, and names in $\mathcal{N}_{\mathrm{lt}}$ in exactly two symbolic roles, as we assume that a long-term key is shared between two parties; however, again, this restriction could easily be lifted. Furthermore, we assume that for every two roles R_i, R_j with $i \neq j$, there exists at most one name in $\mathcal{N}_{\mathrm{lt}}$ that occurs in R_i and R_j. That is, we assume that every two roles share at most one long-term key; again, this restriction could easily be lifted. Since fresh randomness should be used for new encryptions, names r in $\mathcal{N}_{\mathrm{rand}}$ should only occur in at most one subterm and this subterm should be of the form $\{s\}_k^r$. However, this subterm may occur in several places within a symbolic role. The function symbol $\mathrm{sk}(\cdot)$ is meant to be used as a

---

[43]We note that this definition of symbolic protocols is slightly different from the one in [KT09a]. In [KT09a], symbolic protocols where of the form $\mathcal{P} = (\nu \overline{n})(c_{\mathrm{net}}^{\mathrm{in}}(x_1) \ldots c_{\mathrm{net}}^{\mathrm{in}}(x_l).(R_1 \| \cdots \| R_l))$. The variables $x_1, \ldots, x_l$, which have to be set by the adversary before the actual protocol starts, were used to store the party names of the parties that play the respective role (in this protocol session). This allows the adversary to let one party play more than one role (in a protocol session), which requires a more complicated modeling of long-term keys, see Remark 6.2. To avoid this, we assume here that the party names are given by the special names $n_1, \ldots, n_l$ that may be used by all roles $R_1, \ldots, R_l$, see below. Another, minor difference, is that we fix R_1 and R_2 to be the two "main roles" of the protocol (see below). In [KT09a], these two "main roles" were defined by a set $\mathcal{R} \subseteq \{1, \ldots, l\}$ with $|\mathcal{R}| = 2$. Of course, this does not really make a difference because we can reorder the roles in the protocol.

tag for (short- and long-term) keys. Therefore every $n \in \mathcal{N}_{lt} \cup \mathcal{N}_{st}$ should only occur in $\mathcal{P}$ in the form $\mathrm{sk}(n)$, and $\mathrm{sk}(\cdot)$ should not occur in any other form. (Clearly, the adversary will not and cannot be forced to follow this tagging policy.) Long-term keys $\mathrm{sk}(n)$, $n \in \mathcal{N}_{lt}$, are not meant to travel. These keys should therefore only occur as keys for encryption and decryption in $\mathcal{P}$. For example, a subterm of the form $\{\mathrm{sk}(n)\}_k^r$, for $n \in \mathcal{N}_{lt}$, is not allowed in $\mathcal{P}$. We note that instead of using $\mathrm{sk}(\cdot)$ we could have assumed types for symmetric keys. However, since we only need this simple form of types, we decided to emulate such types by $\mathrm{sk}(\cdot)$.

To simplify the definition of corruption of the computational interpretation of symbolic roles, see below, we further assume that the each of two main roles R_1 and R_2 possesses at least one long-term key, i.e., there exist $n, n' \in \mathcal{N}_{lt}$ (possibly $n = n'$, but not necessarily) such that n occurs in R_1 and n' occurs in R_2. This is not really a restriction because if R_1 would not possess any long-term key, it is easy to see that the protocol is either insecure or R_1 never outputs a session key on its I/O channel; analogously for R_2.

Example 6.1. Our Simple Key Exchange Protocol (OSKE), modeled and analyzed in Section 4.4, can be modeled by the following symbolic protocol Π_{oske}:

$$\Pi_{\mathrm{oske}} := (\mathcal{P}_{\mathrm{oske}}, \mathcal{N}_{lt}, \mathcal{N}_{st}, \mathcal{N}_{\mathrm{rand}}, \mathcal{N}_{\mathrm{nonce}}) \ ,$$

with

$$\mathcal{N}_{lt} := \{k_{AB}\} \ , \qquad \mathcal{N}_{st} := \emptyset \ , \qquad \mathcal{N}_{\mathrm{rand}} := \{r\} \ , \qquad \mathcal{N}_{\mathrm{nonce}} := \{k\} \ ,$$
$$\mathcal{P}_{\mathrm{oske}} := (\nu k_{AB}, r, k)(R_1 \parallel R_2) \ ,$$
$$R_1 := c_{\mathrm{net}}^{\mathrm{in},1}(x_1) \cdot \overline{c_{\mathrm{net}}^{\mathrm{out},1}}[\{k\}_{\mathrm{sk}(k_{AB})}^r] \cdot c_{\mathrm{net}}^{\mathrm{in},1}(x_2) \cdot \overline{c_{\mathrm{io}}^{\mathrm{out},1}}[k] \cdot \mathbf{0} \ ,$$
$$R_2 := c_{\mathrm{net}}^{\mathrm{in},2}(y_1) \cdot \overline{c_{\mathrm{io}}^{\mathrm{out},2}}[\mathrm{dec}_{\mathrm{sk}(k_{AB})}(y_1)] \cdot \mathbf{0} \ .$$

In this, R_1 models role A and R_2 role B of the protocol. We note that in OSKE A sends (sid, k) encrypted under the long-term key k_{AB} to B. However, R_1 only encrypts k, i.e., without the SID sid. The reason for this is that SIDs will be added to all plaintext encrypted under long-term keys in the computational interpretation of symbolic protocols (because we will use the joint state realization from Section 5.4). Hence, the computational interpretation of $\mathcal{P}_{\mathrm{oske}}$ will model OSKE precisely, see below.

We refer to Appendix C.2.2 for a much more elaborate example protocol that can be modeled using our class of symbolic protocols.

6.3. Computational Interpretation of Symbolic Protocols

In this section, we briefly describe how a symbolic protocol is executed in the IITM model. This is done in the expected way, we highlight only some aspects, see

Appendix C.1 for details. We note that, compared to [KT09a], there are differences in the computational interpretation of symbolic protocols. These differences are only in the technical formulations and mainly due to the fact that we now use the ideal crypto functionality introduced in Chapter 5 (instead of the functionality for symmetric encryption from [KT09b]). Another difference is that we now follow the modeling of protocols as described in Section 4.1. In particularly, we directly model the protocol in the multi-session setting.

Let $\mathcal{P}$ be a symbolic protocol with roles $R_1, \ldots, R_l$, $l \geq 2$, as in Section 6.2. We assume an injective mapping τ from global constants, i.e., free names in $\mathcal{P}$, to bit strings; except for the special names $n_1, \ldots, n_l$, which represent the party names (they are interpreted using the party names $pid_1, \ldots, pid_l$ that are part of the SID, see below). Then, the protocol system $\llbracket \mathcal{P} \rrbracket^\tau$ of $\mathcal{P}$ is a system of IITMs:

$$\llbracket \mathcal{P} \rrbracket^\tau := \ !M_1 \mid \cdots \mid \ !M_l \mid \ !\mathcal{F}_{\text{crypto}}$$

The IITMs $M_1, \ldots, M_l$ are the computational interpretations $\llbracket R_1 \rrbracket^\tau, \ldots, \llbracket R_l \rrbracket^\tau$ of the symbolic roles $R_1, \ldots, R_l$ and they use the multi-session version of the ideal crypto functionality $\mathcal{F}_{\text{crypto}}$ (see Chapter 5) for encryption and decryption under symmetric keys, as explained below.

The protocol system $\llbracket \mathcal{P} \rrbracket^\tau$ directly defines the multi-session version of the protocol (whereas the symbolic protocol is single-session) and is supposed to realize $!\mathcal{F}_{\text{ke}}$, the multi-session version of the ideal key exchange functionality (see Section 4.3.1).[44] Therefore, $M_1, \ldots, M_l$ are machines as described in Section 4.1 where SIDs are from the following domain: Every SID is of the form $sid = (sid', pid_1, \ldots, pid_l)$ where sid' is an arbitrary bit string and pid_i is the party name of the party playing role i in this session. We require that $pid_i \neq pid_j$ for all $i \neq j$ (i.e., different roles are played by different parties; see Remark 6.2 for a discussion of this restriction) and that pid_i is not in the range of τ for all i (i.e., party names do not collide with global constants).[45] For every such SID sid, there is at most one copy of M_i, denoted by $M_i[sid]$, that is addressed by sid. That is, all messages sent to/by $M_i[sid]$ are prefixed by sid. Furthermore, $\mathcal{F}_{\text{crypto}}$ is the session version of $\mathcal{F}_{\text{crypto}}$ (as defined in Section 2.4 with the domain of SIDs as described above) and the copy $M_i[sid]$ uses the copy $\mathcal{F}_{\text{crypto}}[sid]$ of $\mathcal{F}_{\text{crypto}}$ that is addressed by sid. We note that every session of the protocol uses a different copy of $\mathcal{F}_{\text{crypto}}$, and hence, every session uses fresh long-term keys. This is of course not the desired modeling of the protocol, and hence, we will later replace $!\mathcal{F}_{\text{crypto}}$ by its joint state realization described in Section 5.4. This will give us a protocol that uses the same long-term keys in every session.

---

[44] We note that we omit the extra bit string m that may be part of the Establish requests that are sent to $\mathcal{F}_{\text{ke}}$ (see Section 4.3.1) because it is not needed for our realizations obtained from symbolic protocols.

[45] The restriction that party names must not collide with global constants can easily be enforced by protocols. For example, by using different tags or prefixes for party names and global constants. However, it could also be lifted easily. Then, one would have to define symbolic protocols in such a way that the names of parties may collide with global constants. For example, as explained in Remark 6.2, the (symbolic) adversary could provide the party names before the protocol starts.

Parameters of $\mathcal{F}_{\text{crypto}}$. We now describe the parameters of $\mathcal{F}_{\text{crypto}}$. Note that only symmetric encryption of $\mathcal{F}_{\text{crypto}}$ is used here, so, we only describe the relevant parameters. As expected, $\mathcal{F}_{\text{crypto}}$ is parameterized by the number l so that it has l I/O input and output tapes. Machine M_i connects to the i-th input and output tape. There are only two types of keys: the type t_{st} for short-term keys and the type t_{lt} for long-term keys. Both these types are authenticated encryption types (i.e., $\mathcal{T}_{\text{senc}}^{\text{auth}} = \{t_{\text{st}}, t_{\text{lt}}\}$ and all other sets of types are empty). For simplicity of presentation, we assume that all keys have length η, where η is the security parameter (i.e., $\mathcal{F}_{\text{crypto}}$ is parameterized by the key domains $\mathcal{D}_{\text{keys}}^{t_{\text{st}}} = \mathcal{D}_{\text{keys}}^{t_{\text{lt}}} = \{\{0,1\}^\eta\}_{\eta \in \mathbb{N}}$). This could be easily extended to other key domains. Both leakage algorithms $L_{\text{senc}}^{t_{\text{st}}}$ and $L_{\text{senc}}^{t_{\text{lt}}}$ are the leakage algorithms that return a random bit string of the same length as their input (i.e., upon input 1^η and x, they choose $\bar{x} \in \{0,1\}^{|x|}$ uniformly at random and return $\bar{x}$). These leakage algorithms leak exactly the length of a message (Definition 3.16) and have high entropy (Definition 3.17) for long messages (e.g., collisions among leakages of messages of length $\geq \eta$ occur only with negligible probability in the security parameter η). Furthermore, $\mathcal{F}_{\text{crypto}}$ is parameterized by an arbitrary polynomial p (which is used to bound the runtime of the encryption and decryption algorithms provided by the adversary/simulator).

We define plaintext formatting and parsing in $\mathcal{F}_{\text{crypto}}$ using a very simple tagging method that only distinguishes between *data* (arbitrary bit strings), *keys*, and *pairs* (of data, keys, or pairs). Therefore, let data, key, and pair be arbitrary different bit strings (they might depend on the security parameter, so, in fact, we use bit strings data_η, key_η, and pair_η but, in the following, we omit η). We will tag an arbitrary bit string x that represents data (i.e., global constants, party names, ciphertexts, etc.) as (data, x), which itself is a bit string (for some reasonable encoding of tuples of bit strings). That is, (data, x) represents x of "type" data. Analogously, a key k is tagged as (key, k) and a pair of two bit strings x and y is tagged as (pair, x, y). We say that a bit string x is *well-tagged* if $x = (\text{data}, x')$ for some bit string x', $x = (\text{key}, k)$ for some key k, or (recursively defined) $x = (\text{pair}, x_1, x_2)$ for two well-tagged bit strings x_1 and x_2. We note that well-tagged bit strings will correspond to symbolic terms. Now, plaintexts are formatted as follows. Given a well-tagged plaintext x and a list of typed short-term keys $(t_{\text{st}}, k_1), \ldots, (t_{\text{st}}, k_s)$ such that $|x| \geq \eta$ (see Remark 6.1) and x contains exactly s "dummy" keys of the form $(\text{key}, 0^\eta)$, the formatting functions $\text{format}_{\text{senc}}^{t_{\text{st}}}$ and $\text{format}_{\text{senc}}^{t_{\text{lt}}}$ replace the "dummy" keys in x by the given keys. If the input is not of the above form (e.g., x is not well-tagged), the formatting functions return $\perp$. For example, the message $m = (\text{pair}, (\text{key}, 0^\eta), (\text{pair}, (\text{data}, m'), (\text{key}, 0^\eta)))$ (for some bit string m') is formatted as:

$$\text{format}_{\text{senc}}^{t_{\text{st}}/t_{\text{lt}}}(1^\eta, m, (t_{\text{st}}, k_1), (t_{\text{st}}, k_2)) = (\text{pair}, (\text{key}, k_1), (\text{pair}, (\text{data}, m'), (\text{key}, k_2)))$$

for all keys $k_1, k_2 \in \{0,1\}^\eta$. The corresponding plaintext parsing functions $\text{parse}_{\text{senc}}^{t_{\text{st}}}$ and $\text{parse}_{\text{senc}}^{t_{\text{lt}}}$ are defined as expected: They take a bit string x as input and, if x is well-tagged, they replace all keys in x by the "dummy" key 0^η and return the obtained bit string along with the list of typed keys $(t_{\text{st}}, k_1), \ldots, (t_{\text{st}}, k_n)$ where k_i

is the i-th key in x. If x is not well-tagged, the parsing functions return $\bot$, i.e., parsing fails. It is easy to see that this defines formatting and (corresponding) parsing functions according to Definition 5.2.

To realize $\mathcal{F}_{\text{crypto}}$ (Theorem 5.1), the leakage algorithms $L_{\text{senc}}^{t_{\text{st}}}$ and $L_{\text{senc}}^{t_{\text{lt}}}$ need to be keys hiding w.r.t. $\text{format}_{\text{senc}}^{t_{\text{st}}}/\text{format}_{\text{senc}}^{t_{\text{lt}}}$ (Definition 5.3). To guarantee this, we require that the length of tagged keys and pairs only depends on the length of the input, i.e., that the encoding of tuples of bit strings is *length regular* as defined by: $|(\text{key}, k)| = |(\text{key}, k')|$ and $|(\text{pair}, x, y)| = |(\text{pair}, x', y')|$ for all k, k', x, x', y, y' such that $|k| = |k'|$, $|x| = |x'|$, and $|y| = |y'|$. Then, it is easy to see that the leakage algorithms have the desired properties.

Remark 6.1. The formatting functions in $\mathcal{F}_{\text{crypto}}$, to construct plaintexts, fail if the constructed plaintext would have length less than the security parameter. This means that all constructed plaintexts are guaranteed to have length $\geq \eta$. It is required in the proof of our computational soundness result to guarantee that leakages among ciphertexts occur only with negligible probability (see Lemma 6.1). Of course, there are other ways to guarantee this: For example, we could require that data_η (i.e., the bit string to tag data for security parameter η) has length η. Since keys have length η, this would imply that every well-tagged bit string has length at least η.

Computational interpretation of roles. The IITM $M_i := \llbracket R_i \rrbracket^\tau$, for all $i \leq l$, is derived from its symbolic counterpart R_i in a natural way. It has network tapes for communication with the adversary (who models the network) and it has I/O tapes to connect to $!\mathcal{F}_{\text{crypto}}$ (more precisely, M_i has one I/O input and one I/O output tape to connect to the i-th I/O input and output tape of $!\mathcal{F}_{\text{crypto}}$). The machines M_1 and M_2 additionally have I/O input and output tapes to receive an Establish request, to output the session key, and to allow the environment to obtain the corruption status of this role (just as $!\mathcal{F}_{\text{ke}}$, see Section 4.3.1). We note that only M_1 and M_2 have I/O tapes to the environment because they are the main roles that actually exchange a key. The other roles are just helper roles such as key exchange servers. That is, $\llbracket \mathcal{P} \rrbracket^\tau = !M_1 \mid \cdots \mid !M_l \mid !\mathcal{F}_{\text{crypto}}$ has the same external I/O interface as $!\mathcal{F}_{\text{ke}}$, which it is meant to realize. We already described that there exists one copy $M_i[\textit{sid}]$ per SID $\textit{sid}$. Copies of M_1 and M_2 start by waiting for an Establish request on the I/O tape. They forward this request to the adversary and then follow the protocol, i.e., receive and send messages from/to the adversary. If the protocol accepts and outputs a session key, they output the session key on the I/O tape to the environment. Copies of M_i for $i > 2$ directly start following the protocol, i.e., the first message they expect to receive is from the adversary. A global constant n is computationally interpreted as $(\text{data}, \tau(n))$, the computational interpretation of the special name n_i (the symbolic party name of role i) is $(\text{data}, \textit{pid}_i)$ where $\textit{pid}_i$ is the party name for role i (for every $i \leq l$), and a pair is computationally interpreted as (pair, m_1, m_2) where m_1 and m_2 are the computationally interpretations of the components of the pair. Encryption and decryption is performed via $\mathcal{F}_{\text{crypto}}[\textit{sid}]$ and the ciphertexts are tagged as data, i.e., the computational interpretation of a symbolic ciphertext is $(\mathtt{data}, y)$ where y is the ciphertext (bit string) returned by $\mathcal{F}_{\mathrm{crypto}}[sid]$, see below. Nonces and short-term keys are generated when they are first used. Nonces are tagged as data just as global constants, party names, and ciphertexts. Short-term keys are generated using the KeyGen request of $\mathcal{F}_{\mathrm{crypto}}[sid]$ with the key type t_{st} and tagged as key, i.e., with key, see below. Every long-term key, say for the symbolic name $n \in \mathcal{N}_{\mathrm{lt}}$, is obtained using the GetPSK request of $\mathcal{F}_{\mathrm{crypto}}[sid]$ with the type t_{lt} and the name $name = (\min\{pid_i, pid_j\}, \max\{pid_i, pid_j\})$ (we assume a total order on bit strings, such as lexicographical order) where pid_i is the party name for role i (in this session, i.e., in sid) and pid_j is the party name for role j where j is the role that shares the long-term key n with role i (i.e., the symbolic role R_j uses n). Recall that, by definition of symbolic protocols, every (symbolic) long-term key name occurs in exactly two (symbolic) roles and every two roles share at most one long-term key name. We note that this construction of $name$ guarantees that every two parties use the same pre-shared key name in every session (hence, in the joint state realization, see below, every two parties use the same pre-shared key in every session). The atomic formula $M(s)$ is interpreted as true if the computational interpretation of s does not fail. For example, applying π_1 to a bit string x that is not of the form $(\mathtt{pair}, x_1, x_2)$ for some well-tagged bit strings x_1 and x_2 fails. The atomic formula $\mathrm{EQ}(s_1, s_2)$ is interpreted as true if the computational interpretations of s_1 and s_2 do not fail and yield the same bit strings. The output of the constants 1 and 0 after if-then-else statements is not computationally interpreted, i.e., M_i does not produce such outputs but directly continues with the execution after this output. In other words, the adversary is not given a priori knowledge of the internal evaluation of if-then-else statements, although this could be allowed without changing our results.

We now describe how corruption is defined in $[\![\mathcal{P}]\!]^\tau$. First, we note that corruption of long-term keys is defined in instances of $\mathcal{F}_{\mathrm{crypto}}$. The adversary has the ability to corrupt long-term keys when they are generated (i.e., just before they are used for the first time). In addition to corruption of long-term keys, we allow the adversary to corrupt instances of M_1 and M_2 upon initialization, i.e., corruption is static on a per instance basis. When an instance of M_1 or M_2 forwards the Establish request, to corrupt the instance, the adversary can reply to the Establish request with a special Corr request (later Corr requests are ignored by the instance). We require that, when the adversary corrupts an instance, then its long-term keys must be corrupted, i.e., the long-term keys of this instance (see above) must be corrupted in the corresponding instance of $\mathcal{F}_{\mathrm{crypto}}$ (this restriction is enforced by the instances themselves by checking the corruption status of these long-term keys). As already mentioned in Section 4.4.2 (corruption is defined similarly for OSKE), it is natural to assume that long-term keys are corrupted if an instance that has access to these long-term keys is corrupted. A corrupted instance allows the adversary to determine the session key that is output to the environment. We note that, additionally, a corrupted instance could allow the adversary to use $\mathcal{F}_{\mathrm{crypto}}$ in the name of the instance. However, since all long-term keys of the instance must be corrupted, this would not give additional power to the adversary.

The environment has the ability to ask whether an instance of $\mathcal{F}_{\text{ke}}$ is corrupted, since $\llbracket \mathcal{P} \rrbracket^\tau$ has to provide the same I/O interface as $!\mathcal{F}_{\text{ke}}$, upon such a corruption status request by the environment, instances of M_1 or M_2, respectively, return 1 if and only if they are corrupted or one of the long-term keys in this protocol session (not necessarily a long-term key they use) is corrupted (i.e., the respective long-term key is corrupted in the respective instance of $\mathcal{F}_{\text{crypto}}$). We note that the adversary has the ability to corrupt a long-term key in an instance of $\mathcal{F}_{\text{crypto}}$ without explicitly corrupting the respective instances of M_1 or M_2, and hence, these copies will still follow the protocol. However, these instances report to the environment that they are corrupted if a long-term key is corrupted because a key exchange protocol typically cannot guarantee a secure key exchange in this situation. We further remark that, by our requirement on symbolic protocols that instances of M_1 and M_2 possess at least one long-term key, two instances of M_1 and M_2 that belong to the same session report itself as corrupted iff the other instance reports itself as corrupted, i.e., they agree on the status of corruption that is returned to the environment. Furthermore, corruption can only occur at the beginning of a session (because instances of M_1 and M_2 and keys in instances of $\mathcal{F}_{\text{crypto}}$ are statically corruptible), in particularly, before an instance of M_1 or M_2 has output a session key. These two properties are needed because, otherwise, $\llbracket \mathcal{P} \rrbracket^\tau$ would not realize $!\mathcal{F}_{\text{ke}}$.

Instances of M_i with $i > 2$ are not corruptible. This does not limit the adversary because these instances do not communicate with the environment (they only have network tapes to connect to the adversary and I/O tapes to connect to $!\mathcal{F}_{\text{crypto}}$). Hence, the adversary can take over complete control of these instances by corrupting their long-term keys.

See Appendix C.1 for a definition of the execution of $M_i = \llbracket R_i \rrbracket^\tau$. Here, we only illustrate the execution, with SID $sid = (sid', pid_1, \ldots, pid_l)$, for the symbolic role

$$R_1 = c_{\text{net}}^{\text{in},1}(x) \ . \ \textbf{if } \text{EQ}(\pi_1(\text{dec}_{\text{sk}(k_{AB})}(x)), n_1)$$

$$\textbf{then } \overline{c_{\text{net}}^{\text{out},1}}\langle 1 \rangle \ . \ \overline{c_{\text{net}}^{\text{out},1}}[\{\langle n, \langle \text{sk}(k), a \rangle \rangle\}_{\pi_2(\text{dec}_{\text{sk}(k_{AB})}(x))}^r] \ .$$

$$c_{\text{net}}^{\text{in},1}(x') \ . \ \overline{c_{\text{io}}^{\text{out},1}}[n] \ . \ \mathbf{0}$$

$$\textbf{else } \ldots \ ,$$

where $k_{AB} \in \mathcal{N}_{\text{lt}}$, $k \in \mathcal{N}_{\text{st}}$, $n \in \mathcal{N}_{\text{nonce}}$, $r \in \mathcal{N}_{\text{rand}}$, and $a \in \mathcal{N}$ is a global constant. Recall that the name n_1 is the special name that represents the name of the party that plays role 1 in this session. In this case, after $M_1[sid]$ receives an Establish request on its I/O tape, $M_1[sid]$ forwards it to the network (the adversary) and waits for input from the network. As explained above, the adversary may now corrupt $M_1[sid]$ but let us assume that she decides not to do so. If $M_1[sid]$ receives a message m_x (that is not a Corr request) from the network, then $M_1[sid]$ first checks that m_x is well-tagged (if it is not, then $M_1[sid]$ ignores m_x, produces empty output, and waits for receiving another message from the network) and then assigns m_x to the input variable x. Then, $M_1[sid]$ obtains a pointer (using the GetPSK request), say $ptr_{k_{AB}}$, to the pre-shared key in $\mathcal{F}_{\text{crypto}}[sid]$ corresponding to the long-term key $\text{sk}(k_{AB})$ (as explained above, this is the pre-shared key with type t_{lt} and name $(\min\{pid_1, pid_j\}, \max\{pid_1, pid_j\})$ where j is the role with that role 1 shares the long-term key k_{AB}) and then checks the condition of the if-then-else statement. Therefore, $M_1[sid]$ checks whether the evaluation of $\pi_1(\text{dec}_{\text{sk}(k_{AB})}(x))$ and n_1 is successful, corresponding to checking $M(\pi_1(\text{dec}_{\text{sk}(k_{AB})}(x)))$ and $M(n_1)$. For n_1, which is (data, pid_1) (because every bit string that is not a pair or a key is tagged as data), this is the case. For the former expression, $M_1[sid]$ decrypts m_x (because m_x is assigned to the input variable x) using the pointer $ptr_{k_{AB}}$ and first computes the computational interpretation of $\text{dec}_{\text{sk}(k_{AB})}(x)$. This is done as follows: Assume that $M_1[sid]$ obtains a plaintext, say m, and a (possibly empty) list of pointers from $\mathcal{F}_{\text{crypto}}[sid]$, say $ptr_1, \ldots, ptr_s$. Then, $M_1[sid]$ replaces the i-th (dummy) key in m by (key, ptr_i), for all $i \leq s$. Note that by definition of plaintext formatting and parsing in $\mathcal{F}_{\text{crypto}}$, m is a well-tagged bit string that contains exactly s dummy keys (except if an encryption error occurs, see below). If the interpretation of $\text{dec}_{\text{sk}(k_{AB})}(x)$ succeeds and it yields bit string of the form $\langle m_1, m_2 \rangle$; otherwise the evaluation fails, and the else-branch will be executed. Then, extracting the first component of this pair will also succeed and yields m_1. For $\text{EQ}(\pi_1(\text{dec}_{\text{sk}(k_{AB})}(x)), n_1)$ to be true, it remains to check whether this component coincides with pid_1, i.e., $m_1 = (\text{data}, pid_1)$. If this is the case, the then-branch will be executed. For this, $c_{\text{net}}^{\text{out},i}\langle 1 \rangle$ is skipped. Then, $M_1[sid]$ first generates a nonce $m_n \xleftarrow{\$} \{0,1\}^\eta$ for n and a short-term key (using the KeyGen request). This short-term key corresponds to the key $\text{sk}(k)$. Let ptr_k be the pointer returned by $\mathcal{F}_{\text{crypto}}$. Then, $M_1[sid]$ checks whether the expression $s = \{\langle n, \langle \text{sk}(k), a \rangle \rangle\}_{\pi_2(\text{dec}_{\text{sk}(k_{AB})}(x))}^r$ can be evaluated successfully, which corresponds to checking $M(s)$. The most critical part here is the evaluation of $\pi_2(\text{dec}_{\text{sk}(k_{AB})}(x))$. This is done similarly to the case above. The evaluation should yield a pointer tagged by key, i.e., (key, ptr) for some pointer ptr. This pointer is then used to encrypt, using $\mathcal{F}_{\text{crypto}}[sid]$, the computational interpretation of $\langle n, \langle \text{sk}(k), a \rangle \rangle$ which is $(\text{pair}, (\text{data}, m_n), (\text{pair}, (\text{key}, ptr_k), (\text{data}, \tau(a))))$ (because ptr_k corresponds to the short-term key $\text{sk}(k)$). However, before encryption, $M_1[sid]$ replaces (key, ptr_k) by the dummy key $(\text{key}, 0^\eta)$ and then sends the obtained bit string to $\mathcal{F}_{\text{crypto}}[sid]$ along with the pointer ptr_k. This will trigger $\mathcal{F}_{\text{crypto}}[sid]$ to encrypt the plaintext with the dummy key replaced by the short-term key the pointer ptr_k refers to. Again, $c_{\text{net}}^{\text{out},i}\langle 1 \rangle$ is skipped. The resulting ciphertext is then tagged with data and output on the network. Then, $M_1[sid]$ waits for input from the network. If $M_1[sid]$ receives a well-tagged message $m_{x'}$ from the network ($m_{x'}$ is assigned to the input variable x', but never used), then it is first checked whether the expression n can be evaluated successfully, which corresponds to checking $M(n)$ and will always succeed because the computational interpretation of n is (data, m_n). Again, $c_{\text{net}}^{\text{out},i}\langle 1 \rangle$ is skipped and $(\text{Established}, (\text{data}, m_n))$ is output on the I/O tape, i.e., the nonce m_n (tagged as data) is the session key. Since session keys are tagged as data, we have to assume that keys output by $\mathcal{F}_{\mathrm{ke}}$ are also tagged as data (otherwise $\llbracket \mathcal{P} \rrbracket^{\tau}$ would not realize $!\mathcal{F}_{\mathrm{ke}}$). That is, we assume that $\mathcal{F}_{\mathrm{ke}}$ generates keys as follows: it chooses $k^* \in \{0,1\}^\eta$ uniformly at random and then sets the session key to (data, k^*).

We note that copies of M_i might receive keys in plaintext on the network interface (i.e., receive a bit string that contains (key, k) for some $k \in \{0,1\}^\eta$) or might be asked to output keys in clear. Before the actual parsing, such keys are entered into/extracted from $\mathcal{F}_{\mathrm{crypto}}$ via Store and Retrieve commands. When outputting keys, these keys are tagged with key. Equality tests on keys (i.e., to test whether two pointers refer to the same key) are done using the Equal? request of $\mathcal{F}_{\mathrm{crypto}}$.

We further note that encryption and store requests to $\mathcal{F}_{\mathrm{crypto}}$ might fail, i.e., $\mathcal{F}_{\mathrm{crypto}}$ might return an error message. We call this event an *encryption/store error*. In this case we define M_i to terminate without producing output. For the mapping lemma (see Section 6.5) to hold, there needs to be a corresponding symbolic behavior but such errors do not occur symbolically. Still, there is a corresponding symbolic behavior, namely, that, from the point where the encryption error occurred, no messages are sent to the symbolic role R_i anymore, see Section 6.5.

Remark 6.2. The restriction that no party may play more than one role in the same protocol session corresponds to symbolic protocols where $n_i \neq n_j$ for all $i \neq j$ (recall that the name n_i represents the name of the party playing role R_i). This restriction is quite natural. Nevertheless, it could easily be lifted. Then, one would have to define symbolic protocols in such a way that the names of parties may collide as well. For example, the symbolic protocol could expect the party names as input from the adversary before the actual protocol starts. These party names are then bound to special variables that may be used by the roles R_i. Symbolic protocols then must also model that symbolic long-term key names (i.e., names in $\mathcal{N}_{\mathrm{lt}}$) collide with each other if the corresponding party names collide. For example, if k_{AS} and k_{BS} are long-term keys shared by role A and B with the role S and role A and B are now played by the same party, then k_{AS} and k_{BS} must be the same key. This can, for example, be modeled by a special free functional symbol lk (similar to sk) that takes three arguments. Now, instead of k_{AS} and k_{BS}, $\mathrm{lk}(k, x_A, x_S)$ and $\mathrm{lk}(k, x_B, x_S)$ are used where k is a restricted name and x_A, x_B, and x_S are the special variables that hold the party names for the roles. By our restriction on party names, we avoid this more complicated modeling of long-term keys.

Remark 6.3. It is easy to see that the protocol system $\llbracket \mathcal{P} \rrbracket^{\tau}$ is environmentally strictly bounded.

6.4. The Computational Soundness Result

We now present our computational soundness result. As already mentioned at the beginning of Chapter 6, the symbolic criterion for our computational soundness result consists of two parts: We assume that *(i)* the symbolic protocol is labeled bisimilar (observationally equivalent) to its randomized version in which instead of the actual session key a new nonce is output and that *(ii)* all keys used within one uncorrupted session of the symbolic protocol remain secret. As mentioned above, the second condition is a very natural condition to assume for key exchange protocols. Moreover, it will allow us to deal with dishonestly generated keys, which have been problematic in other works (see also Section 6.6): Intuitively, it implicitly guarantees that keys used by honest principals in a protocol run will be honestly generated.

To formalize the first part of our symbolic criterion, we define the random-world version of a symbolic protocol. The *random-world version* $\mathrm{rand}(\mathcal{P})$ of a symbolic protocol $\mathcal{P}$ as in Section 6.2 is the same as $\mathcal{P}$, except that, instead of outputting the actual session key on channel c_{io}^{out}, a random key (i.e., a new nonce) is output. Formally, we define:

$$\mathrm{rand}(\mathcal{P}) := (\nu n^*)\mathcal{P}_{n^*}$$

where n^* is a name that does not occur in $\mathcal{P}$ and the process $\mathcal{P}_{n^*}$ is obtained from $\mathcal{P}$ by replacing $\overline{c_{io}^{out,i}}\langle s \rangle$ by $\overline{c_{io}^{out,i}}\langle n^* \rangle$ for every term s and $i \in \{1,2\}$ (recall that only role 1 and 2 output a session key). The first part of our symbolic criterion will then simply be $\mathcal{P} \sim_l \mathrm{rand}(\mathcal{P})$. As already mentioned in the introduction, this condition can be checked automatically using existing tools, such as ProVerif [BAF05] (e.g., see Example 6.2 and Appendix C.2.2, where we use ProVerif to prove computational soundness for two example protocols).

To formulate the second part of our symbolic criterion, we first extend our signature Σ by the encryption and decryption symbols encsecret.$(\cdot)$ and decsecret.$(\cdot)$, respectively, and add the equation $\mathrm{decsecret}_y(\mathrm{encsecret}_y(x)) = x$. By adding these symbols, interference with the other encryption and decryption symbols is prevented. We now introduce a protocol secret$(\mathcal{P})$ which is derived from $\mathcal{P}$ as follows: It first generates a new nonce n, used as a secret. It then behaves just as $\mathcal{P}$. However, whenever $\mathcal{P}$ uses a term s as a key for encryption or decryption in the evaluation of a condition in an if-then-else statement or to output a message, then secret$(\mathcal{P})$ outputs $\mathrm{encsecret}_s(n)$.

Now, the second part of our symbolic criterion requires that, when executing secret$(\mathcal{P})$, n can never be derived by the adversary, i.e., for every successor $\mathcal{Q}$ of secret$(\mathcal{P})$, it holds that $\varphi(\mathcal{Q}) \nvdash n$. This exactly captures that all terms used as keys in $\mathcal{P}$ are symbolically secret, i.e., cannot be derived by the adversary. We say that $\mathcal{P}$ *preserves key secrecy*.

There are of course more declarative ways to formulate this condition. However, from the formulation above it is immediately clear that this condition can be checked automatically using existing tools, such as ProVerif.

Now, we are ready to formulate our computational soundness result for universally composable key exchange. As explained above, the symbolic criterion that we use can be checked automatically using existing tools. The proof of this theorem is presented in Section 6.5. The theorem states that the computational interpretation of the protocol, $[\![\mathcal{P}]\!]^\tau$, realizes the ideal multi-session key exchange functionality $!\mathcal{F}_{ke}$ where $\mathcal{F}_{ke}$ is the session version (as defined in Section 2.4 with the same domain of

SIDs as used by $[\![\mathcal{P}]\!]^\tau$) of the standard ideal key exchange functionality $\mathcal{F}_{\text{ke}}$ from Section 4.3.1. The only difference to the formulation in Section 4.3.1 is that we assume here that keys generated by $\mathcal{F}_{\text{ke}}$ are chosen uniformly at random from the set $\{(\texttt{data}, k) \mid k \in \{0,1\}^\eta\}$ (instead of $\{0,1\}^\eta$, where η is the security parameter), i.e., keys are generated normally but are then tagged as data. This reflects that session keys in $[\![\mathcal{P}]\!]^\tau$ are nonces, and hence, tagged as data as well.

Theorem 6.1. *Let $\mathcal{P}$ be a symbolic protocol and let τ be an injective mapping of global constants to bit strings (except for the special names $n_1, \ldots, n_l$, as above). If $\mathcal{P}$ preserves key secrecy and $\mathcal{P} \sim_l \text{rand}(\mathcal{P})$, then $[\![\mathcal{P}]\!]^\tau \leq\, !\mathcal{F}_{\text{ke}}$.*

Recall that $[\![\mathcal{P}]\!]^\tau$ uses $!\mathcal{F}_{\text{crypto}}$ for encryption. That is, a different copy of $\mathcal{F}_{\text{crypto}}$ is used in every session. Hence, using Theorem 5.1 (and the composition theorems) to replace $!\mathcal{F}_{\text{crypto}}$ by its realization $!\mathcal{P}_{\text{crypto}}$ does not yield a practical implementation of the protocol because different long-term keys are used in different sessions. However, as explained in Section 5.4, we can replace $!\mathcal{F}_{\text{crypto}}$ by its joint state realization $\mathcal{P}^{\text{js}}_{\text{crypto}}$; if $[\![\mathcal{P}]\!]^\tau$ (without $!\mathcal{F}_{\text{crypto}}$) is a used-order respecting and non-committing protocol w.r.t. $!\mathcal{F}_{\text{crypto}}$ (see Section 5.4).[46] Let $[\![\mathcal{P}]\!]^\tau_{\text{JS}}$ denote the system obtained from $[\![\mathcal{P}]\!]^\tau$ by replacing $!\mathcal{F}_{\text{crypto}}$ by $\mathcal{P}^{\text{js}}_{\text{crypto}}$. Of course, the parameters of $\mathcal{P}^{\text{js}}_{\text{crypto}}$ need to be chosen such that they are compatible with the parameters of $!\mathcal{F}_{\text{crypto}}$. Furthermore, we assume that the symmetric encryption schemes used in $\mathcal{P}^{\text{js}}_{\text{crypto}}$ are secure authenticated encryption schemes (i.e., IND-CPA and INT-CTXT secure). This yields a practical implementation of the protocol, in which the same long-term keys (per pairs of parties) are used across all sessions. By definition of $\mathcal{P}^{\text{js}}_{\text{crypto}}$, in this realization, SIDs are added to all plaintexts that are encrypted under long-term keys.

We even obtain a stronger result where we do not have to assume that $[\![\mathcal{P}]\!]^\tau$ is non-committing (because this is implied by the criterion "preserves key secrecy"):

Corollary 6.1. *Let $\mathcal{P}$ and τ be as in Theorem 6.1. If $\mathcal{P}$ preserves key secrecy, $\mathcal{P} \sim_l \text{rand}(\mathcal{P})$, and $[\![\mathcal{P}]\!]^\tau$ is used-order respecting w.r.t. $!\mathcal{F}_{\text{crypto}}$, then $[\![\mathcal{P}]\!]^\tau_{\text{JS}} \leq\, !\mathcal{F}_{\text{ke}}$.*

We omit the proof of the above corollary because it is similar to the proof of Corollary 6.2 (see below).

The condition that $[\![\mathcal{P}]\!]^\tau$ is used-order respecting is not a symbolic one. However, there is a simple symbolic criterion which captures the notion of a standard protocol explained in Section 5.3.2.

---

[46]Formally, we need to consider the variant $\mathcal{F}'_{\text{crypto}}$ of $\mathcal{F}_{\text{crypto}}$ that has been introduced in Section 5.4 because only for $!\mathcal{F}'_{\text{crypto}}$ a joint-state realization has been presented. It is however easy to see that Theorem 6.1 remains valid when modifying $[\![\mathcal{P}]\!]^\tau$ (in the obvious way) to use $!\mathcal{F}'_{\text{crypto}}$ instead of $!\mathcal{F}_{\text{crypto}}$. For simplicity of notation, in the following, we always refer to the modified versions of $[\![\mathcal{P}]\!]^\tau$ and $\mathcal{F}_{\text{crypto}}$, without indicating this in our notation.

Definition 6.5. *We call a symbolic protocol* $\mathcal{P}$ *symbolically standard if in every symbolic trace of* $\mathcal{P}$ *no short-term key (i.e.,* $n \in \mathcal{N}_{\mathrm{st}}$*) is encrypted by some other short-term key after it has been used for encryption.*

It is easy to see that this condition can be checked automatically using, for example, ProVerif: The condition can be encoded as a secrecy property where a secret is output to the adversary if the condition is violated. We note that decidability results for detecting key cycles in symbolic protocols were presented in [CZ06]. We obtain the following corollary (see Appendix C.4 for a proof):

Corollary 6.2. *Let* $\mathcal{P}$ *and* τ *be as in Theorem 6.1. If* $\mathcal{P}$ *preserves key secrecy, is symbolically standard, and satisfies* $\mathcal{P} \sim_l \mathrm{rand}(\mathcal{P})$*, then* $[\![\mathcal{P}]\!]_{\mathrm{JS}}^{\tau} \leq !\mathcal{F}_{\mathrm{ke}}$*.*

Altogether, the above results show that if a protocol satisfies our symbolic criterion, which is concerned only with a single protocol session and can be checked automatically, then this protocol satisfies a strong, computational composability property for key exchange. In particular, it can be used as a key exchange protocol in every (probabilistic, polynomial-time) environment and even if polynomially many copies of this protocol run concurrently. This merely assumes that an authenticated encryption scheme is used for symmetric encryption, which is a standard cryptographic assumption, and that SIDs are added to plaintexts before encryption under long-term keys. The latter may not be done explicitly in all protocol implementations, although it is often done implicitly (e.g. in IPsec), and it is, in any case, a good design technique. We note that, in Section 7.6, we present another joint state realization for $\mathcal{F}_{\mathrm{crypto}}$ that does not require SIDs to be added to plaintexts and is thus often more useful when analyzing existing real-world protocols. It might be possible to extend the above computational soundness result such that it makes use of this joint state realization for $\mathcal{F}_{\mathrm{crypto}}$ and becomes applicable to protocols that do not explicitly use SIDs (see Chapter 8).

Example 6.2. In Example 6.1, we modeled OSKE by the symbolic protocol $\mathcal{P}_{\mathrm{oske}}$. We note that the computational interpretation of $\mathcal{P}_{\mathrm{oske}}$, after applying the joint state realization (i.e., $[\![\mathcal{P}_{\mathrm{oske}}]\!]_{\mathrm{JS}}^{\tau}$), is very close to the modeling of OSKE in Section 4.4.2. In Section 4.4.3, it is shown that OSKE is secure, i.e., realizes $!\mathcal{F}_{\mathrm{ke}}$. Using Corollary 6.2, it is easy to obtain basically the same result by only symbolic reasoning about $\mathcal{P}_{\mathrm{oske}}$: Trivially, $\mathcal{P}_{\mathrm{oske}}$ preserves key secrecy (the only key in $\mathcal{P}_{\mathrm{oske}}$ is the long-term key k_{AB} and it is only used for encryption and decryption) and is symbolically standard (there are no short-term keys in $\mathcal{P}_{\mathrm{oske}}$). It is probably easy to show $\mathcal{P}_{\mathrm{oske}} \sim_l \mathrm{rand}(\mathcal{P}_{\mathrm{oske}})$ by hand, but it is even simpler to use ProVerif to do this. We model $\mathcal{P}_{\mathrm{oske}}$ and $\mathrm{rand}(\mathcal{P}_{\mathrm{oske}})$ as a bi-process for ProVerif (the source code is provided in Appendix C.2.1) and use ProVerif to prove $\mathcal{P}_{\mathrm{oske}} \sim_l \mathrm{rand}(\mathcal{P}_{\mathrm{oske}})$. By Corollary 6.2, we obtain that $[\![\mathcal{P}_{\mathrm{oske}}]\!]_{\mathrm{JS}}^{\tau} \leq !\mathcal{F}_{\mathrm{ke}}$.

Similarly, in Appendix C.2.2 we analyze a more elaborate example protocol using ProVerif and Corollary 6.2. This demonstrates the expressiveness of our class of symbolic protocols and the usefulness of our computational soundness result.

6.5. Proof of the Computational Soundness Result

We now prove Theorem 6.1. Throughout this section, we fix a symbolic protocol

$$\mathcal{P} = (\nu \bar{n})(R_1 \parallel \cdots \parallel R_l)$$

that preserves key secrecy and satisfies $\mathcal{P} \sim_l \mathrm{rand}(\mathcal{P})$. We also fix an injective mapping τ of global constants to bit strings (except for the special names $n_1, \ldots, n_l$, as above).

By the composition theorem for unbounded self-composition (Theorem 2.3), it suffices to show that $\llbracket \mathcal{P} \rrbracket^\tau = !M_1 \mid \cdots \mid !M_l \mid !\mathcal{F}_{\mathrm{crypto}}$ realizes $!\mathcal{F}_{\mathrm{ke}}$ for a single protocol session: First, we note that $\llbracket \mathcal{P} \rrbracket^\tau$ and $!\mathcal{F}_{\mathrm{ke}}$ are σ_{prefix}-session versions (sessions are addressed by SIDs of the form $(sid', pid_1, \ldots, pid_l)$ that are prefixed to all messages).[47] Furthermore, $\llbracket \mathcal{P} \rrbracket^\tau$ is environmentally strictly bounded, and hence, $!\llbracket \mathcal{P} \rrbracket^\tau$ is environmentally strictly bounded too (Lemma 2.4). So, by Theorem 2.3, to prove $\llbracket \mathcal{P} \rrbracket^\tau \leq !\mathcal{F}_{\mathrm{ke}}$, it suffices to show that $\llbracket \mathcal{P} \rrbracket^\tau \leq_{\sigma_{\mathrm{prefix}}\text{-single}} !\mathcal{F}_{\mathrm{ke}}$, i.e., to show that there exists a single-session simulator $\mathcal{S}$ such that $\mathcal{E} \mid \llbracket \mathcal{P} \rrbracket^\tau \equiv \mathcal{E} \mid \mathcal{S} \mid !\mathcal{F}_{\mathrm{ke}}$ for all environments $\mathcal{E}$ that only create a single session because they always use the same SID (in all messages to $\llbracket \mathcal{P} \rrbracket^\tau$ or $\mathcal{S} \mid !\mathcal{F}_{\mathrm{ke}}$).

Let $\mathcal{E}$ be such an environment (i.e., $\mathcal{E} \in \mathrm{Env}_{\sigma_{\mathrm{prefix}}\text{-single}}(\llbracket \mathcal{P} \rrbracket^\tau)$). Furthermore, let $sid = (sid', pid_1, \ldots, pid_l)$ be a valid SID, i.e., $pid_i \neq pid_j$ for all $i \neq j$ and pid_i is not in the range of τ for all $i \leq l$ (see Section 6.3). We assume that $\mathcal{E}$ always uses this SID. Of course, $\mathcal{E}$ could arbitrarily generate the SID that it uses (the SID could be randomized or depend on the external input) but this assumption is without loss of generality because $\mathcal{E}$ has to come up with the SID that it uses in this run when it sends the first message to $\llbracket \mathcal{P} \rrbracket^\tau$ (or $\mathcal{S} \mid !\mathcal{F}_{\mathrm{ke}}$).

In the following, we omit the SID sid when we talk about copies of the machines in $\llbracket \mathcal{P} \rrbracket^\tau$ or copies of $\mathcal{F}_{\mathrm{ke}}$. By M_i $(i \leq l)$, $\mathcal{F}_{\mathrm{crypto}}$, and $\mathcal{F}_{\mathrm{ke}}$, we denote the copy of M_i, $\mathcal{F}_{\mathrm{crypto}}$, or $\mathcal{F}_{\mathrm{ke}}$, respectively, with SID sid. Furthermore, we denote by $\mathcal{S}_{\mathrm{real}} := \overline{\mathcal{E} \mid \llbracket \mathcal{P} \rrbracket^\tau}$ the *real* system and by $\mathcal{S}_{\mathrm{ideal}} := \mathcal{E} \mid \mathcal{S} \mid !\mathcal{F}_{\mathrm{ke}}$ the *ideal* system.

We construct the single-session simulator $\mathcal{S}$ as follows: $\mathcal{S}$ simulates the system $\llbracket \mathcal{P} \rrbracket^\tau$, where messages obtained from $\mathcal{F}_{\mathrm{ke}}$ (to start the key exchange for a party) are forwarded to the I/O interface of (the simulated system) $\llbracket \mathcal{P} \rrbracket^\tau$ and all inputs from $\mathcal{E}$ are forwarded to the network interface of $\llbracket \mathcal{P} \rrbracket^\tau$. Network outputs of $\llbracket \mathcal{P} \rrbracket^\tau$ are forwarded to $\mathcal{E}$ and I/O outputs of $\llbracket \mathcal{P} \rrbracket^\tau$ (i.e., of M_1 or M_2), which are Established messages that contain the exchanged session key, are forwarded as Establish messages to $\mathcal{F}_{\mathrm{ke}}$ (i.e., to tell $\mathcal{F}_{\mathrm{ke}}$ to output the session key to the role 1 or 2, respectively) if $\mathcal{F}_{\mathrm{ke}}$ is uncorrupted. If (the simulated instance) M_1 or M_2 would report itself as corrupted upon a corruption status request (i.e., it got corrupted by the adversary upon initialization or a long-term key got corrupted in $\mathcal{F}_{\mathrm{crypto}}$), then $\mathcal{S}$ corrupts $\mathcal{F}_{\mathrm{ke}}$. This always succeeds because corruption can only occur upon initialization

---

[47] Recall from Section 2.4, that σ_{prefix} is the SID function that, for all messages m and tapes c, upon input (m, c) returns sid if $m = (sid, m')$ for some SID sid and message m' and, otherwise, returns $\bot$.

and $\mathcal{F}_{\mathrm{ke}}$ is corruptible as long as no role has obtained a session key. When $\mathcal{F}_{\mathrm{ke}}$ is corrupted, $\mathcal{S}$ can determine the session keys that are output by $\mathcal{F}_{\mathrm{ke}}$ and can thus perfectly simulate $[\![\mathcal{P}]\!]^\tau$.

To prove $\mathcal{S}_{\mathrm{real}} \equiv \mathcal{S}_{\mathrm{ideal}}$, we first prove a so-called mapping lemma, which relates concrete traces to symbolic traces, similar to mapping lemmas in other works on computational soundness. The specific complication we need to deal with in our mapping lemma, unlike other mapping lemmas, is the delicate issue of dishonestly generated keys. For this, we use that $\mathcal{P}$ preserves key secrecy. (The property $\mathcal{P} \sim_l \mathrm{rand}(\mathcal{P})$ is only used later to prove $\mathcal{S}_{\mathrm{real}} \equiv \mathcal{S}_{\mathrm{ideal}}$.) We need a mapping lemma for both systems $\mathcal{S}_{\mathrm{real}}$ and $\mathcal{S}_{\mathrm{ideal}}$.

6.5.1. Mapping Lemmas

Roughly speaking, the mapping lemmas that we want to prove state that, with overwhelming probability, a concrete trace t of $\mathcal{S}_{\mathrm{real}}$ and $\mathcal{S}_{\mathrm{ideal}}$ corresponds to a symbolic trace $\mathrm{symb}(t)$ of $\mathcal{P}$ and $\mathrm{rand}(\mathcal{P})$, respectively. To state such mapping lemmas, we first need to define concrete traces. A concrete trace of a system is given by the definition of runs in the IITM model. However, we provide a definition of concrete traces for $\mathcal{S}_{\mathrm{real}}$ and $\mathcal{S}_{\mathrm{ideal}}$ that highlights the information necessary for the mapping lemma.

A *(concrete) trace* t for $\mathcal{S}_{\mathrm{real}}$ and $\mathcal{S}_{\mathrm{ideal}}$ is a sequence of the following events, where all events contain the index $1 \le i \le l$ of the machine M_i which is involved in the event and the current configuration $\mathcal{C}$ of the system $\mathcal{S}_{\mathrm{real}}$ or $\mathcal{S}_{\mathrm{ideal}}$, respectively.

1. $\mathsf{in}(i, y, m, \mathcal{C})$: $\mathcal{E}$ sent the message m to the network input tape of M_i and M_i stored the input in variable y (note that this implies that m is well-tagged because otherwise M_i would ignore the input m). In the case of $\mathcal{S}_{\mathrm{ideal}}$, m is received by the simulator $\mathcal{S}$ and given to the simulated M_i.

2. $\mathsf{out}(i, m, c, \mathcal{C})$: $\mathcal{E}$ received the message m from the network output tape of M_i in which case $c = c_{\mathrm{net}}^{\mathrm{out},i}$ or from an I/O output tape of M_i in which case $c = c_{\mathrm{io}}^{\mathrm{out},i}$. In the latter case $i \in \{1, 2\}$ and m is an Established message (which contains the session key) that was sent by M_i. In the case of $\mathcal{S}_{\mathrm{ideal}}$, if $c = c_{\mathrm{net}}^{\mathrm{out},i}$, then the simulated M_i sent m. If $c = c_{\mathrm{io}}^{\mathrm{out},i}$, then m is an Established message sent by $\mathcal{F}_{\mathrm{ke}}$.

3. $\mathsf{if}(i, b, \mathcal{C})$: M_i took an internal if-then-else step where the condition was evaluated to $b \in \{0, 1\}$. After every such *if* event, we append the *output* event $\mathsf{out}(i, (\mathsf{data}, \tau(b)), c_{\mathrm{net}}^{\mathrm{out},i}, \mathcal{C}')$ (note that $(\mathsf{data}, \tau(b))$ is the bit string representation of the global constant b). The only difference between the configurations $\mathcal{C}$ and $\mathcal{C}'$ is that the process stored in the configuration of M_i in $\mathcal{C}$ is $\overline{c_{\mathrm{net}}^{\mathrm{out},i}}\langle b \rangle.B$ and the process in M_i in $\mathcal{C}'$ is B.

In the case of $\mathcal{S}_{\mathrm{ideal}}$, the simulated M_i took an internal if-then-else step.

Recall that in the case of a store or encryption error, i.e., $\mathcal{F}_{\text{crypto}}$ returned an error message upon a store or encryption request, M_i terminates with empty output. In this case, we do not record any events during this activation of M_i (i.e., not the *input* event and possible *if* events that occurred before the store or encryption error).

Note that according to the computational interpretation of symbolic protocols (Section 6.3), parties do *not* explicitly output to the environment to what the conditions in if-then-else statements were evaluated. We add the output event after an if event only to facilitate the mapping from concrete to symbolic traces. However, the computational interpretation of symbolic protocols remains unchanged and as expected.

We say that a trace is *uncorrupted* if no pre-shared key in $\mathcal{F}_{\text{crypto}}$ and no machine M_i is corrupted. A trace is called *non-colliding* if it is uncorrupted and no collisions occur between nonces (including the session key output by $\mathcal{F}_{\text{ke}}$ in case of $\mathcal{S}_{\text{ideal}}$), global constants (i.e., the range of τ), the party names $pid_1, \ldots, pid_l$, and ciphertexts which were produced with keys marked unknown (i.e., encryptions of leakages of messages). Almost all uncorrupted traces are non-colliding:

Lemma 6.1. *The probability that a concrete trace t of $\mathcal{S}_{\text{real}}$ is corrupted or t is non-colliding is overwhelming (as a function in the security parameter 1^η and the external input a). The same is true for $\mathcal{S}_{\text{ideal}}$.*

Proof. Global constants do not collide with each other because τ is injective. Also, by definition of the domain of SIDs, the party names $pid_1, \ldots, pid_l$ are disjoint from each other and the global constants (i.e., the range of τ).

Since nonces are chosen independently, at random from $\{0, 1\}^\eta$, the probability that they collide with anything else is negligible. Note also that there is only a fixed number of nonces (which does not depend on the security parameter or the external input).

For a ciphertext c which has been produced with a key marked unknown, not the actual plaintext m but its leakage $\overline{m} \leftarrow L(1^\eta, m)$ is encrypted. By definition of $\mathcal{F}_{\text{crypto}}$ ($\mathcal{F}_{\text{crypto}}$ encrypts $\overline{m}$ instead of m and verifies that the deterministic decryption of c yields $\overline{m}$, i.e., c "contains" the complete information for $\overline{m}$) and because the leakage algorithm has high entropy and plaintexts have at least length η (see Remark 6.1), the probability that c collides with anything else is negligible. Note also that there is only a fixed number of such ciphertexts. □

Given a prefix t of a non-colliding concrete trace of $\mathcal{S}_{\text{real}}$ or $\mathcal{S}_{\text{ideal}}$ (we consider both cases simultaneously), we recursively define a mapping ψ_t from well-tagged bit strings to ground terms (not non-colliding traces are taken care of separately). To this purpose, we fix an injective mapping *Garbage*: $\{0, 1\}^* \to \mathcal{N}$ of bit strings to names such that the names are distinct from all names in $\mathcal{P}$ and $\text{rand}(\mathcal{P})$ (including the special names $n_1, \ldots, n_l$ even if they are not used in $\mathcal{P}$ or $\text{rand}(\mathcal{P})$). The mapping ψ_t will be used to define the symbolic trace $\text{symb}(t)$ corresponding to t. For every well-tagged bit string m, we recursively define:

1. If $m = (\mathtt{pair}, m_1, m_2)$ for some bit strings m_1, m_2: $\psi_t(m) := \langle \psi_t(m_1), \psi_t(m_2) \rangle$.

2. If $m = (\mathtt{key}, k)$ for some bit string k: If k is a short-term key in $\mathcal{F}_{\text{crypto}}$ and corresponds to the name $n \in \mathcal{N}_{\text{st}}$, i.e., for this n some M_i asked $\mathcal{F}_{\text{crypto}}$ to generate a short-term key (i.e., a key of type t_{st}) and this key, stored in $\mathcal{F}_{\text{crypto}}$, is k (where M_i only got a pointer to this key), then $\psi_t(m) := \mathrm{sk}(n)$. Otherwise, $\psi_t(m) := \mathrm{sk}(\mathit{Garbage}(m))$.

3. If $m = (\mathtt{data}, m')$ for some bit string m':

   a) If $m' = \tau(n)$ for some global constant n, then $\psi_t(m) := n$.

   b) If $m' = pid_i$ for some $i \in \{1, \ldots, l\}$, then $\psi_t(m) := n_i$ (recall that n_i is the symbolic party name of the party playing role R_i).

   c) If m' is the random bit string chosen by some M_i for the nonce $n \in \mathcal{N}_{\text{nonce}}$ in t, then $\psi_t(m) := n$.

   d) In case of $\mathcal{S}_{\text{ideal}}$, if m is the session key chosen by $\mathcal{F}_{\text{ke}}$, then $\psi_t(m) := n^*$ where n^* is the extra name introduced by $\mathrm{rand}(\mathcal{P})$.

   e) If m' is a ciphertext recorded in $\mathcal{F}_{\text{crypto}}$ for some plaintext m'' and some (short- or long-term) key k (i.e., in t, some M_i encrypted m'' under k and $\mathcal{F}_{\text{crypto}}$ produced the ciphertext m'), then $\psi_t(m) := \{\psi_t(m'')\}^r_{\mathrm{sk}(n)}$ where $n \in \mathcal{N}_{\text{st}} \cup \mathcal{N}_{\text{lt}}$ is the name corresponding to the key k and $r \in \mathcal{N}_{\text{rand}}$ is the symbolic randomness of the symbolic ciphertext which was evaluated to m' in t.

   f) Otherwise, $\psi_t(m) := \mathit{Garbage}(m)$.

One verifies easily that ψ_t is well-defined and injective, using our tagging convention and that t is non-colliding. We note that ψ_t maps ciphertexts not honestly generated, i.e., not contained in $\mathcal{F}_{\text{crypto}}$, to garbage. For this to make sense, we will use in the proof of the mapping lemmas that $\mathcal{P}$ preserves key secrecy.

Before we can define $\mathrm{symb}(t)$, we define two mappings σ_t^{in} and σ_t^{out} from variables to terms as follows: $\sigma_t^{\text{in}}(y_i) := \psi_t(m_i)$ where y_i, m_i are the variable and message, respectively, in the i-th *input* event of t. Furthermore, we fix a sequence of pairwise distinct variables $z_1, z_2, \ldots$ which do not occur in $\mathcal{P}$ and define $\sigma_t^{\text{out}}(z_i) := \psi_t(m'_i)$ where m'_i is the message contained in the i-th *output* event of t (note that the M_j only output well-tagged messages, so, $\psi_t(m'_i)$ is defined). We define $\varphi_t := (\nu \overline{n'}) \sigma_t^{\text{out}}$ where $\overline{n'}$ are the restricted names of $\mathcal{P}$ and $\mathrm{rand}(\mathcal{P})$, respectively, i.e., $\overline{n'} = \overline{n}$ in case of $\mathcal{P}$ and $\overline{n'} = \overline{n}, n^*$ in case of $\mathrm{rand}(\mathcal{P})$. Note that φ_t will be the frame of the last process of the symbolic trace $\mathrm{symb}(t)$.

We say that *every input in t is derivable* if every input m in an input event is symbolically derivable from all outputs produced before this input. More formally, we require that $\varphi_{t'} \vdash \sigma_t^{\text{in}}(y)$ for every variable y in an input event, where t' is the prefix of t that contains all events before the input event for y.

Obviously, if $(\nu\overline{n'})\sigma \vdash s$, then there exists a term s' such that $\mathrm{fv}(s') \subseteq \mathrm{dom}(\sigma)$, $s'\sigma =_E s$, and $\mathrm{fn}(s') \cap \overline{n'} = \emptyset$. By $dt((\nu\overline{n'})\sigma \vdash s)$, we denote the lexicographically smallest such s' in normal form.

Now, given the prefix t of a non-colliding concrete trace of $\mathcal{S}_{\mathrm{real}}$ (see below for the case $\mathcal{S}_{\mathrm{ideal}}$) such that every input in t is derivable, we inductively define the symbolic trace $\mathrm{symb}(t)$:

1. If $t = \varepsilon$ (empty sequence), then $\mathrm{symb}(t) := \mathcal{P}$.

2. If $t = t', e$ for a prefix of t and an event e, then we define

$$\mathrm{symb}(t) := \mathrm{symb}(t') \xrightarrow{a} (\nu\overline{n}, \overline{y})(R'_1 \| \cdots \| R'_l \| \sigma^{\mathrm{in}}_t \cup \sigma^{\mathrm{out}}_t)$$

where $\overline{y}$ is the sequence of all variables in $\mathrm{dom}(\sigma^{\mathrm{in}}_t)$,

$$a := \begin{cases} \varepsilon & \text{if } e = \mathrm{if}(j, b, \mathcal{C}) \\ (\nu z_r)\overline{c}\langle z_r \rangle & \text{if } e = \mathrm{out}(j, m, c, \mathcal{C}) \text{ is the } r\text{-th } \textit{output} \text{ event in } t \\ c^{\mathrm{in},j}_{\mathrm{net}}(s') & \text{if } e = \mathrm{in}(j, y, m, \mathcal{C}) \ , \end{cases}$$

$s' := dt(\varphi_{t'} \vdash \psi_t(m))$, which is defined because, by assumption, every input in t is derivable, and hence, $\varphi_{t'} \vdash \psi_t(m)$. The process R'_i, $i \le l$, is the process in the configuration of M_i in e which describes the remaining process left for M_i to execute. Note that this is *not* necessarily the process obtained symbolically by taking $\xrightarrow{a}$. (The point of the mapping lemma is to show that the above is in fact a symbolic transition.)

The definition for $\mathcal{S}_{\mathrm{ideal}}$ is as above, except that we replace $\mathcal{P}$ by $\mathrm{rand}(\mathcal{P})$ and $\overline{n}$ by $\overline{n}, n^*$.

We say that a prefix t of a concrete trace of $\mathcal{S}_{\mathrm{real}}$ or $\mathcal{S}_{\mathrm{ideal}}$ is *Dolev-Yao (DY)* if t is non-colliding, every input is derivable, and $\mathrm{symb}(t)$ is a symbolic trace (in terms of Definition 6.1) of $\mathcal{P}$ or $\mathrm{rand}(\mathcal{P})$, respectively.

Because of the assumption that $\mathcal{P}$ preserves key secrecy we obtain that (short- and long-term) keys are always marked unknown in every concrete trace of $\mathcal{S}_{\mathrm{real}}$ or $\mathcal{S}_{\mathrm{ideal}}$ that is DY:

Lemma 6.2. *Let t be a prefix of a concrete trace of $\mathcal{S}_{\mathrm{real}}$. If t is DY, then at any point in t every (long- or short-term) key that is used is marked unknown in $\mathcal{F}_{\mathrm{crypto}}$. The same is true for $\mathcal{S}_{\mathrm{ideal}}$.*

Proof. Because $\mathcal{P}$ preserves key secrecy we have that every key that is used in a symbolic trace of $\mathcal{P}$ is secret. First, we note that it is easy to show that every key that is used in a symbolic trace of $\mathrm{rand}(\mathcal{P})$ is secret too.

Now, the proof is similar in the case for $\mathcal{S}_{\mathrm{real}}$ and $\mathcal{S}_{\mathrm{ideal}}$. Since the trace is uncorrupted, trivially, all pre-shared keys are uncorrupted. Hence, a (short- or long-term) key can only be marked known if *(i)* it was sent out in clear (i.e., the

Retrieve command is used), *(ii)* it was received in clear (i.e., the Store command is used), or *(iii)* it is encrypted by a key that is marked known.

Since long-term keys only occur at key positions in ciphertexts (they are never part of any message), they are never sent or received in clear or encrypted by another key. Hence, all long-term keys always remain marked unknown. (This even holds if $\mathcal{P}/\mathrm{rand}(\mathcal{P})$ would not preserve key secrecy.)

Since every used (short-term) key is (symbolically) secret in $\mathrm{symb}(t)$ ($\mathcal{P}/\mathrm{rand}(\mathcal{P})$ preserves key secrecy) we have that: $(*)$ a short-term key that is used (at some point) is never output in clear and has never been received in clear. By induction on the length of t, we can show that all short-term keys that are used are marked unknown in $\mathcal{F}_{\mathrm{crypto}}$: At first, all keys are marked unknown. By $(*)$, the only way a key can be marked known is by encrypting it with a key that is marked known but this key then is used and marked known, which contradicts the induction hypothesis. $\qquad\square$

Before we state the mapping lemma, we prove that every non-colliding concrete trace of $\mathcal{S}_{\mathrm{real}}$ and $\mathcal{S}_{\mathrm{ideal}}$ where every input is derivable is DY:

Lemma 6.3. *Let t be a prefix of a non-colliding trace of $\mathcal{S}_{\mathrm{real}}$ such that every input in t is derivable. Then, t is DY. The same is true for $\mathcal{S}_{\mathrm{ideal}}$.*

Proof. We concentrate on the case for $\mathcal{S}_{\mathrm{real}}$, the one for $\mathcal{S}_{\mathrm{ideal}}$ is analogous, see below.

We prove this lemma by induction on the length of t. For $t = \varepsilon$ nothing is to show. Now, assume that $t = t', e$ for some event e and t' is DY.

First, given t, we define the computational interpretation $[\![s]\!]_t$ of a term s (which may contain variables). If some machine M_i during the trace t computationally interpreted s to some bit string m, then we define $[\![s]\!]_t := m'$ where m' is obtained from m by replacing every pointer (key, ptr) contained in m by (key, k) where k is the corresponding short-term key stored in $\mathcal{F}_{\mathrm{crypto}}$. Recall that M_i computationally interprets a symbolic short-term key $\mathrm{sk}(n)$ with $n \in \mathcal{N}_{\mathrm{st}}$ as (key, ptr) where ptr is M_i's pointer to the short-term key stored in $\mathcal{F}_{\mathrm{crypto}}$ that corresponds to n. We define $[\![s]\!]_t := \bot$ if the interpretation fails.[48] Otherwise, we say that $[\![s]\!]_t$ is undefined. Note that there is a difference between "$[\![s]\!]_t = \bot$" which holds if the computational interpretation of s failed and "$[\![s]\!]_t$ is undefined" which holds if there was no computational interpretation of s at all. In the case of an encryption error, i.e., where $\mathcal{F}_{\mathrm{crypto}}$ was requested to encrypt a plaintext but returned an error message, $[\![s]\!]_t$ is undefined where s is the symbolic ciphertext that raised the encryption error. Note that, in this case, we do not define $[\![s]\!]_t := \bot$ because we treat encryption errors as if this activation never happened. In particularly, $[\![s]\!]_t = \bot$ would mean that the

---

[48] The computational interpretation $[\![s]\!]^\tau$ of a term s by a machine M_i is defined more rigorous in Appendix C.1. There, τ is a mapping from names and variables to bit strings which is maintained by M_i. Furthermore, $[\![s]\!]^\tau$ maintains state (by having side effects on τ) such that no encryption is done twice, hence, the same symbolic ciphertext yields the same computational ciphertext. These state information is all contained in t and we have that $[\![s]\!]_t$ equals $[\![s]\!]^\tau$ except that pointers are replaced by corresponding keys if, in the trace t, M_i computationally interpreted s with the mapping τ.

interpretation failed, which has no correspondence to the symbolic interpretation, which would have succeeded.

Similarly, by $\llbracket \phi \rrbracket_t \in \{0, 1\}$ we denote the interpretation of a condition ϕ.

Note that all terms s that have been computationally interpreted during the trace t, i.e., where $\llbracket s \rrbracket_t$ is defined, are subterms of the protocol $\mathcal{P}$. For all these terms s we have that:

$$\models M(s\sigma_t^{\text{in}}) \quad \text{if and only if} \quad \llbracket s \rrbracket_t \neq \perp . \tag{6.1}$$

$$\psi_t(\llbracket s \rrbracket_t) =_E s\sigma_t^{\text{in}} \quad \text{if} \quad \llbracket s \rrbracket_t \neq \perp . \tag{6.2}$$

The proof of these statements (see Appendix C.3) is done by induction on the structure of s and based on the induction hypothesis that $\text{symb}(t')$ is a symbolic trace. The main point is to exploit that all keys are used ideally (for encryption and decryption), see Lemma 6.2.

From (6.1) and (6.2) we can easily deduce (see Appendix C.3 for a proof) that every condition ϕ is computationally interpreted (by some machine M_i during the trace t) to true iff $\phi\sigma_t^{\text{in}}$ holds, i.e., for every condition ϕ where $\llbracket \phi \rrbracket_t$ is defined it holds that:

$$\models \phi\sigma_t^{\text{in}} \quad \text{if and only if} \quad \llbracket \phi \rrbracket_t = 1 . \tag{6.3}$$

Next, we prove that $\text{symb}(t)$ is a symbolic trace (of $\mathcal{P}$). In the case $t = \varepsilon$ (the empty sequence), $\text{symb}(t) = \mathcal{P}$, which is a symbolic trace. Otherwise, $t = t', e$ where e is an *input, output*, or *if* event. By definition of $\text{symb}(t')$, the last process of $\text{symb}(t')$ is

$$\mathcal{P}' = (\nu \bar{n}, \overline{y'})(R_1' \parallel \cdots \parallel R_l' \parallel \sigma_{t'}^{\text{in}} \cup \sigma_{t'}^{\text{out}})$$

where $\overline{y'}$ is the sequence of all variables in $\text{dom}(\sigma_{t'}^{\text{in}})$. Note that if $t' = \varepsilon$, then $\text{symb}(t') = \mathcal{P}$, i.e., it is formally not of the above form and, in this case, we choose $\overline{y'}$ to be the empty sequence and $\sigma_{t'}^{\text{in}} = \sigma_{t'}^{\text{out}} = \emptyset$ to be substitutions with empty domains. The process R_i', $i \leq l$, is the process in the configuration of M_i in the last event of t' (if $t' = \varepsilon$ then $R_i' = R_i$). By definition of $\text{symb}(t)$, the last process of $\text{symb}(t)$ is

$$\mathcal{P}'' = (\nu \bar{n}, \overline{y})(R_1'' \parallel \cdots \parallel R_l'' \parallel \sigma_t^{\text{in}} \cup \sigma_t^{\text{out}})$$

where $\overline{y}$ is the sequence of all variables in $\text{dom}(\sigma_t^{\text{in}})$. The process R_i'', $i \leq l$, is the process in the configuration of M_i in the event e. To prove that $\text{symb}(t)$ is a symbolic trace it is left to show that $\mathcal{P}' \xrightarrow{a} \mathcal{P}''$ where

$$a = \begin{cases} \varepsilon & \text{if } e = \text{if}(j, b, \mathcal{C}) \\ (\nu z_r)\bar{c}\langle z_r \rangle & \text{if } e = \text{out}(j, m, c, \mathcal{C}) \text{ is the } r\text{-th } \textit{output} \text{ event in } t \\ c_{\text{net}}^{\text{in}, j}(s') & \text{if } e = \text{in}(j, y, m, \mathcal{C}); \text{ where } s' = dt(\varphi_{t'} \vdash \psi_t(m)) . \end{cases}$$

Depending on the event e, we distinguish the following cases:

1. $e = \text{in}(j, y, m, \mathcal{C})$: M_j received the input m from the network, hence, $R'_j = c^{\text{in},j}_{\text{net}}(y).R''_j$. Furthermore, $R'_i = R''_i$ for all $i \neq j$, $\sigma^{\text{out}}_t = \sigma^{\text{out}}_{t'}$, and $\sigma^{\text{in}}_t = \sigma^{\text{in}}_{t'} \cup \{y \mapsto \psi_t(m)\}$. We conclude

$$\mathcal{P}' \xrightarrow{c^{\text{in},j}_{\text{net}}(s')} (\nu \bar{n}, \bar{y})(R''_1 \| \cdots \| R''_l \| \sigma^{\text{in}}_{t'} \cup \{y \mapsto s'\} \cup \sigma^{\text{out}}_t) \equiv \mathcal{P}'' \ .$$

The process $\mathcal{P}''$ and the process obtained from taking the transition only differ in the substitution which is $\sigma^{\text{in}}_t \cup \sigma^{\text{out}}_t$ and $\sigma^{\text{in}}_{t'} \cup \{y \mapsto s'\} \cup \sigma^{\text{out}}_t$, respectively. The frame of $\mathcal{P}'$ is $\varphi_{t'} = (\nu \bar{n}) \sigma^{\text{out}}_{t'} = (\nu \bar{n}) \sigma^{\text{out}}_t$. Recall that $s' = dt(\varphi_{t'} \vdash \psi_t(m))$, hence, $s' \sigma^{\text{out}}_t = s' \varphi_{t'} =_E \psi_t(m)$. Thus, the substitutions are structurally equivalent. From this it follows easily that the above processes are structurally equivalent.

2. $e = \text{if}(j, b, \mathcal{C})$: M_j took an if-then-else branch and evaluated its condition to $b \in \{0, 1\}$, hence, $R'_j = \textbf{if } \phi \textbf{ then } R^{(1)} \textbf{ else } R^{(0)}$ for some $\phi, R^{(1)}, R^{(0)}$ such that $R^{(b)} = R''_j$. Furthermore, $R'_i = R''_i$ for all $i \neq j$, $\sigma^{\text{out}}_t = \sigma^{\text{out}}_{t'}$, and $\sigma^{\text{in}}_t = \sigma^{\text{in}}_{t'}$. By (6.3), $\models \phi \sigma^{\text{in}}_t$ iff $b = 1$. We conclude $\mathcal{P}' \rightarrow \mathcal{P}''$.

3. $e = \text{out}(j, m, c, \mathcal{C})$: Either M_j produced output m to the network or I/O interface (depending on c) or M_j executed[49] $\overline{c^{\text{out},j}_{\text{net}}}\langle b \rangle$ directly after an if-then-else statement. In any case $R'_j = \bar{c}\langle s \rangle.R''_j$ for some term s such that $\|s\|_t = m$. Furthermore, $R'_i = R''_i$ for all $i \neq j$, $\sigma^{\text{in}}_t = \sigma^{\text{in}}_{t'}$, and $\sigma^{\text{out}}_t = \sigma^{\text{out}}_{t'} \cup \{z_r \mapsto \psi_t(m)\}$ where $r \in \mathbb{N}$ such that e is the r-th output event in t. We conclude

$$\mathcal{P}' \xrightarrow{(\nu z_r)\bar{c}\langle z_r \rangle} (\nu \bar{n}, \bar{y})(R''_1 \| \cdots \| R''_l \| \sigma^{\text{in}}_t \cup \sigma^{\text{out}}_{t'} \cup \{z_r \mapsto s\}) \equiv \mathcal{P}'' \ .$$

As in case 1., the processes only differ in the substitution. The structural equivalence holds because, by (6.2), we have that $\psi_t(m) = \psi_t(\|s\|_t) =_E s \sigma^{\text{in}}_t$. Note that m is well-tagged; by definition of M_j, all output is well-tagged.

The proof in the case for $\mathcal{S}_{\text{ideal}}$ is similar. We basically only have to replace $\mathcal{P}$ and $\bar{n}$ by $\text{rand}(\mathcal{P})$ and $\bar{n}, n^*$, respectively. Note that $\|n^*\|_t$ is undefined because no party actually generates a nonce for n^*. Recall that n^* occurs only in I/O outputs. In particular, (6.1), (6.2), and (6.3) hold in the case for $\mathcal{S}_{\text{ideal}}$ by the same arguments. Furthermore, the cases for the *input* event and *if* event are proven exactly as above. The case for the *output* event where the output is on the network is proven exactly as above too. Finally, the case for an *output* event $\text{out}(j, m, c^{\text{out},j}_{\text{io}}, \mathcal{C})$ is even simpler: By definition of $\mathcal{F}_{\text{ke}}$ and because $\mathcal{F}_{\text{ke}}$ is uncorrupted, m is the session key chosen by $\mathcal{F}_{\text{ke}}$. By definition of ψ_t we have that $\psi_t(m) = n^*$. Since (the simulated) machine M_j produced I/O output, we have that the process in the configuration of M_j is $R'_j = \overline{c^{\text{out},j}_{\text{io}}}\langle s \rangle.R''_j$ for some term s and process R''_j. By definition of $\text{rand}(\cdot)$, $s = n^*$ and, hence, the transition as defined by $\text{symb}(t)$ is a valid transition. $\qquad \square$

---

[49] In fact, M_j did not execute this output instruction because it is an output directly after an if-then-else statement that is only used for the symbolic criteria. Instead M_j skipped this instruction but, nevertheless, it is recorded in the trace.

Now, we state the mapping lemmas for $\mathcal{S}_{\text{real}}$ and $\mathcal{S}_{\text{ideal}}$.

Lemma 6.4 (Mapping Lemmas). *The probability that a concrete trace t of $\mathcal{S}_{\text{real}}$ is corrupted or t is DY is overwhelming (as a function in the security parameter 1^η and the external input a). The same is true for $\mathcal{S}_{\text{ideal}}$.*

Proof. We concentrate on the case for $\mathcal{S}_{\text{real}}$, the one for $\mathcal{S}_{\text{ideal}}$ is analogous, see below.

Because almost every uncorrupted trace is non-colliding (Lemma 6.1) and by Lemma 6.3, it is left to show that in almost every non-colliding trace every input is derivable. More formally, we define the event $B = B(1^\eta, a)$ (for security parameter η and external input a) to be the set of all traces t of $\mathcal{S}_{\text{real}}(1^\eta, a)$ which are non-colliding and where there exists an *input* event, say $\text{in}(j, y, m, \mathcal{C})$, in t such that this input is not derivable, i.e., $\varphi_{t'} \not\vdash \psi_{t'}(m)$ where t' is the prefix of t up to this *input* event. Recall that $\varphi_{t'} = (\nu \bar{n}) \sigma_{t'}^{\text{out}}$ is the frame that contains all outputs in t'. Before we show that the probability of B is negligible (i.e., $\Pr[B(1^\eta, a)]$ is negligible, as a function in 1^η and a) we prove the following statement. Given a well-tagged bit string m, by $\text{PT}(m)$ we denote the set of all *plaintext components* of m, i.e., all bit strings that occur in m only under pairing. Formally, we recursively define: If $m = (\text{pair}, m_1, m_2)$ for some bit strings m_1, m_2, then $\text{PT}(m) := \text{PT}(m_1) \cup \text{PT}(m_2)$. Otherwise, $\text{PT}(m) := \{m\}$.

(∗) Let $t', \text{in}(j, y, m, \mathcal{C})$ be a prefix of a non-colliding trace t of $\mathcal{S}_{\text{real}}$ (i.e., a prefix that ends with an *input* event) and let $m' \in \text{PT}(m)$. Furthermore, assume that in t' every input is derivable and that the term $\psi_t(m')$ is not derivable, i.e., $\varphi_{t'} \not\vdash \psi_t(m')$. Then, there exists $m'' \in \text{PT}(m')$ such that $\varphi_{t'} \not\vdash \psi_t(m'')$ and $\psi_t(m'')$ is either

    (i) a nonce, i.e. $\psi_t(m'') \in \mathcal{N}_{\text{nonce}}$, or

    (ii) a ciphertext, i.e. $\psi_t(m'') = \{s\}_{\text{sk}(n)}^r$ for some term s, (short- or long-term) key $n \in \mathcal{N}_{\text{st}} \cup \mathcal{N}_{\text{lt}}$, and randomness $r \in \mathcal{N}_{\text{rand}}$.

The term $\psi_t(m'')$ is called the *underivable subterm* of $\psi_t(m')$.

We prove (∗) by induction on the structure of $\psi_t(m')$. By definition of ψ_t we only need to consider the following cases:

(a) $\psi_t(m')$ is a nonce, a global constant, the special name n_i for some $i \in \{1, \dots, l\}$, or garbage (i.e., the name $Garbage(m')$): Since $\varphi_{t'} \not\vdash \psi_t(m')$, we have that $\psi_t(m') \in \mathcal{N}_{\text{nonce}}$. Hence, with $m'' := m'$ we are done.

(b) $\psi_t(m') = \{s'\}_{\text{sk}(n)}^r$ for some term s', (short- or long-term) key $n \in \mathcal{N}_{\text{st}} \cup \mathcal{N}_{\text{lt}}$, and randomness $r \in \mathcal{N}_{\text{rand}}$: We can choose $m'' := m'$.

(c) $\psi_t(m') = \text{sk}(n)$ for some short-term key $n \in \mathcal{N}_{\text{st}}$ or $n = Garbage(m')$: We show that this case cannot occur.

    Since $\varphi_{t'} \not\vdash \psi_t(m')$, we have that $n \in \mathcal{N}_{\text{st}}$ and that $\text{sk}(n)$ has never been sent out in clear. Hence, n corresponds to a short-term key k in $\mathcal{F}_{\text{crypto}}$ and the Retrieve command has never been executed on it. Thus, the only way k can be marked known in $\mathcal{F}_{\text{crypto}}$ is because k is encrypted by a key that is marked known. By Lemma 6.3, t' is DY. Hence, by Lemma 6.2, all used keys are marked unknown and we obtain that k is marked unknown too. Now, because m' is the plaintext component of an input, by definition of M_j, the Store command of $\mathcal{F}_{\text{crypto}}$ is called with the short-term key k. Upon this $\mathcal{F}_{\text{crypto}}$ would have returned an error message because k is marked unknown (and $\mathcal{F}_{\text{crypto}}$ would have prevented guessing this key). Hence, M_j would terminate and by the definition of traces this input event would not occur in the trace t. We conclude that this case does not occur.

(d) $\psi_t(m') = \langle \psi_t(m_1), \psi_t(m_2) \rangle$ for some bit strings $m_1, m_2 \in \text{PT}(m')$: Since $\varphi_{t'} \nvdash \psi_t(m')$ we have that $\varphi_{t'} \nvdash \psi_t(m_1)$ or $\varphi_{t'} \nvdash \psi_t(m_2)$. Hence, we can apply the induction hypothesis to m_1 or m_2, respectively, and obtain m''.

Now, given an environment $\mathcal{E}'$ (for $[\![\mathcal{P}]\!]^\tau$) and a ground term s, we consider the following game:

$\text{Exp}^{\mathcal{E}'}_{\text{guess},s}(1^\eta, a)$: Run the system $(\mathcal{E}' \,|\, [\![\mathcal{P}]\!]^\tau)(1^\eta, a)$. (Recall that $\mathcal{S}_{\text{real}} = \mathcal{E} \,|\, [\![\mathcal{P}]\!]^\tau$.) Let t be the trace of this run and let m be the final output of $\mathcal{E}'$. If t is DY, $\psi_t(m) = s$, and $\varphi_t \nvdash s$, then $\mathcal{E}'$ *wins*, otherwise, $\mathcal{E}'$ *looses*.

We construct an environment $\mathcal{E}'$ as follows: Let p be a polynomial (in the security parameter plus the length of the external input) that bounds the maximal number of output messages that $\mathcal{E}$ sends (such a polynomial always exists because $\mathcal{E}$ is universally bounded). First, $\mathcal{E}'$ chooses $i \in \{1, \ldots, p(\eta + |a|)\}$ uniformly at random (where η is the security parameter and a is the external input) and, then, simulates $\mathcal{E}$ up to the i-th output message, say m. Then, $\mathcal{E}'$ chooses a plaintext component $m' \in \text{PT}(m)$ uniformly at random and outputs m'.

By $(*)$ and Lemma 6.3, it is easy to see that if the probability of B is not negligible, then there exists a term $s \in \mathcal{N}_{\text{nonce}} \cup \{\{s'\}^r_{\text{sk}(n)} \mid s' \in \mathcal{T}(\mathcal{N}), n \in \mathcal{N}_{\text{st}} \cup \mathcal{N}_{\text{lt}}, r \in \mathcal{N}_{\text{rand}}\}$ such that $\mathcal{E}'$ wins the game $\text{Exp}^{\mathcal{E}'}_{\text{guess},s}$ with non-negligible probability.

Finally, we show that for any environment $\mathcal{E}'$ and any such term s the probability that $\mathcal{E}'$ wins $\text{Exp}^{\mathcal{E}'}_{\text{guess},s}(1^\eta, a)$ is negligible (as a function in 1^η and a).

Note that if s is not in the range of ψ_t, then $\mathcal{E}'$ looses anyway. Hence, we assume that s is in the range of ψ_t, i.e., there exists a bit string m' such that $\psi_t(m') = s$. Let m be the bit string output by $\mathcal{E}'$. Note that if $m' \neq m$, then $s = \psi_t(m') \neq \psi_t(m)$ and, hence, $\mathcal{E}'$ looses. Since $\varphi_t \nvdash s$, by definition of $\text{symb}(t)$, m' has never been output in clear in t. Furthermore, since t is DY, by Lemma 6.2, every encryption of a plaintext that contains m' is independent of (the actual bits of) m' (it only depends on the length of m' because the leakage algorithms leak at most the length of messages). Hence, it is easy to see that the view of $\mathcal{E}'$ is independent of m'. If $s \in \mathcal{N}_{\text{nonce}}$, then m' is chosen uniformly at random from $\{(\texttt{data}, m'') \mid m'' \in \{0,1\}^\eta\}$, hence, the probability that $m = m'$ is at most $2^{-\eta}$. On the other hand, if s is a (symbolic) ciphertext, then m' is a ciphertext (tagged as data) which has been produced with a key marked unknown (Lemma 6.2). Hence, not the actual plaintext, say m'', but its leakage $\overline{m}'' \leftarrow L(1^\eta, m'')$ is encrypted. By definition of $\mathcal{F}_{\text{crypto}}$ ($\mathcal{F}_{\text{crypto}}$ encrypts $\overline{m}''$ instead of m'' and verifies that the deterministic decryption of m' yields $\overline{m}''$, i.e., m' "contains" the complete information of $\overline{m}''$) and because the leakage algorithm has high entropy and plaintexts have length at least η (see Remark 6.1), the probability that $m = m'$ is negligible.

We conclude that the probability that $\mathcal{E}'$ wins the game is negligible. Hence, the probability that B occurs is negligible.

The proof in the case for $\mathcal{S}_{\text{ideal}}$ is similar. In the definition of the event B we only have to replace $\mathcal{S}_{\text{real}}$ by $\mathcal{S}_{\text{ideal}}$ and $\overline{n}$ by $\overline{n}, n^*$. (Recall that n^* is the restricted name added by $\text{rand}(\mathcal{P})$.) In case (i) of statement $(*)$, we have to add that $\psi_t(m') \in \mathcal{N}_{\text{nonce}} \cup \{n^*\}$. The proof of $(*)$ is similar. In the game $\text{Exp}_{\text{guess},s}^{\mathcal{E}'}(1^\eta, a)$ we have to replace the system $\mathcal{E}' \mid \llbracket \mathcal{P} \rrbracket^\tau$ by $\mathcal{E}' \mid \mathcal{S} \mid !\mathcal{F}_{\text{ke}}$ (recall that $\mathcal{S}_{\text{ideal}} = \mathcal{E} \mid \mathcal{S} \mid !\mathcal{F}_{\text{ke}}$), but the construction of $\mathcal{E}'$ remains the same. Also, the proof that for any $s \in \mathcal{N}_{\text{nonce}} \cup \{n^*\} \cup \{\{s'\}_{\text{sk}(n)}^r \mid s' \in \mathcal{T}(\mathcal{N}), n \in \mathcal{N}_{\text{st}} \cup \mathcal{N}_{\text{lt}}, r \in \mathcal{N}_{\text{rand}}\}$ the probability that $\mathcal{E}'$ wins the game $\text{Exp}_{\text{guess},s}^{\mathcal{E}'}(1^\eta, a)$ is negligible is similar. It is easy to see that also in this case if the event B has non-negligible probability, then $\mathcal{E}'$ wins the game with non-negligible probability. $\qquad\square$

6.5.2. Proof of Theorem 6.1

We can now prove that $\mathcal{S}_{\text{real}} \equiv \mathcal{S}_{\text{ideal}}$ by defining a correspondence relation between (almost) all concretes traces of $\mathcal{S}_{\text{real}}$ and concrete traces of $\mathcal{S}_{\text{ideal}}$, where the final output of $\mathcal{E}$ is the same in corresponding traces.

The case when a concrete trace t of $\mathcal{S}_{\text{real}}$ is corrupted is trivial, since then $\mathcal{S}$ can corrupt $\mathcal{F}_{\text{ke}}$ and mimic the concrete trace of $\mathcal{S}_{\text{real}}$ exactly. The case where in t no session key is output on the I/O interface is also trivial.

If t is not a trace of the above form, then, by the mapping lemma (Lemma 6.4), it is almost certainly DY, and hence, $\text{symb}(t)$ is a symbolic trace of $\mathcal{P}$.

Now, we first observe:

$(*)$ There exists a bit string $m_0 \in \{(\text{data}, m) \mid m \in \{0,1\}^\eta\}$ such that in t, whenever an Established message is sent to the environment, then this message contains m_0 as the session key and $\psi_t(m_0) = n_0$ for some $n_0 \in \mathcal{N}_{\text{nonce}}$, i.e., m_0 corresponds to a nonce in $\text{symb}(t)$.

In traces of $\text{rand}(\mathcal{P})$ the nonce n^* is always output as the session key. So, because $\text{symb}(t)$ is a trace of $\mathcal{P}$ and $\mathcal{P} \sim_l \text{rand}(\mathcal{P})$, it is not hard to show that the session key output in $\text{symb}(t)$ has to be a nonce too and it has to be always the same nonce; otherwise, using the predicates EQ, P_{pair}, P_{enc}, and P_{key}, $\text{symb}(t)$ could be distinguished from all traces of $\text{rand}(\mathcal{P})$. Now, since ψ_t is injective, $(*)$ follows.

Given some value of a nonce $m^* = (\text{data}, m)$ for some $m \in \{0,1\}^\eta$, we define a trace t^* of $\mathcal{S}_{\text{ideal}}$ that will correspond to the trace t of $\mathcal{S}_{\text{real}}$. The randomness used in t and t^* exactly coincide for all system components, except that for the nonce

n_0 (which is output as the session key, see above) used in $\llbracket \mathcal{P} \rrbracket^\tau$ the bit string m^* instead of m_0 is chosen, and in $\mathcal{F}_{\text{ke}}$ the bit string m_0 is chosen as the session key. More formally, the randomness of the environment $\mathcal{E}$, the functionality $\mathcal{F}_{\text{ke}}$, and the simulator $\mathcal{S}$ in t^* is defined such that (i) the randomness of $\mathcal{E}$ is the same in t and t^*, (ii) $\mathcal{F}_{\text{ke}}$ chooses m_0 as the session key, (iii) $\mathcal{S}$ simulates $\llbracket \mathcal{P} \rrbracket^\tau$ such that $\mathcal{F}_{\text{crypto}}$ uses the same randomness in t and t^*, and (iv) $\mathcal{S}$ simulates $\llbracket \mathcal{P} \rrbracket^\tau$ such that for every nonce $n \neq n_0$ the same value is chosen in t and t^* and for the nonce n_0 the value m^* is chosen in t^* (by some simulated M_i).

Note that t^* is uncorrupted because this only depends on the randomness of $\mathcal{E}$ (static corruption), t is uncorrupted, and $\mathcal{E}$ uses the same randomness in t and t^*. By definition, the probability of ρ is 2^η times the probability of ρ^*. By Lemma 6.4, we may assume that t^* is DY, since this is true with overwhelming probability, given that t^* is uncorrupted.

Finally, we prove that the view of $\mathcal{E}$ is the same in t and t^*. In particularly, this implies that the final output of $\mathcal{E}$ is the same in both traces. More precisely, we prove by induction on the length of t:

(a) The event sequence of t coincides with the one of t^* (in particular, input and output, i.e., the view of $\mathcal{E}$, are the same), except for the configurations in the events: The configurations of $M_1, \ldots, M_l$ in t and t^* are equal except for the value of nonce n_0 which is m_0 in t and m^* in t^*. The configuration of $\mathcal{E}$ is the same in both t and t^*.

(b) If $\mathcal{P}_t$ denotes the last process of $\text{symb}(t)$ and $\mathcal{P}_{t^*}$ the last process of $\text{symb}(t^*)$, then $\mathcal{P}_t \sim_l \mathcal{P}_{t^*}$.

For $t = \varepsilon$ the above is obvious. We now consider the possible events that can occur.

Input event.   Assume that $t = \bar{t}, \text{in}(j, y, m, \mathcal{C})$ and (a) and (b) hold for $\bar{t}$ and $\bar{t}^*$. From (a) it follows that $t^* = \bar{t}^*, \text{in}(j, y, m, \mathcal{C}')$ for some $\mathcal{C}'$ (note that the view and randomness of $\mathcal{E}$ is the same in t and t^*). Now, clearly (a) is satisfied for t and t^*. It remains to prove (b) for t and t^*. Because $\mathcal{P}_{\bar{t}} \sim_l \mathcal{P}_{\bar{t}^*}$, it suffices to show that the same labels (module E, see below) are produced in the last step of $\text{symb}(t)$ and $\text{symb}(t^*)$. The label produced by $\text{symb}(t)$ is $c_{\text{net}}^{\text{in},j}(s_m)$ where $s_m = dt(\varphi_{\bar{t}} \vdash \psi_t(m))$ and the one for $\text{symb}(t^*)$ is $c_{\text{net}}^{\text{in},j}(s_m^*)$ where $s_m^* = dt(\varphi_{\bar{t}^*} \vdash \psi_{t^*}(m))$. Next, we show that s_m and s_m^* are basically the same terms.

First, we note the following, which holds in general. The relation $\xrightarrow{a}$ is closed under structural equivalence and structural equivalence allows for replacement of terms by equivalent terms w.r.t. E, hence, it is easy to prove that if $A \xrightarrow{c(s)} B$ where $\text{fn}(s) \cap \text{bn}(A) = \emptyset$ and $\text{fv}(s) \subseteq \text{dom}(A)$, then $A \xrightarrow{c(s')} B$ for every term s' that satisfies $\text{fn}(s') \cap \text{bn}(A) = \emptyset$, $\text{fv}(s') \subseteq \text{dom}(A)$, and $s\varphi(A) =_E s'\varphi(A)$.

Recall that, by definition of dt, we have that both s_m and s_m^* are in normal form, $s_m\varphi_{\bar{t}} =_E \psi_t(m)$, and $s_m^*\varphi_{\bar{t}^*} =_E \psi_{t^*}(m)$. Hence, to prove (b) for t and t^* it remains to prove that $s_m \varphi_{\bar{\imath}^*} =_E s_m^* \varphi_{\bar{\imath}^*}$ because then we can replace s_m^* by s_m in t^*. For this, we prove a more general statement:

(∗∗) For every term s in normal form such that $\mathrm{fn}(s) \cap \{\bar{n}, n^*\} = \emptyset$, $\mathrm{fv}(s) \subseteq \mathrm{dom}(\varphi_{\bar{\imath}})$, and s does not contain $\{\cdot\}$. and dec.$(\cdot)$ and for every well-tagged bit string m such that $s\varphi_{\bar{\imath}} =_E \psi_t(m)$, it holds that $s\varphi_{\bar{\imath}^*} =_E \psi_{t^*}(m)$.

First we note that, by definition of ψ_t and dt, s_m does not contain any restricted names $(\bar{n}, n^*)$. In particular, s_m does not contain symbolic randomness and, hence, s_m does not contain the function symbol $\{\cdot\}$. because $\psi_t(m)$ contains $\{s\}_k^r$ only if r is a restricted name. Furthermore, because all used keys in $\mathrm{symb}(t)$ are secret, it is easy to show that s_m does not contain the function symbol dec.$(\cdot)$: By the definition of ψ_t, $\psi_t(m)$ contains $\mathrm{dec}_k(s)$ only for honest keys k (i.e., where $k = \mathrm{sk}(n)$ for some restricted name $n \in \mathcal{N}_{\mathrm{st}} \cup \mathcal{N}_{\mathrm{lt}}$). Therefore, because all used keys in $\mathrm{symb}(t)$ are secret, the derivation of $\psi_t(m)$ from the frame $\varphi_{\bar{\imath}}$ does not use decryption. Hence, because s_m is in normal form, it does not contain dec.$(\cdot)$. Now, it is easy to see that s_m and m satisfy the precondition of (∗∗), so, we obtain that $s_m \varphi_{\bar{\imath}^*} =_E \psi_{t^*}(m) =_E s_m^* \varphi_{\bar{\imath}^*}$.

Next, we prove (∗∗) by induction on the structure of s:

1. If $s \in \mathcal{N} \setminus \{\bar{n}, n^*\}$, then s is a global constant (i.e., $s \in \mathrm{dom}(\tau)$), $s = n_i$ for some $i \in \{1, \ldots, l\}$, or $s = \mathit{Garbage}(m)$. Hence, $\psi_{t^*}(m) = \psi_t(m) = s$.

2. If $s \in \mathcal{X}$, then $s \in \mathrm{dom}(\varphi_{\bar{\imath}})$. Hence, m is the i-th output message in $\bar{t}$ for some i. By (a), m is the i-th output message in $\bar{t}^*$ too. Hence, by definition, $s\varphi_{\bar{\imath}^*} = \sigma_{\bar{\imath}^*}^{\mathrm{out}}(s) = \psi_{\bar{\imath}^*}(m) = \psi_{t^*}(m)$.

3. If $s = \mathrm{sk}(s')$: Recall that s does not contain restricted names. We have that $s' = \mathit{Garbage}(m)$ because no name from $\mathcal{N}_{\mathrm{st}} \cup \mathcal{N}_{\mathrm{lt}}$ is derivable due to (symbolic) tagging with $\mathrm{sk}(\cdot)$. (At most $\mathrm{sk}(n)$ with $n \in \mathcal{N}_{\mathrm{st}} \cup \mathcal{N}_{\mathrm{lt}}$ is derivable but not n itself.) We conclude that $m = (\mathrm{key}, k)$ for some bit string k that is not a (short- or long-term) key in $\mathcal{F}_{\mathrm{crypto}}$ in t. Because the keys in t and t^* are the same (by (a)), k is not a key in $\mathcal{F}_{\mathrm{crypto}}$ in t^* too. Hence, $\psi_{t^*}(m) = \psi_t(m) = s$.

4. If $s = \langle s_1, s_2 \rangle$: We have that $s\varphi_{\bar{\imath}} =_E \psi_t(m)$, hence, $m = (\mathrm{pair}, m_1, m_2)$ for some bit strings m_1, m_2 and $s_i\varphi_{\bar{\imath}} =_E \psi_t(m_i)$ for $i = 1, 2$. By induction hypothesis, we obtain $s_i\varphi_{\bar{\imath}^*} =_E \psi_{t^*}(m_i)$ for $i = 1, 2$. Hence, $\langle s_1, s_2 \rangle \varphi_{\bar{\imath}^*} =_E \langle \psi_{t^*}(m_1), \psi_{t^*}(m_2) \rangle = \psi_{t^*}(m)$.

5. If $s = \pi_b(s')$: It is easy to see that there exist bit strings m', m_1, m_2 such that $m' = (\mathrm{pair}, m_1, m_2)$, $s'\varphi_{\bar{\imath}} =_E \psi_t(m')$, and $m_b = m$. By induction hypothesis, we obtain $s'\varphi_{\bar{\imath}^*} =_E \psi_{t^*}(m') = \langle \psi_{t^*}(m_1), \psi_{t^*}(m_2) \rangle$. Hence, $\pi_b(s')\varphi_{\bar{\imath}^*} =_E \psi_{t^*}(m_b)$.

Output event. Assume that $t = \bar{t}, \mathrm{out}(j, m, c, \mathcal{C})$ and (a) and (b) hold for $\bar{t}$ and $\bar{t}^*$. Furthermore, assume that $\mathrm{out}(j, m, c, \mathcal{C})$ is not an *output* event that follows directly an *if* event (this is considered in the case for the *if* event, see below). From (a) it follows that $t^* = \bar{t}^*, \mathsf{out}(j, m', c, \mathcal{C}')$ for some bit string m' and some $\mathcal{C}'$. Now, it is easy to see that (b) is satisfied for t and t^*. To prove (a) it remains to show that $m = m'$. If $c = c_{\mathsf{io}}^{\mathsf{out},j}$ (i.e., the session key is output on the I/O interface) then, by (*), $m = m_0$. In t^*, m' is the session key output by $\mathcal{F}_{\mathsf{ke}}$, which, by definition of t^*, is m_0. Now, consider the case $c = c_{\mathsf{net}}^{\mathsf{out},j}$: By (a), we know that M_j performs the same operations to produce the output. More formally, there exists a term s such that $m = \|s\|_t$ and $m' = \|s\|_{t^*}$. We can show that so_t^{in} does not contain n_0 in clear (i.e., if it contains n_0, then only encrypted) because otherwise $\mathcal{P} \not\sim_l \mathsf{rand}(\mathcal{P})$. To prove this, assume that so_t^{in} contains n_0 in clear. Then there exists a variable z such that $z\varphi_t = so_t^{\mathsf{in}}$ (because so_t^{in} is output and therefore accessible in the frame) and, hence, a term s' such that $s'\varphi_t =_E n_0$ and $\mathsf{fn}(s') \cap \{\bar{n}, n^*\} = \emptyset$. Furthermore, let z' be a variable in the frame φ_t that corresponds to the first output on a I/O channel. Such a z' exists and, by (*), we have that $z'\varphi_t = n_0$. Now, the adversary can distinguish between $\mathsf{symb}(t)$ and $\mathsf{symb}(t^*)$ by using the predicate $\mathsf{EQ}(s', z')$ which is always true in $\mathsf{symb}(t)$ (by construction) and never true in $\mathsf{symb}(t^*)$ because $z'\varphi_{t^*} = n^* \neq_E s'\varphi_{t^*}$.

Furthermore, all ciphertexts are obtained from ideal encryption (Lemma 6.2) and, thus, only depend on the length of the plaintext (the leakage algorithms leak at most the length of messages). Hence, the actual bit strings of the ciphertexts depend only on the random coins of $\mathcal{F}_{\mathsf{crypto}}$ (and the length of the plaintext which is the same in t and t^*). From this it is easy to deduce that $m = m'$.

If event.   Assume that $t = \bar{t}, \mathsf{if}(j, b, \mathcal{C}), \mathsf{out}(j, (\mathsf{data}, \tau(b)), c_{\mathsf{net}}^{\mathsf{out},j}, \mathcal{C}')$ and (a) and (b) hold for $\bar{t}$ and $\bar{t}^*$. By (a), it holds $t^* = \bar{t}^*, \mathsf{if}(j, b', \mathcal{C}''), \mathsf{out}(j, (\mathsf{data}, \tau(b')), c_{\mathsf{net}}^{\mathsf{out},j}, \mathcal{C}''')$ for some $b' \in \{0, 1\}$ and some $\mathcal{C}'', \mathcal{C}'''$. From (b) it follows that $\mathcal{P}_{\bar{t}} \sim_l \mathcal{P}_{\bar{t}^*}$ and, hence, $b = b'$. Now, it is easy to show that (a) and (b) hold for t and t^*.

This concludes the proof of Theorem 6.1.

6.6. Related Work

The general approach of this chapter follows the one by Canetti and Herzog [CH06]. However, they considered only the simpler case of public-key encryption. Also, their symbolic criterion is based on patterns [AR00], which is closely related to static equivalence, but more ad hoc.

Comon-Lundh and Cortier [CLC08b] showed that observational equivalence implies computational indistinguishability for a class of protocols similar to the one considered here, but with more restricted if-then-else statements. The main drawback of their result, as already discussed in Section 5.5, is that it makes the unrealistic assumption that the adversary cannot fabricate keys, except for honestly running the key generation algorithm. In other words, dishonestly generated keys are disallowed, an assumption that we do not make. This is one of the reasons why their result does not imply our computational soundness result. Also, the approaches are different in that Comon-Lundh and Cortier consider a game-based setting, while we use a universal composability framework and make intensive use of composition theorems.

As already pointed out in Section 5.5, Backes and Pfitzmann [BP04] proposed a Dolev-Yao style abstraction of symmetric encryption within their cryptographic library [BPW03] but the original proof of the realization of the crypto library in [BP04] is flawed and the examples presented in the full version of the work by Comon-Lundh and Cortier [CLC08a] suggest that dishonestly generated keys also have to be forbidden for the cryptographic library, in case symmetric encryption is considered. Moreover, the realization of this library requires an authenticated encryption scheme which is augmented with extra randomness as well as identifiers for symmetric keys.

As mentioned at the beginning of this chapter, the only work that deals with dishonestly generated symmetric encryption keys without unrealistic assumptions, except for this work, is the one by Comon-Lundh et al. [CLCS12]. However, they use complex deduction rules which may complicate symbolic analysis, especially automation. In contrast, our symbolic criteria are automatically provable using existing tools, such as ProVerif.

Mazaré and Warinschi [MW09] presented a mapping lemma for protocols that use symmetric encryption in a setting with adaptive, rather than only static corruption. However, the protocol class is very restricted: symmetric keys may not be encrypted, and hence, may not "travel", and nested encryption is disallowed.

In [DDMW06], a formal logic that enjoys a computational, game-based semantics is used to reason about protocols that use symmetric encryption. In [Lau04, Bla06], automated methods for reasoning about cryptographic protocols are proposed that are based on transformation of programs and games, and hence, are close to cryptographic reasoning. However, these works do not provide computationally sound symbolic criteria for reasoning about protocols.

As already mentioned in the introduction, computational soundness results for passive or adaptive adversaries have been obtain, for example, in [AR00, KM07].

7. Protocol Analysis Without Pre-Established Session Identifiers

Universal composition theorems, such as the one in the UC model [Can01] and the composition theorems in the IITM model (see Section 2.4), and composition theorems with joint state, such as the ones in [CR03] and [KT08] (see also Sections 4.2.6 and 5.4), allow to obtain security for multiple sessions of a protocol by analyzing just a single protocol session. However, as already mentioned in the introduction, they all assume that parties participating in a protocol session have pre-established a unique session identifier (SID), and as a result (see Section 7.1), make heavy use of this SID in a specific way stipulated by the universal and joint state composition theorems. While using such SIDs is a good design principle and establishing such SIDs is simple (as discussed in [Can05] and [BLR04]), many existing protocols, including most real-world security protocols (e.g., the protocols addressed in our case studies in Section 7.7.2), do not make use of such pre-established SIDs, at least not explicitly and not in the particular way stipulated by the theorems. Hence, these theorems cannot be used for the faithful modular analysis of such protocols. Moreover, it even holds that protocols without pre-established SIDs do *not* realize the multi-session ideal functionalities for which the composition theorems are formulated (e.g., the multi-session version $!\mathcal{F}$ of a functionality $\mathcal{F}$, as in Theorem 2.2), see Section 7.1; except, of course, for trivial, uninteresting functionalities. These problems resulting from pre-established SIDs do not seem to have been brought out in previous work.

In this chapter, we devote ourselves to the modeling and analyses of protocols that do not make use of pre-established SIDs, which allows us to consider a much broader class of protocols, including many real-world protocols, without giving up on precise modeling. As explained above, to analyze these protocols, existing composition theorems cannot be used, and, even if one would be willing to analyze these protocols directly in a multi-session setting, it cannot be shown that they realize the multi-session functionalities used by the composition theorems. Therefore, in Section 7.2, we define new multi-session ideal functionalities, called *multi-session local-SID (ideal) functionalities*. We note that these new multi-session versions of ideal functionalities are similar to the ones by Barak et al. [BLR04] (see Section 7.8 for a discussion of related work). They model the more realistic scenario that a party accesses the functionality simply by a *local* SID which is locally chosen and managed by the party itself, rather than with an SID pre-established with other parties for that session. It is left to the adversary (simulator) to determine which group of local sessions belong to one (global) session. This seemingly harmless modification not only provides a more realistic and more common interface to the functionality (and its realization), but, more importantly, frees the realization from the need to use pre-established SIDs and allows for realizations that faithfully model existing (real-world) protocols.

In the following sections, as mentioned in the introduction, we develop methods to analyze (real-world) protocols in this new multi-session setting, i.e., to show that protocols without pre-established SIDs (we define a general class of such protocols in Section 7.3) realize a multi-session local-SID functionality.

First, in Section 7.4, we develop a (multi-session) criterion to prove that a key exchange protocol that uses our ideal crypto functionality $\mathcal{F}_{\text{crypto}}$ (see Chapter 5) realizes a multi-session local-SID functionality for key exchange. To demonstrate the usefulness of our criterion and $\mathcal{F}_{\text{crypto}}$, we apply it, as a case study, to the 4-Way Handshake (4WHS) protocol of WPA2 (IEEE standard 802.11i [IEE07, IEE04]). We note that the 4WHS protocol does not use pre-established SIDs and cannot be analyzed faithfully using existing composition theorems.

Then, in Sections 7.5 and 7.6, we present our general universal and joint state composition theorems that do not assume pre-established SIDs and their use in cryptographic protocols, and hence, enable fully modular, yet faithful analysis of protocols without the need to modify/idealize these protocols. As mentioned in the introduction, our joint state composition theorem is applicable to protocols that use our ideal functionality $\mathcal{F}_{\text{crypto}}$ (which then constitutes a joint state across sessions) and satisfy the condition *implicit (session) disjointness*. In Section 7.7, we demonstrate the usefulness of our composition theorems and approach and prove implicit disjointness for several real-world security protocols. To now show that these protocols are secure key exchange or secure channel protocols, single-session analysis suffices. Performing this single-session analysis for these protocols is out of the scope of this thesis. The main point of this thesis is to provide a machinery for faithful and highly modular analysis, not to provide a full-fledged, detailed analysis of these protocols.

7.1. On the Role of SIDs in Universal Composition Theorems

Universal composition theorems, such as Theorems 2.2 and 2.3 and Canetti's composition theorem [Can05], allow to obtain security for multiple sessions of a protocol by analyzing just a single session. Such theorems can therefore greatly simplify protocol analysis. However, these theorems rely on the setup assumption that the parties participating in a protocol session agree upon a unique SID and that they invoke their instance of the protocol with that SID. This is due to the way multi-session versions of ideal functionalities are defined in these composition theorems: In a multi-session version of an ideal functionality $\mathcal{F}$ (e.g., as defined in Section 2.4) parties which want to access an instance of $\mathcal{F}$ have to agree on a unique SID in order to be able to all invoke the same instance of $\mathcal{F}$, with that SID. As a consequence, the composition theorems implicitly require that a session of a real protocol with SID *sid* realizes a session of the ideal functionality with SID *sid*. (For example, if a session of the real protocol consists of two instances, e.g., an initiator and a responder instance, then the initiator with SID *sid* and the responder with SID *sid* together have to realize the ideal functionality with SID *sid*.) This, in turn, implies that the real protocol has to use the SID *sid* in some way, since otherwise there is nothing that prevents grouping instances with different SIDs (e.g., an initiator with SID *sid* and a responder with SID *sid'*) into one session. One usage of the SID *sid* is, for example, to access a resource for the specific session, e.g., a functionality (with SID *sid*) that provides the parties with fresh keys or certain communication channels for that specific session. In realizations with joint state such as the ones in Sections 4.2.6 and 5.4, the SID *sid* is used in the protocol messages that are exchanged between parties, in order to prevent interference with other sessions (see also Section 7.6).

Canetti [Can05] discusses three methods of how such unique SIDs could be established, including a method proposed by Barak et al. [BLR04] where parties simply exchange nonces in clear and then form a unique SID by concatenating these nonces and the party names. We will refer to such uniquely established SIDs (using whatever method) by *pre-established* SIDs.[50] The use of pre-established SIDs is certainly a good design principle. However, assuming pre-established SIDs and, as a result, forcing their use in the protocols greatly limits the scope of the composition theorems for the analysis of existing protocols. In particular, they cannot be used for the modular analysis of real-world security protocols since such protocols typically do not make use of SIDs in this explicit and specific way (e.g., the real-world protocols considered in our case studies, see Section 7.7.2). In other words, the composition theorems could only be used to analyze idealized/modified versions of such protocols. However, this is dangerous: While the idealized/modified version of a protocol might be secure, its original version may not be secure (see Section 7.6).

Therefore, in the next section, we propose a new multi-session version of ideal functionalities that allows us to analyze protocols without pre-established SIDs directly in the multi-session setting and, more importantly, to formulate new universal and joint-state composition theorems that are applicable to protocols without pre-established SIDs.

---

[50]In Canetti's second method, the initiator of a protocol gets the SID from the I/O interface in the first message. All other parties get the SID from the first network message. At first glance, it looks as if this might solve some of the problems described above. However, this is not the case. Every party still gets the SID in the first message (from I/O or network) and this is still some kind of prior agreement, namely what we call pre-establishment. The important point—due to the way multi-session ideal functionalities are defined—is that, in the real protocol, parties with the same (pre-established) SID have to use this SID in an essential way to realize the session of the ideal functionality with that SID; the original protocol typically does not use such SIDs (see also the remarks in Section 7.2 and the beginning of Section 7.6). Furthermore, Canetti's second method is impractical: For every SID a party must not run more than one instance. While in the UC model (and other universal composability frameworks such as the IITM model) this is guaranteed by the model, in a real implementation this has to be enforced by other means (otherwise the protocol modeled in the UC model would not represent the real world). So, a responder (who receives the SID to be used from an initiator) would probably have to remember all SIDs used so far to ensure this.

7.2. Multi-Session Local-SID Ideal Functionalities

In this section, we define a new multi-session version of an ideal functionality $\mathcal{F}$ that yields a new multi-session ideal functionality. This functionality, as mentioned above, models the more realistic scenario that a party accesses an instance of $\mathcal{F}$ (i.e., one session) by a *local* SID (locally chosen and managed by the party itself). It is then left to the adversary (simulator) to determine which group of local sessions may use one instance of $\mathcal{F}$, where the grouping into what we call a (global) session is subject to certain restrictions (see below).

Definition of multi-session local-SID functionalities.   Let $\mathcal{F}$ be an ideal functionality that is an σ_{prefix}-session version[51] and has n pairs of input and output I/O tapes, one for each role, and arbitrary network tapes. That is, every message to/from $\mathcal{F}$ is prefixed by an SID and $\mathcal{F}$ models a traditional multi-session ideal functionality. For example, $\mathcal{F} = \underline{\mathcal{F}_{\text{ke}}}$ is the session version of the ideal key exchange functionality from Section 4.3.1.

We now define the new multi-session local-SID functionality that is obtained from $\mathcal{F}$ and that we denote by $\mathcal{F}^{\mathcal{F}}_{\text{session}}$. We call every such functionality (i.e., $\mathcal{F}^{\mathcal{F}}_{\text{session}}$ for some $\mathcal{F}$ as above) a *multi-session local-SID (ideal) functionality*.

Formally, we define $\mathcal{F}^{\mathcal{F}}_{\text{session}}$ to be the protocol system that is the composition of the IITM $\mathcal{F}_{\text{session}}$ and $!\mathcal{F}$:

$$\mathcal{F}^{\mathcal{F}}_{\text{session}} := \mathcal{F}_{\text{session}} \mid !\mathcal{F}$$

where $\mathcal{F}_{\text{session}}$ is described below and defined in pseudocode in Figure 7.1.

For simplicity of presentation, in the following description of $\mathcal{F}^{\mathcal{F}}_{\text{session}}$, we think of $\mathcal{F}$ as a single IITM such that for every SID sid there exists at most one instance of $\mathcal{F}$ that is addressed by sid.[52] As usual, this instance of $\mathcal{F}$ is denoted by $\mathcal{F}[sid]$.

The functionality $\mathcal{F}^{\mathcal{F}}_{\text{session}}$ is parameterized by n (the number of I/O tape pairs of $\mathcal{F}$) and has n pairs of input and output I/O tapes to connect to the environment and I/O tapes to connect to all I/O tapes of $\mathcal{F}$, i.e., $\mathcal{F}^{\mathcal{F}}_{\text{session}}$ provides a similar I/O interface as $\mathcal{F}$. A *user* of $\mathcal{F}^{\mathcal{F}}_{\text{session}}$ is identified within $\mathcal{F}^{\mathcal{F}}_{\text{session}}$ by a pair $(lsid, r)$ where $r \in \{1, \ldots, n\}$ is a role and $lsid$ is a local SID of the form $(lsid', sp)$ for arbitrary bit strings $lsid'$ and sp, that are chosen and managed by the party itself. In particularly, on the tape for role r, $\mathcal{F}^{\mathcal{F}}_{\text{session}}$ expects requests to be prefixed by $lsid$, and conversely, $\mathcal{F}^{\mathcal{F}}_{\text{session}}$ prefixes answers sent on that tape by $lsid$.

The intuition behind a local SID $lsid = (lsid', sp)$ is that sp expresses fixed, pre-established parameters of the session this user participates in and all users of this session agree upon. For example, sp could be the empty bit string, if no

---

[51] Recall from Section 2.4 that σ_{prefix} is the SID function that returns the prefix of every message as the SID. For all messages m and tapes c: $\sigma_{\text{prefix}}(m, c) := sid$ if $m = (sid, m')$ for some sid, m' and $\sigma_{\text{prefix}}(m, c) := \bot$ otherwise.

[52] We note that every system can be simulated by a single machine (Lemma 2.1), so, this view on $\mathcal{F}$ is justified.

Parameters: $n > 0$ *{number of I/O tape pairs*

Tapes: $\forall r \leq n$:   from/to IO_r: $(\mathsf{io}_r^{\mathrm{in}}, \mathsf{io}_r^{\mathrm{out}})$;   from/to IO'_r: $(\mathsf{io}_r^{\mathrm{out}'}, \mathsf{io}_r^{\mathrm{in}'})$;   from/to NET: $(\mathsf{net}^{\mathrm{in}}, \mathsf{net}^{\mathrm{out}})$

State: For all $lsid \in \{0,1\}^*$ and $r \in \{1, \ldots, n\}$:
- $\mathsf{st}(lsid, r) \in \{\text{inactive}, \text{active}, \text{corr}\}$ *{status of user $(lsid, r)$; initially* inactive
- $\mathsf{sid}(lsid, r) \in \{0,1\}^* \cup \{\bot\}$ *{global SID of user $(lsid, r)$; initially* $\bot$

We note that it always holds that $\mathsf{st}(lsid, r) = $ active if $\mathsf{sid}(lsid, r) \neq \bot$.

CheckAddress: Accept every input on every tape.

Compute:

Forward Establish *request from a user $(lsid, r)$ to the adversary, record the user $(lsid, r)$ as active:*
recv $(lsid, \text{Establish})$ **from** IO_r **s.t.** $\mathsf{st}(lsid, r) = $ inactive $\wedge \exists lsid', sp$: $lsid = (lsid', sp)$:
    $\mathsf{st}(lsid, r) := $ active; **send** $(\text{Establish}, lsid, r)$ **to** NET

Forward messages from a user $(lsid, r)$ to role r in $\mathcal{F}[\mathsf{sid}(lsid, r)]$ and vice versa (if SID is set):
recv $(lsid, m)$ **from** IO_r **s.t.** $\mathsf{sid}(lsid, r) \neq \bot$: **send** $(\mathsf{sid}(lsid, r), m)$ **to** IO'_r *⎧ lsid is unique*
recv (sid, m) **from** IO'_r **s.t.** $\exists lsid$: $\mathsf{sid}(lsid, r) = sid$: **send** $(lsid, m)$ **to** IO_r *⎨ because of validity*
                                                                ⎩ test (see below)

Allow the adversary to set a valid SID for an active user $(lsid, r)$:
recv $(\text{Establish}, lsid, r, sid)$ **from** NET **s.t.** $\mathsf{st}(lsid, r) = $ active $\wedge \mathsf{sid}(lsid, r) = \bot$:
    if $(\nexists lsid', sid', sp$: $lsid = (lsid', sp) \wedge sid = (sid', sp)) \vee (\exists lsid''$: $\mathsf{sid}(lsid'', r) = sid)$:
       produce empty output   *{sid is not valid for $(lsid, r)$*
    $\mathsf{sid}(lsid, r) := sid$ *{set SID for user $(lsid, r)$ to sid*
    send $(sid, (\text{Establish}, lsid))$ **to** IO'_r *{send* Establish *request to $\mathcal{F}[sid]$, for role r*

Corruption (we note that $\mathcal{F}$ might define its own corruption mechanism in addition to this one):
recv $(\text{Corr}, lsid, r)$ **from** NET **s.t.** $\mathsf{st}(lsid, r) = $ active $\wedge \mathsf{sid}(lsid, r) = \bot$:
    $\mathsf{st}(lsid, r) := $ corr; **send** Ack **to** NET
recv $(lsid, m)$ **from** IO_r **s.t.** $\mathsf{st}(lsid, r) = $ corr $\wedge m \neq$ Corr?: **send** $(\text{Input}, lsid, r, m)$ **to** NET
recv $(\text{Output}, lsid, r, m)$ **from** NET **s.t.** $\mathsf{st}(lsid, r) = $ corr: **send** $(lsid, m)$ **to** IO_r
recv $(lsid, \text{Corr?})$ **from** IO_r **s.t.** $\mathsf{sid}(lsid, r) = \bot$:   *{corruption status request*
    if $\mathsf{st}(lsid, r) = $ corr: **send** $(lsid, 1)$ **to** IO_r **else: send** $(lsid, 0)$ **to** IO_r

---

Figure 7.1.: The IITM $\mathcal{F}_{\text{session}}$. It is used to define the multi-session local-SID ideal functionality $\mathcal{F}^{\mathcal{F}}_{\text{session}} := \mathcal{F}_{\text{session}} \mid \mathcal{F}$ for an ideal functionality $\mathcal{F}$ which is an σ_{prefix}-session version and has I/O input tapes $\mathsf{io}_1^{\mathrm{in}'}, \ldots, \mathsf{io}_n^{\mathrm{in}'}$ and I/O output tapes $\mathsf{io}_1^{\mathrm{out}'}, \ldots, \mathsf{io}_n^{\mathrm{out}'}$. See Section 3.1 for notational conventions.

pre-established session parameters are needed; *sp* could be a list of party names $pid_1, \ldots, pid_n$, with the intuition that party pid_r plays role r in this session; or *sp* could contain information about a cipher suite or a key distribution server that should be used in this session. In general, the session parameters may contain any session relevant information that is agreed upon before the protocol session starts. The bit string *lsid'* is like a pointer for the user to access a local session with parameters *sp*. It should have nothing to do with the actual protocol, i.e., with the protocol messages that are sent on the network. For example, *lsid'* is a pair (pid, i) of a party name *pid* and a counter i (managed by the party *pid*). Then, the user $(lsid, r)$ with $lsid = ((pid, i), sp)$ would represent party *pid* playing role r in its i-th session with parameters *sp*.

The machine $\mathcal{F}_{\text{session}}$ keeps track of which user belongs to which global session where a global session is identified by a (global) SID which is an arbitrary bit string chosen by the adversary (simulator), see below. First, a user of $\mathcal{F}^{\mathcal{F}}_{\text{session}}$, say $(lsid, r)$, is expected to send an Establish request to $\mathcal{F}^{\mathcal{F}}_{\text{session}}$ (i.e., the request $(lsid, \text{Establish})$ on the tape for role r). Upon such a request, $\mathcal{F}_{\text{session}}$ records the user $(lsid, r)$ as *active* and forwards the request to the adversary. The adversary is expected to provide (global) SIDs for active users. To set the SID sid for an active user $(lsid, r)$, the adversary can send the request $(\text{Establish}, lsid, r, sid)$ to $\mathcal{F}_{\text{session}}$. However, $\mathcal{F}_{\text{session}}$ only accepts it if the SID is *valid* for this user (see below). If $\mathcal{F}_{\text{session}}$ accepts sid for $(lsid, r)$, then it sends $(sid, (\text{Establish}, lsid))$ to the r-th I/O input tape of $\mathcal{F}$, i.e., this message is received by $\mathcal{F}[sid]$ on the tape for role r. (What $\mathcal{F}[sid]$ does with it depends entirely on the definition of $\mathcal{F}$.) From then on, $\mathcal{F}_{\text{session}}$ forwards all input from user $(lsid, r)$ to $\mathcal{F}[sid]$ (for role r) and vice versa. That is, the user has established a (global) session and can now interact with the instance of $\mathcal{F}$ that handles this session. We note that $\mathcal{F}[sid]$ may depend on sid because it is a σ_{prefix}-session version and, of course, on the local SIDs that are contained in the Establish requests it receives.

Of course, $\mathcal{F}^{\mathcal{F}}_{\text{session}}$ should guarantee that there are no two different users that play the same role in the same (global) session (i.e., that have the same global SID). Furthermore, we want $\mathcal{F}^{\mathcal{F}}_{\text{session}}$ to guarantee that all users in one session agree upon the same session parameters (i.e., the sp part of their local SID). Both these requirements are captured by the following notion: We say that a (global) SID sid is *valid for a user* $(lsid, r)$ (w.r.t. a configuration of $\mathcal{F}_{\text{session}}$) if *(i)* there exists no user $(lsid', r')$ such that $lsid \neq lsid'$, $r = r'$, and sid has been recorded for $(lsid', r')$ (in $\mathcal{F}_{\text{session}}$) and *(ii)* $sid = (sid', sp)$ and $lsid = (lsid', sp)$ for some bit strings $sid', lsid'$, and sp. As explained above, $\mathcal{F}_{\text{session}}$ only accepts an SID sid for a user $(lsid, r)$ if sid is valid for $(lsid, r)$. Hence, in runs with $\mathcal{F}^{\mathcal{F}}_{\text{session}}$, $\mathcal{F}_{\text{session}}$ guarantees that all users in one session agree upon the session parameters and that, in every session, there is at most one user per role.

We can define corruption for $\mathcal{F}^{\mathcal{F}}_{\text{session}}$ by defining corruption in $\mathcal{F}$. Then, the adversary might be able to corrupt users (or the session a user belongs to) by corruption mechanisms provided by $\mathcal{F}$. However, with this alone, the adversary can only corrupt users that already belong to a session, i.e., for which she has set an SID. It seems reasonable to allow the adversary to also corrupt users before she has set their SID. Therefore, in addition to what $\mathcal{F}$ provides, we allow the adversary to send a special corrupt message to $\mathcal{F}_{\text{session}}$ to corrupt a user, say $(lsid, r)$, that is active and has not yet obtained an SID. Then, $\mathcal{F}_{\text{session}}$ records $(lsid, r)$ as *corrupted*. For corrupted users, $\mathcal{F}_{\text{session}}$ forwards all messages from the I/O interface to the adversary and vice versa. That is, the adversary completely controls corrupted users. As usual (see Section 4.1.4), we allow the environment to obtain the corruption status of users. When the environment asks whether a user, say $(lsid, r)$, is corrupted, then $\mathcal{F}_{\text{session}}$ returns 1 if $(lsid, r)$ is recorded as corrupted (note that, in this case, $(lsid, r)$ has not obtained an SID) and 0 if $(lsid, r)$ is not recorded as corrupted and has not yet obtained an SID. If $(lsid, r)$ has obtained an SID, then, as all other requests for

$(lsid, r)$, $\mathcal{F}_{\text{session}}$ forwards it to the instance of $\mathcal{F}$ with the SID of $(lsid, r)$. That is, as long as a user has not obtained an SID, corruption status requests are answered by $\mathcal{F}_{\text{session}}$ and, once a user belongs to a session, they are handled by the corresponding instance of $\mathcal{F}$.

Remarks on multi-session local-SID functionalities. For a real protocol, to realize a multi-session local-SID functionality $\mathcal{F} = \mathcal{F}_{\text{session}}^{\mathcal{F}'}$, the simulator must be able to assign a (global) SID to instances of the simulated real protocol before interaction with the instance of $\mathcal{F}'$ for that session is possible. This means that a real protocol needs to allow for this assignment, by whatever mechanism (where the mechanism is typically intertwined with the rest of the protocol). In particular, this SID establishment is part of the protocol, and hence, can now be precisely modeled and analyzed. For example, for authentication, key exchange, secure channel protocols and the like, being able to tell which instances form a session is an essential part of what these protocols (have to) guarantee and different protocols use different mechanisms; these mechanisms should be part of the analysis. Conversely, before there was one fixed mechanism for session building, namely pre-established SIDs. Real protocols needed to make sure that they in fact belong to the session with the SID they obtained, and hence, they had to use the SID in some essential way. Moreover, the SIDs came from outside of the protocol, and hence, their establishment was not part of the protocol.

We note that the multi-session functionalities proposed in [KT11a], also called multi-session local-SID functionalities, are only realizable by protocols that provide mutual authentication because the adversary can only group local session to a (global) session once all local sessions have started the protocol. In the multi-session local-SID functionalities presented above, this restriction on the adversary is lifted, and therefore, they are realizable by protocols that do not provide authentication. Of course, if $\mathcal{F}'$ provides authentication (e.g., $\mathcal{F}' = \mathcal{F}_{\text{ake}}$ where $\mathcal{F}_{\text{ake}}$ is the authenticated key exchange functionality described in Section 4.3.1), then $\mathcal{F}_{\text{session}}^{\mathcal{F}'}$ provides authentication too. So, our multi-session local-SID functionalities still allow to model authentication as a security property.

Often multi-session local-SID functionalities are obtained from ideal functionalities as follows:

Definition 7.1. *Let $\mathcal{F}$ be an arbitrary ideal functionality with n pairs of input and output I/O tapes. Then, we define the* multi-session local-SID version *of $\mathcal{F}$ to be*
$$\widehat{\mathcal{F}} := \mathcal{F}_{\text{session}}^{\underline{\mathcal{F}}}.$$

We note that, in the above definition, $\underline{\mathcal{F}}$ is the session version of $\mathcal{F}$ from Section 2.4, i.e., it is an σ_{prefix}-session version, as required above. Typically, $\mathcal{F}$ is a single-session ideal functionality such as our key exchange, key usability, or secure channel functionalities from Section 4.3.

To conclude the remarks about multi-session local-SID functionalities, we explain why they are very useful ideal functionalities that capture what is typically expected from ideal functionalities for multiple sessions, without being overly restrictive. We explain this for $\widehat{\mathcal{F}}_{ke}$, but our arguments are valid for all sorts of multi-session local-SID functionalities.

Example 7.1. We now motivate the multi-session local-SID functionality $\widehat{\mathcal{F}}_{ke} = \mathcal{F}_{session}^{\mathcal{F}_{ke}}$, which is obtained from the ideal key exchange functionality $\mathcal{F}_{ke}$ (Section 4.3.1). For simplicity of presentation, we consider the case $n = 2$, i.e., two-party/role key exchange.

By definition, users can send Establish requests to $\widehat{\mathcal{F}}_{ke}$ and the local SIDs contain session parameters *sp* (e.g., the names of the parties that are supposed to be playing the two roles in the key exchange). Every such request is forwarded to the adversary (simulator) who can then provide a (global) SID for this user. When this SID, say *sid*, is provided, the Establish request is forwarded to the instance of $\mathcal{F}_{ke}$ for this session, i.e., to $\mathcal{F}_{ke}[sid]$. The adversary can only assign users to the same session if they agree on the session parameters *sp*. This is guaranteed by the definition of $\mathcal{F}_{session}$. The adversary can then send an Establish requests for some role $r \in \{1, 2\}$ to the instance $\mathcal{F}_{ke}[sid]$. Upon such a request, $\mathcal{F}_{ke}[sid]$ will output the session key to $\mathcal{F}_{session}$ which will forward it to the user that belongs to session *sid* and has role r. If $\mathcal{F}_{ke}[sid]$ is uncorrupted, it is guaranteed that the session key is freshly generated and that both roles in this session receive the same session key. Recall that, by definition of $\mathcal{F}_{ke}$, the adversary is free to corrupt instances of $\mathcal{F}_{ke}$ (where no role has established a session key yet) and the environment, in the name of users, can ask for the corruption status of users.

These security guarantees that are provided by $\widehat{\mathcal{F}}_{ke}$ are precisely what we expect from an ideal functionality for multiple sessions of key exchanges where the local SIDs really are local, i.e., not used in the actual protocol. Also, when we want to show that a protocol realizes $\widehat{\mathcal{F}}_{ke}$, the simulator is not overly restricted: Typically, when the protocol outputs a session key in some session, then the protocol has already established some kind of SID during the protocol run, e.g., by exchanging nonces. Then, the simulator can simply use this SID to group users to a (global) session in $\widehat{\mathcal{F}}_{ke}$. For corrupted protocol instances, the simulator can corrupt the corresponding user in $\mathcal{F}_{session}$ and is then free to perfectly simulate the protocol. Or, if the protocol instances gets corrupted after the simulator has set an SID for the corresponding user in $\mathcal{F}_{session}$, then the simulator can still corrupt the corresponding instance of $\mathcal{F}_{ke}$, as long as no role has received a session key.

In particularly, as shown by [BLR04] (see also Section 7.8), if a protocol $\mathcal{P}$ that uses pre-established SIDs realizes $!\mathcal{F}_{ke}$ (i.e., $\mathcal{P} \leq !\mathcal{F}_{ke}$), then $\mathcal{P}' \leq \widehat{\mathcal{F}}_{ke}$ where $\mathcal{P}'$ is a protocol obtained from $\mathcal{P}$ by first exchanging nonces and then using the concatenation of these nonces and the session parameters *sp* instead of the pre-established SID.

7.3. Multi-Session Real Protocols

We now fix some notation and terminology for modeling real protocols without pre-established SIDs. A multi-session real protocol is an arbitrary protocol with

n roles, for some $n \geq 2$, which may use arbitrary subprotocols/functionalities to perform its tasks. It is similar to protocols described in Section 4.1, except that it uses local SIDs instead of global SIDs and that it is meant to realize a multi-session local-SID functionality. More precisely, a *multi-session (real) protocol* $\mathcal{P}$ is a protocol system of the form $\mathcal{P} = !M_1 \mid \cdots \mid !M_n$ for some $n \geq 2$ and machines $M_1, \ldots, M_n$. Every machine M_r represents one role in the protocol and, since these machines are under the scope of a bang operator, there can be multiple instances of each machine in a run of the system (see below). Every machine M_r has *(i)* an I/O input and output tape for communication with the environment (users), *(ii)* a network input and output tape for communication with the adversary (modeling the network), and *(iii)* arbitrary I/O input and output tapes for communication with subprotocols/ideal functionalities. Given arbitrary subprotocols/functionalities $\mathcal{F}_1, \ldots, \mathcal{F}_l$ such that $\mathcal{P}, \mathcal{F}_1, \ldots, \mathcal{F}_l$ connect only via their I/O interfaces and the external I/O tapes of $\mathcal{P} \mid \mathcal{F}_1 \mid \cdots \mid \mathcal{F}_l$ are only the I/O tapes of $\mathcal{P}$, for communication with the environment (users), then we say that $\mathcal{P}$ *uses* $\mathcal{F}_1, \ldots, \mathcal{F}_l$.

Just like a multi-session local-SID functionality, a machine M_r expects inputs to be prefixed by a local SID of the form $lsid = (lsid', sp)$ where $lsid'$ and sp are arbitrary bit string that are chosen and managed by the users themselves (see the explanations in Section 7.2). In a run of $\mathcal{P}$ there is at most one instance of M_r with local SID $lsid$, representing the local session $lsid$ in role r (which corresponds to the user $(lsid, r)$ in a multi-session local-SID functionality). As usual, we denote this instance of M_r by $M_r[lsid]$. Mode CheckAddress of M_r is defined such that the first message that a new instance of M_r receives defines the local SID of this instance. Then, $M_r[lsid]$ only accepts messages of the form $(lsid, m)$ from the adversary or the environment (i.e., its user). Also, every message that is output by $M_r[lsid]$ to the adversary or the environment is prefixed by $lsid$. We note that we do not restrict the format of messages sent between $\mathcal{P}$ and its subprotocols/functionalities $\mathcal{F}_1, \ldots, \mathcal{F}_l$. However, typically, messages there will also contain $lsid$, for addressing purposes.

To model corruption, we assume that every instance of M_r, say $M_r[lsid]$, stores a flag corr $\in \{0, 1\}$ in its state, which initially is 0. At some point, $M_r[lsid]$ might set it to 1 in which case we call $M_r[lsid]$ *corrupted*. We require that once $M_r[lsid]$ sets the flag to 1, it stays 1. Furthermore, whenever the environment sends the message $(lsid, \text{Corr?})$ to $M_r[lsid]$ (on the I/O tape), $M_r[lsid]$ replies with $(lsid, \text{corr})$. This allows the environment to know which instances are corrupted. (As usual, this is necessary in universal composability settings, see Section 4.1.4, and corresponds to the definition of corruption status requests in multi-session local-SID functionalities.) However, we do not fix how $M_r[lsid]$ behaves when corrupted; we leave this entirely up to the definition of M_r. For example, one possible behavior could be that, when corrupted, $M_r[lsid]$ outputs its entire state to the adversary and gives complete control to the adversary by forwarding all messages between the environment and the adversary and also allows the adversary to interact with the subprotocols/functionalities $\mathcal{F}_1, \ldots, \mathcal{F}_l$ in the name of the instance $M_r[lsid]$. See also Section 7.4.3 for an example. We note that the possibility of corrupting single instances of M_r is quite fine-grained and allows for several forms corruption, including complete corruption of a party: the adversary can simply corrupt all instances of that party.

7.4. Analyzing Key Exchange Protocols based on our Crypto Functionality

In this section, we consider a general class of key exchange protocols that use the ideal functionality $\mathcal{F}_{\text{crypto}}$ (or its realization $\mathcal{P}_{\text{crypto}}$), see Chapter 5, and develop a criterion to prove universally composable security for such protocols. Since our criterion is based on $\mathcal{F}_{\text{crypto}}$, proving the criterion merely requires information-theoretic arguments or purely syntactical arguments (without reasoning about probabilities), rather than involved cryptographic reduction proofs. By security of a key exchange protocol, here, we mean that it realizes the ideal functionality $\widehat{\mathcal{F}}_{\text{ke}}$ or $\widehat{\mathcal{F}}_{\text{keyuse}}$. As defined above, $\widehat{\mathcal{F}}_{\text{ke}}$ is the multi-session local-SID version of our ideal key exchange functionality $\mathcal{F}_{\text{ke}}$ from Section 4.3.1. We use $\widehat{\mathcal{F}}_{\text{keyuse}}$ as an abbreviation for $\widehat{\mathcal{F}}_{\text{keyuse}}^{\mathcal{F}_{\text{senc}}^{\text{auth}}}$ ($\mathcal{F}_{\text{senc}}^{\text{auth}}$ and $\mathcal{F}_{\text{keyuse}}^{\mathcal{F}_{\text{senc}}^{\text{auth}}}$ are defined in Section 4.2.3 and 4.3.2, respectively). That is, $\widehat{\mathcal{F}}_{\text{keyuse}}$ is the multi-session local-SID version of our ideal key usability functionality for authenticated symmetric encryption. We note that in contrast to $\widehat{\mathcal{F}}_{\text{ke}}$, $\widehat{\mathcal{F}}_{\text{keyuse}}$ does not output a session key but instead allows users in one session to perform (ideal) authenticated symmetric encryption and decryption. As mentioned in Section 4.3.2, it is often more useful than $\widehat{\mathcal{F}}_{\text{ke}}$ because it allows us to analyze higher-level protocols based on the guarantees provided by ideal encryption and decryption (e.g., in Appendix D.3.2, based on $\widehat{\mathcal{F}}_{\text{keyuse}}$, we show that a generic secure channel protocol realizes the multi-session local-SID ideal secure channel functionality $\widehat{\mathcal{F}}_{\text{sc}}$). Another advantage of $\widehat{\mathcal{F}}_{\text{keyuse}}$ over $\widehat{\mathcal{F}}_{\text{ke}}$ is that it is easier to realize: key exchange protocols that use the session key during the key exchange (e.g., for key confirmation) do not realize $\widehat{\mathcal{F}}_{\text{ke}}$ but they might realize $\widehat{\mathcal{F}}_{\text{keyuse}}$. Furthermore, every key exchange protocol that realizes $\widehat{\mathcal{F}}_{\text{ke}}$ induces a realization of $\widehat{\mathcal{F}}_{\text{keyuse}}$ where the session key is used in a secure authenticated encryption scheme (see Section 4.3.2).

We note that we picked key usability for authenticated symmetric encryption (i.e., $\mathcal{F}_{\text{senc}}^{\text{auth}}$) just for simplicity of presentation. Our class of key exchange protocols and our criterion can easily be adapted to key usability for other long-term key functionalities such as $\mathcal{F}_{\text{senc}}^{\text{unauth}}$, $\mathcal{F}_{\text{mac}}$, or $\mathcal{F}_{\text{derive}}$. They can even be adapted to key usability for much more sophisticated functionalities like $\mathcal{F}_{\text{crypto}}$: the established session key could then be used just like a key in $\mathcal{F}_{\text{crypto}}$, e.g., to encrypt or derive other (ideal) keys, as mentioned in Section 4.3.2. In this case the key exchange protocol, after a session key has been established, would basically provide the interface of $\mathcal{F}_{\text{crypto}}$ (full-fledged or restricted) to its users.

7.4.1. Key Exchange Protocols

We now define the class of key exchange protocols that we consider here. An $\mathcal{F}_{\text{crypto}}$-*key exchange protocol ($\mathcal{F}_{\text{crypto}}$-KE protocol)* $\mathcal{P}$ is a multi-session protocol as defined in Section 7.3 (i.e., $\mathcal{P} = {!}M_1 \mid \cdots \mid {!}M_n$ for some $M_1, \ldots, M_n$) that uses the ideal crypto functionality $\mathcal{F}_{\text{crypto}}$ and (possibly) other arbitrary subprotocols/ideal functionalities $\mathcal{F}_1, \ldots, \mathcal{F}_l$ such that $\mathcal{P} \mid \mathcal{F}_{\text{crypto}} \mid \mathcal{F}_1 \mid \cdots \mid \mathcal{F}_l$ is environmentally bounded.[53]

In the following, we do not distinguish between $\mathcal{P}$ and the system $\mathcal{P} \mid \mathcal{F}_1 \mid \cdots \mid \mathcal{F}_l$, i.e., we omit the functionalities $\mathcal{F}_1, \ldots, \mathcal{F}_l$ in our notation and, for example, just write $\mathcal{P} \mid \mathcal{F}_{\text{crypto}}$ instead of $\mathcal{P} \mid \mathcal{F}_{\text{crypto}} \mid \mathcal{F}_1 \mid \cdots \mid \mathcal{F}_l$.

We note that $\mathcal{P} \mid \mathcal{F}_{\text{crypto}}$ is meant to realize the ideal functionality $\widehat{\mathcal{F}}_{\text{keyuse}}$. (See below for a variant of $\mathcal{P}$ that is meant to realize $\widehat{\mathcal{F}}_{\text{ke}}$.) As explained above, $\widehat{\mathcal{F}}_{\text{keyuse}}$ allows users to ideally encrypt and decrypt messages after a session has been established. Below, we will assume that $\widehat{\mathcal{F}}_{\text{keyuse}}$ (more precisely, $\mathcal{F}_{\text{senc}}^{\text{auth}}$ which is a part of $\widehat{\mathcal{F}}_{\text{keyuse}}$) is parameterized by a polynomial-time decidable domain $D = \{D(\eta)\}_{\eta \in \mathbb{N}}$ of plaintexts such that $\widehat{\mathcal{F}}_{\text{keyuse}}$ only allows to encrypt plaintexts $x \in D(\eta)$ (for security parameter η), i.e., encryption fails for plaintext not in $D(\eta)$ and decryption only returns plaintext from $D(\eta)$ (or $\bot$ if decryption fails). Now, the protocol $\mathcal{P}$ (more precisely, every machine M_i in $\mathcal{P}$) is parameterized by D. In $\mathcal{P}$ this domain is used as follows: When a session key has been established, it can only be used to encrypt plaintexts from $D(\eta)$. However, during the key exchange, the session key may be used to encrypt any plaintext. Our criterion will require that, during the key exchange, only plaintexts not in $D(\eta)$ are encrypted, see below.

We assume that the parameters of $\mathcal{F}_{\text{crypto}}$ are chosen such that there exists a designated key type $t_{\text{sk}} \in T_{\text{senc}}^{\text{auth}}$ which is used as the type of session keys. Furthermore, we assume that the plaintext formatting and parsing functions in $\mathcal{F}_{\text{crypto}}$ for keys of type t_{sk} (i.e., session keys) are basically the identity, without including keys in the messages: $\text{format}_{\text{senc}}^{t_{\text{sk}}}(1^\eta, x, \kappa_1, \ldots, \kappa_l)$ yields x if $l = 0$ and $\bot$ otherwise and $\text{parse}_{\text{senc}}^{t_{\text{sk}}}(1^\eta, x) := (x, \varepsilon)$ (where ε is the empty list), for all x. That is, session keys can only be used to encrypt "raw" plaintexts that are uninterpreted and do not contain keys (of course, the plaintexts may contain keys in plain but these keys cannot be unknown keys in $\mathcal{F}_{\text{crypto}}$).[54]

Recall from Section 7.3 that every machine M_r represents one role in the protocol and for every local SID *lsid*, there exists at most one instance of M_r, denoted by $M_r[\textit{lsid}]$, that is addressed by *lsid*. This instance represents the local session *lsid* in role r, or the user $(\textit{lsid}, r)$. We require that $\mathcal{F}_{\text{crypto}}$ is parameterized such that it has n I/O input and output tapes and that M_r connects to the r-th I/O input and

---

[53] We note that, in typical applications, it is very easy to show that $\mathcal{P} \mid \mathcal{F}_{\text{crypto}} \mid \mathcal{F}_1 \mid \cdots \mid \mathcal{F}_l$ is environmentally bounded (or even environmentally strictly bounded).

[54] As mentioned above, the usage of session keys could be generalized to allow session keys of arbitrary type, e.g., MAC or key derivation keys, and then $M_r[\textit{lsid}]$ could allow the user to perform the corresponding operations. Furthermore, the restriction that no keys can be encrypted under session keys could be lifted.

output tape of $\mathcal{F}_{\text{crypto}}$. Furthermore, we require that $M_r[\textit{lsid}]$ uses $\mathcal{F}_{\text{crypto}}$ only in the name of the user $(\textit{lsid}, r)$, i.e., the user identifier is $\textit{uid} = (\textit{lsid}, r)$ and all message to/from $\mathcal{F}_{\text{crypto}}$ are prefixed by $(\textit{lsid}, r)$. The subprotocols/functionalities $\mathcal{F}_1, \dots, \mathcal{F}_l$ may be used arbitrarily by $M_r[\textit{lsid}]$ (in particularly, messages do not need to be prefixed by $\textit{lsid}$ or $(\textit{lsid}, r)$). They may contain subprotocols or/and additional ideal functionalities such as the ideal digital signature functionality $\mathcal{F}_{\text{sig}}$ from Section 4.2.2 or ideal functionalities for public key certification.

Analogously to $\widehat{\mathcal{F}}_{\text{ke}}$ and $\widehat{\mathcal{F}}_{\text{keyuse}}$, a user $(\textit{lsid}, r)$ initiates a key exchange by sending an Establish request to M_r (on the I/O interface), which creates a new instance of M_r, namely $M_r[\textit{lsid}]$. This instance then enters its *key-exchange phase* to establish a session key. In this phase, $M_r[\textit{lsid}]$ can arbitrarily communicate with the adversary (the network), $\mathcal{F}_{\text{crypto}}$, and $\mathcal{F}_1, \dots, \mathcal{F}_l$, as described above, but $M_r[\textit{lsid}]$ may not produce I/O output to the environment (i.e., to its user), except for answers to corruption status request (as defined in Section 7.3, upon a corruption status request from the environment, the instance directly returns its corruption status which is recorded in its flag corr).

When $M_r[\textit{lsid}]$ gets corrupted (i.e., it sets its flag corr to 1, see Section 7.3), then $M_r[\textit{lsid}]$ enters its *corrupted phase*. In this phase, $M_r[\textit{lsid}]$ may now also produce arbitrary I/O output to its user. We do not fix the behavior of $M_r[\textit{lsid}]$ upon corruption. For example, it may give complete control to the adversary, as described in Section 7.3; see Section 7.4.3 for an example.

The key-exchange phase also ends for $M_r[\textit{lsid}]$ when $M_r[\textit{lsid}]$ outputs an Established message (just as $\widehat{\mathcal{F}}_{\text{keyuse}}$) to the user $(\textit{lsid}, r)$ (i.e., it outputs $(\textit{lsid}, \text{Established})$ on its I/O output tape). When this happens, we assume that $M_r[\textit{lsid}]$ has recorded a distinguished pointer that points to a key of type t_{sk} in $\mathcal{F}_{\text{crypto}}$. We call this key the *established session key* of $M_r[\textit{lsid}]$ and denote it by $\text{key}(\textit{lsid}, r)$. Then, the *key-usage phase* of $M_r[\textit{lsid}]$ starts (note that $M_r[\textit{lsid}]$ is uncorrupted if it enters this phase because, otherwise, it would be in its corrupted phase).

In the key-usage phase, the behavior of $M_r[\textit{lsid}]$ is fixed to be the following (in particularly, it does not anymore communicate with the adversary or $\mathcal{F}_1, \dots, \mathcal{F}_l$): $M_r[\textit{lsid}]$ provides the user $(\textit{lsid}, r)$ with an interface to use the established session key, just as $\widehat{\mathcal{F}}_{\text{keyuse}}$. It allows the user to encrypt and decrypt messages. Upon encryption and decryption requests, the request is performed using $\mathcal{F}_{\text{crypto}}$ with the pointer that points to $\text{key}(\textit{lsid}, r)$. The resulting ciphertext/plaintext is returned to the user. However, upon encryption, if the plaintext is not in the domain of plaintexts $D(\eta)$, then it is not encrypted using $\mathcal{F}_{\text{crypto}}$ but, instead, an error is returned to the user (just as when encryption fails in $\widehat{\mathcal{F}}_{\text{keyuse}}$). Similarly, upon decryption, if the plaintext returned by $\mathcal{F}_{\text{crypto}}$ is not in $D(\eta)$, then an error is returned to the user (just as when decryption fails in $\widehat{\mathcal{F}}_{\text{keyuse}}$). We note that, in the key-usage phase, $M_r[\textit{lsid}]$ cannot be corrupted anymore. That is, either it sets its flag corr to 1 (corrupted) in the key-exchange phase or corr will always remain 0 (uncorrupted).

We also consider a variant $\mathcal{P}^*$ of an $\mathcal{F}_{\text{crypto}}$-KE protocol $\mathcal{P}$ that is defined as follows: Instead of sending $(\textit{lsid}, \text{Established})$ to the user, an uncorrupted instance

$M_r[lsid]$ (for some $lsid, r$) sends $(lsid, (\mathsf{Established}, k))$ to the user (just as $\widehat{\mathcal{F}}_{\mathrm{ke}}$) where $k = \mathsf{key}(lsid, r)$ is the established session key. The key $\mathsf{key}(lsid, r)$ is obtained using the Retrieve request of $\mathcal{F}_{\mathrm{crypto}}$ with the pointer that points to $\mathsf{key}(lsid, r)$. Furthermore, in contrast to $\mathcal{P}$, $\mathcal{P}^*$ basically does not have a key-usage phase: In its key-usage phase, $\mathcal{P}^*$ does not allow the users to perform encryption or decryption requests after the session key has been established. Corruption status requests, as in $\mathcal{P}$, are still possible but no other requests. The corrupted phase of $\mathcal{P}^*$ is the same as the corrupted phase of $\mathcal{P}$.[55]

We note that the protocol $\mathcal{P}^*$ has the same I/O interface as the ideal functionality $\widehat{\mathcal{F}}_{\mathrm{ke}}$; it is in fact meant to realize $\widehat{\mathcal{F}}_{\mathrm{ke}}$ (see below).

7.4.2. A Criterion for Secure Key Exchange Protocols

We now present a sufficient criterion for an $\mathcal{F}_{\mathrm{crypto}}$-KE protocol to realize $\widehat{\mathcal{F}}_{\mathrm{ke}}$ or $\widehat{\mathcal{F}}_{\mathrm{keyuse}}$, respectively.

The criterion is based on partnering functions[56] that group users $(lsid, r)$, more precisely, the corresponding instances of machines M_r in a run of $\mathcal{P} \mid \mathcal{F}_{\mathrm{crypto}}$ with some environment, into sessions. Formally, a *partnering function* τ for an $\mathcal{F}_{\mathrm{crypto}}$-KE protocol $\mathcal{P}$ is a polynomial-time computable function that maps a sequence of configurations of an instance of some machine M_r, in a run of $\mathcal{P} \mid \mathcal{F}_{\mathrm{crypto}}$, to an SID sid (which is an arbitrary bit string) or to the special symbol $\bot$. For every environment $\mathcal{E}$ for $\mathcal{P} \mid \mathcal{F}_{\mathrm{crypto}}$ (i.e., $\mathcal{E} \in \mathrm{Env}(\mathcal{P} \mid \mathcal{F}_{\mathrm{crypto}})$), (partial) run ρ of $(\mathcal{E} \mid \mathcal{P} \mid \mathcal{F}_{\mathrm{crypto}})(1^\eta, a)$ (for some security parameter η and external input a), and every user $(lsid, r)$, we define $\tau_{(lsid, r)}(\rho) := \tau(\alpha)$ where α is the projection of ρ to the sequence of configurations of the instance $M_r[lsid]$. We say that $(lsid, r)$ and $(lsid', r')$ are *partners* or *belong to the same session* (w.r.t. τ) in a (partial) run ρ if $\tau_{(lsid, r)}(\rho) = \tau_{(lsid', r')}(\rho) \neq \bot$.

We say that τ is *valid* for $\mathcal{P}$ if, for every environment $\mathcal{E}$ for $\mathcal{P} \mid \mathcal{F}_{\mathrm{crypto}}$ and every user $(lsid, r)$, the following conditions hold with overwhelming probability, where the probability is taken over runs ρ of $(\mathcal{E} \mid \mathcal{P} \mid \mathcal{F}_{\mathrm{crypto}})(1^\eta, a)$:

1. Once an SID is assigned, it is fixed, i.e., if $\tau_{(lsid, r)}(\rho'') \neq \bot$, then it holds $\tau_{(lsid, r)}(\rho') = \tau_{(lsid, r)}(\rho'')$ for every prefix ρ' of ρ and every prefix ρ'' of ρ'.

---

[55] We note that this definition might not make sense for $\mathcal{P}^*$ (depending on the definition of the corrupted phase of $\mathcal{P}$) because $\mathcal{P}^*$ and $\mathcal{P}$ send/expect different I/O messages. However, in the corrupted phase, $\mathcal{P}$ typically forwards all messages from the environment to the adversary and vice versa and this is also a reasonable corruption behavior for $\mathcal{P}^*$. For simplicity, we leave the corrupted phase unaltered. Anyway, this does not influence our proof where we show that $\mathcal{P}^*$ realizes $\widehat{\mathcal{F}}_{\mathrm{ke}}$ (if our criterion is satisfied) because, in case of corruption, the simulator can corrupt the corresponding user in $\widehat{\mathcal{F}}_{\mathrm{ke}}$ and then perfectly simulate the corrupted protocol instance.

[56] The concept of partnering functions has been used to define security in game-based definitions, which led to discussions whether the obtained security notions are reasonable [BR93, BR95, BPR00, CK01, CH05, KSS09]. Here, we use partnering functions as part of our criteria but not as part of the security definition itself; security means realizing $\widehat{\mathcal{F}}_{\mathrm{ke}}$ or $\widehat{\mathcal{F}}_{\mathrm{keyuse}}$.

2. Corrupted users do not belong to sessions, i.e., if $M_r[\mathit{lsid}]$ set its flag corr to 1 (at some point in ρ), then $\tau_{(\mathit{lsid},r)}(\rho) = \perp$.

3. Every session contains at most one user per role, i.e., for every partner (lsid', r') of (lsid, r) in ρ (i.e., $\tau_{(\mathit{lsid},r)}(\rho) = \tau_{(\mathit{lsid}',r')}(\rho) \neq \perp$), it holds that $r \neq r'$ or $(\mathit{lsid}', r') = (\mathit{lsid}, r)$.

4. The session parameters in the SID correspond to the session parameters in lsid, i.e., $\tau_{(\mathit{lsid},r)}(\rho) = \perp$ or $\tau_{(\mathit{lsid},r)}(\rho) = (\mathit{sid}', \mathit{sp})$ and $\mathit{lsid} = (\mathit{lsid}', \mathit{sp})$ for some bit strings $\mathit{sid}', \mathit{lsid}', \mathit{sp}$.

In practice, partnering functions are typically very simple and validity is easy to see (see, e.g., Section 7.4.3).

We are now ready to state our criterion for $\mathcal{F}_{\mathrm{crypto}}$-KE protocols.

Definition 7.2. *Let D be a polynomial-time decidable domain of plaintexts and $\mathcal{P}$ be an $\mathcal{F}_{\mathrm{crypto}}$-KE protocol that is parameterized by D. We say that $\mathcal{P}$ is a secure $\mathcal{F}_{\mathrm{crypto}}$-KE-protocol if there exists a valid partnering function τ for $\mathcal{P}$ such that for every environment $\mathcal{E} \in \mathrm{Env}(\mathcal{P} \,|\, \mathcal{F}_{\mathrm{crypto}})$ the following holds with overwhelming probability (the probability is taken over runs ρ of $(\mathcal{E} \,|\, \mathcal{P} \,|\, \mathcal{F}_{\mathrm{crypto}})(1^\eta, a)$): For every uncorrupted instance of M_r in ρ (i.e., its flag corr is 0), say $M_r[\mathit{lsid}]$, that has entered its key-usage phase (i.e., it has output Established to its user and $\mathrm{key}(\mathit{lsid}, r)$ is its established session key) it holds that:*

(a) *The user (lsid, r) belongs to some (global) session, i.e., $\tau_{(\mathit{lsid},r)}(\rho) \neq \perp$.*

(b) *The key $\mathrm{key}(\mathit{lsid}, r)$ is marked unknown in $\mathcal{F}_{\mathrm{crypto}}$.*

(c) *If $M_{r'}[\mathit{lsid}']$ for some user (lsid', r') is uncorrupted and has entered its key-usage phase (i.e., $\mathrm{key}(\mathit{lsid}', r')$ is its established session key), then (lsid, r) and (lsid', r') are partners (according to τ) if and only if $\mathrm{key}(\mathit{lsid}, r) = \mathrm{key}(\mathit{lsid}', r')$.*

   That is, uncorrupted partners agree on established session keys and non-partners have established different session keys.

(d) *The key $\mathrm{key}(\mathit{lsid}, r)$ has only been used in $\mathcal{F}_{\mathrm{crypto}}$ as a key by users that belong to the same session as (lsid, r) (according to τ) to encrypt or decrypt messages that do not belong to $D(\eta)$, except in the key-usage phase.*

   More precisely: If $M_{r'}[\mathit{lsid}']$ for some user (lsid', r') has used $\mathrm{key}(\mathit{lsid}, r)$ in $\mathcal{F}_{\mathrm{crypto}}$ as a key to encrypt or decrypt a message, then (lsid', r') and (lsid, r) are partners. Furthermore, if $M_{r'}[\mathit{lsid}']$ encrypted a plaintext x under $\mathrm{key}(\mathit{lsid}, r)$ and $M_{r'}[\mathit{lsid}']$ was in its key-exchange phase at that point in ρ (note that $M_{r'}[\mathit{lsid}']$ is uncorrupted because (lsid', r') and (lsid, r) are partners), then $x \notin D(\eta)$. If $M_{r'}[\mathit{lsid}']$ decrypted a ciphertext with $\mathrm{key}(\mathit{lsid}, r)$, obtained a plaintext $x \in D(\eta)$, and $M_{r'}[\mathit{lsid}']$ was in its key-exchange phase at that point in ρ, then $M_{r'}[\mathit{lsid}']$ rejected the plaintext x, i.e., its output and state does not *depend on x and is the same as if it received the symbol $\perp$ (decryption error) instead of x.*[57]

If, in addition to the above, the following holds:

(e) *The user $(lsid, r)$ belongs to a complete session, i.e., there exist $lsid_1, \ldots, lsid_n$ such that $lsid = lsid_r$ and $\tau_{(lsid_1, 1)}(\rho) = \cdots = \tau_{(lsid_n, n)}(\rho) \neq \perp$.*

Then, we say that $\mathcal{P}$ is a secure authenticated $\mathcal{F}_{\mathrm{crypto}}$-KE protocol.

We note that (d) (in the above definition) requires that plaintexts (and, hence, ciphertexts) are not mixed between key-exchange and key-usage phases: In the key-exchange phase, the protocol may use the session key only to encrypt (and decrypt) plaintexts that are *not* in $D(\eta)$ and in the key-usage phase the protocol allows its users only to encrypt (and decrypt) plaintexts that are in $D(\eta)$. In other words, this condition guarantees that plaintexts of a higher-level protocol that uses the key exchange protocol (i.e., plaintexts from $D(\eta)$) cannot be confused with plaintexts in the key exchange protocol. This is typically the case because different message formats are used in the key exchange and secure channel protocol, e.g., messages are tagged by protocol names. The domain of plaintexts D (in conjunction with (d)) captures this formally. It contains all plaintexts that potentially can occur in the higher-level protocol. Usually, D can be defined based on different message formats in the protocols.

We now explain the special case where D is the domain of all bit strings, i.e., $D(\eta) = \{0, 1\}^*$ for every security parameter η. In this case, (d) basically states that the session keys are never used during the key-exchange phases.[58] As the following theorem shows, we can then prove that the above criterion is indeed sufficient for an $\mathcal{F}_{\mathrm{crypto}}$-KE protocol to realize the multi-session local-SID key exchange functionality $\widehat{\mathcal{F}}_{\mathrm{ke}}$. If the protocol satisfies the stronger criterion with authentication, then it even realizes the variant $\widehat{\mathcal{F}}_{\mathrm{ake}}$ of $\widehat{\mathcal{F}}_{\mathrm{ke}}$ that provides authentication (see Section 4.3.1).

Theorem 7.1. *Let D be the domain of all bit strings (i.e., $D(\eta) = \{0, 1\}^*$ for all $\eta \in \mathbb{N}$), let $\mathcal{P}_{\mathrm{crypto}}$ be the realization of $\mathcal{F}_{\mathrm{crypto}}$ from Section 5.3 (i.e., $\mathcal{Q} \mid \mathcal{P}_{\mathrm{crypto}} \leq \mathcal{Q} \mid \mathcal{F}_{\mathrm{crypto}}$ for every used-order respecting and non-committing protocol $\mathcal{Q}$) such that the domain of keys of type t_{sk} is $\{\{0, 1\}^\eta\}_{\eta \in \mathbb{N}}$ (note that this domain corresponds to the domain of session keys generated by $\widehat{\mathcal{F}}_{\mathrm{ke}}$ and $\widehat{\mathcal{F}}_{\mathrm{ake}}$), and let $\mathcal{P}$ be an $\mathcal{F}_{\mathrm{crypto}}$-KE protocol that is parameterized by D such that $\mathcal{P}^* \mid \mathcal{P}_{\mathrm{crypto}}$ is environmentally bounded and $\mathcal{P}^*$ is used-order respecting and non-committing.*

---

[57] We note that this condition is similar to the concept of tests and successful decryption requests that are introduced in Section 7.6.2. Here, we basically require that $M_{r'}[lsid']$ performs a test after decrypting ciphertexts with $\mathsf{key}(lsid, r)$. The test is simply to verify that the returned plaintext does not belong to $D(\eta)$. This is needed to guarantee that plaintexts encrypted during the key-usage phase of some instance do not leak because they are decrypted in the key-exchange phase of some other instance.

[58] Formally, the key exchange protocol may still use the session key for decryption but then it must behave as if this decryption failed, so, it would be pointless to use it for decryption.

1. *If $\mathcal{P}$ is a secure $\mathcal{F}_{\mathrm{crypto}}$-KE protocol (Definition 7.2), then:*

$$\mathcal{P}^* \,|\, \mathcal{P}_{\mathrm{crypto}} \;\leq\; \widehat{\mathcal{F}}_{\mathrm{ke}} \;.$$

2. *If $\mathcal{P}$ is a secure authenticated $\mathcal{F}_{\mathrm{crypto}}$-KE protocol (Definition 7.2), then:*

$$\mathcal{P}^* \,|\, \mathcal{P}_{\mathrm{crypto}} \;\leq\; \widehat{\mathcal{F}}_{\mathrm{ake}} \;.$$

Before we prove the above theorem, we present another theorem that shows that the above criterion is also sufficient for an $\mathcal{F}_{\mathrm{crypto}}$-KE protocol to realize the multi-session local-SID key usability functionality $\widehat{\mathcal{F}}_{\mathrm{keyuse}}$. We note that now D does not need to be the domain of all bit strings, so, session keys might have been used during the key-exchange phase to encrypt (and decrypt) messages not in D. In this theorem, we assume that $\widehat{\mathcal{F}}_{\mathrm{keyuse}}$ and its authenticated variant $\widehat{\mathcal{F}}_{\mathrm{auth\text{-}keyuse}}$ (see Section 4.3.2) are parameterized by D (more precisely, $\mathcal{F}_{\mathrm{senc}}^{\mathrm{auth}}$, which is part of $\widehat{\mathcal{F}}_{\mathrm{keyuse}}$ and $\widehat{\mathcal{F}}_{\mathrm{auth\text{-}keyuse}}$, is parameterized by D) and that encryption fails for plaintexts not in $D(\eta)$ and decryption only returns plaintexts from $D(\eta)$ (or $\perp$ if decryption fails). This constitutes a slight modification of $\mathcal{F}_{\mathrm{senc}}^{\mathrm{auth}}$, as defined in Section 4.2.3, where the domain of plaintexts was the set of all bit strings.[59] Furthermore, we assume that $\widehat{\mathcal{F}}_{\mathrm{keyuse}}$ and $\widehat{\mathcal{F}}_{\mathrm{auth\text{-}keyuse}}$ are parameterized by the polynomial p and the leakage algorithm $L_{\mathrm{senc}}^{t_{\mathrm{sk}}}$ that are both parameters of $\mathcal{F}_{\mathrm{crypto}}$. The polynomial p is used to bound the runtime of the algorithms provided by the adversary and $L_{\mathrm{senc}}^{t_{\mathrm{sk}}}$ is used for (ideally) encrypting messages under session keys (i.e., keys of type t_{sk}). We also assume that leakages of plaintexts from $D(\eta)$ do not collide with leakages of plaintexts not from $D(\eta)$, except with negligible probability. Formally, we assume that $\Pr\left[\,\overline{x} \leftarrow L_{\mathrm{senc}}^{t_{\mathrm{sk}}}(1^{\eta}, x), \overline{y} \leftarrow L_{\mathrm{senc}}^{t_{\mathrm{sk}}}(1^{\eta}, y) : \overline{x} = \overline{y} \wedge x \in D(\eta) \wedge y \notin D(\eta)\,\right]$ is negligible (as a function in η) for all bit strings x and y (where the probability is over the random coins of $L_{\mathrm{senc}}^{t_{\mathrm{sk}}}$). This property is needed in the proof of the following theorem to guarantee that ciphertexts computed in the key-exchange phase do not collide with ciphertexts computed in the key-usage phase of some instance (except with negligible probability). For example, it is satisfied if D is the domain of all bit strings (as in the above theorem) or if $L_{\mathrm{senc}}^{t_{\mathrm{sk}}}$ has high entropy w.r.t. D (Definition 3.17). The latter is, for example, satisfied if $L_{\mathrm{senc}}^{t_{\mathrm{sk}}}$ returns a random bit string of the same length as the plaintext and all plaintexts in $D(\eta)$ have length at least η.

Theorem 7.2. *Let D be a polynomial-time decidable domain of plaintexts such that $\Pr\left[\,\overline{x} \leftarrow L_{\mathrm{senc}}^{t_{\mathrm{sk}}}(1^{\eta}, x), \overline{y} \leftarrow L_{\mathrm{senc}}^{t_{\mathrm{sk}}}(1^{\eta}, y) : \overline{x} = \overline{y} \wedge x \in D(\eta) \wedge y \notin D(\eta)\,\right]$ is negligible for all $x, y \in \{0,1\}^*$, let $\mathcal{P}$ be an $\mathcal{F}_{\mathrm{crypto}}$-KE protocol that is parameterized by D, and*

---

[59]We note that it is not really required to explicitly restrict the domain of plaintexts in $\mathcal{F}_{\mathrm{senc}}^{\mathrm{auth}}$ because the simulator provides the encryption and decryption algorithms and can thus provide algorithms which fail for plaintexts not in the domain. However, for the proof of Theorem 7.2, it is more convenient to explicitly restrict the domain of plaintexts.

let $\widehat{\mathcal{F}}_{\text{keyuse}}$ and $\widehat{\mathcal{F}}_{\text{auth-keyuse}}$ *be parameterized by* D, *the leakage algorithm* $L_{\text{senc}}^{\text{tsk}}$, *and the polynomial* p *(as described above)*.

1. *If* $\mathcal{P}$ *is a secure* $\mathcal{F}_{\text{crypto}}$-*KE protocol (Definition 7.2), then:*

$$\mathcal{P} \,|\, \mathcal{F}_{\text{crypto}} \;\leq\; \widehat{\mathcal{F}}_{\text{keyuse}} \;.$$

2. *If* $\mathcal{P}$ *is a secure authenticated* $\mathcal{F}_{\text{crypto}}$-*KE protocol (Definition 7.2), then:*

$$\mathcal{P} \,|\, \mathcal{F}_{\text{crypto}} \;\leq\; \widehat{\mathcal{F}}_{\text{auth-keyuse}} \;.$$

We note that, for used-order respecting and non-committing protocols $\mathcal{P}$ (see Section 5.3.2), $\mathcal{F}_{\text{crypto}}$ can be replaced by its realization $\mathcal{P}_{\text{crypto}}$ (Corollary 5.1), i.e., from the above theorem, we obtain that $\mathcal{P} \,|\, \mathcal{P}_{\text{crypto}} \leq \widehat{\mathcal{F}}_{\text{keyuse}}$ or $\mathcal{P} \,|\, \mathcal{P}_{\text{crypto}} \leq \widehat{\mathcal{F}}_{\text{auth-keyuse}}$, respectively.

Now, we prove the above theorems. The proofs nicely demonstrate the usefulness of $\mathcal{F}_{\text{crypto}}$ because $\mathcal{F}_{\text{crypto}}$ allows us to perform purely information theoretic reasoning, without reductions to the underlying cryptographic primitives.

Proof of Theorem 7.1. We first show 1. Let $\mathcal{Q} := \mathcal{P}^* \,|\, \mathcal{S}_{\mathcal{F}_{\text{crypto}}} \,|\, \mathcal{F}_{\text{crypto}}$ where $\mathcal{S}_{\mathcal{F}_{\text{crypto}}}$ is the simulator used to prove Theorem 5.1. We note that, by Corollary 5.1, it holds that $\mathcal{E} \,|\, \mathcal{Q} \equiv \mathcal{E} \,|\, \mathcal{P}^* \,|\, \mathcal{P}_{\text{crypto}}$ for every environment $\mathcal{E}$ for $\mathcal{Q}$ (i.e., $\mathcal{E} \in \text{Env}(\mathcal{Q})$) and that $\mathcal{Q}$ is environmentally bounded (because $\mathcal{P}^* \,|\, \mathcal{P}_{\text{crypto}}$ is environmentally bounded). Next, we define a simulator $\mathcal{S}$ and show that $\mathcal{E} \,|\, \mathcal{Q} \equiv \mathcal{E} \,|\, \mathcal{S} \,|\, \widehat{\mathcal{F}}_{\text{ke}}$ for every environment $\mathcal{E}$ for $\mathcal{Q}$, which completes the proof.

Since $\mathcal{P}$ is a secure $\mathcal{F}_{\text{crypto}}$-KE protocol, there exists a valid partnering function τ. The simulator $\mathcal{S}$ basically emulates $\mathcal{Q}$. More precisely, if $\widehat{\mathcal{F}}_{\text{ke}}$ receives an Establish request, then $\widehat{\mathcal{F}}_{\text{ke}}$ forwards it to $\mathcal{S}$ and $\mathcal{S}$ simulates $\mathcal{Q}$ with this input. In this simulation, $\mathcal{S}$ forwards all network output of $\mathcal{Q}$ to the environment and vice versa. By definition of $\mathcal{F}_{\text{crypto}}$-KE protocols, the simulated $\mathcal{Q}$, i.e., an instance $M_r[lsid]$ in $\mathcal{Q}$, does not produce I/O output until $M_r[lsid]$ is corrupted (i.e., its flag corr is 1) or entered its key-usage phase. During the simulation, $\mathcal{S}$ always checks if one of the simulated instances $M_r[lsid]$ gets corrupted. In this case, $\mathcal{S}$ corrupts the user $(lsid, r)$ in $\widehat{\mathcal{F}}_{\text{ke}}$. If this fails, $\mathcal{S}$ aborts (in this case simulation fails but, since τ is valid, this happens only with negligible probability because an instance $M_r[lsid]$ only gets corrupted as long as τ has not yet assigned an SID to the user $(lsid, r)$). For corrupted instances $M_r[lsid]$, $\mathcal{S}$ also forwards all I/O output to the user $(lsid, r)$ and all I/O input from $(lsid, r)$ to $M_r[lsid]$ (note that $\widehat{\mathcal{F}}_{\text{ke}}$ allows $\mathcal{S}$ to do so because the user $(lsid, r)$ is corrupted in $\widehat{\mathcal{F}}_{\text{ke}}$). Furthermore, for every user $(lsid, r)$, $\mathcal{S}$ always computes $\tau(\alpha)$ where α is the sequence of configurations of the simulated instance $M_r[lsid]$. If this changes from $\bot$ to some SID $sid \neq \bot$, then $\mathcal{S}$ instructs $\widehat{\mathcal{F}}_{\text{ke}}$ to set the SID for user $(lsid, r)$ to sid. When a simulated, uncorrupted instance $M_r[lsid]$ produces I/O output (i.e., it enters its key-usage phase and outputs $(lsid, \text{Established}, k)$ for some session key k), then S instructs $\widehat{\mathcal{F}}_{\mathrm{ke}}[sid]$ (i.e., the instance of $\mathcal{F}_{\mathrm{ke}}$ with SID sid) to output the session key to user $(lsid, r)$ where sid is the SID of the session $(lsid, r)$ belongs to (according to τ). If the SID has not been set (according to τ) for the user $(lsid, r)$ yet (i.e., $(lsid, r)$ does not belong to some session), S aborts (in this case simulation fails but, since $\mathcal{P}$ is secure, this happens only with negligible probability). It is easy to see that $S \,|\, \widehat{\mathcal{F}}_{\mathrm{ke}}$ is environmentally bounded (because $\mathcal{Q}$ is environmentally bounded), and hence, S is a valid simulator (i.e., $S \in \mathrm{Sim}^{\mathcal{P}^* \,|\, \mathcal{P}_{\mathrm{crypto}}}(\widehat{\mathcal{F}}_{\mathrm{ke}})$).

It is now possible to define a mapping from every run ρ of the system $\mathcal{E} \,|\, \mathcal{Q}$ (for any security parameter η and external input a), excluding the (negligible set of) runs for which τ is not valid or one of the conditions in Definition 7.2 is not satisfied, to a set S_ρ of runs of the system $\mathcal{E} \,|\, S \,|\, \widehat{\mathcal{F}}_{\mathrm{ke}}$ such that the probability of ρ is the same as the one for S_ρ and the overall output of ρ (on tape decision) is the same as the overall output of every run in S_ρ. Such a mapping implies that $\mathcal{E} \,|\, \mathcal{Q} \equiv \mathcal{E} \,|\, S \,|\, \widehat{\mathcal{F}}_{\mathrm{ke}}$. The mapping is defined as follows: Let ρ be a run of $\mathcal{E} \,|\, \mathcal{Q}$ which satisfies that the conditions for validity of τ and the conditions in Definition 7.2. We now define S_ρ to be the set of runs of $\mathcal{E} \,|\, S \,|\, \mathcal{F}_{\mathrm{ke}}$ where:

(a) $\mathcal{E}$ uses the same random coins as $\mathcal{E}$ in ρ,

(b) the random coins of $\widehat{\mathcal{F}}_{\mathrm{ke}}$ are defined such that the keys that are generated and output as session keys by $\widehat{\mathcal{F}}_{\mathrm{ke}}$ correspond to the keys generated by $\mathcal{Q}$ and output as session keys by $\mathcal{Q}$ to $\mathcal{E}$ in ρ (this is to make sure that the session keys output in the two systems coincide), and

(c) the random coins of S are defined such that the emulated $\mathcal{Q}$ (within S) uses the same random coins as $\mathcal{Q}$ in ρ, except that we use fresh keys for keys generated by $\mathcal{Q}$ and output as session keys by $\mathcal{Q}$ to $\mathcal{E}$ for (uncorrupted) sessions in ρ, i.e., for every SID sid we choose a fresh key and this is output by the instance $M_r[lsid]$ that belong to this session. Every such fresh key induces one run in S_ρ. Note that for corrupted instance $M_r[lsid]$ $\mathcal{E}$ determines the session keys, and hence, in such a case the two systems behave in the same way.

Note that this mapping is well-defined because ρ satisfies the conditions for validity of τ and the conditions in Definition 7.2. By construction, the probabilities of ρ and S_ρ are equal. Based on the following observations, one can easily show, by induction on the length of runs, that the view of $\mathcal{E}$ in ρ is the same as the view of $\mathcal{E}$ in every run ρ' in S_ρ, and hence, the overall output is the same: The only difference between ρ and ρ' is that for every key that is output as a session key in an (uncorrupted) session in ρ', S does not use this session key in its simulation, but a freshly generated key. By definition of the randomness of ρ', the corresponding session in $\widetilde{\mathcal{F}}_{\mathrm{ke}}$ contains the actual session key. For this reason, output at the I/O interface of ρ and ρ' coincide: The session keys output by (uncorrupted) sessions coincide in both runs, ρ and ρ'. As for the network interface, even though ρ' does not use the actual session key, $\mathcal{E}$ cannot observe this: By assumption, ρ satisfies the conditions in Definition 7.2. Thus, keys output in ρ as session keys in (uncorrupted) sessions are marked unknown, and hence, they have always been encrypted ideally. Moreover, these keys were never used as keys for encryption and decryption always fails (because D is the domain of all plaintexts). So, $\mathcal{E}$ cannot distinguish whether the actual session keys or freshly generated keys have been encrypted.

We now show 2. The proof is identical to the above proof, except that we replace $\widehat{\mathcal{F}}_{\mathrm{ke}}$ by $\widehat{\mathcal{F}}_{\mathrm{ake}}$ and for one difference: When $\mathcal{S}$ instructs $\widehat{\mathcal{F}}_{\mathrm{ake}}[sid]$ to output the session key to user $(lsid, r)$, then this fails if the session sid is not complete (i.e., not every role has sent an Establish request). In this case, the simulation fails. However, it is easy to see that the extra condition that $\mathcal{P}$ is a secure authenticated $\mathcal{F}_{\mathrm{crypto}}$-KE protocol guarantees that this only happens with negligible probability. Hence, when defining the mapping from runs of $\mathcal{E} \mid \mathcal{Q}$ to runs of $\mathcal{E} \mid \mathcal{S} \mid \widehat{\mathcal{F}}_{\mathrm{ake}}$, these runs do not need to be considered. $\qquad\square$

Proof of Theorem 7.2. We first show 1., see below for 2. We now define a simulator $\mathcal{S}$ and show that $\mathcal{E} \mid \mathcal{P} \mid \mathcal{F}_{\mathrm{crypto}} \equiv \mathcal{E} \mid \mathcal{S} \mid \widehat{\mathcal{F}}_{\mathrm{keyuse}}$ for every environment $\mathcal{E}$ for $\mathcal{P} \mid \mathcal{F}_{\mathrm{crypto}}$.

Since $\mathcal{P}$ is a secure $\mathcal{F}_{\mathrm{crypto}}$-KE protocol, there exists a valid partnering function τ. The simulator $\mathcal{S}$ is similar to the simulator defined in the proof of Theorem 7.1. The only difference is that $\mathcal{S}$ simulates the system $\mathcal{P} \mid \mathcal{F}_{\mathrm{crypto}}$ instead of $\mathcal{Q} = \mathcal{P}^* \mid \mathcal{S}_{\mathcal{F}_{\mathrm{crypto}}} \mid \mathcal{P}_{\mathrm{crypto}}$ and that it interacts with $\widehat{\mathcal{F}}_{\mathrm{keyuse}}$ instead of $\widehat{\mathcal{F}}_{\mathrm{ke}}$. In the simulation, $\mathcal{S}$ has to provide encryption and decryption algorithms and keys to $\widehat{\mathcal{F}}_{\mathrm{keyuse}}$. When required, $\mathcal{S}$ provides the key $\mathsf{key}(lsid, r)$ and the corresponding algorithms to $\widehat{\mathcal{F}}_{\mathrm{keyuse}}[sid]$, i.e., to the instance of $\mathcal{F}_{\mathrm{keyuse}}$ for session sid, where $\mathsf{key}(lsid, r)$ is the key in (the simulated) $\mathcal{F}_{\mathrm{crypto}}$ that is the established session key of a user $(lsid, r)$ that belongs to session sid (according to τ). It is easy to see that $\mathcal{S} \mid \widehat{\mathcal{F}}_{\mathrm{keyuse}}$ is environmentally bounded (because $\mathcal{P} \mid \mathcal{F}_{\mathrm{crypto}}$ is environmentally bounded), and hence, $\mathcal{S}$ is a valid simulator (i.e., $\mathcal{S} \in \mathrm{Sim}^{\mathcal{P} \mid \mathcal{F}_{\mathrm{crypto}}}(\widehat{\mathcal{F}}_{\mathrm{keyuse}})$).

Similar to the proof of Theorem 7.1, we can show that $\mathcal{E} \mid \mathcal{P} \mid \mathcal{F}_{\mathrm{crypto}} \equiv \mathcal{E} \mid \mathcal{S} \mid \widehat{\mathcal{F}}_{\mathrm{keyuse}}$ for every environment $\mathcal{E} \in \mathrm{Env}(\mathcal{P} \mid \mathcal{F}_{\mathrm{crypto}})$, by defining a mapping from runs ρ of $\mathcal{E} \mid \mathcal{P} \mid \mathcal{F}_{\mathrm{crypto}}$ (except for the negligible set of runs where the conditions of the validity of τ and Definition 7.2 are violated or ciphertexts computed during the key-exchange phase collide with ciphertexts computed during the key-usage phase of some instance[60]) to runs ρ' of $\mathcal{E} \mid \mathcal{S} \mid \widehat{\mathcal{F}}_{\mathrm{keyuse}}$ such that the probability of ρ equals the probability of ρ' and both runs have the same overall output (on tape decision). This implies that $\mathcal{E} \mid \mathcal{P} \mid \mathcal{F}_{\mathrm{crypto}} \equiv \mathcal{E} \mid \mathcal{S} \mid \widehat{\mathcal{F}}_{\mathrm{keyuse}}$. The proof here is even simpler than the one for Theorem 7.1 because session keys are never output. However, the key-usage phase now has to be taken care of.

In the key-usage phase, in ρ (i.e., in $\mathcal{E} \mid \mathcal{P} \mid \mathcal{F}_{\mathrm{crypto}}$) a message, say x, is encrypted under a session key, say by an uncorrupted instance $M_r[lsid]$ with the session key

---

[60]Since $\Pr\left[\overline{x} \leftarrow L^{tsk}_{\mathrm{senc}}(1^\eta, x), \overline{y} \leftarrow L^{tsk}_{\mathrm{senc}}(1^\eta, y) : \overline{x} = \overline{y} \wedge x \in D(\eta) \wedge y \notin D(\eta)\right]$ is negligible for all $x, y \in \{0,1\}^*$ and $\mathcal{F}_{\mathrm{crypto}}$ performs a decryption test upon encryption to ensure that the ciphertext contains at least the information of the leakage, these ciphertexts collide only with negligible probability.

1. $A \to S$: $pid_A, N_A, c_1[, \text{PMKID}]$
2. $S \to A$: $pid_S, N_S, c_2, \text{mac}_{\text{KCK}}(N_S, c_2)$
3. $A \to S$: $pid_A, N_A, c_3, \text{mac}_{\text{KCK}}(N_A, c_3)$
4. $S \to A$: $pid_S, c_4, \text{mac}_{\text{KCK}}(c_4)$

Figure 7.2.: The 4-Way Handshake protocol of WPA2 (IEEE 802.11i).

$\text{key}(lsid, r)$, using $\mathcal{F}_{\text{crypto}}$. Since $\mathcal{P}$ is secure, $\text{key}(lsid, r)$ is marked unknown in $\mathcal{F}_{\text{crypto}}$, and hence, the leakage is encrypted. However, this fails (without side effects on the state of $M_r[lsid]$) if $x \notin D(\eta)$ (because ρ satisfies (d) in Definition 7.2). By definition of S and $\widehat{\mathcal{F}}_{\text{keyuse}}$, in ρ' (i.e., in $\mathcal{E} \mid S \mid \widehat{\mathcal{F}}_{\text{keyuse}}$) the same happens, i.e., the leakage instead of x is encrypted with the same key and algorithm and encryption also fails if $x \notin D(\eta)$. Similarly, decryption is done in the same way in ρ and in ρ'. We note that in ρ, the decryption table for $\text{key}(lsid, r)$ in $\mathcal{F}_{\text{crypto}}$ (where plaintext/ciphertext pairs are recorded upon encryption) is a superset of the decryption table of $\widehat{\mathcal{F}}_{\text{keyuse}}[sid]$ (where sid is the SID of user $(lsid, r)$ w.r.t. τ) because it may additionally contain the plaintext/ciphertext pairs recorded during the key-exchange phase. However, since ciphertexts computed during the key-exchange phase do not collide with ciphertexts computed during the key-usage phase, the result of decrypting a message in ρ' does not differ from ρ. So, the view of $\mathcal{E}$ in ρ is the same as its view in ρ' and, because in both runs $\mathcal{E}$ uses the same randomness, the overall output of the runs is the same, i.e., $\mathcal{E}$ cannot distinguish. □

7.4.3. Application: Security Analysis of the 4WHS protocol of WPA2

Using our results and methods developed above, as a case study, we now analyze a central protocol of the pre-shared key mode of WPA2 (IEEE standard 802.11i [IEE07, IEE04]), namely the 4-Way Handshake (4WHS) protocol. (We also analyze the CCM Protocol which is a secure channel protocol that uses the 4WHS protocol as a subprotocol, see Appendix D.3.2.) We prove that the 4WHS protocol provides universally composable key exchange. Without $\mathcal{F}_{\text{crypto}}$, our modular approach, and our criteria, the proof would be considerably more complex and would involve non-trivial reduction proofs. In particular, due to $\mathcal{F}_{\text{crypto}}$, our proofs only require syntactic arguments and they illustrate that $\mathcal{F}_{\text{crypto}}$ can be used in an intuitive and easy way for the analysis of real-world security protocols.

We note that, to the best of our knowledge, this constitutes the first rigorous cryptographic analysis of the 4WHS protocol (see Section 7.8 for related work).

The 4-Way Handshake Protocol

The 4-Way Handshake (4WHS) protocol consists of two roles, an authenticator A (e.g., an access point) and a supplicant S (e.g., a laptop) which share a Pairwise

Master Key (PMK). The authenticator may communicate with several supplicants using the same PMK, which in the pre-shared key mode of WPA2 (WPA2-PSK) is a pre-shared key. On an abstract level, the message exchange between an authenticator A and a supplicant S is shown in Figure 7.2, where pid_A and pid_S are the names (Media Access Control addresses) of A and S, respectively, N_A and N_S are nonces generated by A and S, respectively, and $c_1, \ldots, c_4$ are pairwise distinct constants used to indicate different messages. From the PMK, A and S derive a Pairwise Transient Key (PTK) by computing

$$PTK := PRF(PMK, \texttt{"Pairwise key expansion"} \|$$
$$\min(pid_A, pid_S) \| \max(pid_A, pid_S) \| \min(N_A, N_S) \| \max(N_A, N_S))$$

where PRF is an HMAC, which according to the IEEE standard 802.11i is assumed to be pseudorandom. The PTK is then split into the Key Confirmation Key (KCK), the Key Encryption Key (KEK), and the Temporary Key (TK):

$$KCK \| KEK \| TK := PTK \ .$$

We note that the KEK is only used in the Group Key Handshake protocol, that we do not model. The TK is used in the CCM Protocol (CCMP) to establish a secure channel between A and S (see Appendix D.3.2). By $mac_{KCK}(m)$ we denote the MAC of the message m under the KCK. The first message of the 4WHS protocol optionally includes

$$PMKID := PRF(PMK, \texttt{"PMK Name"} \| pid_A \| pid_S)$$

to indicate the corresponding PMK.

Modeling the 4WHS Protocol

Modeling the 4WHS protocol as an $\mathcal{F}_{\text{crypto}}$-KE protocol $\mathcal{P}_{\text{4WHS}}$ is straightforward. We emphasize that, since $\mathcal{F}_{\text{crypto}}$ provides a low-level interface to basic cryptographic primitives, our modeling of the 4WHS protocol, including message formats, the use of cryptographic primitives, and cryptographic assumptions, is very close to the actual standard. We note that in our modeling of 4WHS parties may *not* play both the role of an authenticator and a supplicant with the same pre-shared key. Otherwise, 4WHS would be insecure. Indeed, a reflection attack would be possible [HM05], and our security proof would fail.

The $\mathcal{F}_{\text{crypto}}$-KE protocol $\mathcal{P}_{\text{4WHS}}$ consists of two roles: $\mathcal{P}_{\text{4WHS}} := {!}M_A \,|\, {!}M_S$ and we assume that $\mathcal{P}_{\text{4WHS}}$ uses the ideal functionality $\mathcal{F}_{\text{nonce}}$ for nonces from Section 4.2.7 (in addition to $\mathcal{F}_{\text{crypto}}$). As above, by $\mathcal{P}_{\text{4WHS}} \,|\, \mathcal{F}_{\text{crypto}}$ we denote $\mathcal{P}_{\text{4WHS}} \,|\, \mathcal{F}_{\text{crypto}} \,|\, \mathcal{F}_{\text{nonce}}$, i.e., we omit the functionality $\mathcal{F}_{\text{nonce}}$ in our notation. As defined in Section 7.4.1, there can be multiple instances of M_A and M_S and every instance is addressed by a local SID of the form $lsid = (lsid', sp)$, where sp are the session parameters for this session, see below. Since the session key (TK) is not used in the protocol, we define the domain of plaintexts D (that is a parameter of $\mathcal{P}_{4\text{WHS}}$) to be the domain of all bit strings. We model the optional value PMKID as follows: The adversary will tell an authenticator whether to include PMKID in the first protocol message. Hence, we will obtain that the security of the protocol does not depend on whether PMKID is sent.

We now describe the parameters of $\mathcal{F}_{\text{crypto}}$ that we use here. (Since public-key encryption is not used in the protocol, we omit public-key encryption from our description.) The functionality $\mathcal{F}_{\text{crypto}}$ is parameterized by the following key types: $\mathcal{T}_{\text{derive}} := \{t_{\text{PMK}}\}$ (for key derivation; the PMK will have this type), $\mathcal{T}_{\text{senc}}^{\text{auth}} := \{t_{\text{TK}}, t_{\text{KEK}}, t_{\text{PMKID}}\}$ (for authenticated symmetric encryption; session keys, i.e., the TK, KEK, and PMKID will have this type), $\mathcal{T}_{\text{senc}}^{\text{unauth}} := \emptyset$ (there are no keys for unauthenticated encryption), $\mathcal{T}_{\text{mac}} := \{t_{\text{KCK}}\}$ (for MAC; the KCK will have this type). (We note that it is irrelevant which type the KEK and PMKID have because they are not used as keys in the protocol.) We define the key domains to be $\{0, 1\}^{\eta}$ for security parameter η.[61] The plaintext formatting and parsing functions are defined such that "raw" plaintexts are encrypted that do not contain any keys. For every security parameter η, bit string x, and (typed) keys $\kappa_1, \ldots, \kappa_l$, we define:

$$\text{format}_{\text{senc}}^{t_{\text{TK}}}(1^{\eta}, x, \kappa_1, \ldots, \kappa_l) := \begin{cases} x & \text{if } l = 0 \text{ (i.e., the key list is empty)} \\ \bot & \text{otherwise.} \end{cases}$$

That is, formatting succeeds if and only if no keys are provided. The formatting functions $\text{format}_{\text{senc}}^{t_{\text{KEK}}}$ and $\text{format}_{\text{senc}}^{t_{\text{PMKID}}}$ are defined as $\text{format}_{\text{senc}}^{t_{\text{TK}}}$ (however, this is irrelevant because keys of this type are never used in the protocol). The corresponding parsing functions are defined accordingly. The leakage algorithm $L_{\text{senc}}^{t_{\text{TK}}}$ is defined to return a random bit string of the same length as the plaintext, i.e., $L_{\text{senc}}^{t_{\text{TK}}}(1^{\eta}, x)$ chooses $\overline{x}$ uniformly at random from $\{0, 1\}^{|x|}$ and returns $\overline{x}$. The leakage algorithms $L_{\text{senc}}^{t_{\text{KEK}}}$ and $L_{\text{senc}}^{t_{\text{PMKID}}}$ are defined as $L_{\text{senc}}^{t_{\text{TK}}}$ (however, this is irrelevant again). The way the KCK, KEK, TK, and PMKID are derived from the PMK in the above description of the 4WHS protocol directly induces the definition of the salt parsing function for keys of type t_{PMK} in $\mathcal{F}_{\text{crypto}}$. For every security parameter η and salt x, we define:

$$\text{parse}_{\text{salt}}^{t_{\text{PMK}}}(1^{\eta}, x) := \begin{cases} (t_{\text{KCK}}, t_{\text{KEK}}, t_{\text{TK}}) & \text{if } \exists y\colon x = \text{"Pairwise key expansion"}\|y \\ (t_{\text{PMKID}}) & \text{if } \exists y\colon x = \text{"PMK Name"}\|y \\ \varepsilon & \text{otherwise (where } \varepsilon \text{ is the empty list).} \end{cases}$$

Finally, $\mathcal{F}_{\text{crypto}}$ is parameterized by a polynomial p (that bounds the runtime of the algorithms provided by the adversary/simulator). We choose this polynomial such that it bounds the runtime of the algorithms that we want to use to implement $\mathcal{P}_{\text{crypto}}$ (see Section 5.3.2). We note that the polynomial only becomes relevant when we replace $\mathcal{F}_{\text{crypto}}$ by $\mathcal{P}_{\text{crypto}}$.

---

[61] We note that, since our cryptographic model is asymptotic, the length of keys and nonces depends on the security parameter η whereas keys and nonces in the 4WHS protocol have a fixed length.

A natural way to model the pre-shared key PMK would be the following: At first, every instance (of M_A or M_S) establishes a pre-shared key (in $\mathcal{F}_{\text{crypto}}$) using the party name of the authenticator as the name of the pre-shared key. This way, all supplicants talking to the same authenticator use the same pre-shared key. But this modeling yields that an authenticator, say A, uses the same PMK in every session. For example, A cannot change the PMK. Also, different authenticator would necessarily use different pre-shared keys. Therefore, we model the pre-shared key PMK as follows: We allow the environment to decide which instance uses which pre-shared key. To do so, we require that the session parameters sp (contained in the local SID, see above) are of the form $(pid_A, pid_S, name_{\text{PMK}})$ where pid_A and pid_S are party names and $name_{\text{PMK}}$ is the name of the pre-shared key PMK (they are all arbitrary bit strings). These session parameters describe a session with party pid_A in role A (authenticator) and party pid_S in role S (supplicant) and where both parties use the PMK $name_{\text{PMK}}$. Whenever an instance (of M_A or M_S) is first activated, it verifies that its local SID is of the form $(lsid', sp)$ and that sp is of the form $(pid_A, pid_S, name_{\text{PMK}})$. (If this check fails, the instance terminates.) Then, it obtains a pointer to the pre-shared key with name $name_{\text{PMK}}$ and key type $t_{\text{PMK}} \in \mathcal{T}_{\text{derive}}$ using $\mathcal{F}_{\text{crypto}}$.

After having received an Establish message and established the PMK (as described above), every instance of M_A and M_S forwards this message to the adversary and then waits for input from the adversary (the adversary can now corrupt instance, see below). Then, they execute the 4WHS protocol as expected using $\mathcal{F}_{\text{nonce}}$ to generate nonces and $\mathcal{F}_{\text{crypto}}$ to derive keys, and compute and verify MACs. Finally, the instance records its pointer it obtained to the TK as the pointer that points to the established session key. Then, the instance enters its key-usage phase where its user can now use the TK for encryption and decryption as described in Section 7.4.1. The optional value PMKID is handled as follows: An instance of M_A asks the adversary whether to include the PMKID in the first message. If the adversary tells the instance to do so, the instance derives PMKID using $\mathcal{F}_{\text{crypto}}$ and uses the Retrieve command of $\mathcal{F}_{\text{crypto}}$ to obtain the actual bit string (we note this marks the key PMKID as known in $\mathcal{F}_{\text{crypto}}$ but this is irrelevant to the security of the protocol). Then, the instance of M_A can include the PMKID in plain in the message. An instance of M_B, when it receives the first protocol message and this message contains a PMKID, derives PMKID using $\mathcal{F}_{\text{crypto}}$ and Retrieve (as M_A) and then checks if the received PMKID equals the derived PMKID. It aborts the protocol if this check fails.

As mentioned above, a simple reflection attack on the 4WHS protocol is possible if there is a party playing both the role of an authenticator and a supplicant using the same pre-shared key, see [HM05] and our proof of Theorem 7.3. To prevent such an unusual environment, we use a (polynomial-time computable) predicate on party names which separates party names for authenticators from party names for supplicants. Every instance of M_A and M_S, when it checks that the local SID is of the form $(lsid', sp)$ with $sp = (pid_A, pid_S, name_{\text{PMK}})$ (see above), then additionally checks (using the predicate) that pid_A and pid_S are allowed party names for the role of an authenticator or supplicant, respectively. (If this check fails, the instance terminates.)

We model corruption as follows. The adversary can corrupt an instance of M_A and M_S by sending a special corrupt message to it. This has to be the first message this instance receives from the adversary. A corrupted instance sets its flag corr to 1 and forwards all messages from the user to the adversary and vice versa. Furthermore, it allows the adversary to send requests to $\mathcal{F}_{crypto}$ and $\mathcal{F}_{nonce}$ (the responses are forwarded to the adversary) in the name of the user, except for KeyGen requests to $\mathcal{F}_{crypto}$ to generate new symmetric keys (we note that this does not limit the adversary because she can generate keys herself and insert them into $\mathcal{F}_{crypto}$ using the Store request).

If the instance is corrupted, all pre-shared keys this user (on demand of the adversary) has created in $\mathcal{F}_{crypto}$ should be corrupted (in $\mathcal{F}_{crypto}$) as well. We therefore require that the adversary corrupts all pre-shared keys a corrupted instance creates using $\mathcal{F}_{crypto}$. A corrupted instance always checks (by asking $\mathcal{F}_{crypto}$) if its pre-shared keys created in $\mathcal{F}_{crypto}$ indeed have been corrupted by the adversary and terminates if they have not been corrupted.

An instance also considers itself corrupted (i.e., sets its flag corr to 1) if it has not been corrupted explicitly as above but the pre-shared key PMK it created using $\mathcal{F}_{crypto}$ is corrupted. In this case, the instance still follows the protocol as expected but security will not be provided because the PMK is corrupted.

We note that this modeling (no KeyGen requests and all pre-shared keys are corrupted) implies that a corrupted instance never obtains a pointer to a key marked unknown (in $\mathcal{F}_{crypto}$). Hence, the adversary can use $\mathcal{F}_{crypto}$ (through corrupted instances) only with known keys and it is no problem if the adversary generates key cycles or causes the commitment problem with those known keys. Of course, since the adversary provides all algorithms and keys used in $\mathcal{F}_{crypto}$, she can encrypt and decrypt messages on her own, i.e., outside of $\mathcal{F}_{crypto}$.

In the literature, (static) corruption is often modeled on a per party basis, i.e., if a party is corrupted, then all its keys are corrupted and the adversary is in full control of that party. We note that this is a special case of our modeling of corruption because the adversary can decide to corrupt all keys and instances of a corrupted party.

The messages $c_1, \ldots, c_4$ consist of several fields. For simplicity of the analysis, our modeling ignores some of these fields or fixes them to be constants, as described next (conceptually, it would not be a problem to model these fields precisely): The messages $c_1, \ldots, c_4$ contain counters used for re-keying, which we ignore. The information contained in c_2 and c_3 for negotiating cipher suites and avoiding version rollback attacks is modeled as constants. Finally, we ignore an optional field in c_3 for multicast communication.

We now provide more insight into how message formats of the 4WHS protocol are modeled on the bit level. All four 4WHS messages are *EAPOL-Key frames*, see Figure 7.3, which are defined in the IEEE standard 802.11i, e.g., the field *Key Nonce*

Protocol Version – 1 octet	Packet Type – 1 octet	Packet Body Length – 2 octets	
Descriptor Type – 1 octet			
Key Information – 2 octets		Key Length – 2 octets	
Key Replay Counter – 8 octets			
Key Nonce – 32 octets			
EAPOL-Key IV – 16 octets			
Key RSC – 8 octets			
Reserved – 8 octets			
Key MIC – 16 octets			
Key Data Length – 2 octets		Key Data – n octets	

Figure 7.3.: EAPOL-Key frame [IEE07, Figure 8-23]

contains the nonces of the authenticator or supplicant, respectively, and the field *Key MIC* contains the MACs. Since every instance (of M_A and M_S) knows the bit strings of all parts of an EAPOL-Key frame, e.g., the nonces and MACs, it can easily construct precisely these EAPOL-Key frames. We note that, since our cryptographic model is asymptotic, the length of, e.g., keys and nonces depends on the security parameter η, and hence, we need to generalize EAPOL-Key frames so that the length of some fields depends on η.

Finally, we note that it is easy to see that $\mathcal{P}_{4WHS} \mid \mathcal{F}_{crypto}$ is environmentally strictly bounded.

Security Analysis

We now show that $\mathcal{P}_{4WHS}$ satisfies our criterion for $\mathcal{F}_{crypto}$-KE protocols from Section 7.4.2 (Definition 7.2).

Therefore, we first define a partnering function τ (as in Section 7.4.2) for $\mathcal{P}_{4WHS}$: Let ρ be a partial run of $\mathcal{E} \mid \mathcal{P}_{4WHS} \mid \mathcal{F}_{crypto}$ for some environment $\mathcal{E}$, $(lsid, r)$ be a user in ρ (i.e., $r \in \{A, B\}$), and α be the projection of ρ to the sequence of configurations of the instance $M_r[lsid]$. We define $\tau(\alpha)$ as follows: *(i)* If $M_r[lsid]$ is uncorrupted (i.e., in all configurations in α its flag corr is 0), $r = A$, and $M_r[lsid]$ has received the second protocol message, then $\tau(\alpha) := ((N_A, N_S), sp)$ where N_S is the nonce $M_r[lsid]$ received (in the second protocol message), N_A is the nonce $M_r[lsid]$ generated, and sp are the session parameters contained in $lsid$ (recall that $lsid = (lsid', sp)$ and $sp = (pid_A, pid_B, name_{PMK})$ for some $lsid', pid_A, pid_B, name_{PMK}$). *(ii)* If $M_r[lsid]$ is uncorrupted, $r = S$, and $M_r[lsid]$ has received the first protocol message, then $\tau(\alpha) := ((N_A, N_S), sp)$ where N_A is the nonce $M_r[lsid]$ received (in the first protocol message), N_S is the nonce $M_r[lsid]$ generated, and sp are the session parameters contained in $lsid$. *(iii)* Otherwise, $\tau(\alpha) := \bot$.

It is easy to see that τ is valid for $\mathcal{P}_{\text{4WHS}}$ (as defined in Section 7.4.2) because ideal nonces (i.e., nonces generated using $\mathcal{F}_{\text{nonce}}$) do not collide.

Theorem 7.3. $\mathcal{P}_{\text{4WHS}}$ *is a secure authenticated* $\mathcal{F}_{\text{crypto}}$-*KE protocol.*

Proof. Let τ be the valid partnering function for $\mathcal{P}_{\text{4WHS}}$ that we defined above, let $\mathcal{E} \in \text{Env}(\mathcal{P}_{\text{4WHS}} \,|\, \mathcal{F}_{\text{crypto}})$ be an environment of $\mathcal{P}_{\text{4WHS}} \,|\, \mathcal{F}_{\text{crypto}}$, and let ρ be a run of $\mathcal{E} \,|\, \mathcal{P}_{\text{4WHS}} \,|\, \mathcal{F}_{\text{crypto}}$ (for some security parameter η and external input a). Furthermore, let $M_r[\text{lsid}]$ be some uncorrupted instance (i.e., an instance of M_A or M_B) in ρ which has entered its key-usage phase (i.e., it has output Established to its user and $\text{key}(\text{lsid}, r)$ is its established session key in $\mathcal{F}_{\text{crypto}}$). That is, $M_r[\text{lsid}]$ has obtained a pointer to the pre-shared key PMK (using the GetPSK request) and pointers to the KCK and TK (using the Derive request) in $\mathcal{F}_{\text{crypto}}$.

First, we note that (a) and (d) of Definition 7.2 are trivially satisfied for ρ. The former by definition of τ and the latter because D is the domain of all bit strings.

Then, we observe that, by our modeling of corruption, since $M_r[\text{lsid}]$ is uncorrupted, the PMK is uncorrupted (in $\mathcal{F}_{\text{crypto}}$). Also, every other instance that has a pointer to the same PMK must be uncorrupted as well since keys created by corrupted instances are required to be corrupted. In uncorrupted instances, the PMK is only used to derive keys, hence, it is always marked unknown in $\mathcal{F}_{\text{crypto}}$. In particular, no corrupted instance has a pointer to this PMK. Now, by definition of $\mathcal{F}_{\text{crypto}}$, the KCK and TK can only be derived by instances that have a pointer to the PMK, leaving only uncorrupted instances. Moreover, again by $\mathcal{F}_{\text{crypto}}$, these uncorrupted instances have to use the same salt x as $M_r[\text{lsid}]$, which contains the constant `"Pairwise key expandion"`, two party names, and two nonces. Since nonces generated by $\mathcal{F}_{\text{nonce}}$ are guaranteed to be unique, by the construction of x, it follows that besides $M_r[\text{lsid}]$ at most one other (uncorrupted) instance $M_{r'}[\text{lsid}']$, for some lsid' and r', uses x, and hence, has a pointer to the same KCK and TK by key derivation. By definition of the protocol, the KCK and TK are never encrypted or retrieved and, by definition of $\mathcal{F}_{\text{crypto}}$, it follows that they are always marked unknown in $\mathcal{F}_{\text{crypto}}$ and only $M_r[\text{lsid}]$ and, if present, $M_{r'}[\text{lsid}']$ have pointers to these KCK and TK. This shows that (b) of Definition 7.2 holds for ρ.

We now show that $M_{r'}[\text{lsid}']$ exists and that $M_r[\text{lsid}]$ and $M_{r'}[\text{lsid}']$ are partners (according to τ), which implies that (c) and (e) of Definition 7.2 are satisfied for ρ: We assume that $r = A$; the proof for $r = S$ is similar. So, we have to show that $M_{r'}[\text{lsid}']$ exists, $r' = S$, $M_{r'}[\text{lsid}']$ received the first protocol message, $M_{r'}[\text{lsid}']$ and $M_r[\text{lsid}]$ agree on the nonces, and $sp = sp'$ where $sp = (pid_A, pid_S, \text{name}_{\text{PMK}})$ are the session parameters in lsid and $sp' = (pid_A', pid_S', \text{name}_{\text{PMK}}')$ are the session parameters in lsid'. Then, since we already know that $M_{r'}[\text{lsid}']$ is uncorrupted (if it exists), by definition of τ, this implies that $M_r[\text{lsid}]$ and $M_{r'}[\text{lsid}']$ belong to the same session. The instance $M_r[\text{lsid}]$ successfully verified the MAC in the message $(pid_S, N_S, c_2, \text{mac}_{\text{KCK}}(N_S, c_2))$ where N_S is the nonce $M_r[\text{lsid}]$ received (second protocol message). Since $r = A$ and the constants c_2 and c_3 are distinct, $M_r[\text{lsid}]$ has not created such a MAC itself. By definition of $\mathcal{F}_{\text{crypto}}$, $\text{mac}_{\text{KCK}}(N_S, c_2)$ can only have been created by some instance that has a pointer to KCK, which must be the (uncorrupted) instance $M_{r'}[lsid']$ from above. It follows that $r' = S$ because an uncorrupted instance with $r' = A$ would not create a MAC of such a form. Since $M_{r'}[lsid']$ has a pointer to KCK, it used the same PMK and the same salt (which contains the party names and nonces). Hence, $name_{PMK} = name'_{PMK}$. Furthermore, $pid_A = pid'_A$ and $pid_S = pid'_S$ or $pid_A = pid'_S$ and $pid_S = pid'_A$. By our assumption that a party does not play both the role of A and S with the same pre-shared key PMK, it follows that $pid_A = pid'_A$ and $pid_S = pid'_S$, and hence, $sp = sp'$. (Our assumption, and the implied fact, $pid_A = pid'_A$ and $pid_S = pid'_S$, is crucial; without it the proof would fail and, in fact, a reflection attack would be possible [HM05].) As for party names, we can conclude that $M_r[lsid]$ and $M_{r'}[lsid']$ agree on the nonces, except maybe on the order. More precisely, we conclude that $N_A = N'_A$ and $N_S = N'_S$ or $N_A = N'_S$ and $N_S = N'_A$ where N_A is the nonce generated by $M_r[lsid]$, N_S is the nonce received by $M_r[lsid]$ (in the second protocol message), N'_A is the nonce received by $M_{r'}[lsid']$ (in the first protocol message), and N'_S is the nonce generated by $M_{r'}[lsid']$. Since $M_{r'}[lsid']$ generated the MAC $mac_{KCK}(N_S, c_2)$, we have that $N_S = N'_S$, and hence, also $N_A = N'_A$. We conclude that $M_r[lsid]$ and $M_{r'}[lsid']$ are partners (according to τ). As mentioned above, this implies that (c) and (e) of Definition 7.2 hold for ρ.

We have shown that all conditions of Definition 7.2 are satisfied for every run of $\mathcal{E} \mid \mathcal{P}_{4WHS} \mid \mathcal{F}_{crypto}$ for every environment $\mathcal{E}$. Hence, $\mathcal{P}_{4WHS}$ is a secure authenticated $\mathcal{F}_{crypto}$-KE protocol. □

Using Theorems 7.2 and 7.3, we immediately obtain that $\mathcal{P}_{4WHS} \mid \mathcal{F}_{crypto}$ realizes the multi-session local-SID functionality $\widehat{\mathcal{F}}_{auth\text{-}keyuse} = \widehat{\mathcal{F}}^{\mathcal{F}^{auth}_{senc}}_{auth\text{-}keyuse}$ for authenticated key usability of authenticated symmetric encryption:

Corollary 7.1. $\mathcal{P}_{4WHS} \mid \mathcal{F}_{crypto} \leq \widehat{\mathcal{F}}_{auth\text{-}keyuse}$.

Trivially, $\mathcal{P}_{4WHS}$ is a standard protocol (as defined in Section 5.3.2) because it never encrypts an unknown key after it has been first used. We note that, by our modeling of corruption, corrupted instances do not have pointers to unknown keys, and hence, even upon corruption, no unknown key is encrypted after it has been first used. In fact, no key is encrypted at all by uncorrupted instances. It is therefore easy to see that $\mathcal{P}_{4WHS}$ is used-order respecting and non-committing. Using Corollary 5.1, we can replace $\mathcal{F}_{crypto}$ in $\mathcal{P}_{4WHS} \mid \mathcal{F}_{crypto}$ by its realization $\mathcal{P}_{crypto}$. We obtain:

$$\mathcal{P}_{4WHS} \mid \mathcal{P}_{crypto} \leq \widehat{\mathcal{F}}_{auth\text{-}keyuse} \ .$$

We note that $\mathcal{P}_{4WHS} \mid \mathcal{P}_{crypto}$, as mentioned above, precisely models the 4WHS protocol.

Furthermore, since the domain of plaintexts for $\mathcal{P}_{4WHS}$ is the domain of all bit strings and because $\mathcal{P}^*_{4WHS}$ (recall that $\mathcal{P}^*_{4WHS}$ outputs the session key instead of going entering the key-usage phase) is used-order respecting and non-committing (the argumentation is analogous to the one for $\mathcal{P}_{4WHS}$, see above), using Theorems 7.1

and 7.3, we immediately obtain that $P^*_{\text{4WHS}} \,|\, P_{\text{crypto}}$ realizes the multi-session local-SID functionality $\widehat{\mathcal{F}}_{\text{ake}}$ for authenticated key exchange:

Corollary 7.2. $P^*_{\text{4WHS}} \,|\, P_{\text{crypto}} \leq \widehat{\mathcal{F}}_{\text{ake}}$.

7.5. Universal Composition Without Pre-Established SIDs

In this section, we present a general universal composition theorem that does not assume pre-established SIDs (and their use in protocols). Let $\mathcal{P}$ be a multi-session real protocol using a multi-session local-SID functionality $\mathcal{F}'$ as a subprotocol (or a realization of it) and let $\mathcal{F}$ be a multi-session local-SID functionality. Informally, our theorem states that if $\mathcal{P} \,|\, \mathcal{F}'$ realizes $\mathcal{F}$ in a single-session setting, then $\mathcal{P} \,|\, \mathcal{F}'$ realizes $\mathcal{F}$ in the multi-session setting. The important point here is that, by definition of multi-session local-SID functionalities, no pre-established SIDs (nor their use in the protocol) are required. Before we state the theorem, we describe the class of multi-session real protocols that is considered in the theorem.

7.5.1. Class of Real Protocols

In our universal composition theorem without pre-established SIDs, we consider multi-session real protocols, as defined in Section 7.3, with the following extra restrictions: We only consider multi-session protocols $\mathcal{P}$ (i.e., $\mathcal{P} = !M_1 \,|\, \cdots \,|\, !M_n$ for some machines $M_1, \ldots, M_n$) that use one multi-session local-SID functionality $\mathcal{F}'$ (i.e., as defined in Section 7.2, $\mathcal{F}' = \mathcal{F}^{F'}_{\text{session}}$ for some ideal functionality F' that is a σ_{prefix}-session version) such that $\mathcal{F}'$ also has n roles and the following restrictions are satisfied. Basically, these restrictions only determine some aspects of corruption and that instances of M_r first uses $\mathcal{F}'$, to establish a session, before they do anything else. More precisely, we require the following:

1. $\mathcal{P} \,|\, \mathcal{F}'$ is environmentally strictly bounded.[62]

2. The machine M_r (for any $r \leq n$) connects to the I/O input and output tape of $\mathcal{F}'$ for role r.

3. Whenever an instance of M_r, say $M_r[\mathit{lsid}]$, sends/receives a message, then this message is prefixed by lsid. Hence, $M_r[\mathit{lsid}]$ appears to $\mathcal{F}'$ as the user (lsid, r).

   We note that, by definition of multi-session protocols, this is already required for output to its user (environment) and the adversary (network). Now, we additionally require this for messages to $\mathcal{F}'$.

---

[62] We note that, to prove our universal composition theorem, similar to Theorem 2.3, it would suffice to only assume that $\mathcal{P} \,|\, \mathcal{F}'$ is environmentally *almost* bounded. However, this stronger assumption simplifies the proof and is typically satisfied by real protocols.

4. An instance of M_r, say $M_r[lsid]$, ignores all input (i.e., does not change its internal state and ends an activation with empty output) until it receives the request $(lsid, \mathsf{Establish})$ on its I/O input tape from its user, except for corruption status requests (see below). Then, $M_r[lsid]$ forwards this request to the adversary and waits for a response of the form $(lsid, corr)$ with $corr \in \{0, 1\}$. While waiting for a response, $M_r[lsid]$ ignores all input from its user and other input from the adversary, except for corruption status requests (see below). If $corr = 1$ (the adversary decided to directly corrupt $M_r[lsid]$), then $M_r[lsid]$ sets its flag corr to 1 (recall from the definition of multi-session protocols that every instance of M_r has such a flag to record its corruption status) and returns the acknowledgment message $(lsid, \mathsf{Ack})$ to the adversary. From then on $M_r[lsid]$ forwards all messages from its user to the adversary and vice versa (except for corruption status requests, see below). We say that $M_r[lsid]$ has been *corrupted right from the start*. We note that the adversary is not given access to the ideal functionality $\mathcal{F}'$ in the name of $M_r[lsid]$ if $M_r[lsid]$ is corrupted right from the start. However, M_r may define other forms of corruption where this is possible. If $corr = 0$ (the adversary decided not to corrupt $M_r[lsid]$ right from the start), then $M_r[lsid]$ forwards the request $(lsid, \mathsf{Establish})$ to $\mathcal{F}'$ and waits for a response. Again, while waiting, $M_r[lsid]$ ignores all unexpected input (except for corruption status requests, see below). When it receives a response, $M_r[lsid]$ is not restricted anymore and can arbitrarily communicate with its user, the adversary, and $\mathcal{F}'$ (up to the above restriction that it prefixes all output by $lsid$ and that it must not set corr to 0 once it has been set to 1). This, in particularly, allows $M_r[lsid]$ to define other forms of corruption, e.g., adaptive corruption and/or corruption where the adversary obtains access to $\mathcal{F}'$ (in the name of user $(lsid, r)$). We note that, typically, $M_r[lsid]$ would set its flag corr to 1 if the user $(lsid, r)$ is corrupted in $\mathcal{F}'$ ($M_r[lsid]$ can learn this corruption status by asking $\mathcal{F}'$), but this is up to the definition of M_r.

5. Whenever $M_r[lsid]$ receives the corruption status request $(lsid, \mathsf{Corr?})$ from its user, $M_r[lsid]$ returns $(lsid, \mathsf{corr})$ (without doing anything else, i.e., the state of $M_r[lsid]$ remains unchanged), where corr is the corruption status flag of $M_r[lsid]$, as already mentioned above. This also holds while $M_r[lsid]$ is waiting for an $\mathsf{Establish}$ request from its user or a response from the adversary or $\mathcal{F}'$.

Our intuition is that the protocol $\mathcal{P}$ uses $\mathcal{F}'$ (or a realization of $\mathcal{F}'$) as a sub-protocol/functionality (e.g., to establish a session key or a secure channel) and that $\mathcal{P}$ also makes use of the session establishment process of $\mathcal{F}'$. For such protocols the above restrictions are mild. It is natural to assume that an instance may be corrupted right from the start and, if not corrupted, first starts running its subprotocol. We note that $\mathcal{F}'$ may model the combination of several functionalities (which then share the session establishment mechanism). So, the limitation that $\mathcal{P}$ may only use one ideal functionality is mitigated.

7.5.2. Single-Session Realizability

We now define the single-session realizability relation that is used in our universal composition theorem. Basically, this relation states that $\mathcal{P} \mid \mathcal{F}'$ realizes $\mathcal{F}$ w.r.t. environments that, in every run, create at most one instance of the machines in $\mathcal{P}$ per role such that these instances agree on the session parameters (which are part of the local SIDs) and on the SID (i.e., the corresponding users in $\mathcal{F}'$ have the same SID, if they have one at all). More precisely, this class of environments is defined as follows:

Definition 7.3. *Let* $\mathcal{P} = !M_1 \mid \cdots \mid !M_n$ *be a multi-session real protocol of the above class that uses a multi-session local-SID functionality* $\mathcal{F}' = \mathcal{F}^{F'}_{\text{session}}$. *An environment* $\mathcal{E} \in \text{Env}(\mathcal{P} \mid \mathcal{F}')$ *is called* single-session *(w.r.t.* $\mathcal{P} \mid \mathcal{F}'$*) if, for every run of the system* $(\mathcal{E} \mid \mathcal{P} \mid \mathcal{F}')(1^\eta, a)$ *(for every security parameter* η *and external input* a*), there exists an SID* $sid = (sid', sp)$ *(for some bit strings* sid' *and* sp*) such that:*

1. *For every role* r *at most one instance of* M_r *has been created (in this run) and, if this instance has been created, its local SID is* $(lsid', sp)$ *for some bit string* $lsid'$ *(i.e., all instances agree on the session parameters).*

2. *Every SID that has been set in* $\mathcal{F}_{\text{session}}$ *(in* $\mathcal{F}'$*) for any user (in this run) is* sid.

3. *Every message that* $\mathcal{E}$ *sent to* F' *(in this run) is prefixed by* sid *(i.e., of the form* (sid, m) *for some bit string* m*).*

The set of all environments $\mathcal{E} \in \text{Env}(\mathcal{P} \mid \mathcal{F}')$ *that are single-session is denoted by* $\text{Env}_{\text{single}}(\mathcal{P} \mid \mathcal{F}')$.

Similarly to strong simulatability (Definition 2.3), single-session realizability is now defined as follows:

Definition 7.4. *Let* $\mathcal{P}$ *and* $\mathcal{F}'$ *be as in Definition 7.3. Furthermore, let* $\mathcal{F}$ *be a multi-session local-SID functionality. We say that* $\mathcal{P} \mid \mathcal{F}'$ single-session realizes $\mathcal{F}$ *(denoted by* $\mathcal{P} \mid \mathcal{F}' \leq_{\text{single}} \mathcal{F}$*) if there exists a simulator* $\mathcal{S} \in \text{Sim}^{\mathcal{P} \mid \mathcal{F}'}(\mathcal{F})$ *such that for every single-session environment* $\mathcal{E} \in \text{Env}_{\text{single}}(\mathcal{P} \mid \mathcal{F}')$*:* $\mathcal{E} \mid \mathcal{P} \mid \mathcal{F}' \equiv \mathcal{E} \mid \mathcal{S} \mid \mathcal{F}$.

To be able to prove the composition theorem, we need to slightly restrict the simulator that is used to prove that $\mathcal{P} \mid \mathcal{F}'$ single-session realizes $\mathcal{F}$. Basically, we require that the simulator emulates $\mathcal{P} \mid \mathcal{F}'$ until a user gets corrupted (in $\mathcal{P}$ or in $\mathcal{F}'$) or gets assigned an SID by the environment. From then on, the simulator is not restricted anymore, except that the simulator only uses the SID provided by the environment in its interaction with $\mathcal{F}$ (the simulator does not make up its own SIDs). For this purpose, we define the following class of simulators:

Definition 7.5. *Let* $\mathcal{P}$*,* $\mathcal{F}'$*, and* $\mathcal{F}$ *be as in Definition 7.4, i.e.,* $\mathcal{P} = !M_1 \mid \cdots \mid !M_n$ *for some* $M_1, \ldots, M_n$*,* $\mathcal{F}' = \mathcal{F}^{F'}_{\text{session}} = \mathcal{F}_{\text{session}} \mid !F'$*, and* $\mathcal{F} = \mathcal{F}^{F}_{\text{session}} = \mathcal{F}_{\text{session}} \mid !F$ *for some ideal functionalities* F' *and* F *that are* σ_{prefix}-*session versions. In the following, we refer to* $\mathcal{F}_{\text{session}}$ *in* $\mathcal{F}'$ *by* $\mathcal{F}'_{\text{session}}$ *and to* $\mathcal{F}_{\text{session}}$ *in* $\mathcal{F}$ *by* $\mathcal{F}_{\text{session}}$.

We call a simulator $S \in \text{Sim}^{\mathcal{P} \,|\, \mathcal{F}'}(\mathcal{F})$ well-formed (w.r.t. $\mathcal{P} \,|\, \mathcal{F}'$ and $\mathcal{F}$) if $S \,|\, \mathcal{F}$ is environmentally strictly bounded[63] and S satisfies the following restrictions: S is a single IITM that accepts all messages in mode CheckAddress[64] and it is parameterized by a stateful, probabilistic algorithm A that takes a security parameter 1^η, an input message m, and an input tape name t as input and produces an output message m' and an output tape name t'. This algorithm A basically defines S but it is executed in a "sandbox", which we describe next. For every user $(lsid, r)$, S keeps track of the state of $(lsid, r)$, which initially is inactive. Note that because S will only run together with single-session environments, for every role r, there will be at most one user $(lsid, r)$.

1. Upon input m from $\mathcal{F}_{\text{session}}$:

   a) If $m = (\text{Establish}, lsid, r)$ (i.e., S receives an Establish request forwarded by $\mathcal{F}$), then S records $(lsid, r)$ as waiting-for-corruption and forwards the message $(\text{Establish}, lsid, r)$ to the environment in the name of M_r (i.e., on the network output tape of M_r). (Note that, by definition of our class of protocols, this is what M_r would do. We also note that the algorithm A is not "informed" about this request.)

   b) If $m = (\text{Input}, lsid, r, m')$, then S runs A with input m (and that security parameter and the network output tape name of $\mathcal{F}_{\text{session}}$) and forwards the output of A (i.e., sends the message that is output by A on the tape that is output by A).

   (Note that $\mathcal{F}_{\text{session}}$ will never send other messages to S.)

2. Upon input m from the environment for M_r (i.e., S receives m on its network input tape that corresponds to the one of M_r):

   a) If $m = (lsid, 1)$ and $(lsid, r)$ is waiting-for-corruption (i.e., the environment corrupts $M_r[lsid]$ right from the start), then S records $(lsid, r)$ as corrupted, runs A with input m, and forwards the output of A.

   b) If $m = (lsid, 0)$ and $(lsid, r)$ is waiting-for-corruption, then S records $(lsid, r)$ as waiting-for-$\mathcal{F}'$ and forwards $(\text{Establish}, lsid, r)$ to the environment in the name of $\mathcal{F}'_{\text{session}}$. (Note that, by definition of our class of protocols, this is what $\mathcal{P} \,|\, \mathcal{F}'$ would do and, again, the algorithm A is not "informed" about this request.)

   c) If $m = (lsid, m')$ and $(lsid, r)$ is corrupted or established-sid, then S runs A with input m and forwards the output of A.

   d) Otherwise, S produces empty output (i.e., ends this activation with empty output and waits for new input).

---

[63] We note that, by definition of $\text{Sim}^{\mathcal{P} \,|\, \mathcal{F}'}(\mathcal{F})$, $S \,|\, \mathcal{F}$ is already required to be environmentally *almost* bounded. The extra requirement that $S \,|\, \mathcal{F}$ is environmentally strictly bounded is typically satisfied but does not seem to be essential. It simplifies the proof of the composition theorem.

[64] By Lemma 2.1, this, in fact, is no restriction.

3. *Upon input m from the environment for $\mathcal{F}'_{\text{session}}$:*

     a) *If $m = (\text{Corr}, lsid, r)$ and $(lsid, r)$ is waiting-for-$\mathcal{F}'$ (i.e., the environment corrupts user $(lsid, r)$ in $\mathcal{F}'$), then $\mathcal{S}$ records $(lsid, r)$ as corrupted, runs A with input m, and forwards the output of A.*

     b) *If $m = (\text{Establish}, lsid, r, sid)$ and $(lsid, r)$ is waiting-for-$\mathcal{F}'$ (i.e., the environment sets the SID for user $(lsid, r)$ in $\mathcal{F}'$), then $\mathcal{S}$ records $(lsid, r)$ as established-sid, runs A with input m, and forwards the output of A.*

     c) *If $m = (\text{Output}, lsid, r, m')$ and $(lsid, r)$ is corrupted, then $\mathcal{S}$ runs A with input m and forwards the output of A.*

     d) *Otherwise, $\mathcal{S}$ produces empty output.*

4. *Upon input m from the environment for F': $\mathcal{S}$ runs A with input m and forwards the output of A.*

5. *Upon input m from F: $\mathcal{S}$ runs A with input m and forwards the output of A.*

Furthermore, we require that A only uses the SID that is used by the environment (since the environment is single-session, it uses at most one SID). That is, A does not invent new SIDs. More precisely, we require that (i) A only outputs $(\text{Establish}, lsid, r, sid)$ to $\mathcal{F}_{\text{session}}$ if $(lsid, r)$ is recorded as established-sid and that (ii) A only outputs (sid, m) to F if there exists $(lsid, r)$ such that $(lsid, r)$ is recorded as established-sid (otherwise, $\mathcal{S}$ will produce empty output instead).

We say that $\mathcal{P} \mid \mathcal{F}'$ single-session realizes $\mathcal{F}$ with a well-formed simulator (denoted by $\mathcal{P} \mid \mathcal{F}' \leq_{\text{single}*} \mathcal{F}$) if there exists $\mathcal{S} \in \text{Sim}^{\mathcal{P} \mid \mathcal{F}'}(\mathcal{F})$ such that $\mathcal{S}$ is well-formed and for every $\mathcal{E} \in \text{Env}_{\text{single}}(\mathcal{P} \mid \mathcal{F}')$: $\mathcal{E} \mid \mathcal{P} \mid \mathcal{F}' \equiv \mathcal{E} \mid \mathcal{S} \mid \mathcal{F}$.

Remark 7.1. We note that the algorithm A does not "see" the Establish requests sent from $\mathcal{F}_{\text{session}}$ to $\mathcal{S}$ and the one that $\mathcal{F}'_{\text{session}}$ forwards to the environment. For these messages, $\mathcal{S}$ does exactly what $\mathcal{P} \mid \mathcal{F}'$ would do: it forwards them to the environment. This is a mild restriction on the simulator because, typically, a simulator would simulate the real protocol anyway. In fact, we think that for most applications $\mathcal{P} \mid \mathcal{F}' \leq_{\text{single}} \mathcal{F}$ implies $\mathcal{P} \mid \mathcal{F}' \leq_{\text{single}*} \mathcal{F}$. Moreover, our restriction seems unavoidable in order to prove our composition theorem, as we explain below.

7.5.3. The Universal Composition Theorem

We can now state our universal composition theorem for the protocol class defined above that does not rely on pre-established SIDs (and their use in the protocol).

Theorem 7.4. *Let $\mathcal{P}$ be a multi-session real protocol of the above class that uses a multi-session local-SID functionality $\mathcal{F}'$ and let $\mathcal{F}$ be a multi-session local-SID functionality. If $\mathcal{P} \mid \mathcal{F}'$ single-session realizes $\mathcal{F}$ with a well-formed simulator (i.e., $\mathcal{P} \mid \mathcal{F}' \leq_{\text{single}*} \mathcal{F}$), then $\mathcal{P} \mid \mathcal{F}' \leq \mathcal{F}$.*

We note that Theorem 7.4 can be applied iteratively: For example, if $\mathcal{P}_1 \,|\, \mathcal{F}_1 \leq_{\text{single}*}$ $\mathcal{F}_2$ and $\mathcal{P}_2 \,|\, \mathcal{F}_2 \leq_{\text{single}*} \mathcal{F}_3$, then, by Theorem 7.4 and Theorem 2.1, $\mathcal{P}_2 \,|\, \mathcal{P}_1 \,|\, \mathcal{F}_1 \leq \mathcal{F}_3$.

We mentioned above that our restriction on single-session simulators (well-formedness) seems unavoidable in order to prove the above theorem. We now explain this and, thereby, sketch the proof of Theorem 7.4 (see Appendix D.1 for a full proof).

First, we recall that for the classical universal composition theorems (Theorems 2.2 and 2.3 and Canetti's composition theorem) the proof is by a hybrid argument. In the i-th hybrid system the environment emulates the first $< i$ sessions as real protocols (real sessions) and the last $> i$ sessions as ideal (single-session simulator plus ideal functionality). The i-th session is external. Since every session is identified by a pre-established SID, the environment knows exactly and from the start on which instances of machines form one session. In particular, it knows from the start on whether a session should be emulated as real or ideal and which messages must be relayed to the external session. In our setting, this does not work since we do not assume pre-established SIDs: Initially, the (hybrid) environment does not know to which session an instance $M_r[\text{lsid}]$ will belong. In particular, it does not know whether it will belong to an ideal or real session. This is only determined when the environment sets the SID for the user (lsid, r) in $\mathcal{F}'$ (or $M_r[\text{lsid}]$ gets corrupted right from the start or (lsid, r) gets corrupted in $\mathcal{F}'$ because then $M_r[\text{lsid}]$ does not belong to any session). So, unless an instance $M_r[\text{lsid}]$ does not behave the same in the ideal and real session up to this point, consistent simulation would not be possible. Now, by our assumption on the simulator (at first, it precisely simulates the real protocol), the environment can first simulate the real protocol for the instance $M_r[\text{lsid}]$. Once this instance gets assigned an SID in $\mathcal{F}'$ (more precisely, its corresponding user (lsid, r) gets an SID in $\mathcal{F}'$) or gets corrupted, the environment knows whether the instance belongs to an ideal or real session, and hence, the simulation can be continued accordingly. More concretely, if it turns out that $M_r[\text{lsid}]$ belongs to an ideal session, the environment simulates it using the single-session simulator for that session. This is possible because up to this point the simulator too would have only simulated this instance as the real protocol. For the i-th session, the environment guesses the instances that shall belong to it. Following this idea, we proved our composition theorem (see Appendix D.1 for the proof).

7.6. Joint State Composition Without Pre-Established SIDs

Universal composition theorems, such as Theorem 2.2, Theorem 2.3, and Canetti's composition theorem [Can05], assume that different protocol sessions have disjoint state; in particular, each session has to use fresh randomness. (Theorem 7.4 makes this assumption too, but we exclude this theorem from the following discussion since it does not assume pre-established SIDs.) As already discussed in Section 4.1.5, this can lead to inefficient and impractical protocols because, for example, in every session fresh long-term symmetric and public/private keys have to be used. Canetti and Rabin [CR03] therefore proposed to combine the universal composition theorems with what they called composition theorems with joint state. By now, joint state composition theorems for several cryptographic primitives are available, including joint state composition theorems for digital signatures and public-key encryption [CR03, KT08] (see also Section 4.2.6). In Section 5.4, we also presented a joint state theorem for $\mathcal{F}_{\mathrm{crypto}}$, i.e., for encryption, MAC, and key derivation with long-term symmetric keys. These theorems provide mechanisms that allow to turn a system with independent sessions (i.e., sessions with disjoint state) into a system where the same (long-term symmetric and public/private) keys may be used in different sessions. This joint state comes "for free" in the sense that it does not require additional proof. However, there is a price to pay: Just as the universal composition theorems, the joint state composition theorems assume pre-established SIDs. Moreover, the mechanisms used by the existing joint state theorems for specific cryptographic primitives, such as encryption and digital signatures, prefix *all* plaintexts to be encrypted (with long-term symmetric or public/private keys) and messages to be signed by the unique pre-established SIDs; by this, interference between different sessions is prevented. While this is a good design principle, these theorems are unsuitable for the modular analysis of an existing protocol that does not employ these mechanisms: If such a protocol is secure in the single-session setting, then its multi-session version obtained by combining universal composition with joint state composition, and hence, the version of the protocol in which messages are prefixed with pre-established SIDs, is secure as well. However, from this, in general, it does not follow that the original protocol, which may be drastically different, is also secure in the multi-session setting. In fact, by the above joint-state constructions insecure protocols might be turned into secure ones (see Figure 7.4). In particular, since real-world security protocols typically do not use pre-established SIDs, at least not explicitly and not in the particular way stipulated by the theorems, the joint state composition theorems are unsuitable for the modular and faithful analysis of such protocols; at most idealized/modified protocols, but not the original real-world protocols, can be analyzed in this modular way. For example, in step 3 of the TLS Handshake Protocol (see Figure 7.6 in Section 7.7.2), the client sends the pre-master secret (*PMS*) encrypted under the server's public key. In the variant of TLS obtained by the joint state theorems, a unique SID *sid* would be included in the plaintext as well (i.e., the client would send $\{\!|sid, PMS|\!\}_{k_S}$ instead of $\{\!|PMS|\!\}_{k_S}$). By this alone, unlike the original version of TLS, this message is bound to session *sid*.[65] Another example is the 4WHS protocol of WPA2, that we analyzed in Section 7.4.3: The variant obtained by the joint state theorem for $\mathcal{F}_{\mathrm{crypto}}$ (see Section 5.4) would add a unique SID *sid* to the salt upon key derivation. This alone directly guarantees that

---

[65] We note that the SID would also be added to the message signed by the client, i.e., the client would send $\mathrm{sig}_{k_C}(sid, handshake)$ instead of $\mathrm{sig}_{k_C}(handshake)$. One could argue that this modification of the TLS Handshake Protocol is not severe because *handshake* already contains session specific information (namely the client and server nonces), but it still modifies the original protocol.

	original	modified
1.	$A \rightarrow B$: $\{\!|N_A, pid_A|\!\}_{k_B}$	$\{\!|sid, N_A, pid_A|\!\}_{k_B}$
2.	$B \rightarrow A$: $\{\!|N_A, N_B|\!\}_{k_A}$	$\{\!|sid, N_A, N_B|\!\}_{k_A}$
3.	$A \rightarrow B$: $\{\!|N_B|\!\}_{k_B}$	$\{\!|sid, N_B|\!\}_{k_B}$

Figure 7.4.: The original Needham-Schroeder Public-Key (NSPK) protocol is insecure [Low95]. Its modified version, resulting from the joint-state construction, which prefixes every plaintext with a pre-established SID sid is secure (see Appendix D.3.1 for details).

only parties belonging to the same session derive the same keys. A crucial part in the security proof for the 4WHS protocol (Theorem 7.3) is to establish exactly this, i.e., to show that parties deriving the same session key, in fact, belong to the same session.

In the following, we therefore propose a composition theorem with joint state which does not require to modify the protocol under consideration. In particular, it does not rely on pre-established SIDs and the mechanism of prefixing messages with such SIDs. In this theorem we consider a multi-session real protocol $\mathcal{P}$ which uses the ideal crypto functionality $\mathcal{F}_{\text{crypto}}$ (see Chapter 5) extended by digital signatures and nonces, as described in Remark 5.4. In fact, we use a slightly modified version of $\mathcal{F}_{\text{crypto}}$ (see Section 7.6.1), that we denote by $\widetilde{\mathcal{F}}_{\text{crypto}}$. Every instance of a machine M_r in $\mathcal{P}$ has access to $\widetilde{\mathcal{F}}_{\text{crypto}}$. In other words, $\widetilde{\mathcal{F}}_{\text{crypto}}$ is the joint state of all sessions of $\mathcal{P}$: Different sessions may have access to the same public/private and symmetric keys in $\widetilde{\mathcal{F}}_{\text{crypto}}$. Now, informally speaking, our joint state composition theorem states that under a certain condition on $\mathcal{P}$, which we call *implicit (session) disjointness*, it is sufficient to analyze $\mathcal{P}$ (which may use $\widetilde{\mathcal{F}}_{\text{crypto}}$) in a single-session setting to obtain security in the multi-session setting, where all sessions may use the *same* (instance of the) ideal crypto functionality $\widetilde{\mathcal{F}}_{\text{crypto}}$. (We note that by the universal composition theorems, $\widetilde{\mathcal{F}}_{\text{crypto}}$ can be replaced by its realization.) It seems that most real-world protocols satisfy implicit disjointness and that this property can be verified easily, as illustrated by our case studies in Section 7.7.2.

7.6.1. Preliminaries

Before we state our criterion implicit disjointness and the joint state composition theorem without pre-established SIDs, we introduce some preliminaries.

The Augmented Ideal Crypto Functionality

As mentioned above, for our joint state composition theorem, we consider a slightly modified variant $\widetilde{\mathcal{F}}_{\text{crypto}}$ of our ideal crypto functionality $\mathcal{F}_{\text{crypto}}$ (Chapter 5). The variant $\widetilde{\mathcal{F}}_{\text{crypto}}$ allows users to delete pointers to keys and slightly strengthens the simulator (or adversary), which is needed in our proof of the joint state theorem.

More precisely, a user may send an additional request (Delete, ptr) to $\widetilde{\mathcal{F}}_{\text{crypto}}$ to delete the pointer ptr. Then, $\widetilde{\mathcal{F}}_{\text{crypto}}$ frees the pointer, i.e., ptr does not any longer point to any key. Furthermore, $\widetilde{\mathcal{F}}_{\text{crypto}}$ deletes all keys no pointers point to. (We note that Delete requests are needed by tests upon destruction requests in our criterion implicit disjointness, see Section 7.6.2.) The other modifications give the following extra power to the simulator: The first modification guarantees that the simulator always knows which keys are recorded in $\mathcal{F}_{\text{crypto}}$ and what their status (known/unknown) is. Note that, for $\mathcal{F}_{\text{crypto}}$, the simulator may not know this because the simulator is not informed when a key is marked known (e.g., upon encryption with a known key) or when new known keys are added via the I/O interface (e.g., upon a Store request). The second modification allows the simulator to let a request fail when, during the execution of this request, new keys are recorded, i.e., a key that has not been recorded yet is added as a known or unknown key (e.g., upon a KeyGen request or a decryption request with a known key). The third modification changes the way unauthenticated encryption (i.e., public-key encryption and symmetric encryption under keys of type $t \in \mathcal{T}_{\text{senc}}^{\text{unauth}}$) is performed. If the public/private key pair is uncorrupted or the symmetric key is unknown, respectively, then encryption and decryption are now interactive, i.e., the simulator is asked to provide a ciphertext/plaintext upon encryption/decryption.

We describe the modifications in more detail below. It is easy to see that $\mathcal{P}_{\text{crypto}}$ can be extended, in a natural way, to support Delete requests as well. The other modifications only strengthen the simulator. Hence, it is easy to see that the realization $\mathcal{P}_{\text{crypto}}$ of $\mathcal{F}_{\text{crypto}}$ (extended by Delete requests) is also a realization of $\widetilde{\mathcal{F}}_{\text{crypto}}$, i.e., the results from Section 5.3 (Theorem 5.1 and Corollary 5.1) carry over to $\widetilde{\mathcal{F}}_{\text{crypto}}$. On the other hand, these modifications do not strengthen the simulator too much, $\widetilde{\mathcal{F}}_{\text{crypto}}$ seems to be just as useful as $\mathcal{F}_{\text{crypto}}$ when analyzing protocols. We note that, in Chapter 4, we mentioned that local computation (i.e., non-interactive encryption/decryption as in $\mathcal{F}_{\text{crypto}}$) is useful when reasoning about protocols that use nested encryptions. For example, if a secret message is encrypted under a known key and the ciphertext is then encrypted under an unknown key, then the secret message is still not revealed. This kind of reasoning is still possible with $\widetilde{\mathcal{F}}_{\text{crypto}}$ because interactive encryption/decryption is only performed for unknown keys or uncorrupted public/private keys. Encryption/decryption under known keys or corrupted public/private keys is still non-interactive. We think that, in typical applications, for a protocol $\mathcal{P}$ that uses $\mathcal{F}_{\text{crypto}}$ and an ideal functionality $\mathcal{F}$, $\mathcal{P} \mid \mathcal{F}_{\text{crypto}} \leq \mathcal{F}$ if and only if $\mathcal{P} \mid \widetilde{\mathcal{F}}_{\text{crypto}} \leq \mathcal{F}$.

Delete requests.   A user uid can ask $\widetilde{\mathcal{F}}_{\text{crypto}}$ (more precisely, $\mathcal{F}_{\text{crypto}}^{\text{user}}[uid]$ in $\widetilde{\mathcal{F}}_{\text{crypto}}$) to delete one of its pointers ptr by sending the request (Delete, ptr) to $\widetilde{\mathcal{F}}_{\text{crypto}}$. Upon this request, $\mathcal{F}_{\text{crypto}}^{\text{user}}[uid]$ frees the pointer ptr such that it does not anymore point to any key. Furthermore, $\widetilde{\mathcal{F}}_{\text{crypto}}$ checks whether *(i)* there exists another pointer that points to the (typed) key, say κ, *ptr* points to, *(ii)* κ is a pre-shared key, *(iii)* there exists a recorded plaintext that contains κ, or *(iv)* the instance $\mathcal{F}_{\text{crypto}}^{\text{senc}}[\kappa]$, $\mathcal{F}_{\text{crypto}}^{\text{derive}}[\kappa]$, or $\mathcal{F}_{\text{crypto}}^{\text{mac}}[\kappa]$, respectively, has been created. If this check does not succeed (i.e., no pointer points to κ anymore, κ is not a pre-shared key, and κ only exists as a key in $\widetilde{\mathcal{F}}_{\text{crypto}}$ but has neither been used nor been encrypted under another key), then $\widetilde{\mathcal{F}}_{\text{crypto}}$ removes κ from $\mathcal{K}$ and, if it is marked known, also from $\mathcal{K}_{\text{known}}$. Then, $\widetilde{\mathcal{F}}_{\text{crypto}}$ informs the simulator that it removed κ from $\mathcal{K}$ (so that the simulator knows which keys are recorded in $\mathcal{K}$) and waits for an acknowledgment message from the simulator. Finally, in any case (whether the check succeeded or not), $\widetilde{\mathcal{F}}_{\text{crypto}}$ returns an acknowledgment message to the user.

We note that, the realization $\mathcal{P}_{\text{crypto}}$ of $\widetilde{\mathcal{F}}_{\text{crypto}}$, upon Delete requests, simply frees the pointer and returns an acknowledgment to the user (there is no set $\mathcal{K}$ where keys are recorded, so, there is no need to delete keys). The simulator/adversary is not informed about this request, so, this request is handled locally by $\mathcal{P}_{\text{crypto}}$ (more precisely, by $\mathcal{P}_{\text{crypto}}^{\text{user}}$).

Inform simulator about keys getting marked known. Whenever a key gets marked known in $\widetilde{\mathcal{F}}_{\text{crypto}}$, i.e., a (typed) key κ changes its status from unknown to known (note that this only happens in $\mathcal{F}_{\text{crypto}}^{\text{keys}}$ upon a MarkKnown request), then $\widetilde{\mathcal{F}}_{\text{crypto}}$ (more precisely, $\mathcal{F}_{\text{crypto}}^{\text{keys}}$ in $\widetilde{\mathcal{F}}_{\text{crypto}}$) sends the message (MarkedKnown, κ) to the simulator informing it that κ got marked known. $\widetilde{\mathcal{F}}_{\text{crypto}}$ then waits for receiving an acknowledgment message from the simulator and then continues normally.

Allow simulator to let adding keys fail. Whenever a key that is not yet recorded is recorded, i.e., a (typed) key $\kappa \notin \mathcal{K}$ is added to $\mathcal{K}$, which only happens upon a request of the form (Add, *status*, $\kappa_1, \ldots, \kappa_l$) to $\mathcal{F}_{\text{crypto}}^{\text{keys}}$ where $\kappa = \kappa_i$ for some $i \leq l$, then $\widetilde{\mathcal{F}}_{\text{crypto}}$ (more precisely, $\mathcal{F}_{\text{crypto}}^{\text{keys}}$ in $\widetilde{\mathcal{F}}_{\text{crypto}}$) sends the request (Add?, *status*, κ) to the simulator and waits for receiving *fail* $\in \{0, 1\}$ from the simulator. If *fail* $= 1$, then $\widetilde{\mathcal{F}}_{\text{crypto}}$ lets the request fail and ultimately $\perp$ is returned to the user who's request triggered this (i.e., $\widetilde{\mathcal{F}}_{\text{crypto}}$ continues as if the Add request in $\mathcal{F}_{\text{crypto}}^{\text{keys}}$ fails because an unknown key was guessed by the environment, in case *status* = known, or an unknown key is not fresh, in case *status* = unknown). Otherwise, $\widetilde{\mathcal{F}}_{\text{crypto}}$ continues normally.

Interactive, unauthenticated encryption and decryption with unknown/uncorrupted keys. Upon encryption of a plaintext x under a key κ of type $t \in \mathcal{T}_{\text{senc}}^{\text{unauth}}$ such that κ is marked unknown, $\mathcal{F}_{\text{crypto}}$ (more precisely, the instance $\mathcal{F}_{\text{crypto}}^{\text{senc}}[\kappa]$ in $\mathcal{F}_{\text{crypto}}$) would encrypt the leakage of x (we assume that x is already the formatted plaintext using $\text{format}_{\text{senc}}^t$; plaintext formatting is not changed), record the plaintext/ciphertext pair (x, y) for the key κ (where y is the obtained ciphertext), and returns y to the user. All this happens without interaction with the simulator. Now, $\widetilde{\mathcal{F}}_{\text{crypto}}$ (more precisely, $\mathcal{F}_{\text{crypto}}^{\text{senc}}[\kappa]$) computes the leakage $\overline{x}$ of x (just as $\mathcal{F}_{\text{crypto}}$) but then sends $(\text{Enc}, \kappa, \overline{x})$ to the simulator and waits for receiving a ciphertext y from the simulator. If (x', y) has already been recorded for some x' in $\widetilde{\mathcal{F}}_{\text{crypto}}$ for key κ (i.e., in $\mathcal{F}_{\text{crypto}}^{\text{senc}}[\kappa]$), then $\widetilde{\mathcal{F}}_{\text{crypto}}$ returns an error message to the simulator (i.e., $\widetilde{\mathcal{F}}_{\text{crypto}}$ ideally prevents collisions of ciphertexts) and again waits for receiving a ciphertext y from the simulator. Otherwise, $\widetilde{\mathcal{F}}_{\text{crypto}}$ records (x, y) for the key κ and returns y to the user (just as $\mathcal{F}_{\text{crypto}}$).

Upon decryption of a ciphertext y under a key κ of type $t \in \mathcal{T}_{\text{senc}}^{\text{unauth}}$ such that κ is marked unknown, $\widetilde{\mathcal{F}}_{\text{crypto}}$ (more precisely, $\mathcal{F}_{\text{crypto}}^{\text{senc}}[\kappa]$) checks if (x, y), for some x, has been recorded for some for the key κ. (Note that if this is the case, x is uniquely determined.) If this is the case, $\widetilde{\mathcal{F}}_{\text{crypto}}$ returns x (just as $\mathcal{F}_{\text{crypto}}$). Otherwise (i.e., (x, y) has not been recorded for κ, for any x), $\widetilde{\mathcal{F}}_{\text{crypto}}$ sends (Dec, κ, y) to the simulator and waits for receiving x from the simulator (x might be $\bot$, in which case, decryption fails). (Note that $\mathcal{F}_{\text{crypto}}$ would obtain x by decrypting x using the decryption algorithm provided by the adversary.) Then, just as $\mathcal{F}_{\text{crypto}}$, $\widetilde{\mathcal{F}}_{\text{crypto}}$ parses x, records keys in x as known keys (using the $(\text{Add}, \text{known}, \dots)$ request of $\mathcal{F}_{\text{crypto}}^{\text{keys}}$), and returns x to the user.

Encryption and decryption under public/private keys is changed analogously. Instead of κ being marked unknown, it is required that the public/private key pair *name* is uncorrupted.

We note that encryption and decryption is done exactly as in $\mathcal{F}_{\text{crypto}}$ if the symmetric key κ is of type $t \in \mathcal{T}_{\text{senc}}^{\text{auth}}$, κ is marked known, or the public/private key is corrupted.

Class of Real Protocols

In the following, we consider protocols of this form: $\mathcal{P}$ is a multi-session real protocol (as defined in Section 7.3, i.e., $\mathcal{P} = !M_1 \mid \cdots \mid !M_n$) that uses $\widetilde{\mathcal{F}}_{\text{crypto}}$ such that every instance of M_r (for all $r \leq n$), say $M_r[\textit{lsid}]$, appears to $\widetilde{\mathcal{F}}_{\text{crypto}}$ as the user $(\textit{lsid}, r)$. That is, it uses the user name $\textit{uid} = (\textit{lsid}, r)$ to communicate with $\widetilde{\mathcal{F}}_{\text{crypto}}$: Every message sent to $\widetilde{\mathcal{F}}_{\text{crypto}}$ is prefixed by $\textit{uid}$ and, in mode CheckAddress, a message from $\widetilde{\mathcal{F}}_{\text{crypto}}$ is accepted if and only if it is prefixed by $\textit{uid}$. In particularly, this means that every instance $M_r[\textit{lsid}]$ corresponds to the user $(\textit{lsid}, r)$ in $\widetilde{\mathcal{F}}_{\text{crypto}}$.

Recall from Section 7.3 that every instance of M_r has a flag corr $\in \{0, 1\}$ to record its corruption status and that, upon corruption status requests from the environment (on the I/O input tape), this corruption status is returned.

Furthermore, we require that $\mathcal{P} \mid \mathcal{F}$ is environmentally strictly bounded for every environmentally strictly bounded protocol system $\mathcal{F}$ that has the same I/O interface as $\mathcal{F}_{\text{crypto}}$.[66] Of course, this assumption is stronger than just assuming that $\mathcal{P} \mid \widetilde{\mathcal{F}}_{\text{crypto}}$

---

[66] We note that this assumption does not seem to be necessary to prove our joint state theorem

is environmentally (strictly) bounded. However, does not seem to be too strong for typical applications. In fact, all protocol systems considered in the old IITM model [Küs06] satisfy this assumption because they where assumed to be well-formed (an acyclic condition on the flow of messages). Also, the following class of protocols satisfies the assumption: If $\mathcal{P}$, in any run with any system, sends only a polynomial number of requests of polynomial length on the I/O output tapes to $\widetilde{\mathcal{F}}_{\text{crypto}}$ (and hence to $\mathcal{F}$), where the polynomial is in the security parameter and the length of input received from the environment (but not in the length of the input received on the I/O input tapes from $\widetilde{\mathcal{F}}_{\text{crypto}}$), then it can be shown that $\mathcal{P} \,|\, \mathcal{F}$ is environmentally strictly bounded for every environmentally strictly bounded system $\mathcal{F}$ that has the same I/O interface as $\widetilde{\mathcal{F}}_{\text{crypto}}$. The assumption that $\mathcal{P}$ only sends polynomially many requests of polynomial length is reasonable for most real protocols, e.g., for all protocols considered in our case studies (see Section 7.7.2).

In the following, whenever we say that $\mathcal{P}$ *is a multi-session protocol that uses* $\widetilde{\mathcal{F}}_{\text{crypto}}$ we mean the $\mathcal{P}$ is a protocol of the above form.

Well-Formed Environments

In our joint state composition theorem, we will slightly restrict the environment. We basically assume that it directly replies to network requests from $\widetilde{\mathcal{F}}_{\text{crypto}}$ (e.g., when $\widetilde{\mathcal{F}}_{\text{crypto}}$ asks the adversary, i.e., the environment on its network tapes, to generate a new key). More formally, we define the following class of environments:

Definition 7.6. *Let $\mathcal{P}$ be a multi-session real protocol that uses $\widetilde{\mathcal{F}}_{\text{crypto}}$. An environment $\mathcal{E} \in \text{Env}(\mathcal{P} \,|\, \widetilde{\mathcal{F}}_{\text{crypto}})$ is called* well-formed *(w.r.t. $\mathcal{P} \,|\, \widetilde{\mathcal{F}}_{\text{crypto}}$) if, in every run ρ of $\mathcal{E} \,|\, \mathcal{P} \,|\, \widetilde{\mathcal{F}}_{\text{crypto}}$ (for every security parameter and external input), it holds that: if a request is sent to $\widetilde{\mathcal{F}}_{\text{crypto}}$ on one of its I/O input tapes, at some point in ρ, then, at that point in ρ, $\widetilde{\mathcal{F}}_{\text{crypto}}$ is not waiting for a response on one of its network input tapes.*[67]

Similarly to strong simulatability (Definition 2.3), realizability w.r.t. for well-formed environments is now defined as follows:

Definition 7.7. *Let $\mathcal{P}$ be a multi-session real protocol that uses $\widetilde{\mathcal{F}}_{\text{crypto}}$ and let $\mathcal{F}$ be a multi-session local-SID functionality. We say that $\mathcal{P} \,|\, \widetilde{\mathcal{F}}_{\text{crypto}}$ realizes $\mathcal{F}$ w.r.t. well-formed environments (denoted by $\mathcal{P} \,|\, \widetilde{\mathcal{F}}_{\text{crypto}} \leq^* \mathcal{F}$) if there exists a simulator $\mathcal{S} \in \text{Sim}^{\mathcal{P} \,|\, \widetilde{\mathcal{F}}_{\text{crypto}}}(\mathcal{F})$ such that for every well-formed environment $\mathcal{E} \in \text{Env}(\mathcal{P} \,|\, \widetilde{\mathcal{F}}_{\text{crypto}})$:*
$$\mathcal{E} \,|\, \mathcal{P} \,|\, \widetilde{\mathcal{F}}_{\text{crypto}} \equiv \mathcal{E} \,|\, \mathcal{S} \,|\, \mathcal{F}.$$

---

but, at least, it simplifies the proof. It probably suffices to only assume that $\mathcal{P} \,|\, \widetilde{\mathcal{F}}_{\text{crypto}}$ is environmentally bounded. Then, one needs to show that all systems constructed in the proof are environmentally bounded (which becomes trivial by our assumption), which can probably be done using the same technique as in the proofs of Theorems 2.2 and 2.3, see [KT13].

[67]We note that we could relax the condition on well-formed environments such that it only needs to be satisfied for an overwhelming set of runs. However, this does not seem to make a significant difference.

Remark 7.2. We note that the restrictions we put on well-formed environments are very mild because $\widetilde{\mathcal{F}}_{\text{crypto}}$ only waits for input from the adversary to provide keys upon key generation or key derivation and to provide algorithms for cryptographic primitives. Furthermore, $\widetilde{\mathcal{F}}_{\text{crypto}}$ waits for input from the adversary when it sent one of the added messages that give more power to the adversary (see above). In a real implementation, all these requests correspond to local computations, and hence, it is very natural to assume that the environment directly replies to them. In particularly, given a protocol $\mathcal{P}$ that uses $\widetilde{\mathcal{F}}_{\text{crypto}}$, we are ultimately interested in the security of $\mathcal{P} \,|\, \mathcal{P}_{\text{crypto}}$ (where $\mathcal{P}_{\text{crypto}}$ is the realization of $\widetilde{\mathcal{F}}_{\text{crypto}}$, see above). Now, if we have that $\mathcal{P} \,|\, \widetilde{\mathcal{F}}_{\text{crypto}} \leq^* \mathcal{F}$ and $\mathcal{P}$ is non-committing and used-order respecting (see Section 5.3.2), then we can easily show that $\mathcal{P} \,|\, \mathcal{P}_{\text{crypto}}$ realizes $\mathcal{F}$ w.r.t. all environments that directly reply to network requests from $\mathcal{P}_{\text{crypto}}$. (This is easy to see because the simulator that we defined in the proof of Theorem 5.1, to show that $\mathcal{P}_{\text{crypto}}$ realizes $\mathcal{F}_{\text{crypto}}$, directly replies to most requests from $\mathcal{F}_{\text{crypto}}$.) Since the only network requests from $\mathcal{P}_{\text{crypto}}$ are to model corruption of pre-shared and public/private keys this basically does not restrict the environment.

Single-Session Realizability

Similar to Section 7.5, we now define a single-session realizability relation that is used in our joint state composition theorem. In Section 7.5, to group users into sessions, we used the SIDs provided to the multi-session local SID functionality $\mathcal{F}'$ that $\mathcal{P}$ used. Here, $\mathcal{P}$ uses $\widetilde{\mathcal{F}}_{\text{crypto}}$ instead of $\mathcal{F}'$, so, there is no session building mechanism in a subprotocol that we can use to group users into sessions. Instead, similar to Section 7.4.2, we use partnering functions that group users into sessions as follows.[68]

Partnering functions. A *partnering function* τ for a multi-session protocol $\mathcal{P}$ that uses $\widetilde{\mathcal{F}}_{\text{crypto}}$ is a polynomial-time computable function that maps a sequence $\alpha = (m_1, t_1), \ldots, (m_l, t_l)$ of message/tape pairs (m_i, t_i) sent and received by an instance of a machine M_r in $\mathcal{P}$, say $M_r[\mathit{lsid}]$ (i.e., the instance of M_r with local SID lsid), on its network tapes (i.e., $m_i = (\mathit{lsid}, m_i')$ for some $m_i' \in \{0,1\}^*$ and t_i is a network tape of M_r, for all $i \leq l$), to an SID $\mathit{sid} \in \{0,1\}^*$ (which is an arbitrary bit string), the special symbol corr $\notin \{0,1\}^*$ (which indicates corruption), or to the special symbol $\bot \notin \{0,1\}^* \cup \{\text{corr}\}$ (which indicates that the SID is still undefined).[69] For every environment $\mathcal{E}$ of $\mathcal{P} \,|\, \widetilde{\mathcal{F}}_{\text{crypto}}$, (partial) run ρ of $\mathcal{E} \,|\, \mathcal{P} \,|\, \widetilde{\mathcal{F}}_{\text{crypto}}$ (for any security

---

[68] The concept of partnering functions has been used to define security in game-based definitions, which led to discussions whether the obtained security notions are reasonable [BR93, BR95, BPR00, CK01, CH05, KSS09]. Here, we use partnering functions as part of our criteria but not as part of the security definition itself; security means realizing an ideal functionality.

[69] We note that in [KT11a] the special symbol corr was not used in the definition of partnering functions, instead partnering functions had to return $\bot$ in case of corruption. Using the symbol corr to explicitly signal corruption does not change the result that we obtain, it just allows for slightly more convenient notation. We further note that partnering functions in [KT11a] where defined based on sequences of configurations of $M_r[\mathit{lsid}]$, instead of sequences of the network messages sent/received by $M_r[\mathit{lsid}]$. However, in the proof of the joint state theorem in [KT11a],

parameter and external input), and user $(lsid, r)$, we define $\tau_{(lsid,r)}(\rho) := \tau(\alpha)$ where α is the projection of ρ to the sequence of message/tape pairs sent and received by $M_r[lsid]$ on its network tapes.

Given a (partial) run ρ of $\mathcal{E} \mid \mathcal{P} \mid \widetilde{\mathcal{F}}_{\text{crypto}}$, we say that a user $(lsid, r)$ *is corrupted w.r.t.* τ (in ρ) if $\tau_{(lsid,r)}(\rho) = \text{corr}$. Furthermore, we say that $(lsid, r)$ *belongs to session (with SID)* $sid \in \{0,1\}^*$ (in ρ) if $\tau_{(lsid,r)}(\rho) = sid$ and that $(lsid, r)$ *belongs to some session* (in ρ) if there exists $sid \in \{0,1\}^*$ such that $(lsid, r)$ belongs to session sid (in ρ). Moreover, we say that two users $(lsid, r)$ and $(lsid', r')$ *are partners* (or *belong to the same session*) in ρ if there exists an SID $sid \in \{0,1\}^*$ such that $(lsid, r)$ and $(lsid', r')$ belong to session sid in ρ (i.e., $\tau_{(lsid,r)}(\rho) = \tau_{(lsid',r')}(\rho) = sid$).

A partnering function τ is called *valid* for $\mathcal{P}$ if, for every environment $\mathcal{E}$ for $\mathcal{P} \mid \widetilde{\mathcal{F}}_{\text{crypto}}$ and every user $(lsid, r)$, the following holds with overwhelming probability, where the probability is taken over runs ρ of $(\mathcal{E} \mid \mathcal{P} \mid \widetilde{\mathcal{F}}_{\text{crypto}})(1^\eta, a)$:

1. Once an SID is assigned, it is fixed: If $\tau_{(lsid,r)}(\rho'') \neq \bot$ (i.e., $(lsid, r)$ belongs to a session or is corrupted), then it holds $\tau_{(lsid,r)}(\rho') = \tau_{(lsid,r)}(\rho'')$ for every prefix ρ' of ρ and every prefix ρ'' of ρ'.

2. Every session contains at most one user per role, i.e., for every partner $(lsid', r')$ of $(lsid, r)$ in ρ, it holds that $r \neq r'$ or $(lsid', r') = (lsid, r)$.

3. If $(lsid, r)$ is corrupted in ρ' (i.e., $\tau_{(lsid,r)}(\rho') = \text{corr}$), then $M_r[lsid]$ must have set its flag corr to 1 in ρ', for every every prefix ρ' of ρ.

4. If $M_r[lsid]$ has set its flag corr to 1 in ρ', then $(lsid, r)$ is corrupted or belongs to some session in ρ' (i.e., $\tau_{(lsid,r)}(\rho') \neq \bot$), for every every prefix ρ' of ρ.

5. The session parameters contained in the local SIDs correspond to the session parameters in the SIDs: If $\tau_{(lsid,r)}(\rho) = sid$ for some $sid \in \{0,1\}^*$, then $lsid = (lsid', sp)$ and $sid = (sid', sp)$ for some bit strings $lsid'$, sid', and sp.

We note that this definition of partnering functions is similar to the one in Section 7.4.2. One difference is that corruption is now signaled by τ. The more important difference is that α is now only the sequence of messages received/sent by an instance $M_r[lsid]$ on its network tapes whereas in Section 7.4.2 it is the sequence of configurations of $M_r[lsid]$ (which in particularly includes all sent and received messages). We need this is in the proof of the joint state theorem. For typical applications this does not seem to be a limitation (see, e.g., our case studies in Section 7.7.2).

We further note that the conditions for valid partnering functions require that if a user $(lsid, r)$ is corrupted (according to τ), then the corresponding instance $M_r[lsid]$ must be corrupted (i.e., $M_r[lsid]$ set its flag corr to 1) and that if $M_r[lsid]$ is corrupted, then $(lsid, r)$ is corrupted or belongs to some session (according to τ). So, corruption

---

it was overlooked that the output of the partnering function must be predictable given only the network messages.

according to τ does not exactly correspond to corruption according to $\mathcal{P}$. An instance $M_r[lsid]$ might set its flag corr to 1 after τ has assigned an SID to $(lsid, r)$. Then $(lsid, r)$ would belong to some session and would not be corrupted (according to τ) but $M_r[lsid]$ would be corrupted. This allows more flexibility in modeling corruption (e.g., see Section 7.7.2).

We further note that, in practice, partnering functions are typically very simple. In our case studies (Section 7.7.2), we use conceptually the same partnering function for all protocols; basically partners are determined based on the exchanged nonces.

The single-session realizability relation.   Now, based on partnering functions of the above form, we define single-session realizability. Basically, this relation states that $\mathcal{P} \,|\, \widetilde{\mathcal{F}}_{\mathrm{crypto}}$ realizes $\mathcal{F}$ w.r.t. well-formed environments that only create a single session. Creating only a single session means that the environment only creates one instance of the machines in $\mathcal{P}$ per role and that these instances belong to the same session (according to some partnering function). This class of environments is defined as follows (the definition is similar to Definition 7.3):

Definition 7.8. *Let $\mathcal{P} = !M_1 \,|\, \cdots \,|\, !M_n$ be a multi-session real protocol that uses $\widetilde{\mathcal{F}}_{\mathrm{crypto}}$ and let τ be a valid partnering function for $\mathcal{P}$. We call an environment $\mathcal{E} \in \mathrm{Env}(\mathcal{P} \,|\, \widetilde{\mathcal{F}}_{\mathrm{crypto}})$ single-session w.r.t. τ (and $\mathcal{P} \,|\, \widetilde{\mathcal{F}}_{\mathrm{crypto}}$) if it is well-formed (Definition 7.6) and, for every run ρ of the system $\mathcal{E} \,|\, \mathcal{P} \,|\, \widetilde{\mathcal{F}}_{\mathrm{crypto}}$ (for any security parameter and external input), there exists an SID $sid = (sid', sp)$ (for some bit strings sid' and sp) such that:*

1. *For every role r, at most one instance of M_r has been created (in this run ρ) and if this instance has been created, then its local SID is $(lsid', sp)$ for some bit string $lsid'$ (i.e., all instances agree on the session parameters).*

2. *For every user $(lsid, r)$ it holds that $\tau_{(lsid,r)}(\rho) = \bot$ or $\tau_{(lsid,r)}(\rho) = sid$ (i.e., no user is corrupted and all users belong to the same session or their SID is not determined yet).*

The set of all environments $\mathcal{E} \in \mathrm{Env}(\mathcal{P} \,|\, \widetilde{\mathcal{F}}_{\mathrm{crypto}})$ that are single-session w.r.t. τ is denoted by $\mathrm{Env}_{\tau\text{-single}}(\mathcal{P} \,|\, \widetilde{\mathcal{F}}_{\mathrm{crypto}})$.

We note that single-session environments never corrupt users (at least not according to τ). We could have allowed this. However, disallowing this only makes the environment (which is the distinguisher) weaker, and hence, single-session realizability easier to prove. In the proof of the joint state composition theorem, the case of corruption is simple because the simulator can corrupt the user in $\mathcal{F}$ and then exactly simulate the protocol instance, so, we do not need to consider corruption (according to τ) in the single-session setting.

Similarly to single-session realizability in Section 7.5 (Definition 7.4), single-session realizability w.r.t. a partnering function is defined as follows:

Definition 7.9. *Let $\mathcal{P}$ and τ be as in Definition 7.8 and let $\mathcal{F}$ be a multi-session local-SID functionality. We say that $\mathcal{P} \,|\, \widetilde{\mathcal{F}}_{\mathrm{crypto}}$ single-session realizes $\mathcal{F}$ w.r.t. τ (denoted by $\mathcal{P} \,|\, \widetilde{\mathcal{F}}_{\mathrm{crypto}} \leq_{\tau\text{-single}} \mathcal{F}$) if there exists a simulator $\mathcal{S} \in \mathrm{Sim}^{\mathcal{P} \,|\, \widetilde{\mathcal{F}}_{\mathrm{crypto}}}(\mathcal{F})$ such that for every single-session environment $\mathcal{E} \in \mathrm{Env}_{\tau\text{-single}}(\mathcal{P} \,|\, \widetilde{\mathcal{F}}_{\mathrm{crypto}})$: $\mathcal{E} \,|\, \mathcal{P} \,|\, \widetilde{\mathcal{F}}_{\mathrm{crypto}} \equiv \mathcal{E} \,|\, \mathcal{S} \,|\, \mathcal{F}$.*

As in Section 7.5, to be able to prove the joint state composition theorem, we need to restrict the simulator that is used to prove that $\mathcal{P} \,|\, \widetilde{\mathcal{F}}_{\mathrm{crypto}}$ single-session realizes $\mathcal{F}$ (w.r.t. τ). For this purpose, we define the following class of simulators:

Definition 7.10. *Let $\mathcal{P}$, τ, and $\mathcal{F}$ be as in Definition 7.9. We call a simulator $\mathcal{S} \in \mathrm{Sim}^{\mathcal{P} \,|\, \widetilde{\mathcal{F}}_{\mathrm{crypto}}}(\mathcal{F})$ well-formed (w.r.t. $\mathcal{P} \,|\, \widetilde{\mathcal{F}}_{\mathrm{crypto}}$, τ, and $\mathcal{F}$) if $\mathcal{S}$ is an IITM such that $\mathcal{S} \,|\, \mathcal{F}$ is environmentally strictly bounded[70] and $\mathcal{S}$ operates in two stages as follows: In the first stage, $\mathcal{S}$ simply emulates the system $\mathcal{P} \,|\, \widetilde{\mathcal{F}}_{\mathrm{crypto}}$, where* Establish *messages from $\mathcal{F}$ are forwarded to the emulated $\mathcal{P}$. When $\tau(\alpha_1) = \cdots = \tau(\alpha_n) = sid_0$ for some $sid_0 \in \{0,1\}^*$ (i.e., all users belong to the same session) where α_r is the current sequence of message/tape pairs sent/received by the emulated instances of M_r (there is at most one instance of M_r per role r because the environment is single-session) on its network tapes, then $\mathcal{S}$ enters its second stage. Once in the second stage, $\mathcal{S}$ is not restricted anymore, except that we require that: (i) Whenever $\mathcal{S}$ sends a message of the form* (Establish, $lsid, r, sid$) *to $\mathcal{F}_{\mathrm{session}}$ in $\mathcal{F}$ (to set the SID for user $(lsid, r)$ to sid), then $sid = sid_0$ (where sid_0 is the SID above, when $\mathcal{S}$ entered its second stage), (ii) $\mathcal{S}$ never sends a message of the form* (Corr, $lsid, r$) *to $\mathcal{F}_{\mathrm{session}}$ in $\mathcal{F}$ (to corrupt a user in $\mathcal{F}_{\mathrm{session}}$), and (iii) whenever $\mathcal{S}$ sends a message to F in $\mathcal{F}$ (where $\mathcal{F} = \mathcal{F}^F_{\mathrm{session}} = \mathcal{F}_{\mathrm{session}} \,|\, !F$), then this message is of the form (sid_0, m). (That is, $\mathcal{S}$ does not invent SIDs but uses the SID provided by the partnering function.) If, in the first stage, the emulated $\mathcal{P} \,|\, \widetilde{\mathcal{F}}_{\mathrm{crypto}}$ produces I/O output, then $\mathcal{S}$ terminates. (In this case the simulation fails, see Remark 7.3.)*

We say that $\mathcal{P} \,|\, \widetilde{\mathcal{F}}_{\mathrm{crypto}}$ single-session realizes $\mathcal{F}$ w.r.t. τ with a well-formed simulator (denoted by $\mathcal{P} \,|\, \widetilde{\mathcal{F}}_{\mathrm{crypto}} \leq_{\tau\text{-single}*} \mathcal{F}$) if there exists $\mathcal{S} \in \mathrm{Sim}^{\mathcal{P} \,|\, \widetilde{\mathcal{F}}_{\mathrm{crypto}}}(\mathcal{F})$ such that $\mathcal{S}$ is well-formed and for every $\mathcal{E} \in \mathrm{Env}_{\tau\text{-single}}(\mathcal{P} \,|\, \widetilde{\mathcal{F}}_{\mathrm{crypto}})$: $\mathcal{E} \,|\, \mathcal{P} \,|\, \widetilde{\mathcal{F}}_{\mathrm{crypto}} \equiv \mathcal{E} \,|\, \mathcal{S} \,|\, \mathcal{F}$.

Before we comment on the restrictions on well-formed simulators, we define a property called mutual authentication for protocols and multi-session local-SID functionalities. We will then argue (Remark 7.3) that the restrictions are mild if $\mathcal{P}$ or $\mathcal{F}$ provides mutual authentication.

Let $\mathcal{P}$ and τ be as in the above definitions. We say that $\mathcal{P}$ provides *mutual authentication* w.r.t. τ if, in every run of $(\mathcal{E} \,|\, \mathcal{P} \,|\, \widetilde{\mathcal{F}}_{\mathrm{crypto}})(1^\eta, a)$ for every environment $\mathcal{E} \in \mathrm{Env}(\mathcal{P} \,|\, \widetilde{\mathcal{F}}_{\mathrm{crypto}})$, security parameter η, and external input a (except maybe for a negligible set of runs), every instance of $M_1, \ldots, M_n$, say $M_r[lsid]$, that produced

---

[70] We note that, by definition of $\mathrm{Sim}^{\mathcal{P} \,|\, \widetilde{\mathcal{F}}_{\mathrm{crypto}}}(\mathcal{F})$, $\mathcal{S} \,|\, \mathcal{F}$ is only required to be environmentally almost bounded. The extra requirement that $\mathcal{S} \,|\, \mathcal{F}$ is environmentally strictly bounded does not seem to be essential but simplifies the proof of the joint state composition theorem.

I/O output to $\mathcal{E}$ (except for responses to corruption status requests) in ρ, say just after the partial run ρ', belongs to a complete session or is corrupted (according to τ in ρ'), i.e., $\tau_{(lsid,r)}(\rho') = \mathsf{corr}$ or $\tau_{(lsid_1,1)}(\rho') = \cdots = \tau_{(lsid_n,n)}(\rho') \neq \bot$ for some $lsid_1, \ldots, lsid_n \in \{0,1\}^*$ such that $lsid_r = lsid$.

We say that a multi-session local-SID functionality $\mathcal{F} = \mathcal{F}^F_{\mathrm{session}}$ provides *mutual authentication* if F in $\mathcal{F}$ is defined such that every instance of F only produces I/O output (except for responses to corruption status requests) once it has received an Establish requests for *every* role.[71] For example, if F is a variant of authenticated versions of the ideal functionalities for key exchange, key usability, or secure channel from Section 4.3, then $\mathcal{F}$ provides mutual authentication.[72]

We can show that, basically, if a protocol $\mathcal{P} \,|\, \widetilde{\mathcal{F}}_{\mathrm{crypto}}$ realizes a multi-session local-SID functionality $\mathcal{F}$ that provides mutual authentication, then $\mathcal{P}$ provides mutual authentication too. More precisely, let us assume that $\mathcal{P} \,|\, \widetilde{\mathcal{F}}_{\mathrm{crypto}} \leq \mathcal{F}$ and that τ is a valid partnering function for $\mathcal{P}$ such that the SIDs assigned by τ correspond to the SIDs assigned by a simulator $\mathcal{S}$ for $\mathcal{P} \,|\, \widetilde{\mathcal{F}}_{\mathrm{crypto}} \leq \mathcal{F}$ (i.e., $\mathcal{E} \,|\, \mathcal{P} \,|\, \widetilde{\mathcal{F}}_{\mathrm{crypto}} \equiv \mathcal{E} \,|\, \mathcal{S} \,|\, \mathcal{F}$ for all environments $\mathcal{E}$). That is, in every run of $(\mathcal{E} \,|\, \mathcal{S} \,|\, \mathcal{F})(1^\eta, a)$ (for every environment $\mathcal{E}$, η, a; except maybe for a negligible set of runs), if $\mathcal{S}$ sets the SID of some user $(lsid, r)$ in $\mathcal{F}_{\mathrm{session}}$ in $\mathcal{F}$ to sid, then $\tau(\alpha) = sid$ where α is the sequence of message/tape pairs sent/received by $\mathcal{S}$ on the network tapes of M_r where the messages are all prefixed by $lsid$. Furthermore, if $\mathcal{S}$ corrupts some user $(lsid, r)$ in $\mathcal{F}_{\mathrm{session}}$ in $\mathcal{F}$, then $\tau(\alpha) = \mathsf{corr}$ where α is as above. Then, it is easy to see that $\mathcal{P}$ provides mutual authentication w.r.t. τ if $\mathcal{F}$ provides mutual authentication.

We now comment on the restrictions on well-formed simulators.

Remark 7.3. In the first stage we basically put two restrictions on a well-formed simulator $\mathcal{S}$: First, it has to precisely emulate the real protocol. Second, it has to abort simulation if an emulated instance produces I/O output. However, the first restriction is what simulators typically do anyway. The second restriction of course restricts the simulator. Basically, it requires that the protocol provides mutual authentication (at least in a single-session setting without corruptions). We think that this second restriction could be relaxed such that our joint state composition theorem also becomes useful for analyzing protocols that do not provide mutual authentication, see Chapter 8. However, if $\mathcal{F}$ does provide mutual authentication, then the second restriction is in fact no restriction because then the protocol provides mutual authentication (for some partnering function), as shown above. So, if we

---

[71] We note that in [KT11a], by definition, all multi-session local-SID functionality provide mutual authentication because the simulator can only create complete sessions that consist of active users.

[72] We note that, e.g., $\widehat{\mathcal{F}}_{\mathrm{ake}} = \mathcal{F}^{\mathcal{F}_{\mathrm{ake}}}_{\mathrm{session}}$ (see Section 4.3) does not provide mutual authentication because $\mathcal{F}_{\mathrm{ake}}$ allows corruption. But we could consider a variant of $\widehat{\mathcal{F}}_{\mathrm{ake}}$ that does not allow corruption (corruption is anyway modeled in $\mathcal{F}_{\mathrm{session}}$) and then $\widehat{\mathcal{F}}_{\mathrm{ake}}$ would provide mutual authentication.

restrict ourselves to ideal functionalities (and, hence, protocols) that provide mutual authentication, the simulator is not restricted by this requirement.[73]

Furthermore, we note that partnering functions for practical protocols are typically very simple and decide very fast on the SIDs. For example, all partnering functions that we use in our case studies (Section 7.7.2) determine the SID of an instance after the first two protocol messages (based on the nonces contained in these messages), and hence, the simulator can enter its second phase very early.

In fact, we think that for most applications, if $\mathcal{F}$ provides mutual authentication, then $\mathcal{P} \,|\, \widetilde{\mathcal{F}}_{\mathrm{crypto}} \leq_{\tau\text{-single}} \mathcal{F}$ implies $\mathcal{P} \,|\, \widetilde{\mathcal{F}}_{\mathrm{crypto}} \leq_{\tau\text{-single*}} \mathcal{F}$.

7.6.2. Implicit Disjointness

We now introduce the notion of *implicit (session) disjointness*, already mentioned at the beginning of Section 7.6. Recall that we are interested in the security of the system $\mathcal{P} \,|\, \widetilde{\mathcal{F}}_{\mathrm{crypto}}$, where $\mathcal{P}$ is a multi-session protocol that uses $\widetilde{\mathcal{F}}_{\mathrm{crypto}}$ (i.e., all sessions use the same $\widetilde{\mathcal{F}}_{\mathrm{crypto}}$). As explained before, implicit disjointness is a condition on $\mathcal{P}$ which should allow us to analyze the security of $\mathcal{P}$ in the single-session setting (i.e., w.r.t. single-session environments) in order to obtain security of $\mathcal{P}$ in the multi-session setting, without assuming pre-established SIDs and without modifying $\mathcal{P}$. Intuitively, implicit disjointness is a condition that ensures that different sessions of $\mathcal{P}$ cannot "interfere", even though they share state, in the form of information stored in $\widetilde{\mathcal{F}}_{\mathrm{crypto}}$, including public/private and pre-shared keys, and the information stored along with these keys, e.g., plaintext/ciphertext pairs. In order to define the notion of implicit disjointness, we first introduce some notation and terminology.

Construction and Destruction Requests

We call an encryption, MAC, and sign request (for $\widetilde{\mathcal{F}}_{\mathrm{crypto}}$ by an instance M_r of $\mathcal{P}$, i.e., a user) a *construction* request and a decryption, MAC verification, and signature verification request a *destruction* request.

We say that a construction or destruction request is *ideal* (w.r.t. a configuration of $\widetilde{\mathcal{F}}_{\mathrm{crypto}}$) if the key used in the request is marked unknown in $\widetilde{\mathcal{F}}_{\mathrm{crypto}}$ or is an uncorrupted public/private key in $\widetilde{\mathcal{F}}_{\mathrm{crypto}}$ and, in case of a decryption request, the ciphertext in that request is stored in $\widetilde{\mathcal{F}}_{\mathrm{crypto}}$ (and hence, it was produced by $\widetilde{\mathcal{F}}_{\mathrm{crypto}}$ and the corresponding stored plaintext is returned).

Now, roughly speaking, implicit disjointness says that whenever some user sends a destruction request, then the user who sent the "corresponding" construction request belongs to the same session according to τ. This formulation is, however, too strong. For example, an adversary could send a ciphertext coming from one session to a different session where it is successfully decrypted but further inspection of the plaintext might lead to the rejection of the message (e.g., because excepted nonces

---

[73]We note that [KT11a], by their definition of multi-session local-SID functionalities, restricted themselves to such functionalities.

did not appear or MAC/signature verification failed). We therefore need to introduce the notion of a *successful* destruction request. For this purpose, we introduce what we call *tests*.

Tests and Successful Destruction Requests

We assume that a user $(lsid, r)$ (more precisely, the corresponding instance $M_r[lsid]$ of M_r) after every destruction request runs some deterministic algorithm T which takes as input the response to the destruction request and outputs a bit string or the special error symbol $\bot$. If the test T outputs $\bot$, we say that it *rejected* the response and, otherwise, we say that it *accepted* the response. We now describe the requirements on T informally (see below for a formal definition): If the destruction request is a MAC/signature verification request, then T rejects (i.e., returns $\bot$) if the verification did not succeed (i.e., $\widetilde{\mathcal{F}}_{\text{crypto}}$ did not return 1). If the destruction request is a decryption request, but decryption failed (i.e., $\widetilde{\mathcal{F}}_{\text{crypto}}$ returned $\bot$), then T rejects. Otherwise, i.e., decryption did not fail, and hence, a plaintext was returned, T is free to accept or reject. In the latter case—reject—, we require that, all pointers to keys in $\widetilde{\mathcal{F}}_{\text{crypto}}$ that are returned along with the plaintext are deleted in $\widetilde{\mathcal{F}}_{\text{crypto}}$ (using Delete requests). Furthermore, we always require that the state of $M_r[lsid]$ (i.e., its configuration), after T has rejected, does not depend on the response to the destruction request.

For example, this form of tests allows to check that the returned plaintext contains a particular party name or nonce. However, it does not yet allow to base the result of the test on the result of decrypting nested encryptions or the verification result of embedded MACs/signatures. Therefore, the algorithm T may itself make destruction requests (but no construction requests), which are subject to the same constraints. Also, key derivation requests and tests for equality of keys are allowed within a test. The requirements on T reflect what protocols typically do (see below for examples). Furthermore, we note that the assumption that the protocol does such tests is not a restriction on the protocol because the protocol can always decide to use the test that always accepts and returns the response (Example 7.2 (1)).

Formally, we require that the instances of M_r never directly send construction requests to $\widetilde{\mathcal{F}}_{\text{crypto}}$ but instead call the algorithm send-req that is defined in Figure 7.5 with some inputs req and T. The algorithm send-req is executed without side-effects on the state (i.e., configuration) of the instance of M_r that calls this algorithm. However, it may have side-effects on the state of $\widetilde{\mathcal{F}}_{\text{crypto}}$. Basically, send-req$(req, T)$ sends the request req to $\widetilde{\mathcal{F}}_{\text{crypto}}$ and waits for a response res. Then, it calls T on input res. The bit string T is thereby interpreted as a deterministic algorithm that outputs a tuple of the form (out, req', T') with $out, req', T' \in \{0, 1\}^* \cup \{\bot\}$. More precisely, send-req deterministically emulates T on input res. If this emulation fails, we set the output of T to $(\bot, \bot, \bot)$. The idea is that T has three choices: *(i)* it may accept, in which case T outputs $(out, \bot, \bot)$ and $out \in \{0, 1\}^*$ is the result of the algorithm (e.g., $out = res$); *(ii)* it may reject, in which case T outputs $(\bot, \bot, \bot)$ and $\bot$ is the

function send-req(req, T):
    if req is not a destruction (Dec, Verify, etc.), Derive, or Equal? request:
        return $\bot$ {*reject if req is not an allowed request*
    send req **to** $\widetilde{\mathcal{F}}_{\text{crypto}}$; **recv** res **from** $\widetilde{\mathcal{F}}_{\text{crypto}}$ {*send request req, receive response res*
    if $res = \bot \vee (res = 0 \wedge req$ is a MAC or signature verification request):
        return $\bot$ {*reject the response if it is $\bot$ or verification failed*
    $(out, req', T') := T(res)$ {*run test T on response res*
    if $req' \neq \bot$:   {*T wants to perform another request req' before deciding*
        $out := $ send-req(req', T')   {*recursively call* send-req
    if $out = \bot$:   {*delete all pointers contained in res*
        let $ptr_1, \ldots, ptr_l$ be the pointers contained in res
                 {*this list is empty if req is not a Dec, DecPKE, or Derive request*
        for all $i \in \{1, \ldots, l\}$ **do**: **send** (Delete, ptr_i) **to** $\widetilde{\mathcal{F}}_{\text{crypto}}$; **recv** Ack **from** $\widetilde{\mathcal{F}}_{\text{crypto}}$
    return out

Figure 7.5.: Tests for destruction requests. Formally, when an instance $M_r[lsid]$ runs this algorithm, then all messages to/from $\widetilde{\mathcal{F}}_{\text{crypto}}$ are prefixed by the user identifier $(lsid, r)$ and they are sent/received on the r-th input/output tape of $\widetilde{\mathcal{F}}_{\text{crypto}}$. The inputs req and T are arbitrary bit strings; T is interpreted as a deterministic algorithm that returns tuples of the form (out, req', T') with $out, req', T' \in \{0,1\}^* \cup \{\bot\}$.

result of the algorithm; or *(iii)* it may be undecided and wants to perform another request req' with test T', in which case T outputs $(\bot, req', T')$ and this will trigger the recursive call send-req(req', T') where T' decides whether to accept or reject (or to perform yet another request). The request req' may be a destruction, Derive, or Equal? requests (but no other requests are allowed).[74] If the response is rejected, i.e., send-req returns $\bot$, then, just before it returns $\bot$, send-req deletes all pointers in $\widetilde{\mathcal{F}}_{\text{crypto}}$ that are contained in the response res (of course, at most responses to Dec, DecPKE, or Derive requests contain pointers), using Delete requests. This guarantees that, when a response is rejected, not only the state of the instance of M_r that has sent the request did not change but also the state of $\widetilde{\mathcal{F}}_{\text{crypto}}$ did not change.

We say that a destruction request is *accepted* if the test performed after the request accepts the response. More formally, if the algorithm send-req(req, T) (that is called instead of directly sending req) did not return $\bot$.

We now give a few examples of typical tests.

Example 7.2. 1. This test simply returns the response, i.e., it accepts all responses (except for $\bot$ or, in case of MAC/signature verification, 0):

$$T_{\text{res}}(res) := (res, \bot, \bot) \qquad (\text{for all } res \in \{0,1\}^*).$$

---

[74]We note that we could allow other requests, except for construction requests, as well but they are not needed for defining reasonable tests. For example, it is not needed that a test is based on a new key generated by a KeyGen request. This request can just be sent before or after the test.

This test is typical for responses to MAC/signature verification requests, but it can also be used for decryption requests where any plaintext is acceptable. For verification, it accepts if and only if the response is 1, i.e., verification succeeded. For example, to verify a MAC σ for a message x under the MAC key the pointer ptr refers to, a user (i.e., instance of M_r) could run $out :=$ send-req$((\text{Verify}, ptr, x, \sigma), T_{\text{res}})$.

2. Given a bit string x (e.g., a party name or nonce), this test accepts every response to a decryption request where the plaintext starts with x:

$$T^x_{\text{prefix}}(res) := \begin{cases} (res, \perp, \perp) & \text{if } \exists y, l, ptr_1, \ldots, ptr_l \colon res = (x \| y, ptr_1, \ldots, ptr_l) \\ (\perp, \perp, \perp) & \text{otherwise.} \end{cases}$$

To decrypt a ciphertext y under the symmetric encryption key the pointer ptr refers to and then to check that the decrypted plaintext is prefixed by x, a user could run $out :=$ send-req$((\text{Dec}, ptr, y), T^x_{\text{prefix}})$.

3. Given a pointer ptr to a MAC key, this test for a decryption request checks that the plaintext has the form $x \| \sigma$ for a MAC σ of length l, contains no keys (i.e., the returned list of pointers is empty), and that σ is a valid MAC for x under the key ptr refers to:

$$T_{ptr}(res) := \begin{cases} (\perp, (\text{Verify}, ptr, x, \sigma), T^{x \| \sigma}_{\text{verify}}) & \text{if } \exists x, \sigma \colon |\sigma| = l \wedge res = (x \| \sigma) \\ (\perp, \perp, \perp) & \text{otherwise} \end{cases}$$

where the test $T^{x \| \sigma}_{\text{verify}}$, that is used for the verification request, is defined as follows. For every bit string out (and res):

$$T^{out}_{\text{verify}}(res) := (out, \perp, \perp) \ .$$

That is, T^{out}_{verify} accepts and returns out iff verification succeeds.

For example, to decrypt a ciphertext y under the private key with name $name$ and to check that the message and MAC inside y are valid for the MAC key a pointer ptr refers to, a user could run $out :=$ send-req$((\text{DecPKE}, name, y), T_{ptr})$. If decryption or MAC verification fails, then $out = \perp$. Otherwise, $out = x \| \sigma$ and the user may use x and σ in its following computation.

4. The following test T can be used to test that a decrypted ciphertext contains a message and a key and that a MAC verifies under a key derived from the key contained in the ciphertext:

$$T(res) := \begin{cases} (\perp, (\text{Derive}, ptr, salt), T'_{m,ptr}) & \text{if } \exists m \colon res = (m, ptr) \\ (\perp, \perp, \perp) & \text{otherwise} \end{cases}$$

$$T'_{m,ptr}(res) := \begin{cases} (\perp, (\text{Verify}, ptr', x, \sigma), T^{(m,ptr,ptr')}_{\text{verify}}) & \text{if } \exists ptr' \colon res = (ptr') \\ (\perp, \perp, \perp) & \text{otherwise} \end{cases}$$

where $salt$, x, and σ are some bit strings (which might depend on m) and $T_{\mathrm{verify}}^{out}$ (for any out) is defined above. (We note that the second case in $T'_{m,ptr}$ never occurs if the salt parsing function in $\widetilde{\mathcal{F}}_{\mathrm{crypto}}$ is defined accordingly.) If the tests succeed, then (m, ptr, ptr') is returned where m is the plaintext, ptr is the pointer to the key derivation key contained in the plaintext, and ptr' is the pointer to the MAC key derived from ptr. This plaintext and the pointers may be used in the computation following the test. If the verification does not succeed, then all pointers that where created during the tests are deleted and, hence, cannot be used in the following computation.

Correspondence Between Construction and Destruction Requests

We now define when a construction request corresponds to a destruction request. Let ρ be a run of the system $\mathcal{E} \mid \mathcal{P} \mid \widetilde{\mathcal{F}}_{\mathrm{crypto}}$ and let m_c and m_d be construction and destruction request, respectively, such that m_c was sent by some instance to $\widetilde{\mathcal{F}}_{\mathrm{crypto}}$ before m_d was sent by some (possibly other) instance to $\widetilde{\mathcal{F}}_{\mathrm{crypto}}$ in ρ. Then, we say that m_c *corresponds* to m_d in ρ if *(i)* m_c is an encryption and m_d a decryption request under the same key (for public-key encryption/decryption, under corresponding public/private keys) such that the ciphertext in the response to m_c from $\widetilde{\mathcal{F}}_{\mathrm{crypto}}$ coincides with the ciphertext in m_d or *(ii)* m_c is a MAC/signature generation and m_d a MAC/signature verification request under the same key/corresponding keys such that the message in m_c coincides with the message in m_d (the MACs/signatures do not need to coincide).

Explicitly Shared (Symmetric) Keys

For implicit disjointness, we only impose restrictions on public/private keys and on what we call explicitly shared (symmetric) keys. These are pre-shared symmetric keys or keys (directly or indirectly) derived from such keys in different sessions with the same salt. Recall that symmetric keys in $\widetilde{\mathcal{F}}_{\mathrm{crypto}}$ are typed keys $\kappa = (t, k)$ that consist of a key type t and the actual key k.

Definition 7.11. *Let $\mathcal{P}$ be a multi-session protocol that uses $\widetilde{\mathcal{F}}_{\mathrm{crypto}}$, τ be a valid partnering function for $\mathcal{P}$, and $\mathcal{E}$ be an environment for $\mathcal{P} \mid \widetilde{\mathcal{F}}_{\mathrm{crypto}}$. We (inductively) define that a symmetric (typed) key κ in $\widetilde{\mathcal{F}}_{\mathrm{crypto}}$ is explicitly shared (w.r.t. τ) in a (partial) run ρ of $\mathcal{E} \mid \mathcal{P} \mid \widetilde{\mathcal{F}}_{\mathrm{crypto}}$ (for some security parameter and external input) if there exist two distinct users $(lsid, r)$ and $(lsid', r')$ which are not partners and not both corrupted in ρ (i.e., $\tau_{(lsid,r)}(\rho) \neq \tau_{(lsid',r')}(\rho)$ or $\tau_{(lsid,r)}(\rho) = \tau_{(lsid',r')}(\rho) = \perp$) such that*

1. *both users have sent a GetPSK request to $\widetilde{\mathcal{F}}_{\mathrm{crypto}}$ to get a pre-shared key and both obtained a pointer to κ (i.e., the types and names used in the two requests coincided) or*

2. *both users have sent a* Derive *request to* $\widetilde{\mathcal{F}}_{\text{crypto}}$ *to derive a key from the same explicitly shared key using the same salt and both obtained a pointer to* κ.

We note that in most protocols pre-shared keys are the only explicitly shared keys since keys derived from pre-shared keys are typically derived using salts that are unique to the session.

The Definition of Implicit Disjointness

We are now ready to define the notion of implicit disjointness.

Definition 7.12. *Let* $\mathcal{P}$ *be a multi-session protocol that uses* $\widetilde{\mathcal{F}}_{\text{crypto}}$ *and* τ *be a valid partnering function for* $\mathcal{P} \mid \widetilde{\mathcal{F}}_{\text{crypto}}$. *Then,* $\mathcal{P}$ *satisfies* implicit (session) *disjointness w.r.t.* τ *if, for every environment* $\mathcal{E} \in \text{Env}(\mathcal{P} \mid \widetilde{\mathcal{F}}_{\text{crypto}})$, *the following holds with overwhelming probability, where the probability is taken over runs* ρ *of* $(\mathcal{E} \mid \mathcal{P} \mid \widetilde{\mathcal{F}}_{\text{crypto}})(1^\eta, a)$:

(a) *Every explicitly shared key is either always marked unknown or always marked known in* $\widetilde{\mathcal{F}}_{\text{crypto}}$. *More precisely, for every explicitly shared key* κ *in* ρ, *let* ρ' *be the prefix of* ρ *such that* κ *is an explicitly shared key in* ρ' *but it is not an explicitly shared key in any proper prefix of* ρ'. *Then,* κ *is marked known in (the last configuration of)* ρ *if and only if it is marked known in* ρ'.

(b) *Whenever some user* $(lsid, r)$ *(i.e., the instance* $M_r[lsid]$ *of* M_r*) performed an accepted and ideal destruction request with an explicitly shared key or a public/private key at some point in* ρ, *say just after the partial run* ρ', *then there exists some user* $(lsid', r')$ *that has sent a corresponding construction request such that both users are partners or both users are corrupted in* ρ' *(i.e.,* $\tau_{(lsid,r)}(\rho') = \tau_{(lsid',r')}(\rho') \neq \perp$*).*

Most protocols can easily be seen to satisfy (a) because explicitly shared keys are typically not sent around (i.e., encrypted by other keys), and hence, since they can be corrupted upon generation only, they are either corrupted (i.e., always known) or always unknown. Of course, there are (secure) protocols that do not satisfy (b) (e.g., the Needham-Schroeder-Lowe Public-Key protocol, see Appendix D.3.1) and, hence, cannot be analyzed using our joint state theorem. However, as already mentioned, our case studies (see Section 7.7.2) demonstrate that (b) too is typically satisfied by real-world protocols and can easily be checked. We note that (b) can be interpreted as a specific correspondence assertion, and it might be possible to prove (b) using automated techniques, such as CryptoVerif [Bla07].

7.6.3. The Composition Theorem with Joint State

We now present our joint state composition theorem without pre-established SIDs, with $\widetilde{\mathcal{F}}_{\text{crypto}}$ serving as the joint state. Since our theorem does not assume pre-

established SIDs, protocols analyzed using this theorem do not need to be modi-
fied/idealized by adding SIDs to messages. The usage of our theorem is discussed in
more detail in Section 7.7.

In the theorem, we assume that the leakage algorithms for authenticated symmetric
encryption (i.e., for key types in $\mathcal{T}_{\text{senc}}^{\text{auth}}$) that are used in $\widetilde{\mathcal{F}}_{\text{crypto}}$ have high entropy
(Definition 3.17) w.r.t. the domain of plaintexts produced by the plaintext formatting
functions that are used in $\widetilde{\mathcal{F}}_{\text{crypto}}$.[75] This is, for example, guaranteed if these leakage
algorithms return a random bit string of the same length as the plaintext and all
plaintexts have length $\geq \eta$ (where η is the security parameter). It guarantees that
all ciphertexts generated by $\widetilde{\mathcal{F}}_{\text{crypto}}$ with unknown keys only collide with negligible
probability (see Lemma D.2 in Appendix D.2).

Theorem 7.5. *Let $\mathcal{P}$ be a multi-session protocol that uses $\widetilde{\mathcal{F}}_{\text{crypto}}$ (with leakage
algorithms as described above) and satisfies implicit disjointness w.r.t. a valid part-
nering function τ for $\mathcal{P}$ and let $\mathcal{F}$ be a multi-session local-SID functionality. If
$\mathcal{P} \,|\, \widetilde{\mathcal{F}}_{\text{crypto}}$ single-session realizes $\mathcal{F}$ w.r.t. τ with a well-formed simulator (i.e.,
$\mathcal{P} \,|\, \widetilde{\mathcal{F}}_{\text{crypto}} \leq_{\tau\text{-single*}} \mathcal{F}$), then $\mathcal{P} \,|\, \widetilde{\mathcal{F}}_{\text{crypto}}$ realizes $\mathcal{F}$ w.r.t. well-formed environments
(i.e., $\mathcal{P} \,|\, \widetilde{\mathcal{F}}_{\text{crypto}} \leq^* \mathcal{F}$).*

We note that the restriction on well-formed environments (Definition 7.6) only
requires that environments directly reply to network requests from $\widetilde{\mathcal{F}}_{\text{crypto}}$. This
is natural to assume, as discussed in Remark 7.2. Furthermore, we note that the
restrictions on well-formed simulators (Definition 7.10) basically imply that $\mathcal{P}$ must
provide mutual authentication, see Remark 7.3. To be able to apply the above
theorem to protocols that do not provide mutual authentication, as discussed in
Remark 7.3, the restrictions on well-formed simulators must be loosened. We think
that this is possible, see Chapter 8.

We now briefly sketch our proof of the above theorem (see Appendix D.2 for the
full proof).

Proof sketch. We prove Theorem 7.5 in two steps: We first construct an IITM $\mathcal{Q}_\tau$
that simulates $\mathcal{P} \,|\, \widetilde{\mathcal{F}}_{\text{crypto}}$ except that it uses a different copy of $\widetilde{\mathcal{F}}_{\text{crypto}}$ for every
session (according to τ). Because $\mathcal{P}$ satisfies implicit disjointness w.r.t. τ, we can show
that $\mathcal{E} \,|\, \mathcal{P} \,|\, \widetilde{\mathcal{F}}_{\text{crypto}} \equiv \mathcal{E} \,|\, \mathcal{Q}_\tau$ for every well-formed environment $\mathcal{E}$. More precisely, we
map runs of $\mathcal{E} \,|\, \mathcal{P} \,|\, \widetilde{\mathcal{F}}_{\text{crypto}}$ to runs of $\mathcal{E} \,|\, \mathcal{Q}_\tau$ with the same probability and overall
output. Every sequence of random coins induces a run ρ of $\mathcal{E} \,|\, \mathcal{P} \,|\, \widetilde{\mathcal{F}}_{\text{crypto}}$ and a
corresponding run ρ' of $\mathcal{E} \,|\, \mathcal{Q}_\tau$ where $\mathcal{E}$ uses the same random coins in both systems
and $\mathcal{Q}_\tau$ uses the random coins as $\mathcal{P} \,|\, \widetilde{\mathcal{F}}_{\text{crypto}}$. Then, we only consider runs where the

---

[75]More precisely, we assume that L_{senc}^t has high entropy w.r.t. $\{\text{rng}(\text{format}_{\text{senc}}^t)(\eta)\}_{\eta \in \mathbb{N}}$, the range
of $\text{format}_{\text{senc}}^t$ (see Section 5.1.2 for the definition of $\text{rng}(\text{format}_{\text{senc}}^t)(\eta)$), for all $t \in \mathcal{T}_{\text{senc}}^{\text{auth}}$. We
note that this assumption is not needed for unauthenticated and public-key encryption because
ideal encryption under such keys is interactive in $\widetilde{\mathcal{F}}_{\text{crypto}}$. If ideal authenticated symmetric
encryption in $\widetilde{\mathcal{F}}_{\text{crypto}}$ would be interactive as well, this assumption could be dropped.

criterion in Definition 7.12 (implicit disjointness) is satisfied. This suffices because, by assumption, the probability of this set of runs is overwhelming. By induction on the length of ρ and ρ', we then show that $\mathcal{E}$ has the same view in ρ and ρ', hence, $\mathcal{E}$ will produce the same overall output. Here, the crucial observation is that the only observable (by $\mathcal{E}$) difference between ρ and ρ' occurs if destruction requests are processed differently in ρ and ρ'. For example, in the case that upon decryption of a ciphertext from another session, $\widetilde{\mathcal{F}}_{\text{crypto}}$ returns the plaintext in ρ, while in ρ' for the same request $\widetilde{\mathcal{F}}_{\text{crypto}}$ returns an error message. But since $\mathcal{P}$ satisfies implicit disjointness, we know that the plaintext will be rejected in ρ and, hence, the execution is identical to the one in ρ', where instead of the plaintext an error message is received.

In the second step, we show that $\mathcal{Q}_\tau$ realizes $\mathcal{F}$. We note that $\mathcal{Q}_\tau$ is very similar to a multi-session protocol that uses a multi-session local-SID functionality as in Theorem 7.4. The proof is similar as well: We create a simulator $\mathcal{S}$ using multiple copies of a well-formed single-session simulator $\mathcal{S}_\tau$ for $\mathcal{P} \,|\, \widetilde{\mathcal{F}}_{\text{crypto}} \leq_{\tau\text{-single}*} \mathcal{F}$. The simulator $\mathcal{S}$ uses τ to determine the sessions and emulates one copy of $\mathcal{S}_\tau$ for every session. Because the computation of $\mathcal{S}_\tau$ in its first stage is fixed, this simulation can be done faithfully. By a hybrid argument, we then show that $\mathcal{E} \,|\, \mathcal{Q}_\tau \equiv \mathcal{E} \,|\, \mathcal{S} \,|\, \mathcal{F}$ for every well-formed environment $\mathcal{E}$.

Finally, by transitivity of $\equiv$, we obtain that $\mathcal{E} \,|\, \mathcal{P} \,|\, \widetilde{\mathcal{F}}_{\text{crypto}} \equiv \mathcal{E} \,|\, \mathcal{S} \,|\, \mathcal{F}$ for every well-formed environment $\mathcal{E}$, which concludes the proof. $\qquad\square$

7.7. Applications of our Composition Theorems

In this section, using key exchange and secure channel protocols as examples, we discuss how our results from Sections 7.5 and 7.6, namely Theorems 7.4 and 7.5, can be used to analyze protocols in a modular and faithful way. While our discussion focuses on the analysis of properties of real-world security protocols, our theorems should be useful beyond this domain.

7.7.1. Applications to Key Exchange and Secure Channel Protocols

To illustrate the use of Theorems 7.4 and 7.5, consider, for example, the task of proving that a multi-session protocol $\mathcal{Q}$ which is based on a multi-session key exchange protocol $\mathcal{P}$ realizes the multi-session local-SID secure channel functionality $\widehat{\mathcal{F}}_{\text{sc}}$ (see Section 4.3.3 and Definition 7.1), where both $\mathcal{Q}$ and $\mathcal{P}$ could be real-world security protocols.

While a proof from scratch would, similarly to proofs in a game-based setting, require involved reduction arguments and would be quite complex, using our framework the proof is very modular, with every proof step being relatively small and simple: First, instead of using the actual cryptographic schemes, $\mathcal{P}$ can use $\mathcal{F}_{\text{crypto}}$ (at least for the operations supported by $\mathcal{F}_{\text{crypto}}$). As a result, for the rest of the proof merely information-theoretic reasoning is needed, often not even probabilistic reasoning, in particular no reduction proofs (at least as far as the operations supported by $\mathcal{F}_{\text{crypto}}$ are concerned). The remaining proof steps are to show:

(a) $\mathcal{P} \mid \mathcal{F}_{\text{crypto}}$ satisfies implicit disjointness,

(b) $\mathcal{P} \mid \mathcal{F}_{\text{crypto}}$ single-session realizes $\widehat{\mathcal{F}}_{\text{keyuse}}$, and

(c) $\mathcal{Q} \mid \widehat{\mathcal{F}}_{\text{keyuse}}$ single-session realizes $\widehat{\mathcal{F}}_{\text{sc}}$,

where $\widehat{\mathcal{F}}_{\text{keyuse}}$ is the multi-session local-SID key usability functionality (see Section 4.3.2 and Definition 7.1), say for authentication symmetric encryption, i.e., $\widehat{\mathcal{F}}_{\text{keyuse}} = \widehat{\mathcal{F}}_{\text{keyuse}}^{\mathcal{F}_{\text{senc}}^{\text{auth}}}$, as also considered in Section 7.4. Since, the session key established by $\widehat{\mathcal{F}}_{\text{keyuse}}$ can be used for ideal cryptographic operations, the argument for step (c) is still information-theoretic. We note that only step (a) needs some (information-theoretic) reasoning on multiple sessions, but only to show implicit disjointness. This is easy, as illustrated by our case studies (see below); the proof often merely needs to consider the security properties of a small fraction of the primitives used in the protocol. Now, by (a), (b), and Theorem 7.5, we obtain $\mathcal{P} \mid \mathcal{F}_{\text{crypto}} \leq \widehat{\mathcal{F}}_{\text{keyuse}}$. Theorem 7.4 and (c) imply $\mathcal{Q} \mid \widehat{\mathcal{F}}_{\text{keyuse}} \leq \widehat{\mathcal{F}}_{\text{sc}}$. By Theorem 2.1, we have $\mathcal{Q} \mid \mathcal{P} \mid \mathcal{F}_{\text{crypto}} \leq \mathcal{Q} \mid \widehat{\mathcal{F}}_{\text{keyuse}}$, and hence, $\mathcal{Q} \mid \mathcal{P} \mid \mathcal{F}_{\text{crypto}} \leq \widehat{\mathcal{F}}_{\text{sc}}$, by transitivity of $\leq$.

7.7.2. Case Studies on Real-World Security Protocols

In our case studies, we consider five real-world security protocols: SSL/TLS, WPA2 (IEEE 802.11i), EAP-PSK, SSH, and IPsec. We show that these protocols, for which we model the cryptographic core, satisfy implicit disjointness. That is, we perform step (a) (see above) in the analysis of these protocols. In Appendix D.3.2, we also perform step (c) for a generic secure channel protocol $\mathcal{Q}$ of which many real-world protocols are instances (e.g., the CCM Protocol of IEEE 802.11i is an instance of $\mathcal{Q}$, see Appendix D.3.2). Providing full proofs for step (b) for the key exchange protocols of our case studies (and hence, completing their security analysis) is beyond the scope of this thesis. However, (b) partly follows from existing work, see Section 7.4.3 for WPA2 and [GMP+08] for SSL/TLS. Gajek et al. [GMP+08] showed single-session security of TLS. However, they then used the joint state composition theorem by Canetti and Rabin [CR03], to obtain security in the multi-session setting, which, as discussed, only proves security of a modified, idealized version of TLS (see the remarks on TLS at the beginning of Section 7.6). Using our theorems and the fact that TLS satisfies implicit disjointness, the result by Gajek et al. suggests that security of the (original) version of TLS holds in the multi-session setting, without pre-established SIDs added to plaintexts and signed messages.

In the following, to describe protocols, we use the notation introduced in Table 7.1.

$\{\!|x|\!\}_{k_A}$ –   encryption of message x under the public key of party A

$\text{sig}_{k_A}(x)$ –   signature of message x under the private key of party A

$\{x\}_k$ –   encryption of message x under the symmetric key k

$\text{mac}_k(x)$ –   MAC of message x under the symmetric key k

Table 7.1.: Notation used in protocol descriptions.

The SSL/TLS Protocol

The Transport Layer Security (TLS) protocol [DR08] consists of multiple subprotocols including TLS Handshake Protocols and the TLS Record Protocol.[76] Basically, the Handshake Protocols are used to establish a session key and this session key is used in the Record Protocol to provide a secure channel. There are three Handshake Protocols two thereof are based on Diffie-Hellman key exchange and the third is based on RSA encryption. Here, we only consider the third variant. Also, we only consider the variant of the Handshake Protocol where the client authenticates itself using digital signatures. There also exists a variant where the client is not authenticated but only the server. We note that implicit disjointness would also hold for this variant, see the remark below Theorem 7.6. We further note that all other variants of the Handshake Protocols could also be analyzed using our methods. We assume that the server and client can verify the public key of the other side (e.g., using some kind of public key infrastructure). The cryptographic core of this Handshake Protocol is depicted in Figure 7.6. In this, pid_C and pid_S are the party names of C and S, respectively; N_C and N_S are C's and S's nonce; k_C and k_S are C's and S's public key (pid_C, k_C and pid_S, k_S models the client's and the server's certificate, respectively); the premaster secret PMS is chosen randomly by C; c_1 and c_2 are distinct constants (they are part of the client and server hello messages and used to negotiate algorithms, we model this as constants); PRF is a pseudorandom function; the master secret MS is derived from PMS as follows:

$$MS := \text{PRF}(PMS, \texttt{"master secret"}\|N_C\|N_S) \ ;$$

$\{m\}_{k_1,k_2}^{\text{mac-then-enc}}$ denotes MAC-then-encrypt, i.e., $\{m\}_{k_1,k_2}^{\text{mac-then-enc}} := \{m, \text{mac}_{k_1}(m)\}_{k_2}$; the MAC keys $IKCS$ (client to server) and $IKSC$ (server to client) and the encryption keys $EKCS$ (client to server) and $EKSC$ (server to client) are derived from MS as follows:

$$IKCS\|IKSC\|EKCS\|EKSC := \text{PRF}(MS, \texttt{"key expansion"}\|N_C\|N_S) \ ;$$

---

[76] We note that we consider Version 1.2 of the TLS protocol. There exist security critical differences between the versions of TLS. However, the differences concerning the TLS Handshake Protocol, which we focus on, are only marginal. In particularly, Theorem 7.6 also holds for Versions 1.0 and 1.1 of the TLS Handshake Protocol that we consider.

1. $C \to S$: c_1, N_C
2. $S \to C$: pid_S, k_S, c_2, N_S
3. $C \to S$: $pid_C, k_C, \{\!|PMS|\!\}_{k_S}, \mathrm{sig}_{k_C}(handshake),$
   $$\{\mathrm{PRF}(MS, \texttt{"client finished"} \| handshake')\}_{IKCS,EKCS}^{\text{mac-then-enc}}$$
4. $S \to C$: $\{\mathrm{PRF}(MS, \texttt{"server finished"} \| handshake'')\}_{IKSC,EKSC}^{\text{mac-then-enc}}$

Figure 7.6.: The TLS Handshake Protocol (Key Exchange Method: RSA).

handshake, *handshake'*, and *handshake''* stand for the concatenation of all previous messages, i.e.,

$$handshake := c_1 \| N_C \| pid_S \| k_S \| c_2 \| N_S \| pid_C \| k_C \| \{\!|PMS|\!\}_{k_S} \; ,$$

$$handshake' := handshake \| \mathrm{sig}_{k_C}(handshake) \; , \text{ and}$$

$$handshake'' := handshake \|$$
$$\{\mathrm{PRF}(MS, \texttt{"client finished"} \| handshake')\}_{IKCS,EKCS}^{\text{mac-then-enc}} \; .$$

In step 3 of the protocol, the server performs the following test (as soon as a check fails, the whole message is dropped): It first decrypts the first ciphertext (using $\widetilde{\mathcal{F}}_{\mathrm{crypto}}$). If successful, it checks that the signature is over the expected message. If so, it verifies the signature $\mathrm{sig}_{k_C}(handshake)$ (using $\widetilde{\mathcal{F}}_{\mathrm{crypto}}$). If successful, S derives the keys MS, $EKCS$, etc. and decrypts the second ciphertext (using $\widetilde{\mathcal{F}}_{\mathrm{crypto}}$). If this succeeds, the MAC within the plaintext is verified (using $\widetilde{\mathcal{F}}_{\mathrm{crypto}}$). If successful, the test accepts and S continues the protocol.

Modeling this protocol as a multi-session protocol $\mathcal{P}_{\mathrm{TLS}} = \,!M_C \,|\, !M_S$ that uses $\widetilde{\mathcal{F}}_{\mathrm{crypto}}$ for all cryptographic operations (i.e., public-key and symmetric encryption, digital signatures, key derivation, and MAC) is straightforward. We note that the 4WHS protocol of WPA2 has been modeled in Section 7.4.3 and that our modeling of TLS is similar in many aspects. Therefore, we only mention the most important parts. The protocol $\mathcal{P}_{\mathrm{TLS}}$ is meant to realize $\widehat{\mathcal{F}}_{\mathrm{keyuse}}$ (key usability for authenticated symmetric encryption), i.e., after the keys are established, the parties can send encryption and decryption requests to M_C and M_S which are MACed and encrypted under the corresponding keys. (Note that $\mathcal{P}_{\mathrm{TLS}}$ does not realize $\widehat{\mathcal{F}}_{\mathrm{ke}}$ because the session keys are used for key confirmation.)

The session parameters are of the form $sp = (pid_C, pid_S)$, i.e., all local SIDs are of the form $lsid = (lsid', (pid_C, pid_S))$ for some $lsid'$ and some party names pid_C and pid_S. If an instance of M_C or M_S, respectively, is created with a local SID that does not satisfy the above requirements, it terminates. The instance $M_C[lsid]$ then models the local session $lsid'$ of party pid_C in role C talking to pid_S and $M_S[lsid]$ models the local session $lsid'$ of party pid_S in role S talking to pid_C.

We assume that all public keys are known to all parties. More precisely, if an instance (of M_C or M_S) receives the public key k_S or k_C, respectively, then the instance checks that this public key is in fact the correct public key of the desired partner by comparing the received public key with the public key obtained from $\widetilde{\mathcal{F}}_{\text{crypto}}$ for the desired partner; the public key for party *pid* is obtained from $\widetilde{\mathcal{F}}_{\text{crypto}}$ using *pid* as the public key name. If it is not the correct public key, the instance halts. By this, we model that public keys are either already distributed (in a secure way) or that there is some reliable public key infrastructure.

In step 3 of the protocol, the client computes the finished message, i.e., the message $\{\text{PRF}(MS, \texttt{"client finished"} \| handshake')\}_{IKCS,EKCS}^{\text{mac-then-enc}}$, as follows: First, the client derives the keys MS, $IKCS$, etc. according to the protocol using $\widetilde{\mathcal{F}}_{\text{crypto}}$. Then, the client derives $\text{PRF}(MS, \texttt{"client finished"} \| handshake')$ using $\widetilde{\mathcal{F}}_{\text{crypto}}$, i.e., the client obtains a pointer to this derived key. The client then also asks $\widetilde{\mathcal{F}}_{\text{crypto}}$ (using a Retrieve request) for the actual bit string of this derived key (which will mark this key known in $\widetilde{\mathcal{F}}_{\text{crypto}}$, but this is not a problem). Finally, the client encrypts and MACs the obtained bit string (using $\widetilde{\mathcal{F}}_{\text{crypto}}$). The server similarly computes the message $\{\text{PRF}(MS, \texttt{"server finished"} \| handshake'')\}_{IKSC,EKSC}^{\text{mac-then-enc}}$ in step 4 of the protocol.

Corruption in $\mathcal{P}_{\text{TLS}}$ is modeled as follows: When an instance of M_C or M_S gets activated for the first time (i.e., upon receiving an Establish request), it sends a request to the adversary asking whether it is corrupted. If the adversary decides to corrupt this instance, then this instance sets its flag corr to 1 and we call it *directly corrupted*. The adversary can only corrupt an instance at the beginning, i.e., before the instance starts executing the protocol. If an instance is not directly corrupted, it still sets its flag corr to 1 and we call it *indirectly corrupted* if the public/private key pair of its partner is corrupted. More precisely, an instance of M_C that is not directly corrupted is called *indirectly corrupted* and sets its flag corr to 1 when it is activated for the first time and the server's public/private key pair is corrupted in $\widetilde{\mathcal{F}}_{\text{crypto}}$ (the instance determines the corruption status of the key pair by asking $\widetilde{\mathcal{F}}_{\text{crypto}}$). Similarly, an instance of M_S that is not directly corrupted is called *indirectly corrupted* and sets its flag corr to 1 when it is activated for the first time and the client's public/private key pair is corrupted in $\widetilde{\mathcal{F}}_{\text{crypto}}$. An indirectly corrupted instance will then also inform the adversary that it is indirectly corrupted by sending a special message to her. (Of course, the adversary knows which public/private keys she corrupted, and hence, what instances are indirectly corrupted but this is needed to define the partnering function for implicit disjointness, see below.) An instance that is not directly or indirectly corrupted (i.e., its flag corr is 0) is called *uncorrupted*. An indirectly corrupted or uncorrupted instance follows the protocol normally. Indirect corruption models that this party is honest but the party it wants to talk to is not (or that the adversary somehow obtained the private key of the party it wants to talk to). A directly corrupted instance on the other hand, gives complete control to the adversary by forwarding all messages between the adversary and the environment. Note that, by this definition, directly corrupted instances never send any requests to $\widetilde{\mathcal{F}}_{\text{crypto}}$.[77] For an uncorrupted or indirectly corrupted instance, we assume that its

---

[77]We could allow the adversary to send requests to $\widetilde{\mathcal{F}}_{\text{crypto}}$ in the name of a directly corrupted

public/private key pair is uncorrupted in $\widetilde{\mathcal{F}}_{\text{crypto}}$. More precisely, every instance of M_S checks at the beginning of the protocol that its public/private encryption key is uncorrupted (by asking $\widetilde{\mathcal{F}}_{\text{crypto}}$ for its corruption status) and, if this is not the case, the instance halts (i.e., does not proceed in the protocol). (Since public/private encryption key pairs are only statically corruptible in $\widetilde{\mathcal{F}}_{\text{crypto}}$, this will imply that this key pair remains uncorrupted.) Similarly, every instance of M_C checks at the end of the protocol (i.e., just after receiving the fourth protocol message) that its public/private signature key is uncorrupted and, if this is not the case, the instance halts. (Note that signature keys are adaptively corruptible in $\widetilde{\mathcal{F}}_{\text{crypto}}$, so, these keys might get corrupted later.)

We note that (directly or indirectly) corrupted instances of M_C and M_S will, when realizing $\widehat{\mathcal{F}}_{\text{keyuse}}$, correspond to corrupted users in $\widehat{\mathcal{F}}_{\text{keyuse}}$, i.e., the simulator will corrupt these users in $\widehat{\mathcal{F}}_{\text{keyuse}}$ before they get an SID, and hence, can exactly simulate these instances. This makes sense because even for indirectly corrupted instances, we do not assume any security guarantees to hold. We further remark that an adversary can gain complete control over a whole party by corrupting her public/private key pair in $\widetilde{\mathcal{F}}_{\text{crypto}}$ and all her instances of M_C and M_S.

This concludes the description of the modeling of TLS. It is easy to see that $\mathcal{P}_{\text{TLS}} \,|\, \mathcal{F}$ is environmentally strictly bounded for every environmentally strictly bounded protocol system $\mathcal{F}$ that has the same I/O interface as $\widetilde{\mathcal{F}}_{\text{crypto}}$ because every instance of M_C or M_S, in any run with any system, sends only a polynomial number of requests of polynomial length to $\widetilde{\mathcal{F}}_{\text{crypto}}$ (and hence to $\mathcal{F}$), where the polynomial is in the security parameter and the length of input received from the network (i.e., from the environment). Hence, $\mathcal{P}_{\text{TLS}}$ is in the class of real protocols considered in Section 7.6.

We now prove that $\mathcal{P}_{\text{TLS}}$ satisfies implicit disjointness. The proof does not need to exploit security of symmetric encryption. Moreover, the proof merely requires syntactic arguments (rather than probabilistic reasoning or reduction arguments) since we can use $\widetilde{\mathcal{F}}_{\text{crypto}}$ for the cryptographic primitives.

The partnering function τ_{TLS} for $\mathcal{P}_{\text{TLS}}$ we use is the obvious one: Let ρ be a run of $\mathcal{E} \,|\, \mathcal{P}_{\text{TLS}} \,|\, \widetilde{\mathcal{F}}_{\text{crypto}}$ for some environment $\mathcal{E}$ and $\alpha = (m_1, t_1), \ldots, (m_l, t_l)$ be the projection of ρ to the sequence of messages (with tapes) sent and received by some instance $M_r[lsid]$ on its network tapes, i.e., $r \in \{C, S\}$ and $lsid = (lsid', (pid_C, pid_S))$ for some $lsid', pid_C, pid_S$. If $M_r[lsid]$ is (directly or indirectly) corrupted, then $\tau_{\text{TLS}}(\alpha) := \mathsf{corr}$ (note that this information is contained in α because, if the instance is directly corrupted, the adversary sent a special message to the instance and, if the instance is indirectly corrupted, the instance sent a special message to the adversary). If

---

instance but then, as in Section 7.4.3, all keys this instance creates using $\widetilde{\mathcal{F}}_{\text{crypto}}$ should be corrupted (including the public/private key pair of the party this instance belongs to). Hence, all keys this instance would have pointers to would be marked known in $\widetilde{\mathcal{F}}_{\text{crypto}}$. Since the adversary can perform all operations under known keys herself (outside of $\widetilde{\mathcal{F}}_{\text{crypto}}$), allowing directly corrupted instances access to $\widetilde{\mathcal{F}}_{\text{crypto}}$ would not give more power to the adversary.

$M_r[lsid]$ is uncorrupted and α contains at least the first two protocol messages, then $\tau_{\text{TLS}}(\alpha) := ((N_C, N_S), (pid_C, pid_S))$ where N_C is the nonce contained in the first protocol message and N_S is the nonce contained in the second protocol message. Otherwise, $\tau_{\text{TLS}}(\alpha) := \bot$. It is easy to see that τ_{TLS} is valid for $\mathcal{P}_{\text{TLS}}$ because every instance generated one nonce itself and ideal nonces (i.e., nonces generated using $\widetilde{\mathcal{F}}_{\text{crypto}}$) do not collide (but even if nonces were generated regularly, i.e., without an ideal functionality, this would be easy to see).

Theorem 7.6. $\mathcal{P}_{\text{TLS}}$ *satisfies implicit disjointness w.r.t.* τ_{TLS}.

Proof. Let $\mathcal{E}$ be an environment for $\mathcal{P}_{\text{TLS}} \,|\, \widetilde{\mathcal{F}}_{\text{crypto}}$ and ρ be a run of $\mathcal{E} \,|\, \mathcal{P}_{\text{TLS}} \,|\, \widetilde{\mathcal{F}}_{\text{crypto}}$ (for some security parameter η and external input a). We now show that (a) and (b) of Definition 7.12 (implicit disjointness) are satisfied for ρ. All symmetric keys (i.e., the keys PMS, MS, $EKSC$, etc.) are, by definition, not explicitly shared: PMS is not a pre-shared key but a freshly generated symmetric key; MS is derived from PMS and all other keys are derived from MS. Hence, (a) is trivially satisfied for ρ. Since only uncorrupted or indirectly corrupted instances, which follow the protocol, have access to $\widetilde{\mathcal{F}}_{\text{crypto}}$, the only relevant cases to show (b) are when the server performs a decryption request with k_S (to obtain PMS) or when it performs a verification request to verify the signature of the client.

Assume that an instance of M_S, say $M_S[lsid_S]$ with $lsid_S = (lsid'_S, (pid_C, pid_S))$, performed an accepted and ideal decryption request in ρ with its private key (i.e., the private key of party pid_S). Since corrupted instance do not have access to $\widetilde{\mathcal{F}}_{\text{crypto}}$, $M_S[lsid_S]$ is uncorrupted or indirectly corrupted. Hence, by definition of M_S, $M_S[lsid_S]$ decrypted the first ciphertext, say ct, that it received in the third protocol message and then performed a test, which succeeds. In the test, $M_S[lsid_S]$ verified that: *(i)* the decryption yields (a pointer to) a key PMS, *(ii)* the signature it obtained verifies for the public key of pid_C (this is irrelevant for the following), *(iii)* key derivation of the keys MS, $EKCS$, $IKCS$, etc. succeeds, *(iv)* decryption of the second ciphertext contained in the third protocol with the derived key $EKCS$ succeeds and yields a message m and a MAC σ (two bit strings), and *(v)* verification of the message m and the MAC σ with the derived key $IKCS$ succeeds. Since the decryption request (to decrypt ct) was ideal, (PMS, ct) is recorded in $\widetilde{\mathcal{F}}_{\text{crypto}}$ for public/private key pair of pid_S. Hence, by definition of $\mathcal{P}_{\text{TLS}}$, there exists an uncorrupted or indirectly corrupted instance of M_C, say $M_C[lsid_C]$ with $lsid_C = (lsid'_C, (pid'_C, pid_S))$, that has encrypted PMS under the public key of pid_S (corrupted instances do not have access to $\widetilde{\mathcal{F}}_{\text{crypto}}$, uncorrupted or indirectly corrupted instances of M_S do not encrypt such messages, uncorrupted or indirectly corrupted instances of M_C only encrypt such messages and only with the server's public key). That is, $M_C[lsid_C]$ has sent a corresponding encryption request and it is left to show that $M_C[lsid_C]$ and $M_S[lsid_S]$ are partners. Since $M_S[lsid_S]$ is uncorrupted or indirectly corrupted, its public/private key is uncorrupted, and hence, $M_C[lsid_C]$ is uncorrupted. Now, since $M_C[lsid_C]$ is uncorrupted and it created the key PMS, PMS is marked unknown in $\widetilde{\mathcal{F}}_{\text{crypto}}$ when it was created. By definition of $\widetilde{\mathcal{F}}_{\text{crypto}}$ and $\mathcal{P}_{\text{TLS}}$, only $M_C[lsid_C]$ and uncorrupted or indirectly corrupted instances of M_S can have a pointer to PMS. Hence, PMS will always remain unknown in $\widetilde{\mathcal{F}}_{\text{crypto}}$. By definition of $\widetilde{\mathcal{F}}_{\text{crypto}}$, all keys derived from PMS (i.e., MS, $EKCS$, $IKCS$, etc.) are also marked unknown and only $M_C[\mathit{lsid}_C]$ and uncorrupted or indirectly corrupted instances of M_S can have a pointer to these derived keys ($\widetilde{\mathcal{F}}_{\text{crypto}}$ guarantees that keys derived from an unknown key with different salts are different from any other key). We obtain that the MAC verification by $M_S[\mathit{lsid}_S]$ of message m and MAC σ with the key $IKCS$ was ideal (i.e., $\widetilde{\mathcal{F}}_{\text{crypto}}$ ideally prevented forgery). Since uncorrupted or indirectly corrupted instances of M_S do not use $IKCS$ to MAC messages (they only use it for verification and they use $IKSC$ for MACing), the message m must have been MACed by $M_C[\mathit{lsid}_C]$ with the key $IKCS$. Since $\widetilde{\mathcal{F}}_{\text{crypto}}$ guarantees that keys derived from unknown keys with different salts are different and the message m is $PRF(MS, \texttt{"client finished"} \| handshake')$, we conclude that $M_C[\mathit{lsid}_C]$ and $M_S[\mathit{lsid}_S]$ agree on $handshake'$. In particularly, we obtain that these instances agree on the client's party name (i.e., $pid_C = pid'_C$) and on the nonces N_C and N_S, i.e., $M_C[\mathit{lsid}_C]$ sent N_C in the first protocol message and received N_S in the second and, vice versa, $M_S[\mathit{lsid}_S]$ received N_C in the first protocol message and sent N_S in the second. Since $M_C[\mathit{lsid}_C]$ is uncorrupted, its public/private key is uncorrupted, and hence, $M_S[\mathit{lsid}_S]$ is uncorrupted (because $pid_C = pid'_C$). By definition of τ_{TLS}, we conclude that $M_C[\mathit{lsid}_C]$ and $M_S[\mathit{lsid}_S]$ are partners (it holds that $\tau_{\text{TLS}(\mathit{lsid}_C, C)}(\rho) = \tau_{\text{TLS}(\mathit{lsid}_S, S)}(\rho) = ((N_C, N_S), (pid_C, pid_S)))$.

Now, assume that an instance of M_S, say $M_S[\mathit{lsid}_S]$ with local SID $\mathit{lsid}_S = (\mathit{lsid}'_S, (pid_C, pid_S))$, performed an accepted and ideal signature verification request in ρ. This case is even simpler than the above. Since corrupted instance do not have access to $\widetilde{\mathcal{F}}_{\text{crypto}}$ and the public/private key of pid_C is uncorrupted (otherwise, the request would not have been ideal), $M_S[\mathit{lsid}_S]$ is uncorrupted. Hence, by definition of M_S, $M_S[\mathit{lsid}_S]$ verified a signature of a message $handshake$ with the public key of pid_C (third protocol message). Since this succeeds, $handshake$ must be recorded in $\widetilde{\mathcal{F}}_{\text{crypto}}$ for the key pair of pid_C. Hence, by definition of $\mathcal{P}_{\text{TLS}}$, there exists an uncorrupted or indirectly corrupted instance of M_C, say $M_C[\mathit{lsid}_C]$ with $\mathit{lsid}_C = (\mathit{lsid}'_C, (pid_C, pid_S))$, that has signed $handshake$ (corrupted instances do not have access to $\widetilde{\mathcal{F}}_{\text{crypto}}$, uncorrupted or indirectly corrupted instances of M_S do not sign such messages, uncorrupted or indirectly corrupted instances of M_C only sign messages with their own private key and $handshake$ contains the server's name pid_S). That is, $M_C[\mathit{lsid}_C]$ has sent a corresponding signing request and it is left to show that $M_C[\mathit{lsid}_C]$ and $M_S[\mathit{lsid}_S]$ are partners. Since $M_S[\mathit{lsid}_S]$ is uncorrupted, its public/private key is uncorrupted, and hence, $M_C[\mathit{lsid}_C]$ is uncorrupted. Moreover, since $M_C[\mathit{lsid}_C]$ signed $handshake$, $M_S[\mathit{lsid}_S]$ and $M_C[\mathit{lsid}_C]$ agree on $handshake$. As above, we conclude that $M_C[\mathit{lsid}_C]$ and $M_S[\mathit{lsid}_S]$ agree on the nonces N_C and N_S and that they are partners (according to τ_{TLS}). □

We remark that, in the proof the above theorem, to show (b) of Definition 7.12 (implicit disjointness) for decryption requests under private keys, we did not need to exploit security of digital signatures. The argument is even valid if the client does not send this signature at all. In fact, the TLS protocol without client authentication, appropriately modeled, also satisfies implicit disjointness.[78]

Furthermore, we note that, in SSL/TLS [DR08], to compute the finished messages (the last part of the third protocol message and the fourth protocol message), a hash function is applied to *handshake'* and *handshake''* before they are used in the salt to the PRF. In the above description and modeling of the protocol, we omitted this hash function because we can push it into the definition of the PRF (i.e., into the realization of $\widetilde{\mathcal{F}}_{\text{crypto}}$), and hence, this still constitutes a faithful modeling of the TLS protocol; if the hash function is collision resistant. However, we could have modeled the hash function explicitly. Then, in the proof of Theorem 7.6, we would need to exploit collision resistance of the hash function (to conclude that $M_S[\mathit{lsid}_S]$ and $M_C[\mathit{lsid}_C]$ agree on *handshake'*).

A more detailed analysis and a proof that $\mathcal{P}_{\text{TLS}}$ realizes $\widehat{\mathcal{F}}_{\text{keyuse}}$ is future work. (As mentioned above, the result by [GMP+08] suggests that security of TLS holds in a single-session setting.) It should be quite easy now to prove this because, to show that $\mathcal{P}_{\text{TLS}}$ realizes $\widehat{\mathcal{F}}_{\text{keyuse}}$ in the multi-session setting, i.e., $\mathcal{P}_{\text{TLS}} \,|\, \widetilde{\mathcal{F}}_{\text{crypto}} \leq \widehat{\mathcal{F}}_{\text{keyuse}}$, by Theorem 7.5, it suffices to prove $\mathcal{P}_{\text{TLS}} \,|\, \widetilde{\mathcal{F}}_{\text{crypto}} \leq_{\tau_{\text{TLS}}\text{-single*}} \widehat{\mathcal{F}}_{\text{keyuse}}$. Furthermore, since all cryptographic operations are supported by $\widetilde{\mathcal{F}}_{\text{crypto}}$, proving this should be possible by syntactic reasoning based on $\widetilde{\mathcal{F}}_{\text{crypto}}$ (without reduction arguments or reasoning about probabilities at all).

The 4-Way Handshake Protocol of WPA2 (IEEE 802.11i)

The 4-Way Handshake (4WHS) protocol, which is part of the pre-shared key mode of WPA2 (IEEE standard 802.11i [IEE07, IEE04]), is a key exchange protocol where an authenticator A, e.g., an access point, and a supplicant S, e.g., a laptop, use a pre-shared key to establish a fresh session key. We introduced this protocol in Section 7.4.3. There, we showed that the 4WHS protocol realizes $\widehat{\mathcal{F}}_{\text{keyuse}}$ (key usability for authenticated symmetric encryption) and $\widehat{\mathcal{F}}_{\text{ke}}$; we showed this even for authenticated variants of $\widehat{\mathcal{F}}_{\text{keyuse}}$ and $\widehat{\mathcal{F}}_{\text{ke}}$. However, the analysis in Section 7.4.3 directly considers the multi-session setting. In the following, we demonstrate how we could show that the 4WHS protocol realizes $\widehat{\mathcal{F}}_{\text{keyuse}}$ (or $\widehat{\mathcal{F}}_{\text{ke}}$) using Theorem 7.5, i.e., by only considering a single-session setting. The security of CCMP using 4WHS then follows from our results in Appendix D.3.2.

To analyze the 4WHS protocol using Theorem 7.5, we can model this protocol as in Section 7.4.3, i.e., as the protocol system $\mathcal{P}_{\text{4WHS}} = !M_A \,|\, !M_S$, with two small changes: First, $\mathcal{P}_{\text{4WHS}}$ uses $\widetilde{\mathcal{F}}_{\text{crypto}}$ instead of $\mathcal{F}_{\text{crypto}}$ (but this does not change the

---

[78]We note that single-session realizability w.r.t. well-formed simulators (Definition 7.10) requires that the protocol provides mutual authentication (see Remark 7.3). Hence, although implicit disjointness holds for TLS without client authentication, we cannot use Theorem 7.5 because $\mathcal{P}_{\text{TLS}} \,|\, \widetilde{\mathcal{F}}_{\text{crypto}} \leq_{\tau\text{-single*}} \mathcal{F}$ would not be satisfied (for any appropriate $\mathcal{F}$); except if we extend our results as described in Chapter 8.

definition of M_A and M_S at all). Second, similarly to TLS, an indirectly corrupted instance of M_A or M_S (i.e., an instance that sets its flag corr to 1 because its pre-shared key PMK is corrupted in $\widetilde{\mathcal{F}}_{\text{crypto}}$ but the adversary did not directly corrupt this instance by sending a special message to it), inform the adversary that they are indirectly corrupted by sending a special message to her. (Of course, the adversary knows which pre-shared keys are corrupted, and hence, which instances are indirectly corrupted but this is needed to define the partnering function for implicit disjointness, see below.) The proof that $\mathcal{P}_{\text{4WHS}}$ satisfies implicit disjointness, since we use $\widetilde{\mathcal{F}}_{\text{crypto}}$ for all cryptographic operations, is completely syntactic (i.e., no reduction arguments and not even reasoning about probabilities).

The partnering function τ_{4WHS} for $\mathcal{P}_{\text{4WHS}}$ we use is the obvious one: Let ρ be a run of $\mathcal{E} \mid \mathcal{P}_{\text{4WHS}} \mid \widetilde{\mathcal{F}}_{\text{crypto}}$ for some environment $\mathcal{E}$ and $\alpha = (m_1, t_1), \ldots, (m_l, t_l)$ be the projection of ρ to the sequence of messages (with tapes) sent and received by some instance $M_r[\textit{lsid}]$ on its network tapes, i.e., $r \in \{A, S\}$ and $\textit{lsid} = (\textit{lsid}', (\textit{pid}_A, \textit{pid}_S, \textit{name}_{\text{PMK}}))$ for some $\textit{lsid}', \textit{pid}_A, \textit{pid}_S, \textit{name}_{\text{PMK}}$ (recall that the session parameters are $(\textit{pid}_A, \textit{pid}_S, \textit{name}_{\text{PMK}})$ where $\textit{pid}_A$ and $\textit{pid}_S$ are party names and $\textit{name}_{\text{PMK}}$ is the name of the pre-shared key PMK). If $M_r[\textit{lsid}]$ is corrupted, then $\tau_{\text{4WHS}}(\alpha) :=$ corr (note that this information is contained in α because the adversary sent a special message to the instance to corrupt it or the instance sent a special message to the adversary informing her that it set its flag corr to 1). If $M_r[\textit{lsid}]$ is uncorrupted and α contains at least the first two protocol messages, then $\tau_{\text{4WHS}}(\alpha) := ((N_A, N_S), (\textit{pid}_A, \textit{pid}_S, \textit{name}_{\text{PMK}}))$ where N_A is the nonce contained in the first protocol message and N_S is the nonce contained in the second protocol message. Otherwise, $\tau_{\text{4WHS}}(\alpha) := \bot$. It is easy to see that τ_{4WHS} is valid for $\mathcal{P}_{\text{4WHS}}$ because every instance generated one nonce itself and ideal nonces (i.e., nonces generated using $\widetilde{\mathcal{F}}_{\text{crypto}}$) do not collide (but even if nonces were generated regularly, i.e., without an ideal functionality, this would be easy to see).

Theorem 7.7. $\mathcal{P}_{\text{4WHS}}$ *satisfies implicit disjointness w.r.t.* τ_{4WHS}.

Proof. Let $\mathcal{E}$ be an environment $\mathcal{E} \in \text{Env}(\mathcal{P}_{\text{4WHS}} \mid \widetilde{\mathcal{F}}_{\text{crypto}})$ and ρ be a run of the system $\mathcal{E} \mid \mathcal{P}_{\text{4WHS}} \mid \widetilde{\mathcal{F}}_{\text{crypto}}$ (for some security parameter and external input). First, we show that (a) and (b) of Definition 7.12 (implicit disjointness) hold for PMK (which potentially is an explicitly shared key). This key is never encrypted or retrieved and, hence, it is either corrupted (and always known) or it is unknown, i.e., (a) is satisfied. Furthermore, it is never used to perform a destruction request (which in fact would be impossible because it is a key derivation key) and, hence, (b) is satisfied as well. Trivially, (a) and (b) also hold for PMKID (which is derived from PMK using a constant and the party names $\textit{pid}_A$ and $\textit{pid}_S$ as salt) because PMKID is always marked known (at least before it becomes an explicitly shared key) and never used as a key.

The only other relevant keys in the protocol are the derived keys KCK and TK (we note that we can ignore KEK because, in our modeling, it is never used). If they are not explicitly shared (in ρ), then we are done because implicit disjointness only talks about explicitly shared keys. Recall that KCK and TK are derived from PMK using $\min(pid_A, pid_S) \| \max(pid_A, pid_S) \| \min(N_A, N_S) \| \max(N_A, N_S)$ as part of the salt. If they would instead be derived using $pid_A \| pid_S \| N_A \| N_S$ (i.e., with a fixed order), we could directly conclude that implicit disjointness is satisfied because KCK and TK would not be explicitly shared. All instances that would derive these keys would have SID $((N_A, N_S), (pid_A, pid_S, name_{PMK}))$ (according to τ_{4WHS}) and, hence, they all would belong to the same session. We note that this design decision (to not use a fixed order) has another disadvantage: in a particular (unusual) setting where the same party plays both the role of A and S with the same PMK, it enables a reflection attack on 4WHS, see [HM05] and Section 7.4.3. Next, we show that KCK and TK satisfy (a) and (b) if they are explicitly shared.

First, we note that KCK and TK are known (in $\widetilde{\mathcal{F}}_{crypto}$) iff PMK is known because no user ever encrypts or retrieves these keys. Because PMK is known iff it is corrupted (a) is satisfied for KCK and TK. In the following, we assume that PMK, KCK, and TK are unknown. Assume that there exist two distinct instances $M_{r_1}[lsid_1]$ and $M_{r_2}[lsid_2]$ such that both instances have a pointer to KCK (and TK) and they belong to different sessions, i.e., $\tau_{4WHS(lsid_1, r_1)}(\rho) \neq \tau_{4WHS(lsid_2, r_2)}(\rho)$. Clearly, $M_{r_1}[lsid_1]$ and $M_{r_2}[lsid_2]$ are uncorrupted because PMK is marked unknown.

First, we consider the case that $r_1 = A$ (i.e., $M_{r_1}[lsid_1]$ is an instance of M_A). Let $((N_A, N_S), (pid_A, pid_S, name_{PMK})) := \tau_{4WHS(lsid_1, r_1)}(\rho)$ (i.e., $M_{r_1}[lsid_1]$ generated the nonce N_A and received N_S and $lsid_1 = (lsid_1', (pid_A, pid_S, name_{PMK}))$ for some $lsid_1'$). Since it holds that $\tau_{4WHS(lsid_1, r_1)}(\rho) \neq \tau_{4WHS(lsid_2, r_2)}(\rho)$ but both instances used the same PMK and salt (because they derived the same keys), we have that

$$
\begin{aligned}
\tau_{4WHS(lsid_2, r_2)}(\rho) \in \{ &((N_S, N_A), (pid_A, pid_S, name_{PMK})), \\
&((N_A, N_S), (pid_S, pid_A, name_{PMK})), \\
&((N_S, N_A), (pid_S, pid_A, name_{PMK})) \} \ .
\end{aligned}
$$

By our modeling of 4WHS, the same party never plays both the role of an authenticated and a supplicant with the same PMK (this setting must be excluded because otherwise, as mentioned above, a reflection attack would be possible), and hence, it holds that $\tau_{4WHS(lsid_2, r_2)}(\rho) = ((N_S, N_A), (pid_A, pid_S, name_{PMK}))$. Since ideal nonces do not collide and $M_{r_1}[lsid_1]$ generated N_A, the nonce N_S must have been generated by $M_{r_2}[lsid_2]$ (and N_A is the nonce received by $M_{r_2}[lsid_2]$). By definition of τ_{4WHS}, $r_2 = A$ (i.e., $M_{r_2}[lsid_2]$ is an instance of M_A too). It is easy to see that no other instance has a pointer to KCK (and TK) because ideal nonces do not collide. So, both instances $M_{r_1}[lsid_1]$ and $M_{r_2}[lsid_2]$ play role A, i.e., in the second protocol message, they expect to receive a MAC $mac_{KCK}(N_S, c_2)$ (resp., $mac_{KCK}(N_A, c_2)$) but KCK is never used to MAC a message, hence, the verification always fails (by definition of $\widetilde{\mathcal{F}}_{crypto}$). Hence, (b) is satisfied for KCK and neither $M_{r_1}[lsid_1]$ nor $M_{r_2}[lsid_2]$ complete the protocol. So, TK is never used for encryption or decryption, and hence, (b) is satisfied for TK too.

The case where $r_1 = S$ is similar. We can show that $r_2 = S$, i.e., both $M_{r_1}[lsid_1]$

$$
\begin{aligned}
&1. \quad A \rightarrow B: \quad N_A, pid_A \\
&2. \quad B \rightarrow A: \quad N_A, N_B, \mathrm{mac}_{AK}(pid_B, pid_A, N_A, N_B), pid_B \\
&3. \quad A \rightarrow B: \quad N_A, \mathrm{mac}_{AK}(pid_A, N_B), \{c_1\}_{TEK} \\
&4. \quad B \rightarrow A: \quad N_A, \{c_2\}_{TEK}
\end{aligned}
$$

Figure 7.7.: The EAP-PSK Protocol.

and $M_{r_2}[lsid_2]$ play role S, and that no other instance has a pointer to KCK and TK. Now, $M_{r_1}[lsid_1]$ and $M_{r_2}[lsid_2]$ expect to receive a MAC $\mathrm{mac}_{KCK}(N_A, c_3)$ (resp., $\mathrm{mac}_{KCK}(N_S, c_3)$) but KCK has only been used to MAC messages containing c_2. Since and $c_2 \neq c_3$, we can conclude that (b) is satisfied for KCK and TK. $\qquad\square$

To prove that $\mathcal{P}_{4\text{WHS}}$ realizes $\widehat{\mathcal{F}}_{\text{keyuse}}$ in the multi-session setting, i.e., to show that $\mathcal{P}_{4\text{WHS}} \,|\, \widetilde{\mathcal{F}}_{\text{crypto}} \leq \widehat{\mathcal{F}}_{\text{keyuse}}$, by Theorem 7.5, it now suffices to show that it holds that $\mathcal{P}_{4\text{WHS}} \,|\, \widetilde{\mathcal{F}}_{\text{crypto}} \leq_{\mathcal{T}_{4\text{WHS-single}^*}} \widehat{\mathcal{F}}_{\text{keyuse}}$, which follows from the results shown in Section 7.4.3 (now the proof would be even simpler because only a single-session setting has to be considered). Since this analysis is based on $\widetilde{\mathcal{F}}_{\text{crypto}}$, it can be done by syntactic arguments only (without reasoning about probabilities at all).

The EAP-PSK Protocol

The EAP-PSK protocol [BT07] is an Extensible Authentication Protocol (EAP) which provides mutual authentication and key exchange using a pre-shared key (PSK). It is inspired by AKEP2 [BR93]. The cryptographic core of the EAP-PSK protocol is depicted in Figure 7.7. In this, A is the initiator role; B is the responder role; pid_A is A's party name; pid_B is B's party name; N_A is A's nonce; N_B is B's nonce; c_1 and c_2 are two distinct constants; PRF is a pseudorandom function for key derivation; A and B have a pre-shared key *PSK*; the MAC key AK and the key derivation key KDK are derived from *PSK* using a constant salt:

$$
AK \| KDK := \mathrm{PRF}(PSK, \texttt{"0"}) \ ;
$$

the session key TEK is derived from KDK using the nonce N_B as a salt:

$$
TEK := \mathrm{PRF}(KDK, N_B) \ .
$$

The session key TEK is used in an authenticated symmetric encryption scheme for key confirmation in the last two protocol messages.

Modeling this protocol as a multi-session real protocol $\mathcal{P}_{\text{EAP-PSK}} = !M_A \,|\, !M_B$ that uses $\widetilde{\mathcal{F}}_{\text{crypto}}$ for all cryptographic operations (i.e., key derivation, MAC, symmetric encryption) is straightforward. The key derivation key *PSK* is a pre-shared key with name $(\min\{pid_A, pid_B\}, \max\{pid_A, pid_B\})$ (we assume a total order on party names, e.g., lexicographical order) of some type $t \in \mathcal{T}_{\text{derive}}$ in $\widetilde{\mathcal{F}}_{\text{crypto}}$, i.e., it is shared between the parties pid_A and pid_B. The protocol $\mathcal{P}_{\text{EAP-PSK}}$ is meant to realize $\widehat{\mathcal{F}}_{\text{keyuse}}$, i.e., after the session key TEK is established, the parties can send encryption and decryption requests to M_A and M_B which are encrypted under the session key. (Note that it does not realize $\widehat{\mathcal{F}}_{\text{ke}}$ because the session key is used for key confirmation.)

Similar to $\mathcal{P}_{\text{TLS}}$, the session parameters are of the form $sp = (pid_A, pid_B)$ and all local SIDs are of the form $lsid = (lsid', (pid_A, pid_B))$ for some $lsid'$ and some party names pid_A and pid_B. The instance $M_A[lsid]$ then models the local session $lsid'$ of party pid_A in role A talking to pid_B and $M_B[lsid]$ models the local session $lsid'$ of party pid_B in role B talking to pid_A.

Corruption is modeled as for $\mathcal{P}_{\text{4WHS}}$: An instance of M_A or M_B is corrupted if it is *directly corrupted* (i.e., by a corrupt message from the adversary at the beginning) or *indirectly corrupted* (i.e., the pre-shared key PSK is corrupted in $\widetilde{\mathcal{F}}_{\text{crypto}}$).

This concludes the description of the modeling of EAP-PSK. As for $\mathcal{P}_{\text{TLS}}$, it is easy to see that $\mathcal{P}_{\text{EAP-PSK}} \,|\, \mathcal{F}$ is environment strictly bounded for every environmentally strictly bounded protocol system $\mathcal{F}$ that has the same I/O interface as $\widetilde{\mathcal{F}}_{\text{crypto}}$. Hence, $\mathcal{P}_{\text{EAP-PSK}}$ is in the class of real protocols considered in Section 7.6.

The proof that $\mathcal{P}_{\text{EAP-PSK}}$ satisfies implicit disjointness, since we use $\widetilde{\mathcal{F}}_{\text{crypto}}$ for all cryptographic operations, is completely syntactic (i.e., no reduction arguments and not even reasoning about probabilities).

The partnering function $\tau_{\text{EAP-PSK}}$ for $\mathcal{P}_{\text{EAP-PSK}}$ we use is the obvious one: Let ρ be a run of $\mathcal{E} \,|\, \mathcal{P}_{\text{EAP-PSK}} \,|\, \widetilde{\mathcal{F}}_{\text{crypto}}$ for some environment $\mathcal{E}$ and $\alpha = (m_1, t_1), \ldots, (m_l, t_l)$ be the projection of ρ to the sequence of messages (with tapes) sent and received by some instance $M_r[lsid]$ on its network tapes, i.e., $r \in \{A, B\}$ and $lsid = (lsid', (pid_A, pid_B))$ for some $lsid', pid_A, pid_B$. If $M_r[lsid]$ is (directly or indirectly) corrupted, then we define $\tau_{\text{EAP-PSK}}(\alpha) := \text{corr}$ (note that this information is contained in α because, if the instance is directly corrupted, the adversary sent a special message to the instance and, if the instance is indirectly corrupted, the instance sent a special message to the adversary). If $M_r[lsid]$ is uncorrupted and α contains at least the first two protocol messages, then $\tau_{\text{EAP-PSK}}(\alpha) := ((N_A, N_B), (pid_A, pid_B))$ where N_A is the nonce contained in the first protocol message and N_B is the nonce contained in the second protocol message. Otherwise, $\tau_{\text{EAP-PSK}}(\alpha) := \bot$. It is easy to see that $\tau_{\text{EAP-PSK}}$ is valid for $\mathcal{P}_{\text{EAP-PSK}}$ because every instance generated one nonce itself and ideal nonces (i.e., nonces generated using $\widetilde{\mathcal{F}}_{\text{crypto}}$) do not collide (but even if nonces were generated regularly, i.e., without an ideal functionality, this would be easy to see).

Theorem 7.8. $\mathcal{P}_{\text{EAP-PSK}}$ *satisfies implicit disjointness w.r.t.* $\tau_{\text{EAP-PSK}}$.

Proof. Let $\mathcal{E} \in \text{Env}(\mathcal{P}_{\text{EAP-PSK}} \,|\, \widetilde{\mathcal{F}}_{\text{crypto}})$ be an environment and let ρ be a run of $\mathcal{E} \,|\, \mathcal{P}_{\text{EAP-PSK}} \,|\, \widetilde{\mathcal{F}}_{\text{crypto}}$ (for some security parameter and external input). We now show that implicit disjointness is satisfied for this run, i.e., more precisely, that (a) and (b) of Definition 7.12 (implicit disjointness) are satisfied. Let PSK be a pre-shared key in ρ, say for parties pid_A and pid_B. This key (potentially) is an explicitly shared key.

Since PSK is never encrypted or retrieved, it is either corrupted (i.e., always known) or always unknown in ρ. That is, (a) is satisfied for PSK. Furthermore, if PSK is known, then all (directly or indirectly) derived keys, i.e., AK, KDK, and TEK are always known in ρ. So, (a) is satisfied for all these keys. Also, for known keys (b) is trivially satisfied, i.e., in the following we assume that PSK is unknown.

Since PSK is a key derivation key, it cannot be used for destruction requests and, hence, (b) is trivially satisfied for PSK. We note that AK and KDK (potentially) are explicitly shared keys. Just as PSK, they are never encrypted or retrieved in ρ, i.e., they are always unknown in ρ (because they are derived from the unknown key PSK). So, (a) is satisfied for AK and KDK. Trivially, (b) is satisfied for KDK because it is a key derivation key. Next, we show that (b) is also satisfied for AK and that TEK (which is derived from KDK) is *not* explicitly shared. First, we show that (b) is satisfied for AK, i.e., that AK only successfully verifies MACs for messages which have been MACed in the same session (according to $\tau_{\text{EAP-PSK}}$).

For the MAC in the second protocol message (i.e., $\text{mac}_{AK}(pid_B, pid_A, N_A, N_B)$) this is obvious because it contains the nonces N_A, N_B and the party names pid_A, pid_B. Now, let $M_B[lsid_B]$ with $lsid_B = (lsid'_B, (pid_A, pid_B))$ (for some $lsid'_B, pid_A, pid_B$) be an instance of M_B (i.e., party pid_B in role B talking to pid_A) such that $M_B[lsid_B]$ has successfully verified the MAC in the third protocol message (i.e., $\text{mac}_{AK}(pid_A, N_B)$ where N_B is the nonce generated by $M_B[lsid_B]$) in ρ. Since directly corrupted instances do not have access to $\widetilde{\mathcal{F}}_{\text{crypto}}$ and AK is marked unknown, $M_B[lsid_B]$ is uncorrupted. By definition of $\tau_{\text{EAP-PSK}}$, we have that $\tau_{\text{EAP-PSK}(lsid_B, B)}(\rho) = ((N_A, N_B), (pid_A, pid_B))$ where N_A is the nonce $M_B[lsid_B]$ received in the first protocol message. Such a message is only MACed by an uncorrupted instance $M_A[lsid_A]$ of M_A with $lsid_A = (lsid'_A, (pid_A, pid_B))$ (for some $lsid'_A$ and pid'_B) which previously verified the MAC $\text{mac}_{AK}(pid'_B, pid_A, N'_A, N_B)$ where N'_A is the nonce generated by $M_A[lsid_A]$. Furthermore, only $M_B[lsid_B]$ can have MACed such a message because it contains N_B and, hence, we obtain that $pid'_B = pid_A$ and $N'_A = N'_A$. We conclude that $\tau_{\text{EAP-PSK}(lsid_A, A)}(\rho) = \tau_{\text{EAP-PSK}(lsid_B, B)}(\rho) = ((N_A, N_B), (pid_A, pid_B))$, i.e., $M_A[lsid_A]$ and $M_B[lsid_B]$ are partners in ρ. Hence, (b) is satisfied for AK.

Now, we show that TEK is *not* explicitly shared. Let $M_B[lsid_B]$ with $lsid_B = (lsid'_B, (pid_A, pid_B))$ (for some $lsid'_B, pid_A, pid_B$) be an uncorrupted instance of M_B such that $M_B[lsid_B]$ has derived $TEK := \text{PRF}(KDK, N_B)$. Then, N_B is the nonce generated by $M_B[lsid_B]$ and $\tau_{\text{EAP-PSK}(lsid_B, B)}(\rho) = ((N_A, N_B), (pid_A, pid_B))$ where N_A is the nonce that $M_B[lsid_B]$ received in the first protocol message. Because N_B is the salt, it is easy to see that there exists no other instance of M_B which derived this TEK. Assume that there exists an uncorrupted instance $M_A[lsid_A]$ (for some $lsid_A$) of M_A that derived $TEK := \text{PRF}(KDK, N_B)$. Exactly as above, it can be shown that $\tau_{\text{EAP-PSK}(lsid_A, A)}(\rho) = \tau_{\text{EAP-PSK}(lsid_B, B)}(\rho) = ((N_A, N_B), (pid_A, pid_B))$ (because $M_A[lsid_A]$ verified the MAC in the second protocol message before it derived TEK), i.e., $M_B[lsid_B]$ and $M_A[lsid_A]$ are partners in ρ and, hence, TEK is not explicitly shared.

Altogether, this shows that $\mathcal{P}_{\text{EAP-PSK}}$ satisfies implicit disjointness. $\qquad\square$

We note that showing implicit disjointness of EAP-PSK would be simpler if the MAC in the third protocol message would also contain B's name pid_B and A's nonce N_A (in a way that the message format differs from the one in the second protocol message) and if the salt to derive the session key *TEK* would contain both party names and both nonces (instead of just N_B). Then, it would be trivial to see that the MAC that is verified in the third protocol step has been generated by a partner and that *TEK* is not explicitly shared. But since EAP-PSK takes a somewhat minimalistic approach, as seen in the above proof, more effort is required to show these two statements.

A more detailed analysis and a proof that $\mathcal{P}_{\text{EAP-PSK}}$ realizes $\widehat{\mathcal{F}}_{\text{keyuse}}$ is future work. We only note that it should be quite easy now to prove this because, to show that $\mathcal{P}_{\text{EAP-PSK}}$ realizes $\widehat{\mathcal{F}}_{\text{keyuse}}$ in the multi-session setting, i.e., $\mathcal{P}_{\text{EAP-PSK}} \,|\, \widetilde{\mathcal{F}}_{\text{crypto}} \leq \widehat{\mathcal{F}}_{\text{keyuse}}$, by Theorem 7.5, it suffices to prove $\mathcal{P}_{\text{EAP-PSK}} \,|\, \widetilde{\mathcal{F}}_{\text{crypto}} \leq_{\mathcal{T}\text{EAP-PSK-single*}} \widetilde{\mathcal{F}}_{\text{keyuse}}$. Furthermore, since all cryptographic operations are supported by $\widetilde{\mathcal{F}}_{\text{crypto}}$, proving this should be possible by syntactic reasoning based on $\widetilde{\mathcal{F}}_{\text{crypto}}$ (without reduction arguments or reasoning about probabilities at all).

The SSH Protocol

The Secure Shell (SSH) protocol, consists of several subprotocols. In this section, we analyze two main parts of SSH, see below. The SSH Transport Layer Protocol [YL06b] first runs a key exchange protocol (typically Diffie-Hellman key exchange authenticated by digital signatures) to establishes a unique SID *sid* and a session key K. This session key K is then used to derive encryption and MAC keys which are used to encrypt and MAC all following messages. The Transport Layer Protocol only authenticates the server S (not the client C), therefore, the SSH Authentication Protocol [YL06a] is run (on top of the SSH Transport Layer Protocol) to authenticates the client C, e.g., by the Public Key Authentication Method or the Password Authentication Method. Here, we only consider the Public Key Authentication Method. The cryptographic core of the authenticated Diffie-Hellman key exchange (messages 1 to 4) with following Public Key Authentication Method (messages 5 and 6) is depicted in Figure 7.8. In this, pid_C and pid_S are the party names of C and S, respectively; N_C and N_S denote C's and S's nonces; c_1 and c_2, which are part of first two protocol messages, are used to negotiate algorithms, we model these as constants; p is a publicly known large safe prime; g is a publicly known generator for a subgroup of $\text{GF}(p)$; q is the order of the subgroup; the numbers x and y are chosen (by C and S, respectively) uniformly at random from $\{2, \ldots, q-1\}$; g^x and g^y are computed modulo p; k_S and k_C are S's and C's public key (we note that we identify public keys with party names and always use the pair pid_S, k_S or pid_C, k_C in protocol messages for the public key of S or C, respectively); the session key $K := g^{xy} \bmod p$; the SID

$$sid := H(N_C, N_S, pid_S, k_S, g^x, g^y, K)$$

1. $C \rightarrow S$: c_1, N_C
2. $S \rightarrow C$: c_2, N_S
3. $C \rightarrow S$: g^x
4. $S \rightarrow C$: $pid_S, k_S, g^y, \mathrm{sig}_{k_S}(sid)$
5. $C \rightarrow S$: $\{pid_C, k_C, \mathrm{sig}_{k_C}(sid, pid_C, k_C)\}^{\text{enc-and-mac}}_{EKCS,IKCS}$
6. $S \rightarrow C$: $\{\texttt{"success"}\}^{\text{enc-and-mac}}_{EKSC,IKSC}$

Figure 7.8.: The SSH Key Exchange Protocol (Public Key Authentication Method).

where H is a hash function; by $\{m\}^{\text{enc-and-mac}}_{k_1,k_2}$ we denote encrypt-and-MAC, i.e., we define $\{m\}^{\text{enc-and-mac}}_{k_1,k_2} := (\{m\}_{k_1}, \mathrm{mac}_{k_2}(m))$; the encryption keys $EKCS$ (client to server) and $EKSC$ (server to client) and the MAC keys $IKCS$ (client to server) and $IKSC$ (server to client) are derived from K using H as follows:

$$EKCS := H(K\|sid\|\texttt{"C"}\|sid) \ ,$$
$$EKSC := H(K\|sid\|\texttt{"D"}\|sid) \ ,$$
$$IKCS := H(K\|sid\|\texttt{"E"}\|sid) \ ,$$
$$IKSC := H(K\|sid\|\texttt{"F"}\|sid) \ .$$

After the protocol is completed, a secure channel is established using the keys $EKCS$, $EKSC$, $IKCS$, and $IKSC$.

Modeling this protocol as a multi-session real protocol $\mathcal{P}_{\text{SSH}} = !M_C \,|\, !M_S$ that uses $\widetilde{\mathcal{F}}_{\text{crypto}}$ for digital signatures is straightforward. All other cryptographic operations (i.e., encryption, MAC, hashing) are carried out by M_C and M_S itself because $\widetilde{\mathcal{F}}_{\text{crypto}}$ does not support Diffie-Hellman key exchange and, hence, K (and all derived keys) cannot be a key in $\widetilde{\mathcal{F}}_{\text{crypto}}$. The protocol $\mathcal{P}_{\text{SSH}}$ is meant to realize $\widehat{\mathcal{F}}_{\text{keyuse}}$ (key usability for authenticated symmetric encryption), i.e., after the keys are established, the parties can send encryption and decryption requests to M_C and M_S which are MACed and encrypted under the corresponding keys. (Note that it does not realize $\widehat{\mathcal{F}}_{\text{ke}}$ because the session keys are used for key confirmation.)

The session parameters are of the form $sp = pid_S$ for a party name of a server and the local SIDs contain the client's party name. More precisely, we require that local SIDs are of the form $lsid = ((pid_C, lsid'), pid_S)$ for some party names pid_C and pid_S and some bit string $lsid'$. If an instance of M_C or M_S, respectively, is created with a local SID that does not satisfy the above requirements, it terminates. The instance $M_C[lsid]$ then models the local session $lsid'$ of party pid_C in role C talking to pid_S and $M_S[lsid]$ models the local session $lsid'$ of party pid_S in role S talking to pid_C. We note that, since the client's name is not included in the session parameters (but only in the local part of the local SID), the session grouping mechanism of multi-session local-SID functionalities (i.e., $\mathcal{F}_{\text{session}}$) does not guarantee that servers only belong to sessions where the clients have the intended names. In Remark 7.5, we describe how this can still be guaranteed. The reason the client's name is not included in the session parameters is that it cannot be part of an SID that is assigned by a partnering function that is used for implicit disjointness, see below.

We model public keys here as we did for TLS (see above), i.e., we assume that all public keys are known to all parties and, to refer to the public/private key pair in of a party in $\widetilde{\mathcal{F}}_{\mathrm{crypto}}$, we use her party name.

Corruption in $\mathcal{P}_{\mathrm{SSH}}$ is modeled as follows: When an instance of M_C or M_S gets activated for the first time (i.e., upon receiving an Establish request), it sends a request to the adversary asking whether it is corrupted. If the adversary decides to corrupt this instance, then this instance sets its flag corr to 1 and we call it *corrupted*. The adversary can only corrupt an instance at the beginning, i.e., before the instance starts executing the protocol. A corrupted instance gives complete control to the adversary by forwarding all messages between the adversary and the environment. Note that, by this definition, corrupted instances never send any requests to $\widetilde{\mathcal{F}}_{\mathrm{crypto}}$.[79] An instance that is not corrupted (i.e., its flag corr is 0) is called *uncorrupted*. For an uncorrupted instance, we assume that its own and its intended partner's public/private key are uncorrupted in $\widetilde{\mathcal{F}}_{\mathrm{crypto}}$. More precisely, every instance of M_C and M_S checks that this condition is satisfied (by asking $\widetilde{\mathcal{F}}_{\mathrm{crypto}}$ for the corruption status of the public/private keys) at the end of the protocol (i.e., just before/after sending/receiving the last protocol message) and, if the condition is not met, the instance halts. (Note that signature keys are adaptively corruptible, so, these keys might get corrupted later.) It makes sense to assume that the intended partner's public/private key is uncorrupted because, in this case, we do not assume any security guarantees to hold.

We note that corrupted instances of M_C and M_S will, when realizing $\widehat{\mathcal{F}}_{\mathrm{keyuse}}$, correspond to corrupted users in $\widehat{\mathcal{F}}_{\mathrm{keyuse}}$, i.e., the simulator will corrupt these users in $\widehat{\mathcal{F}}_{\mathrm{keyuse}}$ before they get an SID, and hence, can exactly simulate these instances. We further remark that an adversary can gain complete control over a whole party by corrupting her public/private key pair in $\widetilde{\mathcal{F}}_{\mathrm{crypto}}$ and all her instances of M_C and M_S.

Remark 7.4. Corruption in $\mathcal{P}_{\mathrm{SSH}}$ is modeled differently than for the above protocols. For SSH, we do not distinguish between *directly* and *indirectly* corrupted instances. An instance of M_C or M_S is either corrupted, and then completely controlled by the adversary, or it is uncorrupted, and then both its own and its partner's public/private signature key are uncorrupted. This modeling of corruption has one limitation: It does not model scenarios where an honest party engages in a session with a dishonest party and also in a session with an honest party (at the same time or after each

---

[79]We could allow the adversary to send requests (for digital signatures; no other primitives are modeled using $\widetilde{\mathcal{F}}_{\mathrm{crypto}}$) to $\widetilde{\mathcal{F}}_{\mathrm{crypto}}$ in the name of a corrupted instance but then the public/private signature key of the party of that instance should be corrupted in $\widetilde{\mathcal{F}}_{\mathrm{crypto}}$. Since the adversary could then perform all signature verifications (with any public key) and signature generations (with the corrupted private key of that instance) herself (outside of $\widetilde{\mathcal{F}}_{\mathrm{crypto}}$), allowing corrupted instances access to $\widetilde{\mathcal{F}}_{\mathrm{crypto}}$ would not give more power to the adversary.

other). For example, consider the following scenario: The party pid_C is honest and runs two client instances $M_C[\text{lsid}_1]$ with $\text{lsid}_1 = ((pid_C, \text{lsid}_1'), pid_{S_1})$ (i.e., pid_C in role C talking to pid_{S_1}) and $M_C[\text{lsid}_2]$ with $\text{lsid}_2 = ((pid_C, \text{lsid}_2'), pid_{S_2})$ (i.e., pid_C in role C talking to pid_{S_2}) where $pid_{S_1} \neq pid_{S_2}$, the party pid_{S_1} is corrupted (in particularly, its public/private key is corrupted), and the party pid_{S_2} is uncorrupted (in particularly, its public/private key is uncorrupted). To create this scenario in a run of some environment $\mathcal{E}$ with $\mathcal{P}_{\text{SSH}} \mid \mathcal{P}_{\text{crypto}}$ (where $\mathcal{P}_{\text{crypto}}$ is the realization of $\tilde{\mathcal{F}}_{\text{crypto}}$ from Section 5.3), $\mathcal{E}$ must corrupt the first instance of pid_C, i.e., $M_C[\text{lsid}_1]$, because its intended partner's public/private key (i.e., the key of pid_{S_1}) is corrupted. Then, the environment can completely control $M_C[\text{lsid}_1]$ but, to model it precisely, it needs to compute a signature with pid_C's private key, and hence, $\mathcal{E}$ needs to corrupt pid_C's public/private key. Then, however, $\mathcal{E}$ is forced to corrupt also the second instance of pid_C, i.e., $M_C[\text{lsid}_2]$, although this should be an instance that belongs to an honest session. So, $\mathcal{E}$ cannot create this scenario.

To overcome this limitation, we could define corruption in $\mathcal{P}_{\text{SSH}}$ as for the above protocols, i.e., with the distinction between directly and indirectly corrupted instances. However, then, we could not analyze $\mathcal{P}_{\text{SSH}}$ using Theorem 7.5. We can still prove implicit disjointness for $\mathcal{P}_{\text{SSH}}$. But only for a different partnering function than the one we define below. Basically, the partnering function also assign SIDs to indirectly corrupted instances, just as for uncorrupted instances. Then, we cannot prove $\mathcal{P}_{\text{SSH}} \mid \tilde{\mathcal{F}}_{\text{crypto}} \leq_{\tau\text{-single}*} \mathcal{F}$ for any appropriate ideal functionality $\mathcal{F}$ because our restriction on well-formed simulators (Definition 7.10) requires that the protocol provides mutual authentication (see Remark 7.3) and, clearly, $\mathcal{P}_{\text{SSH}}$ does not provide mutual authentication for indirectly corrupted instances. We think that the requirements on well-formed simulators can be relaxed such that Theorem 7.5 remains valid and protocols $\mathcal{P}$ that do not provide authentication can satisfy $\mathcal{P} \mid \tilde{\mathcal{F}}_{\text{crypto}} \leq_{\tau\text{-single}*} \mathcal{F}$, see Chapter 8. In particularly, we think that this would include $\mathcal{P}_{\text{SSH}}$.

Remark 7.5. Assume that $\mathcal{P}_{\text{SSH}} \mid \tilde{\mathcal{F}}_{\text{crypto}}$ realizes some multi-session local-SID functionality $\mathcal{F} = \mathcal{F}_{\text{session}}^{F}$ (e.g., if $\mathcal{F} = \hat{\mathcal{F}}_{\text{keyuse}}$, then $F = \mathcal{F}_{\text{keyuse}}$). Since the client's name is not included in the session parameters, the session grouping mechanism of $\mathcal{F}$ (more precisely, the one of $\mathcal{F}_{\text{session}}$ in $\mathcal{F}$) does not guarantee that servers (i.e., users in role S) belong to sessions where the client (i.e., the user in role C) has the intended party name (i.e., the party name pid_C contained in the server's local SID). However, this can be guaranteed by F. Recall from the definition of multi-session local-SID functionalities that every instance of F handles one session and that this instance knows all local SIDs of all parties that belong to this session. Hence, F can be defined such that instances of F halt (i.e., terminate the session) if the local SIDs of the client and the server do not correspond on the party names. The ideal functionality $\mathcal{F}$ then guarantees that servers only belong to sessions where the client has the expected party name (except for terminated sessions).

This concludes the description of the modeling of SSH. As for $\mathcal{P}_{\text{TLS}}$, it is easy to see that $\mathcal{P}_{\text{SSH}} \mid \mathcal{F}$ is environment strictly bounded for every environmentally strictly bounded protocol system $\mathcal{F}$ that has the same I/O interface as $\widetilde{\mathcal{F}}_{\text{crypto}}$. Hence, $\mathcal{P}_{\text{SSH}}$ is in the class of real protocols considered in Section 7.6.

We now prove that $\mathcal{P}_{\text{SSH}}$ satisfies implicit disjointness. The proof does not need to exploit security of the encryption scheme, the MAC scheme, or the Diffie-Hellman key exchange. Moreover, in the proof, we can use $\widetilde{\mathcal{F}}_{\text{crypto}}$ for the digital signatures, so, no reduction proofs are necessary for digital signatures. We only need to assume collision resistance for the hash function H (see below).

The partnering function τ_{SSH} for $\mathcal{P}_{\text{SSH}}$ we use is the obvious one: Let ρ be a run of $\mathcal{E} \,|\, \mathcal{P}_{\text{SSH}} \,|\, \widetilde{\mathcal{F}}_{\text{crypto}}$ for some environment $\mathcal{E}$ and $\alpha = (m_1, t_1), \dots, (m_l, t_l)$ be the projection of ρ to the sequence of messages (with tapes) sent and received by some instance $M_r[\textit{lsid}]$ on its network tapes, i.e., $r \in \{C, S\}$ and $\textit{lsid} = ((\textit{pid}_C, \textit{lsid}'), \textit{pid}_S)$ for some $\textit{lsid}', \textit{pid}_C, \textit{pid}_S$. If $M_r[\textit{lsid}]$ is corrupted, then $\tau_{\text{SSH}}(\alpha) := \text{corr}$ (note that this information is contained in α because the adversary sent a special message to the instance to corrupt it). If $M_r[\textit{lsid}]$ is uncorrupted and α contains at least the first two protocol messages, then $\tau_{\text{SSH}}(\alpha) := ((N_C, N_S), \textit{pid}_S)$ where N_C is the nonce contained in the first protocol message and N_S is the nonce contained in the second protocol message. Otherwise, $\tau_{\text{SSH}}(\alpha) := \bot$. It is easy to see that τ_{SSH} is valid for $\mathcal{P}_{\text{SSH}}$ because every instance generated one nonce itself and ideal nonces (i.e., nonces generated using $\widetilde{\mathcal{F}}_{\text{crypto}}$) do not collide (but even if nonces were generated regularly, i.e., without an ideal functionality, this would be easy to see).

Theorem 7.9. *If the hash function H is collision resistant[80], then $\mathcal{P}_{\text{SSH}}$ satisfies implicit disjointness w.r.t. τ_{SSH}.*

Proof. Let $\mathcal{E}$ be an environment for $\mathcal{P}_{\text{SSH}} \,|\, \widetilde{\mathcal{F}}_{\text{crypto}}$. We define the event $B_{\text{coll}}(1^\eta, a)$ that in a run of $\mathcal{E} \,|\, \mathcal{P}_{\text{SSH}} \,|\, \widetilde{\mathcal{F}}_{\text{crypto}}$ (with security parameter η and external input a), two uncorrupted corrupted instances of M_C or M_S compute $\textit{sid} := H(m)$ and $\textit{sid}' := H(m')$ for some $m \neq m'$ such that $\textit{sid} = \textit{sid}'$ (i.e., a collision for H occurs).[81] Since H is collision resistant, it is easy to see that the probability that $B_{\text{coll}}(1^\eta, a)$ occurs is negligible (as a function in 1^η and a).[82] To show implicit disjointness for $\mathcal{P}_{\text{SSH}}$ it now suffices to only consider runs ρ where $B_{\text{coll}}(1^\eta, a)$ does not occur. Therefore, let ρ be a run of $(\mathcal{E} \,|\, \mathcal{P}_{\text{SSH}} \,|\, \widetilde{\mathcal{F}}_{\text{crypto}})(1^\eta, a)$ (i.e., for security parameter

---

[80] Collision resistance for hash function families has been first formalized by Damgård [Dam87]. We model H as a hash function family that is parameterized by a key. We assume that the environment honestly generates this key before the protocol starts and provides it to all instances of M_C and M_S. We recall the definition of collision resistance in Appendix D.3.3.

[81] We note that, formally, the instances of M_C and M_S use the (keyed) hash function h_k^η from the hash function family H, where k is the key honestly generated by $\mathcal{E}$ and provided to the instances.

[82] We can construct an adversary A against H as follows: A simulates a run of $\mathcal{E} \,|\, \mathcal{P}_{\text{SSH}} \,|\, \widetilde{\mathcal{F}}_{\text{crypto}}$ and always checks whether event B_{coll} occurs. If it does, A outputs the collision for H. If the run stops but B_{coll} did not occur, A aborts. A is polynomial time because $\mathcal{P}_{\text{SSH}} \,|\, \widetilde{\mathcal{F}}_{\text{crypto}}$ is environmentally strictly bounded, and hence, $\mathcal{E} \,|\, \mathcal{P}_{\text{SSH}} \,|\, \widetilde{\mathcal{F}}_{\text{crypto}}$ is strictly bounded. It is easy to see that the advantage of A against H (as defined in Appendix D.3.3) is the probability that B_{coll} occurs. Since H is collision resistant, the probability that B_{coll} occurs is negligible.

η and external input a) such that $B_{\mathrm{coll}}(1^\eta, a)$ does not occur. We now show that (a) and (b) of Definition 7.12 (implicit disjointness) are satisfied for ρ. Since only nonce generation and digital signature generation or verification is done using $\widetilde{\mathcal{F}}_{\mathrm{crypto}}$ (corrupted instances do not send requests to $\widetilde{\mathcal{F}}_{\mathrm{crypto}}$), (a) is trivially satisfied and, to show (b), we only have to consider signature verification requests.

Assume that an instance of M_C, say $M_C[\mathit{lsid}_C]$ with $\mathit{lsid}_C = ((\mathit{pid}_C, \mathit{lsid}'_C), \mathit{pid}_S)$, performed an accepted and ideal signature verification request in ρ. Since corrupted instance do not have access to $\widetilde{\mathcal{F}}_{\mathrm{crypto}}$, $M_C[\mathit{lsid}_C]$ is uncorrupted. Hence, by definition of M_C, $M_C[\mathit{lsid}_C]$ verified a signature of a message $\mathit{sid} = H(N_C, N_S, \mathit{pid}_S, k_S, g^x, g^y, K)$ with the public key of pid_S (fourth protocol message). Since this succeeds, sid must be recorded in $\widetilde{\mathcal{F}}_{\mathrm{crypto}}$ for the public/private key of pid_S. Hence, by definition of $\mathcal{P}_{\mathrm{SSH}}$, there exists an uncorrupted instance of M_S, say $M_S[\mathit{lsid}_S]$ with $\mathit{lsid}_S = ((\mathit{pid}'_C, \mathit{lsid}'_S), \mathit{pid}_S)$, that has signed sid (corrupted instances do not have access to $\widetilde{\mathcal{F}}_{\mathrm{crypto}}$, uncorrupted instances of M_C do not sign such messages, uncorrupted instances of M_S only sign messages with their own private key). That is, $M_S[\mathit{lsid}_S]$ has sent a corresponding signing request and it is left to show that $M_C[\mathit{lsid}_C]$ and $M_S[\mathit{lsid}_S]$ are partners. Since $M_S[\mathit{lsid}_S]$ signed sid, $M_S[\mathit{lsid}_S]$ and $M_C[\mathit{lsid}_C]$ agree on sid, i.e., they computed the same hash. Since $B_{\mathrm{coll}}(1^\eta, a)$ does not occur in ρ, we conclude that $M_S[\mathit{lsid}_S]$ and $M_C[\mathit{lsid}_C]$ also agree on the nonces N_C and N_S, i.e., $M_S[\mathit{lsid}_S]$ received N_C in the first protocol message and sent N_S in the second and, vice versa, $M_C[\mathit{lsid}_C]$ sent N_C in the first protocol message and received N_S in the second. By definition of τ_{SSH}, we conclude that $M_C[\mathit{lsid}_C]$ and $M_S[\mathit{lsid}_S]$ are partners (it holds that $\tau_{\mathrm{SSH}(\mathit{lsid}_C, C)}(\rho) = \tau_{\mathrm{SSH}(\mathit{lsid}_S, S)}(\rho) = ((N_C, N_S), \mathit{pid}_S))$. (Note that possibly $\mathit{pid}_C \neq \mathit{pid}'_C$, and hence, the client's party name cannot be a session parameter.)

Now, assume that an instance of M_S, say $M_S[\mathit{lsid}_S]$ with local SID $\mathit{lsid}_S = ((\mathit{pid}_C, \mathit{lsid}'_S), \mathit{pid}_S)$, performed an accepted and ideal signature verification request in ρ. This case is similar to the case above. Analogously, we obtain that $M_S[\mathit{lsid}_S]$ is uncorrupted and verified a signature of a message $(\mathit{sid}, \mathit{pid}_C, k_C)$ with $\mathit{sid} = H(N_C, N_S, \mathit{pid}_S, k_S, g^x, g^y, K)$ with the public key of pid_C (fifth protocol message) and that there exists an uncorrupted instance of M_C, say $M_C[\mathit{lsid}_C]$ with $\mathit{lsid}_C = ((\mathit{pid}_C, \mathit{lsid}'_C), \mathit{pid}'_S)$, that has signed $(\mathit{sid}, \mathit{pid}_C, k_C)$. That is, $M_S[\mathit{lsid}_S]$ has sent a corresponding signing request and it is left to show that $M_C[\mathit{lsid}_C]$ and $M_S[\mathit{lsid}_S]$ are partners. Since $M_C[\mathit{lsid}_C]$ signed $(\mathit{sid}, \mathit{pid}_C, k_C)$, $M_S[\mathit{lsid}_S]$ and $M_C[\mathit{lsid}_C]$ agree on sid, i.e., they computed the same hash. Since $B_{\mathrm{coll}}(1^\eta, a)$ does not occur in ρ, we conclude that $M_S[\mathit{lsid}_S]$ and $M_C[\mathit{lsid}_C]$ also agree on the server's name, i.e., $\mathit{pid}_S = \mathit{pid}'_S$, and on the nonces N_C and N_S. As above, we conclude that $M_C[\mathit{lsid}_C]$ and $M_S[\mathit{lsid}_S]$ are partners (according to τ_{SSH}). $\qquad\square$

A more detailed analysis and a proof that $\mathcal{P}_{\mathrm{SSH}}$ realizes $\widehat{\mathcal{F}}_{\mathrm{keyuse}}$ is future work. We note that to prove that $\mathcal{P}_{\mathrm{SSH}} \,|\, \widetilde{\mathcal{F}}_{\mathrm{crypto}} \leq \widehat{\mathcal{F}}_{\mathrm{keyuse}}$, one would need to do reduction arguments for the Diffie-Hellman key exchange, the hash function H, and the encryption and MAC scheme used for the keys $EKCS, EKSC, IKCS, IKSC$. However,

1. $I \to R$: c_1, g^x, N_I
2. $R \to I$: c_2, g^y, N_R
3. $I \to R$: $\{pid_I, pid_R, \mathrm{sig}_{k_I}(c_1, g^x, N_I, N_R, \mathrm{PRF}(SK_{pi}, pid_I)), c_3\}_{SK_{ei}, SK_{ai}}^{\mathrm{enc\text{-}then\text{-}mac}}$
4. $R \to I$: $\{pid_R, \mathrm{sig}_{k_R}(c_2, g^y, N_R, N_I, \mathrm{PRF}(SK_{pr}, pid_R)), c_4\}_{SK_{er}, SK_{ar}}^{\mathrm{enc\text{-}then\text{-}mac}}$

Figure 7.9.: The IKEv2 Protocol.

because $\mathcal{P}_{\mathrm{SSH}}$ satisfies implicit disjointness, by Theorem 7.5, it suffices to analyze a single session (i.e., to show that $\mathcal{P}_{\mathrm{SSH}} \mid \widetilde{\mathcal{F}}_{\mathrm{crypto}} \leq_{\tau_{\mathrm{SSH}}\text{-single}*} \widehat{\mathcal{F}}_{\mathrm{keyuse}}$) and one can use $\widetilde{\mathcal{F}}_{\mathrm{crypto}}$ for digital signatures. If one would extend $\widetilde{\mathcal{F}}_{\mathrm{crypto}}$ to support Diffie-Hellman key exchange (see Chapter 8), then this analysis would be greatly simplified because all cryptographic operations could be provided by $\widetilde{\mathcal{F}}_{\mathrm{crypto}}$.

The IKEv2 Protocol (IPsec)

The Internet Key Exchange Protocol Version 2 (IKEv2) [KHNE10] is used in the IPsec protocol suite to establish a session key. It uses Diffie-Hellman key exchange, which, e.g., is authenticated by digital signatures. The cryptographic core of the IKEv2 protocol is depicted in Figure 7.9. In this, I is the initiator role; R is the responder role; c_i for $i \leq 4$ are distinct constants which model fields of the messages, e.g., to negotiate algorithms, which we model as constants; p is a publicly known large safe prime; g is a publicly known generator for a subgroup of $\mathrm{GF}(p)$; q is the order of the subgroup; the numbers x and y are chosen (by I and R, respectively) uniformly at random from $\{2, \ldots, q-1\}$; g^x, g^y, and g^{xy} are computed modulo p; pid_I is I's party name; pid_R is R's party name; N_I and N_R denote I's and R's nonce, respectively; k_I is I's public key; k_R is R's public key; PRF is a pseudorandom function; the session key seed is $SKEYSEED := \mathrm{PRF}(N_I \| N_R, g^{xy})$; the key derivation key SK_d (see below), the MAC keys SK_{ai} (for direction I to R) and SK_{ar} (for direction R to I), the encryption keys SK_{ei} and SK_{er}, and the keys SK_{pi} and SK_{pr} (which are used to generate the authentication payload) are derived from $SKEYSEED$:

$$SK_d \| SK_{ai} \| SK_{ar} \| SK_{ei} \| SK_{er} \| SK_{pi} \| SK_{pr} := \mathrm{PRF}(SKEYSEED, N_I \| N_R \| c_1 \| c_2) \ ;$$

by $\{m\}_{k_1, k_2}^{\mathrm{enc\text{-}then\text{-}mac}}$ we denote encrypt-then-MAC, i.e., we define $\{m\}_{k_1, k_2}^{\mathrm{enc\text{-}then\text{-}mac}} :=$ $(\{m\}_{k_1}, \mathrm{mac}_{k_2}(\{m\}_{k_1}))$. The session key $KEYMAT$ is derived from the key derivation key:

$$KEYMAT := \mathrm{PRF}(SK_d, N_I \| N_R) \ .$$

Similar to SSH, modeling this protocol as a multi-session real protocol $\mathcal{P}_{\mathrm{IKEv2}} =$ $!M_I \mid !M_R$ that uses $\widetilde{\mathcal{F}}_{\mathrm{crypto}}$ for digital signatures is straightforward. All other cryptographic operations (i.e., encryption, MAC, key derivation) are carried out by M_I and M_R itself because $\widetilde{\mathcal{F}}_{\mathrm{crypto}}$ does not support Diffie-Hellman key exchange and, hence, g^{xy} (and all derived keys) cannot be a key in $\widetilde{\mathcal{F}}_{\mathrm{crypto}}$. The protocol $\mathcal{P}_{\mathrm{IKEv2}}$

is meant to realize $\widehat{\mathcal{F}}_{\text{keyuse}}$ (key usability for authenticated symmetric encryption), i.e., after the keys are established, the parties can send encryption and decryption requests to M_I and M_R which are encrypted under the session key. (Note that it does not realize $\widehat{\mathcal{F}}_{\text{ke}}$ because the session keys are used for key confirmation.)

In contrast to SSH, the session parameters are the empty bit string $sp = \varepsilon$ and the local SIDs contain the party names of the initiator and responder. More precisely, we require that local SIDs are of the form $lsid = ((pid_I, pid_R, lsid'), \varepsilon)$ for some party names pid_I and pid_R and some bit string $lsid'$. The instance $M_I[lsid]$ then models the local session $lsid'$ of party pid_I in role I talking to pid_R and $M_R[lsid]$ models the local session $lsid'$ of party pid_R in role R talking to pid_I. We note that the difference to SSH is that here the responder's name is not a session parameter but instead only in the local part of the local SID. The reason that we do not model the party names to be session parameters is that, in IKEv2, the agreement on the party names is only established by MACing the last two protocol messages. Hence, to show implicit disjointness for IKEv2 we then would need to exploit security of MACs (and key derivation), which we do not want to do because MACs and key derivation are not modeled using $\widetilde{\mathcal{F}}_{\text{crypto}}$, see below. Of course, this agreement must be established in a proof that $\mathcal{P}_{\text{IKEv2}}$ (single-session) realizes $\widehat{\mathcal{F}}_{\text{keyuse}}$. As discussed in Remark 7.5 for SSH, the ideal functionality that $\mathcal{P}_{\text{IKEv2}}$ realizes must be adjusted to guarantee that only initiators and responders that agree on the party names belong to the same session.

We model public keys here as we did for SSH (see above), i.e., we assume that all public keys are known to all parties and, to refer to the public/private key pair in of a party in $\widetilde{\mathcal{F}}_{\text{crypto}}$, we use her party name.

Also corruption in $\mathcal{P}_{\text{IKEv2}}$ is modeled as for SSH. The adversary can corrupt instances of M_I or M_R at the beginning and then gains complete control over these instances. For an instance that is not corrupted (i.e., its flag corr is 0), we assume that its own and its intended partner's public/private key is uncorrupted in $\widetilde{\mathcal{F}}_{\text{crypto}}$. For more details on modeling corruption, we refer to the remarks given for SSH (see above). As for SSH, this modeling has a limitation but it could be overcome exactly as for SSH, see Remark 7.4.

This concludes the description of the modeling of IKEv2. As for $\mathcal{P}_{\text{TLS}}$, it is easy to see that $\mathcal{P}_{\text{IKEv2}} \mid \mathcal{F}$ is environment strictly bounded for every environmentally strictly bounded protocol system $\mathcal{F}$ that has the same I/O interface as $\widetilde{\mathcal{F}}_{\text{crypto}}$. Hence, $\mathcal{P}_{\text{IKEv2}}$ is in the class of real protocols considered in Section 7.6.

The proof that $\mathcal{P}_{\text{IKEv2}}$ satisfies implicit disjointness, since we use $\widetilde{\mathcal{F}}_{\text{crypto}}$ for digital signatures, is completely syntactic (i.e., no reduction arguments and not even reasoning about probabilities). We note that implicit disjointness of $\mathcal{P}_{\text{IKEv2}}$ does not depend on the security of the encryption scheme, the MAC scheme, the Diffie-Hellman key exchange, or the pseudorandom function.

The partnering function τ_{IKEv2} for $\mathcal{P}_{\text{IKEv2}}$ we use is the obvious one: Let ρ be a run of $\mathcal{E} \mid \mathcal{P}_{\text{IKEv2}} \mid \widetilde{\mathcal{F}}_{\text{crypto}}$ for some environment $\mathcal{E}$ and $\alpha = (m_1, t_1), \ldots, (m_l, t_l)$ be the projection of ρ to the sequence of messages (with tapes) sent and received by some instance $M_r[\mathit{lsid}]$ on its network tapes, i.e., $r \in \{I, R\}$ and $\mathit{lsid} = ((\mathit{pid}_I, \mathit{pid}_R, \mathit{lsid}'), \varepsilon)$ for some $\mathit{pid}_I, \mathit{pid}_R, \mathit{lsid}'$ (recall that the session parameters are the empty bit string ε). If $M_r[\mathit{lsid}]$ is corrupted (note that this information is contained in α because the adversary sent a special message to the instance to corrupt it), then $\tau_{\mathrm{IKEv2}}(\alpha) := \mathsf{corr}$. If $M_r[\mathit{lsid}]$ is uncorrupted and α contains at least the first two protocol messages, then $\tau_{\mathrm{IKEv2}}(\alpha) := ((N_I, N_R), \varepsilon)$ where N_I is the nonce contained in the first protocol message and N_R is the nonce contained in the second protocol message. Otherwise, $\tau_{\mathrm{IKEv2}}(\alpha) := \bot$. It is easy to see that τ_{IKEv2} is valid for $\mathcal{P}_{\mathrm{IKEv2}}$ because every instance generated one nonce itself and ideal nonces (i.e., nonces generated using $\widetilde{\mathcal{F}}_{\mathrm{crypto}}$) do not collide (but even if nonces were generated regularly, i.e., without an ideal functionality, this would be easy to see).

Theorem 7.10. $\mathcal{P}_{\mathrm{IKEv2}}$ *satisfies implicit disjointness w.r.t.* τ_{IKEv2}.

Proof. It is easy to see that $\mathcal{P}_{\mathrm{IKEv2}}$ satisfies implicit disjointness w.r.t. τ_{IKEv2} because the signed messages from I and R contain N_I, N_R and N_R, N_I, respectively. Since only uncorrupted instances have access to $\widetilde{\mathcal{F}}_{\mathrm{crypto}}$, the only relevant cases are when a responder or an initiator performs a verification request to verify the signature of the initiator or responder, respectively.

First, we consider the case of the responder. So, let us assume that some uncorrupted instance of M_R, say $M_R[\mathit{lsid}_R]$, performed an accepted and ideal digital signature verification request (in some run of $\mathcal{E} \,|\, \mathcal{P}_{\mathrm{IKEv2}} \,|\, \widetilde{\mathcal{F}}_{\mathrm{crypto}}$ for some environment $\mathcal{E}$) under some public key of some party. Since the request is accepted and ideal, there exists an instance of M_I or M_R which has created the signature in this request. Since $c_1 \neq c_2$ and only uncorrupted instances have access to $\widetilde{\mathcal{F}}_{\mathrm{crypto}}$, this can only be an uncorrupted instance of M_I, say $M_I[\mathit{lsid}_I]$. Furthermore, since the message over which the signature is computed contains the nonces (N_I and N_R), the instances $M_R[\mathit{lsid}_R]$ and $M_I[\mathit{lsid}_I]$ agree on the nonces and, hence, are partners (according to τ_{IKEv2}).

The case of the initiator, i.e., where an uncorrupted instance of M_I performs an accepted and ideal digital signature verification request, is analogous.   □

A more detailed analysis and a proof that $\mathcal{P}_{\mathrm{IKEv2}}$ realizes $\widehat{\mathcal{F}}_{\mathrm{keyuse}}$ is future work. Similar to $\mathcal{P}_{\mathrm{SSH}}$, we note that to prove that $\mathcal{P}_{\mathrm{IKEv2}} \,|\, \widetilde{\mathcal{F}}_{\mathrm{crypto}} \leq \widehat{\mathcal{F}}_{\mathrm{keyuse}}$, one would need to do reduction arguments for the Diffie-Hellman key exchange, the pseudorandom function PRF, and the encryption and MAC schemes. But, by Theorem 7.5, it suffices to analyze a single session (i.e., to show that $\mathcal{P}_{\mathrm{IKEv2}} \,|\, \widetilde{\mathcal{F}}_{\mathrm{crypto}} \leq_{\tau_{\mathrm{IKEv2}}\text{-single*}} \widehat{\mathcal{F}}_{\mathrm{keyuse}}$) and one can use $\widetilde{\mathcal{F}}_{\mathrm{crypto}}$ for digital signatures. If one would extend $\widetilde{\mathcal{F}}_{\mathrm{crypto}}$ to support Diffie-Hellman key exchange, as we plan in future work, then this analysis would be greatly simplified because all cryptographic operations could be provided by $\widetilde{\mathcal{F}}_{\mathrm{crypto}}$.

We note that an analysis of $\mathcal{P}_{\mathrm{IKEv2}}$ using previous joint state composition theorems (see [CR03] and Section 4.2.6) would be somewhat imprecise because the SID N_I, N_R is not established strictly before the protocol starts but along with first two protocol messages which are also used for algorithm negotiation and Diffie-Hellman key exchange. Furthermore, one of the signed messages does not exactly contain the SID N_I, N_R (as stipulated by these joint state theorems) but contains N_R, N_I instead. We also note that the predecessor of IKEv2, namely IKE, has been analyzed in [CK02a]. In this analysis, although in a game-based setting, pre-established SIDs have been assumed similarly as in the UC model.

7.8. Related Work

Our criterion for universally composable secure key exchange protocols presented in Section 7.4 is related to the concept of secretive protocols proposed by Roy et al. [RDDM07] (see also [KT09b]). However, unlike our criterion, which can be checked based on information-theoretic/syntactical arguments, checking whether a protocol is secretive requires involved cryptographic reduction proofs. Also, Roy et al. do not prove implications for composable security.

The only work we are aware of that attempts to perform a cryptographic analysis of the 4-Way Handshake protocol of WPA2 (IEEE 802.11i) is [ZMM05]; secure channels are not considered. However, this work is quite preliminary: The security assumptions and theorems are not formulated precisely and no security proofs or proof sketches are available. In He et al. [HSD+05], the first *symbolic* analysis of WPA2 has been presented, based on their Protocol Composition Logic (PCL).

As mentioned in the introduction, universal composability approaches have, so far, only very rarely been applied to the analysis of (existing) real-world protocols. The most relevant works are the one by Gajek et al. [GMP+08] and Backes et al. [BCJ+06].

Gajek et al. [GMP+08] use Canetti's UC model to analyze the cryptographic core of TLS. As explained in Section 7.7.2, they show security for a single session of TLS and then, using composition theorems with joint state, obtain security of multiple sessions of a severely modified and idealized version of TLS, where pre-established SIDs are added at various places to the protocol messages.

Backes et al. [BCJ+06] carried out an analysis of Kerberos based on the Dolev-Yao style cryptographic library of Backes, Pfitzmann, and Waidner [BPW03, BP04]. However, it is an open problem whether symmetric encryption in this library has a reasonable realization; the original proof of the realization of the Dolev-Yao library in [BP04] is flawed, as examples presented in [CLC08a] illustrate (see also Section 5.5). Moreover, as already mentioned in Section 5.5, the Dolev-Yao library is only realizable by non-standard encryption schemes and assuming specific message formats. Hence, the modeling of Kerberos in [BCJ+06] is somewhat imprecise.

Game-based protocol analysis, i.e., analysis in a game-based setting, such as, a Bellare-Rogaway style model (see, e.g., [BR93, BR95]), might be advantageous over protocol analysis in a universal composability framework because game-based security definitions provide more flexibility. However, game-based analysis by itself does not support modular protocol analysis. In order to mitigate the complexity of game-based approaches, e.g., when analyzing real-world security protocols, several works aim at *modular* game-based analysis; see, e.g., [MSW10, BFWW11, Wil11] for recent results. However, the results that have been obtained for modular game-based analysis so far provide much less modularity than what can be achieved using our approach (i.e., security analysis based on $\mathcal{F}_{crypto}$ and using the composition and joint state theorems presented in Sections 7.5 and 7.6). Typically, in game-based analysis, even if modular, one still has to analyze multiple session of the lowermost protocol (e.g., a key exchange protocol) at once. Then, higher-level protocols (e.g., protocols that use a key exchange protocol as a subprotocol) might be analyzable using single-session reasoning. However, in any case, one has to perform (complex) reduction proofs to the underlying cryptographic primitives.

Barak et al. [BLR04] consider protocol initialization for the UC model and show how pre-established SIDs can be established in real protocols. For this purpose, they define a multi-session version $\mathcal{F}_{init}$ of an ideal functionality $\mathcal{F}$ which is similar to our multi-session local-SID version. Barak et al. show that, if a protocol $\mathcal{P}$ realizes $\mathcal{F}$, then Π_{init} realizes $\mathcal{F}_{init}$ where Π_{init} is a protocol that first executes an initialization phase (where nonces are exchanged between the participants) to establish an SID and then runs $\mathcal{P}$ with the established SID. However, Barak et al. do not aim at showing that a protocol without pre-established SIDs directly realizes $\mathcal{F}_{init}$, as we do. Also, composition theorems are not consider in [BLR04].

8. Conclusion

In this thesis, we proposed an ideal crypto functionality $\mathcal{F}_{\text{crypto}}$, an ideal functionality for symmetric and public-key encryption, key derivation, and MACs, and have shown that it can be realized based on standard cryptographic assumptions and constructions (Chapter 5). This functionality abstracts from the cryptographic primitives and can therefore be used to simplify the analysis of real-world protocols, without giving up on precise modeling. Based on $\mathcal{F}_{\text{crypto}}$, we identified a criterion which can be checked using merely information theoretic arguments or even syntactic reasoning and is sufficient to show security of key exchange protocols (Section 7.4). Furthermore, we presented a new universal composition theorem (Section 7.5) and a joint state composition theorem for $\mathcal{F}_{\text{crypto}}$ (Section 7.6) that allow us to obtain security of multiple protocol session by only showing security for a single protocol session. What is most important is that they are applicable to real-world protocols because they do not make use of pre-established SIDs.

We demonstrated the usefulness of $\mathcal{F}_{\text{crypto}}$ and the new composition theorems in several applications:

1. In Chapter 6, we obtained a computational soundness result for key exchange protocols that use symmetric encryption and we used $\mathcal{F}_{\text{crypto}}$ to simplify its proof.

2. In Section 7.4.3, using our criterion for secure key exchange protocols, we showed security of the 4-Way Handshake (4WHS) protocol of WPA2-PSK (IEEE 802.11i).

3. In Section 7.7, we demonstrated the applicability of the new composition theorems and $\mathcal{F}_{\text{crypto}}$ to the analysis of several real-world protocols (SSL/TLS, IEEE 802.11i, EAP-PSK, SSH, and IPsec).

These applications demonstrate that our approach enables highly modular, faithful analysis of (real-world) security protocols.

Since $\mathcal{F}_{\text{crypto}}$ does not support Diffie-Hellman (DH) key exchange, when analyzing security protocols that use this method (e.g., SSH, IPsec, and some modes of SSL/TLS), as discussed in Section 7.7.2, $\mathcal{F}_{\text{crypto}}$ is still valuable in this analysis but reduction proofs are necessary for cryptographic operations performed with keys obtained from DH key exchange. It should be possible to extend $\mathcal{F}_{\text{crypto}}$ by operations for DH key exchange. A key established using these operations could then be used for (ideal) cryptographic operations, just as any other symmetric key in $\mathcal{F}_{\text{crypto}}$. Realizing this extension of $\mathcal{F}_{\text{crypto}}$ should be possible under the standard decisional Diffie-Hellman (DDH) assumption if the environment is appropriately (but not overly) restricted.

In our computational soundness result, in Chapter 6, we only consider protocols that use symmetric encryption as their only cryptographic primitive. Since $\mathcal{F}_{crypto}$ not only supports symmetric encryption but also public-key encryption, MACs, and key derivation and $\mathcal{F}_{crypto}$ can be combined with other ideal functionalities for cryptographic primitives (such as digital signatures), it seems possible to extend our result to protocols that use several cryptographic primitives. In particular, it should be easy to extend it to protocols that use both symmetric and public-key encryption because our result should be combinable with the one of Canetti and Herzog [CH06] (we followed the general approach of Canetti and Herzog, who considered the case of public-key encryption). Furthermore, our computational soundness result is only applicable to protocols that use pre-established SIDs (because we use the joint state realization of $\mathcal{F}_{crypto}$ from Section 5.4, that makes use of pre-established SIDs). Using our joint state realization of $\mathcal{F}_{crypto}$ from Section 7.6, i.e., without pre-established SIDs, it should be possible to extend the computational soundness result to protocols without pre-established SIDs. More precisely, similarly to the proof of Theorem 6.1, it should be possible to show that a computational interpretation of a symbolic protocol realizes $\widehat{\mathcal{F}}_{ke}$ w.r.t. single-session environments (as defined in Section 7.6.1), where $\widehat{\mathcal{F}}_{ke}$ is the multi-session local-SID ideal key exchange functionality. If the computational interpretation of the protocol satisfies implicit disjointness, by Theorem 7.5, we then obtain that the protocol realizes $\widehat{\mathcal{F}}_{ke}$ (w.r.t. any environment, i.e., in the multi-session setting). Since implicit disjointness is not a symbolic criterion, this method would not be fully symbolic. However, it might be possible to develop an appropriate symbolic criterion which implies implicit disjointness.

As discussed in Remark 7.3, the joint state composition theorem without pre-established SIDs (Theorem 7.5) is basically only applicable to protocols that provide mutual authentication. This is due to the restrictions that we put on well-formed simulators (Definition 7.10). We think that these restrictions can be loosened (without changing the theorem otherwise) such that the theorem becomes applicable to protocols that do not provide mutual authentication. As discussed in Remark 7.4, this would also allow a better modeling of corruption for SSH and IPsec. More precisely, we require that a well-formed simulator precisely simulates the real protocol and aborts if the protocol produces I/O output before the simulator is in its second stage (i.e., before a complete session has been established). This could probably be relaxed as follows: It should suffice to only require that the simulator simulates every role of the real protocol until the SID of this role is determined. Then, the simulator could be allowed to deviate from the simulation of this role, in particularly, I/O output for these roles could be allowed (although they might not belong to a complete session yet). However, to be able to prove the joint state theorem it seems to be needed that the state of the simulator is somewhat modular such that new simulated roles can be added to the simulation as soon as their SID is set. It would be interesting to see how far our joint state composition theorem can be generalized.

Bibliography

[ABB+05]   A. Armando, D. Basin, Y. Boichut, Y. Chevalier, L. Compagna, J. Cuéllar, P. Drielsma, P.-C. Héam, O. Kouchnarenko, J. Mantovani, S. Mödersheim, D. von Oheimb, M. Rusinowitch, J. Santiago, M. Turuani, L. Viganò, and L. Vigneron. The AVISPA Tool for the Automated Validation of Internet Security Protocols and Applications. In K. Etessami and S. Rajamani, editors, *Computer Aided Verification, 17th International Conference (CAV 2005)*, volume 3576 of *Lecture Notes in Computer Science*, pages 281–285. Springer, 2005.

[AF01]   M. Abadi and C. Fournet. Mobile Values, New Names, and Secure Communication. In *Proceedings of the 28th ACM Symposium on Principles of Programming Languages (POPL 2001)*, pages 104–115. ACM, 2001.

[APW09]   M. R. Albrecht, K. G. Paterson, and G. J. Watson. Plaintext Recovery Attacks against SSH. In *IEEE Symposium on Security and Privacy (S&P 2009)*, pages 16–26. IEEE Computer Society, 2009.

[AR00]   M. Abadi and P. Rogaway. Reconciling Two Views of Cryptography (The Computational Soundness of Formal Encryption). In J. van Leeuwen, O. Watanabe, M. Hagiya, P. Mosses, and T. Ito, editors, *Theoretical Computer Science, Exploring New Frontiers of Theoretical Informatics, International Conference (IFIPTCS 2000)*, volume 1872 of *Lecture Notes in Computer Science*, pages 3–22. Springer, 2000.

[BAF05]   B. Blanchet, M. Abadi, and C. Fournet. Automated Verification of Selected Equivalences for Security Protocols. In *20th IEEE Symposium on Logic in Computer Science (LICS 2005)*, pages 331–340. IEEE Computer Society, 2005.

[Bau05]   M. Baudet. Deciding Security of Protocols Against Off-Line Guessing Attacks. In V. Atluri, C. Meadows, and A. Juels, editors, *Proceedings of the 12th ACM Conference on Computer and Communications Security (CCS 2005)*, pages 16–25. ACM, 2005.

[BCJ+06]   M. Backes, I. Cervesato, A. D. Jaggard, A. Scedrov, and J.-K. Tsay. Cryptographically Sound Security Proofs for Basic and Public-Key Kerberos. In D. Gollmann, J. Meier, and A. Sabelfeld, editors, *Computer Security - ESORICS 2006, 11th European Symposium on Research in Computer Security*, volume 4189 of *Lecture Notes in Computer Science*, pages 362–383. Springer, 2006.

[BDK07]   M. Backes, M. Dürmuth, and R. Küsters. On Simulatability Soundness and Mapping Soundness of Symbolic Cryptography. In *Proceedings of the 27th International Conference on Foundations of Software Technology and Theoretical Computer Science (FSTTCS 2007)*, volume 4855 of *Lecture Notes in Computer Science*, pages 108–120. Springer, 2007.

[BDPR98] M. Bellare, A. Desai, D. Pointcheval, and P. Rogaway. Relations Among Notions of Security for Public-Key Encryption Schemes. In H. Krawczyk, editor, *Advances in Cryptology, 18th Annual International Cryptology Conference (CRYPTO 1998)*, volume 1462 of *Lecture Notes in Computer Science*, pages 549–570. Springer, 1998.

[BFGT06] K. Bhargavan, C. Fournet, A. D. Gordon, and S. Tse. Verified Interoperable Implementations of Security Protocols. In *Proceedings of the 19th IEEE Computer Security Foundations Workshop (CSFW-19 2006)*, pages 139–152. IEEE Computer Society, 2006.

[BFWW11] C. Brzuska, M. Fischlin, B. Warinschi, and S. Williams. Composability of Bellare-Rogaway Key Exchange Protocol. In *Proceedings of the 18th ACM Conference on Computer and Communications Security (CCS 2011)*, pages 51–62. ACM, 2011.

[BGM04]   M. Bellare, O. Goldreich, and A. Mityagin. The Power of Verification Queries in Message Authentication and Authenticated Encryption. Technical Report 2004/309, Cryptology ePrint Archive, 2004. Available at http://eprint.iacr.org/2004/309.

[BGR95]   M. Bellare, R. Guérin, and P. Rogaway. XOR MACs: New Methods for Message Authentication Using Finite Pseudorandom Functions. In D. Coppersmith, editor, *Advances in Cryptology - CRYPTO '95, 15th Annual International Cryptology Conference, Proceedings*, volume 963 of *Lecture Notes in Computer Science*, pages 15–28. Springer, 1995.

[BH04]   M. Backes and D. Hofheinz. How to Break and Repair a Universally Composable Signature Functionality. In *Information Security, 7th International Conference, ISC 2004, Proceedings*, volume 3225 of *Lecture Notes in Computer Science*, pages 61–72. Springer, 2004.

[BHK09]   M. Bellare, D. Hofheinz, and E. Kiltz. Subtleties in the Definition of IND-CCA: When and How Should Challenge-Decryption be Disallowed? Technical Report 2009/418, Cryptology ePrint Archive, 2009. Available at http://eprint.iacr.org/2009/418.

[BKR94]   M. Bellare, J. Kilian, and P. Rogaway. The Security of Cipher Block Chaining. In Y. Desmedt, editor, *Advances in Cryptology - CRYPTO '94, 14th Annual International Cryptology Conference, Proceedings*, volume

839 of *Lecture Notes in Computer Science*, pages 341–358. Springer, 1994.

[BKR00] M. Bellare, J. Kilian, and P. Rogaway. The Security of the Cipher Block Chaining Message Authentication Code. *Journal of Computer and System Sciences*, 61(3):362–399, 2000.

[Bla01] B. Blanchet. An Efficient Cryptographic Protocol Verifier Based on Prolog Rules. In *Proceedings of the 14th IEEE Computer Security Foundations Workshop (CSFW-14)*, pages 82–96. IEEE Computer Society, 2001.

[Bla06] B. Blanchet. A Computationally Sound Mechanized Prover for Security Protocols. In *IEEE Symposium on Security and Privacy (S&P 2006)*, pages 140–154. IEEE Computer Society, 2006.

[Bla07] B. Blanchet. Computationally Sound Mechanized Proofs of Correspondence Assertions. In *20th IEEE Computer Security Foundations Symposium (CSF 2007)*, pages 97–111. IEEE Computer Society, 2007.

[BLR04] B. Barak, Y. Lindell, and T. Rabin. Protocol Initialization for the Framework of Universal Composability. Technical Report 2004/006, Cryptology ePrint Archive, 2004. Available at http://eprint.iacr.org/2004/006.

[BMP05] G. Bella, F. Massacci, and L. Paulson. An Overview of the Verification of SET. *International Journal of Information Security*, 4:17–28, 2005.

[BN00] M. Bellare and C. Namprempre. Authenticated Encryption: Relations among Notions and Analysis of the Generic Composition Paradigm. In T. Okamoto, editor, *Advances in Cryptology - ASIACRYPT 2000, 6th International Conference on the Theory and Application of Cryptology and Information Security, 2000, Proceedings*, volume 1976 of *Lecture Notes in Computer Science*, pages 531–545. Springer, 2000.

[BP04] M. Backes and B. Pfitzmann. Symmetric Encryption in a Simulatable Dolev-Yao Style Cryptographic Library. In *17th IEEE Computer Security Foundations Workshop (CSFW-17 2004)*, pages 204–218. IEEE Computer Society, 2004.

[BPR00] M. Bellare, D. Pointcheval, and P. Rogaway. Authenticated Key Exchange Secure against Dictionary Attacks. In B. Preneel, editor, *Advances in Cryptology – EUROCRYPT 2000*, volume 1807 of *Lecture Notes in Computer Science*, pages 139–155. Springer, 2000.

[BPW03] M. Backes, B. Pfitzmann, and M. Waidner. A Composable Cryptographic Library with Nested Operations. In S. Jajodia, V. Atluri, and T. Jaeger, editors, *Proceedings of the 10th ACM Conference on Computer and Communications Security (CCS 2003)*, pages 220–230. ACM, 2003.

[BR93]   M. Bellare and P. Rogaway. Entity Authentication and Key Distribution. In D. Stinson, editor, *Advances in Cryptology – Crypto '93, 13th Annual International Cryptology Conference*, volume 773 of *Lecture Notes in Computer Science*, pages 232–249. Springer, 1993.

[BR95]   M. Bellare and P. Rogaway. Provably Secure Session Key Distribution: The Three Party Case. In *Proceedings of the Twenty-Seventh Annual ACM Symposium on Theory of Computing (STOC'95)*, pages 57–66. ACM, 1995.

[BRS02]   J. Black, P. Rogaway, and T. Shrimpton. Encryption-Scheme Security in the Presence of Key-Dependent Messages. In K. Nyberg and H. M. Heys, editors, *Selected Areas in Cryptography, 9th Annual International Workshop (SAC 2002)*, volume 2595 of *Lecture Notes in Computer Science*, pages 62–75. Springer, 2002.

[BT07]   F. Bersani and H. Tschofenig. The EAP-PSK Protocol: A Pre-Shared Key Extensible Authentication Protocol (EAP) Method. RFC 4764 (Experimental), January 2007.

[BU08]   M. Backes and D. Unruh. Computational Soundness of Symbolic Zero-Knowledge Proofs Against Active Attackers. In *Proceedings of the 21st IEEE Computer Security Foundations Symposium (CSF 2008)*, pages 255–269. IEEE Computer Society, 2008.

[Can01]   R. Canetti. Universally Composable Security: A New Paradigm for Cryptographic Protocols. In *Proceedings of the 42nd Annual Symposium on Foundations of Computer Science (FOCS 2001)*, pages 136–145. IEEE Computer Society, 2001.

[Can04]   R. Canetti. Universally Composable Signature, Certification, and Authentication. In *Proceedings of the 17th IEEE Computer Security Foundations Workshop (CSFW-17 2004)*, pages 219–233. IEEE Computer Society, 2004.

[Can05]   R. Canetti. Universally Composable Security: A New Paradigm for Cryptographic Protocols. Technical Report 2000/067, Cryptology ePrint Archive, December 2005. Available at http://eprint.iacr.org/2000/067.

[Can06]   R. Canetti. Security and Composition of Cryptographic Protocols: A Tutorial. Technical Report 2006/465, Cryptology ePrint Archive, 2006. Available at http://eprint.iacr.org/2006/465.

[CDNO97]   R. Canetti, C. Dwork, M. Naor, and R. Ostrovsky. Deniable Encryption. In B. S. K. Jr., editor, *Advances in Cryptology - CRYPTO '97, 17th Annual International Cryptology Conference, Proceedings*, volume 1294 of *Lecture Notes in Computer Science*, pages 90–104. Springer, 1997.

[CDPW07]   R. Canetti, Y. Dodis, R. Pass, and S. Walfish. Universally Composable Security with Global Setup. In S. P. Vadhan, editor, *Theory of Cryptography, Proceedings of TCC 2007*, volume 4392 of *Lecture Notes in Computer Science*, pages 61–85. Springer, 2007.

[CF01]   R. Canetti and M. Fischlin. Universally Composable Commitments. In *Advances in Cryptology—CRYPTO 2001, 21st Annual International Cryptology Conference*, volume 2139 of *Lecture Notes in Computer Science*, pages 19–40. Springer, 2001.

[CH05]   K.-K. R. Choo and Y. Hitchcock. Security Requirements for Key Establishment Proof Models: Revisiting Bellare-Rogaway and Jeong-Katz-Lee Protocols. In C. Boyd and J. M. G. Nieto, editors, *Information Security and Privacy, 10th Australasian Conference (ACISP 2005)*, volume 3574 of *Lecture Notes in Computer Science*, pages 429–442. Springer, 2005.

[CH06]   R. Canetti and J. Herzog. Universally Composable Symbolic Analysis of Mutual Authentication and Key-Exchange Protocols. In S. Halevi and T. Rabin, editors, *Theory of Cryptography, Third Theory of Cryptography Conference, TCC 2006*, volume 3876 of *Lecture Notes in Computer Science*, pages 380–403. Springer, 2006.

[CJS+08]   I. Cervesato, A. D. Jaggard, A. Scedrov, J.-K. Tsay, and C. Walstad. Breaking and Fixing Public-key Kerberos. *Inf. Comput.*, 206(2-4):402–424, 2008.

[CK01]   R. Canetti and H. Krawczyk. Analysis of Key-Exchange Protocols and Their Use for Building Secure Channels. In B. Pfitzmann, editor, *Advances in Cryptology – EUROCRYPT 2001*, volume 2045 of *Lecture Notes in Computer Science*, pages 453–474. Springer, 2001.

[CK02a]   R. Canetti and H. Krawczyk. Security Analysis of IKE's Signature-Based Key-Exchange Protocol. In M. Yung, editor, *Advances in Cryptology - CRYPTO 2002, 22nd Annual International Cryptology Conference*, volume 2442 of *Lecture Notes in Computer Science*, pages 143–161. Springer, 2002.

[CK02b]   R. Canetti and H. Krawczyk. Universally Composable Notions of Key Exchange and Secure Channels. In *Advances in Cryptology - EUROCRYPT 2002, International Conference on the Theory and Applications of Cryptographic Techniques, Proceedings*, volume 2332 of *Lecture Notes in Computer Science*, pages 337–351. Springer, 2002.

[CKKW06] V. Cortier, S. Kremer, R. Küsters, and B. Warinschi. Computationally
          Sound Symbolic Secrecy in the Presence of Hash Functions. In *Proceedings of the 26th Conference on Foundations of Software Technology and Theoretical Computer Science (FSTTCS 2006)*, volume 4337 of *Lecture Notes in Computer Science*, pages 176–187. Springer, 2006.

[CLC08a] H. Comon-Lundh and V. Cortier. Computational soundness of observational equivalence. Technical Report INRIA Research Report RR-6508, INRIA, 2008. Available at http://www.loria.fr/~cortier/Papiers/CCS08-report.pdf.

[CLC08b] H. Comon-Lundh and V. Cortier. Computational Soundness of Observational Equivalence. In *Proceedings of the 15th ACM Conference on Computer and Communications Security (CCS 2008)*, pages 109–118. ACM, 2008.

[CLC11]   H. Comon-Lundh and V. Cortier. How to Prove Security of Communication Protocols? A Discussion on the Soundness of Formal Models w.r.t. Computational Ones. In T. Schwentick and C. Dürr, editors, *Proceedings of the 28th International Symposium on Theoretical Aspects of Computer Science (STACS 2011)*, volume 9 of *LIPIcs*, pages 29–44. Schloss Dagstuhl – Leibniz-Zentrum fuer Informatik, 2011.

[CLCS12] H. Comon-Lundh, V. Cortier, and G. Scerri. Security Proof with Dishonest Keys. In P. Degano and J. D. Guttman, editors, *Principles of Security and Trust – First International Conference, POST 2012*, volume 7215 of *Lecture Notes in Computer Science*, pages 149–168. Springer, 2012.

[CR03]   R. Canetti and T. Rabin. Universal Composition with Joint State. In *Advances in Cryptology, 23rd Annual International Cryptology Conference (CRYPTO 2003), Proceedings*, volume 2729 of *Lecture Notes in Computer Science*, pages 265–281. Springer, 2003.

[CW05]   V. Cortier and B. Warinschi. Computationally Sound, Automated Proofs for Security Protocols. In *Proceedings of the 14th European Symposium on Programming (ESOP 2005)*, volume 3444 of *Lecture Notes in Computer Science*, pages 157–171. Springer, 2005.

[CZ06]   V. Cortier and E. Zalinescu. Deciding Key Cycles for Security Protocols. In M. Hermann and A. Voronkov, editors, *Proceedings of the 13th International Conference on Logic for Programming, Artificial Intelligence, and Reasoning (LPAR 2006)*, volume 4246 of *Lecture Notes in Computer Science*, pages 317–331. Springer, 2006.

[Dam87]   I. Damgård. Collision Free Hash Functions and Public Key Signature Schemes. In D. Chaum and W. L. Price, editors, *Advances in Cryptology - EUROCRYPT '87, Workshop on the Theory and Application of Cryptographic Techniques, Proceedings*, volume 304 of *Lecture Notes in Computer Science*, pages 203–216. Springer, 1987.

[DDM+06]   A. Datta, A. Derek, J. C. Mitchell, A. Ramanathan, and A. Scedrov. Games and the Impossibility of Realizable Ideal Functionality. In S. Halevi and T. Rabin, editors, *TCC*, volume 3876 of *Lecture Notes in Computer Science*, pages 360–379. Springer, 2006.

[DDMW06]   A. Datta, A. Derek, J. C. Mitchell, and B. Warinschi. Computationally Sound Compositional Logic for Key Exchange Protocols. In *Proceedings of the 19th IEEE Computer Security Foundations Workshop (CSFW-19 2006)*, pages 321–334. IEEE Computer Society, 2006.

[DP10]   J. P. Degabriele and K. G. Paterson. On the (In)Security of IPsec in MAC-then-Encrypt Configurations. In *17th ACM Conference on Computer and Communications Security (CCS 2010)*, pages 493–504. ACM, 2010.

[DR08]   T. Dierks and E. Rescorla. The Transport Layer Security (TLS) Protocol Version 1.2. RFC 5246 (Proposed Standard), August 2008. Updated by RFCs 5746, 5878, 6176.

[DY83]   D. Dolev and A. Yao. On the Security of Public-Key Protocols. *IEEE Transactions on Information Theory*, 29(2):198–208, 1983.

[GM84]   S. Goldwasser and S. Micali. Probabilistic Encryption. *Journal of Computer and System Sciences*, 28(2):270–299, April 1984.

[GMP+08]   S. Gajek, M. Manulis, O. Pereira, A. Sadeghi, and J. Schwenk. Universally Composable Security Analysis of TLS. In J. Baek, F. Bao, K. Chen, and X. Lai, editors, *Provable Security, Second International Conference (ProvSec 2008)*, volume 5324 of *Lecture Notes in Computer Science*, pages 313–327. Springer, 2008.

[GMR88]   S. Goldwasser, S. Micali, and R. Rivest. A Digital Signature Scheme Secure Against Adaptive Chosen-Message Attacks. *SIAM Journal on Computing*, 17(2):281–308, 1988.

[HM05]   C. He and J. C. Mitchell. Security Analysis and Improvements for IEEE 802.11i. In *Proceedings of the Network and Distributed System Security Symposium (NDSS 2005)*, pages 90–110. The Internet Society, 2005.

[HS11]   D. Hofheinz and V. Shoup. GNUC: A New Universal Composability Framework. Technical Report 2011/303, Cryptology ePrint Archive, 2011. Available at http://eprint.iacr.org/2011/303.

[HSD+05]   C. He, M. Sundararajan, A. Datta, A. Derek, and J. C. Mitchell. A
                Modular Correctness Proof of IEEE 802.11i and TLS. In V. Atluri,
                C. Meadows, and A. Juels, editors, *12th ACM Conference on Computer
                and Communications Security (CCS 2005)*, pages 2–15. ACM, 2005.

[HUMQ09]   D. Hofheinz, D. Unruh, and J. Müller-Quade. Polynomial Runtime and
                Composability. Technical Report 2009/023, Cryptology ePrint Archive,
                2009. Available at http://eprint.iacr.org/2009/023.

[IEE04]   IEEE Standard 802.11i-2004. Medium Access Control (MAC) Secu-
                rity Enhancements, Amendment 6 to IEEE Standard for Information
                technology – Telecommunications and information exchange between
                systems – Local and metropolitan area networks – Specific requirements
                – Part 11: Wireless LAN Medium Access Control (MAC) and Physical
                Layer (PHY) specifications, July 2004.

[IEE07]   IEEE Standard 802.11-2007. Wireless LAN Medium Access Control
                (MAC) and Physical Layer (PHY) Specifications, Part 11 of IEEE Stan-
                dard for Information technology – Telecommunications and information
                exchange between systems – Local and metropolitan area networks –
                Specific requirements, June 2007.

[Jon02]   J. Jonsson. On the Security of CTR + CBC-MAC. In K. Nyberg
                and H. M. Heys, editors, *Selected Areas in Cryptography, 9th Annual
                International Workshop (SAC 2002)*, volume 2595 of *Lecture Notes in
                Computer Science*, pages 76–93. Springer, 2002.

[KHNE10]   C. Kaufman, P. Hoffman, Y. Nir, and P. Eronen. Internet Key Exchange
                Protocol Version 2 (IKEv2). RFC 5996 (Proposed Standard), September
                2010. Updated by RFC 5998.

[KM07]   S. Kremer and L. Mazaré. Adaptive Soundness of Static Equivalence.
                In J. Biskup and J. Lopez, editors, *Proceedings of the 12th European
                Symposium On Research In Computer Security (ESORICS 2007)*, volume
                4734 of *Lecture Notes in Computer Science*, pages 610–625. Springer,
                2007.

[Kra03]   H. Krawczyk. SIGMA: The 'SIGn-and-MAc' Approach to Authenticated
                Diffie-Hellman and Its Use in the IKE-Protocols. In D. Boneh, editor,
                *Advances in Cryptology - CRYPTO 2003, 23rd Annual International
                Cryptology Conference*, volume 2729 of *Lecture Notes in Computer
                Science*, pages 400–425. Springer, 2003.

[Kra10]   H. Krawczyk. Cryptographic Extraction and Key Derivation: The
                HKDF Scheme. In T. Rabin, editor, *Advances in Cryptology - CRYPTO
                2010, 30th Annual Cryptology Conference, Proceedings*, volume 6223 of
                Lecture Notes in Computer Science, pages 631–648. Springer, 2010.

[KSS09]   K. Kobara, S. Shin, and M. Strefler. Partnership in Key Exchange Protocols. In W. Li, W. Susilo, U. K. Tupakula, R. Safavi-Naini, and V. Varadharajan, editors, *Proceedings of the 2009 ACM Symposium on Information, Computer and Communications Security (ASIACCS 2009)*, pages 161–170. ACM, 2009.

[KT08]   R. Küsters and M. Tuengerthal. Joint State Theorems for Public-Key Encryption and Digital Signature Functionalities with Local Computation. In *Proceedings of the 21st IEEE Computer Security Foundations Symposium (CSF 2008)*, pages 270–284. IEEE Computer Society, 2008.

[KT09a]   R. Küsters and M. Tuengerthal. Computational Soundness for Key Exchange Protocols with Symmetric Encryption. In E. Al-Shaer, S. Jha, and A. D. Keromytis, editors, *Proceedings of the 16th ACM Conference on Computer and Communications Security (CCS 2009)*, pages 91–100. ACM, 2009.

[KT09b]   R. Küsters and M. Tuengerthal. Universally Composable Symmetric Encryption. In *Proceedings of the 22nd IEEE Computer Security Foundations Symposium (CSF 2009)*, pages 293–307. IEEE Computer Society, 2009.

[KT11a]   R. Küsters and M. Tuengerthal. Composition Theorems Without Pre-Established Session Identifiers. In Y. Chen, G. Danezis, and V. Shmatikov, editors, *Proceedings of the 18th ACM Conference on Computer and Communications Security (CCS 2011)*, pages 41–50. ACM, 2011.

[KT11b]   R. Küsters and M. Tuengerthal. Ideal Key Derivation and Encryption in Simulation-Based Security. In A. Kiayias, editor, *Topics in Cryptology – CT-RSA 2011, The Cryptographers' Track at the RSA Conference 2011, Proceedings*, volume 6558 of *Lecture Notes in Computer Science*, pages 161–179. Springer, 2011.

[KT13]   R. Küsters and M. Tuengerthal. The IITM Model: a Simple and Expressive Model for Universal Composability. Technical Report 2013/025, Cryptology ePrint Archive, 2013. Available at http://eprint.iacr.org/2013/025.

[Küs06]   R. Küsters. Simulation-Based Security with Inexhaustible Interactive Turing Machines. In *Proceedings of the 19th IEEE Computer Security Foundations Workshop (CSFW-19 2006)*, pages 309–320. IEEE Computer Society, 2006. See [KT13] for a full and revised version.

[Lau04]   P. Laud. Symmetric Encryption in Automatic Analyses for Confidentiality against Active Adversaries. In *IEEE Symposium on Security and Privacy 2004 (S&P 2004)*, pages 71–85. IEEE Computer Society, 2004.

[Low95]   G. Lowe. An Attack on the Needham-Schroeder Public-Key Authentication Protocol. *Information Processing Letters*, 56:131–133, 1995.

[MSC04]   C. Meadows, P. F. Syverson, and I. Cervesato. Formal Specification and Analysis of the Group Domain Of Interpretation Protocol using NPATRL and the NRL Protocol Analyzer. *Journal of Computer Security*, 12(6):893–931, 2004.

[MSS98]   J. Mitchell, V. Shmatikov, and U. Stern. Finite-State Analysis of SSL 3.0. In *Seventh USENIX Security Symposium*, pages 201–216. USENIX, 1998.

[MSW10]   P. Morrissey, N. P. Smart, and B. Warinschi. The TLS Handshake Protocol: A Modular Analysis. *Journal of Cryptology*, 23(2):187–223, 2010.

[MTY11]   T. Malkin, I. Teranishi, and M. Yung. Key Dependent Message Security: Recent Results and Applications. In R. S. Sandhu and E. Bertino, editors, *First ACM Conference on Data and Application Security and Privacy, CODASPY 2011, Proceedings*, pages 3–12. ACM, 2011.

[MW04]   D. Micciancio and B. Warinschi. Soundness of Formal Encryption in the Presence of Active Adversaries. In M. Naor, editor, *First Theory of Cryptography Conference (TCC 2004)*, volume 2951 of *Lecture Notes in Computer Science*, pages 133–151. Springer, 2004.

[MW09]   L. Mazare and B. Warinschi. Separating Trace Mapping and Reactive Simulatability Soundness: The Case of Adaptive Corruption. In *Proceedings of the Joint Workshop on Automated Reasoning for Security Protocol Analysis and Issues in the Theory of Security (ARSPA-WITS'09)*, volume 5511 of *Lecture Notes in Computer Science*, pages 193–210. Springer, 2009.

[NS78]   R. Needham and M. Schroeder. Using Encryption for Authentication in Large Networks of Computers. *Communications of the ACM*, 21(12):993–999, 1978.

[NS87]   R. M. Needham and M. D. Schroeder. Authentication Revisited. *SIGOPS Operating Systems Review*, 21(1):7–7, January 1987.

[OM09]   T. Ohigashi and M. Morii. A Practical Message Falsification Attack on WPA. In *Proceedings of the Fourth Joint Workshop on Information Security (JWIS 2009)*, 2009.

[PW01]   B. Pfitzmann and M. Waidner. A Model for Asynchronous Reactive Systems and its Application to Secure Message Transmission. In *IEEE Symposium on Security and Privacy*, pages 184–201. IEEE Computer Society, 2001.

[RD09]   M. Ray and S. Dispensa. Renegotiating TLS. Available at `http://`
           `extendedsubset.com/Renegotiating_TLS.pdf`, November 2009.

[RDDM07]   A. Roy, A. Datta, A. Derek, and J. C. Mitchell. Inductive Proofs of
           Computational Secrecy. In J. Biskup and J. Lopez, editors, *Proceedings
           of the 12th European Symposium On Research In Computer Security
           (ESORICS 2007)*, volume 4734 of *Lecture Notes in Computer Science*,
           pages 219–234. Springer, 2007.

[RS04]   P. Rogaway and T. Shrimpton. Cryptographic Hash-Function Basics:
           Definitions, Implications, and Separations for Preimage Resistance,
           Second-Preimage Resistance, and Collision Resistance. In B. K. Roy
           and W. Meier, editors, *Fast Software Encryption, 11th International
           Workshop, FSE 2004*, volume 3017 of *Lecture Notes in Computer Science*,
           pages 371–388. Springer, 2004.

[RS09]   P. Rogaway and T. Stegers. Authentication without Elision: Partially
           Specified Protocols, Associated Data, and Cryptographic Models De-
           scribed by Code. In *Proceedings of the 22nd IEEE Computer Security
           Foundations Symposium (CSF 2009)*, pages 26–39. IEEE Computer
           Society, 2009.

[TB09]   E. Tews and M. Beck. Practical Attacks against WEP and WPA. In
           D. A. Basin, S. Capkun, and W. Lee, editors, *Proceedings of the Second
           ACM Conference on Wireless Network Security (WISEC 2009)*, pages
           79–86. ACM, 2009.

[Wil11]   S. C. Williams. Analysis of the SSH Key Exchange Protocol. In L. Chen,
           editor, *13th IMA International Conference of Cryptography and Coding
           (IMACC 2011)*, volume 7089 of *Lecture Notes in Computer Science*,
           pages 356–374. Springer, 2011.

[YL06a]   T. Ylonen and C. Lonvick. The Secure Shell (SSH) Authentication
           Protocol. RFC 4252 (Proposed Standard), January 2006.

[YL06b]   T. Ylonen and C. Lonvick. The Secure Shell (SSH) Transport Layer
           Protocol. RFC 4253 (Proposed Standard), January 2006.

[ZMM05]   F. Zhang, J. Ma, and S. Moon. The Security Proof of a 4-Way Hand-
           shake Protocol in IEEE 802.11i. In Y. Hao, J. Liu, Y. Wang, Y. ming
           Cheung, H. Yin, L. Jiao, J. Ma, and Y.-C. Jiao, editors, *Computational
           Intelligence and Security, International Conference (CIS 2005)*, volume
           3802 of *Lecture Notes in Computer Science*, pages 488–493. Springer,
           2005.

A. Realizations of Long-Term Key Functionalities

In this appendix, we provide proofs of the Theorems 4.3, 4.4, and 4.5 from Section 4.2.

A.1. Proof of Theorem 4.3

In this section, we prove Theorem 4.3, i.e., that a symmetric encryption scheme $\Sigma = (\mathsf{gen}, \mathsf{enc}, \mathsf{dec})$ is IND-CCA2 secure (Definition 3.3) iff $!\mathcal{P}_{\mathrm{senc}} \leq !\mathcal{F}_{\mathrm{senc}}^{\mathrm{unauth}}$ and that Σ is IND-CPA secure and INT-CTXT (Definitions 3.2 and 3.4) iff $!\mathcal{P}_{\mathrm{senc}} \leq !\mathcal{F}_{\mathrm{senc}}^{\mathrm{auth}}$.

"$!\mathcal{P}_{\mathrm{senc}}$ realizes $!\mathcal{F}_{\mathrm{senc}} \Rightarrow \Sigma$ is secure"

This direction is easy to prove: Given any IND-CCA2, IND-CPA, or INT-CTXT adversary A we can easily construct an environment $\mathcal{E}$ for $!\mathcal{P}_{\mathrm{senc}}$ such that the advantage of A is bounded by (a constant fraction of) the advantage of $\mathcal{E}$ distinguishing between $!\mathcal{P}_{\mathrm{senc}}$ and $\mathcal{S} \mid !\mathcal{F}_{\mathrm{senc}}^{\mathrm{unauth}}$ or $\mathcal{S} \mid !\mathcal{F}_{\mathrm{senc}}^{\mathrm{auth}}$, respectively, for every simulator $\mathcal{S}$. The environment $\mathcal{E}$ simply simulates A using one instance of $\mathcal{P}_{\mathrm{senc}}$ (or $\mathcal{F}_{\mathrm{senc}}^{\mathrm{unauth}}$ or $\mathcal{F}_{\mathrm{senc}}^{\mathrm{auth}}$, respectively) for encryption and decryption to simulate the oracles of A.

"Σ is secure $\Rightarrow$ $!\mathcal{P}_{\mathrm{senc}}$ realizes $!\mathcal{F}_{\mathrm{senc}}$"

To show this direction, we first note that both $!\mathcal{P}_{\mathrm{senc}}$ and $!\mathcal{F}_{\mathrm{senc}}$ are σ-session versions (as defined in Section 2.4) for the following SID function σ: For all messages m and tapes c: $\sigma(m, c) := name$ if c is an I/O tape and $m = (id, name, m')$ or c is a network tape and $m = (name, m')$ (for some $id, name, m'$). Otherwise, $\sigma(m, c) := \bot$. Hence, by Theorem 2.3, it suffices to show that $!\mathcal{P}_{\mathrm{senc}} \leq_{\sigma\text{-single}} !\mathcal{F}_{\mathrm{senc}}$, to obtain that $!\mathcal{P}_{\mathrm{senc}} \leq !\mathcal{F}_{\mathrm{senc}}$. That is, it suffices to show that a single instance of $\mathcal{P}_{\mathrm{senc}}$ realizes a single instance of $\mathcal{F}_{\mathrm{senc}}$.

We now define a (single-session) simulator $\mathcal{S}$ and prove $\mathcal{E} \mid !\mathcal{P}_{\mathrm{senc}} \equiv \mathcal{E} \mid \mathcal{S} \mid !\mathcal{F}_{\mathrm{senc}}$ for every single-session environment $\mathcal{E} \in \mathrm{Env}_{\sigma\text{-single}}(!\mathcal{P}_{\mathrm{senc}})$.

The definition of the simulator $\mathcal{S}$ is straightforward (we can use the same simulator for both authenticated and unauthenticated encryption). It forwards the Init request from (one instance of) $\mathcal{F}_{\mathrm{senc}}$ to the environment and when the environment responds with $(name, corr, k)$ then $\mathcal{S}$ forwards $(name, corr, \mathsf{enc}, \mathsf{dec}, k')$ to $\mathcal{F}_{\mathrm{senc}}$ where $k' := k$ if $corr = 1$ (i.e., upon corruption $\mathcal{S}$ provides the key provided by the environment) and $k' \leftarrow \mathsf{gen}(1^\eta)$ if $corr \neq 1$ (i.e., $\mathcal{S}$ generates and provides a fresh key in the uncorrupted case); where η is the security parameter. Upon any other input from the environment, S stops in this activation with empty output. It is easy to see that $S \mid !\mathcal{F}_{\text{senc}}$ is environmentally strictly bounded. In particular, $S \in \text{Sim}_{\sigma\text{-single}}^{!\mathcal{P}_{\text{senc}}}(!\mathcal{F}_{\text{senc}})$.

Unauthenticated encryption. We first show that, if Σ is IND-CCA2 secure, then $\mathcal{E} \mid !\mathcal{P}_{\text{senc}} \equiv \mathcal{E} \mid S \mid !\mathcal{F}_{\text{senc}}^{\text{unauth}}$ for every single-session environment $\mathcal{E}$ for $!\mathcal{P}_{\text{senc}}$. This proves the first statement of the theorem. Therefore, assume that Σ is IND-CCA2 secure and let $\mathcal{E} \in \text{Env}_{\sigma\text{-single}}(\mathcal{P}_{\text{senc}})$.

We define an IND-CCA2 adversary A and show that its advantage against Σ equals the advantage of $\mathcal{E}$ in distinguishing between $!\mathcal{P}_{\text{senc}}$ and $S \mid !\mathcal{F}_{\text{senc}}^{\text{unauth}}$.

The adversary $A^{O_1(\cdot,\cdot),O_2(\cdot)}(1^\eta, a)$ (with encryption oracle O_1 and decryption oracle O_2) simulates a run of $\mathcal{E}$ with security parameter η and external input a as follows:

1. When $\mathcal{E}$ sends the first message to one instance of $\mathcal{P}_{\text{senc}}$, say to $\mathcal{P}_{\text{senc}}[name]$ (recall that $\mathcal{E}$ is single-session, so, it only activates this instance of $\mathcal{P}_{\text{senc}}$), then A records this message and records that (this instance of) $\mathcal{P}_{\text{senc}}$ is *waiting for initialization*. In the following, we omit the name $name$ from all requests and by $\mathcal{P}_{\text{senc}}$ we denote the instance $\mathcal{P}_{\text{senc}}[name]$. Then, A continues the simulation of $\mathcal{E}$ with network input Init from $\mathcal{P}_{\text{senc}}$.

2. When $\mathcal{E}$ sends a message of the form $(corr, k)$ to the network interface of $\mathcal{P}_{\text{senc}}$ and A has recorded $\mathcal{P}_{\text{senc}}$ as waiting for initialization, then A records $\mathcal{P}_{\text{senc}}$ as *initialized*. Furthermore, A records $\mathcal{P}_{\text{senc}}$ as *corrupted* and A records k if $corr = 1$. Then, A continues the simulation of $\mathcal{E}$ as if $\mathcal{E}$ now sends the recorded message to $\mathcal{P}_{\text{senc}}$, see below.

3. When $\mathcal{E}$ sends (Enc, x) to the I/O interface of $\mathcal{P}_{\text{senc}}$ and A has recorded $\mathcal{P}_{\text{senc}}$ as corrupted, then A computes $y \leftarrow \text{enc}(k, x)$ (where k is the recorded key, provided by the environment) and continues the simulation of $\mathcal{E}$ with I/O input y from $\mathcal{P}_{\text{senc}}$.

4. When $\mathcal{E}$ sends (Enc, x) to the I/O interface of $\mathcal{P}_{\text{senc}}$ and A has recorded $\mathcal{P}_{\text{senc}}$ as initialized and not as corrupted, then A computes $y \leftarrow O_1(L(1^\eta, x), x)$, records (x, y), and continues the simulation of $\mathcal{E}$ with I/O input y from $\mathcal{P}_{\text{senc}}$.

5. When $\mathcal{E}$ sends (Dec, y) to the I/O interface of $\mathcal{P}_{\text{senc}}$ and A has recorded $\mathcal{P}_{\text{senc}}$ as corrupted, then A computes $x := \text{dec}(k, y)$ (where k is the recorded key, provided by the environment) and continues the simulation of $\mathcal{E}$ with I/O input x from $\mathcal{P}_{\text{senc}}$.

6. When $\mathcal{E}$ sends (Dec, y) to the I/O interface of $\mathcal{P}_{\text{senc}}$ and A has recorded $\mathcal{P}_{\text{senc}}$ as initialized and not as corrupted, then A checks if there exists x such that (x, y) has been recorded upon encryption. If more than one such x exist (note that this case never occurs if O_1 encrypts the actual plaintext instead of the leakage), then A continues the simulation of $\mathcal{E}$ with I/O input $\bot$ (the error message signaling that decryption failed) from $\mathcal{P}_{\text{senc}}$. If exactly one such x exists, then

A continues the simulation of $\mathcal{E}$ with I/O input x from $\mathcal{P}_{\text{senc}}$. Otherwise, i.e., no such x exists, A computes $x' \leftarrow O_2(y)$ and continues the simulation of $\mathcal{E}$ with I/O input x' from $\mathcal{P}_{\text{senc}}$.

7. When $\mathcal{E}$ sends Corr? (a corruption status request) to the I/O interface of $\mathcal{P}_{\text{senc}}$, then A continues the simulation of $\mathcal{E}$ with I/O input 1 from $\mathcal{P}_{\text{senc}}$ if $\mathcal{P}_{\text{senc}}$ is corrupted and, otherwise, with input 0.

8. When $\mathcal{E}$ sends a message m to the tape decision (i.e., the run would stop with overall output m), then A stops and returns 1 if $m = 1$ and 0 otherwise.

9. When a master IITM in $\mathcal{E}$ produces empty output (which would stop the run with overall all empty output), then A stops and returns 0.

10. When $\mathcal{E}$ sends any message not matching a case above, then A continues the simulation of $\mathcal{E}$ with empty input.

First, we note that A is a valid IND-CCA2 adversary because it runs in polynomial time (because $\mathcal{E}$ is universally bounded) and it never requests O_2 with ciphertexts returned by O_1. We further note that the two messages given to O_1 are always of the same length because L is length preserving.

One easily verifies that (for all security parameter η and external input a)

$$\Pr\left[k \leftarrow \text{gen}(1^\eta) : A^{\text{enc}(k,\text{LR}(\cdot,\cdot,0)),\text{dec}(k,\cdot)}(1^\eta, a) = 1\right]$$
$$= \Pr\left[(\mathcal{E} \,|\, \mathcal{S} \,|\, !\mathcal{F}_{\text{senc}}^{\text{unauth}})(1^\eta, a) = 1\right] \quad \text{(A.1)}$$

because, in this case, $O_1(x_0, x_1) = \text{enc}(k, \text{LR}(x_0, x_1, 0)) = \text{enc}(k, x_0)$ for all x_0, x_1. That is, A precisely simulates a run of $\mathcal{E} \,|\, \mathcal{S} \,|\, !\mathcal{F}_{\text{senc}}^{\text{unauth}}$. Furthermore, one obtains that

$$\Pr\left[k \leftarrow \text{gen}(1^\eta) : A^{\text{enc}(k,\text{LR}(\cdot,\cdot,1)),\text{dec}(k,\cdot)}(1^\eta, a) = 1\right]$$
$$= \Pr\left[(\mathcal{E} \,|\, !\mathcal{P}_{\text{senc}})(1^\eta, a) = 1\right] \quad \text{(A.2)}$$

because, in this case, $O_1(x_0, x_1) = \text{enc}(k, \text{LR}(x_0, x_1, 1)) = \text{enc}(k, x_1)$ for all x_0, x_1 and because $\text{dec}(k, \text{enc}(k, x)) = x$, which implies that if (x, y) is stored then $O_2(y) = x$, for all x, k, y, and hence, for all recorded pairs $(x, y), (x', y')$ we have $x = x'$ if $y = y'$, i.e., A precisely simulates a run of $\mathcal{E} \,|\, !\mathcal{P}_{\text{senc}}$.

Since Σ is IND-CCA2 secure, the IND-CCA2 advantage of A w.r.t. Σ is negligible. That is, by (A.1) and (A.2),

$$\text{adv}_{A,\Sigma}^{\text{ind-cca2}}(1^\eta, a) = \left|\Pr\left[(\mathcal{E} \,|\, !\mathcal{P}_{\text{senc}})(1^\eta, a) = 1\right] - \Pr\left[(\mathcal{E} \,|\, \mathcal{S} \,|\, !\mathcal{F}_{\text{senc}}^{\text{unauth}})(1^\eta, a) = 1\right]\right|$$

is negligible (as a function in 1^η and a). We conclude that $\mathcal{E} \,|\, !\mathcal{P}_{\text{senc}} \equiv \mathcal{E} \,|\, \mathcal{S} \,|\, !\mathcal{F}_{\text{senc}}^{\text{unauth}}$. This proves the first statement of the theorem.

Authenticated encryption. We now prove the second statement of the theorem. Therefore, we assume that the encryption scheme Σ is IND-CPA and INT-CTXT secure. Let $\mathcal{E} \in \mathrm{Env}_{\sigma\text{-single}}(\,!\mathcal{P}_{\mathrm{senc}})$. Similarly to the first statement, we define an IND-CPA adversary A_{cpa} and an INT-CTXT adversary $A_{\mathrm{int\text{-}ctxt}}$ and show that the probability of $\mathcal{E}$ distinguishing between $!\mathcal{P}_{\mathrm{senc}}$ and $\mathcal{S} \,|\, !\mathcal{F}_{\mathrm{senc}}^{\mathrm{auth}}$ is bounded by the sum of the advantages of the two adversaries.

The adversary $A_{\mathrm{cpa}}^{O(\cdot,\cdot)}(1^{\eta}, a)$ (with encryption oracle O) is defined as the IND-CCA2 adversary A (see above), except that, upon decryption of a ciphertext y, if there exists no x such that (x, y) has been recorded upon encryption, then A_{cpa} continues the simulation of $\mathcal{E}$ with I/O input $\perp$ from $\mathcal{P}_{\mathrm{senc}}$. That is, A_{cpa} simulates the run as if decryption fails. In contrast, A used its decryption oracle O_2 in this case. Note that this is the only case where A possibly uses its decryption oracle O_2. Hence, A_{cpa} is a valid IND-CPA adversary.

It is easy to see that (for all security parameter η and external input a):

$$\Pr\left[k \leftarrow \mathrm{gen}(1^{\eta}) : A_{\mathrm{cpa}}^{\mathrm{enc}(k,\mathrm{LR}(\cdot,\cdot,0))}(1^{\eta}, a) = 1\right] = \Pr\left[(\mathcal{E} \,|\, \mathcal{S} \,|\, !\mathcal{F}_{\mathrm{senc}}^{\mathrm{auth}})(1^{\eta}, a) = 1\right]$$
$$(\mathrm{A.3})$$

because, in this case, $O_1(x_0, x_1) = \mathrm{enc}(k, \mathrm{LR}(x_0, x_1, 0)) = \mathrm{enc}(k, x_0)$ for all x_0, x_1 and decryption fails in $\mathcal{F}_{\mathrm{senc}}^{\mathrm{auth}}$ if the ciphertext has not been produced by $\mathcal{F}_{\mathrm{senc}}^{\mathrm{auth}}$ (in the uncorrupted case), i.e., A_{cpa} precisely simulates a run of $\mathcal{E} \,|\, \mathcal{S} \,|\, !\mathcal{F}_{\mathrm{senc}}^{\mathrm{auth}}$.

Let $B(1^{\eta}, a)$ be the event that, in a run of $(\mathcal{E} \,|\, !\mathcal{P}_{\mathrm{senc}})(1^{\eta}, a)$, $\mathcal{E}$ sends (Dec, y) to $\mathcal{P}_{\mathrm{senc}}$'s I/O interface such that $\mathcal{P}_{\mathrm{senc}}$ is not corrupted, $\mathrm{dec}(k, y) \neq \perp$ (where k is the key stored in $\mathcal{P}_{\mathrm{senc}}$), and y has never been output by $\mathcal{P}_{\mathrm{senc}}$ before. Formally, $B(1^{\eta}, a)$ is the set of runs of $(\mathcal{E} \,|\, !\mathcal{P}_{\mathrm{senc}})(1^{\eta}, a)$ that satisfy this condition. It is easy to find an injective mapping from runs ρ of $(\mathcal{E} \,|\, !\mathcal{P}_{\mathrm{senc}})(1^{\eta}, a)$ where $B(1^{\eta}, a)$ does not occur (i.e., $\rho \notin B(1^{\eta}, a)$) to runs ρ' of this probabilistic algorithm:

$$k \leftarrow \mathrm{gen}(1^{\eta}); \; b \leftarrow A_{\mathrm{cpa}}^{\mathrm{enc}(k,\mathrm{LR}(\cdot,\cdot,1))}(1^{\eta}, a); \; \textbf{return } b$$

such that the probability of ρ equals the probability of ρ' and the overall output of ρ is 1 if and only if the output of ρ' is 1. With this, it is easy to see that

$$\left| \Pr\left[k \leftarrow \mathrm{gen}(1^{\eta}) : A_{\mathrm{cpa}}^{\mathrm{enc}(k,\mathrm{LR}(\cdot,\cdot,1))}(1^{\eta}, a) = 1\right] - \Pr\left[(\mathcal{E} \,|\, !\mathcal{P}_{\mathrm{senc}})(1^{\eta}, a) = 1\right] \right|$$
$$\leq \Pr\left[B(1^{\eta}, a)\right]. \quad (\mathrm{A.4})$$

By (A.3) and (A.4), we conclude that

$$\left| \Pr\left[(\mathcal{E} \,|\, !\mathcal{P}_{\mathrm{senc}})(1^{\eta}, a) = 1\right] - \Pr\left[(\mathcal{E} \,|\, \mathcal{S} \,|\, !\mathcal{F}_{\mathrm{senc}}^{\mathrm{auth}})(1^{\eta}, a) = 1\right] \right|$$
$$\leq \mathrm{adv}_{A,\Sigma}^{\mathrm{ind\text{-}cpa}}(1^{\eta}, a) + \Pr\left[B(1^{\eta}, a)\right].$$

Since Σ is IND-CPA secure, $\mathrm{adv}_{A,\Sigma}^{\mathrm{ind\text{-}cpa}}(1^{\eta}, a)$ is negligible (as a function in 1^{η} and a). So, to show that $\mathcal{E} \,|\, !\mathcal{P}_{\mathrm{senc}} \equiv \mathcal{E} \,|\, \mathcal{S} \,|\, !\mathcal{F}_{\mathrm{senc}}^{\mathrm{auth}}$, it suffices to show that $\Pr\left[B(1^{\eta}, a)\right]$ is negligible.

Therefore, we define an adversary $A_{\text{int-ctxt}}^{O_1(\cdot),O_2(\cdot)}(1^\eta, a)$ (with encryption oracle O_1 and decryption oracle O_2) similarly to the IND-CCA2 adversary A (see above). It simulates a run of $\mathcal{E}$ with security parameter η and external input a as follows:

1. When $\mathcal{E}$ sends the first message to (one instance of) $\mathcal{P}_{\text{senc}}$, then $A_{\text{int-ctxt}}$ records this message and records that $\mathcal{P}_{\text{senc}}$ is *waiting for initialization*. Then, $A_{\text{int-ctxt}}$ continues the simulation of $\mathcal{E}$ with network input Init from $\mathcal{P}_{\text{senc}}$ (as above, we omit the name *name* from all requests; since $\mathcal{E}$ is single-session, it activates only one instance of $\mathcal{P}_{\text{senc}}$).

2. When $\mathcal{E}$ sends a message of the form $(corr, k)$ to the network interface of $\mathcal{P}_{\text{senc}}$ and $A_{\text{int-ctxt}}$ has recorded $\mathcal{P}_{\text{senc}}$ as waiting for initialization, then $A_{\text{int-ctxt}}$ records $\mathcal{P}_{\text{senc}}$ as *initialized*. Furthermore, $A_{\text{int-ctxt}}$ records $\mathcal{P}_{\text{senc}}$ as *corrupted* and $A_{\text{int-ctxt}}$ records k if $corr = 1$. Then, $A_{\text{int-ctxt}}$ continues the simulation of $\mathcal{E}$ as if $\mathcal{E}$ now sends the recorded message to $\mathcal{P}_{\text{senc}}$, see below.

3. When $\mathcal{E}$ sends (Enc, x) to the I/O interface of $\mathcal{P}_{\text{senc}}$ and $A_{\text{int-ctxt}}$ has recorded $\mathcal{P}_{\text{senc}}$ as corrupted, then $A_{\text{int-ctxt}}$ computes $y \leftarrow \text{enc}(k, x)$ (where k is the recorded key, provided by the environment) and continues the simulation of $\mathcal{E}$ with I/O input y from $\mathcal{P}_{\text{senc}}$.

4. When $\mathcal{E}$ sends (Enc, x) to the I/O interface of $\mathcal{P}_{\text{senc}}$ and $A_{\text{int-ctxt}}$ has recorded $\mathcal{P}_{\text{senc}}$ as initialized and not as corrupted, then $A_{\text{int-ctxt}}$ computes $y \leftarrow O_1(x)$ and continues the simulation of $\mathcal{E}$ with I/O input y from $\mathcal{P}_{\text{senc}}$.

5. When $\mathcal{E}$ sends (Dec, y) to the I/O interface of $\mathcal{P}_{\text{senc}}$ and $A_{\text{int-ctxt}}$ has recorded $\mathcal{P}_{\text{senc}}$ as corrupted, then $A_{\text{int-ctxt}}$ computes $x := \text{dec}(k, y)$ (where k is the recorded key, provided by the environment) and continues the simulation of $\mathcal{E}$ with I/O input x from $\mathcal{P}_{\text{senc}}$.

6. When $\mathcal{E}$ sends (Dec, y) to the I/O interface of $\mathcal{P}_{\text{senc}}$ and $A_{\text{int-ctxt}}$ has recorded $\mathcal{P}_{\text{senc}}$ as initialized and not as corrupted, then $A_{\text{int-ctxt}}$ computes $x \leftarrow O_2(y)$ and continues the simulation of $\mathcal{E}$ with I/O input x from $\mathcal{P}_{\text{senc}}$.

7. When $\mathcal{E}$ sends Corr? (a corruption status request) to the I/O interface of $\mathcal{P}_{\text{senc}}$, then $A_{\text{int-ctxt}}$ continues the simulation of $\mathcal{E}$ with I/O input 1 from $\mathcal{P}_{\text{senc}}$ if $\mathcal{P}_{\text{senc}}$ is corrupted and, otherwise, with input 0.

8. When $\mathcal{E}$ sends a message m to the tape decision (i.e., the run would stop with overall output m), then $A_{\text{int-ctxt}}$ stops (the output of $A_{\text{int-ctxt}}$ does not matter).

9. When a master IITM in $\mathcal{E}$ produces empty output (which would stop the run with overall all empty output), then $A_{\text{int-ctxt}}$ stops.

10. When $\mathcal{E}$ sends any message not matching a case above, then $A_{\text{int-ctxt}}$ continues the simulation of $\mathcal{E}$ with empty input.

Since $A_{\text{int-ctxt}}$ precisely simulates a run of $\mathcal{E} \mid !\mathcal{P}_{\text{senc}}$, it is easy to see that

$$\text{adv}_{A,\Sigma}^{\text{int-ctxt}}(1^\eta, a) = \Pr[B(1^\eta, a)] \ .$$

Hence, $\Pr[B(1^\eta, a)]$ is negligible (as a function in 1^η and a) because Σ is INT-CTXT secure and $A_{\text{int-ctxt}}$ is a probabilistic, polynomial-time algorithm (because $\mathcal{E}$ is universally bounded). This concludes the proof of Theorem 4.3.

A.2. Proof of Theorem 4.4

In this section, we prove Theorem 4.4, i.e., that a MAC $\Sigma = (\text{gen}, \text{mac})$ is UF-CMA secure (Definition 3.10) iff $!\mathcal{P}_{\text{mac}} \leq !\mathcal{F}_{\text{mac}}$.

"$!\mathcal{P}_{\text{mac}}$ realizes $!\mathcal{F}_{\text{mac}} \Rightarrow \Sigma$ is UF-CMA secure"

This direction is easy to prove: Given any UF-CMA adversary A we can easily construct an environment $\mathcal{E}$ for $!\mathcal{P}_{\text{mac}}$ such that the advantage of A is bounded by the advantage of $\mathcal{E}$ distinguishing between $!\mathcal{P}_{\text{mac}}$ and $\mathcal{S} \mid !\mathcal{F}_{\text{mac}}$ for every simulator $\mathcal{S}$. The environment $\mathcal{E}$ simply simulates A using one instance of $\mathcal{P}_{\text{mac}}$ (resp., $\mathcal{F}_{\text{mac}}$) for MAC generation to simulate the oracles of A. When A outputs a message/MAC pair (m, σ), then $\mathcal{E}$ verifies that m was never MACed by A and that σ verifies for m using $\mathcal{P}_{\text{mac}}$ (or $\mathcal{F}_{\text{mac}}$). In this case, $\mathcal{E}$ outputs 1 on decision. Otherwise, $\mathcal{E}$ outputs 0 on decision. It is easy to see that (for every security parameter η and external input a) $\Pr[(\mathcal{E} \mid !\mathcal{P}_{\text{mac}})(1^\eta, a) = 1] = \text{adv}_{A,\Sigma}^{\text{uf-cma}}(1^\eta, a)$ because $\mathcal{E}$ perfectly simulates a run of A in the experiment of the UF-CMA game and outputs 1 iff A wins. On the other hand, $\Pr[(\mathcal{E} \mid \mathcal{S} \mid !\mathcal{F}_{\text{mac}})(1^\eta, a) = 1] = 0$ because $\mathcal{F}_{\text{mac}}$ ideally prevents forgery. Since $\mathcal{E} \mid !\mathcal{P}_{\text{mac}} \equiv \mathcal{E} \mid \mathcal{S} \mid !\mathcal{F}_{\text{mac}}$ for every simulator $\mathcal{S}$ (because $!\mathcal{P}_{\text{mac}} \leq !\mathcal{F}_{\text{mac}}$), we conclude that $\text{adv}_{A,\Sigma}^{\text{uf-cma}}(1^\eta, a)$ is negligible (as a function in 1^η and a), i.e., Σ is UF-CMA secure.

"Σ is UF-CMA secure $\Rightarrow !\mathcal{P}_{\text{mac}}$ realizes $!\mathcal{F}_{\text{mac}}$"

To show this direction, we first note that both $!\mathcal{P}_{\text{mac}}$ and $!\mathcal{F}_{\text{mac}}$ are σ-session versions (as defined in Section 2.4) for the SID function σ that has been defined above in the proof of Theorem 4.3: For all messages m and tapes c: $\sigma(m, c) := name$ if c is an I/O tape and $m = (id, name, m')$ or c is a network tape and $m = (name, m')$ (for some $id, name, m'$). Otherwise, $\sigma(m, c) := \bot$. Hence, by Theorem 2.3, it suffices to show that $!\mathcal{P}_{\text{mac}} \leq_{\sigma\text{-single}} !\mathcal{F}_{\text{mac}}$, to obtain that $!\mathcal{P}_{\text{mac}} \leq !\mathcal{F}_{\text{mac}}$. That is, it suffices to show that a single instance of $\mathcal{P}_{\text{mac}}$ realizes a single instance of $\mathcal{F}_{\text{mac}}$.

We now define a (single-session) simulator $\mathcal{S}$ and show that $\mathcal{E} \mid !\mathcal{P}_{\text{mac}} \equiv \mathcal{E} \mid \mathcal{S} \mid !\mathcal{F}_{\text{mac}}$ for every single-session environment $\mathcal{E} \in \text{Env}_{\sigma\text{-single}}(!\mathcal{P}_{\text{mac}})$.

The definition of the simulator $\mathcal{S}$ is straight forward. It forwards the Init request from (one instance of) $\mathcal{F}_{\text{mac}}$ to the environment and when the environment responds with $(name, corr, k)$ then $\mathcal{S}$ forwards $(name, corr, \text{mac}, k')$ to $\mathcal{F}_{\text{mac}}$ where $k' := k$ if

$corr = 1$ (i.e., upon corruption S provides the key provided by the environment) and $k' \leftarrow \text{gen}(1^\eta)$ if $corr \neq 1$ (i.e., S generates and provides a fresh key in the uncorrupted case); where η is the security parameter. When the environment sends $(name, \text{Corr})$ to the network interface of $\mathcal{P}_{\text{mac}}$ (to corrupt $\mathcal{P}_{\text{mac}}$), then S forwards $(name, \text{Corr})$ to $\mathcal{F}_{\text{mac}}$ and waits for receiving $(name, \text{Ack})$ (this is the immediate response of $\mathcal{F}_{\text{mac}}$). Then, S sends $(name, k')$ to the environment where k' is the key that S has sent to $\mathcal{F}_{\text{mac}}$ upon initialization. In the case that S has not yet sent k' to $\mathcal{F}_{\text{mac}}$ (i.e., before initialization), S returns $(name, \bot)$ to the environment. Upon any other input from the environment, S stops in this activation with empty output. It is easy to see that $S \mid !\mathcal{F}_{\text{mac}}$ is environmentally strictly bounded. In particular, $S \in \text{Sim}_{\sigma\text{-single}}^{!\mathcal{P}_{\text{mac}}}(!\mathcal{F}_{\text{mac}})$.

We now show that, if Σ is UF-CMA secure, then $\mathcal{E} \mid !\mathcal{P}_{\text{mac}} \equiv \mathcal{E} \mid S \mid !\mathcal{F}_{\text{mac}}$ for every single-session environment $\mathcal{E}$ for $!\mathcal{P}_{\text{mac}}$. This proves the theorem. Therefore, assume that Σ is UF-CMA secure and let $\mathcal{E} \in \text{Env}_{\sigma\text{-single}}(\mathcal{P}_{\text{mac}})$. Let $p_\mathcal{E}$ be a polynomial (in the security parameter plus the length of the external input) that bounds the number of verification requests output by $\mathcal{E}$ in any run. Such a polynomial exists because $\mathcal{E}$ is universally bounded. Using $\mathcal{E}$, we define an UF-CMA adversary A and show that its advantage against Σ is at least $p_\mathcal{E}$ times the advantage of $\mathcal{E}$ in distinguishing between $!\mathcal{P}_{\text{mac}}$ and $S \mid !\mathcal{F}_{\text{mac}}$.

The adversary $A^{O(\cdot)}(1^\eta, a)$ (where O is its MAC oracle) chooses $i \in \{1, \ldots, p_\mathcal{E}(\eta + |a|)\}$ uniformly at random—A tries to guess which verification request of $\mathcal{E}$ constitutes a forgery—and then simulates a run of $\mathcal{E}$ with security parameter η and external input a as the IND-CCA2 adversary A constructed in the proof of Theorem 4.3 (see above), with the following differences (recall that $\mathcal{E}$ only activates a single instance of $\mathcal{P}_{\text{mac}}$, which we denote by $\mathcal{P}_{\text{mac}}$).

1. When $\mathcal{P}_{\text{mac}}$ gets corrupted (i.e., $\mathcal{E}$ corrupts $\mathcal{P}_{\text{mac}}$ upon initialization or later by sending Corr to the network interface of $\mathcal{P}_{\text{mac}}$), then A aborts (i.e., it halts and outputs an arbitrary pair of bit strings, say the pair of empty bit strings).

2. When $\mathcal{E}$ asks $\mathcal{P}_{\text{mac}}$ to MAC a message x and $\mathcal{P}_{\text{mac}}$ is uncorrupted, then A uses its MAC oracle O to compute $\sigma := O(x)$, records (x, σ), and continues the simulation of $\mathcal{E}$ as if $\mathcal{P}_{\text{mac}}$ returned σ.

3. When $\mathcal{E}$ asks $\mathcal{P}_{\text{mac}}$ to verify a MAC σ for a message x and $\mathcal{P}_{\text{mac}}$ is uncorrupted, then A does the following. If this is the i-th verification request, then A halts and outputs (x, σ). Otherwise, A continues the simulation of $\mathcal{E}$ as if $\mathcal{P}_{\text{mac}}$ returned 1 if (x, σ) has been recorded (see above) and 0 otherwise.

4. When the run stops (i.e., $\mathcal{E}$ sends a message to the tape decision or a master IITM in $\mathcal{E}$ produces empty output), then A aborts (as above).

We note that A is a valid UF-CMA adversary because it runs in polynomial time (because $\mathcal{E}$ is universally bounded).

Let $B(1^\eta, a)$ be the event that, in a run of $(\mathcal{E} \mid !\mathcal{P}_{\text{mac}})(1^\eta, a)$, the environment $\mathcal{E}$ sends $(name, \text{Verify}, \sigma, x)$ to $\mathcal{P}_{\text{mac}}$'s I/O interface such that $\mathcal{P}_{\text{mac}}[name]$ is not corrupted,

$\mathsf{mac}(k, x) = \sigma$ (where k is the key stored in $\mathcal{P}_{\mathrm{mac}}[\mathit{name}]$), and x has never been MACed by $\mathcal{P}_{\mathrm{mac}}[\mathit{name}]$ before. Formally, $B(1^\eta, a)$ is the set of runs of $(\mathcal{E} \,|\, !\mathcal{P}_{\mathrm{senc}})(1^\eta, a)$ that satisfy this condition. Since runs of the systems $\mathcal{E} \,|\, !\mathcal{P}_{\mathrm{mac}}$ and $\mathcal{E} \,|\, \mathcal{S} \,|\, !\mathcal{F}_{\mathrm{mac}}$ do not differ until B occurs, it is easy to find an injective mapping from runs ρ of $(\mathcal{E} \,|\, !\mathcal{P}_{\mathrm{mac}})(1^\eta, a)$ where $B(1^\eta, a)$ does not occur (i.e., $\rho \notin B(1^\eta, a)$) to runs ρ' of $(\mathcal{E} \,|\, \mathcal{S} \,|\, !\mathcal{F}_{\mathrm{mac}})(1^\eta, a)$ such that the probability of ρ equals the probability of ρ' and the overall output of ρ equals the one of ρ'. From this, we conclude that (for every security parameter η and external input a):

$$|\Pr\left[(\mathcal{E} \,|\, !\mathcal{P}_{\mathrm{mac}})(1^\eta, a) = 1\right] - \Pr\left[(\mathcal{E} \,|\, \mathcal{S} \,|\, !\mathcal{F}_{\mathrm{mac}})(1^\eta, a) = 1\right]| \leq \Pr\left[B(1^\eta, a)\right] \ . \quad (\text{A.5})$$

By construction of A, A perfectly simulates a run of $\mathcal{E} \,|\, !\mathcal{P}_{\mathrm{mac}}$ until B occurs and if B occurs and A correctly guessed the first verification request sent by $\mathcal{E}$ that triggers B, then A wins (i.e., produces a forgery). That is, we have that:

$$\Pr\left[B(1^\eta, a)\right] \leq p_\mathcal{E}(\eta + |a|) \cdot \mathrm{adv}_{A,\Sigma}^{\mathrm{uf\text{-}cma}}(1^\eta, a) \ . \quad (\text{A.6})$$

Since Σ is UF-CMA secure, the advantage of A is negligible (as a function in 1^η and a). By (A.5) and (A.6) and because $p_\mathcal{E}$ is a polynomial, we obtain that $\mathcal{E} \,|\, !\mathcal{P}_{\mathrm{mac}} \equiv \mathcal{E} \,|\, \mathcal{S} \,|\, !\mathcal{F}_{\mathrm{mac}}$. This concludes the proof of Theorem 4.4.

A.3. Proof of Theorem 4.5

In this section, we prove Theorem 4.5, i.e., that $!\mathcal{P}_{\mathrm{derive}} \leq !\mathcal{F}_{\mathrm{derive}}$ if the VLO-PRF PRF^* used by $\mathcal{P}_{\mathrm{derive}}$ is secure (Definition 3.12).

To show this, we first note that both $!\mathcal{P}_{\mathrm{derive}}$ and $!\mathcal{F}_{\mathrm{derive}}$ are σ-session versions (as defined in Section 2.4) for the SID function σ that has already been introduced above: For all messages m and tapes c: $\sigma(m, c) := \mathit{name}$ if c is an I/O tape and $m = (\mathit{id}, \mathit{name}, m')$ or c is a network tape and $m = (\mathit{name}, m')$ (for some $\mathit{id}, \mathit{name}, m'$). Otherwise, $\sigma(m, c) := \bot$. Hence, by Theorem 2.3, it suffices to show that $!\mathcal{P}_{\mathrm{derive}} \leq_{\sigma\text{-single}} !\mathcal{F}_{\mathrm{derive}}$, to obtain that $!\mathcal{P}_{\mathrm{derive}} \leq !\mathcal{F}_{\mathrm{derive}}$. That is, it suffices to show that a single instance of $\mathcal{P}_{\mathrm{derive}}$ realizes a single instance of $\mathcal{F}_{\mathrm{derive}}$.

We now define a (single-session) simulator $\mathcal{S}$ and then show that $\mathcal{E} \,|\, !\mathcal{P}_{\mathrm{derive}} \equiv \mathcal{E} \,|\, \mathcal{S} \,|\, !\mathcal{F}_{\mathrm{derive}}$ for every single-session environment $\mathcal{E} \in \mathrm{Env}_{\sigma\text{-single}}(!\mathcal{P}_{\mathrm{derive}})$.

The definition of the simulator $\mathcal{S}$ is straight forward. It forwards the Init request from (one instance of) $\mathcal{F}_{\mathrm{derive}}$ to the environment and when the environment responds with $(\mathit{name}, \mathit{corr}, k)$ then $\mathcal{S}$ forwards $(\mathit{name}, \mathit{corr})$ to $\mathcal{F}_{\mathrm{derive}}$. That is, $\mathcal{S}$ corrupts $\mathcal{F}_{\mathrm{derive}}$ iff the environment wants to corrupt $\mathcal{P}_{\mathrm{derive}}$. When $\mathcal{F}_{\mathrm{derive}}$ is corrupted, then it forwards every key derivation request to $\mathcal{S}$. Upon such a request, say with key name name and salt x, $\mathcal{S}$ derives keys just as $\mathcal{P}_{\mathrm{derive}}$ would derive keys from the key k provided by the environment upon initialization. That is, $\mathcal{S}$ computes $(l_1, \ldots, l_n) := \mathsf{parse}(1^\eta, x)$ and $y := \mathrm{PRF}^*(k, x, l_1 + \cdots + l_n)$ and then splits y into keys $k_1, \ldots, k_n$ such that $y = k_1 \| \cdots \| k_n$ and $|k_i| = l_i$ for all $i \leq n$. Then, $\mathcal{S}$ returns

$(name, k_1, \ldots, k_n)$ to $\mathcal{F}_{\text{derive}}$. It is easy to see that $\mathcal{S} \,|\, !\mathcal{F}_{\text{derive}}$ is environmentally strictly bounded. In particular, $\mathcal{S} \in \text{Sim}_{\sigma\text{-single}}^{!\mathcal{P}_{\text{derive}}}(!\mathcal{F}_{\text{derive}})$.

Let $\mathcal{E} \in \text{Env}_{\sigma\text{-single}}(!\mathcal{P}_{\text{derive}})$ (i.e., in every run, $\mathcal{E}$ uses only one name $name$) such that $\mathcal{E}$ satisfies the following assumptions:

1. In any run with any system, upon receiving $(name, \text{Init})$ (for some $name$) on tape $\text{net}_{\mathcal{P}_{\text{derive}}}^{\text{out}}$ ($\mathcal{P}_{\text{derive}}$'s network output tape), $\mathcal{E}$ directly outputs $(name, 0, k)$ for an arbitrary k (this k is ignored by $\mathcal{P}_{\text{derive}}$ and $\mathcal{S} \,|\, \mathcal{F}_{\text{derive}}$ anyway), i.e., $\mathcal{E}$ completes initialization and does not corrupt $\mathcal{P}_{\text{derive}}$ (or $\mathcal{S} \,|\, \mathcal{F}_{\text{derive}}$, respectively).

2. There exists a polynomial p in the security parameter and the length of the external input, such that, in any run with any system and security parameter η and external input a, $\mathcal{E}$ sends exactly $p(\eta + |a|)$ key derivation requests on $\text{io}_{\text{derive}_1}^{\text{in}}$ (the first I/O input of $\mathcal{P}_{\text{derive}}$ or $\mathcal{F}_{\text{derive}}$, respectively) and all these requests use a different salt.

Below, we now show that $\mathcal{E} \,|\, !\mathcal{P}_{\text{derive}} \equiv \mathcal{E} \,|\, \mathcal{S} \,|\, !\mathcal{F}_{\text{derive}}$ for such an environment (we note that these assumptions simplify the construction of the adversary against PRF^*, see below). This implies $\mathcal{E} \,|\, !\mathcal{P}_{\text{derive}} \equiv \mathcal{E} \,|\, \mathcal{S} \,|\, !\mathcal{F}_{\text{derive}}$ for all $\mathcal{E} \in \text{Env}_{\sigma\text{-single}}(!\mathcal{P}_{\text{derive}})$ because every $\mathcal{E} \in \text{Env}_{\sigma\text{-single}}(!\mathcal{P}_{\text{derive}})$ can easily be turned into an environment $\mathcal{E}' \in \text{Env}_{\sigma\text{-single}}(\mathcal{P}_{\text{derive}})$ such that $\mathcal{E}'$ satisfies the above assumptions and $\mathcal{E}'$ has the same advantage in distinguishing between $!\mathcal{P}_{\text{derive}}$ and $\mathcal{S} \,|\, !\mathcal{F}_{\text{derive}}$ as $\mathcal{E}$, i.e., for all η, a:

$$|\Pr\left[(\mathcal{E} \,|\, !\mathcal{P}_{\text{derive}})(1^\eta, a) = 1\right] - \Pr\left[(\mathcal{E} \,|\, \mathcal{S} \,|\, !\mathcal{F}_{\text{derive}})(1^\eta, a) = 1\right]|$$
$$= |\Pr\left[(\mathcal{E}' \,|\, !\mathcal{P}_{\text{derive}})(1^\eta, a) = 1\right] - \Pr\left[(\mathcal{E}' \,|\, \mathcal{S} \,|\, !\mathcal{F}_{\text{derive}})(1^\eta, a) = 1\right]| \ .$$

If $\mathcal{E}$ corrupts $\mathcal{P}_{\text{derive}}$ (or $\mathcal{S} \,|\, \mathcal{F}_{\text{derive}}$, respectively), then $\mathcal{E}'$ simply outputs 0 on decision (note that this terminates the run and the overall output is 0). It is easy to see that this does not change the difference of the above probabilities because, upon corruption, the observable behavior of $!\mathcal{P}_{\text{derive}}$ and $\mathcal{S} \,|\, !\mathcal{F}_{\text{derive}}$ does not differ at all. When $\mathcal{E}$ sends a key derivation request for a salt that has already been sent, then $\mathcal{E}'$ simply recalls the response that was returned when the first request was sent with this salt. Again, this does not change the difference of the above probabilities because both $!\mathcal{P}_{\text{derive}}$ and $\mathcal{S} \,|\, !\mathcal{F}_{\text{derive}}$ always return the same keys upon a second request with the same salt. Finally, when the run would terminate (i.e., $\mathcal{E}$ produces non-empty output on decision or a master IITM in $\mathcal{E}$ stops with empty output), then $\mathcal{E}'$ does the following. It checks if it has sent less exactly $p_\mathcal{E}(\eta + |a|)$ key derivation requests to $!\mathcal{P}_{\text{derive}}$ (or $\mathcal{S} \,|\, !\mathcal{F}_{\text{derive}}$, respectively) where $p_\mathcal{E}$ is a polynomial that bounds the maximal number of key derivation requests output by $\mathcal{E}$ in any run with any system (such a polynomial exists because $\mathcal{E}$ is universally bounded). If this check fails, then $\mathcal{E}'$ sends arbitrary requests (with new salts) to $\mathcal{P}_{\text{derive}}$ until it has sent exactly $p_\mathcal{E}(\eta + |a|)$ requests. Then, $\mathcal{E}'$ terminates the run with the same overall output as $\mathcal{E}$ would have done earlier. Clearly, these extra requests do not change the difference of the above probabilities.

We now show that $\mathcal{E} \,|\, !\mathcal{P}_{\text{derive}} \equiv \mathcal{E} \,|\, \mathcal{S} \,|\, !\mathcal{F}_{\text{derive}}$ for a single-session environment $\mathcal{E} \in \text{Env}_{\sigma\text{-single}}(!\mathcal{P}_{\text{derive}})$ that satisfies the above assumptions. The proof proceeds by a hybrid argument.

For every $i \geq 1$, we define an adversary $A^{(i)} = (A_1^{(i)}, A_2^{(i)})$ against PRF*. Recall from Definition 3.12 that $A_1^{(i)}$ and $A_2^{(i)}$ have access to a key derivation oracle $O(\cdot, \cdot)$ that takes a salt and a length. Furthermore, $A_1^{(i)}$ gets input 1^η and a and $A_2^{(i)}$ gets input x^*, st, and y where x^* is the salt output by $A_1^{(i)}$, st is the status output by $A_1^{(i)}$, and y is a random or a pseudorandom bit string (i.e., chosen uniformly at random or generated by PRF*). It is $A^{(i)}$'s task to try to determine whether y has been generated randomly or pseudorandomly. To do this, $A_1^{(i)}$ simulates a run of $(\mathcal{E} \,|\, \mathcal{S} \,|\, !\mathcal{F}_{\text{derive}})(1^\eta, a)$ until $\mathcal{E}$ sends the i-th key derivation request, say with salt x^*. (We note that this never happens if $i > p_{\mathcal{E}}(\eta + |a|)$. Below it will be guaranteed that $i \leq p_{\mathcal{E}}(\eta + |a|)$, so, this case is irrelevant.) Then, $A_1^{(i)}$ stops and outputs (x^*, l^*, st) where $l^* := l_1 + \cdots + l_n$ with $(l_1, \ldots, l_n) := \text{parse}(1^\eta, x^*)$ and st encodes the state of the simulation of $\mathcal{E} \,|\, \mathcal{S} \,|\, !\mathcal{F}_{\text{derive}}(1^\eta, a)$ such that $A_2^{(i)}$ can continue the simulation.

When $A_2^{(i)}$ is started with input x^*, st, and y, then $A_2^{(i)}$ splits y into the keys $k_1, \ldots, k_n$ such that $y = k_1 \| \cdots \| k_n$ and $|k_j| = l_j$ for all $j \leq n$ (where $l_1, \ldots, l_n$ are as above). Then, $A_2^{(i)}$ continues the simulation of $\mathcal{E}$ by sending $k_1, \ldots, k_n$ to it, in response to the i-th key derivation request. In this simulation of $\mathcal{E}$, when $\mathcal{E}$ sends a key derivation request, say with salt x, then $A_2^{(i)}$ uses its key derivation oracle $O(x, l)$ where l is computed from $\text{parse}(1^\eta, x)$ as above for l^* to obtain a bit string y of length l. Then, as above, $A_2^{(i)}$ splits y into keys of appropriate length and continues the simulation of $\mathcal{E}$. When the simulated run stops with overall output 1 (i.e., $\mathcal{E}$ outputs 1 on decision), then $A_2^{(i)}$ outputs 1. Otherwise, $A_2^{(i)}$ outputs 0 when the simulated run stops.

In addition to $A^{(i)}$, we define the adversary $A^{(\$)}$: $A^{(\$)}$ is defined as $A^{(i)}$ except that, at the beginning, it chooses i uniformly at random from $\{1, \ldots, p_{\mathcal{E}}(\eta + |a|)\}$ and then behaves as $A^{(i)}$.

By our assumptions about $\mathcal{E}$ and because $\mathcal{E}$ is universally bounded and $\mathcal{S} \,|\, !\mathcal{F}_{\text{derive}}$ is environmentally strictly bounded, it is easy to see that $A^{(i)}$, for all i, and $A^{(\$)}$ are valid adversaries against PRF* (i.e., they consist of polynomial-time algorithms and never query their oracle with the salt x^*).

To relate the advantage of $\mathcal{E}$ in distinguishing between $!\mathcal{P}_{\text{derive}}$ and $\mathcal{S} \,|\, !\mathcal{F}_{\text{derive}}$ to the advantage of an adversary against PRF* we first define *success* and *failure* of an adversary against PRF*: By

$$\text{succ}_{A,\text{PRF}^*}(1^\eta, a) := \Pr\left[k \xleftarrow{\$} \{0,1\}^{l(\eta)}; (x^*, l^*, st) \leftarrow A_1^{\text{PRF}^*(k, \cdot, \cdot)}(1^\eta, a); \right.$$
$$\left. y := \text{PRF}^*(k, x^*, l^*); b' \leftarrow A_2^{\text{PRF}^*(k, \cdot, \cdot)}(x^*, st, y) : b' = 1\right]$$

we denote the *success* of $A = (A_1, A_2)$ against PRF^* and by

$$\text{fail}_{A,\text{PRF}^*}(1^\eta, a) := \Pr\left[k \xleftarrow{\$} \{0,1\}^{l(\eta)}; (x^*, l^*, st) \leftarrow A_1^{\text{PRF}^*(k,\cdot,\cdot)}(1^\eta, a);\right.$$
$$\left.y \xleftarrow{\$} \{0,1\}^{l^*}; b' \leftarrow A_2^{\text{PRF}^*(k,\cdot,\cdot)}(x^*, st, y) : b' = 1\right]$$

we denote its *failure*. It is easy to see that

$$\text{adv}_{A,\text{PRF}^*}(1^\eta, a) = \left|\text{succ}_{A,\text{PRF}^*}(1^\eta, a) - \text{fail}_{A,\text{PRF}^*}(1^\eta, a)\right| . \tag{A.7}$$

By definition of $A^{(i)}$, we have that (for all η, a):

$$\text{succ}_{A^{(1)},\text{PRF}^*}(1^\eta, a) = \Pr\left[(\mathcal{E} \mid \mathcal{P}_{\text{derive}})(1^\eta, a) = 1\right] \tag{A.8}$$

$$\text{fail}_{A^{(p_\mathcal{E}(\eta+|a|))},\text{PRF}^*}(1^\eta, a) = \Pr\left[(\mathcal{E} \mid \mathcal{S} \mid \mathcal{F}_{\text{derive}})(1^\eta, a) = 1\right] \tag{A.9}$$

$$\text{fail}_{A^{(i)},\text{PRF}^*}(1^\eta, a) = \text{succ}_{A^{(i+1)},\text{PRF}^*}(1^\eta, a) \tag{A.10}$$

for all $i \in \{1, \ldots, p_\mathcal{E}(\eta + |a|) - 1\}$. Equation (A.8) is easy to see because, in a run of $A^{(1)}$ in the "success game", every key derivation request is handled as in $\mathcal{P}_{\text{derive}}$: the first one because it is the "success game" and all later ones because $i = 1$. Similarly, (A.9) holds because, in a run of $A^{(p_\mathcal{E}(\eta+|a|))}$ in the "failure game", every key derivation request is handled as in $\mathcal{S} \mid \mathcal{F}_{\text{derive}}$: the last one because it is the "failure game" and all previous ones because $i = p_\mathcal{E}(\eta + |a|)$. Also, (A.10) is easy to see: In a run of $A^{(i)}$ in the "failure game" the first i key derivation requests are handled as in $\mathcal{S} \mid \mathcal{F}_{\text{derive}}$ and all later requests as in $\mathcal{P}_{\text{derive}}$. The same happens in a run of $A^{(i+1)}$ in the "success game".

We note that (for all η, a):

$$\sum_{i=1}^{p_\mathcal{E}(\eta+|a|)} \text{succ}_{A^{(i)},\text{PRF}^*}(1^\eta, a) = p_\mathcal{E}(\eta + |a|) \cdot \text{succ}_{A^{(\$)},\text{PRF}^*}(1^\eta, a) \tag{A.11}$$

$$\sum_{i=1}^{p_\mathcal{E}(\eta+|a|)} \text{fail}_{A^{(i)},\text{PRF}^*}(1^\eta, a) = p_\mathcal{E}(\eta + |a|) \cdot \text{fail}_{A^{(\$)},\text{PRF}^*}(1^\eta, a) . \tag{A.12}$$

From the above, we obtain that (for all η, a):

$$\left|\Pr\left[(\mathcal{E} \mid !\mathcal{P}_{\text{derive}})(1^\eta, a) = 1\right] - \Pr\left[(\mathcal{E} \mid \mathcal{S} \mid !\mathcal{F}_{\text{derive}})(1^\eta, a) = 1\right]\right|$$

$$\stackrel{\text{(A.8),(A.9)}}{=} \left|\text{succ}_{A^{(1)},\text{PRF}^*}(1^\eta, a) - \text{fail}_{A^{(p_\mathcal{E}(\eta+|a|))},\text{PRF}^*}(1^\eta, a)\right|$$

$$\stackrel{\text{(A.10)}}{=} \left|\sum_{i=1}^{p_\mathcal{E}(\eta+|a|)} \text{succ}_{A^{(i)},\text{PRF}^*}(1^\eta, a) - \text{fail}_{A^{(i)},\text{PRF}^*}(1^\eta, a)\right|$$

$$\stackrel{\text{(A.11),(A.12)}}{=} p_\mathcal{E}(\eta + |a|) \cdot \left|\text{succ}_{A^{(\$)},\text{PRF}^*}(1^\eta, a) - \text{fail}_{A^{(\$)},\text{PRF}^*}(1^\eta, a)\right|$$

$$\stackrel{\text{(A.7)}}{=} p_\mathcal{E}(\eta + |a|) \cdot \text{adv}_{A^{(\$)},\text{PRF}^*}(1^\eta, a) .$$

Since PRF^* is secure, $\mathrm{adv}_{A^{(\$)},\mathrm{PRF}^*}(1^\eta, a)$ is negligible (as a function in 1^η and a) and, hence, $\mathcal{E} \mid !\mathcal{P}_{\mathrm{derive}} \equiv \mathcal{E} \mid \mathcal{S} \mid !\mathcal{F}_{\mathrm{derive}}$. This concludes the proof of Theorem 4.5.

B. Details and a Proof for our Crypto Functionality

In this appendix, we give a definition of our crypto functionality $\mathcal{F}_{\text{crypto}}$ in pseudocode and provide a proof of Theorem 5.1 ($\mathcal{P}_{\text{crypto}}$ realizes $\mathcal{F}_{\text{crypto}}$).

B.1. Formal Specification of the Ideal Crypto Functionality

Our ideal crypto functionality $\mathcal{F}_{\text{crypto}}$ is formally defined in pseudocode in Figures B.1 to B.8 (see Section 3.1 for notational conventions). As mentioned before, the informal description provided in Section 5.2 contains all necessary details to understand how $\mathcal{F}_{\text{crypto}}$ works. However, the pseudocode is convenient in some proofs.

Parameters: Π *{parameter set, see Section 5.2*

Tapes: from/to IO_r $(r \leq n)$: $(\text{io}^{\text{in}}_{\text{crypto}_r}, \text{io}^{\text{out}}_{\text{crypto}_r})$; from/to $\mathcal{F}^{\text{keys}}_{\text{crypto}}$: $(\text{io}^{\text{out}}_{\text{keys,user}}, \text{io}^{\text{in}}_{\text{keys,user}})$;

from/to $\mathcal{F}^z_{\text{crypto}}$ $(z \in \{\text{keysetup, senc, derive, mac, pke}\})$: $(\text{io}^{\text{out}}_z, \text{io}^{\text{in}}_z)$;

from/to NET: $(\text{net}^{\text{in}}_{\mathcal{F}^{\text{user}}_{\text{crypto}}}, \text{net}^{\text{out}}_{\mathcal{F}^{\text{user}}_{\text{crypto}}})$

State: – uid $\in \{0,1\}^* \cup \{\bot\}$ *{user identifier (used as SID, see mode CheckAddress); initially* $\bot$

    – key: $\mathbb{N} \to \mathcal{D}(\eta) \cup \{\bot\}$ *{mapping of pointers to typed keys; initially* $\forall ptr$: key$(ptr) = \bot$

CheckAddress: *Accept* m *from* IO_r *(for any* r*) iff* $m = (uid, m')$ *for some* $uid, m' \in \{0,1\}^*$ *such that* uid $= \bot$ *or* uid $= uid$. *Accept* m *from* $\mathcal{F}^{\text{keys}}_{\text{crypto}}$ *or* NET *iff* $m = (uid, m')$ *for some* $m' \in \{0,1\}^*$. *Accept* m *from* $\mathcal{F}^z_{\text{crypto}}$ *(for any* z*) iff* $m = (uid, sid, m')$ *for some* $sid, m' \in \{0,1\}^*$.

Initialization: Upon receiving the first message $m = (uid, m')$ from IO_r in mode Compute do:

uid $:= uid$ *{record user identifier*

Then, continue processing the first message in mode Compute.

Compute: The mode Compute of $\mathcal{F}^{\text{user}}_{\text{crypto}}$ is defined in Figure B.2.

In this, we omit uid, i.e., by "**recv/send** m", we denote "**recv/send** (uid, m)". Furthermore, by "$\mathcal{F}^{\text{keys}}_{\text{crypto}} \cdot cmd(m)$", we denote "**send** (uid, cmd, m) to $\mathcal{F}^{\text{keys}}_{\text{crypto}}$; **recv** (uid, m') from $\mathcal{F}^{\text{keys}}_{\text{crypto}}$; **return** m' (as the result)" and, similarly, by "$\mathcal{F}^z_{\text{crypto}}[sid] \cdot cmd(m)$", we denote "**send** (uid, sid, cmd, m) to $\mathcal{F}^z_{\text{crypto}}$; **recv** (uid, sid, m') from $\mathcal{F}^z_{\text{crypto}}$; **return** m'".

The description in Figure B.2 uses this macro to create a new pointer for a typed key κ:

    `create-pointer`(κ): $ptr := \min\{ptr' \in \mathbb{N} \mid \text{key}(ptr') = \bot\}$; key$(ptr) := \kappa$; **return** ptr.

Figure B.1.: The IITM $\mathcal{F}^{\text{user}}_{\text{crypto}}$. As a part of $\mathcal{F}_{\text{crypto}}$, one copy of this IITM serves one user and maintains the pointers of this user.

---

recv (KeyGen, t) **from** IO_r **s.t.** $t \in \mathcal{T}$:

    send (KeyGen, t) **to** NET; **recv** k **from** NET **s.t.** $k \in \mathcal{D}^t_{\mathrm{keys}}(\eta)$ {*obtain key from adversary*

    if $\mathcal{F}^{\mathrm{keys}}_{\mathrm{crypto}}.\mathsf{Add}(\mathrm{unknown}, (t, k)) = \bot$: **send** $\bot$ **to** IO_r {*key is not fresh; return error*

    $ptr := \mathtt{create\text{-}pointer}((t, k))$; **send** ptr **to** IO_r {*create and return pointer*

recv (Store, κ) **from** IO_r **s.t.** $\kappa \in \mathcal{D}(\eta)$:

    if $\mathcal{F}^{\mathrm{keys}}_{\mathrm{crypto}}.\mathsf{Add}(\mathrm{known}, \kappa) = \bot$: **send** $\bot$ **to** IO_r {*key is unknown; return error*

    $ptr := \mathtt{create\text{-}pointer}(\kappa)$; **send** ptr **to** IO_r {*create and return pointer*

recv $(\mathsf{Retrieve}, ptr)$ **from** IO_r **s.t.** $\kappa := \mathsf{key}(ptr) \neq \bot$: $\mathcal{F}^{\mathrm{keys}}_{\mathrm{crypto}}.\mathsf{MarkKnown}(\kappa)$; **send** κ **to** IO_r

recv $(\mathsf{Equal}?, ptr_1, ptr_2)$ **from** IO_r **s.t.** $\forall i \in \{1, 2\}: \kappa_i := \mathsf{key}(ptr_i) \neq \bot$:

    if $\kappa_1 = \kappa_2$: **send** 1 **to** IO_r **else**: **send** 0 **to** IO_r

recv $(\mathsf{GetPSK}, (t, name))$ **from** IO_r **s.t.** $t \in \mathcal{T}$:   {*get pre-shared key*

    $k := \mathcal{F}^{\mathrm{keysetup}}_{\mathrm{crypto}}[t, name].\mathsf{GetPSK}()$; $ptr := \mathtt{create\text{-}pointer}((t, k))$; **send** ptr **to** IO_r

recv $(\mathsf{CorrPSK}?, (t, name))$ **from** IO_r **s.t.** $t \in \mathcal{T}$:   {*corruption status request*

    $corr := \mathcal{F}^{\mathrm{keysetup}}_{\mathrm{crypto}}[t, name].\mathsf{Corr}?()$; **send** $corr$ **to** IO_r

recv $(\mathsf{Enc}, ptr, x, ptr_1, \ldots, ptr_l)$ **from** IO_r **s.t.** $\kappa := \mathsf{key}(ptr) \in \mathcal{D}_{\mathrm{senc}}(\eta) \wedge \forall i \leq l: \mathsf{key}(ptr_i) \neq \bot$:

    $x' := \mathtt{format}^{\kappa.t}_{\mathrm{senc}}(1^\eta, x, \mathsf{key}(ptr_1), \ldots, \mathsf{key}(ptr_l))$ {*construct plaintext*

    if $x' = \bot$: **send** $\bot$ **to** IO_r {*error: constructing plaintext failed*

    $y := \mathcal{F}^{\mathrm{senc}}_{\mathrm{crypto}}[\kappa].\mathsf{Enc}(x')$; **send** y **to** IO_r {*encrypt x', return ciphertext*

recv (Dec, ptr, y) **from** IO_r **s.t.** $\kappa := \mathsf{key}(ptr) \in \mathcal{D}_{\mathrm{senc}}(\eta)$:

    $x := \mathcal{F}^{\mathrm{senc}}_{\mathrm{crypto}}[\kappa].\mathsf{Dec}(y)$ {*decrypt y*

    if $x = \bot \vee \mathtt{parse}^{\kappa.t}_{\mathrm{senc}}(1^\eta, x) = \bot$: **send** $\bot$ **to** IO_r {*error: decryption or parsing failed*

    $(x', \kappa_1, \ldots, \kappa_l) := \mathtt{parse}^{\kappa.t}_{\mathrm{senc}}(1^\eta, x)$ {*parse x; possibly $l = 0$*

    for all $i \in \{1, \ldots, l\}$ **do**: $ptr_i := \mathtt{create\text{-}pointer}(\kappa_i)$ {*create pointer*

    send $(x', ptr_1, \ldots, ptr_l)$ **to** IO_r {*return plaintext and pointer*

recv $(\mathsf{Derive}, ptr, x)$ **from** IO_r **s.t.** $\kappa := \mathsf{key}(ptr) \in \mathcal{D}_{\mathrm{derive}}(\eta)$:

    $(\kappa_1, \ldots, \kappa_l) := \mathcal{F}^{\mathrm{derive}}_{\mathrm{crypto}}[\kappa].\mathsf{Derive}(x)$ {*derive keys*

    for all $i \in \{1, \ldots, l\}$ **do**: $ptr_i := \mathtt{create\text{-}pointer}(\kappa_i)$ {*create pointer*

    send $(ptr_1, \ldots, ptr_l)$ **to** IO_r {*return pointer*

recv (MAC, ptr, x) **from** IO_r **s.t.** $\kappa := \mathsf{key}(ptr) \in \mathcal{D}_{\mathrm{mac}}(\eta)$:

    $\sigma := \mathcal{F}^{\mathrm{mac}}_{\mathrm{crypto}}[\kappa].\mathsf{MAC}(x)$; **send** σ **to** IO_r {*MAC x and return MAC*

recv $(\mathsf{Verify}, ptr, x, \sigma)$ **from** IO_r **s.t.** $\kappa := \mathsf{key}(ptr) \in \mathcal{D}_{\mathrm{mac}}(\eta)$:

    $b := \mathcal{F}^{\mathrm{mac}}_{\mathrm{crypto}}[\kappa].\mathsf{Verify}(x, \sigma)$; **send** b **to** IO_r {*verify MAC σ of x and return result*

recv $(\mathsf{GetPubKey}, name)$ **from** IO_r: {*get public key of name $name$*

    $pk := \mathcal{F}^{\mathrm{pke}}_{\mathrm{crypto}}[name].\mathsf{GetPubKey}()$; **send** pk **to** IO_r

recv $(\mathsf{EncPKE}, name, pk, x, ptr_1, \ldots, ptr_l)$ **from** IO_r **s.t.** $\forall i \leq l: \mathsf{key}(ptr_i) \neq \bot$:

    $x' := \mathtt{format}^{name}_{\mathrm{pke}}(1^\eta, x, \mathsf{key}(ptr_1), \ldots, \mathsf{key}(ptr_l))$ {*construct plaintext*

    if $x' = \bot$: **send** $\bot$ **to** IO_r {*error: constructing plaintext failed*

    $y := \mathcal{F}^{\mathrm{pke}}_{\mathrm{crypto}}[name].\mathsf{Enc}(pk, x')$; **send** y **to** IO_r {*encrypt x', return ciphertext*

recv $(\mathsf{DecPKE}, name, y)$ **from** IO_r:

    As symmetric decryption (Dec) except that $x := \mathcal{F}^{\mathrm{pke}}_{\mathrm{crypto}}[name].\mathsf{Dec}(y)$ and

    $\mathtt{parse}^{\kappa.t}_{\mathrm{senc}}(1^\eta, x)$ is replaced by $\mathtt{parse}^{name}_{\mathrm{pke}}(1^\eta, x)$.

recv $(\mathsf{CorrPKE}?, name)$ **from** IO_r: {*corruption status request*

    $corr := \mathcal{F}^{\mathrm{pke}}_{\mathrm{crypto}}[name].\mathsf{Corr}?()$; **send** $corr$ **to** IO_r

---

Figure B.2.: Mode Compute of $\mathcal{F}^{\mathrm{user}}_{\mathrm{crypto}}$ (see Figure B.1 for notation).

Parameters: Π *{parameter set, see beginning of Section 5.2*

Tapes: from/to $\mathcal{F}^z_{\text{crypto}}$: $(\text{io}^{\text{in}}_{\text{keys},z}, \text{io}^{\text{out}}_{\text{keys},z})$ for all $z \in \{\text{user}, \text{keysetup}, \text{senc}, \text{derive}, \text{mac}, \text{pke}\}$

State: $\mathcal{K} \subseteq \mathcal{D}, \mathcal{K}_{\text{known}} \subseteq \mathcal{K}$ *{sets of (typed) keys and known keys; initially $\emptyset$*

CheckAddress: Accept every input on every tape.

Compute: In the following, by "**recv/send** m **from/to** $\mathcal{F}^z_{\text{crypto}}[sid]$", we denote "**recv/send** (sid, m) **from/to** $\mathcal{F}^z_{\text{crypto}}$" (i.e., communication with the copy of $\mathcal{F}^z_{\text{crypto}}$ that is addressed by sid).

  recv (Status, κ) **from** $\mathcal{F}^z_{\text{crypto}}[sid]$ **s.t.** $\kappa \in \mathcal{K}$:

    if $\kappa \in \mathcal{K}_{\text{known}}$: **send** known **to** $\mathcal{F}^z_{\text{crypto}}[sid]$ **else: send** unknown **to** $\mathcal{F}^z_{\text{crypto}}[sid]$

  recv $(\text{MarkKnown}, \kappa_1, \ldots, \kappa_n)$ **from** $\mathcal{F}^z_{\text{crypto}}[sid]$ **s.t.** $\forall i \leq n \colon \kappa_i \in \mathcal{K}$:

    for all $i \leq n$ **s.t.** $\kappa_i \notin \mathcal{K}_{\text{known}}$ **do: add** κ_i **to** $\mathcal{K}_{\text{known}}$

    send Ack **to** $\mathcal{F}^z_{\text{crypto}}[sid]$

  recv $(\text{Add}, status, \kappa_1, \ldots, \kappa_n)$ **from** $\mathcal{F}^z_{\text{crypto}}[sid]$ **s.t.** $status \in \{\text{known}, \text{unknown}\} \wedge \forall i \leq n \colon \kappa_i \in \mathcal{D}$:

    if $status = $ known:

      if $\exists i \leq n \colon \kappa_i \in \mathcal{K} \setminus \mathcal{K}_{\text{known}}$: **send** $\perp$ **to** $\mathcal{F}^z_{\text{crypto}}[sid]$ *{some key is unknown; return error*

      for all $i \leq n$ **s.t.** $\kappa_i \notin \mathcal{K}_{\text{known}}$ **do: add** κ_i **to** $\mathcal{K}$; **add** κ_i **to** $\mathcal{K}_{\text{known}}$

    else:

      if $\exists i \leq n \colon \kappa_i \in \mathcal{K}$: **send** $\perp$ **to** $\mathcal{F}^z_{\text{crypto}}[sid]$ *{some key is not fresh; return error*

      for all $i \leq n$ **do: add** κ_i **to** $\mathcal{K}$

    send Ack **to** $\mathcal{F}^z_{\text{crypto}}[sid]$

Figure B.3.: The IITM $\mathcal{F}^{\text{keys}}_{\text{crypto}}$. As a part of $\mathcal{F}_{\text{crypto}}$, it keeps track of the known/unknown status of keys.

Parameters: Π   {*parameter set, see beginning of Section 5.2*

Tapes: from/to $\mathcal{F}_{\text{crypto}}^{\text{user}}$: $(\text{io}_{\text{keysetup}}^{\text{in}}, \text{io}_{\text{keysetup}}^{\text{out}})$;

from/to $\mathcal{F}_{\text{crypto}}^{\text{keys}}$: $(\text{io}_{\text{keys,keysetup}}^{\text{out}}, \text{io}_{\text{keys,keysetup}}^{\text{in}})$;

from/to NET: $(\text{net}_{\mathcal{F}_{\text{crypto}}^{\text{keysetup}}}^{\text{in}}, \text{net}_{\mathcal{F}_{\text{crypto}}^{\text{keysetup}}}^{\text{out}})$

$\qquad\qquad\qquad\qquad\qquad\qquad\qquad\qquad\quad$ { *pre-shared key type and name*

State: − psk ∈ {(t, name) | t ∈ 𝒯, name ∈ {0, 1}*} ∪ {⊥}   { *(used as SID); initially* ⊥*

− k ∈ {0, 1}* ∪ {⊥}   {*symmetric key (provided by adversary); initially* ⊥*

− corr ∈ {0, 1}   {*corruption status; initially* 0*

CheckAddress: *Accept input m from* $\mathcal{F}_{\text{crypto}}^{\text{user}}$ *iff* $m = (uid, (t, name), m')$ *for some* $t \in \mathcal{T}$ *and*

uid, name, m' ∈ {0, 1}* *such that* psk = ⊥ *or* psk = (t, name). *Accept input m from* $\mathcal{F}_{\text{crypto}}^{\text{keys}}$ *or*

NET *iff* $m = (\text{psk}, m')$ *for some* $m' \in \{0, 1\}^*$.

Initialization: *Upon receiving the first message* $(uid, (t, name), m')$ *from* $\mathcal{F}_{\text{crypto}}^{\text{user}}$ *in mode*

Compute: *Compute:*

psk := (t, name)   {*record pre-shared key type and name (used as SID)*

repeat   {*let (t, name) such that* psk = (t, name)

  send (psk, Init) **to** NET   {*inform adversary about initialization*

  recv (psk, corr, k) **from** NET **s.t.** $k \in \mathcal{D}_{\text{keys}}^t$ {*receive key from adversary, allow corruption*

  if corr = 1: corr := 1   {*key k is ignored upon corruption*

  else if $\mathcal{F}_{\text{crypto}}^{\text{keys}}$.Add(unknown, (t, k)) ≠ ⊥:[a] k := k   {Add *returns* ⊥ *if the key is not fresh*

until corr = 1 ∨ k ≠ ⊥   {*if corr = 0 and* Add *failed, then repeat, i.e., ask adversary again*

Then, continue processing the first request in mode Compute.

Compute: In the following, "**recv/send** m **from/to** $\mathcal{F}_{\text{crypto}}^{\text{user}}[uid]$", denotes "**recv/send** (uid, psk, m)

from/to $\mathcal{F}_{\text{crypto}}^{\text{user}}$ " (i.e., communication with the copy of $\mathcal{F}_{\text{crypto}}^{\text{user}}$ for user uid).

recv GetPSK **from** $\mathcal{F}_{\text{crypto}}^{\text{user}}[uid]$:   {*let (t, name) s.t.* psk = (t, name)

  if corr = 0:   {*note: corr = 0 implies* k ≠ ⊥ *because of initialization*

    send k **to** $\mathcal{F}_{\text{crypto}}^{\text{user}}[uid]$ {*return recorded key*

  else:

    repeat   {*ask adversary for corrupted key*

      send (psk, GetPSK) **to** NET; **recv** (psk, k) **from** NET **s.t.** $k \in \mathcal{D}_{\text{keys}}^t(\eta)$

    until $\mathcal{F}_{\text{crypto}}^{\text{keys}}$.Add(known, (t, k)) ≠ ⊥   {*if* Add *fails (guessing prevented), then repeat*

    send k **to** $\mathcal{F}_{\text{crypto}}^{\text{user}}[uid]$ {*return key (this key is now marked known)*

recv Corr? **from** $\mathcal{F}_{\text{crypto}}^{\text{user}}[uid]$: **send** corr **to** $\mathcal{F}_{\text{crypto}}^{\text{user}}[uid]$ {*corruption status request*

---

[a]Similar to $\mathcal{F}_{\text{crypto}}^{\text{user}}$, by "$\mathcal{F}_{\text{crypto}}^{\text{keys}}.cmd(m)$", we denote "**send** (psk, cmd, m) **to** $\mathcal{F}_{\text{crypto}}^{\text{keys}}$; **recv** (psk, m') **from** $\mathcal{F}_{\text{crypto}}^{\text{keys}}$; **return** m' (as the result)".

Figure B.4.: The ideal key setup functionality $\mathcal{F}_{\text{crypto}}^{\text{keysetup}}$. It is part of $\mathcal{F}_{\text{crypto}}$.

Parameters: Π {*parameter set, see beginning of Section 5.2*

Tapes: from/to $\mathcal{F}_{\text{crypto}}^{\text{user}}$: $(\text{io}_{\text{senc}}^{\text{in}}, \text{io}_{\text{senc}}^{\text{out}})$; from/to $\mathcal{F}_{\text{crypto}}^{\text{keys}}$: $(\text{io}_{\text{keys,senc}}^{\text{out}}, \text{io}_{\text{keys,senc}}^{\text{in}})$;

    from/to adversary NET: $(\text{net}_{\mathcal{F}\text{senc}}^{\text{in}}, \text{net}_{\mathcal{F}\text{senc}}^{\text{out}})$

State: $- \; \kappa \in \mathcal{D}_{\text{senc}}(\eta) \cup \{\bot\}$ {*typed key (used as SID, see mode* CheckAddress*); initially* $\bot$

    $- \;$ enc, dec $\in \{0,1\}^* \cup \{\bot\}$ {*algorithms, provided by the adversary; initially* $\bot$

    $- \;$ H $\subseteq \{0,1\}^* \times \{0,1\}^*$ {*recorded plaintext/ciphertext pairs; initially* $\emptyset$

CheckAddress: *Accept input* m *from* $\mathcal{F}_{\text{crypto}}^{\text{user}}$ *iff* $m = (uid, (t,k), m')$ *for some* $(t,k) \in \mathcal{D}_{\text{senc}}(\eta)$ *and* $uid, m' \in \{0,1\}^*$ *such that* $\kappa = \bot$ *or* $\kappa = (t,k)$. *Accept input* m *from* $\mathcal{F}_{\text{crypto}}^{\text{keys}}$ *or* NET *iff* $m = (\kappa, m')$ *for some* $m' \in \{0,1\}^*$.

Initialization: *Upon receiving the first message* $(uid, (t,k), m')$ *from* $\mathcal{F}_{\text{crypto}}^{\text{user}}$ *in mode* Compute:

$\kappa := (t,k)$ {*record typed key (used as SID)*

send (κ, Init) **to** NET; **recv** (κ, e, d) **from** NET; enc $:= e$; dec $:= d$ {*get algorithms from adv.*

Then, continue processing the first request in mode Compute.

Compute: In the following, "**recv/send** m **from/to** $\mathcal{F}_{\text{crypto}}^{\text{user}}[uid]$" denotes "**recv/send** (uid, κ, m) **from/to** $\mathcal{F}_{\text{crypto}}^{\text{user}}$" (i.e., communication with the copy of $\mathcal{F}_{\text{crypto}}^{\text{user}}$ for user uid) and "$\mathcal{F}_{\text{crypto}}^{\text{keys}}.cmd(m)$" denotes "**send** (κ, cmd, m) **to** $\mathcal{F}_{\text{crypto}}^{\text{keys}}$; **recv** (κ, m') **from** $\mathcal{F}_{\text{crypto}}^{\text{keys}}$; **return** m' (as the result)".

recv (Enc, x) **from** $\mathcal{F}_{\text{crypto}}^{\text{user}}[uid]$:   {*let* (t,k) *s.t.* $\kappa = (t,k)$

   if $\mathcal{F}_{\text{crypto}}^{\text{keys}}.\text{Status}(\kappa) = \text{unknown}$:   {*i.e.,* κ *is marked unknown*

      $\overline{x} \leftarrow L_{\text{senc}}^t(1^\eta, x)$; $y \leftarrow \text{enc}^{(p)}(k, \overline{x})$; $\overline{x}' := \text{dec}^{(p)}(k, y)$ {*encrypt leakage of* x

      if $y = \bot \vee \overline{x}' \neq \overline{x}$: **send** $\bot$ **to** $\mathcal{F}_{\text{crypto}}^{\text{user}}[uid]$ {*error: encryption or decryption test failed*

      add (x, y) **to** H; **send** y **to** $\mathcal{F}_{\text{crypto}}^{\text{user}}[uid]$ {*record* (x,y) *for decryption, return* y

   else: {*i.e.,* κ *is marked known*

      $(x', \kappa_1, \ldots, \kappa_l) := \text{parse}_{\text{senc}}^t(1^\eta, x)$ {*parse plaintext* x *(never fails by def. of* $\mathcal{F}_{\text{crypto}}^{\text{user}}$*)*

      $\mathcal{F}_{\text{crypto}}^{\text{keys}}.\text{MarkKnown}(\kappa_1, \ldots, \kappa_l)$ {*mark keys in* x *as known*

      $y \leftarrow \text{enc}^{(p)}(k, x)$; **send** y **to** $\mathcal{F}_{\text{crypto}}^{\text{user}}[uid]$ {*encrypt* x, *return* y

recv (Dec, y) **from** $\mathcal{F}_{\text{crypto}}^{\text{user}}[uid]$:   {*let* (t,k) *s.t.* $\kappa = (t,k)$

   if $\mathcal{F}_{\text{crypto}}^{\text{keys}}.\text{Status}(\kappa) = \text{unknown} \wedge (t \in \mathcal{T}_{\text{senc}}^{\text{auth}} \vee \exists x: (x,y) \in \text{H})$:

      if $\exists x, x': x \neq x' \wedge (x,y), (x', y) \in \text{H}$:

         send $\bot$ **to** $\mathcal{F}_{\text{crypto}}^{\text{user}}[uid]$ {*error: unique decryption not possible*

      else if $\exists x: (x, y) \in \text{H}$:

         send x **to** $\mathcal{F}_{\text{crypto}}^{\text{user}}[uid]$ {*this* x *is unique in this case*

      else: {*this case occurs only if authenticated encryption* $(t \in \mathcal{T}_{\text{senc}}^{\text{auth}})$

         send $\bot$ **to** $\mathcal{F}_{\text{crypto}}^{\text{user}}[uid]$ {*error: prevent forgery (ciphertext not recorded)*

   else:

      $x := \text{dec}^{(p)}(k, y)$ {*decrypt* y

      if $x = \bot \vee \text{parse}_{\text{senc}}^t(1^\eta, x) = \bot$: **send** $\bot$ **to** $\mathcal{F}_{\text{crypto}}^{\text{user}}[uid]$ {*decryption or parsing failed*

      $(x', \kappa_1, \ldots, \kappa_l) := \text{parse}_{\text{senc}}^t(1^\eta, x)$ {*parse plaintext* x

      if $\mathcal{F}_{\text{crypto}}^{\text{keys}}.\text{Add}(\text{known}, \kappa_1, \ldots, \kappa_l) = \bot$:

         send $\bot$ **to** $\mathcal{F}_{\text{crypto}}^{\text{user}}[uid]$ {*error:* x *contains unknown keys*

      send x **to** $\mathcal{F}_{\text{crypto}}^{\text{user}}[uid]$ {*return* x

---

Figure B.5.: The ideal symmetric encryption functionality $\mathcal{F}_{\text{crypto}}^{\text{senc}}$. It is part of $\mathcal{F}_{\text{crypto}}$.

Parameters: Π   {*parameter set, see beginning of Section 5.2*

Tapes: from/to $\mathcal{F}_{\text{crypto}}^{\text{user}}$: $(\text{io}_{\text{derive}}^{\text{in}}, \text{io}_{\text{derive}}^{\text{out}})$; from/to $\mathcal{F}_{\text{crypto}}^{\text{keys}}$: $(\text{io}_{\text{keys,derive}}^{\text{out}}, \text{io}_{\text{keys,derive}}^{\text{in}})$;

  from/to adversary NET: $(\text{net}_{\mathcal{F}_{\text{crypto}}^{\text{derive}}}^{\text{in}}, \text{net}_{\mathcal{F}_{\text{crypto}}^{\text{derive}}}^{\text{out}})$

State: – $\kappa \in \mathcal{D}_{\text{derive}}(\eta) \cup \{\bot\}$ {*typed key (used as SID, see mode CheckAddress); initially $\bot$*

  – derived: $\{0,1\}^* \to (\mathcal{D}(\eta))^* \cup \{\bot\}$ {*derived (typed) keys; initially $\forall x\colon$ derived$(x) = \bot$*

CheckAddress: As for $\mathcal{F}_{\text{crypto}}^{\text{senc}}$ (Figure B.5) except that $\mathcal{D}_{\text{senc}}(\eta)$ is replaced by $\mathcal{D}_{\text{derive}}(\eta)$.

Initialization: Upon receiving the first message $(uid, (t,k), m')$ from $\mathcal{F}_{\text{crypto}}^{\text{user}}$ in mode **Compute**:

  $\kappa := (t,k)$ {*record typed key (used as SID)*

  Then, continue processing the first request in mode **Compute**.

Compute: We use the notation $\mathcal{F}_{\text{crypto}}^{\text{user}}[uid]$ and $\mathcal{F}_{\text{crypto}}^{\text{keys}}.cmd(m)$ as introduced for $\mathcal{F}_{\text{crypto}}^{\text{senc}}$.

  recv (Derive, x) **from** $\mathcal{F}_{\text{crypto}}^{\text{user}}[uid]$:   {*let (t,k) s.t. $\kappa = (t,k)$*

   if derived$(x) = \bot$:

    $(t_1, \ldots, t_n) := \text{parse}_{\text{salt}}^t(1^\eta, x)$ {*parse the salt x to get key types*

    $status := \mathcal{F}_{\text{crypto}}^{\text{keys}}.\text{Status}(\kappa)$ {*get known/unknown status of κ*

    repeat

      send $(\kappa, \text{Derive}, x, status)$ **to** NET   {*ask adversary for derived keys*

      recv $(\kappa, k_1, \ldots, k_n)$ **from** NET s.t. $\forall i \leq n\colon k_i \in \mathcal{D}_{\text{keys}}^{t_i}(\eta)$

    until $\mathcal{F}_{\text{crypto}}^{\text{keys}}.\text{Add}(status, (t_1, k_1), \ldots, (t_n, k_n)) \neq \bot$ {*repeat if Add failed*

    derived$(x) := ((t_1, k_1), \ldots, (t_n, k_n))$ {*record derived keys*

  send derived(x) **to** $\mathcal{F}_{\text{crypto}}^{\text{user}}[uid]$ {*return recorded derived keys*

Figure B.6.: Ideal key derivation functionality $\mathcal{F}_{\text{crypto}}^{\text{derive}}$ for $\mathcal{F}_{\text{crypto}}$. It is part of $\mathcal{F}_{\text{crypto}}$.

Parameters: Π {*parameter set, see beginning of Section 5.2*

Tapes: from/to $\mathcal{F}_{\mathrm{crypto}}^{\mathrm{user}}$: $(\mathrm{io}_{\mathrm{mac}}^{\mathrm{in}}, \mathrm{io}_{\mathrm{mac}}^{\mathrm{out}})$; from/to $\mathcal{F}_{\mathrm{crypto}}^{\mathrm{keys}}$: $(\mathrm{io}_{\mathrm{keys,mac}}^{\mathrm{out}}, \mathrm{io}_{\mathrm{keys,mac}}^{\mathrm{in}})$;

     from/to adversary NET: $(\mathrm{net}_{\mathcal{F}_{\mathrm{mac}}}^{\mathrm{in}}, \mathrm{net}_{\mathcal{F}_{\mathrm{mac}}}^{\mathrm{out}})$

State: $-$ $\kappa \in \mathcal{D}_{\mathrm{mac}}(\eta) \cup \{\bot\}$ {*typed key (used as SID, see mode* **CheckAddress***); initially* $\bot$

     $-$ mac $\in \{0,1\}^* \cup \{\bot\}$ {*algorithm (provided by adversary); initially* $\bot$

     $-$ $H \subseteq \{0,1\}^*$ {*recorded messages; initially* $\emptyset$

CheckAddress: As for $\mathcal{F}_{\mathrm{crypto}}^{\mathrm{senc}}$ (Figure B.5) except that $\mathcal{D}_{\mathrm{senc}}(\eta)$ is replaced by $\mathcal{D}_{\mathrm{mac}}(\eta)$.

Initialization: Upon receiving the first message $(uid, (t,k), m')$ from $\mathcal{F}_{\mathrm{crypto}}^{\mathrm{user}}$ in mode **Compute**:

     $\kappa := (t,k)$ {*record typed key (used as SID)*

     send (κ, Init) **to** NET; **recv** (κ, mac) **from** NET; mac $:= mac$ {*get algorithm from adversary*

Then, continue processing the first request in mode **Compute**.

Compute: We use the notation $\mathcal{F}_{\mathrm{crypto}}^{\mathrm{user}}[uid]$ and $\mathcal{F}_{\mathrm{crypto}}^{\mathrm{keys}}.cmd(m)$ as introduced for $\mathcal{F}_{\mathrm{crypto}}^{\mathrm{senc}}$.

     recv (MAC, x) **from** $\mathcal{F}_{\mathrm{crypto}}^{\mathrm{user}}[uid]$:   {*let* (t,k) *s.t.* $\kappa = (t,k)$

         $\sigma := mac^{(p)}(k,x)$ {*compute MAC of* x

         if $\sigma = \bot$: **send** $\bot$ **to** $\mathcal{F}_{\mathrm{crypto}}^{\mathrm{user}}[uid]$ {*error: computing MAC failed*

         add x **to** H; **send** σ **to** $\mathcal{F}_{\mathrm{crypto}}^{\mathrm{user}}[uid]$ {*record* x *for verification and return MAC*

     recv $(\mathsf{Verify}, x, \sigma)$ **from** $\mathcal{F}_{\mathrm{crypto}}^{\mathrm{user}}[uid]$:   {*let* (t,k) *s.t.* $\kappa = (t,k)$

         $\sigma' := mac^{(p)}(k,x)$ {*compute MAC of* x

         if $\sigma = \sigma' \neq \bot$: $b := 1$ **else**: $b := 0$ {b *is the verification result*

         if $\mathcal{F}_{\mathrm{crypto}}^{\mathrm{keys}}.\mathrm{Status}(\kappa) = \mathrm{unknown} \wedge b = 1 \wedge x \notin$ H: **send** $\bot$ **to** $\mathcal{F}_{\mathrm{crypto}}^{\mathrm{user}}[uid]$ {*error: forgery*

     send b **to** $\mathcal{F}_{\mathrm{crypto}}^{\mathrm{user}}[uid]$ {*return verification result*

Figure B.7.: The ideal MAC functionality $\mathcal{F}_{\mathrm{crypto}}^{\mathrm{mac}}$. It is part of $\mathcal{F}_{\mathrm{crypto}}$.

Parameters: Π　　　　　　　　　　　　　　　　{*parameter set, see beginning of Section 5.2*

Tapes: from/to $\mathcal{F}_{\text{crypto}}^{\text{user}}$: $(\text{io}_{\text{pke}}^{\text{in}}, \text{io}_{\text{pke}}^{\text{out}})$; from/to $\mathcal{F}_{\text{crypto}}^{\text{keys}}$: $(\text{io}_{\text{keys},\text{pke}}^{\text{out}}, \text{io}_{\text{keys},\text{pke}}^{\text{in}})$;

　　from/to adversary NET: $(\text{net}_{\mathcal{F}_{\text{crypto}}^{\text{pke}}}^{\text{in}}, \text{net}_{\mathcal{F}_{\text{crypto}}^{\text{pke}}}^{\text{out}})$

State: – name $\in \{0,1\}^* \cup \{\perp\}$　　　　　{*public/private key name (used as SID); initially $\perp$*

　　– enc, dec, pk, sk $\in \{0,1\}^* \cup \{\perp\}$ {*algorithms and key pair (provided by adversary); initially $\perp$*

　　– $H \subseteq \{0,1\}^* \times \{0,1\}^*$　　　　　　{*recorded plaintext/ciphertext pairs; initially $\emptyset$*

　　– corr $\in \{0,1\}$　　　　　　　　　　　　{*corruption status; initially 0*

CheckAddress: *Accept input m from* $\mathcal{F}_{\text{crypto}}^{\text{user}}$ *iff* $m = (uid, name, m')$ *for some $uid, name, m' \in$*
$\{0,1\}^*$ *such that* name $= \perp$ *or* name $=$ *name. Accept input m from* $\mathcal{F}_{\text{crypto}}^{\text{keys}}$ *or* NET *iff*
$m = (name, m')$ *for some $m' \in \{0,1\}^*$.*

Initialization: *Upon receiving the first message $(uid, name, m')$ from* $\mathcal{F}_{\text{crypto}}^{\text{user}}$ *in mode* Compute:
　　name $:=$ *name*　　　　　　　　　　　　{*record public/private key name (used as SID)*
　　send $(name, \text{Init})$ **to** NET　　　　　　　⎧ *get algorithms and*
　　recv $(name, corr, e, d, pk, sk)$ **from** NET **s.t.** $corr \in \{0,1\}$　　⎨ *key pair from adversary,*
　　corr $:=$ *corr*; enc $:= e$; dec $:= d$; pk $:= pk$; sk $:= sk$　　⎩ *allow corruption*

　　Then, continue processing the first request in mode Compute.

Compute: We use the notation $\mathcal{F}_{\text{crypto}}^{\text{user}}[uid]$ and $\mathcal{F}_{\text{crypto}}^{\text{keys}}.cmd(m)$ as introduced for $\mathcal{F}_{\text{crypto}}^{\text{senc}}$
(Figure B.5) except that κ is replaced by name.
　recv GetPubKey **from** $\mathcal{F}_{\text{crypto}}^{\text{user}}[uid]$: **send** pk **to** $\mathcal{F}_{\text{crypto}}^{\text{user}}[uid]$　　　　{*return public key*
　recv (Enc, pk, x) **from** $\mathcal{F}_{\text{crypto}}^{\text{user}}[uid]$:
　　if corr $= 0 \wedge pk = $ pk:　　　　　　{*i.e., uncorrupted and correct public key*
　　　$\bar{x} \leftarrow L_{\text{pke}}^{\text{name}}(1^\eta, x)$; $y \leftarrow \text{enc}^{(p)}(\text{pk}, \bar{x})$; $\bar{x}' := \text{dec}^{(p)}(\text{sk}, y)$　{*encrypt leakage of x*
　　　if $y = \perp \vee \bar{x}' \neq \bar{x}$: **send** $\perp$ **to** $\mathcal{F}_{\text{crypto}}^{\text{user}}[uid]$ {*error: encryption or decryption test failed*
　　　add (x, y) **to** H; **send** y **to** $\mathcal{F}_{\text{crypto}}^{\text{user}}[uid]$　{*record (x,y) for decryption, return y*
　　else:　　　　　　　　　　　　　　　{*i.e., corrupted or wrong public key*
　　　$(x', \kappa_1, \ldots, \kappa_l) := \text{parse}_{\text{pke}}^{\text{name}}(1^\eta, x)$　{*parse plaintext x (never fails by def. of $\mathcal{F}_{\text{crypto}}^{\text{user}}$)*
　　　$\mathcal{F}_{\text{crypto}}^{\text{keys}}.\text{MarkKnown}(\kappa_1, \ldots, \kappa_l)$　　　　{*mark keys in x as known*
　　　$y \leftarrow \text{enc}^{(p)}(\text{pk}, x)$; **send** y **to** $\mathcal{F}_{\text{crypto}}^{\text{user}}[uid]$　{*encrypt x, return y*
　recv (Dec, y) **from** $\mathcal{F}_{\text{crypto}}^{\text{user}}[uid]$:
　　if corr $= 0 \wedge \exists x \colon (x, y) \in$ H:
　　　if $\exists x, x' \colon x \neq x' \wedge (x, y), (x', y) \in$ H:
　　　　send $\perp$ **to** $\mathcal{F}_{\text{crypto}}^{\text{user}}[uid]$　　　　{*error: unique decryption not possible*
　　　let x **s.t.** $(x, y) \in$ H　　　{*this x always exists and is unique in this case*
　　　send x **to** $\mathcal{F}_{\text{crypto}}^{\text{user}}[uid]$　　　　　　　　{*return x*
　　else:
　　　$x := \text{dec}^{(p)}(\text{sk}, y)$　　　　　　　　　　　{*decrypt y*
　　　if $x = \perp \vee \text{parse}_{\text{pke}}^{\text{name}}(1^\eta, x) = \perp$: **send** $\perp$ **to** $\mathcal{F}_{\text{crypto}}^{\text{user}}[uid]$ {*decryption or parsing failed*
　　　$(x', \kappa_1, \ldots, \kappa_l) := \text{parse}_{\text{pke}}^{\text{name}}(1^\eta, x)$　　　{*parse plaintext x*
　　　if $\mathcal{F}_{\text{crypto}}^{\text{keys}}.\text{Add}(\text{known}, \kappa_1, \ldots, \kappa_l) = \perp$:
　　　　send $\perp$ **to** $\mathcal{F}_{\text{crypto}}^{\text{user}}[uid]$　　　{*error: x contains unknown keys*
　　　send x **to** $\mathcal{F}_{\text{crypto}}^{\text{user}}[uid]$　　　　　　　　{*return x*
　recv Corr? **from** $\mathcal{F}_{\text{crypto}}^{\text{user}}[uid]$: **send** corr **to** $\mathcal{F}_{\text{crypto}}^{\text{user}}[uid]$　{*corruption status request*

Figure B.8.: The ideal public-key encryption functionality $\mathcal{F}_{\text{crypto}}^{\text{pke}}$. It is part of
　　　$\mathcal{F}_{\text{crypto}}$.

Parameters: $\mathcal{T}$, $l_t(\eta) \in \mathbb{N}$ for all $t \in \mathcal{T}$ and $\eta \in \mathbb{N}$ {set of key types and key lengths

Tapes: from/to $\mathcal{P}^{\text{user}}_{\text{crypto}}$: ($\text{io}^{\text{in}}_{\text{keysetup}}$, $\text{io}^{\text{out}}_{\text{keysetup}}$); from/to NET: ($\text{net}^{\text{in}}_{\mathcal{F}_{\text{keysetup}}}$, $\text{net}^{\text{out}}_{\mathcal{F}_{\text{keysetup}}}$)

State: {pre-shared key type and name

- psk $\in \{(t, name) \mid t \in \mathcal{T}, name \in \{0,1\}^*\} \cup \{\bot\}$ (used as SID); initially $\bot$
- k $\in \{0,1\}^* \cup \{\bot\}$ {symmetric key; initially $\bot$
- corr $\in \{0,1\}$ {corruption status; initially 0

CheckAddress: *Accept* input m from $\mathcal{P}^{\text{user}}_{\text{crypto}}$ *iff* $m = (uid, (t, name), m')$ *for some* $t \in \mathcal{T}$ *and* $uid, name, m' \in \{0,1\}^*$ *such that* psk $= \bot$ *or* psk $= (t, name)$. *Accept* input m *from* NET *iff* $m = (\text{psk}, m')$ *for some* $m' \in \{0,1\}^*$.

Initialization: *Upon receiving the first message* $(uid, (t, name), m')$ *from* $\mathcal{F}^{\text{user}}_{\text{crypto}}$ *in mode* Compute:

psk $:= (t, name)$ {record pre-shared key type and name (used as SID)
send (psk, Init) **to** NET; **recv** (psk, *corr*) **from** NET   {ask adversary for corruption

if *corr* $= 1$: corr $:= 1$ **else**: k $\xleftarrow{\$} \{0,1\}^{l_t(\eta)}$ {generate fresh key if uncorrupted

Then, continue processing the first request in mode Compute.

Compute: *In the following,* "**recv/send** m **from/to** $\mathcal{P}^{\text{user}}_{\text{crypto}}[uid]$", *denotes* "**recv/send** (uid, psk, m) **from/to** $\mathcal{P}^{\text{user}}_{\text{crypto}}$" *(i.e., communication with the copy of* $\mathcal{P}^{\text{user}}_{\text{crypto}}$ *for user uid).*

recv GetPSK **from** $\mathcal{P}^{\text{user}}_{\text{crypto}}[uid]$:   {let $(t, name)$ s.t. psk $= (t, name)$
    if corr $= 0$:   {note: corr $= 0$ implies k $\neq \bot$ because of initialization
        send k **on** $\mathcal{P}^{\text{user}}_{\text{crypto}}[uid]$ {return recorded key
    else: {ask adversary for corrupted key
        send (psk, GetPSK) **to** NET; **recv** (psk, k) **from** NET s.t. k $\in \{0,1\}^{l_t(\eta)}$
        send k **to** $\mathcal{P}^{\text{user}}_{\text{crypto}}[uid]$ {return key

recv Corr? **from** $\mathcal{P}^{\text{user}}_{\text{crypto}}[uid]$: **send** corr **to** $\mathcal{P}^{\text{user}}_{\text{crypto}}[uid]$ {corruption status request

Figure B.9.: The ideal key setup functionality $\mathcal{F}_{\text{keysetup}}$. It is part of $\mathcal{P}_{\text{crypto}}$.

B.2. Proof of Theorem 5.1

In this section, we prove Theorem 5.1. Statement 2. of Theorem 5.1 follows easily from the proof sketch provided in Section 5.3. We now prove statement 1. of Theorem 5.1 ($\mathcal{F}^* \mid \mathcal{P}_{\text{crypto}} \leq \mathcal{F}^* \mid \mathcal{F}_{\text{crypto}}$), following the proof sketch provided in Section 5.3. That is, we first replace public-key encryption ($\mathcal{P}_{\text{pke}}$) by ideal public-key encryption ($\mathcal{F}_{\text{pke}}$). By Theorem 4.1 and the composition theorem for a constant number of systems (Theorem 2.1), we obtain that

$$\mathcal{F}^* \mid \mathcal{P}_{\text{crypto}} \leq \mathcal{F}^* \mid \mathcal{P}'_{\text{crypto}} \tag{B.1}$$

where

$$\mathcal{P}'_{\text{crypto}} := !\mathcal{P}^{\text{user}}_{\text{crypto}} \mid !\mathcal{F}_{\text{pke}} \mid !\mathcal{F}_{\text{keysetup}} .$$

We note that, formally, we have to consider a variant of $\mathcal{F}_{\text{pke}}$ where the leakage algorithm of $\mathcal{F}_{\text{pke}}$ depends on the public/private key pair name such that the instance $\mathcal{F}_{\text{pke}}[name]$ for the key pair *name* uses the leakage algorithm L^{name}_{pke}. Theorem 4.1 directly carries over to this variant of $\mathcal{F}_{\text{pke}}$.

The simulator S.   Next, we define a simulator $S \in \mathrm{Sim}^{\mathcal{F}^* \mid \mathcal{P}'_{\mathrm{crypto}}}(\mathcal{F}^* \mid \mathcal{F}_{\mathrm{crypto}})$. Then, we show that $\mathcal{E} \mid \mathcal{F}^* \mid \mathcal{P}'_{\mathrm{crypto}} \equiv \mathcal{E} \mid S \mid \mathcal{F}^* \mid \mathcal{F}_{\mathrm{crypto}}$ for every environment $\mathcal{E}$.

We define S to be an IITM that provides the same network interface as $\mathcal{P}'_{\mathrm{crypto}}$ to the environment and has a network interface to connect to all network tapes of $\mathcal{F}_{\mathrm{crypto}}$, i.e., to the network tapes of $\mathcal{F}^{\mathrm{user}}_{\mathrm{crypto}}$, $\mathcal{F}^{\mathrm{keysetup}}_{\mathrm{crypto}}$, $\mathcal{F}^{\mathrm{senc}}_{\mathrm{crypto}}$, $\mathcal{F}^{\mathrm{derive}}_{\mathrm{crypto}}$, $\mathcal{F}^{\mathrm{mac}}_{\mathrm{crypto}}$, and $\mathcal{F}^{\mathrm{pke}}_{\mathrm{crypto}}$. Hence, $S \mid \mathcal{F}^* \mid \mathcal{F}_{\mathrm{crypto}}$ and $\mathcal{F}^* \mid \mathcal{P}'_{\mathrm{crypto}}$ have the same external network and I/O interface.

In mode CheckAddress, S accepts all messages on all tapes. To explain mode Compute, we first note that, in a run with $\mathcal{F}_{\mathrm{crypto}}$ and some environment, S receives the following requests: *(i)* from $\mathcal{F}^{\mathrm{user}}_{\mathrm{crypto}}$ to inform about initialization (Init) and to generate new keys (KeyGen); *(ii)* from $\mathcal{F}^{\mathrm{keysetup}}_{\mathrm{crypto}}$ to inform about initialization (Init) and to provide corrupted pre-shared keys (GetPSK); *(iii)* from $\mathcal{F}^{\mathrm{senc}}_{\mathrm{crypto}}$, $\mathcal{F}^{\mathrm{mac}}_{\mathrm{crypto}}$, and $\mathcal{F}^{\mathrm{pke}}_{\mathrm{crypto}}$ to inform about initialization (Init); and *(iv)* from $\mathcal{F}^{\mathrm{derive}}_{\mathrm{crypto}}$ to inform about initialization (Init) and to provide derived keys (Derive). The network tapes of $\mathcal{P}'_{\mathrm{crypto}}$ are the network tapes of $\mathcal{P}^{\mathrm{user}}_{\mathrm{crypto}}$, $\mathcal{F}_{\mathrm{keysetup}}$, and $\mathcal{F}_{\mathrm{pke}}$ and they are only used to inform the adversary when new copies of $\mathcal{P}^{\mathrm{user}}_{\mathrm{crypto}}$, $\mathcal{F}_{\mathrm{keysetup}}$, and $\mathcal{F}_{\mathrm{pke}}$ are created (in response, the adversary may corrupt the copies of $\mathcal{F}_{\mathrm{keysetup}}$ and $\mathcal{F}_{\mathrm{pke}}$) and to ask the adversary to provide corrupted pre-shared keys. We now explain how S responds to the above mentioned requests:

1. Upon a request Init from $\mathcal{F}^{\mathrm{user}}_{\mathrm{crypto}}[uid]$ (i.e., upon receiving the message (uid, Init) on tape $\mathrm{net}^{\mathrm{out}}_{\mathcal{F}^{\mathrm{user}}_{\mathrm{crypto}}}$), S forwards this request to the adversary (i.e., sends (uid, Init) on $\mathrm{net}^{\mathrm{out}}_{\mathcal{P}^{\mathrm{user}}_{\mathrm{crypto}}}$).

2. Upon a response Continue from the adversary for $\mathcal{P}^{\mathrm{user}}_{\mathrm{crypto}}[uid]$ (i.e., upon receiving $(uid, \mathsf{Continue})$ on $\mathrm{net}^{\mathrm{in}}_{\mathcal{P}^{\mathrm{user}}_{\mathrm{crypto}}}$), S forwards this response to $\mathcal{F}^{\mathrm{user}}_{\mathrm{crypto}}$ (i.e., sends $(uid, \mathsf{Continue})$ on $\mathrm{net}^{\mathrm{in}}_{\mathcal{F}^{\mathrm{user}}_{\mathrm{crypto}}}$).

3. Upon a request (KeyGen, t) from $\mathcal{F}^{\mathrm{user}}_{\mathrm{crypto}}[uid]$, S generates a fresh key k of type t (i.e., chooses k uniformly at random from $\{0,1\}^{l_t(\eta)}$; recall that $l_t(\eta)$ is the length of keys of type t for security parameter η) and sends k to $\mathcal{F}^{\mathrm{user}}_{\mathrm{crypto}}[uid]$.

4. Upon a request Init from $\mathcal{F}^{\mathrm{keysetup}}_{\mathrm{crypto}}[t, name]$ (i.e., upon receiving $((t, name), \mathsf{Init})$ on $\mathrm{net}^{\mathrm{out}}_{\mathcal{F}^{\mathrm{keysetup}}_{\mathrm{crypto}}}$), S forwards this request to the adversary (i.e., sends it on $\mathrm{net}^{\mathrm{out}}_{\mathcal{F}_{\mathrm{keysetup}}}$).

5. Upon a response $corr \in \{0,1\}$ from the adversary for $\mathcal{F}_{\mathrm{keysetup}}[t, name]$ (i.e., upon receiving $((t, name), corr)$ on $\mathrm{net}^{\mathrm{in}}_{\mathcal{F}_{\mathrm{keysetup}}}$), S generates a fresh key k of type t (as above), and sends $(corr, k)$ to $\mathcal{F}^{\mathrm{keysetup}}_{\mathrm{crypto}}[t, name]$ (i.e., sends $((t, name), corr, k)$ on $\mathrm{net}^{\mathrm{in}}_{\mathcal{F}_{\mathrm{keysetup}}}$).

6. Upon a request GetPSK from $\mathcal{F}^{\mathrm{keysetup}}_{\mathrm{crypto}}[t, name]$, S forwards this request to the adversary.

7. Upon a response $k \in \{0,1\}^{l_t(\eta)}$ from the adversary for $\mathcal{F}_{\mathrm{keysetup}}[t, name]$, $\mathcal{S}$ forwards this response to $\mathcal{F}_{\mathrm{crypto}}^{\mathrm{keysetup}}[t, name]$.

8. Upon a request Init from $\mathcal{F}_{\mathrm{crypto}}^{\mathrm{senc}}[(t,k)]$ or $\mathcal{F}_{\mathrm{crypto}}^{\mathrm{mac}}[(t,k)]$ (i.e., upon receiving the message $((t,k), \mathsf{Init})$ on $\mathrm{net}_{\mathcal{F}_{\mathrm{crypto}}^{\mathrm{senc}}}^{\mathrm{out}}$ or $\mathrm{net}_{\mathcal{F}_{\mathrm{crypto}}^{\mathrm{mac}}}^{\mathrm{out}}$), $\mathcal{S}$ sends $(\mathrm{enc}_t, \mathrm{dec}_t)$ to $\mathcal{F}_{\mathrm{crypto}}^{\mathrm{senc}}[(t,k)]$ or mac_t to $\mathcal{F}_{\mathrm{crypto}}^{\mathrm{mac}}[(t,k)]$, respectively.

9. Upon a request $(\mathsf{Derive}, x, status)$ from $\mathcal{F}_{\mathrm{crypto}}^{\mathrm{derive}}[(t,k)]$, $\mathcal{S}$ does the following. If $status = \mathsf{known}$, then $\mathcal{S}$ derives keys as $\mathcal{P}_{\mathrm{crypto}}'$, i.e., $\mathcal{S}$ computes:

$(t_1, \ldots, t_l) := \mathsf{parse}_{\mathrm{salt}}^t(1^\eta, x)$ {*parse the salt x to obtain key types*

$l' := l_{t_1}(\eta) + \cdots + l_{t_l}(\eta)$ {*compute sum of key lengths*

$y \leftarrow \mathsf{PRF}_t^*(k, x, l')$ {*derive y of length l' from k with salt x*

let $k_1, \ldots, k_l$ **s.t.** $y = k_1 \| \cdots \| k_l \wedge \forall i \leq l \colon |k_i| = l_{t_i}(\eta)$ {*split y into keys*

and then sends $(k_1, \ldots, k_l)$ to $\mathcal{F}_{\mathrm{crypto}}^{\mathrm{derive}}[(t,k)]$. Otherwise (i.e., $status = \mathsf{unknown}$), $\mathcal{S}$ also computes $(t_1, \ldots, t_l) := \mathsf{parse}_{\mathrm{salt}}^t(1^\eta, x)$ but then generates l fresh keys: $k_i \xleftarrow{\$} \{0,1\}^{l_{t_i}(\eta)}$ for all $i \leq l$. Then, $\mathcal{S}$ sends $(k_1, \ldots, k_l)$ to $\mathcal{F}_{\mathrm{crypto}}^{\mathrm{derive}}[(t,k)]$.

10. Upon a request Init from $\mathcal{F}_{\mathrm{crypto}}^{\mathrm{pke}}[name]$ (i.e., upon receiving $(name, \mathsf{Init})$ on $\mathrm{net}_{\mathcal{F}_{\mathrm{crypto}}^{\mathrm{pke}}}^{\mathrm{out}}$), $\mathcal{S}$ forwards this request to the adversary (i.e., sends it on $\mathrm{net}_{\mathcal{F}_{\mathrm{pke}}}^{\mathrm{out}}$).

11. Upon a response $(corr, e, d, pk, sk)$ from the adversary for $\mathcal{F}_{\mathrm{pke}}[name]$, $\mathcal{S}$ forwards this response to $\mathcal{F}_{\mathrm{crypto}}^{\mathrm{pke}}[name]$.

Upon any other input, $\mathcal{S}$ produces empty output in this activation and waits for a new request or response. It is easy to see that $\mathcal{S} \,|\, \mathcal{F}^* \,|\, \mathcal{F}_{\mathrm{crypto}}$ is environmentally strictly bounded, and hence, $\mathcal{S} \in \mathrm{Sim}^{\mathcal{F}^* \,|\, \mathcal{P}_{\mathrm{crypto}}'}(\mathcal{F}^* \,|\, \mathcal{F}_{\mathrm{crypto}})$.

The hybrid systems $\mathcal{F}_{\mathrm{crypto}}^{(j)}$. We now define the hybrid systems $\mathcal{F}_{\mathrm{crypto}}^{(j)}$, for all $j \in \mathbb{N}$, that were mentioned in the proof sketch. The system $\mathcal{F}_{\mathrm{crypto}}^{(j)}$ is an IITM that has the same external tapes as $\mathcal{F}_{\mathrm{crypto}}$ and simulates $\mathcal{F}_{\mathrm{crypto}}$. In this simulation $\mathcal{F}_{\mathrm{crypto}}^{(j)}$ keeps track of the order in which unknown encryption and key derivation keys are used (similar to $\mathcal{F}^*$). Furthermore, all these keys with order $< j$ are treated *ideal* (as in $\mathcal{F}_{\mathrm{crypto}}$) but keys with order $\geq j$ are treated *real* (as in the realization $\mathcal{P}_{\mathrm{crypto}}'$). In $\mathcal{F}_{\mathrm{crypto}}$ the adversary was not able to insert keys (upon key generation, store, decryption, or key derivation requests with corrupted or known keys) that collide with unknown keys (in these cases, the Add command with $status = \mathsf{known}$ of $\mathcal{F}_{\mathrm{crypto}}^{\mathrm{keys}}$ is called and this returns an error to prevent guessing of keys that are ideally not known). Here, this is only guaranteed for keys of order $\leq j$ or as long as there are no keys of order $> j$. Also, all MAC keys are treated *real*, they are replaced by *ideal* MACs in another step (Lemma B.3).

More formally: $\mathcal{F}_{\mathrm{crypto}}^{(j)}$ has an additional variable $\mathsf{nextused} \in \mathbb{N}$ (initially 1) and maintains a partial function used from typed keys (the set $\mathcal{K}$ in $\mathcal{F}_{\mathrm{crypto}}^{\mathrm{keys}}$) to natural numbers to keep track of the order in which unknown keys are used. The simulation of $\mathcal{F}^{\text{user}}_{\text{crypto}}$ and $\mathcal{F}^{\text{keys}}_{\text{crypto}}$ is changed as follows.

In $\mathcal{F}^{\text{user}}_{\text{crypto}}$, the commands for symmetric encryption and decryption, MAC and MAC verification, and key derivation are changed as follows:

1. Enc: "$y := \mathcal{F}^{\text{senc}}_{\text{crypto}}[\kappa].\text{Enc}(x')$" (where $\kappa = (t, k)$) is replaced by:

   if $\mathcal{F}^{\text{keys}}_{\text{crypto}}.\text{Status}(\kappa) = \text{unknown}$:
   > **if** $\text{used}(\kappa) = \bot$: $\text{used}(\kappa) := \text{nextused}$; $\text{nextused} := \text{nextused} + 1$
   > **if** $\text{used}(\kappa) < j$: $y := \mathcal{F}^{\text{senc}}_{\text{crypto}}[\kappa].\text{Enc}(x')$ **else:** $y \leftarrow \text{enc}_t(k, x')$

   else:
   > $y := \mathcal{F}^{\text{senc}}_{\text{crypto}}[\kappa].\text{Enc}(x')$

2. Dec: "$x := \mathcal{F}^{\text{senc}}_{\text{crypto}}[\kappa].\text{Dec}(y)$" (where $\kappa = (t, k)$) is replaced by:

   if $t \in \mathcal{T}^{\text{unauth}}_{\text{senc}} \wedge \mathcal{F}^{\text{keys}}_{\text{crypto}}.\text{Status}(\kappa) = \text{unknown}$:
   > **if** $\text{used}(\kappa) = \bot$: $\text{used}(\kappa) := \text{nextused}$; $\text{nextused} := \text{nextused} + 1$
   > **if** $\text{used}(\kappa) < j$: $x := \mathcal{F}^{\text{senc}}_{\text{crypto}}[\kappa].\text{Dec}(y)$ **else:** $x := \text{dec}_t(k, y)$

   else if $t \in \mathcal{T}^{\text{auth}}_{\text{senc}} \wedge \mathcal{F}^{\text{keys}}_{\text{crypto}}.\text{Status}(\kappa) = \text{unknown}$:
   > **if** $\bot \neq \text{used}(\kappa) < j \vee \text{nextused} \leq j$: $x := \mathcal{F}^{\text{senc}}_{\text{crypto}}[\kappa].\text{Dec}(y)$ **else:** $x := \text{dec}_t(k, y)$

   else: $\{i.e.,\ \mathcal{F}^{\text{keys}}_{\text{crypto}}.\text{Status}(\kappa) = \text{known}$
   > $x := \mathcal{F}^{\text{senc}}_{\text{crypto}}[\kappa].\text{Dec}(y)$

3. Derive: "$(\kappa_1, \ldots, \kappa_l) := \mathcal{F}^{\text{derive}}_{\text{crypto}}[\kappa].\text{Derive}(x)$" (where $\kappa = (t, k)$) is replaced by:

   if $\mathcal{F}^{\text{keys}}_{\text{crypto}}.\text{Status}(\kappa) = \text{unknown}$:
   > **if** $\text{used}(\kappa) = \bot$: $\text{used}(\kappa) := \text{nextused}$; $\text{nextused} := \text{nextused} + 1$
   > **if** $\text{used}(\kappa) < j$:
   > > $(\kappa_1, \ldots, \kappa_l) := \mathcal{F}^{\text{derive}}_{\text{crypto}}[\kappa].\text{Derive}(x)$
   >
   > **else:**
   > > $(t_1, \ldots, t_l) := \text{parse}^t_{\text{salt}}(1^\eta, x)$ $\{$parse the salt x to obtain key types
   > > $l' := l_{t_1}(\eta) + \cdots + l_{t_l}(\eta)$ $\{$compute sum of key lengths
   > > $z := \text{PRF}^*_t(k, x, l')$ $\{$derive z of length l' from k with salt x
   > > **let** $k_1, \ldots, k_l$ **s.t.** $z = k_1 \| \cdots \| k_l \wedge \forall i \leq l$: $|k_i| = l_{t_i}(\eta)$ $\{$split z into keys
   > > **for all** $i \in \{1, \ldots, l\}$ **do:** $\kappa_i := (t_i, k_i)$

   else:
   > $(\kappa_1, \ldots, \kappa_l) := \mathcal{F}^{\text{derive}}_{\text{crypto}}[\kappa].\text{Derive}(x)$

4. MAC: "$\sigma := \mathcal{F}^{\text{mac}}_{\text{crypto}}[\kappa].\text{MAC}(x)$" (where $\kappa = (t, k)$) is replaced by "$\sigma := \text{mac}_t(k, x)$".

5. Verify: "$b := \mathcal{F}^{\text{mac}}_{\text{crypto}}[\kappa].\text{Verify}(x, \sigma)$" (where $\kappa = (t, k)$) is replaced by "**if** $\sigma = \text{mac}_t(k, x)$: $b := 1$ **else:** $b := 0$".

In $\mathcal{F}^{\text{keys}}_{\text{crypto}}$, preventing key guessing is relaxed as follows. Upon request Add with *status* = known, the statement

if $\exists i \leq n$: $\kappa_i \in \mathcal{K} \setminus \mathcal{K}_{\text{known}}$: **send** $\bot$ **on** $\mathcal{F}^z_{\text{crypto}}[sid]$

is replaced by

if $\exists i \leq n$: $\kappa_i \in \mathcal{K} \setminus \mathcal{K}_{\text{known}} \wedge (\bot \neq \text{used}(\kappa_i) \leq j \vee \text{nextused} \leq j)$: **send** $\bot$ **on** $\mathcal{F}^z_{\text{crypto}}[sid]$.

This completes the definition of $\mathcal{F}_{\mathrm{crypto}}^{(j)}$.

The ideal external system $\mathcal{F}_{\mathrm{ext}}$ and the real one $\mathcal{P}_{\mathrm{ext}}$. We now define two external systems $\mathcal{F}_{\mathrm{ext}}$ and $\mathcal{P}_{\mathrm{ext}}$ that are used below to show that the j-th hybrid system is indistinguishable from the $(j+1)$-th hybrid system.

The *ideal external system* $\mathcal{F}_{\mathrm{ext}}$ is defined as a single IITM that has only one I/O input tape and one I/O output tape (and no network tapes) and that accepts all messages in CheckAddress. In the first request, $\mathcal{F}_{\mathrm{ext}}$ expects to receive a key type $t \in \mathcal{T}_{\mathrm{senc}} \cup \mathcal{T}_{\mathrm{derive}}$. Then $\mathcal{F}_{\mathrm{ext}}$ generates a key $k \overset{\$}{\leftarrow} \{0,1\}^{l_t(\eta)}$ (recall that $l_t(\eta)$ is the length of keys of type t for security parameter η). This key type and key are recorded and $\mathcal{F}_{\mathrm{ext}}$ outputs an acknowledgment message. Depending on t, $\mathcal{F}_{\mathrm{ext}}$ then provides encryption and decryption requests similar to $\mathcal{F}_{\mathrm{senc}}^{\mathrm{auth}}$ if $t \in \mathcal{T}_{\mathrm{senc}}^{\mathrm{auth}}$ or $\mathcal{F}_{\mathrm{senc}}^{\mathrm{unauth}}$ if $t \in \mathcal{T}_{\mathrm{senc}}^{\mathrm{unauth}}$ or key derivation requests similar to $\mathcal{F}_{\mathrm{derive}}$ if $t \in \mathcal{T}_{\mathrm{derive}}$ (where $\mathcal{F}_{\mathrm{senc}}^{\mathrm{auth}}$, $\mathcal{F}_{\mathrm{senc}}^{\mathrm{unauth}}$, and $\mathcal{F}_{\mathrm{derive}}$ are the long-term key functionalities from Section 4.2), except that there is no corruption, the recorded key is used (instead of using a key provided by the adversary), and (for encryption and decryption) the algorithms from the encryption scheme Σ_t are used (instead of using algorithms provided by the adversary).

More precisely, if $t \in \mathcal{T}_{\mathrm{senc}}^{\mathrm{auth}}$, then $\mathcal{F}_{\mathrm{ext}}$ expects requests of the form (Enc, x) or (Dec, y) and handles them exactly like an uncorrupted $\mathcal{F}_{\mathrm{senc}}^{\mathrm{auth}}(p, L_{\mathrm{senc}}^t)$ with algorithms enc_t and dec_t (where p, L_{senc}^t, enc_t, and dec_t are the parameters of $\mathcal{F}_{\mathrm{crypto}}$). Similarly, if $t \in \mathcal{T}_{\mathrm{senc}}^{\mathrm{unauth}}$, then $\mathcal{F}_{\mathrm{ext}}$ expects requests of the form (Enc, x) or (Dec, y) and handles them exactly like an uncorrupted $\mathcal{F}_{\mathrm{senc}}^{\mathrm{unauth}}(p, L_{\mathrm{senc}}^t)$ with algorithms enc_t and dec_t. If $t \in \mathcal{T}_{\mathrm{derive}}$, then $\mathcal{F}_{\mathrm{ext}}$ expects requests of the form (Derive, x) and handles them exactly like an uncorrupted $\mathcal{F}_{\mathrm{derive}}(\mathsf{parse})$ where the salt parsing function parse is defined as follows: $\mathsf{parse}(1^\eta, x) := (l_{t_1}(\eta), \ldots, l_{t_l}(\eta))$ if $(t_1, \ldots, t_l) = \mathsf{parse}_{\mathrm{salt}}^t(1^\eta, x)$, for all $x \in \{0,1\}^*$.

The *real external system* $\mathcal{P}_{\mathrm{ext}}$ is defined like $\mathcal{F}_{\mathrm{ext}}$ except that instead that it behaves like the ideal functionalities $\mathcal{F}_{\mathrm{senc}}^{\mathrm{auth}}$, $\mathcal{F}_{\mathrm{senc}}^{\mathrm{unauth}}$, or $\mathcal{F}_{\mathrm{derive}}$, it behaves like their realizations $\mathcal{P}_{\mathrm{senc}}$ or $\mathcal{P}_{\mathrm{derive}}$ (where the VLO-PRF PRF_t^* is used for type $t \in \mathcal{T}_{\mathrm{derive}}$). As for $\mathcal{F}_{\mathrm{ext}}$, $\mathcal{P}_{\mathrm{ext}}$ is not corruptible.

Since all encryption schemes and VLO-PRFs are secure, the polynomial is chosen appropriately, and all leakage algorithms are length preserving, it is easy to see that the results from Section 4.2 imply that:

$$\mathcal{E} \,|\, \mathcal{F}_{\mathrm{ext}} \equiv \mathcal{E} \,|\, \mathcal{P}_{\mathrm{ext}} \quad \text{for every } \mathcal{E} \in \mathrm{Env}(\mathcal{F}_{\mathrm{ext}}). \tag{B.2}$$

We note that this is equivalent to $\mathcal{P}_{\mathrm{ext}} \leq \mathcal{F}_{\mathrm{ext}}$ because the systems do not have any network tapes.

The hybrid systems $\widehat{\mathcal{F}}_{\mathrm{crypto}}^{(j)}$ that use an external system. We now define $\widehat{\mathcal{F}}_{\mathrm{crypto}}^{(j)}$. It is an IITM that behaves like $\mathcal{F}_{\mathrm{crypto}}^{(j)}$ except that it connects to the ideal external system $\mathcal{F}_{\text{ext}}$ (or to the real external system $\mathcal{P}_{\text{ext}}$, respectively) such that all requests (i.e., encryption, decryption, or key derivation) for the key with order j (i.e., an encryption or a key derivation key) are relayed out and handled by the external system.

More formally: $\widehat{\mathcal{F}}_{\text{crypto}}^{(j)}$ has additional I/O tapes to connect to $\mathcal{F}_{\text{ext}}$ (or $\mathcal{P}_{\text{ext}}$). When a key gets assigned order j, i.e., $\text{used}(\kappa) := j$ is computed (upon encryption, decryption, or key derivation), $\widehat{\mathcal{F}}_{\text{crypto}}^{(j)}$ sends the type t to $\mathcal{F}_{\text{ext}}$ (which will generate a key, store it, and return an acknowledgment message). Then, $\widehat{\mathcal{F}}_{\text{crypto}}^{(j)}$ continues:

Upon encryption (Enc) everything is exactly as in $\mathcal{F}_{\text{crypto}}^{(j)}$ except that if it holds that $\mathcal{F}_{\text{crypto}}^{\text{keys}}.\text{Status}(\kappa) = \text{unknown}$ and $\text{used}(\kappa) = j$, then the ciphertext y is obtained by sending (Enc, x) to $\mathcal{F}_{\text{ext}}$ and waiting to receive y from $\mathcal{F}_{\text{ext}}$. Similarly, upon decryption (Dec) everything is exactly as in $\mathcal{F}_{\text{crypto}}^{(j)}$ except that if $\mathcal{F}_{\text{crypto}}^{\text{keys}}.\text{Status}(\kappa) = \text{unknown}$ and $\text{used}(\kappa) = j$, then the plaintext x is obtained by sending (Dec, y) to $\mathcal{F}_{\text{ext}}$ and waiting to receive x from $\mathcal{F}_{\text{ext}}$.

Likewise, upon key derivation (Derive) everything is exactly as in $\mathcal{F}_{\text{crypto}}^{(j)}$ except that if $\mathcal{F}_{\text{crypto}}^{\text{keys}}.\text{Status}(\kappa) = \text{unknown}$ and $\text{used}(\kappa) = j$, then the derived keys are obtained by sending (Derive, x) to $\mathcal{F}_{\text{ext}}$ and waiting to receive $(k_1, \ldots, k_l)$ from $\mathcal{F}_{\text{ext}}$. Then, the derived typed keys are $\kappa_1, \ldots, \kappa_l$ with $\kappa_i := (t_i, k_i)$ for all $i \in \{1, \ldots, l\}$ where $t_1, \ldots, t_l$ are the types obtained from $\text{parse}_{\text{salt}}^t(1^\eta, x)$ where t is the type of κ.

Completing the Proof of Theorem 5.1. Let $\mathcal{E} \in \text{Env}(\mathcal{F}^* \mid \mathcal{P}'_{\text{crypto}})$ be an environment for $\mathcal{F}^* \mid \mathcal{P}'_{\text{crypto}}$ and $p_\mathcal{E}$ be a polynomial that bounds the runtime of $\mathcal{E}$ in any run of $\mathcal{E} \mid \mathcal{Q}$ for any system $\mathcal{Q}$. That is, for every security parameter $\eta \in \mathbb{N}$ and initial input $a \in \{0, 1\}^*$, the runtime of $\mathcal{E}$ in any run of $(\mathcal{E} \mid \mathcal{Q})(1^\eta, a)$ is bound from above by $p_\mathcal{E}(\eta + |a|)$. Such a polynomial always exists because $\mathcal{E}$ is an environmental system (i.e., it is universally bounded).

For all $j \in \mathbb{N}$ we define the following *combined* systems:

$$\mathcal{C}^{(j)} := \mathcal{E} \mid \mathcal{S} \mid \mathcal{F}^* \mid \mathcal{F}_{\text{crypto}}^{(j)}$$

and

$$\widehat{\mathcal{C}}^{(j)} := \mathcal{E} \mid \mathcal{S} \mid \mathcal{F}^* \mid \widehat{\mathcal{F}}_{\text{crypto}}^{(j)} \;,$$

where $\mathcal{S}$ is the simulator and $\mathcal{F}_{\text{crypto}}^{(j)}$ and $\widehat{\mathcal{F}}_{\text{crypto}}^{(j)}$ are the hybrid systems that we defined above. By $\mathcal{C}^{(p_\mathcal{E})}$ we denote the system that is defined like $\mathcal{C}^{(j)}$ except that j is set to $p_\mathcal{E}(\eta + |a|)$ (where η is the security parameter). Furthermore, by $\widehat{\mathcal{C}}^{(\$)}$ we denote the system that is defined like $\widehat{\mathcal{C}}^{(j)}$ except that it chooses $j \xleftarrow{\$} \{0, \ldots, p_\mathcal{E}(\eta + |a|) - 1\}$ and then behaves like $\widehat{\mathcal{C}}^{(j)}$. We note that it is easy to see that $\widehat{\mathcal{C}}^{(j)}$ and $\widehat{\mathcal{C}}^{(\$)}$ are universally bounded, and hence, they are environments for $\mathcal{F}_{\text{ext}}$ and $\mathcal{P}_{\text{ext}}$. Hence, by (B.2), we obtain that there exists a negligible function f_{ext} such that:

$$\widehat{\mathcal{C}}^{(\$)} \mid \mathcal{P}_{\text{ext}} \equiv_{f_{\text{ext}}} \widehat{\mathcal{C}}^{(\$)} \mid \mathcal{F}_{\text{ext}} \;. \tag{B.3}$$

Next, we define an error set (i.e., a negligible set of runs we do not want to consider) for collisions of honestly generated symmetric keys. Let $B_{\text{coll}}^{(j)}(1^\eta, a)$ be the set of runs of $\mathcal{C}^{(j)}(1^\eta, a)$ where the simulator $\mathcal{S}$ generates a new key k (i.e., upon a KeyGen request from $\mathcal{F}_{\text{crypto}}^{\text{user}}$, a Init request from $\mathcal{F}_{\text{crypto}}^{\text{keysetup}}$, or a Derive request with $status = $ unknown) of some type, say t, that collides with some already existing (unknown or known) key, i.e., $(t, k) \in \mathcal{K}$ (in $\mathcal{F}_{\text{crypto}}^{\text{keys}}$). We note that upon this event, $\mathcal{F}_{\text{crypto}}^{\text{keys}}$ would not accept the key because of the collision and an error would be triggered.

The following lemma (that is used in the proofs of the following lemmas) shows that $B_{\text{coll}}^{(j)}(1^\eta, a)$ is a negligible set of runs. Importantly, the probability of $B_{\text{coll}}^{(j)}(1^\eta, a)$ can be bound by a negligible function that is independent of j.

Lemma B.1. *There exists a negligible function f_{coll} such that for all $j \in \mathbb{N}$, $\eta \in \mathbb{N}$, and $a \in \{0,1\}^*$:*

$$\Pr\left[B_{\text{coll}}^{(j)}(1^\eta, a)\right] \leq f_{\text{coll}}(\eta + |a|) \ .$$

Proof sketch. Since the cryptographic schemes (symmetric encryption, MACs, and VLO-PRFs) are secure, it is easy to see that collisions among polynomially many keys can only occur with negligible probability (otherwise, adversaries that simply try to guess the key would be successful against the cryptographic schemes). □

The following two lemmas talk about the extreme cases of the hybrid systems and relate them to $\mathcal{E} \,|\, \mathcal{F}^* \,|\, \mathcal{P}_{\text{crypto}}'$ and $\mathcal{E} \,|\, \mathcal{S} \,|\, \mathcal{F}^* \,|\, \mathcal{F}_{\text{crypto}}$, respectively. In the next lemma, only key collisions (which occur with negligible probability as seen above) have to be taken care of.

Lemma B.2. *There exists a negligible function f_0 such that:*

$$\mathcal{C}^{(0)} \equiv_{f_0} \mathcal{E} \,|\, \mathcal{F}^* \,|\, \mathcal{P}_{\text{crypto}}' \ . \tag{B.4}$$

Proof. Note that in every run of $\mathcal{C}^{(0)}(1^\eta, a)$ it always holds that nextused ≥ 1 and for every (typed) key $\kappa \in \mathcal{K}$ it holds that used$(\kappa) = \bot$ or used$(\kappa) > 0$. In particular this implies that the condition $\bot \neq$ used$(\kappa_i) \leq j \vee$ nextused $\leq j$ is always evaluated to false, and hence, the modified $\mathcal{F}_{\text{crypto}}^{\text{keys}}$ (in $\mathcal{C}^{(0)}$) upon request Add with $status = $ known will never return an error (prevent guessing). Thus, the systems $\mathcal{E} \,|\, \mathcal{F}^* \,|\, \mathcal{P}_{\text{crypto}}'$ and $\mathcal{C}^{(0)}$ are equivalent if $B_{\text{coll}}^{(0)}$ does not occur. More formally: One easily verifies that every run of $\mathcal{C}^{(0)}(1^\eta, a)$ where $B_{\text{coll}}^{(0)}(1^\eta, a)$ does not occur corresponds, i.e., can be injectively mapped, to a run of $(\mathcal{E} \,|\, \mathcal{F}^* \,|\, \mathcal{P}_{\text{crypto}}')(1^\eta, a)$ with the same overall output and probability. We conclude that for all η, a:

$$\left|\Pr\left[(\mathcal{E} \,|\, \mathcal{F}^* \,|\, \mathcal{P}_{\text{crypto}}')(1^\eta, a) = 1\right] - \Pr\left[\mathcal{C}^{(0)}(1^\eta, a) = 1\right]\right| \leq \Pr\left[B_{\text{coll}}^{(0)}(1^\eta, a)\right] \ .$$

By Lemma B.1, we conclude $\mathcal{C}^{(0)} \equiv_{f_0} \mathcal{E} \,|\, \mathcal{F}^* \,|\, \mathcal{P}_{\text{crypto}}'$ for a negligible function f_0. □

The next lemma is more involved than the previous one because real MACs have to be replaced by ideal MACs.

Lemma B.3. *There exists a negligible function $f_{p\varepsilon}$ such that:*

$$\mathcal{C}^{(p\varepsilon)} \equiv_{f_{p\varepsilon}} \mathcal{E} \,|\, \mathcal{S} \,|\, \mathcal{F}^* \,|\, \mathcal{F}_{\text{crypto}} \;. \tag{B.5}$$

Proof. First, we define $\mathcal{F}'_{\text{crypto}}$ which is defined exactly like $\mathcal{F}_{\text{crypto}}$ except that MAC and MAC verification is done as in $\mathcal{P}'_{\text{crypto}}$, i.e., in $\mathcal{F}^{\text{user}}_{\text{crypto}}$, "$\sigma := \mathcal{F}^{\text{mac}}_{\text{crypto}}[\kappa].\text{MAC}(x)$" is replaced by "$\sigma \leftarrow \text{mac}_t(k,x)$" and "$b := \mathcal{F}^{\text{mac}}_{\text{crypto}}[\kappa].\text{Verify}(x,\sigma)$" is replaced by "$b := (\sigma = \text{mac}_t(k,x))$". It is easy to see that, as long as key collisions do not occur (i.e., event $B^{(p\varepsilon)}_{\text{coll}}$ does not occur), the systems $\mathcal{C}^{(p\varepsilon)}$ and $\mathcal{E} \,|\, \mathcal{S} \,|\, \mathcal{F}^* \,|\, \mathcal{F}'_{\text{crypto}}$ do not differ (from $\mathcal{E}$'s perspective). Hence, $\mathcal{E} \,|\, \mathcal{S} \,|\, \mathcal{F}^* \,|\, \mathcal{F}'_{\text{crypto}} \equiv_{f_{\text{coll}}} \mathcal{C}^{(p\varepsilon)}$. More formally: In every run of $\mathcal{C}^{(p\varepsilon)}(1^\eta, a)$ it always holds that $\text{nextused} \leq p_\varepsilon(\eta + |a|)$. In particular this implies that the condition $\perp \neq \text{used}(t_i, k_i) \leq j \vee \text{nextused} \leq j$ is always evaluated to true, and hence, the modified $\mathcal{F}^{\text{keys}}_{\text{crypto}}$ (in $\mathcal{C}^{(p\varepsilon)}$) upon request Add with $\text{status} = \text{known}$ returns an error (prevent guessing) if and only if the original $\mathcal{F}^{\text{keys}}_{\text{crypto}}$ (in $\mathcal{F}'_{\text{crypto}}$) returns an error. One easily verifies that every run of $\mathcal{C}^{(p\varepsilon)}(1^\eta, a)$ where $B^{(p_\varepsilon(\eta+|a|))}_{\text{coll}}(1^\eta, a)$ does not occur corresponds, i.e., can be injectively mapped, to a run of $(\mathcal{E} \,|\, \mathcal{S} \,|\, \mathcal{F}^* \,|\, \mathcal{F}'_{\text{crypto}})(1^\eta, a)$ with the same overall output and probability. We conclude that for all η, a:

$$\left| \Pr\left[(\mathcal{E} \,|\, \mathcal{S} \,|\, \mathcal{F}^* \,|\, \mathcal{F}'_{\text{crypto}})(1^\eta, a) = 1 \right] - \Pr\left[\mathcal{C}^{(p\varepsilon)}(1^\eta, a) = 1 \right] \right|$$
$$\leq \Pr\left[B^{(p_\varepsilon(\eta+|a|))}_{\text{coll}}(1^\eta, a) \right] \;.$$

Below, we use that all MAC schemes are UF-CMA secure to show that:

$$\mathcal{E} \,|\, \mathcal{S} \,|\, \mathcal{F}^* \,|\, \mathcal{F}'_{\text{crypto}} \equiv \mathcal{E} \,|\, \mathcal{S} \,|\, \mathcal{F}^* \,|\, \mathcal{F}_{\text{crypto}} \;. \tag{B.6}$$

From this, by Lemma B.1 and transitivity of $\equiv$, we obtain that:

$$\mathcal{C}^{(p\varepsilon)} \equiv \mathcal{E} \,|\, \mathcal{S} \,|\, \mathcal{F}^* \,|\, \mathcal{F}_{\text{crypto}} \;.$$

We now prove (B.6). For all $t \in \mathcal{T}_{\text{mac}}$ (and all η, a), we define $B^t_{\text{forgery}}(1^\eta, a)$ to be the event that, in a run of $(\mathcal{E} \,|\, \mathcal{S} \,|\, \mathcal{F}^* \,|\, \mathcal{F}_{\text{crypto}})(1^\eta, a)$, $\mathcal{F}_{\text{crypto}}$ upon a MAC verification request with a key of type t returns $\perp$ (i.e., prevents a forgery).[83] Since the systems $\mathcal{E} \,|\, \mathcal{S} \,|\, \mathcal{F}^* \,|\, \mathcal{F}'_{\text{crypto}}$ and $\mathcal{E} \,|\, \mathcal{S} \,|\, \mathcal{F}^* \,|\, \mathcal{F}_{\text{crypto}}$ only differ (from $\mathcal{E}$'s perspective) if $B^t_{\text{forgery}}(1^\eta, a)$ occurs for some $t \in \mathcal{T}_{\text{mac}}$, it is easy to see that (for all η, a):

$$\left| \Pr\left[(\mathcal{E} \,|\, \mathcal{S} \,|\, \mathcal{F}^* \,|\, \mathcal{F}'_{\text{crypto}})(1^\eta, a) = 1 \right] - \Pr\left[(\mathcal{E} \,|\, \mathcal{S} \,|\, \mathcal{F}^* \,|\, \mathcal{F}_{\text{crypto}})(1^\eta, a) = 1 \right] \right|$$
$$\leq \Pr\left[\bigcup_{t \in \mathcal{T}_{\text{mac}}} B^t_{\text{forgery}}(1^\eta, a) \right] \leq \sum_{t \in \mathcal{T}_{\text{mac}}} \Pr\left[B^t_{\text{forgery}}(1^\eta, a) \right] \;.$$

---

[83] Formally, $B^t_{\text{forgery}}(1^\eta, a)$ is the set of runs of $(\mathcal{E} \,|\, \mathcal{S} \,|\, \mathcal{F}^* \,|\, \mathcal{F}_{\text{crypto}})(1^\eta, a)$ with the mentioned property.

Next, we show that the event $B_{\text{forgery}}^t(1^\eta, a)$, for every $t \in \mathcal{T}_{\text{mac}}$, occurs only with negligible probability, which proves (B.6) (because $\mathcal{T}_{\text{mac}}$ is finite and its size is constant, i.e., does not depend on the security parameter).

Therefore, let $t \in \mathcal{T}_{\text{mac}}$. Recall that $p_{\mathcal{E}}$ is the polynomial that bounds the overall runtime of $\mathcal{E}$, i.e., there are at most $p_{\mathcal{E}}(\eta)$ MAC keys and at most $p_{\mathcal{E}}(\eta)$ MAC verification requests in every run of $(\mathcal{E} \,|\, \mathcal{S} \,|\, \mathcal{F}^* \,|\, \mathcal{F}_{\text{crypto}})(1^\eta, a)$ (for every security parameter η and external input a). We define an adversary A_t against the MAC scheme $\Sigma_t = (\text{gen}_t, \text{mac}_t)$ as follows: At first, A_t chooses j and i from $\{1, \ldots, p_{\mathcal{E}}(\eta + |a|)\}$ both uniformly at random. (Intuitively, A_t guesses that the i-th verification request with the j-th key of type t triggers the event B_{forgery}^t, i.e., this verification request contains a forgery.) Then A_t simulates a run of $(\mathcal{E} \,|\, \mathcal{S} \,|\, \mathcal{F}^* \,|\, \mathcal{F}_{\text{crypto}})(1^\eta, a)$ but, upon MAC generation for the j-th unknown key of type t (see below), A_t uses its MAC oracle instead of the algorithm mac_t. Upon verification with the j-th unknown key of type t, say of message m and MAC σ, A_t checks if this is the i-th verification request with this key. If this is the case, A_t halts and returns (m, σ) (because A_t assumes that it guessed correctly and that this is a forgery). Otherwise, if A_t has previously asked its MAC oracle to obtain a MAC for m and this MAC was σ, then A_t continues the simulation as if verification succeeded. Otherwise, A_t continues the simulation as if verification failed. If the simulation stops (e.g., because $\mathcal{E}$ outputs some message on tape decision), then A_t aborts (note that this only happens if, in the simulated run, less than i verification requests are sent for the j-th unknown MAC key).

More precisely, this j-th unknown key of type t, which we denote by k^*, is the j-th key of type t that is generated in $\mathcal{S}$ upon key generation (KeyGen), key derivation (Derive) from an unknown key, or key generation of an uncorrupted pre-shared key (GetPSK). Hence, at the moment of generation of the key k^* it is unknown (more precisely, (t, k^*) is marked unknown in $\mathcal{F}_{\text{crypto}}^{\text{keys}}$, i.e., $(t, k^*) \in \mathcal{K} \setminus \mathcal{K}_{\text{known}}$) but it may become known later (the commitment problem is only prevented by $\mathcal{F}^*$ for encryption and key derivation keys but not for MAC keys). If this happens, A_t aborts (in this case A_t looses).

Now, we analyze the advantage of A_t against the MAC Σ_t. Let ρ be a run of $(\mathcal{E} \,|\, \mathcal{S} \,|\, \mathcal{F}^* \,|\, \mathcal{F}_{\text{crypto}})(1^\eta, a)$ where $B_{\text{forgery}}^t(1^\eta, a)$ occurs,[84] and let $j^*, i^* \in \{1, \ldots, p_{\mathcal{E}}(\eta + |a|)\}$ such that the first MAC verification request that returns $\perp$ (prevent guessing) in ρ is with the j^*-th unknown key of type t and this is the i^*-th MAC verification request with this key. Such j^* and i^* always exists because $B_{\text{forgery}}^t(1^\eta, a)$ occurs and $\mathcal{E}$'s runtime is bounded by $p_{\mathcal{E}}(\eta)$ (i.e., there are at most $p_{\mathcal{E}}(\eta + |a|)$ keys and $p_{\mathcal{E}}(\eta + |a|)$ MAC verification requests). Then, the run ρ' of the MAC game with A_t and Σ_t where $j = j^*$, $i = i^*$, and A_t uses the same random coins as in ρ to simulate $\mathcal{E} \,|\, \mathcal{S} \,|\, \mathcal{F}^* \,|\, \mathcal{F}_{\text{crypto}}(1^\eta, a)$ is a winning run for A_t against Σ_t, i.e., A_t outputs a forgery and wins the game. We note that A_t perfectly simulates the run: (i) k^* is generated as in the MAC game, by definition of $\mathcal{S}$, it is chosen uniformly at random from $\mathcal{D}_{\text{keys}}^t$. (ii) k^* never becomes known (i.e., A_t never aborts) because, otherwise,

---

[84]Formally, this just means: Let $\rho \in B_{\text{forgery}}^t(1^\eta, a)$.

the verification request to $\mathcal{F}_{\text{crypto}}$ would not return $\perp$ for this key. *(iii)* k^* is always encrypted ideally, i.e., only its leakage is encrypted. Hence, because the leakage algorithm is keys hiding, $\mathcal{E}$ does not see a difference whether the key k^* is used or A_t's oracles are used to MAC or verify messages.[85] In other words, if A_t guesses j^* and i^* correctly and $B^t_{\text{forgery}}(1^\eta, a)$ occurs in the simulated run, then A_t wins the game against Σ_t. We conclude that (for all η, a):

$$\Pr\left[B^t_{\text{forgery}}(1^\eta, a)\right] \leq p^2_{\mathcal{E}}(\eta + |a|) \cdot \text{adv}^{\text{uf-cma}}_{A, \Sigma_t}(1^\eta, a) \ .$$

Since A_t is a PPT algorithm ($\mathcal{E} \,|\, \mathcal{S} \,|\, \mathcal{F}^* \,|\, \mathcal{F}_{\text{crypto}}$ is strictly bounded) and Σ_t is UF-CMA secure, we have that $\text{adv}^{\text{uf-cma}}_{A_t, \Sigma_t}(1^\eta, a)$ is negligible (as a function in 1^η and a). We obtain that $\Pr[B^t_{\text{forgery}}(1^\eta, a)]$ is negligible, which concludes the proof. $\qquad\square$

The next lemma is used to show that the j-th hybrid is indistinguishable from the $(j+1)$-th hybrid.

Lemma B.4. *There exist negligible functions* f_{real} *and* f_{ideal} *such that for all* $j \in \mathbb{N}$:

$$\mathcal{C}^{(j)} \equiv_{f_{\text{real}}} \widehat{\mathcal{C}}^{(j)} \,|\, \mathcal{P}_{\text{ext}} \tag{B.7}$$

and

$$\mathcal{C}^{(j+1)} \equiv_{f_{\text{ideal}}} \widehat{\mathcal{C}}^{(j)} \,|\, \mathcal{F}_{\text{ext}} \ . \tag{B.8}$$

Proof. We only show (B.7), the proof of (B.8) is similar. First, we note that the two systems $\mathcal{C}^{(j)}$ and $\widehat{\mathcal{C}}^{(j)} \,|\, \mathcal{P}_{\text{ext}}$ are already very close to each other because every key (including the j-th key) is treated in the same way (real or ideal) in the two systems. The only difference is that in $\mathcal{C}^{(j)}$ the j-th key is handled inside $\mathcal{F}^{(j)}_{\text{crypto}}$ while in $\widehat{\mathcal{C}}^{(j)} \,|\, \mathcal{P}_{\text{ext}}$ cryptographic operations with the j-th key are handled inside $\mathcal{P}_{\text{ext}}$ and $\widehat{\mathcal{F}}^{(j)}_{\text{crypto}}$ encrypts a different key than the key in $\mathcal{P}_{\text{ext}}$ if the j-th key is encrypted. Since the used-order is respected, the j-th key is always encrypted ideally, i.e., not the key itself is encrypted but its leakage. Hence, the actual value of the key when encrypted does not matter (the leakage algorithm is keys hiding). Furthermore, even if the j-th key is a derived key, it has been derived ideally, i.e., chosen uniformly at random, and hence, it is distributed just like the key in $\mathcal{P}_{\text{ext}}$. Thus, the only difference between $\mathcal{C}^{(j)}$ and $\widehat{\mathcal{C}}^{(j)} \,|\, \mathcal{P}_{\text{ext}}$ occurs upon key collisions (if a fresh key generated by $\mathcal{S}$ collides with some other key) or if the environment is able to guess the j-th key (see below). But because this keys was only encrypted ideally, we can show that this probability is negligible.

More formally, to show (B.7), we define a mapping from every run ρ of $\mathcal{C}^{(j)}$, excluding a negligible set $B^{(j)}$ of error runs (see below), to a set S_ρ of runs of $\widehat{\mathcal{C}}^{(j)} \,|\, \mathcal{P}_{\text{ext}}$ such that the probability of ρ is the same as the one for S_ρ and the overall output of ρ (on tape decision) is the same as the overall output of every run in S_ρ. Such a mapping implies that $\mathcal{C}^{(j)} \equiv \widehat{\mathcal{C}}^{(j)} \,|\, \mathcal{P}_{\text{ext}}$.

---

[85] Formally, one would have to do a mapping of runs of the MAC game with A_t and Σ_t to runs of $\mathcal{E} \,|\, \mathcal{S} \,|\, \mathcal{F}^* \,|\, \mathcal{F}_{\text{crypto}}$ where one replaces the key k^* by the key generated in the MAC game.

We define the error set $B^{(j)}$ to be $B^{(j)}_{\text{coll}} \cup B^{(j)}_{\text{guess}}$. The set $B^{(j)}_{\text{coll}}$ is defined above and its probability is shown to be negligible in Lemma B.1, with a bound that is independent of j. The set $B^{(j)}_{\text{guess}}$ is the set of runs of $\mathcal{C}^{(j)}$ where $\mathcal{E}$ "guesses" the j-th key, i.e., where at some point during the run (i) $\mathcal{E}$ wants to use the j-th key as a corrupted pre-shared key, (ii) $\mathcal{E}$ wants to store the j-th key, (iii) $\mathcal{E}$ derives the j-th key from a known key, or (iv) $\mathcal{E}$ decrypts a ciphertext with a known symmetric key or a corrupted private key and where the decryption contains the j-th key. If the probability for $B^{(j)}_{\text{guess}}$ were not negligible, one could easily construct a successful adversary against the encryption and pseudorandom function games in question: The adversary would simulate the system $\mathcal{C}^{(j)}$ using his oracles to perform operations with the j-th key and guesses the position (among polynomially many possible positions) where $\mathcal{E}$ guesses the j-th key. This simulation corresponds to the actual system $\mathcal{C}^{(j)}$ because the j-th key is only encrypted ideally and if it is a derived key, it was derived ideally, and hence, its distribution corresponds to the one in the game. Thus, if the guesses of the adversary and the emulated $\mathcal{E}$ are correct, the adversary can easily win the game. It follows that the probability for $B^{(j)}_{\text{guess}}$ must be negligible. To obtain a bound which is independent of j, one can consider an adversary that first guesses j and then proceeds as above. Altogether, we obtain a negligible function, which is independent of j, and bounds the probability for $B^{(j)}$.

Now, the mapping is defined in the obvious way as follows: Let ρ be a run of $\mathcal{C}^{(j)}$ which is not in $B^{(j)}$. We now define S_ρ to be the set of runs of $\widehat{\mathcal{C}}^{(j)} \,|\, \mathcal{P}_{\text{ext}}$ where the key in $\mathcal{P}_{\text{ext}}$ is defined to be the j-th key in ρ and where we use a freshly generated key as the j-th key in $\widehat{\mathcal{F}}^{(j)}_{\text{crypto}}$ (in $\widehat{\mathcal{C}}^{(j)}$). Every such freshly generated key induces one run in S_ρ. By construction, the probabilities of ρ and S_ρ are equal. Now, with the observations made above (the j-th key is ideally encrypted and uniformly distributed) and the fact that collisions and guessing does not occur, one can easily show, by induction on the length of runs, that the view of $\mathcal{E}$ in ρ is the same as the view of $\mathcal{E}$ in every run ρ' in S_ρ, and hence, the overall output is the same.

Since the probability of $B^{(j)}$ is bounded by a negligible function independently of j, we obtain that there exists a negligible function f_{real} such that $\mathcal{C}^{(j)} \equiv_{f_{\text{real}}} \widehat{\mathcal{C}}^{(j)} \,|\, \mathcal{P}_{\text{ext}}$ for all $j \in \mathbb{N}$. $\qquad\square$

Finally, using the lemmas above, we complete the proof of Theorem 5.1. In the following, for better readability, we omit the security parameter η and the external input a (e.g., we write $\Pr\left[(\widehat{\mathcal{C}}^{(j)} \,|\, \mathcal{P}_{\text{ext}}) = 1\right]$ instead of $\Pr\left[(\widehat{\mathcal{C}}^{(j)} \,|\, \mathcal{P}_{\text{ext}})(1^\eta, a) = 1\right]$ and $p_{\mathcal{E}}$ instead of $p_{\mathcal{E}}(\eta + |a|)$). First, we note that for all $\eta \in \mathbb{N}$ and $a \in \{0,1\}^*$:

$$\sum_{j < p_{\mathcal{E}}} \Pr\left[(\widehat{\mathcal{C}}^{(j)} \,|\, \mathcal{P}_{\text{ext}}) = 1\right] = \sum_{j < p_{\mathcal{E}}} \Pr\left[(\widehat{\mathcal{C}}^{(\$)} \,|\, \mathcal{P}_{\text{ext}}) = 1 \,|\, \widehat{\mathcal{C}}^{(\$)} \text{ chooses } j\right]$$

$$= p_{\mathcal{E}} \cdot \sum_{j < p_{\mathcal{E}}} \Pr\left[(\widehat{\mathcal{C}}^{(\$)} \,|\, \mathcal{P}_{\text{ext}}) = 1 \wedge \widehat{\mathcal{C}}^{(\$)} \text{ chooses } j\right] \quad (\text{B.9})$$

$$= p_{\mathcal{E}} \cdot \Pr\left[(\widehat{\mathcal{C}}^{(\$)} \,|\, \mathcal{P}_{\text{ext}}) = 1\right] \ .$$

Analogously, for all $\eta \in \mathbb{N}$ and $a \in \{0,1\}^*$:

$$\sum_{j<p_{\mathcal{E}}} \Pr\left[(\widehat{\mathcal{C}}^{(j)} \mid \mathcal{F}_{\text{ext}}) = 1\right] = p_{\mathcal{E}} \cdot \Pr\left[(\widehat{\mathcal{C}}^{(\$)} \mid \mathcal{F}_{\text{ext}}) = 1\right] . \qquad (\text{B.10})$$

Then, for all $\eta \in \mathbb{N}$ and $a \in \{0,1\}^*$:

$$\left|\Pr\left[(\mathcal{E} \mid \mathcal{F}^* \mid \mathcal{P}'_{\text{crypto}}) = 1\right] - \Pr\left[(\mathcal{E} \mid \mathcal{S} \mid \mathcal{F}^* \mid \mathcal{F}_{\text{crypto}}) = 1\right]\right|$$

$$\overset{(\text{B.4}),(\text{B.5})}{\leq} \left|\Pr\left[\mathcal{C}^{(0)} = 1\right] - \Pr\left[\mathcal{C}^{(p_{\mathcal{E}})} = 1\right]\right| + f_0 + f_{p_{\mathcal{E}}}$$

$$= \left|\sum_{j<p_{\mathcal{E}}} \Pr\left[\mathcal{C}^{(j)} = 1\right] - \Pr\left[\mathcal{C}^{(j+1)} = 1\right]\right| + f_0 + f_{p_{\mathcal{E}}}$$

$$\overset{(\text{B.7}),(\text{B.8})}{\leq} \left|\sum_{j<p_{\mathcal{E}}} \Pr\left[(\widehat{\mathcal{C}}^{(j)} \mid \mathcal{P}_{\text{ext}}) = 1\right] - \Pr\left[(\widehat{\mathcal{C}}^{(j)} \mid \mathcal{F}_{\text{ext}}) = 1\right]\right|$$

$$+ f_0 + f_{p_{\mathcal{E}}} + p_{\mathcal{E}} \cdot (f_{\text{real}} + f_{\text{ideal}})$$

$$\overset{(\text{B.9}),(\text{B.10})}{=} p_{\mathcal{E}} \cdot \left|\Pr\left[(\widehat{\mathcal{C}}^{(\$)} \mid \mathcal{P}_{\text{ext}}) = 1\right] - \Pr\left[(\widehat{\mathcal{C}}^{(\$)} \mid \mathcal{F}_{\text{ext}}) = 1\right]\right|$$

$$+ f_0 + f_{p_{\mathcal{E}}} + p_{\mathcal{E}} \cdot (f_{\text{real}} + f_{\text{ideal}})$$

$$\overset{(\text{B.3})}{\leq} p_{\mathcal{E}} \cdot f_{\text{ext}} + f_0 + f_{p_{\mathcal{E}}} + p_{\mathcal{E}} \cdot (f_{\text{real}} + f_{\text{ideal}}) .$$

Since this is negligible, we obtain that $\mathcal{E} \mid \mathcal{F}^* \mid \mathcal{P}'_{\text{crypto}} \equiv \mathcal{E} \mid \mathcal{S} \mid \mathcal{F}^* \mid \mathcal{F}_{\text{crypto}}$, and hence, $\mathcal{F}^* \mid \mathcal{P}'_{\text{crypto}} \leq \mathcal{F}^* \mid \mathcal{F}_{\text{crypto}}$. By (B.1) ($\mathcal{F}^* \mid \mathcal{P}_{\text{crypto}} \leq \mathcal{F}^* \mid \mathcal{P}'_{\text{crypto}}$) and transitivity of $\leq$, this concludes the proof of Theorem 5.1.

C. Details and Proofs for our Computational Soundness Result

In this appendix, we provide more details and proofs concerning Chapter 6.

C.1. Computational Interpretation of Symbolic Protocols

We now give a more formal definition of the computational interpretations of symbolic protocols (which was only informally described in Section 6.3).

Definition of the IITMs M_i. Let $\mathcal{P}$ be a symbolic protocol with roles $R_1, \ldots, R_l$, $l \geq 2$, and τ an injective mapping τ from global constants (except for $n_1, \ldots, n_l$) to bit strings, as in Section 6.3. We now define the execution of (an instance of) the IITM $M_i = [\![R_i]\!]^\tau$, for all $i \leq l$. More precisely, the execution of $M_i[sid]$ (i.e., the instance of M_i with SID sid) where $sid = (sid', pid_1, \ldots, pid_l)$ is a valid SID (i.e., as described in Section 6.3, $pid_j \neq pid_k$ for all $j \neq k$ and pid_j is not in the range of τ). First, we note, that $M_i[sid]$ interacts with $!\mathcal{F}_{\text{crypto}}$ in session sid with user identifier $uid := i$. That is, all messages sent to $!\mathcal{F}_{\text{crypto}}$ are of the form $(sid, (i, m))$ and will be received by the instance of $\mathcal{F}_{\text{crypto}}$ with SID sid for the user i.[86] In the following, we denote the instance of $\mathcal{F}_{\text{crypto}}$ with SID sid by $\mathcal{F}_{\text{crypto}}[sid]$.

For the first message, we distinguish the cases $i \in \{1, 2\}$ and $i \notin \{1, 2\}$.

1. If $i \in \{1, 2\}$, then $M_i[sid]$ waits for receiving $(sid, \text{Establish})$ from I/O (i.e., on its I/O input tape to the environment). (All other messages are ignored, i.e., $M_i[sid]$ produces empty output, until this message is received; except for corruption status requests, see below.) Then, $M_i[sid]$ forwards $(sid, \text{Establish})$ to the network (i.e., sends it on its network output tape) and waits for receiving (sid, Corr) or $(sid, \text{Continue}, m)$ (for some bit string m) from the network (again all other messages are ignored, except for corruption status requests). When $M_i[sid]$ receives (sid, Corr), then $M_i[sid]$ verifies, by asking $\mathcal{F}_{\text{crypto}}$, that all long-term keys that occur in R_i are corrupted in $\mathcal{F}_{\text{crypto}}[sid]$. More precisely, for every symbolic long-term key $n \in \mathcal{N}_{\text{lt}}$ that occurs in R_i, $M_i[sid]$ asks $\mathcal{F}_{\text{crypto}}[sid]$ whether the long-term key with name $name(n, sid) := (\min\{pid_i, pid_j\}, \max\{pid_i, pid_j\})$

---

[86] We note that instead of i, $M_i[sid]$ could have used a different user identifier (e.g., pid_i). It only has to be guaranteed that the other roles in this session (i.e., the instances $M_j[sid]$ for $j \neq i$) use a different user identifier.

and type t_{lt} is corrupted, where $j \neq i$ is such that R_j contains n (by our assumptions on symbolic protocols there exists exactly one other role that contains n). If one of these keys is not corrupted, $M_i[sid]$ sends $(sid, \bot)$ to the network and waits for receiving $(sid, \mathsf{Continue}, m)$ from the network. Otherwise, $M_i[sid]$ records itself as corrupted and sends (sid, Ack) to the network. Then, $M_i[sid]$ waits for receiving a key $k \in \{0,1\}^\eta$ from the network and then outputs $(sid, (\mathsf{Established}, (\mathtt{data}, k)))$ on its I/O output tape, i.e., to the environment. That is, the adversary can determine the session key that is output. From then on $M_i[sid]$ ignores all other input messages; except for corruption status requests, which are now always answered with $(sid, 1)$ (meaning "corrupted"). When $M_i[sid]$ receives $(sid, \mathsf{Continue}, m)$, instead of (sid, Corr), then $M_i[sid]$, similarly to above, checks whether there exists $n \in \mathcal{N}_{lt}$ such that the long-term key corresponding to n is corrupted in $\mathcal{F}_{\mathrm{crypto}}[sid]$. If this is the case, then $M_i[sid]$ will, from then on, answer all corruption status requests with $(sid, 1)$. Otherwise, it will answer all corruption status requests with $(sid, 0)$ (meaning "uncorrupted"). We emphasize that $M_i[sid]$ reports itself as corrupted if any long-term key has been corrupted even if this is a long-term key that is not used by $M_i[sid]$ (i.e., n does not occur in R_i). In any case, since $M_i[sid]$ has not received a Corr message, $M_i[sid]$ then follows the prescribed protocol and processes the network input message m as described below.

2. If $i \notin \{1, 2\}$ (recall that, in this case, M_i does not have I/O tapes to the environment), then $M_i[sid]$ waits for receiving $(sid, \mathsf{Continue}, m)$ from the network (all other messages are ignored) and then processes the network input as described below.

In the case $i \in \{1, 2\}$, we now assume that $M_i[sid]$ has not been corrupted (otherwise it forwards messages between network and I/O as described above). We now describe how $M_i[sid]$ processes network input of the form $(sid, \mathsf{Continue}, m)$.

To record its state, the instance $M_i[sid]$ uses two variables: a symbolic role R and a (partial) mapping τ from (symbolic) names and variables to well-tagged bit strings (their computational interpretation). Initially, $M_i[sid]$ sets $\mathsf{R} := R_i$ and $\tau(n) := (\mathtt{data}, \tau(n))$ for every n in the domain of τ (recall that τ is a mapping from global constants to bit strings, except for the special names $n_1, \ldots, n_l$) and $\tau(n_i) := (\mathtt{data}, pid_i)$ for every $i \leq l$.

When receiving $(sid, \mathsf{Continue}, m)$ from the network for some bit string m, $M_i[sid]$ does the following:

1. $M_i[sid]$ parses m and verifies that it is well-tagged. If this is not the case, $M_i[sid]$ ignores m, produces empty output, and waits for receiving another $\mathsf{Continue}$ message that is processed in the same way. Otherwise, $M_i[sid]$ parses m and translates all keys that occur in m to pointers using the Store command of $\mathcal{F}_{\mathrm{crypto}}[sid]$, i.e., for every $(\mathtt{key}, k)$ in m, $M_i[sid]$ stores the key k with type t_{st} in $\mathcal{F}_{\mathrm{crypto}}[sid]$ and obtains a pointer ptr. Then, $M_i[sid]$ replaces $(\mathtt{key}, k)$ by $(\mathtt{key}, ptr)$ in m.

If storing fails for some key (i.e., $\mathcal{F}_{\text{crypto}}[sid]$ returns $\perp$ instead of a pointer), $M_i[sid]$ terminates, i.e., it produces empty output in this and every following activation (except for corruption status requests, see below), see Remark C.1.

2. Since R is a symbolic role, $R = \mathbf{0}$ or $R = c_{\text{net}}^{\text{in},i}(x).R'$ for some variable x and process R'. If $R = \mathbf{0}$, then $M_i[sid]$ terminates (as above). Otherwise, $M_i[sid]$ sets $\tau(x) := m$ and computes $(R', m', c') \leftarrow \|R\|^{\tau}$ (see below). Then, $M_i[sid]$ sets $R := R'$.

3. $M_i[sid]$ translates all pointers that occur in m' to keys using the Retrieve command of $\mathcal{F}_{\text{crypto}}[sid]$, i.e., for every (key, ptr) in m', $M_i[sid]$ obtains the key k corresponding to pointer ptr. Then, M_i replaces (key, ptr) by (key, k) in m'.

4. $M_i[sid]$ outputs m' to the network if $c' = c_{\text{net}}^{\text{out},i}$ and outputs $(sid, (\text{Established}, m'))$ to I/O if $c' = c_{\text{io}}^{\text{out},i}$. (Note that in the latter case $M_i[sid]$ outputs m' as the session key.)

5. $M_i[sid]$ then waits for receiving another Continue message that is processed in the same way.

Computational interpretation of symbolic roles. We recursively define the algorithm $\|R\|^{\tau}$:

1. If $R = \textbf{if } \phi \textbf{ then } \overline{c_{\text{net}}^{\text{out}}}\langle 1\rangle.R^{(1)} \textbf{ else } \overline{c_{\text{net}}^{\text{out}}}\langle 0\rangle.R^{(0)}$, compute $b \leftarrow \|\phi\|^{\tau}$ (see below) and $(R', m, c) \leftarrow \|R^{(b)}\|^{\tau}$. Then, return (R', m, c).

2. If $R = \overline{c}\langle s\rangle.R'$, compute $m \leftarrow \|s\|^{\tau}$ (see below). Then, return (R', m, c).

Note that by the definition of symbolic roles we do not need to consider the case of inputs (i.e., $R = c(s).R'$) or other if-then-else statements because the algorithm $\|R\|^{\tau}$ is never called with such processes. Furthermore, we note that the returned process R' is always a symbolic role.

Computational interpretation of terms. Next, we recursively define the algorithm $\|s\|^{\tau}$ for a term s. We note that this algorithm has side effects on the variable τ that is stored in the state of $M_i[sid]$. We note that $\|s\|^{\tau}$ always returns either $\perp$ or a well-tagged bit string.

1. If s is a name or a variable: If s is in the domain of τ, return $\tau(s)$. Otherwise, by our definition of symbolic protocols, s must be a nonce, i.e., $s \in \mathcal{N}_{\text{nonce}}$. (Since keys are always wrapped using $\text{sk}(\cdot)$, $\|s\|^{\tau}$ is never called for short- or long-term keys or symbolic randomnesses.) Then, choose $m \in \{0,1\}^{\eta}$ uniformly at random, set $\tau(s) := (\text{data}, m)$, and return (data, m).

2. If $s = \langle t, t'\rangle$ for some terms t, t': Compute $m \leftarrow \|t\|^{\tau}$ and $m' \leftarrow \|t'\|^{\tau}$. If $m = \perp$ or $m' = \perp$ then return $\perp$. Otherwise, return (pair, m, m').

3. If $s = \pi_b(t)$ for some $b \in \{1, 2\}$ and term t: Compute $m \leftarrow \llbracket t \rrbracket^\tau$. Return m_b if $m = (\text{pair}, m_1, m_2)$ for some bit strings m_1, m_2, otherwise, return $\bot$.

4. If $s = \{t\}_k^r$ for some terms r, t, k: By our assumptions on symbolic protocols, we have that r is a symbolic randomness (i.e., $r \in \mathcal{N}_{\text{rand}}$). If r is in the domain of τ (in this case the ciphertext has been computed previously and was stored in $\tau(r)$), return $\tau(r)$. Otherwise, compute $m \leftarrow \llbracket t \rrbracket^\tau$. If $m = \bot$, return $\bot$. Otherwise, compute $k' \leftarrow \llbracket k \rrbracket^\tau$. If $k' \neq (\text{key}, ptr)$ for any pointer ptr, return $\bot$. If $k' = (\text{key}, ptr)$ for some pointer ptr, then replace all pointers in m by "dummy" keys (i.e., every (key, ptr) in m is replaced by $(\text{key}, 0^\eta)$). Then, encrypt m along with the pointers that where contained in m under the key the pointer ptr refers to using $\mathcal{F}_{\text{crypto}}[sid]$ (note that the plaintext formatting function in $\mathcal{F}_{\text{crypto}}[sid]$ will replace all dummy keys by the actual keys the pointers refer to). Let c be the ciphertext returned by $\mathcal{F}_{\text{crypto}}[sid]$. If $c \neq \bot$, then set $\tau(r) := (\text{data}, c)$ (i.e., record the ciphertext, tagged as data, under the symbolic randomness r) and return (data, c). Otherwise (i.e., encryption fails), $M_i[sid]$ terminates (as above), see Remark C.1.

5. If $s = \text{dec}_k(t)$ for some terms t, k: Compute $c \leftarrow \llbracket t \rrbracket^\tau$. If $c \neq (\text{data}, c')$ for any bit string c', return $\bot$ (ciphertexts are always tagged as data). If $c = (\text{data}, c')$ for some bit string c', compute $k' \leftarrow \llbracket k \rrbracket^\tau$. If $k' \neq (\text{key}, ptr)$ for any pointer ptr, return $\bot$. If $k' = (\text{key}, ptr)$ for some pointer ptr, then decrypt c' with the pointer ptr using $\mathcal{F}_{\text{crypto}}[sid]$. Let m be the plaintext and $ptr_1, \ldots, ptr_r$ be the (possibly empty) list of pointers returned by $\mathcal{F}_{\text{crypto}}[sid]$. If $m = \bot$, return $\bot$. Otherwise, replace the j-th "dummy" key (i.e., $(\text{key}, 0^\eta)$) in m by (key, ptr_j). (By the definition of plaintext formatting and parsing, m is either $\bot$ or well-tagged and contains exactly r "dummy" keys). Then, return the obtained bit string.

6. If $s = \text{sk}(s')$ for some term s': By our assumptions on symbolic protocols, $s' \in \mathcal{N}_{\text{lt}} \cup \mathcal{N}_{\text{st}}$.

   If s' is a long-term key name (i.e., $s' \in \mathcal{N}_{\text{lt}}$) and $\tau(s')$ is not defined, then obtain a pointer, say ptr, to the long-term key corresponding to s' using $\mathcal{F}_{\text{crypto}}[sid]$ (i.e., for the long-term key with name $name(s', sid)$ and type t_{lt}, as defined above) and set $\tau(s') := ptr$.

   If s' is short-term key name (i.e., $s' \in \mathcal{N}_{\text{st}}$) and $\tau(s')$ is not defined, then generate a new key of type t_{st} in $\mathcal{F}_{\text{crypto}}[sid]$ (using the request KeyGen) and set $\tau(s') := ptr$ where ptr is the pointer returned by $\mathcal{F}_{\text{crypto}}[sid]$.

   Finally, return $\tau(s')$.

Computational interpretation of conditions.   We recursively define the algorithm $\llbracket \phi \rrbracket^\tau$ for a condition ϕ:

1. If $\phi = M(s)$ for some term s: Compute $m \leftarrow [\![s]\!]^\tau$. If $m \neq \bot$, return 1, otherwise, return 0.

2. If $\phi = EQ(s,t)$ for some terms s, t: Compute $m \leftarrow [\![s]\!]^\tau$ and $m' \leftarrow [\![t]\!]^\tau$. If $m = \bot$ or $m' = \bot$, return 0. Otherwise, check the the bit strings m and m' are equal where pointers (tagged as keys in m and m') are equal if the equality test using $\mathcal{F}_{\mathrm{crypto}}[sid]$ returns 1. More precisely, interpret the bit strings m and m' (which are well-tagged by definition of $[\![\cdot]\!]^\tau$) as rooted, binary trees T and T' where the inner nodes are labeled by **pair** and the leaf nodes are labeled by (**data**, x) or (**key**, ptr) (for bit strings x and keys ptr). Then, check that *(i)* the trees have the same structure, *(ii)* for every leaf node (labeled) (**data**, x) in T, the corresponding leaf node in T' has the same label (**data**, x), and *(iii)* for every leaf node (labeled) (**key**, ptr) in T, the corresponding leaf node in T' has the label (**key**, ptr') for some ptr' such that ptr and ptr' point to the same key in $\mathcal{F}_{\mathrm{crypto}}[sid]$ (this is tested using the **Equal** command of $\mathcal{F}_{\mathrm{crypto}}[sid]$). Return 1 if this check succeeds, otherwise, return 0.

3. If $\phi = \phi_1 \wedge \phi_2$ for some conditions ϕ_1, ϕ_2: Compute $b_1 \leftarrow [\![\phi_1]\!]^\tau$ and $b_2 \leftarrow [\![\phi_2]\!]^\tau$. Return 1 if $b_1 = b_2 = 1$, otherwise, return 0.

4. If $\phi = \neg \phi'$ for some condition ϕ': Compute $b' \leftarrow [\![\phi']\!]^\tau$. Return 1 if $b' = 0$, otherwise, return 0.

Remark C.1. In the interaction with $M_i[sid]$, $\mathcal{F}_{\mathrm{crypto}}[sid]$ might return an error message ($\bot$) upon storing a key ($\mathcal{F}_{\mathrm{crypto}}[sid]$ does this to prevent guessing a key that is marked unknown) or upon encryption (e.g., because the decryption test in $\mathcal{F}_{\mathrm{crypto}}[sid]$ does not succeed or because the length of the plaintext is less than η, and hence, formatting fails) In such a case, $M_i[sid]$ will terminate, i.e., abort the current computation, produce empty output, and, from then on, produce empty output upon every activation (except for corruption status requests).

C.2. Applications

C.2.1. Our Simple Key Exchange Protocol (OSKE)

The symbolic process $\mathcal{P}_{\mathrm{oske}}$ from Example 6.1 models OSKE from Section 4.4.1. Below, we provide ProVerif source code that models $\mathcal{P}_{\mathrm{oske}}$ and its randomized version rand($\mathcal{P}_{\mathrm{oske}}$) as a bi-process. For this code, ProVerif[87] quickly proves observational equivalence. As shown in Example 6.2, this proves that the computational interpretation of $\mathcal{P}_{\mathrm{oske}}$ realizes an ideal key exchange functionality.

---

[87] We used ProVerif version 1.86pl4, which is available from `http://prosecco.gforge.inria.fr/personal/bblanche/proverif/`.

```
(* Our Simple Key Exchange Protocol (OSKE)
     A -> B:  {K}_Kab                                    *)

(* Pairing *)
fun pair/2.
reduc fst(pair(x,y)) = x.
reduc snd(pair(x,y)) = y.

(* Key tagging *)
fun sk/1.

(* Randomized symmetric key encryption *)
fun enc/3.
reduc dec(enc(x,y,z),y) = x.

(* Constants *)
fun true/0.
fun false/0.

(* Modeling predicates *)
reduc Pkey(sk(x)) = true.
reduc Penc(enc(x,y,z)) = true.
reduc Ppair(pair(x,y)) = true.

(* Channel names *)
free netinA, netoutA, iooutA, netinB, netoutB, iooutB.

free n1,n2. (* name of A and B, respectively *)

let processA =
    in(netinA, y1);
    (* omitted test M(enc(K, sk(Kab),R)),
         it would always succeed anyway *)
    out(netoutA, enc(K, sk(Kab), R));
    in(netinA, y2);
    (* omitted test M(K), it would always succeed anyway *)
    out(iooutA, choice[K,NK]).

let processB =
    in(netinB, z1);
    (* corresponds to test M(dec(z1, sk(Kab))): *)
    let k = dec(z1, sk(Kab)) in (
        out(netoutB, true);
        out(iooutB, choice[k,NK])
    ) else (
        out(netoutB, false)
    ).
```

process
 new NK; (∗ *the fresh session key* n^∗ ∗)
 new Kab; (∗ *long−term key* ∗)
 new K;   (∗ *nonce (used as session key)* ∗)
 new R;   (∗ *randomness for encryption* ∗)
 (processA | processB)

C.2.2. The ANSSK' Protocol

In this section, we model and analyze the ANSSK' protocol, a variant of the Amended Needham Schroeder Symmetric Key (ANSSK) protocol [NS87] that has been proposed in [KT09b]. This demonstrates the expressiveness of our class of symbolic protocols and the usefulness of our computational soundness result. The ANSSK' protocol is depicted in Figure C.1.

We model the ANSSK' protocol as the following symbolic protocol $\Pi_{\mathrm{anssk'}}$. As for OSKE (see Example 6.1), we omit the SID *sid* in the modeling of the protocol because it is added by the joint state realization of $\mathcal{F}_{\mathrm{crypto}}$, when we apply Corollary 6.2 (see below).

$$\Pi_{\mathrm{anssk'}} := (\mathcal{P}_{\mathrm{anssk'}}, \mathcal{N}_{\mathrm{lt}}, \mathcal{N}_{\mathrm{st}}, \mathcal{N}_{\mathrm{rand}}, \mathcal{N}_{\mathrm{nonce}}) \ ,$$

with

$$\mathcal{N}_{\mathrm{lt}} := \{k_{AS}, k_{BS}\} \ , \qquad \mathcal{N}_{\mathrm{st}} := \{k_A\} \ ,$$
$$\mathcal{N}_{\mathrm{rand}} := \{r_1, r_2, r_3\} \ , \qquad \mathcal{N}_{\mathrm{nonce}} := \{N_B, k_{AB}\} \ ,$$
$$\mathcal{P}_{\mathrm{anssk'}} := (\nu k_{AS}, k_{BS}, k_A, r_1, r_2, r_3, N_B, k_{AB})(R_1 \parallel R_2 \parallel R_3) \ ,$$

$$R_1 := c_{\mathrm{net}}^{\mathrm{in},1}(x_1) \cdot \overline{c_{\mathrm{net}}^{\mathrm{out},1}}[\{\langle n_2, \mathrm{sk}(k_A)\rangle\}_{\mathrm{sk}(k_{AS})}^{r_1}] \cdot c_{\mathrm{net}}^{\mathrm{in},1}(x_2) \cdot$$
$$\quad \textbf{if } \mathrm{EQ}(n_2, \pi_2(\mathrm{dec}_{\mathrm{sk}(k_A)}(x_2))) \textbf{ then } \overline{c_{\mathrm{net}}^{\mathrm{out},1}}\langle 1\rangle \cdot \overline{c_{\mathrm{io}}^{\mathrm{out},1}}[k'_{AB}] \cdot \mathbf{0} \ ,$$
$$\qquad\qquad\qquad\qquad\qquad\qquad\qquad\qquad k'_{AB} := \pi_1(\mathrm{dec}_{\mathrm{sk}(k_A)}(x_2))$$

$$R_2 := c_{\mathrm{net}}^{\mathrm{in},2}(y_1) \cdot \overline{c_{\mathrm{net}}^{\mathrm{out},2}}[\langle n_1, \langle n_2, \langle N_B, y_1\rangle\rangle\rangle] \cdot c_{\mathrm{net}}^{\mathrm{in},2}(y_2) \cdot$$
$$\quad \textbf{if } \mathrm{EQ}(N_B, \pi_1(\mathrm{dec}_{\mathrm{sk}(k_{BS})}(y_2))) \ \wedge \ \mathrm{EQ}(n_1, \pi_1(\pi_2(\mathrm{dec}_{\mathrm{sk}(k_{BS})}(y_2))))$$
$$\quad \textbf{then } \overline{c_{\mathrm{net}}^{\mathrm{out},2}}\langle 1\rangle \cdot \overline{c_{\mathrm{net}}^{\mathrm{out},2}}[ct] \cdot c_{\mathrm{net}}^{\mathrm{in},2}(y_3) \cdot \overline{c_{\mathrm{io}}^{\mathrm{out},2}}[k''_{AB}] \cdot \mathbf{0} \ ,$$
$$\qquad\qquad ct := \pi_2(\pi_2(\pi_2(\mathrm{dec}_{\mathrm{sk}(k_{BS})}(y_2)))) \qquad k''_{AB} := \pi_1(\pi_2(\pi_2(\mathrm{dec}_{\mathrm{sk}(k_{BS})}(y_2))))$$

$$R_3 := c_{\mathrm{net}}^{\mathrm{in},3}(z_1) \cdot$$
$$\quad \textbf{if } \mathrm{EQ}(n_1, \pi_1(z_1)) \ \wedge \ \mathrm{EQ}(n_2, \pi_1(\pi_2(z_1))) \ \wedge$$
$$\qquad \mathrm{EQ}(n_2, \pi_1(\mathrm{dec}_{\mathrm{sk}(k_{AS})}(\pi_2(\pi_2(\pi_2(z_1))))))$$
$$\quad \textbf{then } \overline{c_{\mathrm{net}}^{\mathrm{out},3}}\langle 1\rangle \cdot \overline{c_{\mathrm{net}}^{\mathrm{out},3}}[\{\langle N'_B, \langle n_1, \langle k_{AB}, \{\langle k_{AB}, n_2\rangle\}_{k'_A}^{r_2}\rangle\rangle\rangle\}_{\mathrm{sk}(k_{BS})}^{r_3}] \cdot \mathbf{0} \ .$$
$$\qquad\qquad N'_B := \pi_1(\pi_2(\pi_2(z_1))) \qquad k'_A := \pi_2(\mathrm{dec}_{\mathrm{sk}(k_{AS})}(\pi_2(\pi_2(\pi_2(z_1)))))$$

1. $A \rightarrow B$: $\{sid, pid_B, k_A\}_{k_{AS}}$
2. $B \rightarrow S$: $pid_A, pid_B, N_B, \{sid, pid_B, k_A\}_{k_{AS}}$
3. $S \rightarrow B$: $\{sid, N_B, pid_A, k_{AB}, \{k_{AB}, pid_B\}_{k_A}\}_{k_{BS}}$
4. $B \rightarrow A$: $\{k_{AB}, pid_B\}_{k_A}$

sid: unique pre-established SID
pid_A, pid_B: party names of A and B, respectively
k_{AS}, k_{BS}: pre-shared symmetric encryption keys, shared between A/B and S
k_A: symmetric encryption key, generated by A
N_B: nonce, generated by B
k_{AB}: session key to be established between A and B, generated by S

Figure C.1.: The ANSSK' Protocol.

In this, R_1 models role A, R_2 role B, and R_3 role S of the protocol. Furthermore, we omitted the else branch: We use **if** ϕ **then** $\overline{c_{net}^{out,j}}\langle 1\rangle$. R as an abbreviation of **if** ϕ **then** $\overline{c_{net}^{out,j}}\langle 1\rangle$. R **else** $\overline{c_{net}^{out,j}}\langle 0\rangle$. **0**. Recall that the special names n_1, n_2, and n_3 (n_3 is not used in the protocol) represent the party names of the roles.

To prove observational equivalence of the protocol $\mathcal{P}_{anssk'}$ and its randomized version rand($\mathcal{P}_{anssk'}$), we use the following ProVerif source code; it models these symbolic processes as a bi-process. For this code, ProVerif[88] quickly proves observational equivalence. For simplicity of presentation, in this code, we omitted the output of 1 or 0, respectively, after if-then-else statements. Since the protocol has observationally different behavior after if-then-else statements anyway (if a condition is evaluated to false, the role terminates and otherwise it continues), this does not make a difference.

So, by Corollary 6.2, to show that the computational interpretation of $[\![\mathcal{P}_{anssk'}]\!]_{JS}$ (which precisely models the ANSSK' protocol in the IITM model) is secure (i.e., realizes $!\mathcal{F}_{ke}$), it is left to show that $\mathcal{P}_{anssk'}$ preserves key secrecy and is symbolically standard. These two properties are easy to see for $\mathcal{P}_{anssk'}$ but we omit their proof.

```
(* ANSSK' Protocol
    A -> B: {B,Ka}_Kas
    B -> S: B,A,Nb,{B,Ka}_Kas
    S -> B: {Nb,A,Kab,{Kab,B}_Ka}_Kbs
    B -> A: {Kab,B}_Ka                              *)


(* Pairing *)
fun pair/2.
reduc fst(pair(x,y)) = x.
reduc snd(pair(x,y)) = y.
```

---

[88] We used ProVerif version 1.86pl4, which is available from http://prosecco.gforge.inria.fr/personal/bblanche/proverif/.

```
(* Key tagging *)
fun sk/1.

(* Randomized symmetric key encryption *)
fun enc/3.
reduc dec(enc(x,y,z),y) = x.

(* Constants *)
fun true/0.
fun false/0.

(* Modeling predicates *)
reduc Pkey(sk(x)) = true.
reduc Penc(enc(x,y,z)) = true.
reduc Ppair(pair(x,y)) = true.

(* Channel names *)
free netinA, netoutA, iooutA, netinB, netoutB, iooutB, netinS, netoutS.

free n1,n2,n3. (* name of A, B, and S, respectively *)

let processA =
    in(netinA, y1);
    out(netoutA, enc(pair(n2,sk(Ka)),sk(Kas),R1));
    in(netinA, y2);
    if n2 = snd(dec(y2,sk(Ka))) then
    let kab = fst(dec(y2,sk(Ka))) in
    out(iooutA, choice[kab,NK]).

let processB =
    in(netinB, z1);
    out(netoutB, pair(n2,pair(n1,pair(Nb,z1))));
    in(netinB, z2);
    if Nb = fst(dec(z2,sk(Kbs))) then
    if n1 = fst(snd(dec(z2,sk(Kbs)))) then
    let kab = fst(snd(snd(dec(z2,sk(Kbs))))) in
    let z3 = snd(snd(snd(dec(z2,sk(Kbs))))) in
    out(netoutB, z3);
    out(iooutB, choice[kab,NK]).

let processS =
    in(netinS, u1);
    if n2 = fst(u1) then
    if n1 = fst(snd(u1)) then
    let nb = fst(snd(snd(u1))) in
    let u2 = snd(snd(snd(u1))) in
```

```
if n2 = fst(dec(u2,sk(Kas))) then
let ka = snd(dec(u2,sk(Kas))) in
let ct1 = enc(pair(Kab,n2),ka,R2) in
let ct2 = enc(pair(nb,pair(n1,pair(Kab,ct1))),sk(Kbs),R3) in
out(netoutS, ct2).
```

process
new NK;	(* *the fresh session key* n^* *)
new Kas; **new** Kbs;	(* *long−term keys* *)
new Ka;	(* *short−term key* *)
new Nb; **new** Kab;	(* *nonces* *)
new R1; **new** R2; **new** R3;	(* *randomness for encryption* *)
(processA | processB | processS)	

C.3. Proof of Lemma 6.3

In this section, we complete the proof of Lemma 6.3 in Section 6.5.1, i.e., we prove the statements (6.1), (6.2), and (6.3).

C.3.1. Proof of (6.1) and (6.2)

Under the preconditions of Lemma 6.3, for all terms s where $\llbracket s \rrbracket_t$ is defined, it holds:

$$\models M(s\sigma_t^{\text{in}}) \quad \text{if and only if} \quad \llbracket s \rrbracket_t \neq \perp . \tag{6.1}$$

$$\psi_t(\llbracket s \rrbracket_t) =_E s\sigma_t^{\text{in}} \quad \text{if} \quad \llbracket s \rrbracket_t \neq \perp . \tag{6.2}$$

Proof of (6.1) and (6.2). We prove (6.1) and (6.2) by induction on the structure of s.

1. $s \in \mathcal{N}$: Names for randomness and keys are never computationally interpreted (at most $\text{sk}(n)$ for $n \in \mathcal{N}_{\text{lt}} \cup \mathcal{N}_{\text{st}}$ is interpreted but not n itself), hence, s is a nonce (i.e., $s \in \mathcal{N}_{\text{nonce}}$), a global constant, or $s = n_i$ for some $i \in \{1, \dots, l\}$. We conclude that $\llbracket s \rrbracket_t \neq \perp$ and $\models M(s) = M(s\sigma_t^{\text{in}})$.

   Furthermore, $\psi_t(\llbracket s \rrbracket_t) = s = s\sigma_t^{\text{in}}$, by definition of ψ_t.

2. $s \in \mathcal{X}$: By definition of $\mathcal{P}$ and $\llbracket \mathcal{P} \rrbracket^\tau$, all variables correspond to input variables and are interpreted to the received message. Hence, $\llbracket s \rrbracket_t \neq \perp$ and, by definition of σ_t^{in}, $\psi_t(\llbracket s \rrbracket_t) = s\sigma_t^{\text{in}}$. Also, $\models M(s\sigma_t^{\text{in}})$ because $M(s')$ holds for any s' produced by ψ_t.

3. $s = \text{sk}(s')$: By definition of $\mathcal{P}$ we have that s' is a short-term key, i.e., $s' \in \mathcal{N}_{\text{st}}$. Note that long-term keys are never computationally interpreted and that only keys are tagged as keys. Hence, $\llbracket s \rrbracket_t = (\textbf{key}, k)$ for some bit string k which is a short-term key in $\mathcal{F}_{\text{crypto}}$. On the other hand, $\models M(s)$ because $s' \in \mathcal{N}_{\text{st}}$.

   Furthermore, by definition of ψ_t, $\psi_t(\llbracket s \rrbracket_t) = s = s\sigma_t^{\text{in}}$.

4. $s = \langle s_1, s_2 \rangle$: By induction hypotheses (IH), (6.1) and (6.2) hold for both s_1 and s_2. We have that $\llbracket s \rrbracket_t \neq \bot$ iff $\llbracket s_1 \rrbracket_t, \llbracket s_2 \rrbracket_t \neq \bot$ iff (IH) $\models M(s_1 \sigma_t^{\text{in}})$ and $\models M(s_2 \sigma_t^{\text{in}})$ iff $\mathcal{M} \models M(s)$.

   Furthermore, if $\llbracket s \rrbracket_t \neq \bot$ then $\psi_t(\llbracket s \rrbracket_t) \overset{\text{def. of } \llbracket \cdot \rrbracket_t}{=} \psi_t((\texttt{pair}, \llbracket s_1 \rrbracket_t, \llbracket s_2 \rrbracket_t)) \overset{\text{def. of } \psi_t}{=}$
   $\langle \llbracket s_1 \rrbracket_t, \llbracket s_2 \rrbracket_t \rangle \overset{\text{IH}}{=}_E \langle s_1 \sigma_t^{\text{in}}, s_2 \sigma_t^{\text{in}} \rangle = s \sigma_t^{\text{in}}$.

5. $s = \pi_b(s')$ $(b \in \{1,2\})$: By IH, (6.1) and (6.2) hold for s'.

   Assume that $\llbracket s \rrbracket_t \neq \bot$. Then $\llbracket s' \rrbracket_t = (\texttt{pair}, m_1, m_2)$ for some $m_1, m_2 \in \{0,1\}^*$. By IH, $\models M(s' \sigma_t^{\text{in}})$ and $s' \sigma_t^{\text{in}} =_E \psi_t(\llbracket s' \rrbracket_t) = \langle \psi_t(m_1), \psi_t(m_2) \rangle$. Hence, $\models M(s \sigma_t^{\text{in}})$.

   Furthermore, $\llbracket s \rrbracket_t = m_b$ and, hence, $\psi_t(\llbracket s \rrbracket_t) = \psi_t(m_b) =_E \pi_b(\langle \psi_t(m_1), \psi_t(m_2) \rangle)$ $=_E s \sigma_t^{\text{in}}$.

   Assume that $\models M(s \sigma_t^{\text{in}})$. Then $\models M(s' \sigma_t^{\text{in}})$ and $s' \sigma_t^{\text{in}} =_E \langle s_1, s_2 \rangle$ for some terms s_1, s_2. By IH, $\psi_t(\llbracket s' \rrbracket_t) =_E s' \sigma_t^{\text{in}} =_E \langle s_1, s_2 \rangle$. By definition of ψ_t we have that $\psi_t(\llbracket s' \rrbracket_t) = \langle s_1', s_2' \rangle$ for some terms s_1', s_2'. Hence, $\llbracket s' \rrbracket_t = (\texttt{pair}, m_1, m_2)$ for some bit strings m_1, m_2. Hence, $\llbracket s \rrbracket_t = m_b \neq \bot$.

6. $s = \{s_1\}_{s_2}^{s_3}$: By definition of $\mathcal{P}$ we have that s_3 is randomness, i.e., $s_3 \in \mathcal{N}_{\text{rand}}$.

   First, we consider the case where s_2 is a long-term key, i.e., $s_2 = \text{sk}(n)$ for some name $n \in \mathcal{N}_{\text{lt}}$. Because $\mathcal{P}$ preserves key secrecy and by Lemma 6.2, the long-term key (associated with) n is marked unknown in $\mathcal{F}_{\text{crypto}}$. By IH, (6.1) and (6.2) hold for s_1.

   Assume that $\llbracket s \rrbracket_t \neq \bot$. Then, $\llbracket s_1 \rrbracket_t \neq \bot$ and the plaintext/ciphertext pair $(\llbracket s_1 \rrbracket_t, \llbracket s \rrbracket_t)$ is stored in $\mathcal{F}_{\text{crypto}}$ for the long-term key n. By IH, $\models M(s_1 \sigma_t^{\text{in}})$ and, hence, $\models M(s \sigma_t^{\text{in}})$. Furthermore, $\psi_t(\llbracket s \rrbracket_t) \overset{\text{def. of } \psi_t}{=} \{\psi_t(\llbracket s_1 \rrbracket_t)\}_{s_2}^{s_3} \overset{\text{IH}}{=}_E$ $\{s_1 \sigma_t^{\text{in}}\}_{s_2}^{s_3} = s \sigma_t^{\text{in}}$.

   Now, assume that $\llbracket s \rrbracket_t = \bot$. By definition of $\llbracket \cdot \rrbracket_t$ we have that $\llbracket s_1 \rrbracket_t = \bot$. Recall that if $\mathcal{F}_{\text{crypto}}$ returned an error message upon encryption then $\llbracket s \rrbracket_t$ is undefined and not $\llbracket s \rrbracket_t = \bot$. This case does not need to be considered here because we only consider terms s where $\llbracket s \rrbracket_t$ is defined. By IH, $\not\models M(s_1 \sigma_t^{\text{in}})$ and, hence, $\not\models M(s \sigma_t^{\text{in}})$.

   Next, we consider the case where s_2 is not a long-term key.

   Assume that $\llbracket s \rrbracket_t \neq \bot$. Then, $\llbracket s_2 \rrbracket_t = (\texttt{key}, k)$ for some bit string k which is a short-term key in $\mathcal{F}_{\text{crypto}}$ and $\llbracket s_1 \rrbracket_t \neq \bot$. Because $\mathcal{P}$ preserves key secrecy and by Lemma 6.2, k is marked unknown in $\mathcal{F}_{\text{crypto}}$. Hence, the plaintext/ciphertext pair $(\llbracket s_1 \rrbracket_t, \llbracket s \rrbracket_t)$ is stored in $\mathcal{F}_{\text{crypto}}$ for the short-term key k. By definition of ψ_t, $\psi_t(\llbracket s_2 \rrbracket_t) = \text{sk}(n)$ for some short-term key $n \in \mathcal{N}_{\text{st}}$. By IH, (6.1) and (6.2) hold for both s_1 and s_2, hence, $\models M(s_1 \sigma_t^{\text{in}})$, $\psi_t(\llbracket s_1 \rrbracket_t) =_E s_1 \sigma_t^{\text{in}}$, $\models M(s_2 \sigma_t^{\text{in}})$, and $\text{sk}(n) = \psi_t(\llbracket s_2 \rrbracket_t) =_E s_2 \sigma_t^{\text{in}}$. We conclude that $\models M(s \sigma_t^{\text{in}})$. Furthermore, $\psi_t(\llbracket s \rrbracket_t) \overset{\text{def. of } \psi_t}{=} \{\psi_t(\llbracket s_1 \rrbracket_t)\}_{\text{sk}(n)}^{s_3} \overset{\text{IH}}{=}_E \{s_1 \sigma_t^{\text{in}}\}_{s_2 \sigma_t^{\text{in}}}^{s_3} = s \sigma_t^{\text{in}}$.

Now, assume that $\llbracket s \rrbracket_t = \bot$. By definition of $\llbracket \cdot \rrbracket_t$ we have that $\llbracket s_1 \rrbracket_t = \bot$ or $\llbracket s_2 \rrbracket_t \neq (\text{key}, k)$ for any bit string k that is a short-term key in $\mathcal{F}_{\text{crypto}}$. As above, recall that if $\mathcal{F}_{\text{crypto}}$ returned an error message upon encryption then $\llbracket s \rrbracket_t$ is undefined and not $\llbracket s \rrbracket_t = \bot$. This case does not need to be considered here because we only consider terms s where $\llbracket s \rrbracket_t$ is defined. In fact, if $\llbracket s_2 \rrbracket_t \neq (\text{key}, k)$ for any such k, then $\llbracket s_2 \rrbracket_t \neq (\text{key}, k)$ for any bit string k. This follows from the way pointers are handled. If $\llbracket s_2 \rrbracket_t \neq (\text{key}, k)$ for any k, then $\psi_t(\llbracket s_2 \rrbracket_t) \neq \text{sk}(s')$ for any term s'. By IH, (6.1) and (6.2) hold for s_2, hence, $\not\models M(s_2 \sigma_t^{\text{in}})$ or $s_2 \sigma_t^{\text{in}} =_E \psi_t(\llbracket s_2 \rrbracket_t) \neq \text{sk}(s')$ for any term s'. In both cases we conclude $\not\models M(s \sigma_t^{\text{in}})$. Otherwise, if $\llbracket s_2 \rrbracket_t = (\text{key}, k)$ for some bit string k which is a short-term key in $\mathcal{F}_{\text{crypto}}$, then $\llbracket s_1 \rrbracket_t = \bot$. By IH, (6.1) and (6.2) hold for s_1 and, hence, $\not\models M(s_1 \sigma_t^{\text{in}})$. In particular, $\not\models M(s \sigma_t^{\text{in}})$.

7. $s = \text{dec}_{s_2}(s_1)$: First, we consider the case where s_2 is a long-term key, i.e., $s_2 = \text{sk}(n)$ for some name $n \in \mathcal{N}_{\text{lt}}$. Because $\mathcal{P}$ preserves key secrecy and by Lemma 6.2, the long-term key (associated with) n is marked unknown in $\mathcal{F}_{\text{crypto}}$. By IH, (6.1) and (6.2) hold for s_1.

Assume that $\llbracket s \rrbracket_t \neq \bot$. Then, the plaintext/ciphertext pair $(\llbracket s \rrbracket_t, \llbracket s_1 \rrbracket_t)$ is stored in $\mathcal{F}_{\text{crypto}}$ for the long-term key n. Hence, there exists a name $r \in \mathcal{N}_{\text{rand}}$ and a term s' such that $\llbracket \cdot \rrbracket_t$ had been called with the term $\{s'\}_{\text{sk}(n)}^r$, $\llbracket s' \rrbracket_t = \llbracket s \rrbracket_t$, and $\llbracket \{s'\}_{\text{sk}(n)}^r \rrbracket_t = \llbracket s_1 \rrbracket_t$. By IH, $\models M(s_1 \sigma_t^{\text{in}})$ and $\psi_t(\llbracket s_1 \rrbracket_t) =_E s_1 \sigma_t^{\text{in}}$. By definition of ψ_t, $\{\psi_t(\llbracket s \rrbracket_t)\}_{\text{sk}(n)}^r = \psi_t(\llbracket s_1 \rrbracket_t) =_E s_1 \sigma_t^{\text{in}}$. Hence, $\models M(s \sigma_t^{\text{in}})$. Furthermore, we have that $\psi_t(\llbracket s \rrbracket_t) = \psi_t(\llbracket s' \rrbracket_t) =_E \text{dec}_{\text{sk}(n)}(\{\psi_t(\llbracket s' \rrbracket_t)\}_{\text{sk}(n)}^r) =_E \text{dec}_{\text{sk}(n)}(s_1 \sigma_t^{\text{in}}) = s \sigma_t^{\text{in}}$.

Now, assume that $\llbracket s \rrbracket_t = \bot$. By definition of $\llbracket \cdot \rrbracket_t$ we have that $\llbracket s_1 \rrbracket_t = \bot$ or $\llbracket s_1 \rrbracket_t$ is not stored as a ciphertext in $\mathcal{F}_{\text{crypto}}$ for the long-term key n. If $\llbracket s_1 \rrbracket_t = \bot$, then, by IH, $\not\models M(s_1 \sigma_t^{\text{in}})$ and, hence, $\not\models M(s \sigma_t^{\text{in}})$. Otherwise, $\psi_t(\llbracket s_1 \rrbracket_t) \neq_E \{s'\}_{\text{sk}(n)}^{s''}$ for any terms s' and s''. On the other hand, by IH, $\psi_t(\llbracket s_1 \rrbracket_t) =_E s_1 \sigma_t^{\text{in}}$. Hence, $\not\models M(s \sigma_t^{\text{in}})$.

Next, we consider the case where s_2 is not a long-term key.

Assume that $\llbracket s \rrbracket_t \neq \bot$. Then, $\llbracket s_2 \rrbracket_t = (\text{key}, k)$ for some bit string k which is a short-term key in $\mathcal{F}_{\text{crypto}}$ and $\llbracket s_1 \rrbracket_t \neq \bot$. Because $\mathcal{P}$ preserves key secrecy and by Lemma 6.2, k is marked unknown in $\mathcal{F}_{\text{crypto}}$. Hence, the plaintext/ciphertext pair $(\llbracket s \rrbracket_t, \llbracket s_1 \rrbracket_t)$ is stored in $\mathcal{F}_{\text{crypto}}$ for the short-term key k and there exists a name $r \in \mathcal{N}_{\text{rand}}$ and terms s', s'' such that $\llbracket \cdot \rrbracket_t$ had been called with the term $\{s'\}_{s''}^r$, $\llbracket s' \rrbracket_t = \llbracket s \rrbracket_t$, $\llbracket s'' \rrbracket_t = (\text{key}, k)$, and $\llbracket \{s'\}_{s''}^r \rrbracket_t = \llbracket s_1 \rrbracket_t$. Because k is marked unknown in $\mathcal{F}_{\text{crypto}}$, by definition of $\mathcal{F}_{\text{crypto}}$ (only honestly generated keys are marked unknown), k corresponds to some short-term key $n \in \mathcal{N}_{\text{st}}$. By definition of ψ_t, $\psi_t(\llbracket s_2 \rrbracket_t) = \text{sk}(n)$. By IH, (6.1) and (6.2) hold for both s_1 and s_2, hence, $\models M(s_1 \sigma_t^{\text{in}})$, $\psi_t(\llbracket s_1 \rrbracket_t) =_E s_1 \sigma_t^{\text{in}}$, $\models M(s_2 \sigma_t^{\text{in}})$, and $\text{sk}(n) = \psi_t(\llbracket s_2 \rrbracket_t) =_E s_2 \sigma_t^{\text{in}}$. We conclude $s_1 \sigma_t^{\text{in}} \overset{\text{IH}}{=}_E \psi_t(\llbracket s_1 \rrbracket_t) \overset{\text{def. of } \psi_t}{=} \{\psi_t(\llbracket s' \rrbracket_t)\}_{\text{sk}(n)}^r \overset{\text{IH}}{=}_E \{\psi_t(\llbracket s' \rrbracket_t)\}_{s_2 \sigma_t^{\text{in}}}^r$.

Hence, $\models M(s\sigma_t^{\mathrm{in}})$. Furthermore, we have that $\psi_t(\lVert s \rVert_t) = \psi_t(\lVert s' \rVert_t) =_E$ $\mathrm{dec}_{s_2\sigma_t^{\mathrm{in}}}(\{\psi_t(\lVert s' \rVert_t)\}_{s_2\sigma_t^{\mathrm{in}}}^r) =_E \mathrm{dec}_{s_2\sigma_t^{\mathrm{in}}}(s_1\sigma_t^{\mathrm{in}}) = s\sigma_t^{\mathrm{in}}$.

Now, assume that $\lVert s \rVert_t = \bot$. By definition of $\lVert \cdot \rVert_t$ we have that $\lVert s_2 \rVert_t \neq (\mathsf{key}, k)$ for any bit string k that is a short-term key in $\mathcal{F}_{\mathrm{crypto}}$, $\lVert s_1 \rVert_t = \bot$, or $\lVert s_1 \rVert_t$ is not stored as a ciphertext in $\mathcal{F}_{\mathrm{crypto}}$ for the short-term key k where $\lVert s_2 \rVert_t = (\mathsf{key}, k)$. In fact, if $\lVert s_2 \rVert_t \neq (\mathsf{key}, k)$ for any bit string k which is a short-term key in $\mathcal{F}_{\mathrm{crypto}}$, then $\lVert s_2 \rVert_t \neq (\mathsf{key}, k)$ for any bit string k. This follows from the way pointers are handled. If $\lVert s_2 \rVert_t \neq (\mathsf{key}, k)$ for any bit string k, then, by IH for s_2 and definition of ψ_t, $s_2\sigma_t^{\mathrm{in}} \neq \mathrm{sk}(s')$ for any term s' and, hence, $\not\models M(s\sigma_t^{\mathrm{in}})$. Otherwise if $\lVert s_1 \rVert_t = \bot$, then, by IH for s_1, $\not\models M(s_1\sigma_t^{\mathrm{in}})$ and, hence, $\not\models M(s\sigma_t^{\mathrm{in}})$. Otherwise, because $\mathcal{P}$ preserves key secrecy and by Lemma 6.2, k is marked unknown in $\mathcal{F}_{\mathrm{crypto}}$ and, by definition of $\mathcal{F}_{\mathrm{crypto}}$ (only honestly generated keys are marked unknown), k corresponds to some short-term key $n \in \mathcal{N}_{\mathrm{st}}$. By IH for s_2 and definition of ψ_t, $s_2\sigma_t^{\mathrm{in}} =_E \psi_t(\lVert s_2 \rVert_t) = \mathrm{sk}(n)$. Because $\lVert s_1 \rVert_t$ is not stored as a ciphertext in $\mathcal{F}_{\mathrm{crypto}}$ for the short-term key k, $\psi_t(\lVert s_1 \rVert_t) \neq_E \{s'\}_{\mathrm{sk}(n)}^{s''}$ for any terms s' and s''. On the other hand, by IH for s_1, $\psi_t(\lVert s_1 \rVert_t) =_E s_1\sigma_t^{\mathrm{in}}$. Hence, $\not\models M(s\sigma_t^{\mathrm{in}})$. $\qquad\square$

C.3.2. Proof of (6.3)

Under the preconditions of Lemma 6.3, for all conditions ϕ where $\lVert \phi \rVert_t$ is defined, it holds:

$$\models \phi\sigma_t^{\mathrm{in}} \quad \text{if and only if} \quad \lVert \phi \rVert_t = 1 \ . \tag{6.3}$$

Now, we prove (6.3) using (6.1) and (6.2).

Proof of (6.3). First, we note that the machines M_i in fact do not compute $\lVert s \rVert_t$ for a term s because we replace pointers by the corresponding keys. For example, consider the case where M_i evaluates $\mathrm{EQ}(s_1, s_2)$ and $\lVert s_1 \rVert_t = \lVert s_2 \rVert_t = (\mathsf{key}, k)$ for some short-term key k in $\mathcal{F}_{\mathrm{crypto}}$. In fact, M_i evaluates s_1 and s_2 to some pointers (key, ptr_1) and (key, ptr_2), respectively, which are both associated with the short-term key k. Then, to test if the pointers ptr_1 and ptr_2 point to the same key, M_i uses the Equal command of $\mathcal{F}_{\mathrm{crypto}}$. By definition, $\mathcal{F}_{\mathrm{crypto}}$ returns 1 because they point to the same key. Hence, $\mathrm{EQ}(s_1, s_2)$ is interpreted to true by M_i, i.e., $\lVert \mathrm{EQ}(s_1, s_2) \rVert_t = 1$. In general, we can prove that $\lVert \mathrm{EQ}(s_1, s_2) \rVert_t = 1$ iff $\lVert s_1 \rVert_t = \lVert s_2 \rVert_t \neq \bot$. Similarly, we obtain that $\lVert M(s) \rVert_t = 1$ iff $\lVert s \rVert_t \neq \bot$.

We prove (6.3) by induction on the structure of ϕ:

1. $\phi = M(s)$: We have $\lVert M(s) \rVert_t = 1$ iff $\lVert s \rVert_t \neq \bot$ which, by (6.1), holds iff $\models M(s\sigma_t^{\mathrm{in}})$.

2. $\phi = \mathrm{EQ}(s_1, s_2)$: First, assume that $\lVert \mathrm{EQ}(s_1, s_2) \rVert_t = 1$. Then, $\lVert s_1 \rVert_t = \lVert s_2 \rVert_t \neq \bot$ and, hence, by (6.1), $\models M(s_1\sigma_t^{\mathrm{in}})$ and $\models M(s_2\sigma_t^{\mathrm{in}})$. Furthermore, by (6.2), $s_1\sigma_t^{\mathrm{in}} =_E \psi_t(\lVert s_1 \rVert_t) = \psi_t(\lVert s_2 \rVert_t) =_E s_2\sigma_t^{\mathrm{in}}$. Hence, $\models \mathrm{EQ}(s_1\sigma_t^{\mathrm{in}}, s_2\sigma_t^{\mathrm{in}})$.

On the other hand, assume that $\models EQ(s_1\sigma_t^{in}, s_2\sigma_t^{in})$. Then, $\models M(s_1\sigma_t^{in})$, $\models M(s_2\sigma_t^{in})$, and $s_1\sigma_t^{in} =_E s_2\sigma_t^{in}$. By (6.1) and (6.2), $s_1\sigma_t^{in} =_E \psi_t(\llbracket s_1 \rrbracket_t)$ and $s_2\sigma_t^{in} =_E \psi_t(\llbracket s_2 \rrbracket_t)$. By definition of ψ_t, this implies that $\psi_t(\llbracket s_1 \rrbracket_t) = \psi_t(\llbracket s_2 \rrbracket_t)$. Because ψ_t is injective, we conclude $\llbracket s_1 \rrbracket_t = \llbracket s_2 \rrbracket_t \neq \perp$ and, hence, $\llbracket EQ(s_1, s_2) \rrbracket_t = 1$.

3. $\phi = \phi_1 \wedge \phi_2$: We have that $\models \phi\sigma_t^{in}$ iff $\models \phi_1\sigma_t^{in}$ and $\models \phi_2\sigma_t^{in}$ iff (induction hypotheses) $\llbracket \phi_1 \rrbracket_t = \llbracket \phi_2 \rrbracket_t = 1$ iff $\llbracket \phi \rrbracket_t = 1$.

4. $\phi = \neg\phi'$: We have that $\models \phi\sigma_t^{in}$ iff $\not\models \phi'\sigma_t^{in}$ iff (induction hypotheses) $\llbracket \phi' \rrbracket_t \neq 1$ iff $\llbracket \phi \rrbracket_t = 1$. $\square$

C.4. Proof of Corollary 6.2

We now prove Corollary 6.2 ($\llbracket P \rrbracket_{JS}^\tau \leq !\mathcal{F}_{ke}$). From Section 5.4, recall that $\mathcal{F}'_{crypto} = \mathcal{F}_{crypto}^{ST} \mid !\mathcal{F}_{crypto}^{LT\text{-senc}}$ (we omit key derivation and MACs) is the variant of $\mathcal{F}_{crypto}$ that uses $\mathcal{F}_{crypto}^{LT\text{-senc}}$ for long-term encryption keys and that $\mathcal{P}_{crypto}^{js} = !\mathcal{P}_{crypto}^{ST} \mid !\mathcal{P}_{senc}^{js} \mid !\mathcal{P}_{senc}$ is its joint state realization (again, we omit key derivation and MACs), where $!\mathcal{P}_{senc}^{js} \mid !\mathcal{P}_{senc}$ is the joint state realization for symmetric encryption with long-term keys. In Section 5.4 it has been shown that $\mathcal{P} \mid \mathcal{P}_{crypto}^{js} \leq \mathcal{P} \mid !\mathcal{F}'_{crypto}$ if the protocol system $\mathcal{P}$ is non-committing and used-order respecting w.r.t. $!\mathcal{F}'_{crypto}$. Also, recall from Section 6.4 that $\llbracket P \rrbracket^\tau = !M_1 \mid \cdots \mid !M_l \mid !\mathcal{F}'_{crypto}$ (note that, for Corollary 6.2, we replaced $!\mathcal{F}_{crypto}$ by $!\mathcal{F}'_{crypto}$) and that $\llbracket P \rrbracket_{JS}^\tau = !M_1 \mid \cdots \mid !M_l \mid \mathcal{P}_{crypto}^{js}$. By Theorem 6.1, we have that $\llbracket P \rrbracket^\tau \leq !\mathcal{F}_{ke}$.

Hence, to prove Corollary 6.2, it would suffice to show that $\llbracket P \rrbracket^\tau$ (without $!\mathcal{F}'_{crypto}$, i.e., $!M_1 \mid \cdots \mid !M_l$) is non-committing and used-order respecting. However, this might not be the case because it is not clear what happens in corrupted sessions. For uncorrupted sessions, we can use the mapping lemma (and the fact that the symbolic protocol is symbolically standard and preserves key secrecy) and can hence deduce that nothing bad happens. This is not possible for corrupted sessions because there the mapping lemma does not hold. Fortunately, corrupted sessions are easy to deal with: the simulator can corrupt this session of $\mathcal{F}_{ke}$ and then precisely simulate the protocol. We now use this idea to prove Corollary 6.2.

First, we show that one session of $!M_1 \mid \cdots \mid !M_l \mid !\mathcal{P}_{crypto}^{ST} \mid !\mathcal{F}_{senc}$, i.e., short-term keys are treated in the *real* way (as in $\mathcal{P}_{crypto}$) but long-term keys are still treated *ideally* (as in $\mathcal{F}_{crypto}$), realizes one session of $!\mathcal{F}_{ke}$. More precisely, we show that

$$!M_1 \mid \cdots \mid !M_l \mid !\mathcal{P}_{crypto}^{ST} \mid !\mathcal{F}_{senc} \leq_{\sigma_{prefix}\text{-single}} !\mathcal{F}_{ke} .$$

Then, using Corollary 4.3 ($!\mathcal{P}_{senc}^{js} \mid !\mathcal{P}_{senc} \leq !\mathcal{F}_{senc}$) and the composition theorems, we obtain the statement of the corollary: $\llbracket P \rrbracket_{JS}^\tau \leq !\mathcal{F}_{ke}$.

As described in Section 5.4, it holds that $\mathcal{F}^* \mid \mathcal{P}^{\text{ST}}_{\text{crypto}} \mid !\mathcal{F}_{\text{senc}} \leq \mathcal{F}^* \mid \mathcal{F}'_{\text{crypto}}$. That is, we find a simulator $\mathcal{S}_{\mathcal{F}_{\text{crypto}}}$ such that for every non-committing and used-order respecting environment $\mathcal{E}$ (i.e., $\mathcal{E}$ triggers the error flag in $\mathcal{F}^*$ only with negligible probability, see Section 5.3.2 for details):

$$\mathcal{E} \mid \mathcal{P}^{\text{ST}}_{\text{crypto}} \mid !\mathcal{F}_{\text{senc}} \equiv \mathcal{E} \mid \mathcal{S}_{\mathcal{F}'_{\text{crypto}}} \mid \mathcal{F}'_{\text{crypto}} . \tag{C.1}$$

By definition of $\mathcal{F}'_{\text{crypto}}$ (because it supports corruption status requests) it follows that, with overwhelming probability, $\mathcal{S}_{\mathcal{F}'_{\text{crypto}}}$ corrupts keys in $\mathcal{F}_{\text{crypto}}$ only if instructed by $\mathcal{E}$.[89] By Lemma 2.1, we may assume that $\mathcal{S}_{\mathcal{F}'_{\text{crypto}}}$ is a single IITM that accepts all messages in mode CheckAddress.

By Theorem 6.1 (as mentioned above, the proof of this theorem can be adapted to work with the variant $\mathcal{F}'_{\text{crypto}}$ instead of $\mathcal{F}_{\text{crypto}}$), we find a simulator $\mathcal{S}_{\mathcal{F}_{\text{ke}}}$ such that for every environment $\mathcal{E}$:

$$\mathcal{E} \mid !M_1 \mid \cdots \mid !M_l \mid !\underline{\mathcal{F}'_{\text{crypto}}} \equiv \mathcal{E} \mid \mathcal{S}_{\mathcal{F}_{\text{ke}}} \mid !\underline{\mathcal{F}_{\text{ke}}} . \tag{C.2}$$

As the proofs of Theorem 6.1 and the composition theorem for unbounded self-composition (Theorem 2.3) reveal, we may assume that $\mathcal{S}_{\mathcal{F}_{\text{ke}}}$ is of the form $\mathcal{S}_{\mathcal{F}_{\text{ke}}} = !M$ for some IITM M such that for every session (with SID) sid there is one instance of M, denoted by $\mathcal{S}_{\mathcal{F}_{\text{ke}}}[sid]$, that simulates that session.

Now, we define a simulator $\mathcal{S}$, to show that for all single-session environments $\mathcal{E}$ (more precisely, for all $\mathcal{E} \in \text{Env}_{\sigma_{\text{prefix-single}}}(!M_1 \mid \cdots \mid !M_l \mid !\mathcal{P}^{\text{ST}}_{\text{crypto}} \mid !\mathcal{F}_{\text{senc}})$):

$$\mathcal{E} \mid !M_1 \mid \cdots \mid !M_l \mid !\underline{\mathcal{P}^{\text{ST}}_{\text{crypto}}} \mid !\mathcal{F}_{\text{senc}} \equiv \mathcal{E} \mid \mathcal{S} \mid !\underline{\mathcal{F}_{\text{ke}}} . \tag{C.3}$$

As shown above, this will conclude the proof of Corollary 6.2.

We define the simulator $\mathcal{S}$ as follows. Recall that it only needs to work for a single session. If the (single-session) environment corrupts a long-term key (i.e., some instance of $\mathcal{F}_{\text{senc}}$) or a role (i.e., M_1 or M_2), then $\mathcal{S}$ corrupts $\mathcal{F}_{\text{ke}}[sid]$, where sid is the SID of the protocol session initiated by the environment, and precisely simulates $!M_1 \mid \cdots \mid !M_l \mid !\underline{\mathcal{P}^{\text{ST}}_{\text{crypto}}} \mid !\mathcal{F}_{\text{senc}}$ (since $\mathcal{F}_{\text{ke}}[sid]$ is corrupted it allows $\mathcal{S}$ to produce arbitrary output to its I/O interface). Otherwise, $\mathcal{S}$ simulates $!\mathcal{S}_{\mathcal{F}'_{\text{crypto}}} \mid \mathcal{S}_{\mathcal{F}_{\text{ke}}}$ (in fact, only one instance of $\mathcal{S}_{\mathcal{F}'_{\text{crypto}}}$ and $\mathcal{S}_{\mathcal{F}_{\text{ke}}}$, namely $\mathcal{S}_{\mathcal{F}'_{\text{crypto}}}[sid]$ and $\mathcal{S}_{\mathcal{F}_{\text{ke}}}[sid]$, need to be simulated because the environment is single-session). Note that because of static corruption, $\mathcal{S}$ knows whether it is in the corrupted or uncorrupted case.

Now, let $\mathcal{E} \in \text{Env}_{\sigma_{\text{prefix-single}}}(!M_1 \mid \cdots \mid !M_l \mid !\mathcal{P}^{\text{ST}}_{\text{crypto}} \mid !\mathcal{F}_{\text{senc}})$ be any single-session environment. We need to show (C.3). Since the cases where $\mathcal{E}$ corrupts (any long-term key or role) are trivial (because then $\mathcal{S}$ precisely simulates the protocol) and corruption is static, it is easy to see that, if (C.3) holds for environments that do not

---

[89]We note that the simulator constructed in Section 5.3.2 corrupts keys in $\mathcal{F}_{\text{crypto}}$ only if instructed by the environment, so, we could also just take this simulator.

corrupt, this implies that (C.3) holds for all single-session environments. Hence, we now assume that $\mathcal{E}$ never corrupts (any long-term key or role).

Since $\mathcal{E}$ does not corrupt, by definition of $\mathcal{S}$ we have that

$$\mathcal{E} \,|\, \mathcal{S} \,|\, !\underline{\mathcal{F}_{\text{ke}}} \equiv \mathcal{E} \,|\, !\mathcal{S}_{\mathcal{F}'_{\text{crypto}}} \,|\, \mathcal{S}_{\mathcal{F}_{\text{ke}}} \,|\, !\underline{\mathcal{F}_{\text{ke}}} \qquad \text{(definition of } \mathcal{S})$$

$$\equiv \mathcal{E} \,|\, !\mathcal{S}_{\mathcal{F}'_{\text{crypto}}} \,|\, !M_1 \,|\, \cdots \,|\, !M_l \,|\, !\underline{\mathcal{F}'_{\text{crypto}}} \qquad \text{(C.2).}$$

The latter equivalence follows with the composition theorems and (C.2) (and taking $\mathcal{E} = \mathcal{E} \,|\, !\mathcal{S}_{\mathcal{F}'_{\text{crypto}}}$).

Now, we know that (almost) all traces t of $\mathcal{E} \,|\, !\mathcal{S}_{\mathcal{F}_{\text{crypto}}} \,|\, !M_1 \,|\, \cdots \,|\, !M_l \,|\, !\underline{\mathcal{F}'_{\text{crypto}}}$ are uncorrupted because $\mathcal{E}$ does not corrupt and $!\mathcal{S}_{\mathcal{F}'_{\text{crypto}}}$ only corrupts if $\mathcal{E}$ corrupts (except with negligible probability), and hence, by Lemma 6.4, are DY. Now, since $\mathcal{P}$ preserves key secrecy it follows with Lemma 6.2 (all used keys are always marked unknown) that the commitment problem does not occur. Hence, the environment $\mathcal{E}' := \mathcal{E} \,|\, !M_1 \,|\, \cdots \,|\, !M_l$ is non-committing. Moreover, the used-order can only be violated if a used short-term key is later encrypted by another short-term key. Assume that this happens, i.e., that there exist bit strings k, k' which are short-term keys in $\mathcal{F}_{\text{crypto}}$ such that k has been used for encryption and is later encrypted by k'. Then, by definition of the M_i's, there exist terms $s_1, s_2, r, s_1', s_2', r'$ such that $\llbracket s_2 \rrbracket_t = (\text{key}, k)$, $\llbracket s_2' \rrbracket_t = (\text{key}, k')$, and $\llbracket s_1' \rrbracket_t$ contains (key, k). Furthermore, some M_i computed the computational interpretation of $\{s_1\}_{s_2}^r$, i.e., $\llbracket \{s_1\}_{s_2}^r \rrbracket_t$, and later some $M_{i'}$ computed the computational interpretation of $\{s_1'\}_{s_2'}^{r'}$, i.e., $\llbracket \{s_1'\}_{s_2'}^{r'} \rrbracket_t$. Let $n, n' \in \mathcal{N}_{\text{st}}$ be the names corresponding to the short-term keys k and k', respectively. By (6.1) and (6.2) in the proof of Lemma 6.3 and by the definition of ψ_t we have that:

$$s_2 \sigma_t^{\text{in}} =_E \psi_t(\llbracket s_2 \rrbracket_t) = \psi_t((\text{key}, k)) = \text{sk}(n) \ ,$$

$$s_2' \sigma_t^{\text{in}} =_E \psi_t(\llbracket s_2' \rrbracket_t) = \psi_t((\text{key}, k')) = \text{sk}(n') \ , \text{ and}$$

$$s_1' \sigma_t^{\text{in}} =_E \psi_t(\llbracket s_1' \rrbracket_t) \ .$$

Furthermore, because $\llbracket s_1' \rrbracket_t$ contains (key, k), by definition of ψ_t, we have that $\psi_t(\llbracket s_1' \rrbracket_t)$ contains $\text{sk}(n)$ in clear (i.e., only under pairing). By definition of $\text{symb}(t)$ we can conclude that in $\text{symb}(t)$ the short-term key n was used for encryption (in the term $\{s_1\}_{s_2}^r$) before n was encrypted by n' (in the term $\{s_1'\}_{s_2'}^{r'}$). This contradicts our assumption that $\mathcal{P}$ is symbolically standard, hence, used-order violations never occur in t. Thus, $\mathcal{E}'$ is used-order respecting.

Since $\mathcal{E}'$ is non-committing and used-order respecting, we obtain that:

$$\mathcal{E} \,|\, !M_1 \,|\, \cdots \,|\, !M_l \,|\, !\underline{\mathcal{P}_{\text{crypto}}^{\text{ST}}} \,|\, !\underline{\mathcal{F}_{\text{senc}}} \equiv \mathcal{E}' \,|\, !\underline{\mathcal{P}_{\text{crypto}}^{\text{ST}}} \,|\, !\underline{\mathcal{F}_{\text{senc}}} \qquad \text{(definition of } \mathcal{E}')$$

$$\equiv \mathcal{E}' \,|\, !\mathcal{S}_{\mathcal{F}'_{\text{crypto}}} \,|\, !\underline{\mathcal{F}_{\text{crypto}}'} \qquad \text{(C.1).}$$

The latter equivalence follows with the composition theorems and (C.1). Since it holds that $\mathcal{E}' \,|\, !\mathcal{S}_{\mathcal{F}'_{\text{crypto}}} \,|\, !\underline{\mathcal{F}'_{\text{crypto}}} \equiv \mathcal{E} \,|\, \mathcal{S} \,|\, !\underline{\mathcal{F}_{\text{ke}}}$ (see above), (C.3) follows. This concludes the proof of Corollary 6.2.

D. Details and Proofs for Protocol Analysis Without Pre-Established SIDs

In this appendix, we provide proofs of the general composition theorem without pre-established SIDs (Theorem 7.4) and the joint state composition theorem without pre-established SIDs (Theorem 7.5) and more details concerning our applications in Section 7.7.

D.1. Proof of Theorem 7.4

In this section, we prove Theorem 7.4 from Section 7.5. Therefore, as in the theorem, let $\mathcal{P}$ be a multi-session real protocol of the protocol class defined in Section 7.5 that uses a multi-session local-SID functionality $\mathcal{F}'$. Furthermore, let $\mathcal{F}$ be a multi-session local-SID functionality such that $\mathcal{P} \mid \mathcal{F}'$ single-session realizes $\mathcal{F}$ with a well-formed simulator (i.e., $\mathcal{P} \mid \mathcal{F}' \leq_{\text{single}*} \mathcal{F}$). That is, there exists a simulator $\mathcal{S}' \in \text{Sim}^{\mathcal{P} \mid \mathcal{F}'}(\mathcal{F})$ such that $\mathcal{S}'$ is well-formed and for every single-session environment $\mathcal{E} \in \text{Env}_{\text{single}}(\mathcal{P} \mid \mathcal{F}')$:

$$\mathcal{E} \mid \mathcal{P} \mid \mathcal{F}' \equiv \mathcal{E} \mid \mathcal{S}' \mid \mathcal{F} . \tag{D.1}$$

We now use this "single-session" simulator $\mathcal{S}'$ to define a simulator $\mathcal{S} \in \text{Sim}^{\mathcal{P} \mid \mathcal{F}'}(\mathcal{F})$ and then show that $\mathcal{E} \mid \mathcal{P} \mid \mathcal{F}' \equiv \mathcal{E} \mid \mathcal{S} \mid \mathcal{F}$ for every environment $\mathcal{E} \in \text{Env}(\mathcal{P} \mid \mathcal{F}')$, which proves Theorem 7.4. Without loss of generality, we may assume that $\mathcal{S}'$ is a single IITM that accepts every message in mode CheckAddress (Lemma 2.1).

The simulator. Recall that $\mathcal{F}$ and $\mathcal{F}'$ are multi-session local-SID functionalities, i.e., they are of the form $\mathcal{F} = \mathcal{F}_{\text{session}}^{F} = \mathcal{F}_{\text{session}} \mid !F$ and $\mathcal{F}' = \mathcal{F}_{\text{session}}^{F'} = \mathcal{F}_{\text{session}}' \mid !F'$ for some σ_{prefix}-session versions F and F' and all messages to/from F and F' are prefixed by SIDs. To easily distinguish between $\mathcal{F}_{\text{session}}$ in $\mathcal{F}$ and $\mathcal{F}'$, respectively, we refer to $\mathcal{F}_{\text{session}}$ in $\mathcal{F}'$ by $\mathcal{F}_{\text{session}}'$ and to $\mathcal{F}_{\text{session}}$ in $\mathcal{F}$ by $\mathcal{F}_{\text{session}}$.

The simulator $\mathcal{S}$ is an IITM that has the same network interface as $\mathcal{P} \mid \mathcal{F}'$ and connects to the network interface of $\mathcal{F}$ (i.e., $\mathcal{S} \mid \mathcal{F}$ has the same external interface as $\mathcal{P} \mid \mathcal{F}'$). It accepts all messages in mode CheckAddress and operates as follows in mode Compute. Basically, $\mathcal{S}$ just emulates the system $\mathcal{P} \mid \mathcal{F}'$ for every user until this user gets assigned an SID in $\mathcal{F}'$ (i.e., in $\mathcal{F}_{\text{session}}'$) or gets corrupted. Furthermore, $\mathcal{S}$ emulates one copy of the "single-session" simulator $\mathcal{S}'$ for every SID and one copy for every corrupted user. When a user gets assigned an SID or gets corrupted, then the respective copy of $\mathcal{S}'$ is used to continue the simulation for this user.

More formally, S maintains a status for every user and copies of S' that are denoted by $S'[sid]$ for SID sid and by $S'[(lsid, r)]$ for the corrupted user $(lsid, r)$. In the following description, when we say that S emulates one of these copies of S' (with some input), then we implicitly assume that, if this copy does not already exist, S initializes it by a new copy of S'. Furthermore, when the emulation stops, say with output m (to the environment or $\mathcal{F}$), then S forwards this output. If the output is the empty output, then S produces empty output too. The recorded configuration of every copy is updated after every emulation, so that the next emulation of this copy resumes in the old configuration. Now, we describe S in mode Compute:

1. For every message m that S receives from $\mathcal{F}_{\text{session}}$, S does the following. Note that, by definition of $\mathcal{F}_{\text{session}}$, m is of the form (Establish, $lsid, r$) or (Input, $lsid, r, m'$) (or Ack but this input is treated below).

   a) If $m =$ (Establish, $lsid, r$) for some user $(lsid, r)$ (i.e., the Establish request from user $(lsid, r)$ has been forwarded by $\mathcal{F}_{\text{session}}$ to S), then S sets the status of $(lsid, r)$ to waiting-for-corruption and outputs $(lsid, \text{Establish})$ on the network output tape of M_r.

   b) If $m =$ (Input, $lsid, r, m'$) for some user $(lsid, r)$ and message m' (i.e., the user $(lsid, r)$ is corrupted in $\mathcal{F}_{\text{session}}$ and its input m' has been forwarded by $\mathcal{F}_{\text{session}}$ to S), then S emulates $S'[(lsid, r)]$ with input m from $\mathcal{F}_{\text{session}}$ (and forwards the output as described above). (Note that, since $(lsid, r)$ is corrupted in $\mathcal{F}_{\text{session}}$, the status of $(lsid, r)$ must be corrupted and, hence, we use the copy of S' for the corrupted user $(lsid, r)$.)

2. For every message (sid, m) that S receives from F, S emulates $S'[sid]$ with input (sid, m) from F (and forwards the output as described above). (Note that every message from F is of the form (sid, m) because F is an σ_{prefix}-session version.)

3. For every message m that S receives from the environment on the network input tape of M_r (for some $r \leq n$), S does the following:

   a) If $m =$ ($lsid$, corr) for some $lsid$ and corr $\in \{0, 1\}$ and the status of user $(lsid, r)$ is waiting-for-corruption, then S does the following. If corr $= 1$ (i.e., the environment wants to corrupt $M_r[lsid]$ right from the start), then S sets the status of $(lsid, r)$ to corrupted, emulates $S'[(lsid, r)]$ with input m on the network input tape of M_r (and forwards the output as described above). Otherwise (i.e., corr $= 0$), S sets the status of $(lsid, r)$ to waiting-for-$\mathcal{F}'$ and outputs (Establish, $lsid, r$) on the network output tape of $\mathcal{F}'_{\text{session}}$.

   b) If $m =$ ($lsid, m'$) for some $lsid, m'$ and the status of user $(lsid, r)$ is established-sid for some SID sid, then S emulates $S'[sid]$ with input m on the network input tape of M_r (and forwards the output as described above).

   c) If $m =$ ($lsid, m'$) for some $lsid, m'$ and the status of user $(lsid, r)$ is corrupted, then S emulates $S'[(lsid, r)]$ with input m on the network input tape of M_r (and forwards the output as described above).

   d) Otherwise (i.e., no case above applies), S produces empty output.

4. For every message m that S receives from the environment on the network input tape of $\mathcal{F}'_{\text{session}}$, S does the following:

   a) If $m = (\text{Establish}, lsid, r, sid)$ for some $lsid, r, sid$, the status of user $(lsid, r)$ is waiting-for-$\mathcal{F}'$, and this is a valid request to set this SID for this user (i.e., $\mathcal{F}'_{\text{session}}$ would accept it, which means that $lsid$ and sid contain the same session parameters and that no user in role r has status established-sid), then S sets the status of $(lsid, r)$ to established-sid and emulates $S'[sid]$ with input m on the network input tape of $\mathcal{F}'_{\text{session}}$ (and forwards output as described above).

   b) If $m = (\text{Corr}, lsid, r)$ for some $lsid, r$ and the status of user $(lsid, r)$ is waiting-for-$\mathcal{F}'$, then S sets the status of $(lsid, r)$ to corrupted and emulates $S'[(lsid, r)]$ with input m on the network input tape of $\mathcal{F}'_{\text{session}}$ (and forwards output as described above).

   c) If $m = (\text{Output}, lsid, r, m')$ for some $lsid, r, m'$ and the status of user $(lsid, r)$ is corrupted, then S emulates $S'[(lsid, r)]$ with input m on the network input tape of $\mathcal{F}'_{\text{session}}$ (and forwards output as described above).

   d) Otherwise (i.e., no case above applies), S produces empty output.

5. For every message m that S receives from the environment on a network input tape of F', S does the following: If $m = (sid, m')$ for some sid, m', then S emulates $S'[sid]$ with input m on the same network input tape of F' (and forwards the output as described above). Otherwise, S produces empty output.

   We note that some messages are held back from the emulated copies of S': Establish messages from users are directly forwarded by S to the environment (see case 1. a)) and the responses to these where the environment decided not to corrupt the user right from the start are also directly handled by S, without using S' (see case 3. a)). In both these cases, it is not clear to S what copy of S' should be used because no SID has been set for this user and it is not yet corrupted. However, by our assumption that S' is well-formed (Definition 7.5), we know exactly what S' would do in these cases, namely what S does. Furthermore, the state of S' does not depend on whether it received these messages or not, so, the emulation of S' by S is faithful, as we see below.

   Since $S' \,|\, \mathcal{F}$ is environmentally strictly bounded (S' is well-formed) and all sessions in a run of $S \,|\, \mathcal{F}$ are basically disjoint, similar to Lemma 2.4, it is easy to show that $S \,|\, \mathcal{F}$ is environmentally strictly bounded. Hence, we have that $S \in \text{Sim}^{\mathcal{P} \,|\, \mathcal{F}'}(\mathcal{F})$.

Fixing an environment. For the rest of the proof, we fix an environment $\mathcal{E} \in \text{Env}(\mathcal{P} \,|\, \mathcal{F}')$. Without loss of generality, we may assume that $\mathcal{E}$ is a single IITM that accepts all messages in mode CheckAddress (Lemma 2.2). Furthermore, we assume that $\mathcal{E}$ has the external tapes start and decision (otherwise, $\mathcal{E} \,|\, \mathcal{P} \,|\, \mathcal{F}' \equiv \mathcal{E} \,|\, S \,|\, \mathcal{F}$ would be satisfied trivially). Let $p_{\mathcal{E}}$ be a polynomial (in the security parameter η plus the length of the external input a) that bounds the overall runtime (i.e., taken steps) of $\mathcal{E}$. (By definition of environmental systems such a polynomial exists.) Since only $\mathcal{E}$ can create new instances of machines in $\mathcal{P}$ by sending requests to them, the overall number of these instances is bounded by $p_{\mathcal{E}}(\eta + |a|)$ (η is the security parameter and a is the external input, which we often omit in the following).

Hybrid systems. Next, we define hybrid systems $\mathcal{H}_i$ for all $i \in \mathbb{N}$. Basically, $\mathcal{H}_i$ emulates $\mathcal{E}$ interacting with $\mathcal{P} \,|\, \mathcal{F}'$ and $\mathcal{S} \,|\, \mathcal{F}$, respectively, such that the first $i - 1$ sessions are handled by $\mathcal{P} \,|\, \mathcal{F}'$ and all later sessions are handled by $\mathcal{S} \,|\, \mathcal{F}$. We note that every corrupted user (more precisely, a user which became corrupted before it obtained a SID) is treated as its own session, see below.

The hybrid system $\mathcal{H}_i$, for every $i \in \mathbb{N}$, is an IITM that has only two external tapes: start and decision. It maintains a list L. This list, which is initially empty, is used to record all sessions where a session is identified by a SID sid or a corrupted user $(lsid, r)$. The systems $\mathcal{E}$, $\mathcal{P} \,|\, \mathcal{F}'$, and $\mathcal{S} \,|\, \mathcal{F}$ are emulated as follows. When activated for the first time (i.e., with some external input a on tape start), $\mathcal{H}_i$ starts the simulation of $\mathcal{E}$ (with the same external input a and the same security parameter). The simulation continues as follows:

1. When $\mathcal{E}$ sends a message of the form $(lsid, \mathsf{Establish})$ to a role r in $\mathcal{P}$ (i.e., to $M_r[lsid]$) on the I/O tape such that this message has not been sent before (i.e., the user $(lsid, r)$ is inactive in $\mathcal{F}'$), then $\mathcal{H}_i$ does the following. It simulates $\mathcal{P} \,|\, \mathcal{F}'$ with input of this message. By definition of our class of protocols, this will trigger $M_r[lsid]$ to forward this request to its network interface. Then, $\mathcal{H}_i$ also simulates $\mathcal{S} \,|\, \mathcal{F}$ with input of the same message and this will trigger $\mathcal{S}$ to also forward this request. Finally, $\mathcal{H}_i$ continues the simulation of $\mathcal{E}$ as if $\mathcal{E}$ received this Establish request from $M_r[lsid]$. (We note that now in both systems $\mathcal{P} \,|\, \mathcal{F}'$ and $\mathcal{S} \,|\, \mathcal{F}$ the user $(lsid, r)$ is now active and waiting for "corruption right from the start". Of course, if this user will be corrupted, this will only happen in one of the two systems, see below.)

2. When $\mathcal{E}$ sends a message of the form $(lsid, corr)$ with $corr \in \{0, 1\}$ to a role r in $\mathcal{P}$ (i.e., to $M_r[lsid]$) on the network tape such that this user is "waiting for corruption right from the start" (see above), then we distinguish two cases:

   If $corr = 1$ (i.e., this user is corrupted right from the start), then $\mathcal{H}_i$ appends $(lsid, r)$ to the end of L and records the user $(lsid, r)$ as *corrupted*. Let $j \geq 1$ be the position where $(lsid, r)$ occurs in L (starting to count from 1). Then:

   a) If $j < i$, then $\mathcal{H}_i$ forwards $(lsid, corr)$ to $\mathcal{P} \,|\, \mathcal{F}'$.

   b) If $j \geq i$, then $\mathcal{H}_i$ forwards $(lsid, corr)$ to $\mathcal{S} \,|\, \mathcal{F}$.

   If $corr = 0$, $\mathcal{H}_i$ simulates $\mathcal{P} \,|\, \mathcal{F}'$ with input of the message $(lsid, corr)$. By definition of our class of protocols, this will trigger $M_r[lsid]$ to send an Establish request to $\mathcal{F}'$ and, by definition of multi-session local-SID functionalities, $\mathcal{F}'$

(more precisely, $\mathcal{F}'_{\text{session}}$ in $\mathcal{F}'$) will forward this Establish request to its network interface. Then, $\mathcal{H}_i$ also simulates $\mathcal{S}\,|\,\mathcal{F}$ with input of the same message $(lsid, corr)$ and this will trigger $\mathcal{S}$ to output the same Establish request. Finally, $\mathcal{H}_i$ continues the simulation of $\mathcal{E}$ as if $\mathcal{E}$ received this Establish request from $\mathcal{F}'$. (We note that now in both systems $\mathcal{P}\,|\,\mathcal{F}'$ and $\mathcal{S}\,|\,\mathcal{F}$ the user $(lsid, r)$ is active and waiting for $\mathcal{F}'$, i.e., an SID can be set for this user in $\mathcal{F}'$ or it can be corrupted in $\mathcal{F}'$. (Of course, this will only happen in one of the two systems, see below.)

3. When $\mathcal{E}$ sends an Establish request, say $(\mathsf{Establish}, lsid, r, sid)$, to the network interface of ($\mathcal{F}'_{\text{session}}$ in) $\mathcal{F}'$ to set the SID for a user and this request is valid (i.e., $\mathcal{F}'$ and $\mathcal{S}$ would not ignore it and produce empty output), then $\mathcal{H}_i$ records the SID sid for user $(lsid, r)$ and does the following. If sid does not occur in L, $\mathcal{H}_i$ appends sid at the end of L. Let $j \geq 1$ be the position where sid occurs in L. Then:

   a) If $j < i$, then $\mathcal{H}_i$ forwards the Establish request to $\mathcal{P}\,|\,\mathcal{F}'$.

   b) If $j \geq i$, then $\mathcal{H}_i$ forwards the Establish request to $\mathcal{S}\,|\,\mathcal{F}$.

4. When $\mathcal{E}$ sends a Corr request, say $(\mathsf{Corr}, lsid, r)$, to the network interface of ($\mathcal{F}'_{\text{session}}$ in) $\mathcal{F}'$ to corrupt a user and this request is valid (i.e., $\mathcal{F}'$ and $\mathcal{S}$ would not ignore it and produce empty output), then $\mathcal{H}_i$ records the user $(lsid, r)$ as *corrupted* and appends $(lsid, r)$ to the end of L. Let $j \geq 1$ be the position where $(lsid, r)$ occurs in L. Then:

   a) If $j < i$, then $\mathcal{H}_i$ forwards the Corr request to $\mathcal{P}\,|\,\mathcal{F}'$.

   b) If $j \geq i$, then $\mathcal{H}_i$ forwards the Corr request to $\mathcal{S}\,|\,\mathcal{F}$.

5. When $\mathcal{E}$ sends an Output request, say $(\mathsf{Output}, lsid, r, m)$, to the network interface of ($\mathcal{F}'_{\text{session}}$ in) $\mathcal{F}'$ to produce output for a corrupted user and this request is valid (i.e., this user has in fact been corrupted by a Corr request to $\mathcal{F}'$, see above), then $\mathcal{H}_i$ does the following. Let $j \geq 1$ be the position where $(lsid, r)$ occurs in L (it must occur in L because $(lsid, r)$ is corrupted). Then:

   a) If $j < i$, then $\mathcal{H}_i$ forwards the Output request to $\mathcal{P}\,|\,\mathcal{F}'$.

   b) If $j \geq i$, then $\mathcal{H}_i$ forwards the Output request to $\mathcal{S}\,|\,\mathcal{F}$.

6. When $\mathcal{E}$ sends a message of the form (sid, m) to the network interface of $\mathcal{F}'$ (recall that $\mathcal{F}' = \mathcal{F}^{\mathcal{F}'}_{\text{session}} = \mathcal{F}'_{\text{session}}\,|\,!\mathcal{F}'$), then $\mathcal{H}_i$ does the following. As above, if sid does not occur in L, $\mathcal{H}_i$ appends sid at the end of L. Let $j \geq 1$ be the position where sid occurs in L. Then:

   a) If $j < i$, then $\mathcal{H}_i$ forwards (sid, m) to $\mathcal{P}\,|\,\mathcal{F}'$.

   b) If $j \geq i$, then $\mathcal{H}_i$ forwards (sid, m) to $\mathcal{S}\,|\,\mathcal{F}$.

7. When $\mathcal{E}$ sends a message of the form $(lsid, m)$ to role r in $\mathcal{P}$ (i.e., to $M_r[lsid]$) on the I/O or network tape (and this is not one of the messages mentioned above), then $\mathcal{H}_i$ does the following.

   If the user $(lsid, r)$ is not recorded as corrupted and there is no recorded SID for user $(lsid, r)$, then $\mathcal{H}_i$ continues the simulation of $\mathcal{E}$ as if $M_r[lsid]$ produces empty output (i.e., $\mathcal{E}$ is triggered with empty input because it is the master IITM); except if this is a corruption status request (i.e., send on the I/O tape and $m = \mathsf{Corr?}$), in this case, $\mathcal{H}_i$ continues the simulation of $\mathcal{E}$ as if $M_r[lsid]$ returned $(lsid, 0)$ to $\mathcal{E}$ (i.e., reports its status as being uncorrupted).

   Otherwise, $(lsid, r)$ is recorded as corrupted or an SID has been recorded for $(lsid, r)$. In the former case, let $j \geq 1$ be the position where $(lsid, r)$ occurs in L (it must occur in L because $(lsid, r)$ is corrupted). In the latter case, let $j \geq 1$ be the position where the SID recorded for $(lsid, r)$ occurs in L (it must occur in L because it has been recorded for $(lsid, r)$). Then:

   a) If $j < i$, then $\mathcal{H}_i$ forwards $(lsid, m)$ to $\mathcal{P} \,|\, \mathcal{F}'$.

   b) If $j \geq i$, then $\mathcal{H}_i$ forwards $(lsid, m)$ to $\mathcal{S} \,|\, \mathcal{F}$.

8. When $\mathcal{E}$ sends a message to decision or produces empty output in its activation, then $\mathcal{H}_i$ outputs this message on decision or stops with empty output, respectively. In any case, this terminates the run because $\mathcal{E}$ is the master IITM.

9. When $\mathcal{E}$ sends a message different from any message mentioned above, then $\mathcal{H}_i$ continues the simulation of $\mathcal{E}$ as if the receiver of this message produces empty output (i.e., $\mathcal{E}$ is triggered with empty input because it is the master IITM).

10. When $\mathcal{P} \,|\, \mathcal{F}'$ or $\mathcal{S} \,|\, \mathcal{F}$ sends a message (on some I/O or network tape) to $\mathcal{E}$ (or ends its activation with empty output), then $\mathcal{H}_i$ forwards this message to $\mathcal{E}$ (or triggers $\mathcal{E}$ with empty input, respectively).

Since $\mathcal{P} \,|\, \mathcal{F}'$ and $\mathcal{S} \,|\, \mathcal{F}$ are environmentally strictly bounded and these two systems are simulated by $\mathcal{H}_i$ as if they have disjoint tapes (all communication between them goes through $\mathcal{E}$), similar to Lemma 2.3 and because $\mathcal{E}$ is universally bounded, it is easy to see that $\mathcal{H}_i$ is strictly bounded for all $i \in \mathbb{N}$.

Additionally to the above hybrid systems, we define $\mathcal{H}_{p_\mathcal{E}+1}$ to be the IITM that is defined just as $\mathcal{H}_i$ except that it uses $p_\mathcal{E}(\eta + |a|) + 1$ instead of i. That is, all sessions are handled by $\mathcal{P} \,|\, \mathcal{F}'$ because $\mathcal{E}$ creates at most $p_\mathcal{E}(\eta + |a|)$ sessions. In particularly, we have that:

$$\mathcal{H}_{p_\mathcal{E}+1} \equiv \mathcal{E} \,|\, \mathcal{P} \,|\, \mathcal{F}' \ . \tag{D.2}$$

Similarly, by construction, $\mathcal{H}_1$ forwards all sessions to $\mathcal{S} \,|\, \mathcal{F}$ and we have that:

$$\mathcal{H}_1 \equiv \mathcal{E} \,|\, \mathcal{S} \,|\, \mathcal{F} \ . \tag{D.3}$$

We note that the above two statements require that $\mathcal{P}$ is from the class of real world protocols defined in Section 7.5 and that the "single-session" simulator $\mathcal{S}'$

(that is used in the construction of $\mathcal{S}$) is well-formed. If $\mathcal{P}$ would not belong to this class of protocols, $\mathcal{H}_{p_\mathcal{E}+1}$ might deviate from $\mathcal{E} \mid \mathcal{P} \mid \mathcal{F}'$ upon messages from $\mathcal{E}$ to instances of the machines in $\mathcal{P}$ if their SID is not yet set or they are not yet corrupted ($\mathcal{H}_{p_\mathcal{E}+1}$ simply produces empty output and this is required from $\mathcal{P}$ too). If the simulator would not be well-formed, $\mathcal{H}_1$ might deviate from $\mathcal{E} \mid \mathcal{S} \mid \mathcal{F}$ upon $(lsid, \mathsf{Establish})$ requests and upon network messages to instances of the machines in $\mathcal{P}$ if their SID is not yet set or they are not yet corrupted ($\mathcal{H}_1$ simply produces empty output and this is required from well-formed simulators too).

To show that $\mathcal{H}_i$ is indistinguishable from $\mathcal{H}_{i+1}$, for all $i \in \mathbb{N}$, we introduce hybrid systems $\mathcal{H}^*_{i,i_1,\ldots,i_n}$, for all $i \in \mathbb{N}$ and $i_1, \ldots, i_n \in \mathbb{N} \cup \{\bot\}$, which are supposed to be single-session environments for $\mathcal{P} \mid \mathcal{F}'$ (i.e., $\mathcal{H}^*_{i,i_1,\ldots,i_n} \in \mathrm{Env}_{\mathrm{single}}(\mathcal{P} \mid \mathcal{F}')$) and to distinguish between $\mathcal{P} \mid \mathcal{F}'$ and $\mathcal{S}' \mid \mathcal{F}$. First, we define the notion of the "i'-th user" (similar to the notion of the i-th session). The i'-th user for $i' \in \mathbb{N}$ in a run of $\mathcal{H}_i$ is the user $(lsid, r)$ if $M_r[lsid]$ is the i'-th instance (of the machines in $\mathcal{P}$) that has been created during the emulation of $\mathcal{H}_i$. (If such a user does not exist, then the i'-th user is undefined.) For example, if the first request of the form $(lsid_1, \mathsf{Establish})$ is sent to role r_1 by $\mathcal{E}$, then $(lsid_1, r_1)$ is the first user in this run of $\mathcal{H}_i$. The second such request (to any role) defines the second user and so on.

Similar to $\mathcal{H}_i$, $\mathcal{H}^*_{i,i_1,\ldots,i_n}$ emulates $\mathcal{E}$ interacting with $\mathcal{P} \mid \mathcal{F}'$ and $\mathcal{S} \mid \mathcal{F}$ but the i-th session (where we count corrupted users as sessions, i.e., everything that is recorded in the list L) is now handled by the external system $\mathcal{P} \mid \mathcal{F}'$ or $\mathcal{S}' \mid \mathcal{F}$, respectively. To successfully outsource the i-th session, $\mathcal{H}^*_{i,i_1,\ldots,i_n}$ has to know which users belong to this session even before the SIDs of the users have been set. Therefore, $\mathcal{H}^*_{i,i_1,\ldots,i_n}$ is additionally parametrized by $i_1, \ldots, i_n$ which tells $\mathcal{H}^*_{i,i_1,\ldots,i_n}$ that the i_r-th user plays role r in the i-th session. If $i_r = \bot$, then this means that there is no user in role r in the i-th session.

The hybrid system $\mathcal{H}^*_{i,i_1,\ldots,i_n}$, for every $i \in \mathbb{N}$ and $i_1, \ldots, i_n \in \mathbb{N} \cup \{\bot\}$, is an IITM that has tapes start and decision and tapes to connect to $\mathcal{P} \mid \mathcal{F}'$ (and hence, to $\mathcal{S} \mid \mathcal{F}$). When $\mathcal{H}^*_{i,i_1,\ldots,i_n}$ sends/receives messages on the tapes that connect to $\mathcal{P} \mid \mathcal{F}'$, we say that it sends/receives messages to/from the *external system*. The machine $\mathcal{H}^*_{i,i_1,\ldots,i_n}$ maintains a list L (just as $\mathcal{H}_i$) and additionally a list of users L' and emulates $\mathcal{E}$, $\mathcal{P} \mid \mathcal{F}'$, and $\mathcal{S} \mid \mathcal{F}$ as $\mathcal{H}_i$, with the following exceptions:

1. When $\mathcal{E}$ sends a message of the form $(lsid, \mathsf{Establish})$ to a role r in $\mathcal{P}$ (i.e., to $M_r[lsid]$) on the I/O tape such that this message has not been sent before, then $\mathcal{H}^*_{i,i_1,\ldots,i_n}$ does the following. It first appends the user $(lsid, r)$ at the end of L'. Let $j' \geq 1$ be the position where $(lsid, r)$ occurs in L' (starting to count from 1). If $j' \neq i_r$, then $\mathcal{H}^*_{i,i_1,\ldots,i_n}$ continues the emulation as $\mathcal{H}_i$. If $j' = i_r$, then $\mathcal{H}^*_{i,i_1,\ldots,i_n}$ forwards the output to the external system if this does not violate the requirements for being a single-session environment (e.g., $\mathcal{H}^*_{i,i_1,\ldots,i_n}$ must not create two instances $M_{r_1}[lsid_1]$ and $M_{r_2}[lsid_2]$ such that these instances do not agree on the session parameters). If it does violate these requirements, $\mathcal{H}^*_{i,i_1,\ldots,i_n}$ outputs a special error message on the tape decision (i.e., the run stops and the

overall output is this error message); we say that $\mathcal{H}^*_{i,i_1,\ldots,i_n}$ terminates with an error.

2. When $\mathcal{H}_i$ would forward a message to $\mathcal{S}\,|\,\mathcal{F}$ where $j = i$ (i.e., for the i-th session or corrupted user), then $\mathcal{H}^*_{i,i_1,\ldots,i_n}$ instead forwards the message to the external system if this does not violate the requirements for being a single-session environment (e.g., $\mathcal{H}^*_{i,i_1,\ldots,i_n}$ must not set different SIDs for the users in the external system). If it does violate these requirements, as above, $\mathcal{H}^*_{i,i_1,\ldots,i_n}$ terminates with an error.

3. When $\mathcal{H}^*_{i,i_1,\ldots,i_n}$ receives a message from the external system, then it emulates $\mathcal{E}$ with this input.

4. When the emulated run stops with overall output m (i.e., $\mathcal{E}$ produced output m on tape decision or $\mathcal{E}$ stopped with empty output and $m = \varepsilon$ is the empty message), then $\mathcal{H}^*_{i,i_1,\ldots,i_n}$ does the following. It verifies that $i_1,\ldots,i_n \in \mathbb{N} \cup \{\bot\}$ correctly specify the i-th session: Let x be the element in the list L at position i, if L has less than i elements, then let $x = \bot$. (Note that x is either an SID sid, a corrupted user $(lsid, r)$, or $\bot$.) We say that $i_1,\ldots,i_n$ correctly specify the i-th session if $x \neq \bot$ and the following holds:

   a) If $x = sid$ is an SID, then, for every user $(lsid, r)$ in L', let i' be its position in L' (i.e., $(lsid, r)$ is the i'-th user), it holds that the SID of this user has been set to sid (i.e., a message $(\mathsf{Establish}, lsid, r, sid)$ has been sent by $\mathcal{E}$) if and only if $i' = i_r$. (That is, the i_r-th user, if $i_r \neq \bot$, actually got the SID of the i-th session sid. Furthermore, no other user got the SID of the i-th session sid.)

   b) If $x = (lsid, r)$ is a corrupted user, then $i_r \neq \bot$ and $i_{r'} = \bot$ for all $r' \neq r$ and $(lsid, r)$ is the i_r-th user (i.e., occurs on position i_r in L') and has been corrupted in the external session (i.e., $\mathcal{H}^*_{i,i_1,\ldots,i_n}$ sent a message to the external system to corrupt this user right from the start or in $\mathcal{F}'$).

   If $i_1,\ldots,i_n$ correctly specify the i-th session, then $\mathcal{H}^*_{i,i_1,\ldots,i_n}$ outputs m on tape decision, which stops the run with overall output m. Otherwise, $\mathcal{H}^*_{i,i_1,\ldots,i_n}$ terminates with an error (i.e., outputs a special error message on decision). (We note that we use this in the proof of Lemma D.1.)

Since $\mathcal{H}_i$ are strictly bounded and $\mathcal{E}$ is universally bounded, it is easy to see that $\mathcal{H}^*_{i,i_1,\ldots,i_n}$ is universally bounded. Hence, $\mathcal{H}^*_{i,i_1,\ldots,i_n} \in \mathrm{Env}(\mathcal{P}\,|\,\mathcal{F}')$.

Next, we basically show that, under the condition that $\mathcal{H}^*_{i,i_1,\ldots,i_n}$ does not terminate with an error (i.e., $i_1,\ldots,i_n$ correctly specify the i-th session), $\mathcal{H}_i$ is indistinguishable from $\mathcal{H}^*_{i,i_1,\ldots,i_n}\,|\,\mathcal{S}'\,|\,\mathcal{F}$ and that $\mathcal{H}_{i+1}$ is indistinguishable from $\mathcal{H}^*_{i,i_1,\ldots,i_n}\,|\,\mathcal{P}\,|\,\mathcal{F}'$.

First, we define events to reason about the i-th session in a run of the hybrid systems and we develop further notation: For all $i, i' \in \mathbb{N}$, we define $B_{\mathcal{H}_{i'}}(i)$ to be the set of runs of $\mathcal{H}_{i'}$ where the i-th session is never created (i.e., where, at the end of the run, L contains less than i elements) and, for all $i, i' \in \mathbb{N}$ and $i_1,\ldots,i_n \in \mathbb{N} \cup \{\bot\}$, we define $B_{\mathcal{H}_{i'}}(i, i_1, \ldots, i_n)$ to be the set of runs of $\mathcal{H}_{i'}$ where $i_1, \ldots, i_n$ correctly specify the i-th session.[90] The latter is similar to the definition "correctly specify the i-th session" above but now is formulated for the system $\mathcal{H}_{i'}$ instead of $\mathcal{H}^*_{i,i_1,\ldots,i_n}$. More precisely, $B_{\mathcal{H}_{i'}}(i, i_1, \ldots, i_n)$ is the set of runs of $\mathcal{H}_{i'}$ where, at the end of the run, the following holds:

1. The i-th session exists, i.e., the list L in $\mathcal{H}_{i'}$ has at least i elements. Let x be the element in L at position i. (Note that x is either an SID sid or a corrupted user $(lsid, r)$.)

2. If $x = sid$ is an SID, then, for every $i'' \in \mathbb{N}$ such that the i''-th user exists, say it is $(lsid, r)$, it holds that: the SID of this user has been set to sid (i.e., a message $(\text{Establish}, lsid, r, sid)$ has been sent by $\mathcal{E}$) if and only if $i'' = i_r$. (That is, the i_r-th user, if $i_r \neq \perp$, actually got the SID of the i-th session sid. Furthermore, no other user got the SID of the i-th session sid.)

3. If $x = (lsid, r)$ is a corrupted user, then $i_r \neq \perp$ and $i_{r'} = \perp$ for all $r' \neq r$ and $(lsid, r)$ is the i_r-th user and has been corrupted (i.e., $\mathcal{E}$ sent a message to corrupt this user right from the start or in $\mathcal{F}'$).

Since the i-th session either exists or not (in runs of $\mathcal{H}_{i'}$) and, if it exists, there is only one combination of $i_1, \ldots, i_n$ that specifies the i-th session, it is easy to see that, for all $i, i' \in \mathbb{N}$, the following sets are pairwise disjoint: $B_{\mathcal{H}_{i'}}(i)$ and $B_{\mathcal{H}_{i'}}(i, i_1, \ldots, i_n)$ for all $i_1, \ldots, i_n \in \mathbb{N} \cup \{\perp\}$. On the other hand, every run of $\mathcal{H}_{i'}$ belongs to one of these sets. Hence, $B_{\mathcal{H}_{i'}}(i) \cup \bigcup_{i_1,\ldots,i_n \in \mathbb{N} \cup \{\perp\}} B_{\mathcal{H}_{i'}}(i, i_1, \ldots, i_n)$ is the disjoint union of all runs of $\mathcal{H}_{i'}$. Furthermore, since $\mathcal{E}$ is bounded by $p_\mathcal{E}$, at most $p_\mathcal{E}(\eta + |a|)$ many users are created in every run of $\mathcal{H}_{i'}$ and, hence, $B_{\mathcal{H}_{i'}}(i, i_1, \ldots, i_n) = \emptyset$ for all $i, i', i_1, \ldots, i_n$ such that $\perp \neq i_r > p_\mathcal{E}(\eta + |a|)$ for some $r \leq n$. We conclude that, for all $i, i' \in \mathbb{N}$, security parameter η, and external input a:

$$
\begin{aligned}
&\Pr\left[\mathcal{H}_{i'}(1^\eta, a) = 1\right] \\
&= \Pr\left[\mathcal{H}_{i'}(1^\eta, a) = 1 \cap B_{\mathcal{H}_{i'}}(i)\right] \\
&\quad + \sum_{\substack{i_1,\ldots,i_n \in \\ \{1,\ldots,p_\mathcal{E}(\eta+|a|)\} \cup \{\perp\}}} \Pr\left[\mathcal{H}_{i'}(1^\eta, a) = 1 \cap B_{\mathcal{H}_{i'}}(i, i_1, \ldots, i_n)\right] .
\end{aligned}
\tag{D.4}
$$

As mentioned above, if $i_1, \ldots, i_n$ correctly specify the i-th session (which can now be expressed by the above set of runs), then $\mathcal{H}_i$ is indistinguishable from $\mathcal{H}^*_{i,i_1,\ldots,i_n} \mid \mathcal{S}' \mid \mathcal{F}$ and $\mathcal{H}_{i+1}$ is indistinguishable from $\mathcal{H}^*_{i,i_1,\ldots,i_n} \mid \mathcal{P} \mid \mathcal{F}'$ as the next lemma states.

---

[90]Note that we omit the security parameter η and external input a here. Formally, for every η, a, $B_{\mathcal{H}_{i'}}(i)(1^\eta, a)$ and $B_{\mathcal{H}_{i'}}(i, i_1, \ldots, i_n)(1^\eta, a)$ are the sets of runs of $\mathcal{H}_{i'}(1^\eta, a)$ that have the desired properties.

Lemma D.1. *For every security parameter $\eta \in \mathbb{N}$, external input $a \in \{0,1\}^*$, $i \in \mathbb{N}$, and $i_1, \ldots, i_n \in \mathbb{N} \cup \{\bot\}$ it holds that:*

$$\Pr\left[(\mathcal{H}^*_{i,i_1,\ldots,i_n} \mid \mathcal{S}' \mid \mathcal{F})(1^\eta, a) = 1\right] = \Pr\left[\mathcal{H}_i(1^\eta, a) = 1 \cap B_{\mathcal{H}_i}(i, i_1, \ldots, i_n)\right] \quad (D.5)$$

$$\Pr\left[(\mathcal{H}^*_{i,i_1,\ldots,i_n} \mid \mathcal{P} \mid \mathcal{F}')(1^\eta, a) = 1\right] = \Pr\left[\mathcal{H}_{i+1}(1^\eta, a) = 1 \cap B_{\mathcal{H}_{i+1}}(i, i_1, \ldots, i_n)\right] \,.$$
$$(D.6)$$

Proof. We first show (D.5). In both systems $\mathcal{H}_i$ and $\mathcal{H}^*_{i,i_1,\ldots,i_n} \mid \mathcal{S}' \mid \mathcal{F}$, the i-th session (treating corrupted users as sessions, as above) is treated as $\mathcal{S}' \mid \mathcal{F}$. It is thus easy to define an injective mapping β from $B_{\mathcal{H}_i}(i, i_1, \ldots, i_n)$ (i.e., the set of runs of $\mathcal{H}_i$ where the i-th session exists and is specified by $i_1, \ldots, i_n$) to runs of $\mathcal{H}^*_{i,i_1,\ldots,i_n} \mid \mathcal{S}' \mid \mathcal{F}$ such that for every run $\rho \in B_{\mathcal{H}_i}(i, i_1, \ldots, i_n)$, the probability of ρ and $\beta(\rho)$ is the same and ρ outputs 1 (i.e., the overall output on the tape decision is 1) if and only if $\beta(\rho)$ outputs 1. The run $\beta(\rho)$ is obtained from ρ by outsourcing the i-th session to $\mathcal{S}' \mid \mathcal{F}$. This can be done without changing the view of the environment or anything else because it is independent from any other session. Let $\operatorname{rng}(\beta)$ be the range of β, i.e., $\operatorname{rng}(\beta)$ is the set of runs ρ' of $\mathcal{H}^*_{i,i_1,\ldots,i_n} \mid \mathcal{S}' \mid \mathcal{F}$ such that there exists a run $\rho \in B_{\mathcal{H}_i}(i, i_1, \ldots, i_n)$ with $\beta(\rho) = \rho'$. That is, by β, we have shown that (for all η, a):

$$\Pr\left[\mathcal{H}_i(1^\eta, a) = 1 \cap B_{\mathcal{H}_i}(i, i_1, \ldots, i_n)\right]$$
$$= \Pr\left[(\mathcal{H}^*_{i,i_1,\ldots,i_n} \mid \mathcal{S}' \mid \mathcal{F})(1^\eta, a) = 1 \cap \operatorname{rng}(\beta)\right] \,. \quad (D.7)$$

Note that not every run of $\mathcal{H}^*_{i,i_1,\ldots,i_n} \mid \mathcal{S}' \mid \mathcal{F}$ is in the range of β, i.e., β is not surjective. Next, we show that every such run does not output 1: Therefore, let ρ' be a run of $\mathcal{H}^*_{i,i_1,\ldots,i_n} \mid \mathcal{S}' \mid \mathcal{F}$ such that $\rho' \notin \operatorname{rng}(\beta)$, i.e., there does not exist a run $\rho \in B_{\mathcal{H}_i}(i, i_1, \ldots, i_n)$ with $\alpha(\rho) = \rho'$. First, we note that if the i-th session does not exists in ρ', then by definition of $\mathcal{H}^*_{i,i_1,\ldots,i_n}$, $\mathcal{H}^*_{i,i_1,\ldots,i_n}$ never outputs 1. So, in the following, assume that the i-th session exist. If the i-th session in ρ' would be specified by $i_1, \ldots, i_n$, then there would exist $\rho \in B_{\mathcal{H}_i}(i, i_1, \ldots, i_n)$ with $\alpha(\rho) = \rho'$. (This ρ could easily be constructed from ρ'.) Hence, we can conclude that, by definition of $\mathcal{H}^*_{i,i_1,\ldots,i_n}$, $\mathcal{H}^*_{i,i_1,\ldots,i_n} \mid \mathcal{S}' \mid \mathcal{F}$ terminates with an error. In particular, the output of ρ' is not 1. We have now shown that (for all η, a):

$$\Pr\left[(\mathcal{H}^*_{i,i_1,\ldots,i_n} \mid \mathcal{S}' \mid \mathcal{F})(1^\eta, a) = 1 \cap \overline{\operatorname{rng}(\beta)}\right] = 0 \,, \quad (D.8)$$

where $\overline{\operatorname{rng}(\beta)}$ denotes the complement of $\operatorname{rng}(\beta)$, i.e., the set of runs of the system $(\mathcal{H}^*_{i,i_1,\ldots,i_n} \mid \mathcal{S}' \mid \mathcal{F})(1^\eta, a)$ that are not in $\operatorname{rng}(\beta)$. Since the probability that a run of $\mathcal{H}^*_{i,i_1,\ldots,i_n} \mid \mathcal{S}' \mid \mathcal{F}$ outputs 1 (i.e., $\Pr\left[(\mathcal{H}^*_{i,i_1,\ldots,i_n} \mid \mathcal{S}' \mid \mathcal{F})(1^\eta, a) = 1\right]$) is the sum of the probability that a run in the range of β outputs 1 plus the probability that a run of $\mathcal{H}^*_{i,i_1,\ldots,i_n} \mid \mathcal{S}' \mid \mathcal{F}$ that is not in the range of β outputs 1, by the above, we conclude as follows (for all η, a):

$$\Pr\left[(\mathcal{H}^*_{i,i_1,\ldots,i_n} \mid \mathcal{S}' \mid \mathcal{F})(1^\eta, a) = 1\right]$$

$$= \Pr\left[(\mathcal{H}^*_{i,i_1,\ldots,i_n} \mid \mathcal{S}' \mid \mathcal{F})(1^\eta, a) = 1 \cap \mathrm{rng}(\beta)\right]$$
$$+ \Pr\left[(\mathcal{H}^*_{i,i_1,\ldots,i_n} \mid \mathcal{S}' \mid \mathcal{F})(1^\eta, a) = 1 \cap \overline{\mathrm{rng}(\beta)}\right]$$
$$\overset{(\mathrm{D.7}),(\mathrm{D.8})}{=} \Pr\left[\mathcal{H}_i(1^\eta, a) = 1 \cap B_{\mathcal{H}_i}(i, i_1, \ldots, i_n)\right] .$$

The proof of (D.6) is similar to the proof of (D.5). We only have to replace the external system $\mathcal{S}' \mid \mathcal{F}$ by $\mathcal{P} \mid \mathcal{F}'$. $\qquad\square$

Putting everything together. Finally, we show that $\mathcal{E} \mid \mathcal{P} \mid \mathcal{F}' \equiv \mathcal{E} \mid \mathcal{S} \mid \mathcal{F}$. First, we note that, for all $i \in \mathbb{N}$:

$$\Pr\left[\mathcal{H}_i(1^\eta, a) = 1 \cap B_{\mathcal{H}_i}(i)\right] = \Pr\left[\mathcal{H}_{i+1}(1^\eta, a) = 1 \cap B_{\mathcal{H}_{i+1}}(i)\right] \qquad (\mathrm{D.9})$$

because, if there is no i-th session (i.e., there are at most $i-1$ sessions), then $\mathcal{H}_i$ and $\mathcal{H}_{i+1}$ do not differ.

Next, we define an environment $\mathcal{H}^*_\$ \in \mathrm{Env}_{\mathrm{single}}(\mathcal{P} \mid \mathcal{F}')$. We define $\mathcal{H}^*_\$$ to an IITM similar to $\mathcal{H}^*_{i,i_1,\ldots,i_n}$ but $\mathcal{H}^*_\$$ chooses $i \in \{1,\ldots,p_\mathcal{E}(\eta + |a|)\}$ and $i_1,\ldots,i_n \in \{1,\ldots,p_\mathcal{E}(\eta+|a|)\}\cup\{\bot\}$ uniformly at random and $\mathcal{H}^*_\$$ then emulates $\mathcal{H}^*_{i,i_1,\ldots,i_n}$. Since $\mathcal{H}^*_{i,i_1,\ldots,i_n}$ is universally bounded and $\mathcal{H}^*_\$$ is universally bounded too. Furthermore, it is easy to see that $\mathcal{H}^*_\$$ is a single-session environment (Definition 7.3).

Since $\mathcal{H}^*_\$ \in \mathrm{Env}_{\mathrm{single}}(\mathcal{P} \mid \mathcal{F}')$, by (D.1) ($\mathcal{P} \mid \mathcal{F}'$ and $\mathcal{S}' \mid \mathcal{F}$ are indistinguishable for every single-session environment):

$$f(1^\eta, a) := \left|\Pr\left[(\mathcal{H}^*_\$ \mid \mathcal{P} \mid \mathcal{F}')(1^\eta, a) = 1\right] - \Pr\left[(\mathcal{H}^*_\$ \mid \mathcal{S}' \mid \mathcal{F})(1^\eta, a) = 1\right]\right| \qquad (\mathrm{D.10})$$

is negligible (as a function in 1^η and a).

To simplify notation, in the following, we omit the security parameter η and the external input a (e.g., we write $\Pr\left[\mathcal{H}^*_\$ \mid \mathcal{P} \mid \mathcal{F}' = 1\right]$ for $\Pr\left[(\mathcal{H}^*_\$ \mid \mathcal{P} \mid \mathcal{F}')(1^\eta, a) = 1\right]$ and $p_\mathcal{E}$ for $p_\mathcal{E}(\eta + |a|)$). Furthermore, by I we denote the set $I := \{(i_1,\ldots,i_n) \mid i_1,\ldots,i_n \in \{1,\ldots,p_\mathcal{E}(\eta+|a|)\}\cup\{\bot\}\}$ and we write $\bar{i}$ instead of $i_1,\ldots,i_n \in I$ (e.g., we write $\mathcal{H}^*_{i,\bar{i}}$ for $\mathcal{H}^*_{i,i_1,\ldots,i_n}$) and by $|I|$ its size, i.e., $|I| = (p_\mathcal{E}(\eta + |a|) + 1)^n$, which is a polynomial in $\eta + |a|$ (because the number of roles n is a constant, it does not depend on η or a).

With this notation, we finally conclude that, for every security parameter η and external input a:

$$f(1^\eta, a) \overset{(\mathrm{D.10})}{=} \left|\Pr\left[\mathcal{H}^*_\$ \mid \mathcal{P} \mid \mathcal{F}' = 1\right] - \Pr\left[\mathcal{H}^*_\$ \mid \mathcal{S}' \mid \mathcal{F} = 1\right]\right|$$

$$= \frac{1}{p_\mathcal{E} \cdot |I|} \cdot \left|\sum_{i=1}^{p_\mathcal{E}} \sum_{\bar{i}\in I} \Pr\left[\mathcal{H}^*_{i,\bar{i}} \mid \mathcal{P} \mid \mathcal{F}' = 1\right] - \Pr\left[\mathcal{H}^*_{i,\bar{i}} \mid \mathcal{S}' \mid \mathcal{F} = 1\right]\right|$$

$$\overset{(\mathrm{D.5}),(\mathrm{D.6})}{=} \frac{1}{p_\mathcal{E} \cdot |I|} \cdot \left|\sum_{i=1}^{p_\mathcal{E}} \sum_{\bar{i}\in I} \Pr\left[\mathcal{H}_{i+1} = 1 \cap B_{\mathcal{H}_{i+1}}(i,\bar{i})\right]\right.$$

$$\left. - \Pr\left[\mathcal{H}_i = 1 \cap B_{\mathcal{H}_i}(i,\bar{i})\right]\right|$$

$$\stackrel{\text{(D.9)}}{=} \frac{1}{p_{\mathcal{E}} \cdot |I|} \cdot \left| \sum_{i=1}^{p_{\mathcal{E}}} \Big(\Pr\left[\mathcal{H}_{i+1} = 1 \cap B_{\mathcal{H}_{i+1}}(i)\right] - \Pr\left[\mathcal{H}_i = 1 \cap B_{\mathcal{H}_i}(i)\right] \right.$$

$$\left. + \sum_{\bar{i} \in I} \Pr\left[\mathcal{H}_{i+1} = 1 \cap B_{\mathcal{H}_{i+1}}(i, \bar{i})\right] - \Pr\left[\mathcal{H}_i = 1 \cap B_{\mathcal{H}_i}(i, \bar{i})\right] \Big) \right|$$

$$\stackrel{\text{(D.4)}}{=} \frac{1}{p_{\mathcal{E}} \cdot |I|} \cdot \left| \sum_{i=1}^{p_{\mathcal{E}}} \Pr\left[\mathcal{H}_{i+1} = 1\right] - \Pr\left[\mathcal{H}_i = 1\right] \right|$$

$$= \frac{1}{p_{\mathcal{E}} \cdot |I|} \cdot \left| \Pr\left[\mathcal{H}_{p_{\mathcal{E}}+1} = 1\right] - \Pr\left[\mathcal{H}_1 = 1\right] \right|$$

$$\stackrel{\text{(D.2),(D.3)}}{=} \frac{1}{p_{\mathcal{E}} \cdot |I|} \cdot \left| \Pr\left[\mathcal{E} \,|\, \mathcal{P} \,|\, \mathcal{F}' = 1\right] - \Pr\left[\mathcal{E} \,|\, \mathcal{S} \,|\, \mathcal{F} = 1\right] \right| \ .$$

This shows that $\mathcal{E} \,|\, \mathcal{P} \,|\, \mathcal{F}' \equiv \mathcal{E} \,|\, \mathcal{S} \,|\, \mathcal{F}$ because f is negligible and $p_{\mathcal{E}} \cdot |I|$ is a polynomial in $\eta + |a|$ (as mentioned above $|I|$ is a polynomial in $\eta + |a|$ because the number of roles n is constant). This concludes the proof of Theorem 7.4.

D.2. Proof of Theorem 7.5

In this section, we prove Theorem 7.5 in two steps: First, we define an IITM $\mathcal{Q}_\tau$ that simulates $\mathcal{P} \,|\, \tilde{\mathcal{F}}_{\text{crypto}}$ except that it uses a different copy of $\tilde{\mathcal{F}}_{\text{crypto}}$ for every session (according to τ) and we show that $\mathcal{P} \,|\, \tilde{\mathcal{F}}_{\text{crypto}}$ is indistinguishable from an IITM $\mathcal{Q}_\tau$ for every well-formed environment $\mathcal{E}$ (i.e., $\mathcal{E} \,|\, \mathcal{P} \,|\, \tilde{\mathcal{F}}_{\text{crypto}} \equiv \mathcal{E} \,|\, \mathcal{Q}_\tau$). So, in this step we split $\tilde{\mathcal{F}}_{\text{crypto}}$ such that every session uses its own copy of $\tilde{\mathcal{F}}_{\text{crypto}}$, and hence, every session has a disjoint state. Second, we show that $\mathcal{Q}_\tau$ realizes $\mathcal{F}$ (i.e., that there exists a simulator $\mathcal{S}$ such that $\mathcal{E} \,|\, \mathcal{Q}_\tau \equiv \mathcal{E} \,|\, \mathcal{S} \,|\, \mathcal{F}$ for every environment $\mathcal{E}$). We note that these two steps are independent of each other. The first step only requires that $\mathcal{P}$ satisfies implicit disjointness but not that $\mathcal{P} \,|\, \tilde{\mathcal{F}}_{\text{crypto}}$ single-session realizes $\mathcal{F}$. In contrast, the second step only requires that $\mathcal{P} \,|\, \tilde{\mathcal{F}}_{\text{crypto}}$ single-session realizes $\mathcal{F}$ but not that $\mathcal{P}$ satisfies implicit disjointness. We also note that $\mathcal{Q}_\tau$ is similar to a multi-session protocol that uses a multi-session local-SID functionality as in Theorem 7.4. The proof that $\mathcal{Q}_\tau$ realizes $\mathcal{F}$ is indeed similar to the proof of Theorem 7.4.

Throughout this proof, as in the theorem, we fix a multi-session protocol $\mathcal{P}$ that uses $\tilde{\mathcal{F}}_{\text{crypto}}$ and a partnering function τ that is valid for $\mathcal{P}$. Furthermore, let $\mathcal{E} \in \text{Env}(\mathcal{P} \,|\, \tilde{\mathcal{F}}_{\text{crypto}})$ be a well-formed environment and let $p_{\mathcal{E}}$ be a polynomial (in the security parameter η and the length of the external input a) that bounds the overall runtime (i.e., taken steps) of $\mathcal{E}$. (By definition of environmental systems such a polynomial exists.) By Lemma 2.2, we may assume that $\mathcal{E}$ is a single IITM that accepts all messages in mode CheckAddress. Since only $\mathcal{E}$ can create new instances of machines in $\mathcal{P}$ by sending requests to them, the overall number of these instances is bounded by $p_{\mathcal{E}}$. In the following, we explicitly mention where the assumptions that $\mathcal{P}$ satisfies implicit disjointness and that $\mathcal{P} \,|\, \widetilde{\mathcal{F}}_{\text{crypto}}$ single-session realizes $\mathcal{F}$ ($\mathcal{P} \,|\, \widetilde{\mathcal{F}}_{\text{crypto}} \leq_{\tau\text{-single*}} \mathcal{F}$) are needed.

D.2.1. Step 1: $\mathcal{E} \,|\, \mathcal{P} \,|\, \widetilde{\mathcal{F}}_{\text{crypto}} \equiv \mathcal{E} \,|\, \mathcal{Q}_\tau$

Before we define $\mathcal{Q}_\tau$ and show that $\mathcal{E} \,|\, \mathcal{P} \,|\, \widetilde{\mathcal{F}}_{\text{crypto}} \equiv \mathcal{E} \,|\, \mathcal{Q}_\tau$, we prove a general lemma about collisions of ciphertexts and a lemma about "implicitly shared keys".

Collisions of ciphertexts. We now prove a general lemma that shows that ciphertext produced by $\widetilde{\mathcal{F}}_{\text{crypto}}$ do not collide in our setting (except with negligible probability). We say that an instance of $\widetilde{\mathcal{F}}_{\text{crypto}}$ is *(ciphertext) collision free* if there does not exist bit strings x, x', y such that $x \neq x'$, (x, y) is recorded (upon ideal encryption, i.e., under a unknown/uncorrupted key) for the some (symmetric or public/private) key, and (x', y) is recorded for some (possibly different) key. The next lemma shows that $\widetilde{\mathcal{F}}_{\text{crypto}}$ is collision free with overwhelming probability.

Lemma D.2. *The probability that, in a run of $\mathcal{E} \,|\, \mathcal{P} \,|\, \widetilde{\mathcal{F}}_{\text{crypto}}$ (for some security parameter and external input), $\widetilde{\mathcal{F}}_{\text{crypto}}$ is always collision free is overwhelming (in the security parameter).*

Proof. First, we note that we do not need to consider non-ideally produced ciphertext (i.e., ciphertexts provided by the environment) because they are not stored in $\widetilde{\mathcal{F}}_{\text{crypto}}$. Only ideally produced ciphertexts, i.e., ciphertexts which are the encryption of the leakage of a message, are stored in $\widetilde{\mathcal{F}}_{\text{crypto}}$. Since ideal encryption under unauthenticated symmetric keys (i.e., keys of some type $t \in \mathcal{T}_{\text{senc}}^{\text{unauth}}$) or public keys is interactive and $\widetilde{\mathcal{F}}_{\text{crypto}}$ only accepts ciphertexts provided by the adversary if they do not collide with already recorded ciphertexts (this is one of the modifications of $\widetilde{\mathcal{F}}_{\text{crypto}}$ compared to $\mathcal{F}_{\text{crypto}}$), such ciphertexts never collide. Finally, we consider ideal authenticated symmetric encryption. The following argumentation is similar to the one at the end of Section 3.3 (usefulness of leakage algorithms with high entropy). By assumption, the leakage algorithms for authenticated symmetric encryption in $\widetilde{\mathcal{F}}_{\text{crypto}}$ have high entropy (Definition 3.17) for the domain of plaintexts. Hence, the probability that two leakages (i.e., messages returned by the leakage algorithm) are the same is negligible (in the security parameter). Since the decryption of an encryption of a leakage yields the leakage (decryption test in $\widetilde{\mathcal{F}}_{\text{crypto}}$), different leakages encrypt to different ciphertexts. So, such ciphertexts collide only with negligible probability. □

No implicitly shared (symmetric) keys. The next lemma basically says that unknown symmetric keys that are not explicitly shared are not shared among sessions. This lemma holds because an unknown symmetric (typed) key κ which is not explicitly shared is either a freshly generated key or derived (directly or indirectly) from a freshly generated key. Hence, κ originates from one user. Since κ is unknown, another user can only obtain a pointer to κ by decrypting a ciphertext which contains

κ (or a key in the chain of derivations). Implicit disjointness guarantees that only users in the same session decrypt a ciphertext containing κ and accept. Hence, only users of the same session can have a pointer to κ.

Lemma D.3. *If $\mathcal{P}$ satisfies implicit disjointness w.r.t. τ, then the following holds with overwhelming probability, where the probability is over runs ρ of $\mathcal{E} \,|\, \mathcal{P} \,|\, \widetilde{\mathcal{F}}_{\text{crypto}}$ (for some security parameter and external input): If two distinct users $(lsid, r)$ and $(lsid', r')$ both have a pointer to a (typed) key κ which is marked unknown in $\widetilde{\mathcal{F}}_{\text{crypto}}$ and κ is not explicitly shared (in ρ), then both users are partners or both users are corrupted in ρ (i.e., $\tau_{(lsid,r)}(\rho) = \tau_{(lsid',r')}(\rho) \neq \perp$).*

Proof. Let ρ be a run of $\mathcal{E} \,|\, \mathcal{P} \,|\, \widetilde{\mathcal{F}}_{\text{crypto}}$ (for some security parameter and external input) such that $\widetilde{\mathcal{F}}_{\text{crypto}}$ in ρ is always collision free and (a) and (b) in Definition 7.12 are satisfied. We show that for ρ the statement of the lemma holds. By Lemma D.2 and because $\mathcal{P}$ satisfies implicit disjointness w.r.t. τ, we then have shown the statement of the lemma for an overwhelming set of runs.

We show this by the method of considering a minimal counterexample. Assume that there exist a symmetric (typed) key κ (in $\widetilde{\mathcal{F}}_{\text{crypto}}$ in ρ) such that:

(1) κ is marked unknown in $\widetilde{\mathcal{F}}_{\text{crypto}}$,

(2) κ is not explicitly shared,

(3) there exists two distinct users $(lsid, r)$ and $(lsid', r')$ that both have a pointer to κ, and

(4) not both users are partners or not both users are corrupted in ρ (that is, $\tau_{(lsid,r)}(\rho) \neq \tau_{(lsid',r')}(\rho)$ or $\tau_{(lsid,r)}(\rho) = \tau_{(lsid',r')}(\rho) = \perp$).

Furthermore, we assume that κ is the first such key in ρ, i.e., for every other such a key κ', it holds that κ' has been added to $\mathcal{K}$ (the set of all keys in $\mathcal{F}_{\text{crypto}}^{\text{keys}}$ in $\widetilde{\mathcal{F}}_{\text{crypto}}$) after κ has been added to $\mathcal{K}$. We will lead this to a contradiction, which proves the lemma.

Let $(lsid, r)$ be the user that obtained the first pointer to κ in ρ. Furthermore, let m be the request that $(lsid, r)$ sent to $\widetilde{\mathcal{F}}_{\text{crypto}}$ such that the response of $\widetilde{\mathcal{F}}_{\text{crypto}}$ contained the first pointer to κ. Furthermore, let $(lsid', r') \neq (lsid, r)$ be the first user that obtained a pointer to κ in ρ such that $(lsid', r')$ and $(lsid, r)$ are not partners or not both $(lsid', r')$ and $(lsid, r)$ are corrupted in ρ (i.e., $\tau_{(lsid,r)}(\rho) \neq \tau_{(lsid',r')}(\rho)$ or $\tau_{(lsid,r)}(\rho) = \tau_{(lsid',r')}(\rho) = \perp$). (By assumption such a user $(lsid', r')$ exists.) Let m' be the first request that $(lsid', r')$ sent to $\widetilde{\mathcal{F}}_{\text{crypto}}$ such that the response of $\widetilde{\mathcal{F}}_{\text{crypto}}$ contained the first pointer to κ for $(lsid', r')$. By definition of $\widetilde{\mathcal{F}}_{\text{crypto}}$, new pointers are only created upon the following requests: (KeyGen, t), (Store, κ''), (GetPSK, $(t, name)$), (Derive, ptr, x), (Dec, ptr, y), or (DecPKE, $name, y$). Next, we show that m' cannot be such a requests, which is the desired contradiction.

Of course, by definition of $\widetilde{\mathcal{F}}_{\text{crypto}}$ and because κ is unknown, m' is not of the form (KeyGen, t) or $(\mathsf{Store}, \kappa'')$.

If m' is of the form $(\mathsf{GetPSK}, (t, name))$, then, by definition of $\widetilde{\mathcal{F}}_{\text{crypto}}$ and because κ is unknown, m is of the form $(\mathsf{GetPSK}, (t, name))$ too, because the response of m contained the first pointer to κ. Since κ is not explicitly shared, $(lsid, r)$ and $(lsid', r')$ are partners or both are corrupted. Contradiction. Hence, m' is not of the form $(\mathsf{GetPSK}, (t, name))$.

If m' is of the form $(\mathsf{Derive}, ptr', x)$, then, by definition of $\widetilde{\mathcal{F}}_{\text{crypto}}$ and because κ is unknown, m is of the form $(\mathsf{Derive}, ptr, x)$ and the pointers ptr (of $(lsid, r)$) and ptr' (of $(lsid', r')$) point to the same key, say κ', in $\widetilde{\mathcal{F}}_{\text{crypto}}$. Furthermore, κ' is unknown, i.e., (1) holds for κ'. If κ' would be explicitly shared, then κ also would be explicitly shared. Hence, (2) holds for κ'. Also, (3) and (4) hold for κ' because $(lsid, r)$ and $(lsid', r')$ have a pointer to κ'. But this contradicts the minimality of κ. Hence, m' is not of the form $(\mathsf{Derive}, ptr', x)$.

If m' is of the form $(\mathsf{DecPKE}, name, y)$, then, by definition of $\widetilde{\mathcal{F}}_{\text{crypto}}$ and because κ is unknown, the decryption request m' was performed ideally by $\widetilde{\mathcal{F}}_{\text{crypto}}$, i.e., m' is an ideal destruction request. Furthermore, m' is an accepted destruction request of user $(lsid', r')$. By (b) in Definition 7.12 (implicit disjointness), there exists some user $(lsid'', r'')$ that has sent a corresponding (to m') construction request such that $(lsid', r')$ and $(lsid'', r'')$ are partners or both $(lsid', r')$ and $(lsid'', r'')$ are corrupted. That is, $(lsid'', r'')$ has a pointer to κ and encrypted κ under the public key of pid'. Since $(lsid', r')$ does not has a pointer to κ before it receives the response to m', it holds that $(lsid'', r'') \neq (lsid', r')$. Since $(lsid', r')$ and $(lsid'', r'')$ are partners or both $(lsid', r')$ and $(lsid'', r'')$ are corrupted, it holds that $(lsid, r)$ and $(lsid'', r'')$ are not partners or not both $(lsid, r)$ and $(lsid'', r'')$ are corrupted. But this contradicts the assumption that $(lsid', r')$ is the first such user. Hence, m' is not of the form $(\mathsf{DecPKE}, name, y)$.

Similar to the case of public-key encryption, if m' is of the form (Dec, ptr, y), then, by definition of $\widetilde{\mathcal{F}}_{\text{crypto}}$ and because κ is unknown, the decryption request m' was performed ideally by $\widetilde{\mathcal{F}}_{\text{crypto}}$, i.e., m' is an ideal destruction request; in particular, the key, say κ', pointer ptr points to is unknown. Furthermore, m' is an accepted destruction request of user $(lsid', r')$. If κ' is an explicitly shared key, then (b) in Definition 7.12 (implicit disjointness) holds for κ' and exactly as above, we can show that m' is not of the form (Dec, ptr, y). Now, assume that κ' is not an explicitly shared key. Then (1) and (2) hold for κ'. Also, (3) and (4) hold for κ' because $(lsid, r)$ and $(lsid', r')$ have a pointer to κ'. But this contradicts the minimality of κ. Hence, m' is not of the form (Dec, ptr, y).

Altogether, we conclude that m' is not a request of the form (KeyGen, t), $(\mathsf{Store}, \kappa'')$, $(\mathsf{GetPSK}, (t, name))$, $(\mathsf{Derive}, ptr, x)$, (Dec, ptr, y), or $(\mathsf{DecPKE}, name, y)$, which is a contradiction. $\qquad\square$

Definition of $\mathcal{Q}_\tau$. Before we define $\mathcal{Q}_\tau$ we introduce additional notation. We say that two collision free copies $\widetilde{\mathcal{F}}_{\text{crypto}}[z]$ and $\widetilde{\mathcal{F}}_{\text{crypto}}[z']$ of $\widetilde{\mathcal{F}}_{\text{crypto}}$ (z and z' are just used to denote different copies of $\widetilde{\mathcal{F}}_{\text{crypto}}$) have *compatible states* if they do not have conflicting values for the recorded algorithms (provided by the environment), the status of keys (known/unknown or corrupted/uncorrupted, respectively), and the information recorded for the keys (e.g., the list of plaintext/ciphertext pairs for encryption keys). More formally, we say that $\widetilde{\mathcal{F}}_{\text{crypto}}[z]$ and $\widetilde{\mathcal{F}}_{\text{crypto}}[z']$ have *compatible states* if the following holds:

1. $\widetilde{\mathcal{F}}_{\text{crypto}}[z]$ and $\widetilde{\mathcal{F}}_{\text{crypto}}[z']$ correspond on all algorithms (e.g., for symmetric and public-key encryption/decryption) which have been provided by the environment.

2. For every public/private key name *name*, *name* is corrupted in $\widetilde{\mathcal{F}}_{\text{crypto}}[z]$ iff it is corrupted in $\widetilde{\mathcal{F}}_{\text{crypto}}[z']$. Furthermore, ciphertexts do not collide, i.e., there does not exist bit strings x, x', y such that $x \neq x'$, (x, y) is recorded for *name* in $\widetilde{\mathcal{F}}_{\text{crypto}}[z]$, and (x', y) is recorded for *name* in $\widetilde{\mathcal{F}}_{\text{crypto}}[z']$.

3. For every symmetric (typed) key κ that exists in both $\widetilde{\mathcal{F}}_{\text{crypto}}[z]$ and $\widetilde{\mathcal{F}}_{\text{crypto}}[z']$, κ is known in $\widetilde{\mathcal{F}}_{\text{crypto}}[z]$ iff κ is known in $\widetilde{\mathcal{F}}_{\text{crypto}}[z']$. Furthermore, ciphertexts do not collide, i.e., if κ is an encryption key, then there does not exist bit strings x, x', y such that $x \neq x'$, (x, y) is recorded for κ in $\widetilde{\mathcal{F}}_{\text{crypto}}[z]$, and (x', y) is recorded for κ in $\widetilde{\mathcal{F}}_{\text{crypto}}[z']$.

4. There is no nonce that occurs in both $\widetilde{\mathcal{F}}_{\text{crypto}}[z]$ and $\widetilde{\mathcal{F}}_{\text{crypto}}[z']$.

5. For every pre-shared key name $(t, name)$ (where t is the key type) that exists in both $\widetilde{\mathcal{F}}_{\text{crypto}}[z]$ and $\widetilde{\mathcal{F}}_{\text{crypto}}[z']$, it holds that $(t, name)$ is corrupted in $\widetilde{\mathcal{F}}_{\text{crypto}}[z]$ iff $(t, name)$ is corrupted in $\widetilde{\mathcal{F}}_{\text{crypto}}[z']$ and it holds that $\widetilde{\mathcal{F}}_{\text{crypto}}[z]$ and $\widetilde{\mathcal{F}}_{\text{crypto}}[z']$ correspond on the value of the key (in case it is not corrupted).

6. If the keys $\kappa_1, \ldots, \kappa_l$ are derived from a key κ in $\widetilde{\mathcal{F}}_{\text{crypto}}[z]$ using salt x and $\kappa'_1, \ldots, \kappa'_l$ are derived from κ in $\widetilde{\mathcal{F}}_{\text{crypto}}[z']$ using the same salt x, then $\kappa_i = \kappa'_i$ for all $i \leq l$.

7. At most one instance $\widetilde{\mathcal{F}}_{\text{crypto}}[z]$ or $\widetilde{\mathcal{F}}_{\text{crypto}}[z']$ is waiting for input from the environment but not both (i.e., waiting for a reply to a KeyGen, Init, etc. requests that this instance has sent to the environment on its network tape).

Two collision free copies of $\widetilde{\mathcal{F}}_{\text{crypto}}$ that have compatible states can be merged in the obvious way. The merged copy just contains all keys and, e.g., all recorded pairs of plaintexts/ciphertexts. By definition, the merged copy is collision free as well. Furthermore, several collision free instances of $\widetilde{\mathcal{F}}_{\text{crypto}}$ that have pairwise compatible states can all be merge into one copy of $\widetilde{\mathcal{F}}_{\text{crypto}}$.

Now, we define the IITM $\mathcal{Q}_\tau$. It has the same I/O and network interface as $\mathcal{P} \mid \tilde{\mathcal{F}}_{\text{crypto}}$ and emulates $\mathcal{P}$ and several copies of $\tilde{\mathcal{F}}_{\text{crypto}}$ (basically one for every session). For every instance $M_r[\textit{lsid}]$ ($M_r[\textit{lsid}]$ denotes the emulated instance of M_r in $\mathcal{P}$ with local SID $\textit{lsid}$), $\mathcal{Q}_\tau$ creates a copy of $\tilde{\mathcal{F}}_{\text{crypto}}$, denoted by $\tilde{\mathcal{F}}_{\text{crypto}}[(\textit{lsid}, r)]$.

Whenever some (emulated) copy of $\tilde{\mathcal{F}}_{\text{crypto}}$ produces (I/O or network) output, $\mathcal{Q}_\tau$ checks that all copies of $\tilde{\mathcal{F}}_{\text{crypto}}$ are collision free and have pairwise compatible states. If this is not the case, $\mathcal{Q}_\tau$ terminates. (In this case the environment could distinguish between $\mathcal{P} \mid \tilde{\mathcal{F}}_{\text{crypto}}$ and $\mathcal{Q}_\tau$ but, as we will see, this happens only with negligible probability.)

Whenever $M_r[\textit{lsid}]$ produces (I/O or network) output, $\mathcal{Q}_\tau$ checks whether $(\textit{lsid}, r)$ is corrupted or $(\textit{lsid}, r)$ belongs to some session w.r.t. τ, i.e., $\tau(\alpha) = \text{corr}$ or $\tau(\alpha) = \textit{sid}$ for some $\textit{sid} \in \{0, 1\}^*$ where α is the sequence of messages (along with tapes) sent and received by $M_r[\textit{lsid}]$ on network tapes so far. If this is the case, $\mathcal{Q}_\tau$ sets $s := \tau(\alpha)$ (i.e., $s = \text{corr}$ or $s = \textit{sid}$). If $\tilde{\mathcal{F}}_{\text{crypto}}[(\textit{lsid}, r)]$ exists (i.e., it has not been merged with some other copies of $\tilde{\mathcal{F}}_{\text{crypto}}$ and removed afterwards) and $\tilde{\mathcal{F}}_{\text{crypto}}[s]$ does not exist, then $\mathcal{Q}_\tau$ sets $\tilde{\mathcal{F}}_{\text{crypto}}[s] := \tilde{\mathcal{F}}_{\text{crypto}}[(\textit{lsid}, r)]$ and removes $\tilde{\mathcal{F}}_{\text{crypto}}[(\textit{lsid}, r)]$. Otherwise, if $\tilde{\mathcal{F}}_{\text{crypto}}[(\textit{lsid}, r)]$ and $\tilde{\mathcal{F}}_{\text{crypto}}[s]$ exist, then $\mathcal{Q}_\tau$ merges $\tilde{\mathcal{F}}_{\text{crypto}}[(\textit{lsid}, r)]$ and $\tilde{\mathcal{F}}_{\text{crypto}}[s]$ and replaces $\tilde{\mathcal{F}}_{\text{crypto}}[s]$ by the merged instance. (If $\tilde{\mathcal{F}}_{\text{crypto}}[(\textit{lsid}, r)]$ does not exists, then $\mathcal{Q}_\tau$ does nothing because it already has been merged with $\tilde{\mathcal{F}}_{\text{crypto}}[s]$ and removed afterwards.)

Considering the above, $\mathcal{Q}_\tau$ performs the emulation as follows:

1. *Messages from environment to $M_r[\textit{lsid}]$:* If $\mathcal{Q}_\tau$ receives (I/O or network) input from the environment for $M_r[\textit{lsid}]$, then it just forwards it to $M_r[\textit{lsid}]$.

2. *Messages from $M_r[\textit{lsid}]$ to the environment:* If $M_r[\textit{lsid}]$ sends a message m to the environment, then $\mathcal{Q}_\tau$ first merges instances of $\tilde{\mathcal{F}}_{\text{crypto}}$ as described above and then forwards m to the environment.

3. *Requests of $M_r[\textit{lsid}]$ to $\tilde{\mathcal{F}}_{\text{crypto}}$:* Upon a request m of $M_r[\textit{lsid}]$ to $\tilde{\mathcal{F}}_{\text{crypto}}$, $\mathcal{Q}_\tau$ first merges copies of $\tilde{\mathcal{F}}_{\text{crypto}}$ as described above and then forwards m to the copy of $\tilde{\mathcal{F}}_{\text{crypto}}$ corresponding to $M_r[\textit{lsid}]$ (i.e., to $\tilde{\mathcal{F}}_{\text{crypto}}[\text{corr}]$ if $(\textit{lsid}, r)$ is corrupted according to τ, to $\tilde{\mathcal{F}}_{\text{crypto}}[\textit{sid}]$ if $(\textit{lsid}, r)$ has SID $\textit{sid}$ according to τ, or to $\tilde{\mathcal{F}}_{\text{crypto}}[(\textit{lsid}, r)]$ otherwise).

4. *Responses of $\tilde{\mathcal{F}}_{\text{crypto}}$ to $M_r[\textit{lsid}]$:* If some instance of $\tilde{\mathcal{F}}_{\text{crypto}}$ produces I/O output to $M_r[\textit{lsid}]$, then $\mathcal{Q}_\tau$ just forwards it to $M_r[\textit{lsid}]$.

5. *Messages from $\tilde{\mathcal{F}}_{\text{crypto}}$ to the environment:* If some copy $\tilde{\mathcal{F}}_{\text{crypto}}[z]$ of $\tilde{\mathcal{F}}_{\text{crypto}}$ (i.e., $z = \text{corr}$, $z = \textit{sid}$ for some SID $\textit{sid}$, or $z = (\textit{lsid}, r)$ for some user $(\textit{lsid}, r)$) produces network output m to the environment, then $\mathcal{Q}_\tau$ does the following:

   (a) If $m = ((\textit{lsid}, r), \text{KeyGen}, t)$ (for some user $(\textit{lsid}, r)$ and key type t) was sent by $\mathcal{F}_{\text{crypto}}^{\text{user}}[(\textit{lsid}, r)]$ in $\tilde{\mathcal{F}}_{\text{crypto}}[z]$ (i.e., the instance of $\mathcal{F}_{\text{crypto}}^{\text{user}}$ in $\tilde{\mathcal{F}}_{\text{crypto}}[z]$

that is addressed by the user name $(lsid, r)$), then $\mathcal{Q}_\tau$ forwards m to the environment.

(b) If $m = (psk, \mathsf{Init})$ was sent by $\mathcal{F}_{\text{crypto}}^{\text{keysetup}}[psk]$ in $\widetilde{\mathcal{F}}_{\text{crypto}}[z]$, then $\mathcal{Q}_\tau$ checks if there exists another copy of $\widetilde{\mathcal{F}}_{\text{crypto}}$ that contains an instance $\mathcal{F}_{\text{crypto}}^{\text{keysetup}}[psk]$ such that $\text{corr} = 1$ or $\mathsf{k} \neq \bot$ in this instance (i.e., in this instance, the pre-shared key with name psk has been corrupted or provided by the environment). (We note that because all copies of $\widetilde{\mathcal{F}}_{\text{crypto}}$ have pairwise compatible states, if there exist more than one such copy, they agree on the values of corr and k.)

If this is the case and $\text{corr} = 1$, then $\mathcal{Q}_\tau$ sends $(psk, 1, k)$ to $\mathcal{F}_{\text{crypto}}^{\text{keysetup}}[psk]$ in $\widetilde{\mathcal{F}}_{\text{crypto}}[z]$ (to corrupt the pre-shared key psk) where k is an arbitrary key from the domain of keys of the type of psk (it will be ignored anyway upon corruption).

If this is the case and $\text{corr} = 0$, then $\mathcal{Q}_\tau$ sends $(psk, 0, \mathsf{k})$ to $\mathcal{F}_{\text{crypto}}^{\text{keysetup}}[psk]$ in $\widetilde{\mathcal{F}}_{\text{crypto}}[z]$ (to set the same pre-shared key). This might trigger $\widetilde{\mathcal{F}}_{\text{crypto}}[z]$ to directly send an $\mathsf{Add?}$ request (this is one of the notification message added to $\widetilde{\mathcal{F}}_{\text{crypto}}$ that does not exist in $\mathcal{F}_{\text{crypto}}$) of the form $(\mathsf{Add?}, \mathsf{unknown}, (t, k))$ to the environment. Upon this request, $\mathcal{Q}_\tau$ replies with 1. This will trigger $\widetilde{\mathcal{F}}_{\text{crypto}}[z]$ to proceed normally.

Otherwise (i.e., the pre-shared key psk is not corrupted or set in any copy of $\widetilde{\mathcal{F}}_{\text{crypto}}$), $\mathcal{Q}_\tau$ forwards m to the environment.

(c) If $m = (psk, \mathsf{GetPSK})$ was sent by $\mathcal{F}_{\text{crypto}}^{\text{keysetup}}[psk]$ in $\widetilde{\mathcal{F}}_{\text{crypto}}[z]$ (note that this is only done if the pre-shared key psk is corrupted, i.e., $\mathcal{F}_{\text{crypto}}^{\text{keysetup}}[psk]$ is corrupted), then $\mathcal{Q}_\tau$ forwards m to the environment.

(d) If $m = (\kappa, \mathsf{Init})$ was sent by $\mathcal{F}_{\text{crypto}}^{\text{senc}}[\kappa]$ in $\widetilde{\mathcal{F}}_{\text{crypto}}[z]$, then (similarly to Init requests from $\mathcal{F}_{\text{crypto}}^{\text{keysetup}}$) $\mathcal{Q}_\tau$ checks if there exists another copy of $\widetilde{\mathcal{F}}_{\text{crypto}}$ that contains an instance $\mathcal{F}_{\text{crypto}}^{\text{senc}}[\kappa]$ such that $\text{enc} \neq \bot$ and $\text{dec} \neq \bot$ in this instance (i.e., this instance has received encryption and decryption algorithms from the environment). (We note that because all copies of $\widetilde{\mathcal{F}}_{\text{crypto}}$ have pairwise compatible states, if there exist more than one such copy, they agree on the algorithms.)

If this is the case, then $\mathcal{Q}_\tau$ sends $(\kappa, \text{enc}, \text{dec})$ to $\mathcal{F}_{\text{crypto}}^{\text{senc}}[\kappa]$ in $\widetilde{\mathcal{F}}_{\text{crypto}}[z]$ (to provide the same algorithms). Otherwise, $\mathcal{Q}_\tau$ forwards m to the environment.

(e) If $m = (\kappa, \mathsf{Init})$ or $m = (name, \mathsf{Init})$ was sent by $\mathcal{F}_{\text{crypto}}^{\text{mac}}[\kappa]$, $\mathcal{F}_{\text{crypto}}^{\text{pke}}[name]$, or $\mathcal{F}_{\text{crypto}}^{\text{sig}}[name]$, respectively, in $\widetilde{\mathcal{F}}_{\text{crypto}}[z]$, then, just as for Init requests from $\mathcal{F}_{\text{crypto}}^{\text{senc}}[\kappa]$ (see above), $\mathcal{Q}_\tau$ provides the same algorithms that have been provided to some other copy of $\widetilde{\mathcal{F}}_{\text{crypto}}$, if they have been provided, and, otherwise, forwards m to the environment.

(f) If $m = (\kappa, \mathsf{Derive}, x, \textit{status})$ was sent by $\mathcal{F}_{\text{crypto}}^{\text{derive}}[\kappa]$ in $\widetilde{\mathcal{F}}_{\text{crypto}}[z]$, then (similarly to Init requests from $\mathcal{F}_{\text{crypto}}^{\text{keysetup}}$) $\mathcal{Q}_{\tau}$ checks if there exists another copy of $\widetilde{\mathcal{F}}_{\text{crypto}}$ that contains an instance $\mathcal{F}_{\text{crypto}}^{\text{derive}}[\kappa]$ such that $\mathsf{derived}(x) \neq \perp$ in this instance (i.e., in this instance keys have been derived using the same salt x). (We note that because all copies of $\widetilde{\mathcal{F}}_{\text{crypto}}$ have pairwise compatible states, if there exist more than one such copy, they agree on $\mathsf{derived}(x)$.)

If this is the case, then $\mathcal{Q}_{\tau}$ sends $(\kappa, k_1, \ldots, k_l)$ to $\mathcal{F}_{\text{crypto}}^{\text{derive}}[\kappa]$ in $\widetilde{\mathcal{F}}_{\text{crypto}}[z]$ (to provide the same derived keys) where $k_1, \ldots, k_l$ are the keys recorded in $\mathsf{derived}(x)$. This might trigger $\widetilde{\mathcal{F}}_{\text{crypto}}[z]$ to directly send an Add? request to the environment. Upon this request, $\mathcal{Q}_{\tau}$ replies with 1. This will trigger $\widetilde{\mathcal{F}}_{\text{crypto}}[z]$ to proceed normally.

Otherwise, $\mathcal{Q}_{\tau}$ forwards m to the environment.

(g) If $m = (\mathsf{MarkedKnown}, \kappa)$ was sent by $\mathcal{F}_{\text{crypto}}^{\text{keys}}$ (this is the first notification message added to $\widetilde{\mathcal{F}}_{\text{crypto}}$ that does not exist in $\mathcal{F}_{\text{crypto}}$), then $\mathcal{Q}_{\tau}$ forwards m to the environment.

(h) If $m = (\mathsf{Add}?, \textit{status}, \kappa)$ was sent by $\mathcal{F}_{\text{crypto}}^{\text{keys}}$ (this is the other notification message added to $\widetilde{\mathcal{F}}_{\text{crypto}}$ that does not exist in $\mathcal{F}_{\text{crypto}}$), then $\mathcal{Q}_{\tau}$ does the following. (We note that some cases where an Add? request is sent by $\mathcal{F}_{\text{crypto}}^{\text{keys}}$ have already been treated above. Here, we consider only the remaining cases.)

If $\textit{status} = \mathsf{known}$ (i.e., the key κ is supposed to be added to the set of all keys in $\mathcal{F}_{\text{crypto}}^{\text{keys}}$ as a known key), it checks if κ exists in some other copy of $\widetilde{\mathcal{F}}_{\text{crypto}}$ and is marked unknown therein. If this is the case, $\mathcal{Q}_{\tau}$ sends the response 0 to $\mathcal{F}_{\text{crypto}}^{\text{keys}}$ in $\widetilde{\mathcal{F}}_{\text{crypto}}[z]$. (See below for remarks.) Otherwise, $\mathcal{Q}_{\tau}$ forwards m to the environment.

If $\textit{status} = \mathsf{unknown}$ (i.e., the key κ is supposed to be added to the set of all keys in $\mathcal{F}_{\text{crypto}}^{\text{keys}}$ as an unknown key), it checks if κ exists in some other copy of $\widetilde{\mathcal{F}}_{\text{crypto}}$ (it does not matter whether it is marked known or unknown therein). If this is the case, $\mathcal{Q}_{\tau}$ sends the response 0 to $\mathcal{F}_{\text{crypto}}^{\text{keys}}$ in $\widetilde{\mathcal{F}}_{\text{crypto}}[z]$. Otherwise, $\mathcal{Q}_{\tau}$ forwards m to the environment.

We note that when $\mathcal{Q}_{\tau}$ replies with 0, this will trigger $\widetilde{\mathcal{F}}_{\text{crypto}}[z]$ to proceed as if Add failed (i.e., $\mathcal{F}_{\text{crypto}}^{\text{keys}}$ returns $\perp$) because an unknown key was guessed (in case $\textit{status} = \mathsf{known}$) or a key is not fresh (in case $\textit{status} = \mathsf{unknown}$). So, the Add request is processed as it would be processed in the copy of $\widetilde{\mathcal{F}}_{\text{crypto}}$ obtained from merging all copies of $\widetilde{\mathcal{F}}_{\text{crypto}}$.

(i) If $m = (\kappa, \mathsf{Enc}, \overline{x})$ or $m = (\textit{name}, \mathsf{EncPKE}, pk, \overline{x})$ was sent by $\mathcal{F}_{\text{crypto}}^{\text{senc}}[\kappa]$ or $\mathcal{F}_{\text{crypto}}^{\text{pke}}[\textit{name}]$, respectively, in $\widetilde{\mathcal{F}}_{\text{crypto}}[z]$ (i.e., the environment is asked to provide a ciphertext that is the encryption of the leakage $\overline{x}$; these requests were added to $\widetilde{\mathcal{F}}_{\text{crypto}}$ and do not exist in $\mathcal{F}_{\text{crypto}}$), then $\mathcal{Q}_\tau$ forwards m to the environment.

(j) If $m = (\kappa, \text{Dec}, y)$ was sent by $\mathcal{F}^{\text{senc}}_{\text{crypto}}[\kappa]$ in $\widetilde{\mathcal{F}}_{\text{crypto}}[z]$ (i.e., $\mathcal{F}^{\text{senc}}_{\text{crypto}}[\kappa]$ asks for the decryption of a ciphertext y; this request was added to $\widetilde{\mathcal{F}}_{\text{crypto}}$ and does not exist in $\mathcal{F}_{\text{crypto}}$), then $\mathcal{Q}_\tau$ checks if there exists a plaintext x and another copy of $\widetilde{\mathcal{F}}_{\text{crypto}}$ such that (x, y) has been recorded therein upon encryption for the key κ (i.e., this other copy of $\widetilde{\mathcal{F}}_{\text{crypto}}$ contains an instance $\mathcal{F}^{\text{senc}}_{\text{crypto}}[\kappa]$ such that (x, y) has been recorded therein).

If this is the case, then $\mathcal{Q}_\tau$ sends $(\kappa, \perp)$ to $\mathcal{F}^{\text{senc}}_{\text{crypto}}[\kappa]$ in $\widetilde{\mathcal{F}}_{\text{crypto}}[z]$ (to let decryption fail in $\mathcal{F}^{\text{senc}}_{\text{crypto}}[\kappa]$). Otherwise, $\mathcal{Q}_\tau$ forwards m to the environment.

(k) If $m = (name, \text{DecPKE}, y)$ was sent by $\mathcal{F}^{\text{pke}}_{\text{crypto}}[name]$ in $\widetilde{\mathcal{F}}_{\text{crypto}}[z]$ (that is, $\mathcal{F}^{\text{pke}}_{\text{crypto}}[name]$ asks for the decryption of a ciphertext y; this request was added to $\widetilde{\mathcal{F}}_{\text{crypto}}$ and does not exist in $\mathcal{F}_{\text{crypto}}$), then, just as for Dec requests from $\mathcal{F}^{\text{senc}}_{\text{crypto}}[\kappa]$ (see above), $\mathcal{Q}_\tau$ provides the plaintext that is recorded for y in some other copy of $\widetilde{\mathcal{F}}_{\text{crypto}}$ for the same public/private key $name$, if such a plaintext exists, and, otherwise, forwards m to the environment.

(By definition of $\widetilde{\mathcal{F}}_{\text{crypto}}$, other cases cannot occur.) We note that the above might lead to incompatible states in two cases: First, if a key is getting marked known (this triggers the message MarkedKnown) in one copy of $\widetilde{\mathcal{F}}_{\text{crypto}}$ and this key also exists in another copy of $\widetilde{\mathcal{F}}_{\text{crypto}}$ but there it is marked unknown, then the states of these copies are incompatible. Second, if $\mathcal{Q}_\tau$ forwards m to the environment and there is another copy of $\widetilde{\mathcal{F}}_{\text{crypto}}$ that is already waiting for a response from the environment (i.e., there would now be two copies of $\widetilde{\mathcal{F}}_{\text{crypto}}$ that are waiting for input from the environment), then the states of these copies are incompatible. In both these cases, $\mathcal{Q}_\tau$ terminates.[91]

6. *Messages from the environment to $\widetilde{\mathcal{F}}_{\text{crypto}}$:* If $\mathcal{Q}_\tau$ receives network input m from the environment for $\widetilde{\mathcal{F}}_{\text{crypto}}$, then $\mathcal{Q}_\tau$ does the following:

(a) If m is the response to a KeyGen, Init, GetPSK, Derive, MarkedKnown, or Add? request, then $\mathcal{Q}_\tau$ forwards m to the copy of $\widetilde{\mathcal{F}}_{\text{crypto}}$ that is waiting for this response. $\mathcal{Q}_\tau$ knows which this copy is because they all have pairwise compatible states, and hence, at most one such copy can wait for this response from the environment.

---

[91] We will later see that this happens only with negligible probability. For the first case this basically follows from Lemma D.3 and (a) in Definition 7.12 (implicit disjointness). For the second case this holds because we assume that the environment is well-formed, i.e., it always answers these requests before another request is sent.

(b) If m is the response to a Enc or EncPKE request, i.e., $m = (\kappa, y)$ or $m = (name, y)$ (where κ is a symmetric key, $name$ is a public/private key name, and y is a ciphertext), respectively, then $\mathcal{Q}_\tau$ checks if (x, y), for some x, has been recorded in some (emulated) copy of $\widetilde{\mathcal{F}}_{\text{crypto}}$ for the key $\kappa/name$.

If this is the case, $\mathcal{Q}_\tau$ returns an error message to the environment signaling a ciphertext collision. We note that this is the same as what would happen if the copy of $\widetilde{\mathcal{F}}_{\text{crypto}}$ that is obtained from merging all copies of $\widetilde{\mathcal{F}}_{\text{crypto}}$ would receive m.

Otherwise, $\mathcal{Q}_\tau$ forwards m to the copy of $\widetilde{\mathcal{F}}_{\text{crypto}}$ that is waiting for this response (as explained above, $\mathcal{Q}_\tau$ knows which copy is waiting for this response).

(c) If m is the response to a Dec or DecPKE request, i.e., $m = (\kappa, x)$ or $m = (name, x)$ (where κ is a symmetric key, $name$ is a public/private key name, and x is a plaintext), respectively, then $\mathcal{Q}_\tau$ forwards m to the copy of $\widetilde{\mathcal{F}}_{\text{crypto}}$ that is waiting for this response (as explained above $\mathcal{Q}_\tau$ knows which copy is waiting for this response).

(d) Otherwise (i.e., no instance of $\widetilde{\mathcal{F}}_{\text{crypto}}$ is waiting for this response), $\mathcal{Q}_\tau$ stops in this activation with empty output (i.e., the master IITM in the environment will be triggered with empty input).

Since $\widetilde{\mathcal{F}}_{\text{crypto}}$ is environmentally strictly bounded and $\mathcal{P} \,|\, \mathcal{F}$ is environmentally strictly bounded for every environmentally strictly bounded system $\mathcal{F}$ with the same I/O interface as $\widetilde{\mathcal{F}}_{\text{crypto}}$, it is easy to see that $\mathcal{Q}_\tau$ is environmentally strictly bounded. Hence, $\mathcal{E} \,|\, \mathcal{Q}_\tau$ is strictly bounded.

Next, we show that $\mathcal{P} \,|\, \widetilde{\mathcal{F}}_{\text{crypto}}$ is indistinguishable from $\mathcal{Q}_\tau$. As mentioned above, this does not require that $\mathcal{P} \,|\, \widetilde{\mathcal{F}}_{\text{crypto}}$ single-session realizes $\mathcal{F}$ but only that $\mathcal{P}$ satisfies implicit disjointness.

Lemma D.4. *If $\mathcal{P}$ satisfies implicit disjointness w.r.t. τ, then $\mathcal{E} \,|\, \mathcal{P} \,|\, \widetilde{\mathcal{F}}_{\text{crypto}} \equiv \mathcal{E} \,|\, \mathcal{Q}_\tau$.*

Proof. To prove Lemma D.4, we define a one-to-one mapping between runs (or at least an overwhelming set of runs) of $\mathcal{E} \,|\, \mathcal{P} \,|\, \widetilde{\mathcal{F}}_{\text{crypto}}$ and runs of $\mathcal{E} \,|\, \mathcal{Q}_\tau$ such that corresponding runs have the same probability and overall output.

Therefore, let ρ be a run of $\mathcal{E} \,|\, \mathcal{P} \,|\, \widetilde{\mathcal{F}}_{\text{crypto}}$ (for some security parameter and external input) such that $\widetilde{\mathcal{F}}_{\text{crypto}}$ in ρ is always collision free, (a) and (b) of Definition 7.12 (implicit disjointness) are satisfied for ρ, and there exists no implicitly shared keys that are marked unknown in $\widetilde{\mathcal{F}}_{\text{crypto}}$ in ρ, i.e., the statement of Lemma D.3 holds for ρ. Given such a run ρ, we first define the corresponding run ρ' of $\mathcal{E} \,|\, \mathcal{Q}_\tau$. Then, we show that the probability of ρ is the same as the probability of ρ' and that the overall output (i.e., the output on tape decision) is the same in ρ and ρ'. By Lemma D.2, Lemma D.3, and because $\mathcal{P}$ satisfies implicitly disjointness w.r.t. τ, the set of runs of $\mathcal{E} \mid \mathcal{P} \mid \widetilde{\mathcal{F}}_{\text{crypto}}$ that we consider has overwhelming probability and, hence, we can conclude that $\mathcal{E} \mid \mathcal{P} \mid \widetilde{\mathcal{F}}_{\text{crypto}} \equiv \mathcal{E} \mid \mathcal{Q}_\tau$.

We define ρ' to be the run of $\mathcal{E} \mid \mathcal{Q}_\tau$ where the following holds:

1. $\mathcal{E}$ uses the same random coins as $\mathcal{E}$ in ρ.

2. The random coins of $\mathcal{Q}_\tau$ are defined such that:

   a) The emulated $\mathcal{P}$ uses the same random coins as $\mathcal{P}$ in ρ.

   b) The emulated copies of $\widetilde{\mathcal{F}}_{\text{crypto}}$ jointly use the same random coins as $\widetilde{\mathcal{F}}_{\text{crypto}}$ in ρ.

By construction, the probabilities of ρ and ρ' are equal. W.l.o.g., in the following, we assume that $\mathcal{P} \mid \widetilde{\mathcal{F}}_{\text{crypto}}$ in the run ρ is a single IITM (in Lemma 2.1, it has been shown that every system of IITMs can be emulated by a single IITM). This simplifies the proof because $\mathcal{Q}_\tau$ is a single IITM in ρ' and, hence, the structure of ρ and ρ' is more similar. In particular, now, every configuration in ρ is either $\mathcal{E}$ sending output to $\mathcal{P} \mid \widetilde{\mathcal{F}}_{\text{crypto}}$ or tape decision (which of course can only be the last configuration of ρ), $\mathcal{P} \mid \widetilde{\mathcal{F}}_{\text{crypto}}$ sending output to $\mathcal{E}$, or $\mathcal{E}$ or $\mathcal{P} \mid \widetilde{\mathcal{F}}_{\text{crypto}}$ producing empty output. Otherwise, we would have to talk about intermediate configurations, e.g., where $\mathcal{P}$ sends requests to $\widetilde{\mathcal{F}}_{\text{crypto}}$, which do not exist in ρ'.

By induction on the length of prefixes of ρ, we show that the following holds for every prefix $\hat{\rho}$ of ρ (the corresponding prefix $\hat{\rho}'$ of ρ' is defined analogously to ρ'):

($*$) (a) The view of $\mathcal{E}$ in $\hat{\rho}$ is the same as the view of $\mathcal{E}$ in $\hat{\rho}'$.

   (b) The last configuration of $\mathcal{E}$ in $\hat{\rho}$ is the same as the last configuration of $\mathcal{E}$ in $\hat{\rho}'$.

   (c) The last configuration of $\mathcal{P}$ in $\hat{\rho}$ is the same as the configuration of the emulated $\mathcal{P}$ in the last configuration of $\mathcal{Q}_\tau$ in $\hat{\rho}'$.

   (d) All emulated copies of $\widetilde{\mathcal{F}}_{\text{crypto}}$ in the last configuration of $\mathcal{Q}_\tau$ in $\hat{\rho}'$ have compatible states.

   (e) The last configuration of $\widetilde{\mathcal{F}}_{\text{crypto}}$ in $\hat{\rho}$ is the same as the configuration of $\widetilde{\mathcal{F}}_{\text{crypto}}$ that is obtained from merging (see above) all emulated copies of $\widetilde{\mathcal{F}}_{\text{crypto}}$ in the last configuration of $\mathcal{Q}_\tau$ in $\hat{\rho}'$.

After we have shown this, we can conclude as follows: Since ($*$) in particularly holds for $\hat{\rho} = \rho$, only $\mathcal{E}$ might produce output to decision, and $\mathcal{E}$ uses the same randomness in both runs, the overall output of ρ is the same as the one of ρ'. Furthermore, it is easy to see that the overall runtime of all machines in ρ' is polynomially bounded by the overall runtime of all machines in ρ (for a fixed polynomial that does not depend on ρ).

Clearly, ($*$) holds if $\hat{\rho}$ has length 1, i.e., where $\mathcal{P} \mid \widetilde{\mathcal{F}}_{\text{crypto}}$ has never been activated in $\hat{\rho}$. Now, let $\hat{\rho}$ be a prefix of ρ of length > 1 and assume that ($*$) holds for the prefix $\tilde{\rho}$ of $\hat{\rho}$ which is by one shorter than $\hat{\rho}$. There are two cases: In the last configuration

of $\tilde{\rho}$ the last IITM that has been active (and possibly produced output) is either
(i) $\mathcal{P} \,|\, \tilde{\mathcal{F}}_{\text{crypto}}$ or *(ii)* $\mathcal{E}$. In the first case, by $(*)$ for $\tilde{\rho}$, it trivially follows that the
output of $\mathcal{P} \,|\, \tilde{\mathcal{F}}_{\text{crypto}}$ in $\tilde{\rho}$ equals the output of $\mathcal{Q}_\tau$ in $\hat{\rho}'$. Hence, $(*)$ holds for $\hat{\rho}$. Next,
we consider the second case. If $\mathcal{E}$ produces empty output or output to tape decision,
then the run stops and nothing is to show. Now, assume that $\mathcal{E}$ produces output,
say m, to $\mathcal{P} \,|\, \tilde{\mathcal{F}}_{\text{crypto}}$. Note that the message m might trigger $\mathcal{P}$ and $\tilde{\mathcal{F}}_{\text{crypto}}$ to send
multiple messages between each other before $\mathcal{P}$ or $\tilde{\mathcal{F}}_{\text{crypto}}$ outputs a message m' to
$\mathcal{E}$. We show that $(*)$ is satisfied for every such in-between message.

If m is sent to $\mathcal{P}$, then $(*)$ trivially holds for the configuration that is reached when
$\mathcal{P}$ outputs a message (either to $\mathcal{E}$ or to $\tilde{\mathcal{F}}_{\text{crypto}}$) because of $(*)\,(c)$ for $\tilde{\rho}$ and $\mathcal{P}$ uses
the same randomness in ρ and ρ'.

On the other hand, if m is sent to $\tilde{\mathcal{F}}_{\text{crypto}}$ (i.e., to the network interface of $\tilde{\mathcal{F}}_{\text{crypto}}$),
then, of course $(*)\,(a)$, $(*)\,(b)$, and $(*)\,(c)$ hold because the configuration of $\mathcal{E}$ and $\mathcal{P}$
did not change at all. To show that $(*)\,(d)$ and $(*)\,(e)$ hold as well, we first note that,
by definition of $\mathcal{Q}_\tau$ (5.(h)) and by $(*)\,(e)$ for $\tilde{\rho}$, Add requests in $\mathcal{F}_{\text{crypto}}^{\text{keys}}$ in $\tilde{\mathcal{F}}_{\text{crypto}}$
in ρ are handled just as Add requests in $\mathcal{F}_{\text{crypto}}^{\text{keys}}$ in copies of $\tilde{\mathcal{F}}_{\text{crypto}}$ in ρ', i.e., they
return the error $\perp$ in ρ iff they return $\perp$ in ρ'. We distinguish the following cases:

1. Since Add requests are handled identically in ρ and ρ', as mentioned above, it
   is easy to see that $(*)\,(d)$ and $(*)\,(e)$ remain satisfied if m is the response to a
   KeyGen, Init, GetPSK, Derive, MarkedKnown, or Add? request.

2. If m is the response to an Enc or EncPKE request (i.e., contains a ciphertext y),
   then $\mathcal{Q}_\tau$ lets encryption fail in ρ' (i.e., sends $\perp$) if it fails in ρ (i.e., the provided
   ciphertext y has already been recorded in $\tilde{\mathcal{F}}_{\text{crypto}}$ in ρ). Otherwise, $\mathcal{Q}_\tau$ simply
   forwards m to the copy of $\tilde{\mathcal{F}}_{\text{crypto}}$ that is waiting for this response. So, it is
   easy to see that $(*)\,(d)$ and $(*)\,(e)$ remain satisfied.

3. If m is the response to a Dec or DecPKE request, then $\mathcal{Q}_\tau$ simply forwards m
   to the copy of $\tilde{\mathcal{F}}_{\text{crypto}}$ that is waiting for this response. Since Add requests are
   handled identically in ρ and ρ', as mentioned above, $(*)\,(d)$ and $(*)\,(e)$ remain
   satisfied.

4. Otherwise (i.e., no instance of $\tilde{\mathcal{F}}_{\text{crypto}}$ is waiting for the response m), $\mathcal{Q}_\tau$ stops
   in this activation with empty output and the master IITM in the environment
   will be triggered with empty input in ρ'. The same happens in ρ because $\tilde{\mathcal{F}}_{\text{crypto}}$
   in ρ is also not waiting for this response.

Now, if $\mathcal{P}$ sends a request m' to $\tilde{\mathcal{F}}_{\text{crypto}}$, then we have to show that $(*)$ holds after
$\tilde{\mathcal{F}}_{\text{crypto}}$ has processed this request and either returned a response to $\mathcal{P}$ or sent a
message to $\mathcal{E}$. Since $\mathcal{E}$ is well-formed, $\tilde{\mathcal{F}}_{\text{crypto}}$ will not wait for a response on a network
tape, i.e., it will process the request m' as expected. Hence, also no instance of $\tilde{\mathcal{F}}_{\text{crypto}}$
in $\mathcal{Q}_\tau$ will be waiting for a response on a network tape. It is then easy to see that $(*)$
is satisfied if m' is not a destruction request (i.e., m' is not of the form (Dec, ptr, y),

(DecPKE, *name*, y), (Verify, *ptr*, x, σ), or (VerifySig, *name*, *pk*, x, σ)). For construction requests, e.g., m' is an encryption request, it holds because $\widetilde{\mathcal{F}}_{\text{crypto}}$ in ρ and the corresponding copy of $\widetilde{\mathcal{F}}_{\text{crypto}}$ in ρ' use the same randomness to produce the ciphertext. Requests of the form (Retrieve, *ptr*), (Enc, *ptr*, x), and (EncPKE, *name*, *pk*, x) might turn unknown keys into known keys in $\widetilde{\mathcal{F}}_{\text{crypto}}$. By (a) in Definition 7.12 (i.e., explicitly shared keys do not change the known/unknown status) and because there are no implicitly shared keys (Lemma D.3), we can conclude that if a key, say κ, in ρ changes from unknown to known in $\widetilde{\mathcal{F}}_{\text{crypto}}$, then κ only exists in ρ' in the emulated copy of $\widetilde{\mathcal{F}}_{\text{crypto}}$ that receives m' and, hence, it remains true that the copies of $\widetilde{\mathcal{F}}_{\text{crypto}}$ in ρ' have compatible states $((*)\,(d))$. Next, we distinguish the remaining cases:

1. *MAC verification*, i.e., m' is of the form (Verify, *ptr*, x, σ): Let (lsid, r) be the user that sent m' to $\widetilde{\mathcal{F}}_{\text{crypto}}$. By $(*)\,(e)$, we have that the key, say κ, *ptr* points to for user (lsid, r) is marked unknown in ρ iff it is marked unknown in ρ'. If κ is marked known, then the same happens in ρ and ρ'. So, in the following, we assume that κ is marked unknown.

   First, consider the case where verification in ρ succeeds, i.e., x is recorded as MACed under κ in ρ (i.e., x is recorded in the instance $\mathcal{F}^{\text{mac}}_{\text{crypto}}[\kappa]$). If κ is an explicitly shared key, then, by (b) in Definition 7.12 (implicit disjointness), x has been MACed by a user in the same session as (lsid, r) (or both users are corrupted) and, hence, x is recorded as MACed under κ in the copy of $\widetilde{\mathcal{F}}_{\text{crypto}}$ that (lsid, r) uses. It follows that m' is processed equally in ρ and ρ' and, hence, $(*)$ remains satisfied. If κ is not an explicitly shared key, then it is not shared at all (Lemma D.3). Hence, similarly, x is recorded as MACed under κ in the copy of $\widetilde{\mathcal{F}}_{\text{crypto}}$ that (lsid, r) uses and, hence, $(*)$ remains satisfied.

   Second, consider the case where verification in ρ does not succeed. Then, either $\widetilde{\mathcal{F}}_{\text{crypto}}$ prevents forgery (i.e., the MAC verification algorithm says that the MAC verifies but x is not recorded as MACed under κ) or the MAC verification algorithm does not verify the MAC (i.e., returns 0). If x is not recorded as MACed for x in ρ, then it is not recorded as MACed for x in any copy of $\widetilde{\mathcal{F}}_{\text{crypto}}$ in ρ'. Furthermore, if the MAC verification algorithm does not verify the MAC in ρ, then it does not verify it in ρ' because the same algorithm is run.

   Altogether, we conclude that $(*)$ remains satisfied after $\mathcal{F}_{\text{crypto}}$ has processed the request m'.

2. *Signature verification*, i.e., m' is of the form (VerifySig, *pid'*, *pk*, x, σ): This case is analog to MAC verification, see above.

3. *Symmetric authenticated decryption*, i.e., m' is of the form (Dec, *ptr*, y) and *ptr* points to a key $\kappa \in \mathcal{D}^{\text{auth}}_{\text{senc}}(\eta)$ (i.e., a typed key of type $t \in \mathcal{T}^{\text{auth}}_{\text{senc}}$) in $\widetilde{\mathcal{F}}_{\text{crypto}}$ for the user (lsid, r) that sent m' to $\widetilde{\mathcal{F}}_{\text{crypto}}$: By $(*)\,(e)$, we have that κ is marked unknown in ρ iff it is marked unknown in ρ'. If κ is marked known, then, in ρ,

y is decrypted using the algorithm provided the adversary. Then, the plaintext is parsed and all keys are recorded as known keys (if this fails because guessing of unknown keys is prevented, an error is returned as if decryption fails). The same happens in ρ' because, by $(*)$ (e), the same algorithm is used and $\mathcal{Q}_\tau$ replies with 0 to the Add? request if a key is "guessed" that is marked unknown in some emulated copy of $\widetilde{\mathcal{F}}_{\text{crypto}}$. So, in the following, we assume that κ is marked unknown, i.e., that decryption is performed ideally by $\widetilde{\mathcal{F}}_{\text{crypto}}$.

Since ciphertexts do not collide, there are two cases in ρ: There exists a unique x' such that (x', y) is stored in $\widetilde{\mathcal{F}}_{\text{crypto}}$ for key κ (i.e., in the instance $\mathcal{F}^{\text{senc}}_{\text{crypto}}[\kappa]$), or there does not exist such an x'. In the latter case, also in ρ' it holds that there does not exist an x' such that (x', y) is stored for κ in the copy of $\widetilde{\mathcal{F}}_{\text{crypto}}$ used by $(lsid, r)$. Hence, in both runs ρ and ρ', an error (signaling that decryption failed) is returned to the user $(lsid, r)$. So, $(*)$ remains satisfied.

If there exists a unique x' such that (x', y) is stored in $\mathcal{F}_{\text{crypto}}$ for key κ in ρ and $(lsid, r)$ accepts the response of $\widetilde{\mathcal{F}}_{\text{crypto}}$ (which contains x') in ρ, i.e., the algorithm send-req which is run by $M_r[lsid]$ to determine whether to accept or reject the response of $\widetilde{\mathcal{F}}_{\text{crypto}}$ returns some bit string $\neq \perp$, then: If κ is an explicitly shared key, then, by (b) in Definition 7.12 (implicit disjointness), y has been produced by a user in the same session as $(lsid, r)$ (or both users are corrupted) and, hence, (x', y) is stored for κ in the copy of $\widetilde{\mathcal{F}}_{\text{crypto}}$ that $(lsid, r)$ uses. It follows that m' is processed equally in ρ and ρ' and, hence, $(*)$ remains satisfied. If κ is not an explicitly shared key, then it is not shared at all (Lemma D.3). Hence, similarly, (x', y) is stored for κ in the copy of $\widetilde{\mathcal{F}}_{\text{crypto}}$ that $(lsid, r)$ uses and, hence, $(*)$ remains satisfied.

On the other hand, if there exists a unique x' such that (x', y) is stored in $\widetilde{\mathcal{F}}_{\text{crypto}}$ for key κ in ρ but $M_r[lsid]$ rejects the response of $\mathcal{F}_{\text{crypto}}$ (which contains x') in ρ, i.e., the algorithm send-req which is run by $M_r[lsid]$ to determine whether to accept or reject the response of $\widetilde{\mathcal{F}}_{\text{crypto}}$ returns $\perp$, then: If (x', y) is stored for κ in the copy of $\widetilde{\mathcal{F}}_{\text{crypto}}$ that $(lsid, r)$ uses in ρ', then the same happens in ρ and ρ'. If (x', y) is not stored for κ in the copy of $\widetilde{\mathcal{F}}_{\text{crypto}}$ that $(lsid, r)$ uses in ρ' (i.e., it is stored in some other copy of $\widetilde{\mathcal{F}}_{\text{crypto}}$), then in ρ' the user $(lsid, r)$ receives an error message (signaling that decryption failed). By definition of tests and because send-req rejected the response in ρ, the state of $M_r[lsid]$ in ρ after send-req rejected the response is the same as the state of $M_r[lsid]$ if an error message would have been received. Hence, the state of $M_r[lsid]$ is the same in ρ and ρ'. Furthermore, since all created pointers are deleted, also the state of $\widetilde{\mathcal{F}}_{\text{crypto}}$ in ρ did not change (just as the state of the copy of $\widetilde{\mathcal{F}}_{\text{crypto}}$ that $(lsid, r)$ uses did not change in ρ'). So, $(*)$ remains satisfied.

4. *Symmetric unauthenticated decryption*, i.e., m' is of the form (Dec, ptr, y) and ptr points to a key $\kappa \in \mathcal{D}^{\text{unauth}}_{\text{senc}}(\eta)$ (i.e., a typed key of type $t \in \mathcal{T}^{\text{unauth}}_{\text{senc}}$) in

$\widetilde{\mathcal{F}}_{\text{crypto}}$ for the user $(lsid, r)$ that sent m' to $\widetilde{\mathcal{F}}_{\text{crypto}}$: This case is similar to symmetric authenticated decryption, only the following cases differ:

a) If κ is marked unknown and there does not exist an x' such that (x', y) is stored in $\widetilde{\mathcal{F}}_{\text{crypto}}$ for key κ in ρ, then also in ρ' there does not exist an x' such that (x', y) is stored for κ in any copy of $\widetilde{\mathcal{F}}_{\text{crypto}}$. Then, in both cases the environment is asked to provide a plaintext for y. In ρ', $\mathcal{Q}_\tau$ forwards this request because (x', y) is not stored in any copy of $\widetilde{\mathcal{F}}_{\text{crypto}}$ for any x'. So, $(*)$ remains satisfied.

b) If κ is marked unknown, there exists a unique x' such that (x', y) is stored for κ in $\widetilde{\mathcal{F}}_{\text{crypto}}$ in ρ, $M_r[lsid]$ rejects the response of $\widetilde{\mathcal{F}}_{\text{crypto}}$ (which contains x') in ρ, and (x', y) is not stored for κ in the copy of $\widetilde{\mathcal{F}}_{\text{crypto}}$, say $\widetilde{\mathcal{F}}_{\text{crypto}}[z]$, that $M_r[lsid]$ uses in ρ' (note that in this case there does not exist any x'' such that (x'', y) is stored for key κ in $\widetilde{\mathcal{F}}_{\text{crypto}}[z]$), then, in ρ', $\widetilde{\mathcal{F}}_{\text{crypto}}[z]$ asks the environment to provide a plaintext for y. By definition of $\mathcal{Q}_\tau$ (5. (j)), $\mathcal{Q}_\tau$ returns $\bot$ to $\widetilde{\mathcal{F}}_{\text{crypto}}[z]$ instead of a plaintext, i.e., decryption fails in $\widetilde{\mathcal{F}}_{\text{crypto}}[z]$ and $M_r[lsid]$ rejects the response of $\widetilde{\mathcal{F}}_{\text{crypto}}[z]$ in ρ'. As already mentioned above, by definition of tests and because $M_r[lsid]$ rejected the response in ρ, the state of $M_r[lsid]$ in ρ after it rejected the response is the same as the state of $M_r[lsid]$ if an error message would have been received. Hence, the state of $M_r[lsid]$ is the same in ρ and ρ'. Furthermore, since all created pointers are deleted, also the state of $\widetilde{\mathcal{F}}_{\text{crypto}}$ in ρ did not change (just as the state $\widetilde{\mathcal{F}}_{\text{crypto}}[z]$ did not change in ρ'). So, $(*)$ remains satisfied.

5. *Public-key decryption*, i.e., m' is of the form (DecPKE, y): This case is analog to symmetric unauthenticated decryption, see above.

This concludes the proof of Lemma D.4. $\qquad\qquad\qquad\qquad\qquad\qquad\square$

D.2.2. Step 2: $\mathcal{E}\,|\,\mathcal{Q}_\tau \equiv \mathcal{E}\,|\,\mathcal{S}\,|\,\mathcal{F}$

Next, we show that $\mathcal{Q}_\tau$ realizes $\mathcal{F}$. Therefore, we first define a simulator $\mathcal{S}$ (that does not depend on the environment $\mathcal{E}$) and then show the following lemma. As mentioned above, this does not require that $\mathcal{P}$ satisfies implicit disjointness but only that $\mathcal{P}\,|\,\widetilde{\mathcal{F}}_{\text{crypto}}$ single-session realizes $\mathcal{F}$.

Lemma D.5. *If* $\mathcal{P}\,|\,\widetilde{\mathcal{F}}_{\text{crypto}} \leq_{\tau\text{-single}*} \mathcal{F}$, *then* $\mathcal{E}\,|\,\mathcal{Q}_\tau \equiv \mathcal{E}\,|\,\mathcal{S}\,|\,\mathcal{F}$.

Before we define $\mathcal{S}$ and prove the above lemma, we note that if $\mathcal{P}$ satisfies implicit disjointness w.r.t. τ and $\mathcal{P}\,|\,\widetilde{\mathcal{F}}_{\text{crypto}} \leq_{\tau\text{-single}*} \mathcal{F}$, then Lemma D.4 ($\mathcal{E}\,|\,\mathcal{P}\,|\,\widetilde{\mathcal{F}}_{\text{crypto}} \equiv \mathcal{E}\,|\,\mathcal{Q}_\tau$) and Lemma D.5, by transitivity of $\equiv$, directly imply $\mathcal{E}\,|\,\mathcal{P}\,|\,\widetilde{\mathcal{F}}_{\text{crypto}} \equiv \mathcal{E}\,|\,\mathcal{S}\,|\,\mathcal{F}$ (for the simulator $\mathcal{S}$ defined below). Hence, this proves Theorem 7.5.

The simulator. We now define the simulator $\mathcal{S}$ that occurs in Lemma D.5. Therefore, let $\mathcal{S}_\tau \in \text{Sim}^{\mathcal{P}\,|\,\widetilde{\mathcal{F}}_{\text{crypto}}}(\mathcal{F})$ be a "single-session" simulator for $\mathcal{P}\,|\,\widetilde{\mathcal{F}}_{\text{crypto}} \leq_{\tau\text{-single*}} \mathcal{F}$, i.e., $\mathcal{S}_\tau$ is well-formed (Definition 7.10) and

$$\mathcal{E}'\,|\,\mathcal{P}\,|\,\widetilde{\mathcal{F}}_{\text{crypto}} \equiv \mathcal{E}'\,|\,\mathcal{S}_\tau\,|\,\mathcal{F} \tag{D.11}$$

for every single-session environment $\mathcal{E}' \in \text{Env}_{\tau\text{-single}}(\mathcal{P}\,|\,\widetilde{\mathcal{F}}_{\text{crypto}})$.

The simulator $\mathcal{S}$ is an IITM that uses several copies of $\mathcal{S}_\tau$ (basically one for every session). It has the same network interface as $\mathcal{Q}_\tau$, connects to the network interface of $\mathcal{F}$ (i.e., $\mathcal{S}\,|\,\mathcal{F}$ has the same external interface as $\mathcal{Q}_\tau$), and simulates the IITM $\mathcal{Q}_\tau$ as follows.

Every Establish message for a user (which is forwarded by $\mathcal{F}$ to $\mathcal{S}$), is forwarded by $\mathcal{S}$ to $\mathcal{Q}_\tau$. Also, $\mathcal{S}$ forwards all network output/input from/to $\mathcal{Q}_\tau$ to/from the environment.

During the simulation of $\mathcal{Q}_\tau$, $\mathcal{S}$ always checks whether there exists a new complete session, i.e., instances $M_1[lsid_1], \ldots, M_n[lsid_n]$ of the machines $M_1, \ldots, M_n$ in $\mathcal{P}$ (which are emulated by $\mathcal{Q}_\tau$) such that they are partners according to τ (i.e., $\tau(\alpha_1) = \cdots = \tau(\alpha_n) = sid \in \{0,1\}^*$ for some SID sid where α_r is the sequence of messages (along with tapes) sent and received by $M_r[lsid_r]$ on network tapes in this run so far). If $\mathcal{S}$ finds such a new complete session, then $\mathcal{S}$ continues the simulation of $\mathcal{Q}_\tau$ such that this session (i.e., the instances $M_1[lsid_1], \ldots, M_n[lsid_n]$ and $\widetilde{\mathcal{F}}_{\text{crypto}}[sid]$, which is the corresponding copy of $\widetilde{\mathcal{F}}_{\text{crypto}}$) is now handled by a new copy of the "single-session" simulator $\mathcal{S}_\tau$. The initial state of this new copy of $\mathcal{S}_\tau$ is set as if this session has always been handled by $\mathcal{S}_\tau$. Because $\mathcal{S}_\tau$ is well-formed (Definition 7.10), and hence, in its first stage, it exactly simulated $\mathcal{P}\,|\,\widetilde{\mathcal{F}}_{\text{crypto}}$ (by definition of well-formedness for Definition 7.10), $\mathcal{S}$ can adjust the state of $\mathcal{S}_\tau$ appropriately. Then, $\mathcal{S}$ forwards all output/input from/to $\mathcal{S}_\tau$ to/from $\mathcal{F}$.

Furthermore, $\mathcal{S}$ always checks whether a user an instance $M_r[lsid]$ of M_r in $\mathcal{P}$ gets corrupted according to τ (i.e., $\tau(\alpha) = \text{corr}$ where α is the sequence of messages (along with tapes) sent and received by $M_r[lsid]$ on network tapes in this run so far). If this is the case, then $\mathcal{S}$ corrupts $(lsid, r)$ in $\mathcal{F}_{\text{session}}$ in $\mathcal{F}$ (by sending $(\text{Corr}, lsid, r)$) and, from then on, $\mathcal{S}$ forwards all I/O output/input from/to $M_r[lsid]$ to/from $\mathcal{F}_{\text{session}}$ in $\mathcal{F}$ for the user $(lsid, r)$ (using the Output request). Note that $\mathcal{F}_{\text{session}}$ in $\mathcal{F}$ forwards this output to the user $(lsid, r)$ as desired.

Once an uncorrupted instance $M_r[lsid]$ (according to τ) belongs to a complete session, it does not produce I/O output because it is not anymore simulated as it is but instead it is handled by a copy of $\mathcal{S}_\tau$ which directly interfaces with $\mathcal{F}$. But an uncorrupted instance $M_r[lsid]$ that does not belong to a complete session might produce I/O output. If this happens, then $\mathcal{S}$ terminates. (In this case the simulation fails but this happens only with negligible probability, as we will see.)

Since $\mathcal{S}_\tau\,|\,\mathcal{F}$ is environmentally strictly bounded ($\mathcal{S}_\tau$ is well-formed), as for $\mathcal{Q}_\tau$, it is easy to see that $\mathcal{S}\,|\,\mathcal{F}$ is environmentally strictly bounded. Hence, we have that $\mathcal{S} \in \text{Sim}^{\mathcal{Q}_\tau}(\mathcal{F}) = \text{Sim}^{\mathcal{P}\,|\,\widetilde{\mathcal{F}}_{\text{crypto}}}(\mathcal{F})$.

Proof of Lemma D.5. By definition, $\mathcal{S}$ terminates if an emulated instance $M_r[lsid]$ produces I/O output although it is not corrupted or does not belong to a complete session (according to τ). We now show that such "early output" happens only with negligible probability in runs of $\mathcal{E} \,|\, \mathcal{Q}_\tau$, and hence, as we will see, also in runs of $\mathcal{S} \,|\, \mathcal{F}$.

Lemma D.6. *If $\mathcal{P} \,|\, \widetilde{\mathcal{F}}_{\mathrm{crypto}} \leq_{\tau\text{-single*}} \mathcal{F}$, then the following holds with overwhelming probability, where the probability is over runs ρ of $\mathcal{E} \,|\, \mathcal{Q}_\tau$ (for some security parameter and external input): If an instance $M_r[lsid]$ (emulated by $\mathcal{Q}_\tau$), for some $r, lsid$, produces I/O output to $\mathcal{E}$ (except for responses to corruption status requests of the form $(lsid, \mathsf{Corr?})$) at some point in ρ, then either*

1. *$(lsid, r)$ is corrupted at that point in ρ, i.e., $\tau_{(lsid,r)}(\rho') = \mathsf{corr}$ where ρ' is the prefix of ρ up to the point where $M_r[lsid]$ produces the first I/O output to $\mathcal{E}$, or*

2. *$(lsid, r)$ belongs to a complete session, i.e., there exist sid, $lsid_1$, $\ldots$, $lsid_n$ such that $lsid_r = lsid$ and $\tau_{(lsid_1,1)}(\rho') = \cdots = \tau_{(lsid_n,n)}(\rho') = sid \in \{0,1\}^*$ where ρ' is as above.*

Proof. The idea to prove this lemma is simple: We define a single-session environment $\mathcal{E}'$ for $\mathcal{P} \,|\, \widetilde{\mathcal{F}}_{\mathrm{crypto}}$ that simulates a run of $\mathcal{E} \,|\, \mathcal{Q}_\tau$ but first guesses the session that contains the instance $M_r[lsid]$ that produces this "early output" and relays this session out to the external system $\mathcal{P} \,|\, \widetilde{\mathcal{F}}_{\mathrm{crypto}}$ or $\mathcal{S}_\tau \,|\, \mathcal{F}$, respectively. When this "early output" happens, $\mathcal{E}'$ produces overall output 1. Otherwise, it produces overall output 0. Since $\mathcal{S}_\tau$ is well-formed and by definition of $\mathcal{F}$, the probability that $\mathcal{E}' \,|\, \mathcal{S}_\tau \,|\, \mathcal{F}$ produces overall output 1 is zero. Since $\mathcal{E}' \,|\, \mathcal{P} \,|\, \widetilde{\mathcal{F}}_{\mathrm{crypto}} \equiv \mathcal{E}'\mathcal{S}_\tau \,|\, \mathcal{F}$ (because $\mathcal{P} \,|\, \widetilde{\mathcal{F}}_{\mathrm{crypto}} \leq_{\tau\text{-single*}} \mathcal{F}$), the probability that $\mathcal{E}' \,|\, \mathcal{P} \,|\, \widetilde{\mathcal{F}}_{\mathrm{crypto}}$ produces overall output 1 is negligible. Since $\mathcal{E}'$ correctly guesses the external session with non-negligible probability, we can conclude that the probability that an instance $M_r[lsid]$ produces "early output" in a run of $\mathcal{E} \,|\, \mathcal{Q}_\tau$ is negligible.

More precisely, $\mathcal{E}'$ is an IITM that connects to $\mathcal{P} \,|\, \widetilde{\mathcal{F}}_{\mathrm{crypto}}$ such that $\mathcal{E}' \,|\, \mathcal{P} \,|\, \widetilde{\mathcal{F}}_{\mathrm{crypto}}$ has the same external interface as $\mathcal{P} \,|\, \widetilde{\mathcal{F}}_{\mathrm{crypto}}$. First, $\mathcal{E}'$ chooses $(i_1, \ldots, i_n) \in I$ where $I := \{(i'_1, \ldots, i'_n) \mid i'_1, \ldots, i'_n \in \{1, \ldots, p_\mathcal{E}(\eta + |a|)\} \cup \{\bot\}\}$ uniformly at random. Recall that $p_\mathcal{E}$ is the polynomial that bounds the runtime of $\mathcal{E}$ and, hence, the number of users in a run of $\mathcal{E} \,|\, \mathcal{Q}_\tau$. Then, $\mathcal{E}'$ emulates a run of $\mathcal{E} \,|\, \mathcal{Q}_\tau$ but, for all r such that $i_r \neq \bot$, the i_r-th user (the i'-th user is just the user/instance of some M_r that sent the i'-th Establish message in the run) is handled by the *external* system $\mathcal{P} \,|\, \widetilde{\mathcal{F}}_{\mathrm{crypto}}$ or $\mathcal{S} \,|\, \mathcal{F}$, respectively. That is, all messages for this user and its corresponding copy of $\widetilde{\mathcal{F}}_{\mathrm{crypto}}$ are sent to the external system. Note that if $i_r = \bot$, then there exits no user in role r in the external system. If $\mathcal{E}'$ would violate the conditions of being a single-session environment for $\mathcal{P} \,|\, \widetilde{\mathcal{F}}_{\mathrm{crypto}}$ (Definition 7.8) at some point, then $\mathcal{E}'$ terminates with overall output 0 (on tape decision). We note that $\mathcal{E}'$ can observe when this happens because τ only depends on the messages that have been sent on the network interface of $\mathcal{P}$.

If a user in the external system, say the i_r-th user for some r, produces "early output", i.e., it produces I/O output to the environment but it does not belong to a complete session or is not corrupted (according to τ), then $\mathcal{E}'$ does the following. First, note that the i_r-th user cannot be corrupted (according to τ) because then $\mathcal{E}'$ would not be single-session. If the i_r-th user does not belong to any session (i.e., τ returns $\bot$ for this user), then $\mathcal{E}'$ verifies that $i_{r'} = \bot$ for all $r' \neq r$. If this is the case, i.e., the external system only contains the i_r-th user which does not belong to any session, then $\mathcal{E}'$ produces overall output 1 (i.e., outputs 1 on tape decision). Otherwise, $\mathcal{E}'$ produces overall output 0. On the other hand, if the i_r-th user belongs to some session, say with SID sid, then $\mathcal{E}'$ verifies that all external users (i.e., $i_{r'}$-th user for all r' such that $i_{r'} \neq \bot$) belong to the same session sid and that no other user belong to this session sid. If this is the case, i.e., $i_1, \ldots, i_n$ correctly specifies a session, then $\mathcal{E}'$ produces overall output 1. Otherwise, $\mathcal{E}'$ produces overall output 0.

Since $\mathcal{S}_\tau$ is well-formed (Definition 7.10) and by definition of $\mathcal{F}$, it is easy to see that (for every security parameter η and external input a):

$$\Pr\left[(\mathcal{E}' \,|\, \mathcal{S}_\tau \,|\, \mathcal{F})(1^\eta, a) = 1\right] = 0 \ .$$

Since $\mathcal{E} \,|\, \mathcal{Q}_\tau$ is strictly bounded, it is easy to see that $\mathcal{E}'$ is universally bounded. By definition, it is also single-session w.r.t. τ. Hence, $\mathcal{E}' \in \mathrm{Env}_{\tau\text{-single}}(\mathcal{P} \,|\, \widetilde{\mathcal{F}}_{\mathrm{crypto}})$. By (D.11) ($\mathcal{P} \,|\, \widetilde{\mathcal{F}}_{\mathrm{crypto}} \leq_{\tau\text{-single}*} \mathcal{F}$ with simulator $\mathcal{S}_\tau$), we obtain that:

$$\mathcal{E}' \,|\, \mathcal{P} \,|\, \widetilde{\mathcal{F}}_{\mathrm{crypto}} \equiv \mathcal{E}' \,|\, \mathcal{S}_\tau \,|\, \mathcal{F} \ .$$

We obtain that there exists a negligible function f such that:

$$\Pr\left[(\mathcal{E}' \,|\, \mathcal{P} \,|\, \widetilde{\mathcal{F}}_{\mathrm{crypto}})(1^\eta, a) = 1\right] \leq f(\eta) \ .$$

Let B be the event that, in a run of $\mathcal{E} \,|\, \mathcal{Q}_\tau$, some instance $M_r[lsid]$ produces "early output". Since $\mathcal{E}' \,|\, \mathcal{P} \,|\, \widetilde{\mathcal{F}}_{\mathrm{crypto}}$ precisely simulates such a run of $\mathcal{E} \,|\, \mathcal{Q}_\tau$ and produces overall outputs 1 if $\mathcal{E}'$ guessed the external session correctly, we conclude that:

$$|I|^{-1} \cdot \Pr[B] \leq \Pr\left[(\mathcal{E}' \,|\, \mathcal{P} \,|\, \widetilde{\mathcal{F}}_{\mathrm{crypto}})(1^\eta, a) = 1\right] \leq f(\eta) \ .$$

Since $|I| = (p_\mathcal{E}(\eta) + 1)^n$ is a polynomial in η (the number of roles n is constant and does not depend on η), we obtain that $\Pr[B]$ is negligible, which concludes the proof. $\qquad\qquad\square$

The proof proceeds similarly to the proof of Theorem 7.4 because $\mathcal{Q}_\tau$ is similar to $\mathcal{P} \,|\, \mathcal{F}'$ for some multi-session local-SID functionality $\mathcal{F}'$.

We define hybrid systems $\mathcal{H}_i$ for all $i \in \mathbb{N}$. They are similar to the ones in the proof of Theorem 7.4. Basically, $\mathcal{H}_i$ emulates $\mathcal{E}$ interacting with $\mathcal{Q}_\tau$ and $\mathcal{S} \,|\, \mathcal{F}$ such that the first $i-1$ sessions are handled by $\mathcal{Q}_\tau$ and all later session are handled by $\mathcal{S} \,|\, \mathcal{F}$. Here, the *i-th session* is simply the i-th complete session that τ signals (i.e., the i-th SID sid where there exist n users, one for each role, that belong to session sid according to τ). We note that, as long as an instance $M_r[lsid]$ is not corrupted and does not belong to a complete session, it is treated identically in $\mathcal{Q}_\tau$ and $\mathcal{S} \,|\, \mathcal{F}$, except that $\mathcal{S}$ would terminate if $M_r[lsid]$ produces I/O to $\mathcal{E}$ (except for responses to corruption status requests). In such an "early output" occurs, we define $\mathcal{H}_i$ to terminate with output 0 on decision. We further note that corrupted instances (i.e., where τ signals corr) are not counted as sessions. They are unproblematic anyway because they are treated identically in $\mathcal{Q}_\tau$ and $\mathcal{S}\,|\,\mathcal{F}$. In $\mathcal{S}\,|\,\mathcal{F}$, the corresponding user gets corrupted in $\mathcal{F}$ and is then perfectly simulated.

Since $\mathcal{Q}_\tau$ and $\mathcal{S}\,|\,\mathcal{F}$ are environmentally strictly bounded and these two systems are simulated by $\mathcal{H}_i$ almost as if they have disjoint tapes (basically all communication between them goes through $\mathcal{E}$), similar to Lemma 2.3 and because $\mathcal{E}$ is universally bounded, it is easy to see that $\mathcal{H}_i$ is strictly bounded for all $i \in \mathbb{N}$.

Additionally to the above hybrid systems, we define $\mathcal{H}_{p_\mathcal{E}+1}$ to be the IITM that is defined just as $\mathcal{H}_i$ except that it uses $p_\mathcal{E}(\eta)$ instead of i (η is the security parameter). That is, all sessions are handled by $\mathcal{Q}_\tau$ because $\mathcal{E}$ creates at most $p_\mathcal{E}(\eta)$ sessions. In particularly, using that $\mathcal{Q}_\tau$ never produces I/O output for an instance $M_r[lsid]$ that is not corrupted and does not belong to a complete session (Lemma D.6), we obtain that:

$$\mathcal{H}_{p_\mathcal{E}+1} \equiv \mathcal{E}\,|\,\mathcal{Q}_\tau \ . \tag{D.12}$$

Similarly, by construction, $\mathcal{H}_1$ forwards all sessions to $\mathcal{S}\,|\,\mathcal{F}$ and we have that:

$$\mathcal{H}_1 \equiv \mathcal{E}\,|\,\mathcal{S}\,|\,\mathcal{F} \ . \tag{D.13}$$

Similarly to the proof of Theorem 7.4, we define hybrid systems $\mathcal{H}^*_{i,i_1,\dots,i_n}$, for all $i \in \mathbb{N}$ and $i_1,\dots,i_n \in \mathbb{N} \cup \{\bot\}$, which are supposed to be single-session environments for $\mathcal{P}\,|\,\widetilde{\mathcal{F}}_{\text{crypto}}$ (i.e., $\mathcal{H}^*_{i,i_1,\dots,i_n} \in \text{Env}_{\tau\text{-single}}(\mathcal{P}\,|\,\widetilde{\mathcal{F}}_{\text{crypto}})$). The hybrid $\mathcal{H}^*_{i,i_1,\dots,i_n}$ is similar to $\mathcal{H}_i$, i.e., it emulates $\mathcal{E}$ interacting with $\mathcal{Q}_\tau$ and $\mathcal{S}\,|\,\mathcal{F}$, but the i-th session is handled by the *external system* $\mathcal{P}\,|\,\widetilde{\mathcal{F}}_{\text{crypto}}$ or $\mathcal{S}_\tau\,|\,\mathcal{F}$, respectively. To successfully outsource the i-th session, $\mathcal{H}^*_{i,i_1,\dots,i_n}$ has to know which users belong to this session even before this session is created. Therefore, $\mathcal{H}^*_{i,i_1,\dots,i_n}$ is additionally parametrized by $i_1,\dots,i_n$ which tells $\mathcal{H}^*_{i,i_1,\dots,i_n}$ that the i_r-th user plays role r in the i-th session (the i'-th user is just the user $(lsid,r)$ that sent the i'-th Establish message in the run). If $i_r = \bot$, then there is no user in role r in the external session.

Recall from the definition of $\mathcal{Q}_\tau$ that $\mathcal{Q}_\tau$ needs information about the internal states of the copies of $\widetilde{\mathcal{F}}_{\text{crypto}}$ that it emulates. For example, to keep the states compatible, it needs to know which keys exist in which instance and what their status is (known or unknown). For another example, because $\mathcal{Q}_\tau$ lets decryption fail if a ciphertext is decrypted under a private key or an unauthenticated symmetric encryption key and this ciphertext is recorded in some other copy of $\widetilde{\mathcal{F}}_{\text{crypto}}$ (rule 5. (j) in the definition of $\mathcal{Q}_\tau$), $\mathcal{Q}_\tau$ needs to know which ciphertext is recorded in which copy of $\widetilde{\mathcal{F}}_{\text{crypto}}$ for public/private keys and unauthenticated symmetric encryption keys. Now, $\mathcal{H}^*_{i,i_1,\dots,i_n}$ has to do the same things but of course it cannot directly inspect the state of $\widetilde{\mathcal{F}}_{\text{crypto}}$ in the external session. But due to our modifications of $\widetilde{\mathcal{F}}_{\text{crypto}}$ (adding MarkedKnown and Add? requests and that the adversary provides the ciphertext in case of unauthenticated encryption), $\mathcal{H}^*_{i,i_1,\dots,i_n}$ knows which keys are known and which are unknown in the external session and which ciphertexts have been recorded in the external session for unauthenticated encryption. This tells $\mathcal{H}^*_{i,i_1,\ldots,i_n}$ exactly the information about the state of the external session that it needs to emulate $\mathcal{Q}_\tau$.

If $\mathcal{H}^*_{i,i_1,\ldots,i_n}$ would violate the conditions of being a single-session environment for $\mathcal{P} \,|\, \widetilde{\mathcal{F}}_{\text{crypto}}$ at some point, then $\mathcal{H}^*_{i,i_1,\ldots,i_n}$ instead terminates with error, i.e., the overall output (on tape decision) is some error message $\neq 1$. For example, this happens if two users in the external session have different SIDs (according to τ). We note that $\mathcal{H}^*_{i,i_1,\ldots,i_n}$ can observe when this happens because τ only depends on the messages that have been sent on the network interface of $\mathcal{P}$ (and not on the internal state of the external session). Furthermore, if the run stops with overall output m, say, then $\mathcal{H}^*_{i,i_1,\ldots,i_n}$ checks if the i-th session exists and, for all $i' \in \mathbb{N}$, if the i'-th user exists then it has SID sid if and only if $i' = i_r$ for some r (i.e., the i'-th user is the user in role r in the external session) where sid is the SID of the i-th session. (That is, all users that exist in the external session have SID sid and no other users have SID sid.) If this is the case, $\mathcal{H}^*_{i,i_1,\ldots,i_n}$ produces overall output m. Otherwise, $\mathcal{H}^*_{i,i_1,\ldots,i_n}$ terminates with an error (as above). If $\mathcal{H}^*_{i,i_1,\ldots,i_n}$ does not terminate with an error, we say that $i_1, \ldots, i_n$ *correctly specify the i-th session.*

As in the proof of Theorem 7.4, for all $i, i' \in \mathbb{N}$, $i_1, \ldots, i_n \in \mathbb{N} \cup \{\bot\}$, we define $B_{\mathcal{H}_{i'}}(i, i_1, \ldots, i_n)$, to be the set of runs of $\mathcal{H}_{i'}$ where the i-th complete session exists and $i_1, \ldots, i_n$ correctly specify the i-th session.

Similarly to Lemma D.1 in the proof of Theorem 7.4, for all $i \in \mathbb{N}$, $i_1, \ldots, i_n \in \mathbb{N} \cup \{\bot\}$, we can show that (for every security parameter η and external input a):

$$\Pr\left[(\mathcal{H}^*_{i,i_1,\ldots,i_n} \,|\, \mathcal{S}_\tau \,|\, \mathcal{F})(1^\eta, a) = 1\right] = \Pr\left[\mathcal{H}_i(1^\eta, a) = 1 \cap B_{\mathcal{H}_i}(i, i_1, \ldots, i_n)\right]$$
$$(\text{D.14})$$

$$\Pr\left[(\mathcal{H}^*_{i,i_1,\ldots,i_n} \,|\, \mathcal{P} \,|\, \widetilde{\mathcal{F}}_{\text{crypto}})(1^\eta, a) = 1\right] = \Pr\left[\mathcal{H}_{i+1}(1^\eta, a) = 1 \cap B_{\mathcal{H}_{i+1}}(i, i_1, \ldots, i_n)\right].$$
$$(\text{D.15})$$

That is, the probability that a run of $\mathcal{H}^*_{i,i_1,\ldots,i_n} \,|\, \mathcal{S}_\tau \,|\, \mathcal{F}$ (resp., $\mathcal{H}^*_{i,i_1,\ldots,i_n} \,|\, \mathcal{P} \,|\, \widetilde{\mathcal{F}}_{\text{crypto}}$) produces overall output 1 equals the probability that a run of $\mathcal{H}_i$ (resp., $\mathcal{H}_{i+1}$) produces overall output 1 where the i-th session is specified by $i_1, \ldots, i_n$.

Finally, as for Theorem 7.4, using (D.14) and (D.15), we conclude that $\mathcal{H}_1 \equiv \mathcal{H}_{p_{\mathcal{E}}+1}$. By (D.12) and (D.13), we further conclude that $\mathcal{E} \,|\, \mathcal{S} \,|\, \mathcal{F} \equiv \mathcal{E} \,|\, \mathcal{Q}_\tau$. This concludes the proof of Lemma D.5.

D.3. Applications

In this appendix, we present more details for Section 7.7.

$$
\begin{array}{lll}
1. & A \rightarrow B: & \{\!|N_A, pid_A|\!\}_{k_B} \\
2. & B \rightarrow A: & \{\!|N_A, N_B|\!\}_{k_A} \\
3. & A \rightarrow B: & \{\!|N_B|\!\}_{k_B}
\end{array}
$$

Figure D.1.: The Needham-Schroeder Public-Key (NSPK) protocol.

$$
\begin{array}{lll}
1. & A \rightarrow B: & N_A' \\
2. & B \rightarrow A: & N_B' \\
3. & A \rightarrow B: & \{\!|(pid_A, pid_B, N_A', N_B'), N_A, pid_A|\!\}_{k_B} \\
4. & B \rightarrow A: & \{\!|(pid_A, pid_B, N_A', N_B'), N_A, N_B|\!\}_{k_A} \\
5. & A \rightarrow B: & \{\!|(pid_A, pid_B, N_A', N_B'), N_B|\!\}_{k_B}
\end{array}
$$

Figure D.2.: The idealized NSPK protocol.

D.3.1. The Needham-Schroeder Public-Key Protocol

We now present an example of an *insecure* protocol, namely the Needham-Schroeder Public-Key (NSPK) protocol, which is turned into a *secure* protocol when prefixing messages with pre-established SIDs as done in classical joint state theorems for encryption. We also give an example of a secure protocol that does not satisfies implicit disjointness, namely the Needham-Schroeder-Lowe (NSL) protocol.

The NSPK Protocol.   The Needham-Schroeder Public-Key (NSPK) protocol [NS78] is sketched in Figure D.1. In this, pid_A is A's party name and N_A and N_B are nonces chosen by A and B, respectively. It can be shown that this protocol (appropriately modeled as a protocol in the IITM or UC model) is secure in a single-session setting (e.g., realizes a single-session ideal key exchange functionality), e.g., $\mathcal{F}_{\mathrm{ke}}$ (see Section 4.3.1). Using joint state composition theorems for public-key encryption (see Section 4.2.6), we obtain security in the multi-session setting of an idealized NSPK protocol which assumes and uses pre-established SIDs, i.e., that it realizes the multi-session ideal key exchange functionality $!\mathcal{F}_{\mathrm{ke}}$. A concrete instance of such an idealized NSPK protocol where these SIDs are established by exchanging nonces (N_A' and N_B'), as discussed in [BLR04], is the protocol depicted in Figure D.2. As can be seen, this changes the NSPK protocol dramatically; in particular, while NSPK is insecure in the multi-session setting, in particularly, it does not realize $!\mathcal{F}_{\mathrm{ke}}$ or the multi-session local-SID ideal key exchange functionality $\widehat{\mathcal{F}}_{\mathrm{ke}}$, (the protocol in) Figure D.2 is secure. We note that Figure D.2 in particularly applies Lowe's fix [Low95] (namely adding B's name pid_B to the second plaintext, see Figure D.3) but it does much more; also, it trivially satisfies implicit disjointness.

The NSL Protocol.   The Needham-Schroeder-Lowe (NSL) protocol [Low95] is depicted in Figure D.3. In this, pid_A and pid_B are A's and B's party name, respectively, and N_A and N_B are the nonces chosen by A and B, respectively. This protocol

$$
\begin{array}{lll}
1. & A \to B: & \{\!| N_A, pid_A |\!\}_{k_B} \\
2. & B \to A: & \{\!| N_A, N_B, pid_B |\!\}_{k_A} \\
3. & A \to B: & \{\!| N_B |\!\}_{k_B}
\end{array}
$$

Figure D.3.: The Needham-Schroeder-Lowe (NSL) protocol.

(appropriately modeled as a multi-session protocol that uses $\mathcal{F}_{\text{crypto}}$ for public-key encryption) does not satisfy implicit disjointness because B would decrypt the first message (i.e., $\{\!| N_A, pid_A |\!\}_{k_B}$) in any session. The reason that this protocol is still secure is because the link between the first message and the session is established by the third protocol message (i.e., $\{\!| N_B |\!\}_{k_B}$), see also [CH06]. Fortunately, as demonstrated by our case studies in Section 7.7.2, most real-world protocols do not use such kind of authentication but establish a link between every message (that contains ciphertexts, MACs, or signatures) and the session.

D.3.2. Building Secure Channels from Key Exchange Protocols

We now define two generic secure channel multi-session real protocols $\mathcal{P}_{\text{sc}}$ and $\mathcal{P}_{\text{sc}}^+$ that belong to the class of protocols defined in Section 7.5.1 (i.e., they can be analyzed using Theorem 7.4, our universal composition theorem without pre-established SIDs). As a subprotocol/functionality they use the multi-session local-SID functionality $\widehat{\mathcal{F}}_{\text{keyuse}} = \widehat{\mathcal{F}}_{\text{keyuse}}^{\mathcal{F}_{\text{senc}}^{\text{auth}}}$ for key usability, where the session key can be used for ideal authenticated symmetric encryption (see Section 4.2.3 for the functionality $\mathcal{F}_{\text{senc}}^{\text{auth}}$, Section 4.3.2 for the key usability functionality $\mathcal{F}_{\text{keyuse}}$, and Definition 7.1 for multi-session local-SID functionalities).[92] Then, we show that $\mathcal{P}_{\text{sc}} \,|\, \widehat{\mathcal{F}}_{\text{keyuse}}$ realizes $\widehat{\mathcal{F}}_{\text{sc}}$ and that $\mathcal{P}_{\text{sc}}^+ \,|\, \widehat{\mathcal{F}}_{\text{keyuse}}$ realizes $\widehat{\mathcal{F}}_{\text{sc}}^+$, where $\widehat{\mathcal{F}}_{\text{sc}}$ and $\widehat{\mathcal{F}}_{\text{sc}}^+$ are the multi-session local-SID versions (see Definition 7.1) of the ideal secure channel functionalities $\mathcal{F}_{\text{sc}}$ and $\mathcal{F}_{\text{sc}}^+$ from Section 4.3.3.

We note that, if we would replace $\widehat{\mathcal{F}}_{\text{keyuse}}$ by its authenticated variant $\widehat{\mathcal{F}}_{\text{auth-keyuse}}$ (see Section 4.3.2), i.e., the key exchange protocol now must provide authentication, then these protocols realize the variant of $\widehat{\mathcal{F}}_{\text{sc}}$ or $\widehat{\mathcal{F}}_{\text{sc}}^+$, respectively, that provides authentication (see Section 4.3.3).

For many real-world secure channel protocols these secure channel protocols can be instantiated appropriately such that $\mathcal{P}_{\text{sc}}$ (or $\mathcal{P}_{\text{sc}}^+$) faithfully models the secure channel protocol. For example, the CCM Protocol (CCMP), which is part of IEEE standard 802.11i [IEE07, IEE04] and uses the 4WHS protocol (see Section 7.4.3) to establish a secure channel, can be modeled by $\mathcal{P}_{\text{sc}}$, as we will see below. Together

---

[92]We note that (variants of) the protocols $\mathcal{P}_{\text{sc}}$ and $\mathcal{P}_{\text{sc}}^+$ have been analyzed in [KT11b] in a different setting. It was shown, directly in the multi-session setting (i.e., without using composition theorems), that $\mathcal{P}_{\text{sc}}$ (resp., $\mathcal{P}_{\text{sc}}^+$), under certain assumptions on the underlying key exchange protocol, realizes a multi-session ideal secure channel functionality which is similar to $\mathcal{F}_{\text{sc}}$ (resp., $\mathcal{F}_{\text{sc}}^+$).

with the results from Section 7.4.3 (where we showed that the 4WHS protocol realizes $\widehat{\mathcal{F}}_{\text{auth-keyuse}}$) and the composition theorems, we obtain that CCMP combined with 4WHS realizes $\widehat{\mathcal{F}}_{\text{sc}}$ (as mentioned above, it even realizes the variant of $\widehat{\mathcal{F}}_{\text{sc}}$ that provides authentication), i.e., is a *secure* secure channel protocol.

Generic Secure Channel Protocols

In a nutshell, a session of $\mathcal{P}_{\text{sc}}$ (and also of $\mathcal{P}_{\text{sc}}^+$) runs a session of $\widehat{\mathcal{F}}_{\text{keyuse}}$ to establish a session key. This session key is then used to establish secure channels between the parties of the session, one channel for each pair of parties in that session. For this purpose, before a message is encrypted under the session key, a counter is added to the plaintext as well as some information indicating the sender and the receiver (e.g., party names). While $\mathcal{P}_{\text{sc}}$ tolerates message loss, $\mathcal{P}_{\text{sc}}^+$ does not.

We define the leakage function of $\mathcal{F}_{\text{senc}}^{\text{auth}}$ in $\widehat{\mathcal{F}}_{\text{keyuse}}$ (see above) to be the leakage function $L(1^\eta, m)$ that returns a random bit string of length $|m|$, i.e., it leaks exactly the length of a message. Furthermore, as in Section 7.4.2, we consider a variant of $\mathcal{F}_{\text{senc}}^{\text{auth}}$ that is parametrized by a polynomial-time decidable domain of plaintexts $D = \{D(\eta)\}_{\eta \in \mathbb{N}}$ such that only plaintexts from this domain can be encrypted/decrypted using $\mathcal{F}_{\text{senc}}^{\text{auth}}$.

The protocols $\mathcal{P}_{\text{sc}}$ and $\mathcal{P}_{\text{sc}}^+$ are of the form $!M_1 \mid \cdots \mid !M_n$ where the machine M_r, for all $r \leq n$, models role r of the protocol. These machines are parametrized by a (polynomial-time decidable) domain of session parameters $SP = \{SP(\eta)\}_{\eta \in \mathbb{N}}$ and a domain of natural numbers $V = \{V(\eta)\}_{\eta \in \mathbb{N}}$ (these numbers bound the counter values, see below). Furthermore, to format and parse plaintexts, the machines are parametrized by two polynomial-time computable functions f and p. The *formatting* function f takes as inputs a security parameter 1^η, two different roles $r, r' \in \{1, \ldots, n\}$ (i.e., $r \neq r'$), session parameters $sp \in SP(\eta)$, a counter $v < V(\eta)$, and a message $m \in \{0,1\}^*$ and outputs a plaintext $m' \in D(\eta)$ (recall that D is the domain of plaintexts of $\mathcal{F}_{\text{senc}}^{\text{auth}}$). We require that $|f(1^\eta, sp, r, r', v, m)| = |f(1^\eta, sp, r, r', v, \hat{m})|$ for all $\eta, sp, r, r', v, m, \hat{m}$ such that $|m| = |\hat{m}|$. That is, the length of the plaintext returned by f only depends on the length of m (and possibly on the other arguments), but not on the actual bits of m (we need this to guarantee that plaintext formatting does not leak information about the message m, see the proof of Theorem D.1). The *parsing* function p takes as inputs a security parameter 1^η, session parameters $sp \in SP(\eta)$, and a plaintext $m' \in D(\eta)$ and outputs $\bot$ (signaling an error) or a tuple of the form (r, r', v, m) where $r, r' \leq n$ are two different roles, $v < V(\eta)$ is a counter, and $m \in \{0,1\}^*$ is a message. Basically, we require that parsing inverts formatting. More formally, we require that, for all η, sp, r, r', v, m, it holds that $p(1^\eta, sp, f(1^\eta, sp, r, r', v, m)) = (r, r', v, m)$. That is, given a plaintext and the security parameter and session parameters that where used to construct this plaintext, p reconstructs the other arguments of f. These functions are used as follows in our protocol: In a session of the protocol with parameters sp, when role r wants to send the v-th message, say m, to role r', then it will compute m' and send it, encrypted under the session key, to the network (with the intention that it reaches role r' in the same session). Upon receiving a ciphertext, an instance (i.e., some role in some session) will decrypt it with the session key and use the parsing function to reconstruct the original message (see below).

For example, the parameters can be instantiated as follows: $n := 2$ (i.e., a secure channel with two roles), $D(\eta) := \{0\|x \mid x \in \{0,1\}^*, |x| \geq 3\eta\}$ (i.e., all plaintexts start with 0 and have length at least $3\eta + 1$),[93] $SP(\eta) := \{(pid_1, pid_2) \mid pid_1, pid_2 \in \{0,1\}^\eta, pid_1 \neq pid_2\}$ (i.e., session parameters are pairs of different party names of length η, the party playing role 1 and role 2, respectively), and $V(\eta) := 2^\eta$ (i.e., counters are smaller than 2^η). Furthermore, $f(1^\eta, (pid_1, pid_2), r, r', v, m) := 0\|pid_r\|pid_{r'}\|\langle v\rangle_\eta\|m$ where $x\|y$ denotes concatenation the of two bit strings x and y and $\langle v\rangle_\eta$, for all $\eta \in \mathbb{N}$ and $v < 2^\eta$, denotes the encoding of v as a bit string of length η. That is, plaintexts are constructed by concatenating the party names, in the order "sender, receiver", the counter (in its bit string representation of length η), and the actual message m that the sender wants to send to the receiver. Since party names are different and party names and the encoding of counters have a fixed length, the original arguments can be reconstructed:

$$p(1^\eta, (pid_1, pid_2), m') := \begin{cases} (1, 2, v, m) & \text{if } \exists v, m\colon m' = 0\|pid_1\|pid_2\|\langle v\rangle_\eta\|m \\ (2, 1, v, m) & \text{if } \exists v, m\colon m' = 0\|pid_2\|pid_1\|\langle v\rangle_\eta\|m \\ \bot & \text{otherwise.} \end{cases}$$

Now, we describe $\mathcal{P}_{sc} = !M_1 \mid \cdots \mid !M_n$ in more detail. Recall from Section 7.5.1, the parts of $\mathcal{P}_{sc}$ that are fixed (e.g., an instance of M_r waits for an Establish request, then asks the adversary whether it is directly corrupted, and, if not, forwards the Establish request to $\widehat{\mathcal{F}}_{\text{keyuse}}$ and waits for receiving a response). We now describe the parts of $\mathcal{P}_{sc}$ that are not fixed. For every instance of a machine in $\mathcal{P}_{sc}$, say $M_r[lsid]$ with $lsid = (lsid', sp)$, this starts with receiving an Established message from $\widehat{\mathcal{F}}_{\text{keyuse}}$ (more precisely, $M_r[lsid]$ receives $(lsid, \text{Established})$, by definition of $\widehat{\mathcal{F}}_{\text{keyuse}}$), signaling that a session key has been established that can now be used for encryption and decryption. First, $M_r[lsid]$ verifies if its session is corrupted in $\widehat{\mathcal{F}}_{\text{keyuse}}$ (i.e., it sends the corruption status request $(lsid, \text{Corr?})$ to $\widehat{\mathcal{F}}_{\text{keyuse}}$). If it is corrupted, then $M_r[lsid]$ sets its flag corr to 1. Otherwise, the flag remains 0. Then, $M_r[lsid]$ checks if the session parameters are in the domain of session parameters (i.e., $sp \in SP(\eta)$ where η is the security parameter). If this is not the case, then $M_r[lsid]$ basically terminates: from then on, $M_r[lsid]$ ignores all input (i.e., it ends an activation with empty output), except for corruption status request which are answered as usual (i.e., by returning corr).[94] Otherwise (i.e., the session parameters are correct), $M_r[lsid]$ initializes two counters $S_{r'} := 0$ and $R_{r'} := 0$ for every role $r' \neq r$ (for counting

---

[93] Since the domain of plaintexts is not the domain of all bit strings, a key exchange protocol that realizes $\widehat{\mathcal{F}}_{\text{keyuse}}$ (see below) may have used the session key (e.g., for key confirmation) to encrypt messages not in D (e.g., messages prefixed by 1).

[94] We note that, alternatively, we could have defined that only instance with correct session

messages send to/received from role r'), outputs ($lsid$, Established) on its I/O output tape (i.e., just like $\widehat{\mathcal{F}}_{sc}$ when a session has been established), and then waits for receiving a Send request on its I/O input tape (just like $\widehat{\mathcal{F}}_{sc}$) or a message from the adversary (network) which is handled as follows:

- Upon receiving a request to send a message m to some role $r' \neq r$ (i.e., the message ($lsid$, (Send, r', m)); other I/O input is ignored), $M_r[lsid]$ does the following. If $S_{r'} \geq V(\eta)$ (i.e., the counter has hit its bound), then $M_r[lsid]$ ends this activation with empty output and waits for new input (that is handled analogously). Otherwise, $M_r[lsid]$ computes the plaintext $m' := f(1^\eta, sp, r, r', S_{r'}, m)$, encrypts m' using $\widehat{\mathcal{F}}_{keyuse}$ (i.e., $M_r[lsid]$ sends ($lsid$, (Enc, m')) to $\widehat{\mathcal{F}}_{keyuse}$), and obtains a ciphertext c (or the error symbol $\bot$) from $\widehat{\mathcal{F}}_{keyuse}$. If encryption fails, $M_r[lsid]$ ends this activation with empty output and waits for new input. Otherwise, it increases $S_{r'}$ by one, sends ($lsid$, Send, r', c) to the adversary (network), and waits for new input.

- Upon receiving a message from the adversary (i.e., from the network) of the form ($lsid$, Recv, r', c) for some role $r' \neq r$ and some bit string c (other network input is ignored, i.e., $M_r[lsid]$ ends this activation with empty output and waits for new input), $M_r[lsid]$ tries to decrypt c using $\widehat{\mathcal{F}}_{keyuse}$ (i.e., $M_r[lsid]$ sends ($lsid$, (Dec, c)) to $\widehat{\mathcal{F}}_{keyuse}$). If the decryption succeeds, i.e., $M_r[lsid]$ obtains a plaintext $m' \neq \bot$ from $\widehat{\mathcal{F}}_{keyuse}$, and $p(1^\eta, sp, m') = (r', r, v, m)$ for some number $v \geq R_{r'}$ and some message m, then $M_r[lsid]$ sets $R_{r'} := v+1$, outputs ($lsid$, (Received, r', m)) on its I/O output tape, and waits for new input. Otherwise (i.e., decryption or parsing fails or parsing succeeds but the other conditions are not satisfied), $M_r[lsid]$ ends this activation with empty output and waits for new input.

Unlike $\mathcal{P}_{sc}$, $\mathcal{P}_{sc}^+$ discards messages from the adversary if, when decrypted, they do not satisfy $p(1^\eta, sp, m') = (r', r, v, m)$ for $v = R_{r'}$, i.e., the counter $R_{r'}$ (maintained by the receiving instance) has to correspond to the counter contained in m' (the counter used by the sending instance); this will guarantee that message loss is not tolerated by $\mathcal{P}_{sc}^+$.

It is easy to see that $\mathcal{P}_{sc} \mid \widehat{\mathcal{F}}_{keyuse}$ and $\mathcal{P}_{sc}^+ \mid \widehat{\mathcal{F}}_{keyuse}$ are environmentally strictly bounded.

The next theorem shows that $\mathcal{P}_{sc}$ realizes $\widehat{\mathcal{F}}_{sc}$ and that $\mathcal{P}_{sc}^+$ realizes $\widehat{\mathcal{F}}_{sc}^+$. We note that, due to the use of $\widehat{\mathcal{F}}_{keyuse}$, the proof is completely syntactical and, by Theorem 7.4, we only need to consider the single session case.

Theorem D.1. $\mathcal{P}_{sc} \mid \widehat{\mathcal{F}}_{keyuse} \leq \widehat{\mathcal{F}}_{sc}$ *and* $\mathcal{P}_{sc}^+ \mid \widehat{\mathcal{F}}_{keyuse} \leq \widehat{\mathcal{F}}_{sc}^+$.

Before we prove the above theorem we note that, by this theorem, Theorem 2.1, and the transitivity of $\leq$, it follows that every protocol $\mathcal{P}$ that realizes $\widehat{\mathcal{F}}_{keyuse}$, e.g.,

---

parameters can be created. Then, $\widehat{\mathcal{F}}_{sc}$ must be parameterized by the same domain of session parameters because, otherwise, $\mathcal{P}_{sc}$ would not realize $\widehat{\mathcal{F}}_{sc}$.

every secure $\mathcal{F}_{\mathrm{crypto}}$-KE protocol that is parameterized by the domain D of plaintexts (see Theorem 7.1), such as the 4-Way Handshake (4WHS) protocol $\mathcal{P}_{\mathrm{4WHS}} \,|\, \mathcal{F}_{\mathrm{crypto}}$ of IEEE 802.11i (see Theorem 7.3), can be used as a lower-level protocol for $\mathcal{P}_{\mathrm{sc}}$ (or $\mathcal{P}_{\mathrm{sc}}^{+}$). More precisely, if $\mathcal{P} \leq \widehat{\mathcal{F}}_{\mathrm{keyuse}}$, then $\mathcal{P}_{\mathrm{sc}} \,|\, \mathcal{P} \leq \widehat{\mathcal{F}}_{\mathrm{sc}}$ and $\mathcal{P}_{\mathrm{sc}}^{+} \,|\, \mathcal{P} \leq \widehat{\mathcal{F}}_{\mathrm{sc}}^{+}$.

Proof sketch of Theorem D.1. By Theorem 7.4, we only need to consider a single session, i.e., it suffices to show $\mathcal{P}_{\mathrm{sc}} \,|\, \widehat{\mathcal{F}}_{\mathrm{keyuse}} \leq_{\mathrm{single}*} \widehat{\mathcal{F}}_{\mathrm{sc}}$ and $\mathcal{P}_{\mathrm{sc}}^{+} \,|\, \widehat{\mathcal{F}}_{\mathrm{keyuse}} \leq_{\mathrm{single}*} \widehat{\mathcal{F}}_{\mathrm{sc}}^{+}$.

First, we consider the case of $\widehat{\mathcal{F}}_{\mathrm{sc}}$, see below for the case of $\widehat{\mathcal{F}}_{\mathrm{sc}}^{+}$. Therefore, we first define a well-formed simulator $\mathcal{S} \in \mathrm{Sim}^{\mathcal{P}_{\mathrm{sc}} \,|\, \widehat{\mathcal{F}}_{\mathrm{keyuse}}}(\widehat{\mathcal{F}}_{\mathrm{sc}})$.

The simulator $\mathcal{S}$ is the natural simulator that basically emulates the system $\mathcal{P}_{\mathrm{sc}} \,|\, \widehat{\mathcal{F}}_{\mathrm{keyuse}}$. More precisely, $\mathcal{S}$ emulates the system $\mathcal{P}_{\mathrm{sc}} \,|\, \widehat{\mathcal{F}}_{\mathrm{keyuse}}$ (recall that the environment is single-session and, hence, $\mathcal{S}$ only has to emulate one instance of the machines in $\mathcal{P}_{\mathrm{sc}}$ and one instance of $\mathcal{F}_{\mathrm{keyuse}}$ in $\widehat{\mathcal{F}}_{\mathrm{keyuse}}$, say $\mathcal{F}_{\mathrm{keyuse}}[sid]$, i.e., the environment uses the SID sid). The simulator forwards all Establish requests, that it receives from $\widehat{\mathcal{F}}_{\mathrm{sc}}$, to (the emulated) $\mathcal{P}_{\mathrm{sc}} \,|\, \widehat{\mathcal{F}}_{\mathrm{keyuse}}$. Also, $\mathcal{S}$ forwards all network messages from the environment to $\mathcal{P}_{\mathrm{sc}} \,|\, \widehat{\mathcal{F}}_{\mathrm{keyuse}}$ and vice versa. If a (simulated) machine M_r in $\mathcal{P}_{\mathrm{sc}}$ gets corrupted (i.e., it sets its flag corr to 1), then $\mathcal{S}$ corrupts the corresponding user in $\mathcal{F}_{\mathrm{session}}$ in $\widehat{\mathcal{F}}_{\mathrm{sc}}$. (Note that this is always possible because corruption in $\mathcal{P}_{\mathrm{sc}} \,|\, \widehat{\mathcal{F}}_{\mathrm{keyuse}}$ is static.) For corrupted users, $\mathcal{F}_{\mathrm{session}}$ in $\widehat{\mathcal{F}}_{\mathrm{sc}}$ gives complete control to $\mathcal{S}$. Hence, $\mathcal{S}$ can precisely simulate corrupted machines M_r: Whenever a corrupted machine produces I/O output, $\mathcal{S}$ instructs $\mathcal{F}_{\mathrm{session}}$ in $\widehat{\mathcal{F}}_{\mathrm{sc}}$ to produces this output. Vice versa, upon input from $\mathcal{F}_{\mathrm{session}}$ in $\widehat{\mathcal{F}}_{\mathrm{sc}}$ for corrupted users, $\mathcal{S}$ forwards this input to the corresponding corrupted machine. If a machine M_r that is not corrupted produces the first I/O output (note that, by definition of $\mathcal{P}_{\mathrm{sc}}$, this must be an Established message), then $\mathcal{S}$ sets the SID of the corresponding user in $\mathcal{F}_{\mathrm{session}}$ in $\widehat{\mathcal{F}}_{\mathrm{sc}}$ to the SID, say sid, that this user has in $\widehat{\mathcal{F}}_{\mathrm{keyuse}}$ (this user must have an SID because it is not corrupted and it produced I/O output) and then instructs $\mathcal{F}_{\mathrm{sc}}[sid]$ in $\widehat{\mathcal{F}}_{\mathrm{sc}}$ to output an Established message for role r. When $\mathcal{S}$ receives a message $(sid, \mathsf{Send}, r, r', 0^l)$ from $\mathcal{F}_{\mathrm{sc}}[sid]$ (because role r instructed $\widehat{\mathcal{F}}_{\mathrm{sc}}$ to send a message of length l to role r'), then $\mathcal{S}$ emulates M_r with input $(lsid, \mathsf{Send}, r', 0^l)$ where $lsid$ is the local SID of the instance M_r. When a machine M_r that is not corrupted produces I/O output of the form $(lsid, \mathsf{Received}, r', m)$, then, by definition of M_r, it must have computed $p(1^\eta, sp, m') = (r', r, v, m)$ for some plaintext m' and counter $v \geq R_{r'}$. Then, $\mathcal{S}$ instructs $\mathcal{F}_{\mathrm{sc}}[sid]$ in $\widehat{\mathcal{F}}_{\mathrm{sc}}$ to drop $v - R_{r'}$ many messages from role r' to r (by sending $v - R_{r'}$ many Drop requests to $\mathcal{F}_{\mathrm{sc}}[sid]$; note that possibly $v = R_{r'}$, in which case $\mathcal{S}$ does not send any Drop requests) and then $\mathcal{S}$ instructs $\mathcal{F}_{\mathrm{sc}}[sid]$ to deliver the next message from role r' to r (by sending a Deliver request to $\mathcal{F}_{\mathrm{sc}}[sid]$). It is easy to see that $\mathcal{S}$ can be defined such that it is a well-formed simulator.

Now, we show that $\mathcal{E} \,|\, \mathcal{P}_{\mathrm{sc}} \,|\, \widehat{\mathcal{F}}_{\mathrm{keyuse}} \equiv \mathcal{E} \,|\, \mathcal{S} \,|\, \widehat{\mathcal{F}}_{\mathrm{sc}}$ for every single-session environment $\mathcal{E} \in \mathrm{Env}_{\mathrm{single}}(\mathcal{P}_{\mathrm{sc}} \,|\, \widehat{\mathcal{F}}_{\mathrm{keyuse}})$. We only sketch the proof. It is easy to see that corrupted instances of M_r are perfectly simulated. Hence, in the following we only consider the case of uncorrupted instances. We note that for uncorrupted instances, $\widehat{\mathcal{F}}_{\mathrm{keyuse}}$ is uncorrupted and, hence, these instances perform ideal encryption and decryption. The systems $\mathcal{P}_{sc} \,|\, \widehat{\mathcal{F}}_{\text{keyuse}}$ and $\mathcal{S} \,|\, \widehat{\mathcal{F}}_{sc}$ potentially only differ *(i)* upon a Send request for some message, say m, because in $\mathcal{P}_{sc} \,|\, \widehat{\mathcal{F}}_{\text{keyuse}}$ the plaintext $f(1^\eta, sp, r, r', v, m)$ gets encrypted while in $\mathcal{S} \,|\, \widehat{\mathcal{F}}_{sc}$ the plaintext $f(1^\eta, sp, r, r', v, 0^{|m|})$ gets encrypted or *(ii)* upon delivery of messages to the parties because $\mathcal{P}_{sc} \,|\, \widehat{\mathcal{F}}_{\text{keyuse}}$ outputs the decrypted received message while $\mathcal{S} \,|\, \widehat{\mathcal{F}}_{sc}$ (possibly) drops messages and outputs the next message in the queue. Next, we show that the systems in fact do not differ.

ad (i): By definition of $\mathcal{F}_{\text{keyuse}}$ it follows that in $\mathcal{P}_{sc} \,|\, !\mathcal{F}_{\text{keyuse}}$ not the plaintext $f(1^\eta, sp, r, r', v, m)$ but its leakage, which is a random bit string of the same length, is encrypted. Similarly, in $\mathcal{S} \,|\, \widehat{\mathcal{F}}_{sc}$ not $f(1^\eta, sp, r, r', v, 0^{|m|})$ but its leakage is encrypted. Since $|f(1^\eta, sp, r, r', v, m)| = |f(1^\eta, sp, r, r', v, 0^{|m|})|$ (by our assumption on f), the distribution of the produced ciphertext is the same in both systems.

ad (ii): Assume that $\mathcal{E}$ sends a network message that contains a ciphertext c to M_r. In this case, both systems $\mathcal{P}_{sc} \,|\, \widehat{\mathcal{F}}_{\text{keyuse}}$ and $\mathcal{S} \,|\, \widehat{\mathcal{F}}_{sc}$ decrypt c using (an instance of) $\mathcal{F}_{\text{keyuse}}$ (or the emulated $\mathcal{F}_{\text{keyuse}}$ in $\mathcal{S}$). If the obtained plaintext, say m', does not satisfy $p(1^\eta, sp, m') = (r', r, v, m)$ for some r', m, and $v \geq R_{r'}$ (where sp are the session parameters of the instance of M_r), then both systems discard this message. Otherwise, $\mathcal{P}_{sc} \,|\, \widehat{\mathcal{F}}_{\text{keyuse}}$ delivers m while $\mathcal{S}$ instructs $\widehat{\mathcal{F}}_{sc}$ to drop $v - R_{r'}$ messages and to deliver the next message, say $\tilde{m}$. We need to show that $m = \tilde{m}$. By definition of $\mathcal{F}_{\text{keyuse}}$, only plaintexts are returned that have been previously encrypted using $\mathcal{F}_{\text{keyuse}}$. By definition of $\mathcal{P}_{sc}$, it must have been the user in role r' who produced c when sending the v-th message to role r. (Otherwise, the plaintext would not satisfy $p(1^\eta, sp, m') = (r', r, v, m)$ because all instances use the same session parameters sp.) Note that $R_{r'}$ is exactly the number of messages role r has already received from r'. Since $v - R_{r'}$ messages are dropped, $\widehat{\mathcal{F}}_{sc}$ will deliver the $R_{r'} + (v - R_{r'}) = v$-th message that role r' has sent to r. We conclude that $m = \tilde{m}$.

In the case of $\mathcal{F}_{sc}^+$, we can use the same simulator $\mathcal{S}$ except that it emulates $\mathcal{P}_{sc}^+ \,|\, \widehat{\mathcal{F}}_{\text{keyuse}}$ instead of $\mathcal{P}_{sc} \,|\, \widehat{\mathcal{F}}_{\text{keyuse}}$. Note that $\mathcal{S}$ will never instruct $\widehat{\mathcal{F}}_{sc}^+$ to drop messages because, by definition of $\mathcal{P}_{sc}^+$, $v = R_{r'}$ if a message is delivered. The rest of the proof is analogous to the case of $\mathcal{F}_{sc}$. $\qquad\square$

The CCM Protocol of IEEE 802.11i

The protocol WPA2 (see Section 7.4.3) uses the CCM Protocol (CCMP) with the Temporal Key (TK) which has been exchanged by the 4-Way Handshake (4WHS) protocol to establish a secure channel between the authenticator and the supplicant. In CCMP, both parties maintain and use counters for the messages they send and received just like $\mathcal{P}_{sc}$. Encryption is done using the block cipher AES (with the key TK) in the CCM (Counter with CBC-MAC) encryption mode.

We model CCMP as the protocol $\mathcal{P}_{\text{CCMP}} := \mathcal{P}_{sc}$ using a formatting function f and a parsing function p that closely models the message formats of CCMP. More precisely, we define the domain D of plaintexts to be the domain of all bit strings, the domain SP of session parameters such that session parameters are as in Section 7.4.3, i.e., they have the form $(pid_A, pid_S, name_{PMK})$ where pid_A and pid_S are allowed party names for the role of an authenticator or supplicant, respectively; in particularly, $pid_A \neq pid_S$. We define the formatting function f such that the plaintexts $f(1^\eta, (pid_A, pid_S, name_{PMK}), r, r', v, m)$ (recall that $r \in \{1, 2\}$ where role 1 is the role of an applicant and role 2 is the role of a supplicant) precisely model the format of plaintexts in the CCMP protocol, see [IEE07, Section 8.3.3] for a definition of these message formats. Since the plaintexts in the CCMP protocol, in particularly, contain the party names pid_A and pid_S, the counter v, and the actual message m, it is easy to define the corresponding parsing function p. The CCM encryption mode is a secure authenticated encryption mode [Jon02] and, hence, it is reasonable to assume that it provides a secure authenticated encryption scheme. Altogether, the protocol $\mathcal{P}_{CCMP} \,|\, \mathcal{P}_{4WHS} \,|\, \mathcal{P}_{crypto}$ (where $\mathcal{P}_{crypto}$ is the realization of $\mathcal{F}_{crypto}$) is very close to an actual cryptographic implementation of CCMP using the 4WHS protocol for key exchange.

As shown in Section 7.4.3, it holds that $\mathcal{P}_{4WHS} \,|\, \mathcal{P}_{crypto} \leq \widehat{\mathcal{F}}_{keyuse}$. Hence, by Theorem D.1 (and the composition theorems), we obtain that $\mathcal{P}_{CCMP} \,|\, \mathcal{P}_{4WHS} \,|\, \mathcal{P}_{crypto}$ is secure, i.e., realizes $\widehat{\mathcal{F}}_{sc}$:

Corollary D.1. $\mathcal{P}_{CCMP} \,|\, \mathcal{P}_{4WHS} \,|\, \mathcal{P}_{crypto} \leq \widehat{\mathcal{F}}_{sc}$

We note it has been shown that the 4WHS protocol with TKIP (instead of CCMP) is insecure [TB09, OM09]. The attacks exploit that TKIP uses the stream cipher RC4 in an encryption mode which does not yield a secure authenticated encryption scheme.

D.3.3. Collision Resistant Hash functions

Collision resistance for (families of) cryptographic hash functions has been first formalized by Damgård [Dam87]. We now define families of hash functions and collision resistance following the definitions of [RS04], adapted to the asymptotic setting.

Definition D.1. *A hash function family* $H = \{h^\eta\}_{\eta \in \mathbb{N}}$ *is a family of functions* $h^\eta \colon K_\eta \times \{0,1\}^* \to \{0,1\}^{l_\eta}$ *such that there exist polynomials* p *and* q *such that* $l_\eta = p(\eta)$ *and* $K_\eta = \{0,1\}^{q(\eta)}$ *for all* $\eta \in \mathbb{N}$. *We require that* $h^\eta(k, x)$ *is computable in time polynomial in* η *and* $|x|$ *for all* $\eta \in \mathbb{N}$, $x \in \{0,1\}^*$, *and* $k \in K_\eta$.

We often write the first argument of h^η as a subscript, i.e., $h_k^\eta(x) = h^\eta(k, x)$ for all η, k, x. This is the (keyed) hash function for security parameter η and key k.

Definition D.2. *A hash function family* H *is called* collision resistant *if, for every probabilistic, polynomial-time algorithm* A, *the advantage of* A *against* H

$$\mathrm{adv}_{A,H}^{cr}(1^\eta, a) := \Pr\left[k \xleftarrow{\$} K_\eta; (x, y) \leftarrow A(1^\eta, a, k) : (x \neq y) \wedge (h_k^\eta(x) = h_k^\eta(y))\right]$$

is negligible (as a function in 1^η *and* a*).*